C000320098

the Backpackers Ultimate Guide

Australia 2004

BUG Australia 2004

Second edition – February 2004

Published by:
BUG Backpackers Guide
ABN 47 801 693 475
Kilcunda, VIC 3995, Australia
www.backpackersultimateguide.com

Printed in Canada

National Library of Australia
Cataloguing in Publication data:

BUG Australia 2004.

2nd ed.
Includes index.
ISBN 0 9581796 1 1.

1. Backpacking - Australia - Guidebooks. 2. Australia -
Guidebooks. 3. Australia - Description and travel.

919.4

copyright BUG Backpackers Guide © 2003-2004

Cover photographs
Front cover: Brachina Gorge, Flinders Ranges, South Australia
Photo copyright Australian Tourism Commission *(website www.australia.com)*.

Back cover: Camel Riding at Silverton, Outback New South Wales
Photo copyright Hamilton Lund, Tourism New South Wales *(website www.sydneyaustralia.com)*.

Maps
Maps are created by BUG Backpackers Guide using data and base maps supplied by the following organisations: Department of Lands (NSW & ACT); Department of Infrastructure, Planning and Environment (NT); Department of Natural Resources and Mines (QLD); RAA (SA & NT); TASMAP (TAS); TUMAS (VIC); DLI (WA). Full map acknowledgements are on page 363.

Contents

3

4 Contents

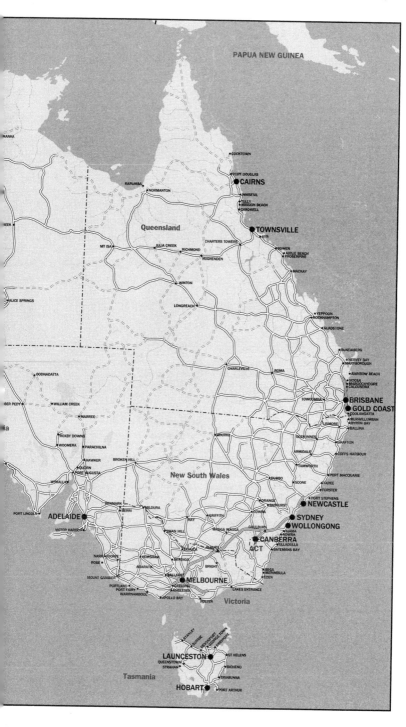

Welcome

Welcome to BUG

BUG is the Backpackers' Ultimate Guide and we believe this is the best guidebook available for anyone backpacking around Australia. We set out to publish a guidebook dedicated solely for backpackers (independent budget travellers). You won't find any information about fancy hotels in this book and because of this we can better concentrate on giving you honest and detailed information about hostels and budget travel options across Australia. Compare us with other guides, you'll find that we have more details on more hostels for any given destination.

This is the second edition of BUG Australia and it's the first year that BUG's star rating system has been incorporated into its guidebooks. Over time BUG will grow to fill a major niche in the guidebook market, but we don't plan on emulating other guidebook publishers and bringing out hundreds of different titles. Instead we will stick to a small number of guidebooks, fill them with accurate and honest information and keep them updated with a new edition every year.

How to use this book

We've travelled extensively and know what should be in a guidebook and what you can find out for yourself. We've kept this in mind when putting this book together to ensure that it's packed with lots of useful information and not weighed down with stuff you don't need.

The book won't bore you with trivial details such as history or politics, which often turn out to be just a soapbox for the author to air his or her views. Instead of making you lug around an extra 100 or more pages we jump straight into the useful stuff.

The Essentials chapter has information on passports and visas, discount cards and money. Boring, but important things that you need to know before you arrive.

The next chapter is Getting Around – we don't tell you how to get to Australia because that's what travel agents are for. The Getting Around chapter has the low-down on transport options in Australia including details on bus and train passes, hitchhiking, flying and driving. Read this before you go to buy your ticket so you know whether you're getting a good deal when the travel agent tries to sell you a travel pass.

After these introductory chapters it's straight into the destination chapters. There's a chapter for each state, with each one organised geographically starting with the state capital. These chapters are in alphabetical order.

When you arrive in a new destination you generally want to find a place to stay, take your backpack off and start exploring. We have put details on local transport and accommodation at the start of each destination guide, so you can choose where you want to stay and find your way there.

Once you've checked into a hostel you'll find that the staff behind the front desk are experts on the local area and will be able to help you with any little questions such as where to do your laundry, check your email or grab a bite to eat. For this reason we cut out the crap such as restaurant reviews and shopping information to make room for much more comprehensive accommodation reviews.

We have organised the information on accommodation and attractions so that every listing is followed by the address, a list of which bus or tram routes stop nearby, telephone number, website address, prices and opening hours (reception hours for accommodation listings).

A lot of hostels give discounts to holders of Nomads, VIP or YHA hostel cards. When we list accommodation prices the discounted price is shown after the full price as follows: Dorm bed $18.50 ($17.50 VIP/YHA). Just because a hostel offers a discount to someone holding a card from a particular hostel organisation is no indication that that hostel is affiliated with it. Where a price range is specified, for example: (Dorm bed $17-22), the low price is often the cheapest bed off-season and the high price the most expensive in the peak season. In a lot of hostels the cheapest beds are in the largest dormitories and the more expensive ones in the small dorms.

In BUG, we define a dormitory bed (or dorm bed) as any bed in a room that you share with other people who you are not travelling with. In Australia most dorms have four to six beds. We quote the price per person for a dorm bed and the price per room for single, double and twin rooms.

We classify a double room as a private room with one double, queen or king-size bed in it. A twin room is a private room with two single beds.

Some small hostels don't keep regular reception hours, in this case we don't list any hours. If the reception is unattended there is usually a phone number to call to speak with the manager who usually isn't far away. If you're arriving late it's a good idea to call in advance to arrange a bed for the night, in some cases you may be able to check in after reception hours if this is arranged in advance.

BUG's hostel ratings

Last year's BUG Australia travel guide highlighted the best hostel(s) in each major destination. Although this was a good way for travellers to quickly pinpoint the best hostel, it wasn't much help if all the best places were booked and it also did give credit to a lot of excellent hostels if they were the only place in town.

We wanted to provide the most comprehensive resource that could quickly describe a hostel while also providing more in depth information on hostels than any other guidebook. To achieve this we set about creating our own star rating system that highlighted the maintenance and cleanliness, facilities, atmosphere and character and security of each hostel while also providing an overall rating.

BUG's hostel reviewers fill out a two page form that collects information about various features, which are then rated to calculate that hostel's star rating. In addition to determining an objective star rating, the BUG hostel reviewer also writes a more subjective review of each hostel.

The individual ratings for particular characteristics are a handy way for travellers to choose a hostel based on what is important to them. For instance if a place with a great atmosphere is more important to you than cleanliness and maintenance, then you can just look at the atmosphere & character star rating rather than the other ratings.

When we set about creating our hostel rating system, we used what we believe are the best hostels as a benchmark for being awarded five stars. For instance we looked at the hostel we thought offered the most facilities to calculate our scoring system for this category. We did the same for security, cleanliness and atmosphere. It is very rare to find a hostel that excels in each area and because of this we have yet to award a full five stars to any hostel but any place with an overall score of four stars or higher can be considered outstanding.

The 'cleanliness and maintenance' rating shows how clean and well maintained the hostel is. A brand new purpose built place should score five stars and recently renovated hostels shouldn't be too far behind. The 'facilities' rating indicates the extent, but not necessarily the quality, of the facilities and amenities. The 'atmosphere and character' rating combines the charm of the building with the fun factor of staying at the hostel. The 'security' rating indicates the degree of security precautions that the hostel has taken.

The overall rating is calculated by averaging the other four ratings, but this is weighted to give priority to the more important aspects of the hostel.

There are other rating systems out there. AAA Tourism, an independent rating agency that is affiliated with the Australian state motoring organisations, also produces a star rating system for hostels. The AAA star rating focuses mostly on the hostel's facilities but very little emphasis is placed on the hostel's atmosphere or character. The main differences are that we developed our rating system from the ground up as a hostel rating (rather than an adaptation of a hotel or motel rating), we rate every hostel and the BUG score is broken into categories so you can see how the overall score is awarded. Unlike the AAA Tourism score, hostels don't choose to be rated and we certainly don't charge them for a rating or give advance warning that we are coming so they can make their hostel look nice for us.

We use the same criteria to rate hostels regardless of where they are in the world. No other hostel rating system has the same international consistency and you can be confident that a 3½ star hostel in Barcelona will offer a similar standard of accommodation as a hostel in Brisbane that has the same BUG rating.

Help keep us up-to-date

Although we update everything every year it is impossible to keep everything current for the entire life of this guide.

If you find something wrong please let us know so we can keep everyone up-to-date; you can email us at editor@bugaustralia.com or fax us at +61 3 5678 7033 or (03) 5678 7033 from within Australia. If you think one our hostel reviews is way off track, you can write your own review on our website (www.bugaustralia.com).

We update our website with the correct details as soon as we know them. Check our website (www.bugaustralia.com) for up-to-date facts.

Visit us on the Web

BUG started out in 1997 with a small website about budget travel in Europe and we have grown to become an extensive network of websites that can be accessed from our homepage (www.bug.co.uk). This guide is online (www.bugaustralia.com) and features interactive hostel reviews where you can write your own reviews of hostels all over Australia (and also in New Zealand, Pacific islands and in Europe). There are also forums where you can share travel tips with other travellers and a ride sharing service (http://australia.bugride.com) where you can organise a lift across the country.

Our network of websites extends beyond Australia and includes budget travel information on New Zealand, the Pacific and Europe.

If you're also planning on visiting New Zealand and other Pacific islands such as Fiji or Hawaii; then take a look at BUG Pacific (www.bugpacific.com). BUG Europe (www.bugeurope.com) is useful if you're planning to travel in Europe.

cost £42 for a 32-page passport and £54.50 for a 48-page passport; an additional £5 fee applies when lodging your application at a High Street partner. For expedited applications lodged in person at a Passport Office passports cost £70 (32-pages) to £71 (48-pages) for a one-week service or £89 (32-pages) to £95.50 (48-pages) for same day service.

Passport applications lodged at post offices and travel agents are normally issued in around three weeks, while applications lodged at UK Passport Offices are processed in two weeks. You can apply for a passport online at https://www.passport-application.gov.uk, however online applications are not recommended if you need your application processed within four weeks.

British passports are valid for 10 years.

United States

US citizens can apply for a passport at over 5,000 public places that accept passport applications, which include courthouses, and many post offices. Applications can take longer than eight weeks to be processed but applications lodged at one of 13 passport offices are processed quicker – usually within five weeks. Passports cost US$55 plus a US$30 execution fee.

For more information, contact the US Passport office (☎ *(202) 647 0518;* **website** *http://travel.state.gov/passport_services.html).*

Tourist Visas

Everyone except New Zealanders requires a visa to visit Australia.

There are two types of tourist visa issued to visitors to Australia. Most visitors are issued with an Electronic Travel Authority (ETA), however citizens of some countries must apply for an old fashioned stamp in their passport that is valid for visits of either three or six months and costs $65.

See the Working in Australia section later in this chapter for information on work visas.

Electronic Travel Authority (ETA)

If you are planning on visiting Australia on a three-month tourist visa you may be given an electronic visa known as an Electronic Travel Authority (ETA). The majority of tourist visas issued to visitors to Australia are ETAs. An ETA is similar to a visa, however there is no stamp in your passport and you do not need to visit an Australian embassy, consulate or high commission to get your ETA.

ETAs are issued to citizens of the following countries: Andorra, Austria, Belgium, Brunei, Canada, Denmark, Finland, France, Germany, Greece, Hong Kong SAR, Iceland, Ireland, Italy, Japan, Liechtenstein, Luxembourg, Malaysia, Malta, Monaco, Netherlands, Norway, Portugal, San Marino, Singapore, South Korea, Spain, Sweden, Switzerland, United Kingdom, United States of America and Vatican City.

Most applications for ETAs are submitted through travel agents or airlines but you can also apply for them online. Online applications can be made directly at the Australian Department of Immigration and Multicultural Affairs' website *(www.eta.immi.gov.au)* for $20, which is charged even if your application is unsuccessful. Alternatively you can apply for an ETA through the eVisas website *(www.evisas.com)* – this costs a lot more, US$20 rather than A$20, although you are not charged if your application is unsuccessful.

ETAs are issued within a few seconds from making an application, either online or through a travel agent, however in rare cases you may be asked to provide additional information before an ETA is issued.

Australian Embassies, Consulates & High Commissions
Austria
Australian Embassy, 3rd Floor, Winterthur House, Mattiellistraße 2, Vienna. ☎ *(01) 50674.* **Website** *www.australian-embassy.at.* **Open** *Mon-Fri 9.30am-noon.*

Canada
Australian High Commission, Suite 710, 50 O'Connor Street, Ottawa, Ontario K1P 6L2.

☎ *1 (613) 236 0841.*
Website www.ahc-ottawa.org.
Open Mon-Fri 10am-noon.

Germany
Australian Embassy, Philip Johnson House, Sixth Floor, Friedrichstrasse 200, 10117 Berlin.
☎ *(030) 8800 880.*
Website www.australian-embassy.de.
Open Mon-Fri 9am-noon.

Ireland
Australian Embassy, 7th Floor, Fitzwilton House, Wilton Terrace, Dublin 2.
☎ *(01) 6645 300; 24-hour information line (01) 6645 345.*
Website www.australianembassy.ie.

The visa section of the Australian Embassy in Dublin has closed. If you cannot make an application online or through a travel agent, you should contact the Australian High Commission in London or Visa Australia in Dublin:
Visa Australia, 12 Anglesea Street, Temple Bar, Dublin 2.
☎ *(01) 679 5452.*
Website www.australianvisas.ie.
Open Mon-Fri 9.30am-5.30pm.

Malta
Australian High Commission, Ta' Xbiex Terrace, Ta'Xbiex MSD 11, Malta GC.
☎ *33 8201.*
Website www.embassy.gov.au/mt.html.
Open Mon 8am-4pm, Tue 7.30am-5pm, Wed 8am-4pm, Thu 7.30am-5pm, Fri 8am-4pm.

The Netherlands
Australian Embassy, Carnegielaan 4, The Hague 2517 KH.
☎ *(070) 310 8200.*
Website www.australian-embassy.nl.
Open Mon-Fri 10am-12.30pm.

New Zealand
Australian Consulate-General, Level 7, PricewaterhouseCoopers Building, 186-194 Quay Street, Auckland.
☎ *(09) 921 8800.*
Website www.australia.org.nz.
Open Mon-Fri 9am-noon & 1.30pm-3.30pm.

South Africa
Australian High Commission, 292 Orient Street, Arcadia, Pretoria 0083.
☎ *(012) 342 3781.*
Website www.australia.co.za.
Open Mon-Fri 8.45am-11.30pm.

United Kingdom
Australian High Commission, Australia House, The Strand, London WC2B 4LA.
☎ *(020) 7379 4334.*
Website www.australia.org.uk.
Open Mon-Fri 9am-11am.

United States of America
Australian Embassy, 1601 Massachusetts Avenue NW, Washington DC 20036-2273.
☎ *(202) 797 3000 or 1800 990 8888.*
Website www.austemb.org.
Open Mon-Fri 9am-11am.

Australian Consulate-General (Chicago), Suite 1330, 123 North Wacker Drive, Chicago, IL 60606.
☎ *(312) 419 1480 or 1800 990 8888.*
Open Mon-Fri 8.40am-4pm.

Australian Consulate-General (Los Angeles), 19th Floor, Century Plaza Towers, 2049 Century Park East, Los Angeles, CA 90067-3238.
☎ *(310) 229 4800 or 1800 990 8888.*
Open Mon-Fri 8.45am-5pm.

Customs & Quarantine

Australia's customs regulations are much like those of other countries but it has some of the toughest quarantine policies in the world.

Customs

Visitors aged over 18 are allowed to bring 1125ml of alcohol and 250 cigarettes or 250 grams of tobacco into Australia without paying import duties. You are also allowed to import up to A$400 of other goods such as cameras, electronic goods etc which have been purchased duty free.

The duty free limit for travellers aged under 18 is $200.

Like many other countries, you are not allowed to bring weapons, steroids or many drugs into Australia.

Visit the Australian Customs Service website *(www.customs.gov.au)* for more information.

Quarantine

Because of Australia is free of many pests and diseases that plague other countries, the Australian Quarantine and Inspection Service *(website www. aqis.gov.au)* are extremely vigilant about keeping these out of Australia.

You will have to declare any food and animal or plant products that you have with you and most unpackaged food will not be allowed into the country. Quarantine officers will also check for dirty boots or shoes as well as camping equipment that may contain dirt that may introduce pests and diseases into Australia. You will also be questioned if you have visited a farm or engaged in any outdoor activity or if you have visited certain African or South American countries within the past week.

Working

Because of the common language and availability of working holiday permits, Australia is a popular spot for travellers to find work.

Working Holiday Visas

Australia allows citizens of Canada, Cyprus, Denmark, Finland, Germany, Hong Kong SAR, Ireland, Japan, Malta, the Netherlands, Norway, South Korea, Sweden and the United Kingdom to work on a temporary basis through the Working Holiday Maker programme.

A Working Holiday Maker visa allows citizens of the above countries aged 18-30 with no dependent children to spend up to one year in Australia taking casual and temporary work to supplement their funds. The programme specifically implies that work is of a casual/part-time or temporary nature and you may not work at one job for longer than three months.

You must apply for the visa before you arrive in Australia. Citizens of Cyprus, Germany, Hong Kong SAR, Japan, Malta and South Korea must apply in their home country, while citizens of Canada, Denmark, Finland, Ireland, the Netherlands, Norway, Sweden and the United Kingdom may apply from any Australian consulate, embassy or high commission outside Australia.

Applications for the working holiday visa can also be made online *(www.immi.gov.au/e_visa/visit.htm)*. If you make an online application you will be granted an electronic working holiday visa, which is similar to an ETA.

There is a limit to the number of Working Holiday Visas issued each year. 85,200 Working Holiday Visas were issued during 2001-2002.

You will need to fill in Form 1150 that is available from Australian consulates, embassies or high commissions or which can be downloaded from the Australian Department of Immigration and Multicultural Affairs' website *(www.immi.gov.au)*. It may also be necessary to be interviewed and you may be asked to show evidence of a return ticket or sufficient funds for a return or onward airfare plus evidence of sufficient funds to support yourself during the initial stage of your time in Australia. Generally you are expected to provide bank statements showing that you have access to at least $5000.

Once issued, a Working Holiday Visa gives you 12 months to travel to Australia and then allows you to stay in Australia for 12 months from your date of entry.

CIEE Work Exchange Programmes for US Citizens

US citizens can also work in Australia, however they have to apply through the Council on International Educational Exchange *(CIEE; ☎ 1 207 553 7600 from USA; website www.ciee.org)* and the requirements are much more restrictive. Like the Working Holiday Visa, this programme requires you to undertake short-term, temporary and casual work but the visa is only four months in length (you do not need to change your job after three months).

The programme is for US citizens between the ages of 18 and 30. There is no student status requirement to work in Australia through CIEE and you must be in the United States at the time of application.

The exchange programme costs US$500 plus an additional US$40 per month insurance fee. You may be asked to prove that you have access to at least US$1500 to show that you can support yourself before you get your first pay cheque.

Allow four weeks to be accepted into the programme, after which time you will have to apply for your work visa though the Australian Embassy, which will take an additional three weeks. The visa will incur an application fee of US$110 plus approximately US$20 shipping costs.

Tax

If you're working in Australia, you will have to pay tax on your income there. As a traveller on a working holidaymaker visa, you are not entitled to as many government services as Australians and you also have to pay tax from the very first dollar you earn, while Australians enjoy a $6,000 tax-free threshold.

You will be taxed at a rate of 29% on the first $21,600 you earn, with the tax rate rising to a maximum of 47% once you earn over $62,500.

You will need to get a Tax File Number to avoid paying a higher tax rate than you need to. You'll need to quote this number when applying for work. If you have a Working Holiday Visa and an Australian address you can apply for a Tax File Number online at the Australian Taxation Office's web-site (*www.ato.gov.au*).

At the end of the Australian tax year (30 June) and before you return home, you will need to complete a tax return. In Australia this is much more complex than in the UK and many travellers get an accountant or tax agent to do this for them. An accountant will charge around $120 for this service, but they are familiar with Australian tax law and will often be able to get you a better refund than you could get yourself.

Superannuation

If you are earning over $450 per month, you employer will pay 9% of your earn-ings into a superannuation fund (retirement savings fund).

Normally you cannot access this money until you reach 55, but temporary residents and visitors on a Working Holiday Maker visa can reclaim their money when they leave Australia. Money in your super fund is subject to withholding tax.

Contact the Australian Taxation Office (☎ 13 10 20; *website www.ato.gov.au/super/*) for further information on superannuation.

Finding Work

Your best option for work is to register at temporary employment agencies. This fits within the scope of your working holiday permit and also lines you up for reasonably well paying work. You could try one of the following agencies, which have a job search function on their website and offices throughout Australia:

Adecco

With more than 6000 offices world-wide, Adecco has all sorts of office work available.
Level 2, 280 George Street, Sydney.
☎ *13 29 93.*
***Website** www.adecco.com.au.*

Hamilton James & Bruce

This is a recruitment firm specialising in executive, middle management and office support roles.
Level 8, 275 George Street, Sydney.
☎ *(02) 9299 2711.*
***Website** www.hjb.com.au.*

Hays Personnel

This large international agency has a focus on accountancy, banking, IT and call centre jobs.
Level 11, Chifley Tower, 2 Chifley Square, Sydney.
☎ *(02) 8226 9700.*
***Website** www.hays.com.au.*

NurseWorldwide

This nursing agency has offices in Melbourne, Sydney, Brisbane and the Gold Coast.
Suite 1, Mezzanine Level, 234 Sussex Street, Sydney.

☎ *1300 132 190.*
Website *www.nurseworldwide.com.*

Nursing Australia
Nursing Australia is one Australia's largest specialist nursing agencies.
Level 1, 580 Church Street, Richmond, VIC.
☎ *13 10 95.*
Website *www.nursingagency.com.*

Recruitment Solutions
This agency has a wide selection of accountancy, finance and customer support positions and offices in Adelaide, Brisbane, Melbourne, Perth and Sydney.
Level 12, 2 Park Street, Sydney.
☎ *(02) 9269 8666.*
Website *www.recruitment-solutions.com.au.*

Summit Recruitment
This Sydney-based employment agency specialises in nursing positions.
Level 25, St Martins Tower, 31 Market Street, Sydney.
☎ *(02) 9286 375.*
Website *www.sumrecruit.com*

United Recruitment
This Melbourne-based agency specialises in hospitality, nursing, retail and secretarial positions.
2nd Floor, 3 Wellington Street, Windsor.
☎ *1300 360 362.*
Website *www.ur.com.au.*

West Australian Nursing Agency
This Perth-based nursing agency has positions throughout Western Australia and features work in more remote locations.
242 Railway Parade, West Leederville.
☎ *(08) 9382 2888.*
Website *www.wana.com.au.*

There are a few good general-purpose employment websites that are a good starting point. These include: employment.com.au, JobNet *(www.jobnet.com.au)*, MyCareer *(www.mycareer.com.au)* and Seek *(www.seek.com.au)*.
To get a good idea about the availability of work, long-term accommodation and costs of living, check the classified ads in the main Australian newspapers. The Saturday editions of *the Age* (Melbourne), the *Courier Mail* (Brisbane) and the *Sydney Morning Herald* are particularly good places to look for work.
Fruit picking is a popular backpackers job in Australia. It is hard work, but it's a good way to keep fit and get a tan. This sort of work is usually in small rural towns that you wouldn't otherwise want to visit, however there is work available in most parts of Australia. A lot of hostels in fruit-picking destinations will find work for you and a quick phone call before arriving can give you a quick rundown on the work situation.
Employment National (☎ *1300 720 126; website www.employmentnational.com.au/go_harvest.htm)* is a good place to start as they have a regularly updated database on where harvest work is available. It's a good idea to contact them before leaving for the area where you want to work as conditions can quickly change.

Health Cover

Finland, Ireland, Italy, Malta, the Netherlands, New Zealand, Sweden and the UK have reciprocal health agreements with Australia. If you are from one of these countries you may be entitled to free emergency health care although this sometimes limited if you are on a Working Holiday Visa.
Visitors from Ireland and New Zealand are entitled to subsidised medicine under the Pharmaceutical Benefits Scheme and free treatment at public hospitals. Irish and New Zealand travellers do not have access to Medicare benefits for non-hospital care and are not issued with a Medicare card. You simply show your passport at the hospital or pharmacy.
Residents of Finland, Italy, Malta, the Netherlands, Sweden and the UK who visit Australia are entitled to subsidised medicine under the Pharmaceutical Benefits Scheme, free treatment at public hospitals and Medicare benefits for treatment by doctors in private surgeries.

The reciprocal health care agreements don't cover other medical expenses such as dental and chiropractic services, glasses and contact lenses, elective surgery or hospital treatment that is not considered necessary before returning home.

Travellers from countries covered by this scheme, except visitors from Italy and Malta, are covered for the duration of their permitted stay. Visitors from Italy and Malta are covered for six months from the date of arrival in Australia.

Contact Medicare (☎ *13 20 11; website www.hic.gov.au/yourhealth/services _for_travellers/vtta.htm)* for more information on the reciprocal health scheme.

If you are not covered by a reciprocal health agreement you may want to take out comprehensive travel insurance or sign up with an Australian private health insurer. Australian Unity (☎ *13 29 39; website www.austunity.com.au)* has a private health insurance policy for international visitors called Healthy Travel, which you may want to consider; although some travel insurance policies are better value.

Money

Australia is a fairly cheap country to travel around, particularly when taking into account the quality of hostel accommodation. However prices can come as a shock if you've arrived here after a couple of months on the road in Asia.

Work out your daily budget by tripling your accommodation cost. Multiply this by the number of days you're planning on travelling for and add the cost of your airfare and bus/travel passes and you get a pretty good idea of the costs of travelling around Australia.

You should be able to save some money by cooking all your own meals and not drinking, however there are lots of easy ways to blow through a wad of cash such as a few big nights out on the town or adventure activities such as scuba diving, bungee jumping or white water rafting.

Travellers' Cheques

Travellers' cheques used to be the best way to carry travel money, however they're not as common now that ATMs and credit cards are so widespread.

It is worthwhile taking some of your money as travellers' cheques since it is a great backup if you lose your wallet with all your credit cards or if you arrive to discover that your cash card won't work in the ATM.

The beauty of travellers' cheques is that they can be replaced if they're lost or stolen. It helps if you keep a record of your travellers' cheque numbers in a safe place, preferably a copy with you (but not with your cheques) and another copy at home (or somewhere where someone can fax them to you if you need to make a claim for lost cheques).

Many travellers buy travellers cheques in British pounds, euros or US dollars, which is fine if you're travelling through lots of different countries. However travellers' cheques in Australian dollars have the advantage of being able to be used as an alternative to cash as long as you can find someone willing to accept them.

If you bring travellers' cheques with you, make sure that you sign them when you buy them, but do not countersign them until you are ready to cash them. You may also need to have identification such as your passport with you when you cash your cheques.

The most widely accepted brands of travellers' cheques are American Express, Thomas Cook and Visa. Don't travel with anything else as many people will not recognise or accept them.

ATMs, Credit Cards & EFTPOS

Over the past few years, plastic has quickly become the preferred way to access your cash while you're on the road and most cards are widely accepted throughout Australia.

There are several types of cards, each with their advantages. Most travellers have at least one credit card, and also a card to draw cash from an ATM (either from an account at home or from an Australian bank account).

CREDIT CARDS

Credit cards are great for getting out of trouble and are often tied to a frequent flyer programme. One of the main advantages of credit cards is the favourable currency exchange rate as well the freedom to spend more money than you have. Of course this spending can get out of hand and you'll end up paying for it later on.

The most useful cards in Australia are MasterCard and Visa, followed by Bankcard (only issued by banks in Australia, New Zealand and some Pacific Islands), American Express and Diners Club. In tourist areas you may find some places that accept JCB card, but Discover card is not accepted in Australia.

Most credit cards can be replaced quickly if they are lost or stolen. Call one of the following numbers if you need a new card:

American Express
☎ *1300 132 639.*
Website www.americanexpress.com.

Diners Club
☎ *1300 360 060.*
Website www.dinersclub.com.

MasterCard
☎ *1800 120 113.*
Website www.mastercard.com.

Visa
☎ *1800 450 346.*
Website www.visa.com.

ATM & EFTPOS CARDS

ATM cards are a popular way to access your cash, particularly if your card is part of an international network allowing you to use Australian Automatic Teller Machines (ATMs). If the bank that issued your card is part of the Plus, Cirrus or Visa networks you should find plenty of ATMs in Australia where you can withdraw money.

Despite the favourable exchange rate and the ease of drawing your money from a cash dispenser, there are sometimes problems using your cash card abroad. Before leaving home you should check with your bank whether it is possible to use your card in Australia. In some cases you may need to change your PIN or even have a new card issued.

Cards issued by Australian banks are a lot more useful, working in virtually all ATMs and also at EFTPOS terminals in most shops, hotels, service stations and pubs.

Electronic Funds Transfer at Point of Sale (EFTPOS) terminals at cash registers at most Australian shops allow you to use an Australian issued ATM card to pay for things and withdraw cash from your account. The combination of ATMs and EFTPOS terminals everywhere makes getting an Aussie bank account essential if you're planning on staying in the country for more than a few months.

Australian Bank Accounts

If you're planning on spending a lot of time in Australia, your own bank account will make things a lot easier, particularly if you're planning on finding work.

The four biggest banks in Australia are ANZ *(website www.anz.com)*, Commonwealth Bank *(website www.commbank.com.au)*, National Australia Bank *(website www.national.com.au)* and Westpac *(website www.westpac.com.au)*. Since you'll be on the road, it makes sense to open an account with one of the bigger banks as they have branches everywhere.

If you've just arrived you can open an Australian bank account by presenting your passport as identification, but you may be asked for additional identification if you try to open an account after spending more than six weeks in the country.

GST & the Tourist Refund Scheme

Australia has a 10% goods and services tax on most retail purchases, and there is a scheme where travellers can reclaim the GST on some purchases.

The Tourist Refund Scheme (TRS) enables you to claim a refund of the Goods and Services Tax (GST) and Wine Equalisation Tax (WET) that you pay on goods you buy in Australia.

The refund only applies to goods you take with you as hand luggage or wear onto the plane when you leave the country. It does not apply to services or goods consumed or partly consumed in Australia. Unlike other tourist shopping schemes, such as duty free shopping, you can use the goods before leaving Australia.

It is essential that you get a tax invoice when you buy the goods you want to claim a refund on and take this with you to the airport. There are TRS booths at the departure areas of Sydney, Brisbane, Melbourne, Perth, Cairns, Adelaide, Darwin and Coolangatta airports where you need to show the goods you want to claim the refund on, the tax invoice, your passport and boarding pass. In most cases you will be able to get a cash refund on the spot. If you're leaving from an international airport that doesn't have a TRS booth, such as Broome, you will need to present these items to a customs officer who should be able to process your refund; however in this case you will not get a cash refund.

Contact the Customs Service (☎ 1300 363 263; *website www. customs.gov.au*) for more information on the scheme.

Tipping & Bribery

Bribery in exchange for good service isn't very widely practised in Australia although tipping is starting to catch on, particularly in fancy restaurants in trendy inner-city neighbourhoods.

Ten years ago it would be rare to find an Australian who would regularly tip, but now there are many people who regularly tip 10% in restaurants and who even self-righteously promote this custom.

Despite the increasing number of people tipping, the average Aussie doesn't tip and even in more expensive restaurants it is quite normal to pay the exact change for your meal. You never tip in a pub or bar, which also means that pub meals are tip-free. Because cafés are basically pubs with a different drinks menu and décor, don't feel you need to tip there either even if some people do.

When paying taxi fares it is commonplace to round up the fare, such as paying $10 for a $9.60 fare; but it is not uncommon for a taxi driver to round a $10.20 fare down to an even $10.

Discount Cards

If you're travelling on a budget you're crazy to pay full price if there is a cheaper option. Armed with a wallet full of discount cards you should be able to drastically cut the cost of travel. Discount cards come in two varieties – hostel cards and student/youth cards. Both types of cards are worth taking, particularly if you're travelling for a while. Student cards are generally best for getting cut-price admission to museums and other attractions and often allow for cut-price transport; with hostel cards, the emphasis is on cheaper accommodation although these also give you excellent discounts on buses, trains and domestic airfares.

Student & Youth Cards

It's worth bringing along several student cards if you're a student, if you're not a student but are aged under 26 you can get a youth discount card that gives you similar discounts.

Most sightseeing attractions including museums, wildlife parks and zoos allow substantial discounts for students. Many attractions throughout Australia refer to the discounted price as the concession rate. Some hostels will also extend the VIP/YHA discount to you if you have a student card. In many cases just flashing the card issued by your university will get you these discounts, however some attractions require an internationally recognised card such as the ISIC or ISE card. This is a good reason why you should have at least two student cards.

Both ISIC and ISE publish a list of available discounts, however virtually all establishments that offer discounts will grant the discount for either card even if it that establishment is not listed in the card's discount guide.

The concession rate on the public transport networks in most Australian cities is not available with these cards and in most cases it is restricted to students enrolled in local schools.

ISE

The International Student Exchange (ISE) card is a good option with loads of discounts. Although this card is not as established as the ISIC, many establishments that give discounts to the ISIC will also provide the same discounts to ISE cardholders. The ISE card costs US$25 and you can order it online. See the ISE website *(www.isecards.com)* for more information.

ISIC, IYTC & ITIC

The International Student Travel Confederation *(ISTC; website www.isiccard.com)* produces three discount cards that give discounts to students; teachers and travellers aged under 26. Some of these cards include basic travel insurance although this is dependant on where the card is issued. ISIC, IYTC and ITIC cards each cost US$22 or £7.

The International Student Identity Card (ISIC) is the most widely accepted of the student cards. Many travellers buy fake ISIC cards while they're travelling through Asia which means non-students can sometimes pick one up; because of this the cards aren't quite as good for big discounts as they used to be and you may sometimes be asked for a secondary identification such as your student ID from your university at home. This is yet another reason why you should have a couple of student ID cards.

The International Youth Travel Card (IYTC) is an alternative for travellers aged under 26 who do not qualify for an ISIC. There is a wide range of discounts, although it is not as good as a student card.

The International Teacher Identity Card (ITIC) is a good alternative if you are a full-time teacher. Like the IYTC this isn't quite as good as a student card but it's worthwhile if you don't qualify for anything else.

Hostel Cards

Cards issued by the different hostelling organisations offer excellent discounts, particularly for transport and accommodation. Many travellers take along two cards, a YHA or Hostelling International card and one issued by an independent hostelling organisation such as VIP Backpackers Resorts or Nomads. There is more information about hostel cards in the following hostel section.

In our accommodation listings we list the price without a hostel card followed by the price charged if you have a card. Just because a hostel offers a discount to someone with a card from a particular hostel network does not mean that that hostel is part of the network.

Hostels

Hostels are a great cheap accommodation option, however they have much more to offer than a cheap bed. A good backpackers' hostel is also a place to party, meet new friends from around the world and get information on other cool places to go.

Hostels provide dormitory accommodation, along with shared shower and kitchen facilities. Generally there are four to six people sharing a room and there is somewhere like a TV room or bar where you can meet other travellers. Often the people running the hostel are backpackers themselves, and are a mine of information about places to see, things to do and transport and accommodation options elsewhere in Australia.

Australia has some of the world's best hostels and they often include facilities that you would seldom find in hostels in Europe or North America such as spas, swimming pools and courtesy buses. The Australian backpacking industry is very competitive and this keeps the standard of accommodation relatively high.

The best hostels are usually either small hostels in historic buildings that are full of character or newer purpose-built places with first-class facilities. Hostels in popular destinations such as Airlie Beach, Byron Bay, Mission Beach, Noosa and Port Douglas tend to be excellent as the competition between hostels in these places drives up the standard of accommodation. However hostels in bigger cities and less visited regional centres aren't as predictable.

A good hostel should provide a way for travellers to meet each other with common areas and a design that is conducive to meeting other people. This is one of the main features that distinguish hostels from hotels and motels, which are designed to offer their guests privacy. For this reason, many hostels with self-contained facilities (usually those that are former motels or apartment complexes) don't have as much atmosphere as your average backpackers hostel.

Hostels that are located above pubs are among the worst. In many of these places the bar downstairs is the main business and a lot less attention is paid to the accommodation.

Hostels catering to working holidaymakers are usually not that great either, existing solely to provide accommodation to backpackers picking fruit and they do little for travellers that happen to be passing through town and only staying a night or two. However the management of workers' hostels do have a lot of employment contacts and sometimes also provide transport to and from work. These hostels work for the employers as much as the backpackers and they have more rules than your standard hostel. Often there are restrictions on alcohol consumption in workers' hostels as local farms rely on them to provide a reliable, hard-working and sober workforce. Despite the overall lower standard of workers' hostels, there are a few that stand out from the crowd such as the Atherton Travellers Lodge (Atherton, Queensland) and Codge Lodge (Innisfail, Queensland).

Although we believe that the hostel reviews in this book are more comprehensive than any other guidebook, the reviews on our website *(www.bugaustralia.com)* are even more detailed and allow you to write your own hostel reviews and read reviews submitted by other travellers. A lot of the hostels reviewed on our website also allow online booking; where this is possible there will be a 'Book this Hostel' button next to the address on the review.

Hostel Chains

There are three main groups of hostels in Australia. Each of which offers its own discount/membership card that gives discounts on accommodation and transport.

Nomads

Nomads *(website www.nomadsworld.com)* started out by setting up hostels above pubs and the overall quality of their hostels wasn't all that great. However they seem to be really cleaning up their act and in the past couple of years have opened some excellent hostels. Nomads is the smallest of the three hostel chains.

The Nomads travel card offers over 600 discounts in Australia including around $1 off Nomads hostels. Transport discounts include 10% off McCafferty's/Greyhound buses, 5% off Oz Experience and the Wayward bus and discounts on trains operated by Great Southern Railway. The Nomads card costs $29 and is available from Nomads hostels.

Nomads also offer some very good welcome packages that include a Nomads card, airport transfers, tours and a few nights accommodation. This is good value and it is nice to have no worries about accommodation when you first arrive in the country. These packages *(website www.nomads.com.au/ oz.asp?Agent_ID=21)* are available for Adelaide, Brisbane, Cairns, Darwin, Gold Coast, Melbourne, Perth and Sydney.

VIP

VIP Backpackers Resorts *(website www.vipbackpackers.com)* is a group of independently run hostels that vary enormously as far as facilities are concerned.

The VIP card is one of the most useful hostel cards and a lot of backpackers buy one. Hundreds of hostels in Australia, New Zealand and other countries give discounts to VIP cardholders. Most of the hostels give a $1 discount per night. The card also has excellent transport discounts such as 10-15% discounts on McCafferty's/ Greyhound buses, discounts on trains operated by Great Southern Railway and discounts on rental cars. A VIP card costs $38.50 for one year or $50 for two years and is available online and from VIP hostels.

Youth Hostels Association (YHA)

The Youth Hostel Association *(website www.yha.org.au)* is the Australian branch of Hostelling International (HI) and its hostels have a fairly consistent standard. In Australia the YHA's main market are independent travellers as opposed to school groups that fill a lot of European hostels and consequently youth hostels in Australia have a much better atmosphere than the institutional hostels that you find in Europe. The competition between hostels in Australia has also forced the YHA to clean up its act and you won't find any YHA hostels in Australia with chores, a curfew or a lockout. Although YHA hostels in Australia are better than Hostelling International hostels elsewhere, they still have a reputation as a dull and relatively boring place to stay and very few YHA hostels fit the description of 'party hostel'.

Most travellers take along a YHA or Hostelling International card. This hostel card allows the biggest accommodation discounts with savings of around $3.50 per night. The card is good at any of the thousands of hostels around the world, including over 140 in Australia, that are part of the Hostelling International organisation. Most YHA youth hostels only give discounts on this card so it is essential if you are planning on staying at a lot of YHA hostels. Many independent backpackers hostels will also extend the Nomads or VIP discount to YHA members making this a good card to bring along. YHA cards are available through many student travel agencies as well as at YHA offices and hostels and costs US$28/£13.50/€25 although you can collect stamps towards a membership for every night you stay at a YHA hostel at the non-member rate, which can work out cheaper than buying a card in advance. The YHA card also has good discounts on transport including discounts on car rental, bus and train travel.

Getting Around

Air

The past couple of years have seen a lot of changes in the Australian airline industry that have had a big impact on the budget traveller. The result of fierce competition has left Australia with two large airlines in addition to a number of smaller regional carriers.

The two main airlines are the long-established Qantas and newcomer Virgin Blue. Qantas has the most extensive flight network, while Virgin Blue is quickly expanding to meet demand. Both airlines have relatively young fleets. Generally Virgin Blue (☎13 67 89; website www.virginblue.com.au) offer the cheapest fares of the two airlines but Qantas (☎13 13 13; website www.qantas.com.au) has good value red e-deals advertised on its website.

Regional Express, also known as Rex Airlines (☎ 13 17 13; website www.rex.com.au) flies to around 30 regional destinations in New South Wales, South Australia, Tasmania and Victoria. The main cities that Rex flies to are Adelaide, Canberra, Melbourne and Sydney; the most northern destination on the Rex network is Ballina/Byron Bay and they also fly to outback towns like Broken Hill, Olympic Dam and Coober Pedy. Rex has introduced two excellent value backpacker travel passes that allow either one month unlimited standby travel for $499 or two months for $949. These passes are only available to international travellers with a ISIC, IYTC, VIP or YHA card and you cannot use this pass to accrue frequent flyer points. Despite the limited reach of the Rex network, this is probably Australia's best value travel pass.

Other regional airlines include SkyWest (☎ 1300 66 00 88; website www.skywest.com.au) and Alliance Airlines (☎1300 13 00 92; website www.allianceairlines.com.au). These regional airlines operate flights to smaller cities and some of their fares are competitive with the bigger carriers, particularly on the busier routes.

Qantas is part of the One World network along with American Airlines and British Airways. If you're not already a member of a OneWorld airline's frequent flyer programme you can join American Airlines' programme for free and earn points with Qantas flights, rather than paying to join the Qantas frequent flyer programme. You can sign up for the American Airlines frequent flyer programme on their website (www.aa.com).

Train

Train travel is the most comfortable way to travel overland, but trains don't run as frequently or operate to as many destinations as buses.

Trains go to the most popular destinations along the east coast including the popular Sydney-Cairns route and also along major inter-city lines including Sydney to Adelaide, Canberra and Melbourne and onwards to Perth on the west coast. From Adelaide, there are also trains running north to Darwin.

Great Southern Railway (GSR; ☎ 13 21 47; website www.gsr.com.au) runs most of Australia's great classic rail journeys, which include the long-distance Indian Pacific between Sydney and Perth and the legendary Ghan, running from Sydney and Melbourne to Adelaide and up to Darwin. Great Southern Railway offers backpackers discounts of up to 50%. Just show your Nomads, VIP or YHA card and the train becomes a cheap alternative to bus travel. Some of the fares with the backpacker discount include Melbourne-Adelaide ($42), Adelaide-Alice Springs ($105), Adelaide-Darwin ($220) and Sydney-Perth ($252).

Railway companies that serve their home state operate most other train services in Australia. These include Countrylink (☎ 13 22 32; website www.countrylink.nsw.gov.au), which operates trains in New South Wales; QR (☎ 13 22 32; website www.qr.com.au), which runs train services in Queensland; V/line (☎ *13 61 96; website www.vl inepassenger.com.au*) and West Coast Railway (☎ *(03) 5221 8966; website www.wcr.com.au*), which operate trains in Victoria. Westrail (☎ *13 10 53; web-site www.wagr.wa.gov.au*) has limited train services in Western Australia.

There are a number of rail passes available that make train travel a little easier and more affordable.

These rail passes are available from student and backpacker travel agents or contact the railway companies listed above for more information.

Australian rail passes include:

Great Southern Railway Pass

The Great Southern Railway Pass is one of the best deals, particularly if you have a backpackers card. This pass allows six months unlimited travel on the Ghan, Indian Pacific and Overland trains. It costs $590 or $450 if you have a Nomads, VIP or YHA card. This pass is not available to Australian passport holders.

Backtracker Rail Pass

This Backtracker Rail Pass (☎ *13 22 32; website www.backpackerrailpass. info*) is good for economy travel on all Countrylink trains and buses in New South Wales and includes travel on Countrylink trains to Brisbane and Melbourne.

This pass is only available to travellers in possession of a valid international passport.

Validity	Price
14 days	$217.80
1 month	$250.80
2 months	$272.80
3 months	$382.80

East Coast Discovery Pass

The East Coast Discovery Pass is the most economical way to explore the East Coast by train. The pass is valid for six months travel on Countrylink and QR trains between Melbourne and Cairns.

There are passes available for shorter segments of this route.

This East Coast Discovery Pass is not valid on the Kuranda Scenic Railway.

Route	Price
Brisbane-Cairns	$224.40
Sydney-Cairns	$312.40
Melbourne-Brisbane/ Surfers Paradise	$176.00
Melbourne-Cairns	$393.80
Sydney-Melbourne	$93.50
Sydney-Brisbane	$93.50

Bus

Bus travel is the most popular way to get around Australia. Buses go virtually everywhere and many bus tickets allow you to hop on and off en route to your destination.

There is a fairly comprehensive network of bus routes with lots of competition on the more heavily travelled routes between Adelaide, Melbourne and Sydney and up the east coast to Cairns making it a cheap way to get around.

Once you start to head west from Adelaide, there is less competition between various bus companies and the distances between towns are much longer making it a less cost effective transport option.

Bus travel is split between scheduled bus operators such as Firefly, Premier Motor Services and McCafferty's/ Greyhound and backpacker buses such as Easyrider, Groovy Grape, Oz Experience and the Wayward Bus. Scheduled buses are usually cheaper and run more frequently but the specialist backpacker buses often go to out of the way places that you would otherwise miss out on. Unfortunately some backpacker buses are too organised and feel a lot more like tours, which goes against the whole spirit of backpacking and independent travel.

Scheduled Buses

Scheduled buses are the cheapest and most common way to get around. This is everyday travel for many Australians and is often a good way to meet the locals. These bus services are operated by loads of small companies covering regional areas but there are a few bigger companies that operate a national network.

Some of the bigger regional operators include Firefly (☎ 1800 631 164; website *www.fireflyexpress.com.au*), which runs good value Adelaide-Melbourne and Adelaide-Sydney services and V/line (☎ 13 61 96; *website www.vlinepassenger.com.au*), which operates regional services within Victoria.

McCafferty's/Greyhound

McCafferty's/Greyhound (☎ 13 20 30; *website www.mccaffertys.com.au*) offer an extensive route network covering all of mainland Australia, but not Tasmania. They offer the following passes:

AUSSIE EXPLORER PASSES

These passes allow you to travel along a pre-set route getting on and off at stops along the way. Some passes allow free tours and transfers to places like Kakadu and Uluru National Parks. Passes are valid from two to 12 months.

Various Aussie Explorer Passes are listed below. Discount fares apply to holders of Euro 26, ISIC, Nomads, VIP and YHA cards.

All Australian

Covers the whole country except Tasmania. This pass includes trips to Kakadu and Uluru National Parks.
Full fare $2,403; *discount fare* $2,163.
Distance approx 22,000km
Days required 48
Validity 365 days.

Aussie Highlights

The east coast plus the Northern Territory, South Australia and Victoria.
Full fare $1,434; *discount fare* $1,291.
Distance 12,600km
Days required 32 days
Valid 365 days

Best of the East

The east coast plus Alice Springs, Uluru National Park, South Australia and Victoria.
Full fare $1,173; *discount fare* $1,056.
Distance 10,100km

Days required 22 days
Valid 365 days

Best of the Outback

Sydney to Darwin, via Adelaide, Alice Springs and Uluru National Park.
Full fare $799; *discount fare* $719.
Distance 5,234km
Days required 14 days
Valid 183 days

Best of the West

The west coast plus Northern Territory and South Australia; includes Kakadu and Uluru National Parks.
Full fare $1,444; *discount fare* $1,156.
Distance 14,000km
Days required 22 days
Valid 365 days

Central Coaster

Sydney to Brisbane
Full fare $107; *discount fare* $96.
Distance 1,022km
Valid 90 days

Central Explorer (ex Melbourne)

Melbourne to Alice Springs; including Kings Canyon and Uluru National Park.
Full fare $499; *discount fare* $449.
Distance 3,828km
Valid 183 days

Central Explorer (ex Sydney)

Sydney to Alice Springs; includes Kings Canyon and Uluru National Park.
Full fare $580; *discount fare* $522.
Distance 4,785km
Valid 183 days

Clean Sweep

Broome to Darwin; including Kakadu National Park.
Full fare $360; *discount fare* $324.
Distance 2,650km
Valid 183 days

Coast to Coast

Sydney to Perth via Adelaide and either Melbourne or Canberra.
Full fare $485; *discount fare* $437.
Distance 4,600km
Days required 10 days
Valid 183 days

Country Road

Sydney to Cairns, via the outback. Includes Adelaide, Alice Springs, Kings Canyon, Uluru National Park, Mt Isa and Townsville.
Full fare $814; discount fare $732.
Distance 7,207km
Days required 14 days
Valid 183 days

Exmouth Explorer

Perth to Exmouth with transfers to Monkey Mia and Kalbarri.
Full fare $483; discount fare $386.
Distance 1,294km
Days required 8 days
Valid 90 days

Mini Travellers Pass

Sydney to Cairns (also available ex Melbourne and ex Brisbane).
Full fare $299; discount fare $269.
Distance 2,955km
Days required 3 days
Valid 30 days

Monkey Mia Explorer

Perth to Monkey Mia including transfer to Kalbarri.
Full fare $339; discount fare $271.
Distance 1,011km
Days required 8 days
Valid 90 days

Outback & Reef Explorer

Sydney to Cairns and Darwin; includes Kakadu National Park.
Full fare $830; discount fare $747.
Distance 6,563km
Days required 12 days
Valid 183 days

Pearl Diver

Perth to Broome.
Full fare $434; discount fare $348.
Distance 4,100km
Days required 9 days
Valid 183 days

Reef & Rock (ex Brisbane)

Brisbane to Cairns, then across to the Northern Territory via Townsville; includes Darwin, Alice Springs, Kakadu and Uluru National Parks.
Full fare $1022; discount fare $920.
Distance 9,041km
Days required 16 days
Valid 183 days

Reef & Rock (ex Cairns)

Cairns to the Northern Territory via Townsville; includes Darwin, Alice Springs, Kakadu and Uluru National Parks.
Full fare $682; discount fare $614.
Distance 6,986km
Days required 12 days
Valid 183 days

Rock Track

Darwin to Alice Springs including Uluru and Kakadu National Parks.
Full fare $455; discount fare $410.
Distance 3,800km
Days required 8 days
Valid 183 days

Rocker

Cairns to Alice Springs including Kings Canyon and Uluru National Park.
Full fare $512; discount fare $460.
Distance 3,981km
Valid 183 days

Sunseeker (ex Melbourne)

Melbourne to Cairns.
Full fare $470; discount fare $422.
Distance 4,701km
Days required 8 days
Valid 183 days

Sunseeker (ex Sydney)

Sydney to Cairns.
Full fare $374; discount fare $337.
Distance 2,955km
Days required 8 days
Valid 183 days

Top End Explorer

Darwin to Cairns; including Kakadu National Park.
Full fare $461; discount fare $415.
Distance 3,608km
Days required 10 days
Valid 183 days

Travellers Pass

Areas covered Sydney to Cairns.
Full fare $318; discount fare $228.
Distance 2,955km
Days required 8 days
Valid 90 days

Western Explorer

Areas covered Perth to Darwin along the west coast; includes Kakadu National Park and transfers to Monkey Mia, Kalbarri and Exmouth.

Full fare $674; discount fare $540.
Distance 9,600km
Days required 13 days
Valid 183 days

AUSSIE KILOMETRE PASSES

McCafferty's/Greyhound's Aussie Kilometre Pass offers more flexibility than the predetermined routes covered by their Aussie Explorer Passes.

Travel is purchased in kilometre blocks starting at 2000km and increasing in blocks of 1000km to a maximum of 20,000km.

This pass allows you to visit any destination on the McCafferty's/ Greyhound network. Aussie Kilometre Passes are valid for 12 months.

Validity	Full fare	Discount
2,000km	$391	$289
3,000km	$431	$387
4,000km	$545	$490
5,000km	$666	$599
6,000km	$777	$699
7,000km	$886	$797
8,000km	$995	$895
9,000km	$1,111	$1,000
10,000km	$1,231	$1,108

Premier Motor Service

Premier (☎ *13 34 10; website www.premierms.com.au*) is the biggest of the small coach operators and has scheduled services along the east coast. They operate buses on the popular Sydney to Cairns route and also along the coastal route between Melbourne and Sydney. Premier offers several travel passes that allow three months travel along a specified route: these include Melbourne to Cairns, Melbourne to Sydney, Sydney to Cairns and Sydney to Brisbane.

Backpacker Buses

Australia has a multitude of specialised bus services operated specifically for backpackers. Some of these include very useful services stopping off at hostels and also making detours to attractions that the express coaches miss. However some of these so-called backpacker buses are simply tours, and this runs against the spirit of backpacking and independent travel.

Oz Experience is biggest backpacker bus operator and has routes covering most of the country. It represents a good travel option.

Some smaller companies also offer excellent transport options within a particular region and they often have the benefit of local knowledge.

If you're thinking about buying a pass for one of the smaller backpacker bus companies, first check whether it really caters for independent travellers – allowing you to get on and off as you please – if it doesn't offer this sort of flexibility then it is nothing but a tour.

Autopia Tours

Autopia Tours (☎ *(03) 9326 5536; website www.autopiatours.com.au*) is a tour company in the same mould as Wildlife Tours and the Wayward Bus that has a good Melbourne-Adelaide trip ($165) and also a Melbourne-Sydney trip ($180) that runs via the Snowy Mountains, Canberra and the Blue Mountains.

Autopia also runs several excellent day trips from Melbourne that are worth considering if you don't have your own car. These include Phillip Island ($70), Great Ocean Road ($65) and the Grampians National Park ($65).

Easyrider Backpacker Tours

Easyrider Backpacker Tours (☎ *(08) 9226 0307; website www. easyriderbp.com.au*) operates tours and hop-on hop-off buses in Western Australia.

Easyrider's hop-on hop-off buses have two main routes. The northwest route runs between Perth and Broome ($579, $559 with ISIC/VIP/YHA discount), although you have the option of only travelling Perth-Exmouth ($329, $319 with ISIC/VIP/YHA discount) or Exmouth-Broome ($289, $279 with ISIC/VIP/YHA discount). The southwest route ($239, $229 with ISIC/VIP/ YHA discount) runs a circuit covering southwestern WA, including Albany, Margaret River and Walpole.

Nullarbor Traveller

Nullarbor Traveller (☎ (08) 8364 0407; *website www.the-traveller.com.au)* runs seven and nine-day tours between Adelaide and Perth.

Although the Nullabor Traveller is a tour rather than a hop-on hop-off bus there are very few places on the Nullarbor that most travellers would want to stay for longer than a day if they were travelling independently so it is an excellent way of covering this vast distance while seeing all the interesting bits en route. The tours cost $945 Adelaide to Perth and $735 Perth-Adelaide.

Oz Experience

Oz Experience (☎ (02) 8356 1766; *website www.ozexperience.com)* is the biggest of the backpacker bus operators. They go everywhere except Western Australia and their passes allow you to hop on and off at stops along the way. Most passes are valid for six months although some are valid for 12 months.

Oz Experience includes a lot of extras on its trips such as visits to National Parks and sheep and cattle stations.

Because they offer so many different passes it can be confusing working out which one is best for you.

Ox Experience passes include:

Big Blue Hill
Blue Mountains day trip.
Full fare $75; discount fare $70.
Minimum trip 1 day.

Bruce (ex Adelaide)
Adelaide to Cairns.
Full fare $641; discount fare $609.
Minimum trip 15 days.
Valid 12 months.

Bruce (ex Melbourne)
Melbourne to Cairns.
Full fare $515; discount fare $489.
Minimum trip 12 days.
Valid 12 months.

Bruce (ex Sydney)
Sydney to Cairns.
Full fare $386; discount fare $367.
Minimum trip 9 days.
Valid 12 months.

Cobber (ends Adelaide)
Cairns to Adelaide.
Full fare $641; discount fare $609.
Minimum trip 15 days.
Valid 12 months.

Cobber (ends Melbourne)
Cairns to Melbourne.
Full fare $515; discount fare $489.
Minimum trip 12 days.
Valid 12 months.

Cobber (ends Sydney)
Cairns to Sydney.
Full fare $386; discount fare $367.
Minimum trip 9 days.
Valid 12 months.

Donga
Adelaide to Alice Springs, via Ayers Rock.
Full fare $520; discount fare $495.
Minimum trip 6 days.
Valid 12 months.

Dunny Door
Brisbane to Sydney.
Full fare $163.
Minimum trip 4 days.
Valid 12 months.

Fair Dinkum
Sydney-Cairns-Darwin-Alice Springs-Adelaide-Melbourne-Sydney
Full fare $1727; discount fare $1641.
Minimum trip 27 days.
Valid 12 months.

Fish Hook
Sydney-Melbourne-Adelaide-Alice Springs-Darwin.
Full fare $1019; discount fare $968.
Minimum trip 15 days.
Valid 12 months.

Goanna
Melbourne-Adelaide-Darwin.
Full fare $919; discount fare $873.
Minimum trip 12 days.
Valid 12 months.

Grouse

Sydney-Melbourne-Adelaide-Alice Springs-Cairns.
Full fare $1143; discount fare $1086.
Minimum trip 15 days.
Valid 12 months.

Knobs & Bells

Sydney-Melbourne-Adelaide-Alice Springs-Cairns-Brisbane-Sydney.
Full fare $1452; discount fare $1379.
Minimum trip 24 days.
Valid 12 months.

Matey (ex Melbourne)

Melbourne to Sydney.
Full fare $240; discount fare $228.
Minimum trip 4 days.
Valid 6 months.

Matey (ex Sydney)

Sydney to Melbourne.
Full fare $194; discount fare $184.
Minimum trip 3 days.
Valid 12 months.

Strewth

Byron Bay to Cairns.
Full fare $236; discount fare $203.
Minimum trip 7 days.
Valid 12 months.

Troppo

Adelaide-Alice Springs-Cairns.
Full fare $783.
Minimum trip 9 days.
Valid 6 months.

U-Bolt

Cairns-Sydney-Melbourne-Adelaide-Alice Springs-Darwin.
Full fare $1381; discount fare $1312.
Minimum trip 27 days.
Valid 12 months.

Vegemight

Sydney to Brisbane.
Full fare $226.
Minimum trip 4 days.
Valid 12 months.

Victa

Adelaide to Melbourne.
Full fare $194; discount fare $184.
Minimum trip 3 days.
Valid 12 months.

Victa/Matey

Adelaide-Melbourne-Sydney.
Full fare $336; discount fare $319.
Minimum trip 6 days.
Valid 6 months.

Whipper Snapper (ex Melbourne)

Melbourne-Sydney-Cairns-Alice Springs-Darwin.
Full fare $1112; discount fare $1056.
Minimum trip 18 days.
Valid 12 months.

Whipper Snapper (ex Sydney)

Sydney-Cairns-Alice Springs-Darwin.
Full fare $955; discount fare $907.
Minimum trip 15 days.
Valid 12 months.

Oz Experience also have a range of Air-Bus passes which include bus travel plus a Qantas flight back to either the starting point or another destination. See the table on the opposite page for more information on Oz Experience travel passes.

Wayward Bus

Wayward Bus (☎ *(08) 8410 8833; website www.waywardbus.com.au)* is more a tour company than an independent travel option, however they do have some excellent trips that allow you to discover some great out-of-the-way places including the Flinders Ranges, Central Australia and Kangaroo Island. They're also well known for their Great Ocean Road trip in Victoria.

Wildlife Tours

Wildlife Tours (☎ *(03) 9534 8868; website www.wildlifetours.com.au)* run Melbourne-Sydney and Melbourne-Adelaide trips as well as tours from Melbourne to the Grampians and the Great Ocean Road in Victoria.

Driving

Driving is the best way to travel around Australia. Having access to your own set of wheels frees you from the constraints of routes and schedules and allows you to visit places off the beaten track.

Anyone over 18 can drive in Australia with their local licence, providing it is valid and that you've been in the country for less than six months. If you're spending longer in Australia you should bring along an international driving permit or apply for an Australian driver's licence.

Driving in Australia is easy. Traffic drives on the left and roads are generally well-maintained but motorways are usually restricted to the approaches to major cities and heavily travelled routes such as Melbourne-Sydney and Sunshine Coast-Brisbane-Gold Coast. A regular car will take you virtually everywhere in Australia, but a four-wheel-drive is essential for beach driving or if you want to explore Fraser Island and the Cape York Peninsula.

There are some very long and boring stretches of road in Australia and fatigue is a big killer – make plenty of rest stops, drink plenty of coffee or cola and share the driving with someone else. If you've got a spare seat or two, you may want to offer a lift on BUG Ride *(website http://australia.bugride.com)*, BUG's online ride sharing service. Offering a lift is a good way to split your fuel costs as well as avoiding spending too much time behind the wheel.

Speed limits on most country roads are 100-110km/h. On motorways the limit is usually 110km/h outside cities and 100km/h in built up areas. Minor roads in towns and cities are usually either 50km/h or 60km/h with an increasing number of towns adopting the lower speed limit. On highways in the Northern Territory you can drive as fast as your car and common sense allow. It is compulsory to wear seat belts and it's illegal to talk on a mobile phone while driving. You must not park facing oncoming traffic.

Watch out for road trains if you're driving in the outback. These 50-metre-long semi-trailers can't stop as quickly as a regular car so keep out of their way and make sure that you allow plenty of room to overtake one. Also be alert if you're driving in the countryside around dusk – kangaroos are active at this time and are unpredictable – often jumping into the path of an oncoming vehicle.

Motoring organisations

If you're a member of a motoring organisation you can use the facilities of their Australian counterpart. Each state has its own motoring organisation, although they all fall under the umbrella of the Australian Automobile Association (AAA).

If you're not a member of an auto club at home it's worth joining one in Australia, particularly for the peace of mind and the potential savings of the roadside assistance.

Roadside assistance can be contacted by calling 13 11 11 in any state.

AANT (Automobile Association of Northern Territory)
81 Smith Street, Darwin.
☎ *(08) 8981 3837*
Website *www.aant.com.au*

NRMA (National Roads & Motorists Association)
74 -76 King Street, Sydney.
🚇 *Martin Place, Wynyard*
☎ *13 21 32*
Website *www.nrma.com.au*

RAA (Royal Automobile Association)
41 Hindmarsh Square, Adelaide
☎ *(08) 8202 4600*
Website *www.raa.com.au*

RACT (Royal Automobile Club of Tasmania)
Corner Murray & Patrick Streets, Hobart.
☎ *13 11 11*
Website *www.ract.com.au*

RACQ (Royal Automobile Club of Queensland)
300 St Pauls Terrace, Fortitude Valley
🚌 *Brunswick Street*
☎ *(07) 3361 2444*
Website *www.racq.com.au*

RACV (Royal Automobile Club of Victoria)
360 Bourke Street, Melbourne
🚌 *19, 57, 59, 68, 86, 96;* 🚇 *Flinders Street, Melbourne Central*
☎ *13 19 55*
Website *www.racv.com.au*

RAC of WA (Royal Automobile Club of Western Australia)
228 Adelaide Terrace, Perth.
☎ *(08) 9421 4444*
Website www.racwa.com.au

Renting a Car

Although expensive over a long period, renting a car is a good option if your time is limited and if you want to explore a particular region in depth. Car rental companies with branches nation-wide are generally the most expensive although these companies do offer advantages such as airport pick-up and drop-off points, frequent flyer points and long-distance one-way rentals.

The standard insurance cover that comes with most car rental companies requires that you pay an excess of around $2000 before the insurance company pays out. Rental car companies will try and sell you insurance to cover this excess, but at around $20 a day this is overpriced and can substantially increase the cost of your car rental. A much better idea is to take out travel insurance that covers this excess or arrange rental car excess insurance before leaving home. This works out a lot cheaper than paying the excess cover that rental car companies charge.

Car rental companies include:

Avis
220 William Street, Kings Cross.
🚇 *Kings Cross.*
☎ *(02) 9357 2000.*
Website www.avis.com/au/

Budget
93 William Street, East Sydney.
🚇 *Kings Cross, Museum.*
☎ *(02) 8255 9600*
Website www.budget.com.au

Delta Europcar
77-83 William Street, East Sydney.
🚇 *Museum.*
☎ *1800 626 186.*
Website www.deltaeuropcar.com.au

Hertz
Corner Riley & William Streets, East Sydney.
🚇 *Museum.*

☎ *13 30 39*
Website www.hertz.com.au.

Thrifty
75 William Street, East Sydney.
🚇 *Museum.*
☎ *1300 367 227.*
Website www.thrifty.com.au.

Renting a Campervan

Campervans are a popular alternative to a rental car since they give you somewhere to stay. However they are more expensive than regular car rental and you'll often have to pay to stay in a caravan park so you can have a shower.

Because you spend a lot of time sleeping in your campervan, you generally miss out on being part of the backpacker scene.

Several companies that rent fully equipped campervans complete with camping gear and prices are quite reasonable for longer rentals. Campervan rental companies include:

Backpacker Campervans
653 Gardeners Road, Mascot, NSW.
☎ *(02) 9667 0402*
Website www.backpackercampervans.com

Britz
9 Ashley Street, Braybrook, VIC
☎ *(03) 8379 8890*
Website www.britz.com.au

Integra
☎ *1800 067 414*
Website www.integracampervan.com.au

NQ
96-102 Princes Highway, Arncliffe, NSW.
🚇 *Arncliffe*
☎ *1800 079 529.*
Website www.nqrentals.com.au

Travellers Autobarn
177 William Street, Kings Cross, NSW.
🚇 *Kings Cross.*
☎ *1800 674 374.*
Website www.travellersautobarn.com.au

Wicked Campers
79 McLachlan Street, Fortitude Valley, Brisbane.

🅿 *Brunswick Street.*
☎ *1800 246 869.*
Website *www.wickedcampers.com.au.*

Buying a car

If you're going to be travelling around Australia for several months it may be worth the trouble to buy your own car and sell it before you leave. Cheap reliable cars are generally large cars such as the Ford Falcon and Holden Commodore, which can cost a lot to run but are generally cheap to fix and service.

Ideally it's a good idea to check hostel notice boards and buy your car from another traveller as it may come with camping equipment and you should be able to get a good bargain, considering that other travellers have a flight home to catch and are in a hurry to sell. Other good places to look are the classified ads in Friday's *Sydney Morning Herald* and *Herald Sun* (Melbourne) and Saturday's *the Age* (Melbourne). *The Trading Post* is also a good spot to find a bargain. Buying a car privately, either from another traveller or through classified advertisements is usually the cheapest option, although it's not always the best choice if your time is limited. Buying from a used car dealer is easier and the dealer will organise the paperwork to get the car transferred into your name. There are loads of used car dealers in the suburbs of the big cities.

Some car dealers that do a lot of business with backpackers offer a buy-back guarantee, where they offer to buy the car back from you at an agreed (lower) price at the end of your trip. You can usually get a much better price selling the car yourself although a buy-back guarantee is handy if you don't want to waste precious time trying to sell the car when you have finished with it. If you buy from a car dealer that offers a buy-back guarantee, read the fine print and make sure that you are not required to pass a roadworthy inspection. Very few vehicles can pass a roadworthy after a trip around Australia and a buy-back guarantee with this condition is virtually worthless. The biggest of the car dealers that offer a buy-back guarantee is Travellers Autobarn (☎ *1800 674 374; website www.travellersautobarn.com.au).*

Used cars need a certificate of roadworthiness before they can be sold – don't buy a car without one as you'll need to show it when you transfer the registration. You will also need to get a certificate of roadworthiness before you sell the car at the end of your trip. Many mechanics can assess your car and issue the certificate.

Once you have a roadworthiness certificate, take it along with the receipt, your driver's licence and passport to the local department of transport; this department is known by different names in different states (refer to the list at the end of this paragraph). You will need to pay a fee, which is calculated according to the value of the car. If the annual vehicle registration is due, or if you are buying a car in a different state to which it is registered, this will also need to be paid. The registration (or rego) includes the minimum legal third-party insurance. You can count on these fees running to several hundred dollars. Each state's laws vary, check with the department of transport in the state where you plan on buying or selling your car.

Department of Transport & Works (Northern Territory)
Cavenagh Street, Darwin.
☎ *(08) 8924 7296*
Website *www.nt.gov.au/dtw/aboutus/ branches/transport/roadtransport/*

DIER – Transport Division (Tasmania)
134 Macquarie Street, Hobart
☎ *13 11 05*
Website *www.transport.tas.gov.au*

RTA (New South Wales)
Centennial Plaza Motor Registry, Ground Floor, Centennial Plaza, 260 Elizabeth Street, Sydney.
🚇 *Central.*
☎ *13 22 13.*
Website *www.rta.nsw.gov.au*

Transport Queensland
229 Elizabeth Street, Brisbane.
☎ *13 23 80.*
Website *www.transport.qld.gov.au/ driving*

Transport Roads & Traffic (Australian Capital Territory)
Dickson Motor Registry, 13-15 Challis Street, Dickson.
☎ *(02) 6207 7000.*
Website *www.canberraconnect.act. gov.au.*

Transport SA (South Australia)
Ground Floor, EDS Centre, 108 North Terrace, Adelaide.
☎ *13 10 84.*
Website *www.transport.sa.gov.au/rls/.*

Transport Western Australia
13 Wickham Street, East Perth
☎ *13 11 56.*
Website *www.transport.wa.gov.au/ licensing/.*

VicRoads (Victoria)
459 Lygon Street, Carlton
☎ *13 11 71.*
Website *www.vicroads.vic.gov.au.*

Hitchhiking

Hitchhiking is a great way to travel that allows you to really get to know the locals. Many people prefer hitching to other forms of transport because it you can get dropped off anywhere, allowing you to discover places you may never have dreamt of visiting.

Unfortunately hitchhiking gets a lot of bad press, particularly since the widely publicised hitchhiker murders several years ago. It seems that there are a lot of people who think that you'll get murdered if you hitch. This attitude has two negative effects – people are too frightened to pick you up and a lot of other travellers are scared to hitchhike meaning less hitchers on the road, which ultimately leads to hitchhiking becoming a dying art.

Where to hitch

It is important to choose a good spot to hitchhike. A good spot makes it easier to get a ride and more importantly it is safer for both you and the driver.

If you are leaving a big city it is a good idea to take a bus or train to the outskirts of town to get to a road lead-ing to a motorway and then choose a spot with plenty of room for the driver to safely stop. If possible try and stand in a spot where the traffic isn't too fast. It is much safer and also most drivers want to size you up before they decide whether to give you a lift.

If you've got a lift on a motorway, try and get dropped off at a service area rather than in town. If you're dropped off in town you have to wait hours in local traffic before getting a lift back on to the motorway. If you hitch at a service area you have facilities like a restaurant, shop and toilets; you can chat to truck drivers and ask about getting a lift and you can get a good safe spot to stand where all the traffic is long distance.

Don't hitchhike on motorways, stick to the entrance ramps and service areas. Not only is hitching on motorways dangerous, it is difficult for cars to safely stop and in most places it is illegal.

Signs

A lot of hitchers debate whether to use signs or not. Some argue that drivers won't stop if they don't know where you want to go, while other hitchers say that it is safer to avoid using a sign. If you don't use a sign you can ask the driver where they are going before accepting a lift – the driver won't be able to lie about his destination to get you into the car.

A good compromise is to use a sign indicating the name of the road you want to travel on. This is especially useful if you are on a busy road before a major intersection, without a sign you may get a lift going in the wrong direction.

Tips for getting a ride

You'll find a lot of rides come from regular stoppers – people who've hitchhiked themselves and are repaying the favour and frequent solo travellers, like couriers and truck drivers who want some company. Although you'll find that different people have different reasons for picking you up, there are a number of things you can do to improve your chances of getting a lift.

- Look neat and respectable. Not only should you look non-threatening to any passing driver, but you also help to improve other people's impression of hitchhiking.
- Face the oncoming traffic and smile. It is important that people can see you, so avoid wearing sunglasses.
- Try and look smart and clean.
- When a car stops ask the driver where they are going to. At this point it is easy to decline the lift if you don't like the look of the driver or if they aren't going your way.
- Never smoke in someone else's car.
- Travel light. The lighter your load, the quicker you travel.
- Take an international drivers licence. Many people stop because they want someone to share the driving.

Safety

Although hitchhiking is more hazardous than bus or train travel, it's still safer than other forms of transport such as cycling.

The most dangerous thing about hitchhiking is the possibility of being involved in a car accident or being hit by a car if you stand too close to the side of the road.

There is also a very small danger posed by accepting a lift with a driver that you do not know. The driver could either be a dangerous character or simply a bad driver.

Despite the perceived danger, there are plenty of ways to minimise your risk.

If you're a single female you'll travel quickly, however you'll also attract your fair share of obnoxious drivers. It is a good idea to travel with someone else, preferably a guy. This way you will be perceived as a couple which means that you shouldn't have any sleazy old men trying to come on to you, and if they do at least there is someone to help you out.

Many hitchhikers travel with a mobile phone and only hitch where there is coverage. Being able to call for help makes hitching a safer transport option. For this to work you need to keep your phone charged and in your pocket and you need to know the emergency number (112 is the international emergency number from GSM mobile phones, although the Australian emergency number 000 also works on many networks).

Don't let the driver put your backpack in the car boot. Try and keep all your stuff with you, even when you stop for food and fuel.

Don't feel compelled to accept a lift just because someone has stopped for you. If it doesn't feel right, don't get in. Another ride will come along.

Ride sharing

Ride sharing agencies are a good alternative to hitchhiking. These agencies act as a matchmaker between drivers and riders and cost around half what the bus fare would be.

Ride sharing agencies aren't as common in Australia as they are in Europe, however you can log on to BUG Ride (*website http://australia. bugride.com*). This is BUG's own Internet-based ride sharing agency where you can offer lifts to other travellers or search for a lift. The lift is often free although it's also common to split fuel expenses with the driver.

Australian Capital Territory

While Australia's state capitals owe their existence to Britain, convicts, trade, defence or simple geography, Canberra owes its origin to political necessity. It was created because Australia decided, soon after it became a unified nation in 1901, that it needed an independent capital free from political or commercial domination by any one state.

New South Wales and Victoria (always strong rivals) were jockeying at the time for the privilege of housing Federal Parliament. NSW favoured Sydney; Victoria preferred Melbourne. An independently sited capital, surrounded by a neutral buffer zone, was the logical, diplomatic solution. The Australian Capital Territory (ACT) was established in 1911 as an administrative territory to encompass Australia's proposed new capital.

The ACT is surrounded entirely by New South Wales.

Canberra

Canberra is a modern city – there is no old quarter and few restored buildings. The city was designed by Chicago architect Walter Burley Griffin, who submitted the design without visiting the site. Burley Griffin planned that his creation should blend with nature rather than imposing itself on the landscape.

Canberra is often overlooked by many backpackers, bypassing the capital in favour of more exciting destinations. Although the city doesn't have much charm or atmosphere, there are a lot of things to see.

In 1988, Canberra's main landmark – Parliament House – opened, replacing an earlier building dating from 1927. Other attractions include the Australian War Memorial, the High Court, National Gallery of Australia, Old Parliament House and the new National Museum of Australia.

Practical Information
INFORMATION CENTRES & USEFUL ADDRESSES
Canberra Tourism
330 Northbourne Avenue, Canberra.
🚌 *30, 31, 32, 39, 50, 80*
☎ *(02) 6205 0044 or 1300 554 114*
Website www.canberratourism.com.au
Open Mon-Fri 9am-5.30pm, Sat-Sun 9am-4pm

American Express
Shop 1, Centrepoint, 185 City Walk, Canberra.
🚌 *All buses.*
☎ *(02) 6247 2333*
Website www.americanexpress.com
Open Mon-Fri 9am-5pm, Sat 9am-noon

EMBASSIES & CONSULATES
British Embassy
Level 10, SAP House, Corner Akuna & Bunda Streets, Canberra.
🚌 *All buses.*
☎ *(02) 6270 6666.*
Website www.uk.emb.gov.au.
Open Mon-Fri 9am-3pm.

Canadian Embassy
Commonwealth Avenue, Yarralumba.
🚌 *29, 31, 32.*
☎ *(02) 6270 4000.*
Open Mon-Fri 8.30am-12.30pm & 1pm-4.30pm.

Irish Embassy
20 Arkana Street, Yarralumba.
🚌 *29, 31, 32.*
☎ *(02) 6273 3022.*
Open Mon-Fri 9.30am-12.45pm & 2pm-4pm.

New Zealand High Commission
Commonwealth Avenue, Yarralumba.
🚌 *29, 31, 32.*
☎ *(02) 6270 4211.*
Open Mon-Fri 8.45am-5pm.

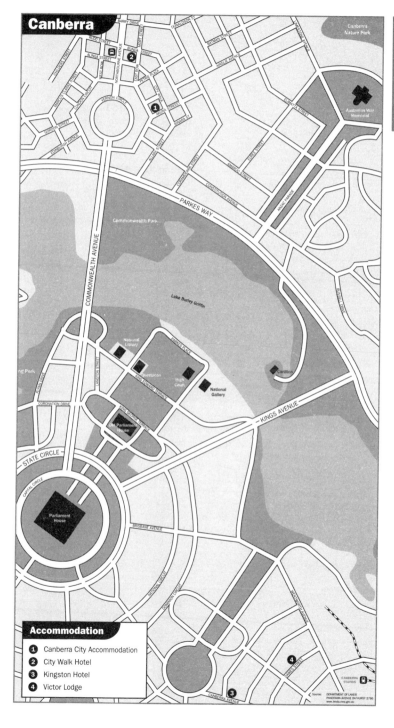

Canberra

ACT

Accommodation

1. Canberra City Accommodation
2. City Walk Hotel
3. Kingston Hotel
4. Victor Lodge

Source: DEPARTMENT OF LANDS
PANORAMA AVENUE BATHURST 2795
www.lands.nsw.gov.au

ACT

South African Embassy
Corner Rhodes Place & State Circle,
Yarralumba.
🚌 *29, 31, 32.*
☎ *(02) 6273 2424.*
Website www.rsa.emb.gov.au.
Open Mon-Fri 8.30am-1pm.

USA Embassy
1 Moonah Place, Yarralumba.
🚌 *29, 31, 32.*
☎ *(02) 6214 5600.*
Website www.usis-australia.gov.
Open Mon-Fri 8am-5pm.

Coming & Going
AIR
Canberra's airport (☎ *(02) 6275 2236; website www.canberraairport. com.au)* has frequent flights to most major Australian destinations although backpackers rarely use it.

The airport is located 7km east of the city centre and is served by an airport shuttle bus operated by Deane's Bus Lines (☎ *(02) 6299 3722; website www. deanesbuslines.com.au)*, which costs $5 each way.

BUS
Buses terminate at the Jolimont Transit Centre at 65-57 Northbourne Avenue. There are direct buses to Adelaide, Melbourne, Sydney and country destinations in New South Wales including the ski resorts in the Snowy Mountains.

TRAIN
Trains between Canberra and Sydney use the train station on Wentworth Avenue in Kingston. Buses 39, 80, 83 and 84 run between the station and the city centre.

HITCHHIKING
There are a few good hitching spots that are relatively easy to get to by public transport. It is usually not too difficult to get a lift out of Canberra.

Northbourne Avenue runs north from the city centre and splits into the Barton and Federal Highways that join the Hume Freeway, which runs between Melbourne and Sydney. Hitching from Canberra is best on one of these two roads.

If you're heading to Melbourne, it's best to get to the Barton Highway, which meets the Hume Freeway near Yass. Buses 51, 52, 56, 251, 252 or 253 take you to where the Barton Highway branches off from Northbourne Avenue.

The Federal Highway is your best bet for a lift to Sydney. This road joins the Hume Highway near Goulburn. Take bus 36 to get to the Federal Highway.

Local Transport
Canberra is a sprawling city and most attractions are spaced too far apart for walking to be a practical option. You're best off with a car or bicycle although Canberra has an extensive bus network.

Canberra's buses, run by ACTION (☎ *13 17 10; website www.action.act. gov.au)*, provide a good coverage of the city although the frequency of the services makes it a time consuming way to get around.

A single bus ride costs $2.40. Ask the driver for a transfer ticket if you need to transfer to another bus route; transfer tickets cost no more than regular tickets and allow you to change to other bus routes within a one-hour period. Ten-ride tickets are available from newsagents for $21 and weekly passes cost $23.50. Day passes are available on board buses or from newsagents for $6 or $3.50 for off-peak travel (Mon-Fri 9am-4.30pm & after 6pm, Sat-Sun all day).

Accommodation
Canberra City Accommodation
Canberra City Accommodation is a big well-appointed and centrally located hostel. Facilities include a fully equipped kitchen and several TV lounges plus a lot of things you wouldn't expect in a city centre hostel like a swimming pool, spa, sauna and gymnasium. Each floor has a lounge area with a TV and the whole place is air-conditioned and there is wheelchair access to most parts of the hostel (even to the swimming pool). Although parts of the hostel feel a little sterile, the atmosphere is as good as you can expect from a big 350-bed hostel in Canberra.

ACT

7 Akuna Street, Canberra.
All buses.
☎ (02) 6229 0888 or 1800 300 488.
Website www.canberrabackpackers.
com.au.
Dorm bed $22-26; **single room** $55;
double room $80; **twin room** $70.
Credit cards MC, Visa.
Reception open 24 hours.

Maintenance & cleanliness	★★★★★
Facilities	★★★★⯪
Atmosphere & character	★⯪
Security	★★★★
Overall rating	★★★★

Canberra YHA
This is a well-equipped hostel with a nice balcony overlooking the car park. There is a huge kitchen as well as a pool table, Internet access and a TV lounge. Groups are kept separated from backpackers and are usually checked into the older building, which has more atmosphere than the main building. The hostel is on a quiet suburban street away from the city centre.
191 Dryandra Street, Canberra.
35.
☎ (02) 6248 9155.
Dorm bed $23.50-25.50 ($20-22 YHA); **double/twin room** $63-71 ($56-64 YHA).
Credit cards MC, Visa.
Reception open 7am-10pm daily.

Maintenance & cleanliness	★★★★⯪
Facilities	★★⯪
Atmosphere & character	★★⯪
Security	★★
Overall rating	★★★

City Walk Hotel
This budget hotel in the city centre has some dormitories for backpackers. The TV room feels very institutional and alcohol is not allowed here and it lacks atmosphere, even by Canberra's standards.
2 Mort Street, Canberra.
All buses.
☎ (02) 6257 0124.
Website www.citywalkhotel.citysearch.
com.au.
Dorm bed $22-24; **single room** $70;
double/twin room $60-80.

Credit cards MC, Visa.
Reception open Mon-Sat 8am-10pm;
Sun 8am-8pm.

Maintenance & cleanliness	★★⯪
Facilities	★
Atmosphere & character	-
Security	★★
Overall rating	★★⯪

Kingston Hotel
This big suburban pub offers basic backpackers accommodation. Facilities are very limited and the only shared area is the very basic kitchen. It is relatively close to the train station.
73 Canberra Avenue, Kingston.
39, 83, 84.
☎ (02) 6295 0123.
Dorm bed 16.50-22.50.
Reception open 8am-midnight.

Maintenance & cleanliness	★★⯪
Facilities	★
Atmosphere & character	★
Security	★⯪
Overall rating	★⯪

Victor Lodge
Victor Lodge is a good accommodation option. It is clean with good facilities that include a kitchen, TV lounge and Internet access. They provide a good buffet breakfast. It has a quiet location on a residential street between the train station and the new Parliament House. The Kingston shops, which include pubs, cafés and restaurants, are just behind the hostel.
29 Dawes Street, Kingston.
39, 83, 84.
☎ (02) 6295 7777.
Dorm bed $23 ($22 VIP); **single room** $49 ($48 VIP); **double/twin room** $65 ($63 VIP).
Credit cards MC, Visa.
Reception open 7.30am-9.30pm daily.

Maintenance & cleanliness	★★★★
Facilities	★★
Atmosphere & character	★⯪
Security	★⯪
Overall rating	★★★⯪

Eating & Drinking
Although Canberra has a reasonably good restaurant scene for such a small

city, most of the really good restaurants cater to diplomats and politicians. There are some budget dining options in the city centre including several fast food places, but your best option is to prepare a picnic lunch to eat in one of the city's parks.

There's a good fresh food market and a big Supabarn supermarket on Bunda Street in the city centre.

Sights
NORTH OF LAKE BURLEY GRIFFIN

The area north of Lake Burley Griffin is home to the city centre, the War Memorial and the city's main lookouts.

Australian War Memorial

This is the most impressive of Australia's many war memorials. The memorial is home to a small museum with exhibits on Australia's military involvement.
Anzac Parade, Reid.
🚌 *33, 40.*
☎ *(02) 6243 4211.*
Website www.awm.gov.au.
Admission free.
Open 10am-5pm daily.

Canberra Museum & Gallery

This museum has displays on the city's history and cultural diversity.
Corner Civic Square & London Circuit, Canberra.
🚌 *all buses.*
☎ *(02) 6207 3968.*
Website www.museumsandgalleries.act. gov.au/museum/.
Admission free.
Open Jan-May Tue-Thu 10am-5pm, Fri 10am-7pm, Sat-Sun noon-5pm; Jun-Aug Tue-Fri 10am-5pm, Sat-Sun noon-4pm; Sep-Dec Tue-Thu 10am-5pm, Fri 10am-7pm, Sat-Sun noon-5pm.

Discovery

Discovery is a science museum showcasing the CSIRO's achievements in science and technology. The complex includes working science laboratories where visitors can view research in progress.
North Science Road at CSIRO Black Mountain laboratories, Clunies Ross Street, Canberra.
🚌 *34.*
☎ *(02) 6243 4646.*

Admission $6.
Open Mon-Fri 9am-5pm.

Mt Ainslie

This hill behind the War Memorial offers great views of the city. It is accessible via walking tracks from the War Memorial.

National Capital Exhibition

The National Capital Exhibition is a small museum showing the planning, construction and growth of the city. This should be the first thing you see in Canberra as it gives you a good understanding of how the city is laid out.
Regatta Point, Commonwealth Park.
🚌 *any Intertown route.*
☎ *(02) 6257 1068.*
Admission free.
Open 9am-5pm daily.

National Museum of Australia

The new National Museum of Australia features a variety of exhibits on Australian culture with a significant part of the Museum devoted to the history, culture and contemporary issues of Australia's Aboriginal and Torres Strait Islander peoples. The Museum is located on Acton Peninsula with views across Lake Burley Griffin.
Acton Peninsula, Acton.
🚌 *34.*
☎ *(02) 6208 5000.*
Website www.nma.gov.au.
Admission free, charge for special exhibits.
Open 9am-5pm daily.

National Zoo & Aquarium

Canberra's small zoo has a good selection of Australian and African wildlife including the world's only walk-through puma cave and Australia's only tigons (a cross between a lion and tiger).
Lady Denham Drive, Scrivener Dam.
☎ *(02) 6287 1211.*
Website www.zooquarium.com.au.
Admission $18.50, students $15.50.
Open 9am-5.30pm daily.

Screensound Australia

ScreenSound Australia, the National Film and Sound Archive, is located

ACT

on the campus of the Australian National University. Set in a beautiful Art Deco building, it includes much of the nation's film, radio and television history, including recordings of many early programmes.
McCoy Circuit, Acton.
🚌 *34.*
☎ *(02) 6248 2000.*
Website www.screensound.gov.au.
Admission free
Open Mon-Fri 9am-5pm, Sat-Sun 10am-5pm.

Telstra Tower (Black Mountain)
The Telstra Tower at the summit of Black Mountain offers fantastic views of the city.
Black Mountain.
☎ *1800 806 718.*
Admission $3.30.
Open 9am-10pm daily.

SOUTH OF LAKE BURLEY GRIFFIN
The area immediately south of Lake Burley Griffin is an area known as the Parliamentary Triangle. This area contains many of Canberra's most important buildings including the new and old Parliament Houses as well as the High Court, National Gallery and National Library. Heading further south takes you through Yarralumba, where many of the embassies are located.

High Court of Australia
The High Court of Australia is the pinnacle of Australia's legal system. The building is modern architecture at its most daring. It has been branded an architectural monstrosity, and Gar's Mahal after former Chief Justice Sir Garfield Barwick who presided over its opening. A dramatic interior features a public hall that's seven stories high.
King Edward Terrace, Parkes.
🚌 *34.*
☎ *(02) 6270 6811.*
Website www.hcourt.gov.au.
Admission free.
Open Mon-Fri 9.45am-4.30pm.

National Gallery of Australia
Canberra's National Gallery houses Australia's most extensive art collec-

tion. The collection is eclectic enough to span Aboriginal masterpieces, Monet's *Water Lilies* and Jackson Pollock's *Blue Poles.*
King Edward Terrace, Parkes.
🚌 *30, 34.*
☎ *(02) 6240 6411.*
Website www.nga.gov.au.
Admission free.
Open 10am-5pm daily.

National Library of Australia
The National Library aims to hold copies of everything published either in or about Australia. The library is adding to its collection at the rate of 500 items every day.
King Edward Terrace, Parkes.
🚌 *31, 34, 36, 39.*
☎ *(02) 6262 1156.*
Admission free.
Open Mon-Thu 9am-9pm, Fri-Sat 9am-5pm, Sun 1.30pm-5pm.

Old Parliament House
Situated in front of the new Parliament House, is a more traditional building that was originally built as a temporary structure and served as Australia's seat of government from 1927 until 1988. The building now houses the National Portrait Gallery, the Australian Archives Gallery and a museum chronicling Australia's political history.
King George Terrace, Parkes.
🚌 *31, 34, 36, 39.*
☎ *(02) 6270 8222.*
Website www.dcita.gov.au/oph.html & www.portrait.gov.au.
Admission $2.
Open 9am-5pm daily; tours 9.30am, 10.15am, 11am, 11.45am, 12.45pm, 1.30pm, 2.30pm, 3.15pm.

Parliament House
An 81m flag mast that has become the city's major landmark crowns Parliament House. Visitors can join a guided tour, stroll through its public galleries, walk around its striking exterior – or roll down the grassy slopes that are part of its design. You can watch a session of parliament, if it is sitting. This enormous building took half a century to conceive and a decade to build.
Capital Hill, Parkes.

ACT

📷 *31, 34, 39.*
☎ *(02) 6277 5399.*
Website www.aph.gov.au.
Admission free.
Open 9am-5pm daily; tours every 30 minutes.

Questacon

This excellent hands-on science museum has a lot of exhibits geared towards kids.
King Edward Terrace, Parkes.
📷 *34.*
☎ *02) 6270 2800.*
Website www.questacon.edu.au.

Admission $10.
Open 10am-5pm daily.

Royal Australian Mint

This is where most coins are minted and offers fascinating tours where you can see money being made.
Denison Street, Deakin.
📷 *30, 31, 32.*
☎ *(02) 6202 6999.*
Website www.ramint.gov.au.
Admission free.
Open Mon-Fri 9am-4pm, Sat-Sun 10am-4pm but you can only see coins being produced on weekday afternoons.

Traveller's Contact Point
Level 7, The Dymocks building, 428 George Street, Sydney.
🚇 *Park Plaza;* 🚇 *Town Hall.*
☎ *(02) 9221 8744.*
Website www.travellers.com.au.
Open Mon-Fri 9am-6pm, Sat 10am-4pm.

Well Connected Cafe
35 Glebe Point Road, Glebe.
🚌 *431, 432, 433, 434; T Glebe.*
☎ *(02) 9566 2655*
Open Mon-Fri 7am-midnight, Sat-Sun 8am-7.30pm.

Coming & Going

Sydney is the country's main international gateway and has good transport connections with destinations around Australia. The city has a thriving backpacker scene and several travel agents that cater to backpackers who should be able to fix you up with cheap bus or train passes.

AIR

Sydney is a good spot to get a cheap domestic flight up and down the coast with good deals to Brisbane and Melbourne. Check billboards and local papers for the latest specials.

Sydney Airport (☎ *(02) 9667 9111; website www.sydneyairport.com.au)* is located about 8 km south of the city centre and is easily accessible by train from Central Station. The airport is split into domestic and international terminals that are located several kilometres apart. The international terminal is all contained in one building, while the domestic terminal is comprised of separate buildings that are used for Qantas, Rex and Virgin Blue flights.

The easiest way to the airport is the new Airport train line *(website www.airportlink.com.au)* that whisks you to the airport in around ten minutes. Trains leave from Central Station and less frequently from other stations on the City Circle line. The one-way fare from the Domestic Terminal to Central Station or Kings Cross is $11; one-way fares from the International Terminal are $10.60 to Central Station and $11.80 to Kings Cross.

You can combine your airport train ticket with a Day Tripper or TravelPass ticket, which works out considerably cheaper than buying the tickets separately. A Day Tripper with a single airport station access costs $23.80 and allows you to travel to most parts of the city. A Red weekly TravelPass with single airport access costs $40.80 or $44.50 with return airport access and a Green weekly TravelPass with single airport access is $48.80 or $52.50 with return airport access.

Bus route 400 connects the airport with Bondi Junction station. This is the cheapest way to and from the airport and is handy if you're staying at Bondi Beach.

BUS

Sydney has good bus connections to the rest of the country with the majority of buses departing from Eddy Avenue near Central Station.

TRAIN

Central Station is Sydney's hub for train travel with long-distance services departing upstairs from the bus station in front of the SLR tram stop. The station has all the facilities that you would expect including bars, shops, fast food outlets and lockers.

Countrylink and CityRail both offer intercity train services although CityRail's network extends only as far south as Goulburn and Nowra, west to the Blue Mountains and north to Newcastle and Scone. Countrylink goes further afield within New South Wales and also runs a few interstate services. Really long-distance train journeys are operated by Great Southern Railway and include the *Indian Pacific* to Perth (via Broken Hill and Adelaide) and *the Ghan* to Alice Springs and Darwin (also via Broken Hill and Adelaide).

HITCHHIKING

There are a few good hitching spots that are relatively easy to get to by public transport. However it can take a while to hitch a lift out of town because there is so much local traffic.

There are motorways leaving Sydney to the north, south and west although they don't go all the way into the city centre, which means there are some good hitchhiking spots right before the motorway entrance with a lot of long-distance traffic. These roads also carry a lot of local traffic so you'll need a sign indicating that you're looking for a longer ride.

The Sydney-Newcastle Freeway goes to Newcastle and also has a lot of traffic heading further up the coast and towards Queensland. Take the train to Wahroonga (on the North Shore line), walk down Coonanbarra Road and take the footbridge across the Pacific Highway and wait in front of the Abbotsleigh School for a lift. Use a sign with either your destination or North written on it.

There are a couple of options heading south to Melbourne. The Hume Highway is the easiest and quickest option while the more scenic coastal route via Wollongong may take you a little longer but there is plenty to see en route.

For the Hume Highway, take a train to Beverly Hills and walk up King Georges Road to the start of the South Western Motorway. This road gets a lot of local traffic so you'll need a sign.

Because there is less local traffic it may be easier to get a lift on the coastal route to Melbourne, although it will be a longer trip. There are a couple of good hitching spots accessible by train. The cheapest is to take the train to either Heathcote or Waterfall (on the Illawarra line) and try your luck on the Princes Highway before the motorway begins. Alternatively you can take the train further south to Berry and completely bypass Wollongong and all the local traffic between Sydney and Wollongong. This will cost you a bit more than hitching at the northern end of the motorway, although you'll be on a regular road rather than a motorway and will have a better choice of spots to wait for a lift and if you have no luck, at least Berry is a nice town to get stranded in.

If you're heading west, you'll want to get on Parramatta Road before the start of the Western Motorway. Take the train to Strathfield, walk up Mosely Street and try your luck. You could also try Parramatta Road closer to the city centre although you'll have a longer wait, as there will be more local traffic. In any case you'll need a destination sign to avoid shorter lifts.

An easier option is to use a web-based ride sharing service such as BUG Ride (*website* http://australia.bugride.com), which allows travellers to both offer lifts and search for rides throughout Australia.

Local Transport

Sydney has an extensive transport network comprised of buses, trains, ferries, monorail and a tram. It is pretty easy to get around the city on public transport although it's an expensive system if you don't have a weekly TravelPass.

TRAIN

CityRail (☎ *13 15 00 Transport Infoline; website* www.cityrail.info) is Sydney's comprehensive suburban train network, which has a good coverage of the western suburbs and the city centre. Most travellers use the Airport, City Circle and Eastern Suburbs lines, which run mostly underground and connect the city centre to Bondi Junction and the airport.

Four stations on the Airport Line (*website* www.airportlink.com.au) are not run by CityRail and require either an individual ticket or payment of a GatePass (station access fee). A GatePass costs $8.80 for the Domestic and International airport terminals and $1.80 for Green Square and Mascot stations. It is possible to buy a weekly GatePass or a DayTripper or TravelPass with the GatePass included.

At around $2.20 for a ride in the city centre and increasing to $4 for the short hop between the domestic and international airport terminals it can be an expensive way to get around if you don't buy a CityHopper, DayTripper or a weekly TravelPass. See the facing page for more information on fares.

BUS

Sydney's buses (☎ *13 15 00 Transport Infoline; website* www.sydneybuses.nsw .gov.au) are a handy way to get to all the spots not covered by the train network, which includes most of Sydney's beaches and some neighbourhoods in the inner west such as Balmain and Glebe. Although traffic can hold them up, buses run frequently and are generally a reliable way to get around.

Bus fares are calculated by distance. The cheapest bus fare is $1.60 and the most expensive is $4.80. Most of the bus routes popular with travellers cost $2.70.

There are also the Bondi and Sydney Explorer buses that are operated specifically for tourists and run a circuit between the main sights. Forget about these, they're way overpriced at $30 for a day pass – it's cheaper to buy a weekly TravelPass.

FERRY

Sydney's ferries are the nicest way to get around and a cheaper alternative to the touristy harbour cruises. All ferries terminate at Circular Quay in the city centre with frequent departures to destinations around the harbour. Most ferries depart at half-hourly intervals.

Ferry fares start at $4.50 for a short hop in the inner harbour and increase to $7.50 for the JetCat to Manly. The most popular ferry route with travellers is the Manly ferry, which costs $5.80 each way.

MONORAIL

The monorail (*website www.metromonorail.com.au*) looks cool and runs right through the city centre, but it is almost completely useless as a way to get around. It runs a circular route in only one direction taking in Pitt Street, Chinatown and Darling Harbour. It is good fun to take a joy ride around the city, but the $4 fare is a bit overpriced considering you can walk between Pitt Street and Darling Harbour in about 10 minutes.

The monorail is not included in any TravelPass ticket but you can buy a day pass for $9.

TRAM (LIGHT RAIL)

Sydney's light rail is a tram route designed to complement the monorail. However it is a much more useful transport option than the monorail as

it actually goes somewhere. The route starts right outside Central Station and trams run through Chinatown, Darling Harbour, Pyrmont, Glebe and Rozelle Bay to Lilyfield. The Glebe and Jubilee Park stops are handy for travellers staying at hostels in the Glebe area.

The tram is quite expensive compared to the bus with fares ranging from $2.80 to $3.80. Day passes cost $8.40 but the $20 weekly pass is better value. The Sydney Light Rail (SLR) tram is not included in any TravelPass ticket.

MULTIPLE TRIP TICKETS

Multiple trip tickets are a good deal if you're staying in Sydney for a while, but don't travel regularly enough on public transport to get value from a weekly TravelPass.

Various multiple trip tickets include:

TravelTen

The TravelTen pass is valid for ten bus trips. There is a colour coded range of TravelTen passes based on the number of sections travelled. Prices range from $11.80 for a Blue TravelTen that allows ten short trips of up to two sections to $41.80 for an Orange TravelTen for ten long trips of 16 sections or more. The Brown TravelTen pass is probably the most useful for most travellers and is good for ten rides of three to five sections, which is basically ten trips between Glebe and the city centre. The Brown TravelTen costs $19.70 whereas ten separate bus tickets would cost you $27.

DAY PASSES

Although these aren't as good value as the weekly tickets, the limited range of day passes is worth considering if you're only in Sydney for a day or two. However if you're going to be in Sydney for more than two days, it is cheaper to buy a weekly Red or Green TravelPass.

The various day passes include:

CityHopper 🚃

This ticket is good for one day unlimited train travel between the 11 stations in the central Sydney area that is bounded by Kings Cross, North Sydney and Redfern. The CityHopper costs $6.80.

New South Wales

DayTripper 🚌🚊⛴

The DayTripper allows you to travel all day on buses, trains and ferries for $15. The area covered by this pass corresponds with that of the Purple TravelPass, but you need to pay a station access fee if you want to get off at stations on the Airport line.

A DayTripper is a good deal if you're only in Sydney for a day or two.

SydneyPass 🚌🚊⛴

This is the most extensive of the day passes but it is also priced out of reach of most budget travellers. It includes unlimited travel almost everywhere on buses, trains and ferries and includes the Bondi and Sydney Explorer buses and train stations on the Airport line.

A three-day SydneyPass costs a whopping $90, a five-day pass is $120.

TRAVELPASS TICKETS

There are a number of passes for regular commuters to bring down the otherwise high cost of travelling around Sydney. The TravelPass tickets are available in various configurations including bus only, bus & ferry and train, bus and ferry. The monorail and SLR tram are not covered by the TravelPass.

Most travellers will find the Red and Green TravelPasses the most useful although the Bus & Ferry and Bus only passes offer a slightly cheaper alternative. The various TravelPasses include:

Red TravelPass 🚌🚊⛴

This is probably the most handy pass. It allows travel on trains in the central area as far north as Chatswood, west to Croydon, Canterbury and Bardwell Park and south to Rockdale. It also allows travel on Sydney Buses in zones 1, 3, 6, & 7 which covers most of the nearby beaches including Bondi and Coogee. Travel on inner harbour ferries is also included, but you cannot take ferries as far afield as Manly or Parramatta. There is an extra charge for stations on the Airport line. A weekly Red TravelPass is $32.

Green TravelPass 🚌🚊⛴

This pass covers a slightly larger area than the red pass and is handy if you're staying in Manly. Train travel on this pass can go as far north as Chatswood or Epping, west to Lidcombe, Regents Park or Kingsgrove and south to Kogarah. You can travel on Sydney Buses in zones 1 to 8 and all ferries except the Manly JetCat. There is an extra charge for stations on the Airport line. A weekly Green TravelPass is $40.

Yellow TravelPass 🚌🚊⛴

This pass is similar to the Green Travel-Pass but you can take the train as far as Parramatta. A weekly Yellow Travel-Pass is $44.

Pink TravelPass 🚌🚊⛴

This pass is the same as the Yellow TravelPass but you can take the train as far as Liverpool, Seven Hills, Hornsby, Holsworthy, Engadine or Carringbah. A weekly Pink TravelPass is $47.

Purple TravelPass 🚌🚊⛴

This pass is good for unlimited train travel in the area bounded by Bondi Junction, Cowan, Carlingford, Richmond, Emu Plains, Macarthur, Otford, Cronulla and Olympic Park stations. It is also good for travel on all buses and ferries in zones 1 to 11 (except the Manly Jetcat before 7pm). A weekly Purple TravelPass is $54.

Blue TravelPass 🚌⛴

This pass allows travel on buses in zones 1, 3, 6 and 7 and inner harbour ferries. A weekly Blue TravelPass is $29.

Orange TravelPass 🚌⛴

This pass allows travel on buses in zones 1 to 8 and all ferries except the Manly JetCat. A weekly Orange TravelPass is $36.

Pittwater TravelPass 🚌⛴

This pass allows travel on buses in all zones and all ferries except the Manly JetCat. A weekly Pittwater TravelPass is $49.

Two Zone TravelPass 🚌

This pass allows travel on buses in two adjacent zones but is not valid in Zone 1. A weekly Two Zone TravelPass is $29.

Accommodation
BONDI
Bondi is the closest real beach to the city centre and it is a popular spot with travellers. The quickest way from the city centre is by train to Bondi Junction and then a connecting bus to the beach.

Biltmore on Bondi
The Biltmore is situated in an older building and there are obvious signs of decay. There aren't a lot of common facilities but there is a fridge and sink in every room. It's right across the road from the beach – the best located of the Bondi hostels.
110 Campbell Parade, Bondi Beach.
380, 381, 382, L82.
(02) 9130 4660.
Dorm bed *$17-25;* **double room** *$44-60;* **twin room** *$40-55; prices include breakfast.*
Credit cards *MC, Visa.*
Reception open *7.30am-12.30pm & 2.30pm-7.30pm daily.*

Maintenance & cleanliness	★
Facilities	★★
Atmosphere & character	★★★☆
Security	★★☆
Overall rating	★☆

Bondi Beach Guesthouse
The Bondi Beach Guesthouse consists of a ramshackle old house with a TV lounge and a tiny kitchen plus a small outdoor barbecue area. It caters mostly to long-term guests.
11 Consett Avenue, Bondi Beach.
380, 381, 382, L82.
(02) 9300 9310.
Dorm bed *$15-20;* **single room** *$30;* **double/twin room** *$40-50.*
Reception open *8am-7pm daily.*

Maintenance & cleanliness	★☆
Facilities	★
Atmosphere & character	★★★★☆
Security	★
Overall rating	★★

Bondi Beachouse YHA
Bondi's YHA hostel is in a big art deco building several blocks south of the beach. There's a good kitchen, several TV lounges, Internet access plus a rooftop deck with a spa and sweeping ocean views. Security is excellent with key card access and lockers in all dorms.
Corner Dellview & Fletcher Streets, Bondi.
380, 381, 382, L82.
(02) 9365 2088.
Dorm bed *$27;* **double room** *$70-80;* **family room** *$110-130.*
Reception open *7am-10pm daily.*

Maintenance & cleanliness	★★★★
Facilities	★★☆
Atmosphere & character	★★★★☆
Security	★★★★
Overall rating	★★★★☆

Indy's Bondi Beach Backpackers
Indy's Backpackers has a great vibe and it boasts the best atmosphere of Bondi's hostels. It features an outdoor area with a barbecue plus the usual kitchen and TV lounge with a big screen telly. Guests have free use of bicycles and body boards and surfboards are available to rent.
35A Hall Street, Bondi Beach.
380, 381, 382, L82.
(02) 9365 4900.
Dorm bed *$25 ($22 VIP/$23 YHA/$24 ISIC); price includes breakfast.*
Credit cards *Amex, Diners, MC, Visa.*
Reception open *Mon-Sat 7.30am-11am & 4pm-8pm, Sun 8am-11am.*

Maintenance & cleanliness	★★
Facilities	★★☆
Atmosphere & character	★★★★★☆
Security	★★☆
Overall rating	★★★

Lamrock Lodge
Lamrock Lodge is a clean hostel that is popular with surfers. There are loads of vending machines scattered throughout the hostel but there aren't many shared facilities. The atmosphere here could be better.
19 Lamrock Avenue, Bondi Beach.
380, 381, 382, L82.
(02) 9130 5063 or 1800 625 063.
Website *www.lamrocklodge.com.*
Dorm bed *$26.*

Maintenance & cleanliness	★★★
Facilities	★
Atmosphere & character	★★
Security	★★☆
Overall rating	★★

New South Wales

Noah's Bondi Beach

This is a good clean hostel with a good atmosphere. Facilities include the usual kitchen and TV lounge plus a rooftop terrace. All rooms have lockers and double/twin rooms also have a fridge and TV. It is the only hostel in Bondi with its own bar, which has happy hours and cheap food.
2 Campbell Parade, Bondi Beach.
▣ *380, 381, 382, L82.*
☎ *(02) 9365 7100.*
***Dorm bed** $22-25 ($21-14 VIP);*
***double room** $55-60 ($53-58 VIP);*
***twin room** $55 ($53 VIP).*
***Credit cards** MC, Visa.*
***Reception open** 24 hours.*

Maintenance & cleanliness	★★★
Facilities	★★☆
Atmosphere & character	★★★☆
Security	★★☆
Overall rating	★★★

CITY CENTRE & SURRY HILLS

The hostels in the city centre are close to all the action. There are also plenty of budget accommodation options in the quieter inner city neighbourhood of Surry Hills, which is located near Central Station.

Alfred Park Accommodation

This is a quiet place that appeals more to couples, families and backpackers looking for a bit of privacy. Facilities include a kitchen, Internet access and a big courtyard. All rooms have a TV and fridge and some of the dormitories have an en suite. It's located across the road from Prince Alfred Park, south of Central Station.
207 Cleveland Street, Strawberry Hills.
▣ *352, 372, 393, 395;* ▣ *Central, Redfern.*
☎ *(02) 9319 4031.*
***Website** www.g-day.com.au.*
***Dorm bed** $22-25;* ***double room** $80-90.*
***Credit cards** MC, Visa.*
***Reception open** 7.30am-10pm daily.*
▣

Maintenance & cleanliness	★★★
Facilities	★
Atmosphere & character	★★☆
Security	★★
Overall rating	★★

Big on Elizabeth

This big modern hostel is clean with good quality fittings. Amenities include a fully equipped kitchen and a TV lounge with a big screen projection TV.
212 Elizabeth Street, Sydney.
▣ *308, 309, 310, 311, 339, 343, 372, 378, 393, 395;* ▣ *Central;* ▣ *Central.*
☎ *(02) 9281 6030 or 1800 212 244.*
***Website** www.bigonelizabeth.com.*
Dorm bed** $25-34;* ***single room** $72;
***double room** $92; includes breakfast.*
***Credit cards** MC, Visa.*
***Reception open** 24 hours.*

Maintenance & cleanliness	★★★★☆
Facilities	★★
Atmosphere & character	★★★
Security	★★★★
Overall rating	★★★☆

City Central Backpackers

This hostel is located in an old building that feels a little worn, but amenities are OK and the location is great. There are groovy murals winding up the staircase but furnishings are old and worn. Shower and toilet facilities are limited.
752 George Street, Sydney.
▣ *412, 413, 431, 432, 433, 436, 437, 438, 440, 461, 470, 480, 483, 501, L38, L88, L90;* ▣ *Capitol Square;* ▣ *Central, Town Hall.*
☎ *(02) 9212 4833.*
***Website** www.ccbackpack.com.au.*
***Dorm bed** $25 ($23 VIP/YHA);*
***double room** $65 ($60 VIP/YHA).*
***Credit cards** MC, Visa.*
***Reception open** 7am-10pm daily.*

Maintenance & cleanliness	★☆
Facilities	★★☆
Atmosphere & character	★★★☆
Security	★★★
Overall rating	★★

Downtown City Backpackers

Downtown City Backpackers is a centrally located hostel with a funky atmosphere with murals painted on the walls. The bathrooms are clean enough, but the kitchen facilities are limited. There's also a TV lounge and a balcony. The location near the corner of George and Goulburn Streets is excellent. The entrance is on Goulburn Street.
611 George Street, Sydney.
▣ *412, 413, 431, 432, 433, 436, 437,*

in the city centre. It is professionally run and features spacious dormitories with new furnishings and beds are made up with real mattresses. The ground floor features an in-house employment agency, travel agency and Internet access and there's also a basement with a bar, TV lounge, kitchen and even a solarium. It has very good security with key card access and coin-operated lockers.

477 Kent Street, Sydney.

 441, 442, 443, 501, 506, 507, 515, 518, 520, L20, L88, L90; *Town Hall.*

☎ *(02) 9267 7718.*

Website *www.wanderersonkent.com.au.*

Dorm bed *$24-32.50 ($23-31.50 Nomads);* ***single/double/twin room*** *$84 ($82 Nomads).*

Credit cards *Amex, Diners, JCB, MC, Visa.*

Reception open *24 hours.*

Maintenance & cleanliness	★★★★★
Facilities	★★
Atmosphere & character	★★★★☆
Security	★★★★
Overall rating	★★★★

COOGEE

This suburban beach is a popular alternative to Bondi and it has a good selection of budget accommodation geared towards long-term guests. It is an inconvenient location if you're only in Sydney for a few days to see the sights.

The Beachhouse

This clean hostel has the usual amenities such as a kitchen and TV lounge, but there are TVs in some rooms which detract from the atmosphere.

171 Arden Street, Coogee Beach.

 313, 314, 353, 370, 372, 373, 374, X73, X74.

☎ *(02) 9665 1162.*

Dorm bed *$20-25;* ***double room*** *$50-60;* ***twin room*** *$45-50; includes breakfast.*

Credit cards *Amex, Diners, MC, Visa.*

Reception open *8am-1pm & 3pm-8pm daily.*

Maintenance & cleanliness	★★★★
Facilities	★★☆
Atmosphere & character	★★☆
Security	★★
Overall rating	★★★☆

The Castle

The Castle is a good hostel that is popular with travellers on a working holiday. Facilities include two kitchens, two TV lounges and there are several outdoor decks with lovely sea views. There rooms are clean with good quality beds.

272 Clovelly Beach Road, Clovelly Beach.

 339, X39, 360, 353.

☎ *(02) 9665 1824 or 0800 857 004.*

Website *www.castlebackpackers.com.*

Dorm bed *$17-30;* ***double/twin room*** *$55-85.*

Credit cards *Amex, MC, Visa.*

Reception open *8am-1pm & 4pm-8pm daily.*

Maintenance & cleanliness	★★★
Facilities	★★★
Atmosphere & character	★★★
Security	★★☆
Overall rating	★★★

Coogee Beachside

Coogee Beachside is a very clean and quiet hostel that caters mostly to backpacking couples. Common areas are limited and there is no lounge, just a kitchen. There are TVs in the rooms.

178 Coogee Beach Road, Coogee.

 313, 314, 353, 370, 372, 373, 374, X73, X74.

☎ *(02) 9315 8511.*

Dorm bed *$23-27;* ***double room*** *$55.*

Credit cards *MC, Visa.*

Reception open *8am-noon & 5pm-8pm daily.*

Maintenance & cleanliness	★★★★☆
Facilities	★
Atmosphere & character	★
Security	★★☆
Overall rating	★★★☆

Surfside Backpackers

Surfside Backpackers has the best location in Coogee, across the road from the beach. It has been recently renovated and has a TV lounge and a good kitchen with brand new appliances. There are great sea views from the TV lounge and balconies.

186 Arden Street, Coogee.

 313, 314, 353, 370, 372, 373, 374, X73, X74.

☎ *(02) 9315 7888.*

Website www.surfsidebackpackers.
com.au.
Dorm bed $23-27 ($21-25 VIP, $22-
26 YHA, 23-27 ISIC); *double/twin
room* $58-60 ($54-56 VIP, $56-58
YHA).
Credit cards MC, Visa.
Reception open 8am-1pm & 5pm-8pm
daily.

Maintenance & cleanliness	★★★★⯪
Facilities	★⯪
Atmosphere & character	★★⯪
Security	★★
Overall rating	★★★

Wizard of Oz

This clean hostel is in a nicely renovated
house that is close to shops. It has the
usual kitchen and TV lounge and a
great atmosphere.
172 Coogee Beach Road, Coogee.
🚌 313, 314, 353, 370, 372, 373, 374,
X73, X74.
☎ (02) 9315 7876.
Website www.wizardofoz.com.au.
Dorm bed $23-27.
Credit cards MC, Visa.
Reception open 8am-1pm & 5pm-8pm
daily.

Maintenance & cleanliness	★★★★⯪
Facilities	★⯪
Atmosphere & character	★★★★⯪
Security	★⯪
Overall rating	★★★⯪

DARLINGHURST
& WOOLLOOMOOLOO

These two inner-city neighbourhoods
are located to the east of the city
centre. Woolloomooloo is the harbour
side area in the valley between the city
centre and Kings Cross and is home to
a naval base while Darlinghurst is the
area south of William Street with a
diverse atmosphere that encompasses
everything from prostitution to quaint
Victorian architecture. The Kings
Cross end of William Street can feel a
little threatening at times, however this
area is a convenient area to base yourself and is within walking distance of
both Kings Cross and the city centre.

Australian Backpackers

Australian Backpackers is in an older
building and has a rooftop terrace with

great city views plus the usual kitchen
and TV lounge. This hostel is geared
mostly for travellers on a working holiday visa and the staff can help you find
work. It has a fantastic party atmosphere, particularly when they host free
barbecues on the roof.
132 Bourke Street, Woolloomooloo.
🚌 200, 311, 324, 325, 326, 327;
🚉 Kings Cross, Museum.
☎ (02) 9331 0822.
Website www.australianbackpackers.
com.au.
Dorm bed $20-22; *double/twin
room* $55; price includes breakfast.
Credit cards Amex, MC, Visa.
Reception open Mon-Sat 8am-1pm
& 3pm-7.30pm, Sun 8am-noon &
3pm-7pm.

Maintenance & cleanliness	★★★
Facilities	★⯪
Atmosphere & character	★★★★⯪
Security	★⯪
Overall rating	★★★

Boomerang Backpackers

Boomerang Backpackers is a nice
clean hostel handy to both the city
centre and the Cross. There are clean
bathrooms and a rooftop sundeck with
table tennis, barbecue and great views
of the city.
141 William Street, Darlinghurst.
🚌 200, 311, 324, 325, 326, 327;
🚉 Kings Cross, Museum.
☎ (02) 8354 0488.
Website www.boomerangbackpackers
.com.
Dorm bed $18-26; *double/twin
room* $50-60.
Credit cards MC, Visa.
Reception open 7am-12.30pm & 4pm-
10pm daily.

Maintenance & cleanliness	★★★⯪
Facilities	★★
Atmosphere & character	★★★★⯪
Security	★★
Overall rating	★★★

City Resort Hostel

This hostel is tired looking, but clean,
and it offers only basic facilities. All the
rooms have fridges and TVs, which keep
people from hanging out in the small
common room and consequently it has
no atmosphere. It is located on a busy

New South Wales

street that leads to a motorway entrance and there is a lot of traffic noise. It's just off William Street behind the Westfield Tower about midway between Kings Cross and the city centre.
103 Palmer Street, Woolloomooloo.
🚌 *200, 311, 324, 325, 326, 327;*
🚆 *Kings Cross.*
☎ *(02) 9357 3333 or 1800 688 335.*
Dorm bed $22; double room $50.
Credit cards *Amex, MC, Visa.*
Reception open *Mon-Sat 7am-10pm, Sun 7.30am-10pm.*

Maintenance & cleanliness	★★★
Facilities	★
Atmosphere & character	-
Security	★★★☆
Overall rating	★★

Forbes Terrace

Forbes Terrace is a nice clean place with a pleasant shady courtyard. All rooms have a fridge and TV and come with made up beds.
153 Forbes Street, Woolloomooloo.
🚌 *200, 311, 324, 325, 326, 327;*
🚆 *Kings Cross.*
☎ *(02) 9358 4327.*
Website *www.g-day.com.au.*
Dorm bed $19.80-22; single/double/ twin room $44-88.
Credit cards *MC, Visa.*
Reception open *8am-10pm daily.*

Maintenance & cleanliness	★★★
Facilities	★
Atmosphere & character	★★
Security	★★★☆
Overall rating	★★

Harbour City Hotel

This is a big hostel with plenty of facilities that include two TV lounges and a large kitchen. Accommodation consists of four, six and eight-bed dorms and it has excellent security with key card access and lockers in all rooms. It is on a busy road in Woolloomooloo, across the road from the Domain and just a short walk to either the city centre or Kings Cross.
50 Sir John Young Crescent, Woolloomooloo.
🚌 *200, 311, 324, 325, 326, 327;*
🚆 *St James.*
☎ *(02) 9380 2922.*
Website *www.harbourcityhotel.com.*

Dorm bed $25 ($24 VIP); double/ twin room $75.
Credit cards *MC, Visa.*
Reception open *8am-10pm daily.*

Maintenance & cleanliness	★★★★☆
Facilities	★★☆
Atmosphere & character	★★★
Security	★★★★
Overall rating	★★★☆

Hotel Altamont

This former boutique hotel has been converted to an upmarket backpackers hostel although many double rooms remain for the previous clientele. It is a very trendy place with modern industrial/medieval décor. Facilities include a big commercial kitchen, a bar, Internet access and a big rooftop sundeck. All rooms have TV and en suite bathrooms. It has a great friendly atmosphere and is excellent value.
207 Darlinghurst Road, Darlinghurst.
🚌 *200, 311, 324, 325, 326, 327;*
🚆 *Kings Cross.*
☎ *(02) 9360 6000.*
Website *www.altamont.com.au.*
Dorm bed $20; double room $90.
Credit cards *Amex, JCB, MC, Visa.*
Reception open *8am-8pm daily.*

Maintenance & cleanliness	★★★★★
Facilities	★★★
Atmosphere & character	★★★★☆
Security	★★
Overall rating	★★★★

The Wood Duck Inn

The Wood Duck Inn is a small hostel, but it's big enough to have a good atmosphere. It features a roof top sundeck with great city views plus a barbecue, kitchen and TV lounge. The hostel organises activities and runs trips to the beach, which encourages interaction between guests and makes it a good place to meet other travellers. It is located near the Australian Museum at the nicer end of William Street and it's just a two minute walk into the city centre and about five minutes to Kings Cross.
49 William Street, East Sydney.
🚌 *200, 311, 324, 325, 326, 327, 389;*
🚆 *Museum.*
☎ *(02) 9358 5856 or 1800 110 025.*
Website *www.woodduckinn.com.au.*
Dorm bed $20-22; includes breakfast.

Credit cards Amex, Diners, MC, Visa.
Reception open 8am-1pm & 4pm-9pm daily.

Maintenance & cleanliness	★★★
Facilities	★★★
Atmosphere & character	★★★★★
Security	★★★
Overall rating	★★★★☆

GLEBE

This is a quiet area with a sizable student population a short distance west of the city centre. Although it isn't served by Sydney's rail system, there are plenty of buses and the SLR tram stops here.

Alishan International Guest House

This hostel is located in a beautiful building that has been tastefully decorated. There is a very nice common room with Internet access and a clean kitchen. The bathrooms are spotless. There is also a backyard with a barbecue and picnic tables and a balcony overlooking the street. It is a quiet hostel with a pleasant relaxed atmosphere. It has the best location of Glebe's hostels right in Glebe's main shopping area.

100 Glebe Point Road, Glebe.
🚌 431, 432, 433, 434; 🚆 Glebe.
☎ (02) 9566 4048.
Website www.alishan.com.au.
Dorm bed $25; **single room** $85-95; **double room** $95-105; **family room** $154.
Credit cards Amex, MC, Visa.
Reception open 8am-10.30pm daily.

Maintenance & cleanliness	★★★★☆
Facilities	★★
Atmosphere & character	★★★★
Security	★★☆
Overall rating	★★★★☆

Forest Lodge Hotel

This clean hostel is above a pub on a quiet street near Glebe. The accommodation is split between drab rooms in the original building and very nice rooms in the newer building. Facilities include a TV lounge, kitchen and a café.

117 Arundel Street, Forest Lodge.
🚌 413, 435, 436, 437, 438, 440, 461, 470, 480, 483.
☎ (02) 9660 1872.

Website www.forestlodgehotel.com.au.
Dorm bed $20; **single room** $45; **double room** $55.
Credit cards MC, Visa.
Reception open Mon-Sat 7.30am-midnight, Sun 7.30am-9pm.

Maintenance & cleanliness	★★★★
Facilities	★★
Atmosphere & character	★★★☆
Security	★★
Overall rating	★★★

Glebe Point YHA

Although a little institutional, this is better than many other YHA hostels. Everything here is very clean and the common areas have good facilities that include a games room with pinball and a pool table, a huge kitchen plus a TV/video room. There's also a rooftop barbecue area. All the bunk beds have their own locker and reading light and there's a sink in each room.

262 Glebe Point Road, Glebe.
🚌 431, 432, 433, 434; 🚆 Glebe.
☎ (02) 9692 8418.
Dorm bed $27.50-31.50 ($24-28 YHA); **double/twin room** $75 ($68 YHA).
Credit cards MC, Visa.
Reception open 7am-10.45pm daily.

Maintenance & cleanliness	★★★★
Facilities	★★
Atmosphere & character	★★★☆
Security	★★★
Overall rating	★★★

Glebe Village Backpackers

Glebe Village backpackers consists of four big old buildings. It is old and looks a little worn from the outside however it is reasonably clean inside and it has the best atmosphere of the Glebe hostels. The best feature is the laid back front yard with picnic tables and table tennis. It's located next to the YHA at the quiet end of Glebe Point Road.

256 Glebe Point Road, Glebe.
🚌 431, 432, 433, 434; 🚆 Glebe.
☎ (02) 9660 8133 or 1800 801 983.
Website www.bakpak.com/glebevillage/.
Dorm bed $25; **double room** $75; includes breakfast.
Credit cards MC, Visa.
Reception open 7.30am-8.30pm daily.

Maintenance & cleanliness	★★★
Facilities	★★☆
Atmosphere & character	★★★★★
Security	★★★☆
Overall rating	★★★

Wattle House

Accommodating a maximum of 26 guests, Wattle House is one of Sydney's smallest hostels and definitely one of the best. The attention to detail is a big thing here with towels, linen and duvets on all beds and bathrobes in twin and double rooms. There are even teddy bears on the beds. Communal areas include a well-equipped kitchen, a book exchange and reading room and a nice back garden with tables and market umbrellas. This is the best budget accommodation option for couples visiting Sydney.

44 Hereford Street, Glebe.
🚌 *431, 432, 433, 434;* 🚆 *Glebe.*
☎ *(02) 9552 4997.*
Website *www.wattlehouse.com.au.*
Dorm bed *$25-30;* ***double room*** *$75-85.*
Credit cards *MC, Visa.*
Reception open *Mon-Fri 9am-lunchtime & 6pm-7pm, Sat-Sun 10am-lunchtime.*

Maintenance & cleanliness	★★★★★
Facilities	★★
Atmosphere & character	★★★★★
Security	★★☆
Overall rating	★★★★

KINGS CROSS

Kings Cross is backpacker central with loads of hostels, particularly along quiet tree-lined Victoria Street. Many of the hostels in Kings Cross have rooftop sundecks with amazing city views. The neighbourhood has plenty of cheap eats; great transport connections and is only a 15-minute walk from the heart of the city. However the Cross is also Sydney's red light district and some people may not feel comfortable walking around alone at night among the brothels and sex shops.

Ambassador Backpackers

This hostel doesn't have many common areas – just a kitchen and a rooftop deck with nice views. There's no TV lounge and all the rooms have TVs, which keep travellers in their room and kills any chance of a social atmosphere. Apart from that, it's a clean hostel with en suites in most rooms.

15 Earl Place, Kings Cross.
🚌 *311, 324, 325, 326, 327;* 🚆 *Kings Cross.*
☎ *(02) 9331 6664 or 1800 005 331.*
Dorm bed *$25-30;* ***double/twin room*** *$80;* ***triple room*** *$75; includes breakfast.*
Credit cards *MC, Visa.*
Reception open *8am-noon & 4pm-8pm daily.*

Maintenance & cleanliness	★★★
Facilities	★★★☆
Atmosphere & character	☆
Security	★★
Overall rating	★★☆

Backpackers Headquarters

This is a very nice hostel that is kept clean and well maintained. The hostel features a nice bright TV lounge, a kitchen, Internet access and a rooftop sundeck with a barbecue. Accommodation is of a high standard and beds are made up and feature real mattresses. It is at the quiet Rushcutters Bay end of Kings Cross.

79 Bayswater Road, Kings Cross.
🚌 *311, 324, 325, 326, 327;* 🚆 *Kings Cross.*
☎ *(02) 9331 6180.*
Website *www.backpackershqhostel.com.au.*
Dorm bed *$21-22 ($20-21 VIP);* ***double/twin room*** *$66 ($64 VIP).*
Credit cards *MC, Visa.*
Reception open *Mon-Fri 7am-11pm, Sat-Sun 8am-11pm daily.*

Maintenance & cleanliness	★★★★☆
Facilities	★★☆
Atmosphere & character	★★★
Security	★★★☆
Overall rating	★★★

Bernly Private Hotel

The Bernly Private Hotel is a very nice hotel that also has backpackers' dormitories. Because it doesn't cater exclusively to backpackers there is not the same sort of atmosphere as many other hostels in the Cross, but some travellers prefer the quieter feel of this place. It

has good facilities that include a small kitchen with limited facilities and a nice rooftop terrace with great city views. It is located down a small alleyway in one of the seedier areas of Kings Cross. At night you will feel safer entering from the relatively well lit square near Hungry Jacks, rather than walking down Earl Place from Victoria Street.
15 Springfield Avenue, Kings Cross.
🚌 *311, 324, 325, 326, 327;* 🚉 *Kings Cross.*
☎ *(02) 9358 3122.*
Website www.bernlyprivatehotel. com.au.
Dorm bed *$20;* **single room** *$50-70;* **double/twin room** *$55-80.*
Credit cards *Amex, Diners, JCB, MC, Visa.*
Reception open *24 hours.*

Maintenance & cleanliness	★★★★
Facilities	★★
Atmosphere & character	★★½
Security	★★★
Overall rating	★★★

Blue Parrot Backpackers

The Blue Parrot is one of the better hostels in Kings Cross. It is very clean and most of the facilities are brand new. There are the usual amenities such as a kitchen and TV lounge plus a nice courtyard with a barbecue. It has a good atmosphere for a quiet hostel.
87 Macleay Street, Kings Cross.
🚌 *311, 324, 325, 326, 327;* 🚉 *Kings Cross.*
☎ *(02) 9356 4888 or 1800 252 299.*
Website www.blueparrot.com.au.
Dorm bed *$25-27;* **double/twin room** *$65.*
Credit cards *MC, Visa.*
Reception open *8.30am-8.30pm daily.*

Maintenance & cleanliness	★★★★½
Facilities	★★
Atmosphere & character	★★★★½
Security	★★★
Overall rating	★★★½

Cooee Travellers Accommodation

Cooee Travellers Accommodation is a new, clean hostel with a small kitchen and several lounges, including one with a projection screen TV, plus a big sundeck with great views. All rooms have lockers and reading lamps and there

are hairdryers in the bathroom. It is very centrally located next door to the entrance to Kings Cross station.
107-109 Darlinghurst Road, Kings Cross.
🚌 *311, 324, 325, 326, 327;* 🚉 *Kings Cross.*
☎ *(02) 9331 0009 or 1800 200 793.*
Website www.cooeetravellers.com.
Dorm bed *$24-26;* **double room** *$70;* **twin room** *$70-80; includes a free evening meal.*
Credit cards *MC, Visa.*
Reception open *24 hours.*

Maintenance & cleanliness	★★★½
Facilities	★★★
Atmosphere & character	★★★½
Security	★★★½
Overall rating	★★★½

Eva's Backpackers

This is a nice hostel with the usual facilities plus a nice rooftop sundeck with a barbecue and fantastic views of Sydney.
6-8 Orwell Street, Kings Cross.
🚌 *311, 324, 325, 326, 327;* 🚉 *Kings Cross.*
☎ *(02) 9358 2185.*
Dorm bed *$24-26;* **double/twin room** *$60-65; includes breakfast.*
Credit cards *MC, Visa.*
Reception open *Mon-Sat 7am-2pm & 5pm-7pm, Sun 7am-2pm.*

Maintenance & cleanliness	★★★½
Facilities	★★½
Atmosphere & character	★★★★★½
Security	★★
Overall rating	★★★★½

Funk House Backpackers

This is a fun hostel with a convenient, if a little seedy, location. The place has a great atmosphere and a colourful and unique décor with murals everywhere. Facilities are good and include a rooftop sundeck with a barbecue as well as the usual kitchen and TV lounge.
23 Darlinghurst Road, Kings Cross.
🚌 *311, 324, 325, 326, 327;* 🚉 *Kings Cross.*
☎ *(02) 9358 6455 or 1800 247 600.*
Website www.funkhouse.com.au.
Dorm bed *$23-24 ($22-23 VIP);* **double/twin room** *$62 ($60 VIP).*
Credit cards *MC, Visa.*

New South Wales

Reception open Mon-Sat 7am-10pm, Sun 8am-8pm.

Maintenance & cleanliness	★★
Facilities	★⯪
Atmosphere & character	★★★★★
Security	★★⯪
Overall rating	★★⯪

The Globe Backpackers

This hostel has a good TV lounge with a big screen TV, free Internet access and a small barbecue area. The Darlinghurst Road location won't appeal to everyone.

40 Darlinghurst Road, Kings Crosss.
⊞ *311, 324, 325, 326, 327;* ⊞ *Kings Cross.*
☎ *(02) 9326 9675.*
Dorm bed $19-25; includes breakfast.
Credit cards MC, Visa.
Reception open 8.30am-9pm; late check in by prior arrangement.

Maintenance & cleanliness	★★⯪
Facilities	★★
Atmosphere & character	★★★
Security	★★⯪
Overall rating	★★⯪

Great Aussie Backpackers

Great Aussie Backpackers offers similar facilities to other hostels on Victoria Street. This includes a small kitchen, a TV lounge and a courtyard barbecue area.

174 Victoria Street, Kings Cross.
⊞ *311, 324, 325, 326, 327;* ⊞ *Kings Cross.*
☎ *(02) 9356 4551.*
Dorm bed $20; double room $55; includes breakfast.
Credit cards MC, Visa.
Reception open 7am-8pm daily.

Maintenance & cleanliness	★★★
Facilities	★⯪
Atmosphere & character	★★★
Security	★★
Overall rating	★★⯪

Hancock Dury House

This hostel in the midst of Darlinghurst Road is a quiet place that lacks atmosphere. It has minimal facilities that include a tiny kitchen and a smoke-filled lounge, but there are fridges and TVs in the rooms. It is a popular hostel with Asian backpackers.

48A Darlinghurst Road, Kings Cross.
⊞ *311, 324, 325, 326, 327;* ⊞ *Kings Cross.*
☎ *(02) 9357 2255 or 1800 778 282.*
Website www.duryhouse.com.
Dorm bed $18-22.
Credit cards MC, Visa.
Reception open 7.30am-12.30pm & 5pm-10pm daily.

Maintenance & cleanliness	★★★⯪
Facilities	★
Atmosphere & character	⯪
Security	★★★⯪
Overall rating	★★⯪

Jolly Swagman

The Jolly Swagman is a lively place with a god atmosphere. The accommodation here is much the same as other hostels in the Cross and there are plenty of common areas where you can meet other travellers.

27 Orwell Street, Kings Cross.
⊞ *311, 324, 325, 326, 327;* ⊞ *Kings Cross.*
☎ *(02) 9358 6400.*
Website www.jollyswagman.com.au.
Dorm bed $23-24 ($22-24 VIP); double room $60-65 ($58-63 VIP); includes breakfast.
Credit cards MC, Visa.
Reception open 24 hours.

Maintenance & cleanliness	★★★
Facilities	★⯪
Atmosphere & character	★★★★⯪
Security	★★★
Overall rating	★★★

Kanga House

Kanga House is a good hostel with a handy location. It is clean and facilities are similar to other hostels in the Cross. Facilities include a kitchen and TV lounge plus free Internet access.

141 Victoria Street, Kings Cross.
⊞ *311, 324, 325, 326, 327;* ⊞ *Kings Cross.*
☎ *(02) 9357 7897.*
Website www.kangahouse.com.au.
Dorm bed $20-22; double room $55-60; twin room $50.
Credit cards MC, Visa.
Reception open 8am-3pm & 4pm-7pm daily.

Maintenance & cleanliness	★★★
Facilities	★★

Atmosphere & character	★★★★
Security	★★
Overall rating	★★★

Kings Cross Budget Motel

This place on Darlinghurst Road has basic facilities including a small common room with a TV and pool table.

39-41 Darlinghurst Road, Kings Cross.
🚌 *311, 324, 325, 326, 327;* 🚇 *Kings Cross.*
☎ *(02) 9360 4444.*
Dorm bed *$20.*
Credit cards *MC, Visa.*
Reception open *7am-10pm daily.*

Maintenance & cleanliness	★★★
Facilities	★★
Atmosphere & character	★★
Security	★★★
Overall rating	★★★

Kings Cross Palace

This hostel offers very basic facilities that include a TV lounge and a crappy kitchen. It calls itself a party hostel, but it just felt depressing when we visited.

34B Darlinghurst Road, Kings Cross.
🚌 *311, 324, 325, 326, 327;* 🚇 *Kings Cross.*
☎ *(02) 9368 0188 or 1800 688 336.*
Website *www.duryhouse.com.*
Dorm bed *$16-22.*
Reception open *7am-10pm daily.*

Maintenance & cleanliness	★★
Facilities	★
Atmosphere & character	★★
Security	★★★
Overall rating	★★

The Original Backpackers Lodge

Established in 1982, the Original Backpackers Lodge is one of Sydney's longest established hostels and is reputed to be the first hostel to call itself a 'backpackers'. This hostel is clean and tidy with very good facilities including a large kitchen, Internet access, a good TV lounge and a nice garden area with a barbecue.

160-162 Victoria Street, Kings Cross.
🚌 *311, 324, 325, 326, 327;* 🚇 *Kings Cross.*
☎ *(02) 9356 3232.*
Website *www.originalbackpackers. com.au.*

Dorm bed *$21-25 ($20-24 VIP); single room $45 ($43 VIP); double/ twin room $65 ($63 VIP).*
Credit cards *Amex, MC, Visa.*
Reception open *24 hours.*

Maintenance & cleanliness	★★★
Facilities	★★
Atmosphere & character	★★★★
Security	★★★★
Overall rating	★★★

The Palms

The Palms is a good hostel with a leafy front garden. It features a couple of kitchens, a barbecue area, TV lounge and free Internet access. They run regular trips to the beach.

23 Hughes Street, Kings Cross.
🚌 *311, 324, 325, 326, 327;* 🚇 *Kings Cross.*
☎ *(02) 9357 1199.*
Dorm bed *$18-22; double/twin room $45-50; includes breakfast.*
Credit cards *MC, Visa.*
Reception open *8am-noon & 5pm-8pm daily.*

Maintenance & cleanliness	★★★
Facilities	★★★
Atmosphere & character	★★★
Security	★★★
Overall rating	★★★

The Pink House

This is a big old house with loads of character. It has the usual facilities including a kitchen and TV lounge plus free Internet access and several quiet shady courtyard areas including one with a barbecue.

6-8 Barncleuth Square, Kings Cross.
🚌 *311, 324, 325, 326, 327;* 🚇 *Kings Cross.*
☎ *(02) 9358 1689 or 1800 806 384.*
Website *www.pinkhouse.com.au.*
Dorm bed *$22-24; double room $60-70; twin room $60; includes breakfast.*
Credit cards *MC, Visa.*
Reception open *Mon-Fri 8.30am-12.30pm & 2pm-9pm, Sat-Sun 9am-12.30pm & 1.30pm-9pm.*

Maintenance & cleanliness	★★★
Facilities	★★
Atmosphere & character	★★★
Security	★★★
Overall rating	★★★

Potts Point House

This hostel isn't as well maintained as others in the area, but it is one of the cheapest places to stay in Sydney.
154 Victoria Street, Kings Cross.
🚌 *311, 324, 325, 326, 327;* 🚊 *Kings Cross.*
☎ *(02) 9368 0733.*
Dorm bed *$15; double room $45.*
Reception open *8am-1pm & 3pm-9pm daily.*

Maintenance & cleanliness	★★
Facilities	★
Atmosphere & character	★★⯪
Security	★★★⯪
Overall rating	★★⯪

Sydney Central Backpackers

This hostel has polished floorboards in the reception and nice clean bathrooms. It also has a good kitchen area, a TV lounge and a brilliant rooftop sundeck with spectacular views of the Opera House and Sydney Harbour Bridge.
16 Orwell Street, Kings Cross.
🚌 *311, 324, 325, 326, 327;* 🚊 *Kings Cross.*
☎ *(02) 9358 6600 or 1800 440 202.*
Website *www.sydneybackpackers. com.au.*
Dorm bed *$24; double room $55.*
Credit cards *MC, Visa.*
Reception open *Mon-Sat 7am-9pm, Sun 8am-1pm.*

Maintenance & cleanliness	★★★⯪
Facilities	★★
Atmosphere & character	★★★★⯪
Security	★★⯪
Overall rating	★★★

Travellers Rest

Travellers Rest is a quiet hostel that is well suited to backpacking couples. The only communal area is the shared kitchen, but all rooms have a TV and fridge. The lack of communal areas along with the 'no alcohol' rule means that this place doesn't have much atmosphere, however the owners are very helpful.
156 Victoria Street, Kings Cross.
🚌 *311, 324, 325, 326, 327;* 🚊 *Kings Cross.*
☎ *(02) 9380 2044.*
Dorm bed *$18; double room $50-55; twin room $45.*

Reception open *8am-noon & 4.3-pm-6pm daily.*

Maintenance & cleanliness	★★★
Facilities	★★⯪
Atmosphere & character	★
Security	★★★⯪
Overall rating	★★

V Backpackers

V Backpackers has a good common room with polished floorboards, foosball and a TV plus an adjoining courtyard with a barbecue. Accommodation is similar to other hostels in the Cross and the rooms have lockers and there are fridges in the double and twin rooms.
144 Victoria Street, Kings Cross.
🚌 *311, 324, 325, 326, 327;* 🚊 *Kings Cross.*
☎ *(02) 9357 4733 or 1800 667 225.*
Website *www.vbackpackers.com.*
Dorm bed *$18-26; double room $55-65.*
Credit cards *Amex, Diners, JCB, MC, Visa.*
Reception open *8am-8pm daily.*

Maintenance & cleanliness	★★★
Facilities	★
Atmosphere & character	★★★★
Security	★★★★⯪
Overall rating	★★⯪

MANLY

Although a half-hour ferry ride from the centre of Sydney, this beachside suburb is a nice spot with a lively atmosphere, good pubs and a great beach. There are frequent ferries from Circular Quay.

Boardrider Backpacker

Boardrider is the best of Manly's hostels. It is a clean, purpose-built hostel with a brilliant location. The facilities include a big TV lounge with Internet access, a nice rooftop barbecue area and also a balcony overlooking the Corso. Security here is very good with key card access and lockers in the rooms.
63 The Corso, Manly.
🚌 *151, 169, E69, E71;* 🚢 *Manly.*
☎ *(02) 9977 6077.*
Website *www.boardrider.com.au.*
Dorm bed *$25-28 ($24-27 VIP); double/twin room $60-85 ($58-83 VIP).*

New South Wales

Credit cards MC, Visa.
Reception open Mon-Fri 8am-8pm,
Sat-Sun 9am-6pm.

Maintenance & cleanliness	★★★★★
Facilities	★★
Atmosphere & character	★★★☆
Security	★★★★☆
Overall rating	★★★★☆

Manly Backpackers Beachside

Everything at this hostel is clean and it
has a big fully-equipped kitchen and a
nice courtyard.
28 Raglan Street, Manly.
▣ 151, 169, E69, E71; ▣ *Manly.*
☎ (02) 9977 3411 or 1800 656 299.
Dorm bed $22; double room $50.
Credit cards MC, Visa.
Reception open Mon-Fri 9am-1pm &
4pm-7pm; Sat-Sun 9am-2pm.

Maintenance & cleanliness	★★★★☆
Facilities	★★☆
Atmosphere & character	★★★★
Security	★★★
Overall rating	★★★

Manly Beach Resort

Manly Beach Resort is a good hostel
with a TV lounge with Internet access
plus a swimming pool and spa. There
is also a motel on site and some motel
facilities (such as parking) aren't available to backpackers.
6 Carlton Street, Manly.
▣ 151, 169, E69, E71; ▣ *Manly.*
☎ (02) 9977 4188.
Website www.manlyview.com.au.
*Dorm bed $22 ($21 VIP); double
room $50 ($48 VIP).*
Credit cards Amex, Diners, JCB, MC,
Visa.
Reception open Mon-Thu 7am-11pm,
Fri-Sat 24 hours, Sun 7am-11pm.

Maintenance & cleanliness	★★★
Facilities	★★★☆
Atmosphere & character	★★★☆
Security	★★☆
Overall rating	★★★☆

Manly Bunkhouse

This is a nice place with a good TV
lounge with Internet access and a sunny
backyard with a barbecue. The hostel is
generally clean and well maintained
and it has a pretty good atmosphere
despite the 'no alcohol' rule.

35 Pine Street, Manly.
▣ 151, 169, E69, E71; ▣ *Manly.*
☎ (02) 9976 0472 or 1800 657 122.
*Dorm bed $25 ($24 VIP); double/
twin room $65 ($64 VIP).*
Credit cards MC, Visa.
Reception open Mon-Fri 8.30am-1pm
& 4pm-8pm; Sat-Sun 9am-noon &
6pm-7pm.

Maintenance & cleanliness	★★★
Facilities	★★☆
Atmosphere & character	★★★☆
Security	★★☆
Overall rating	★★★☆

Manly Cottage Inn

This is a small hostel inside a cute old
house on busy Pittwater Road. It has a
friendly atmosphere and a small garden
area in the front but the facilities are
basic and it has a manky smell.
25 Pittwater Road, Manly.
▣ 151, 169, E69, E71; ▣ *Manly.*
☎ (02) 9976 0297.
Website www.users.bigpond.com/
manlycottage/.
Dorm bed $25; twin room $70.

Maintenance & cleanliness	★★☆
Facilities	★
Atmosphere & character	★★★★☆
Security	★★☆
Overall rating	★★

Manly Travellers Hostel

This is a very basic hostel in an old
house. It is poorly maintained with old
furnishings and old bed sheets however
it is relatively clean.
56 Whistler Street, Manly.
▣ 151, 169, E69, E71; ▣ *Manly.*
☎ 0423 218 250.
Dorm bed $20; single room $50.

Maintenance & cleanliness	★★☆
Facilities	★
Atmosphere & character	★★
Security	★
Overall rating	★★☆

NEWTOWN

Newtown is a vibrant neighbourhood
with lots of pubs, restaurants and cafés.
It is about 10 minutes from the city
centre by bus or train. Parking is very
difficult to find here so you may want
to avoid staying here if you're travelling
by car.

Open *Mon-Fri 9am-9pm, Sat-Sun 11am-5pm.*

Sydney Opera House
The Sydney Opera House was designed by Danish architect Jørn Utzon and built over a 14-year period. It was finally completed, way over budget, in 1973. The Opera House is one of Australia's two internationally recognised urban landmarks (the Harbour Bridge is the other) and is widely recognised for its unique design and imposing position overlooking the harbour at the tip of Bennelong Point. The Opera House has four auditoria and features ballet, classical music, theatre and opera performances. Front of house tours run frequently but backstage tours run less often and need to be booked in advance.
Bennelong Point, Sydney.
🚌 *all Circular Quay buses;* 🚢 *Circular Quay;* 🚃 *Circular Quay.*
☎ *(02) 9250 7777.*
Website *www.soh.nsw.gov.au.*
Tours cost *$16.20-25.*
Tours depart *9am-5pm daily.*

Town Hall
Sydney's Town Hall is a fine example of Victorian architecture and features a clock tower while the interior contains a concert hall with an impressive 8,500-pipe organ.
483 George Street, Sydney.
🚌 *151, 169, 175, 178, 180, 183, 184, 190, 200, 247, 254, 261, 264, 286, 288, 289, 290, 291, 292, 293, 294, 441, 442, 461;* 🚢 *Park Plaza;*
🚃 *Town Hall.*
☎ *(02) 9265 9007.*
Admission *free.*
Open *Mon-Fri 8am-6pm.*

DARLING HARBOUR
Just a short walk from the heart of the city centre, this harbour side precinct has been developed as new tourist area with hotels, museums, parks, shopping centres and plenty of fast food shops. Everything in Darling Harbour was built in the last 15 years and parts of it seem quite sterile, however the area is home to several attractions including the Sydney Aquarium, the

Sydney Art Gallery, the National Maritime Museum and the Powerhouse Museum.

Australian National Maritime Museum
An excellent maritime museum with exhibits which include the submarine HMAS Onslow.
2 Murray Street, Pyrmont.
🚌 *888;* 🚢 *Darling Harbour;* 🚢 *Harbourside;* 🚃 *Pyrmont Bay.*
☎ *(02) 9298 3777.*
Website *www.anmm.gov.au.*
Admission *$10 museum, $20 museum, boats & submarine.*
Open *Jan 9.30am-6pm daily, Feb-Dec 9.30am-5pm daily.*

Powerhouse Museum
One of Australia's largest museums has some excellent interactive displays and is host to a number of very good temporary exhibits. It is definitely one of Australia's more enjoyable museums.
500 Harris Street, Ultimo.
🚌 *501;* 🚢 *Darling Harbour;* 🚢 *Haymarket;* 🚃 *Haymarket.*
☎ *(02) 9217 0100 or 9217 0444.*
Website *www.phm.gov.au.*
Admission *$10, $3 students, free first Sat of every month.*
Open *10am-5pm daily.*

Sydney Aquarium
This aquarium is excellent and shows underwater life in different ecosystems from mangrove swamps to rivers and the Great Barrier Reef and features glass tunnels where you are surrounded by water.
Wheat Street, Sydney.
🚢 *Darling Harbour;* 🚢 *Darling Park;* 🚃 *Town Hall.*
☎ *(02) 9262 2300.*
Website *www.sydneyaquarium.com.au.*
Admission *$24, $16 students; combined ferry and admission tickets available.*
Open *9am-10pm daily, seal sanctuary closes at sunset.*

THE ROCKS
This area near the southern end of the Harbour Bridge is Sydney's oldest neighbourhood and it is a welcome departure

from the towers of glass and steel just a few minutes walk away. Much of the area has been renovated with plenty of expensive restaurants and boutiques. The Rocks is also home to some of the city's best pubs and can get quite busy on a Friday or Saturday night.

Museum of Contemporary Art

With an enviable location overlooking Sydney Cove from Circular Quay West, the Museum of Contemporay Art has a good collection of artworks including a number of excellent temporary exhibits.

140 George Street, The Rocks.
 435, 436, 437, 438, 440, 443, 470, 500, 501, 504, 506, 508, 510, 520, 888; *Circular Quay;* *Circular Quay.*
 (02) 9252 4033.
Website *www.mca.com.au.*
Admission *free.*
Open *10am-5pm daily.*

Sydney Harbour Bridge

The world's largest, but not the longest, steel arch bridge opened in 1932 becoming Sydney's first internationally recognised landmark. The bridge is such an enduring symbol of the city that it deserves more than just a quick look. Walking across is the cheapest and one of the best ways to experience the bridge, although you can also take a bus or train across. If you've got the money the best experience by far is the BridgeClimb. One of the bridge's southern pylons houses the Harbour Bridge Museum that has great views from the top.

Access to the pedestrian lane is via the Bridge Stairs on Cumberland Street between Argyle and Gloucester Streets, The Rocks.
 X39, 339, X43, 343, 431, 432, 433, 434; *Wynyard, Milsons Point.*

BridgeClimb

The BridgeClimb offers a once in a lifetime opportunity to climb the outer arch of the Sydney Harbour Bridge. Although expensive and out of many backpackers' budgets the BridgeClimb is widely established as Sydney's top attraction. The BridgeClimb bills itself as an adventure activity although it's not in the same league as skydiving or bungee jumping. The experience lasts for three hours and gives you a fantastic view of the city and an appreciation of the Sydney Harbour Bridge.

All climbers are fitted with a bridge suit and safety harness and given a safety briefing before heading out on to the bridge. Then small groups of around ten climb a series of ladders to the lower area of the top arch, from where they climb to the top of the bridge. There's a photo session at the top, then you walk across a walkway to the other side where you descend back to street level. Bookings are essential and don't go out on the town the night before as everyone is breathalysed before the climb.

5 Cumberland Street, The Rocks.
 all Wynyard & Circular Quay buses; *Circular Quay;* *Circular Quay.*
 (02) 8274 7777.
Website *www.bridgeclimb.com.au.*
Admission *$155-225.*
Open *8am-5pm daily.*

Harbour Bridge Pylon Lookout

The climb up the stairs inside one of the bridge's southern pylons is a cheaper alternative to the BridgeClimb although the experience isn't quite the same. There are great views from the top and the museum inside the pylon has exhibits about the bridge's construction.

Hickson Road, Dawes Point. South East Pylon (access is via the pedestrian pathway on the Eastern side of the bridge).
 X39, 339, X43, 343, 431, 432, 433, 434, 435, 436, 437, 438, 440, 443, 470, 500, 504, 506, 888; *Circular Quay;* *Circular Quay.*
 (02) 9240 1100.
Website *www.pylonlookout.com.au.*
Admission *$8.50.*
Open *10am-5pm.*

Sydney Observatory

Australia's oldest observatory features an exhibition on astronomy and its context in Australian history.

Watson Road, Observatory Hill, The Rocks.
 X39, 339, X43, 343, 431, 432, 433,

434; ⊠ *Circular Quay;* ⊠ *Circular Quay.*
☎ *(02) 9217 0485.*
Website *www.phm.gov.au/observe/.*
Admission *$6 during the day, $12 at night (bookings essential).*
Open *10am-5pm daily.*

OTHER AREAS
Sydney's suburbs go on and on and on so allow plenty of travelling time to get to the city's more far-flung sights.

Sydney Jewish Museum
This is an excellent small museum that presents Jewish history and includes moving exhibits on the Holocaust.
148 Darlinghurst Road, Darlinghurst.
⊠ *311, 378, 380, 382, 389;*
⊠ *Kings Cross.*
☎ *(02) 9360 7999.*
Website *www.sjm.com.au.*
Admission *$10, $7 students.*
Open *Sun-Thu 10am-4pm, Fri 10am-2pm.*

Taronga Zoo
Taronga Zoo is one of Sydney's most popular attractions. It is known as the zoo with a view and is one of the world's more enjoyable zoos, partly because of its lovely harbourside setting. The zoo has the usual collection of animals from around the globe and a couple of good picnic and barbecue areas.
Bradleys Head Road, Mosman.
⊠ *Taronga Zoo.*
☎ *(02) 9969 2777.*
Website *www.zoo.nsw.gov.au.*
Admission *$25, $17.50 students, combined ferry and admission tickets available.*
Open *9am-5pm daily.*

Wonderland
Wonderland is a big amusement park in Sydney's western suburbs that features roller coasters, waterslides, a wildlife park and various themed areas.
Wallgrove Road, Eastern Creek.
⊠ *Rooty Hill then bus transfer.*
☎ *(02) 9830 9100.*
Website *www.wonderland.com.au.*
Admission *$48.40 theme park, $17.60 wildlife park.*
Open *10am-5pm daily.*

Around Sydney
There are plenty of interesting excursions that can be made from Sydney and most can be made as either a day trip or a weekend getaway.

Attractions around Sydney range from medium-sized industrial cities including Newcastle and Wollongong to the vineyards of the Hunter Valley and hiking in the Blue Mountains and Ku-Ring-Gai Chase National Park.

Newcastle
Newcastle is Australia's sixth largest city and the state's second largest. Most travellers overlook Newcastle but this industrial city has some good surf beaches and other attractions. Although Newcastle is a major industrial port it's a good base for exploring the nearby Hunter Valley while the city centre has enough attractions to keep you busy for half a day or so. Newcastle's attractions include a couple of museums and the excellent Fort Scratchley.

Practical Information
Tourist Information Centre
363 Hunter Street, Newcastle.
☎ *(02) 4974 2999.*
Website *www.newcastletourism.com.*
Open *Mon-Fri 9am-5pm, Sat-Sun 10am-3.30pm.*

Coming & Going
Newcastle is part of the CityRail network with frequent trains to Sydney. The train journey between Newcastle and Sydney Central should take around three hours. Trains heading further north stop at Broadmeadow station, which is about five stations out of town on the CityRail system. The train from Sydney Central to Newcastle costs $17 one-way and $21 for an off-peak return.

The bus terminal is located behind the train station. There are buses to destinations all the way up the east coast as far as Cairns as well as buses to Sydney. Generally the train is the cheaper way to get to Sydney whereas the bus is cheaper for destinations to the north.

New South Wales

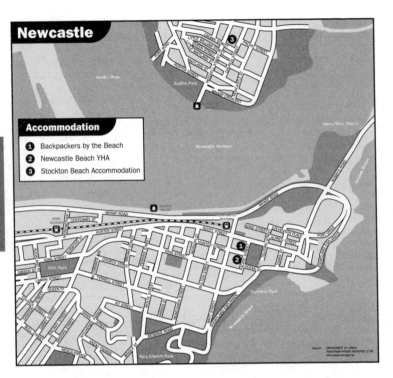

Local Transport

Newcastle has a good public transport network that is made up of buses, trains and ferries. Buses *(website www.newcastlebuses.info)* are the most common form of transport for most travellers.

All bus tickets are good for unlimited rides within a one-hour, four-hour or all day period. A one-hour ticket is $2.60, four-hour tickets cost $5.10 and an all day ticket costs $7.80. A ten-trip ticket is also available and costs $21.50. Weekly passes cost $36 for bus and ferry travel and $44-47 for bus, ferry and train travel.

Ferries run at half-hour intervals between Queens Wharf near the main train station and Stockton on the north shore of the Hunter River. The ferry costs $1.90 one-way.

The CityRail network serves the western and southern suburbs. Train fares in the Newcastle area generally cost between $2.20 and $4.40 for a one-way ticket. Return tickets cost twice the one-way fare with the exception of off-peak return tickets that cost between $2.60 and $5.20. Off-peak return tick-

ets are equivalent to a cheap day return and must be purchased after 9am.

Accommodation
Backpackers by the Beach

This clean hostel has a kitchen and dining room on the ground floor with big windows facing the street. Downstairs there's a TV lounge with Internet access and there is another TV room upstairs. It has good security with lockers in the rooms. *34-36 Hunter Street, Newcastle.*
🚌 *100, 101, 103, 104, 107, 108, 111, 201, 222, 224, 225, 226, 230, 231, 235, 310, 317, 322, 334, 349, 350, 351, 363;* 🚆 *Newcastle.*
☎ *(02) 4926 3472.*
Dorm bed *$24 ($22 Nomads/ISIC/VIP/YHA);* ***double room*** *$53 ($50 Nomads/ISIC/VIP/YHA);* ***triple room*** *$71 ($65 Nomads/ISIC/VIP/YHA).*
Reception open *7am-11pm daily.*

Maintenance & cleanliness	★★★
Facilities	★
Atmosphere & character	★★
Security	★★★
Overall rating	★★★☆

Backpackers Newcastle

This friendly hostel is set in two old houses and facilities include a big common room with a pool table, TV and kitchen plus a courtyard with table tennis. It's the only hostel in Newcastle that has a swimming pool.

42-44 Denison Street, Hamilton.
🚌 *201, 222, 226, 230, 231, 317, 322, 334, 349, 350, 363;* 🚉 *Hamilton.*
☎ *(02) 4969 3436 or 1800 33 34 36.*
Dorm bed *$19-25;* **double/twin room** *$46-60.*
Credit cards *MC, Visa.*
Reception open *8am-10am & 4pm-8pm daily.*

Maintenance & cleanliness	★★☆
Facilities	★★☆
Atmosphere & character	★★★★
Security	★
Overall rating	★★☆

Newcastle Beach YHA

Newcastle's YHA hostel is housed in a heritage building with plenty of comfy leather couches and a big fireplace, which gives it a lot of charm. Facilities include a good kitchen, a pool table and a big lounge. Accommodation is a high standard, but some of the dorms are larger than average. This hostel boasts a great location in the heart of the city centre.

30 Pacific Street, Newcastle.
🚌 *100, 101, 103, 104, 107, 108, 111, 201, 222, 224, 225, 226, 230, 231, 235, 310, 317, 322, 334, 349, 350, 351, 363;* 🚉 *Newcastle*
☎ *(02) 4925 3544.*
Dorm bed *$27.50-28.50 ($24-25 YHA);* **single room** *$45.50-46.50 ($42-43 YHA);* **double/twin room** *$67-69 ($60-62 YHA).*
Credit cards *MC, Visa.*
Reception open *7am-10.30pm daily.*

Maintenance & cleanliness	★★★
Facilities	★★★
Atmosphere & character	★★★★☆
Security	★★
Overall rating	★★★

Stockton Beach Accommodation

This is an extremely clean hostel with first class facilities that include a spa and sauna, lots of common areas including a TV lounge and kitchen. It

used to be a squash court so some of the common areas have very high ceilings and there's a rooftop sundeck with great views of Newcastle city centre and Stockton Beach.

68 Mitchell Street, Stockton.
🚉 *Stockton.*
☎ *(02) 4928 4333.*
Website *www.stocktonbeachbackpackers.com.au.*
Dorm bed *$25;* **double room** *$63-80.*
Credit cards *Amex, Diners, JCB, MC, Visa.*
♿

Maintenance & cleanliness	★★★★★
Facilities	★★★☆
Atmosphere & character	★★★☆
Security	★★★
Overall rating	★★★★☆

West End Guest House

This former pub offers budget accommodation, but it isn't really geared for backpackers and there isn't much atmosphere. It is clean and facilities include a small kitchen and a small TV lounge behind the reception.

775 Hunter Street, Newcastle.
🚌 *100, 106, 111, 201, 226, 230, 231, 235, 317, 322, 334, 349, 350, 351, 363;* 🚉 *Wickham.*
☎ *(02) 4961 4446.*
Dorm bed *$30;* **single room** *$60;* **double room** *$70.*
Credit cards *MC, Visa.*

Maintenance & cleanliness	★★★
Facilities	★
Atmosphere & character	★
Security	★☆
Overall rating	★★

Sights
Fort Scratchley

Built in the 1880s, this former defence post now contains a military and maritime museum. The fort offers good views of both the harbour and city centre. There is an extensive system of tunnels linking the complex.

Corner Nobbys & Wharf Roads, Newcastle East.
🚌 *100, 101, 103, 104, 107, 108, 111, 201, 222, 224, 225, 226, 230, 231, 235, 310, 317, 322, 334, 349, 350, 351, 363;* 🚉 *Newcastle.*
☎ *(02) 4929 2588.*

Admission *Maritime Museum free,
Military Museum free, tours of the
tunnel system $1.50.*
Open *Maritime Museum Tue-Fri
10am-4pm, Sat-Sun noon-4pm, Military Museum Sat-Sun noon-4pm.*

Newcastle Region Art Gallery

This isn't bad for a regional art gallery
and there is a decent collection of Australian and international exhibits.
Laman Street, Newcastle.
■ *100, 101, 103, 104, 107, 111, 201,
222, 225, 226, 230, 231, 235, 317,
322, 334, 349, 350, 351, 363;*
■ *Civic.*
☎ *(02) 4974 5100.*
Admission *free.*
Open *Tue-Sun 10am-5pm.*

Newcastle Regional Museum

A good museum with exhibits on
regional history alongside hands-on
science displays.
787 Hunter Street, Newcastle.
■ *100, 101, 103, 104, 107, 111, 201,
222, 224, 230, 231, 235, 317, 322,
334, 349, 350, 363;* ■ *Wickham.*
☎ *(02) 4974 1400.*
Website *www.nrmuseum.com.au.*
Admission *free.*
Open *Tue-Sun 10am-5pm.*

Wetlands Centre

More than 170 bird species have been
recorded in this 45-hectare wildlife
sanctuary in the suburbs. There are
hiking trails and canoes can also be
rented.
Sandgate Road, Shortlands.
■ *103, 108;* ■ *Sandgate.*
☎ *(02) 4951 6466.*
Website *www.wetlands.org.au.*
Admission *$4.50.*
Open *Mon-Fri 9am-3pm, Sat-Sun
9am-5pm.*

Hunter Valley

The Hunter Valley is the closest major
wine-producing region to Sydney.
Located west of Newcastle, the region
is home to many of Australia's top
wineries most of which are centred
around Polkobin although much larger
Cessnock is the area's major town. Like

other wine producing regions such as
the Barossa Valley, the main attraction
here is visiting the wineries and sampling their products.

Practical Information
Wine and Visitors Centre

111 Main Road, Polkolbin.
☎ *(02) 4990 4477.*
Website *www.winecountry.com.au.*
Open *Mon-Thu 9am-5pm, Fri 9am-
6pm, Sat 9.30am-5pm, Sun 9.30am-
3.30pm.*

Coming & Going

Cessnock is most easily accessible from
Newcastle. If you're visiting Newcastle
you can make the Hunter Valley a day
trip, catching a bus from there or alternatively taking a train to Maitland and
the getting a connecting bus.

Coming from Sydney you have
the option of going via Newcastle or
Maitland or catching a less frequent
direct bus. Keans Travel Express
(☎ *(02) 9281 9366)* runs a daily service to Scone, which passes through the
Hunter Valley.

Local Transport

There's no public transport between
the wineries in the Hunter Valley,
so your best bet is to tag along with
someone who's driving or rent a
bike. Bicycle rental is available from
Grapemobile (☎ *(02) 4991 2339;
website* *www.grapemobile.com.au)* in
Polkobin.

Ku-Ring-Gai Chase National Park

Ku-Ring-Gai Chase National Park is
just 24km north of central Sydney. It is
Australia's second-oldest national park
and features numerous coves and inlets
along Broken Bay. The park is easily
accessible by public transport making it
a great day-trip or weekend destination.
The park has some good bush walks,
including a couple of easy 20-minute
walks.

The Pittwater YHA hostel is located
here, making the national park a popular destination with backpackers.

Practical Information
Bobbin Head Visitor Centre
Bobbin Head, Ku-Ring-Gai Chase National Park.
☎ *(02) 9472 8949.*
Open Mon-Fri 1pm-4pm, Sat-Sun 10am-5pm.

Kalkari Visitor Centre
Ku-Ring-Gai Chase Road, Ku-Ring-Gai Chase National Park.
☎ *(02) 9472 9300.*
Open 9am-5pm daily.

Coming & Going
Ku-Ring-Gai Chase National Park is unique in its easy accessibility by public transport.

To get to the Bobbin Head entrance at the southern end of the park take a train to Turramurra (on the North Shore line) and then transfer to bus 577.

If you want to get to the Pittwater YHA hostel at the eastern end of the national park, take bus E86 from Wynyard Station, or bus 156 from Manly, to Church Point and then take the ferry to the hostel. The ferry costs $4.50 each way and runs approximately every 45 minutes.

Accommodation
Pittwater YHA Hostel
Pittwater YHA is one of Australia's most beautifully located hostels. It is on a secluded hilltop overlooking Pittwater and the surrounding area is home to wildlife including wallabies and cockatoos. The hostel's facilities include a big common room with piano and plenty of books. There is also a big kitchen and an outdoor area with a barbecue. Accommodation is in small dorms with balconies that allow you to enjoy stunning views. This hostel closed for renovation after it was last reviewed so it doesn't have a current BUG star rating.
Halls Wharf via Church Point, Pittwater.
☐ *156, E86 to Church Point then C to Halls Wharf.*
☎ *(02) 9999 5748.*
Dorm bed $26.50 ($23 YHA);
double/twin room $67 ($60 YHA).
Credit cards MC, Visa.

Reception open 8am-11am & 5pm-8pm daily.
Not yet rated.

Blue Mountains
Named for their distinctive blue haze, a result of eucalyptus oil evaporating from gum trees, the Blue Mountains have long been a popular destination. They are famous for their scenery that features spectacular rock formations, vast gorges and sandstone cliffs hundreds of metres high. Situated on the Great Dividing Range at an average altitude of 1,000 metres above sea level, the Blue Mountains is a vast and rugged natural wilderness area containing three National Parks totalling almost 250,000 hectares; for which a World Heritage listing has been proposed.

The Blue Mountains were initially perceived as an impenetrable barrier for early explorers and a route through them was not found until 1813. Today the Great Western Highway closely follows the route blazed by the early explorers, winding its way along a string of 26 mountain townships and it is now easily accessible by train from Sydney.

The Three Sisters rock formation is the most famous Blue Mountains attraction and there are plenty of hiking trails in the surrounding area.

Other attractions include the world's steepest railway, the Katoomba Scenic Railway, which travels from the cliff top at Katoomba down into the Jamison Valley. Above, the Skyway carries passengers along a ropeway 206 metres above the valley floor.

Katoomba is the major town in the Blue Mountains and caters to day-trippers from Sydney with plenty of pricey boutiques, craft shops and cafés. Katoomba is the best place to base yourself in the Blue Mountains and it has easy access to the Scenic Railway, scenic lookouts and hiking trails and good rail access from Sydney.

Practical Information
Blue Mountains Visitor Centre
Echo Point Road, Katoomba.
☎ *1300 653 408.*

New South Wales

Website www.bluemountainstourism.org.au
Open 9am-5pm daily

Coming & Going

CityRail operate an hourly train service between Sydney Central station and the Blue Mountains with stops at Katoomba, Leura and Wentworth Falls. The train from Sydney Central costs $11.40 one-way and $14 for an off-peak return.

Local Transport

Mountainlink and the Blue Mountains Bus Company (☎ (02) 4782 4213) operate local public transport with regular bus services through most of the day, although services become much less frequent after 6pm. If you arrive at Katoomba station, walk down Katoomba Street, which will take you to the cliff-face overlooking Jamison Valley. This is where most of the hiking trails depart from and it's also where you'll find the Scenic Skyway, Scenic Railway, the Three Sisters lookout and the information centre at Echo Point.

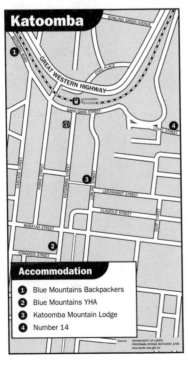

Katoomba

Accommodation
1. Blue Mountains Backpackers
2. Blue Mountains YHA
3. Katoomba Mountain Lodge
4. Number 14

Source: DEPARTMENT OF LANDS
PANORAMA AVENUE BATHURST 2795
www.lands.nsw.gov.au

Accommodation

Blue Mountains Backpackers

This small clean hostel is in an old house. It is a friendly place with a cosy TV lounge and a small kitchen.
190 Bathurst Road, Katoomba.
☎ *(02) 4782 4226.*
Dorm bed $19-22 ($17-20 VIP, $17-22 YHA); *double/twin room* $54-58 ($52-54 VIP, $52-58 YHA); *camping* $13-14 per person.
Credit cards MC, Visa.
Reception open Mon-Thu 9am-noon & 5.30pm-8pm, Fri 9am-noon & 5.30pm-9pm, Sat-Sun 9am-noon & 8pm.

Maintenance & cleanliness	★★★
Facilities	★★☆
Atmosphere & character	★★★★☆
Security	★★☆
Overall rating	★★★

Blue Mountains YHA

The Blue Mountains YHA is a big new youth hostel housed in an historic building that was home to a cabaret club in the 1930s and has been renovated retaining its art deco character. This hostel has top quality fittings and facilities include a fully equipped kitchen, big dining area/common room with pool table and foosball and a big screen TV in the downstairs TV lounge. There is excellent security with key card access and a locker for each bed.
207 Katoomba Street, Katoomba.
☎ *(02) 4782 1416.*
Dorm bed $24.50-28.50 ($21-25 YHA); *double room* $73-81 ($66-74 YHA).
Credit cards MC, Visa.
Reception open 7am-10pm daily.

Maintenance & cleanliness	★★★★★
Facilities	★★☆
Atmosphere & character	★★★★☆
Security	★★★★
Overall rating	★★★★

Katoomba Mountain Lodge

This big old building has a good atmosphere but the décor is a little drab. It has a kitchen, a cosy common room with a piano, log fire and TV and a big balcony at the front of the building with lovely views.

31 Lurline Street, Katoomba.
☎ (02) 4782 3933.
Dorm bed $20 ($19 VIP/YHA).
Credit cards MC, Visa.
Reception open 8am-10pm daily.
🚗

Maintenance & cleanliness	★★★
Facilities	★★
Atmosphere & character	★★★
Security	★☆
Overall rating	★★☆

Number 14
Number 14 is a small hostel in a tastefully decorated old house with nice polished floorboards and a cosy atmosphere. Accommodation is in mostly double and twin rooms but there are also a few small dormitories.
14 Lovel Street, Katoomba.
☎ (02) 4782 7104.
Website www.bluemts.com.au/no14/.
Dorm bed $20-25; **double/twin room** $55-60.
Credit cards MC, Visa.
Reception open 9am-11am & 5pm-8.30pm daily.

Maintenance & cleanliness	★★★★☆
Facilities	★
Atmosphere & character	★★★★☆
Security	★★☆
Overall rating	★★★

Sights & Activities
Hiking
There are some excellent hiking trails around the Blue Mountains with most of the walks originating around Katoomba.

The most popular include the Giant Stairway Walk that descends the Jamison Valley from Echo Point and the Federal Pass Trail that passes along the floor of the valley and includes the Katoomba Falls and Orphan Rock.

Scenic Railway
The world's steepest inclined railway is more like a short roller coaster ride. It is a very popular and thrilling ride.
Corner Violet Street & Cliff Drive, Katoomba.
☎ (02) 4752 2699.
Website www.scenicworld.com.au.
Tickets $6 one-way, $12 return.
Open 9am-5pm daily.

Scenic Skyway
This cable gondola provides an impressive view of Katoomba and the Blue Mountains from above Jamison Valley.
Corner Violet Street & Cliff Drive, Katoomba.
☎ (02) 4752 2699.
Website www.scenicworld.com.au.
Tickets $10.
Open 9am-5pm daily.

Wollongong
Less than two hours south of Sydney is Wollongong, the state's third largest city. Wollongong has a busy port and coal and steel industries but the city also has a few attractions including centrally located surf beaches. It makes a good base for exploring the surrounding Illawarra region.

Practical Information
Tourism Wollongong
93 Crown Street, Wollongong.
☎ (02) 4227 5545.
Website www.tourismwollongong.com.
Open Mon-Fri 9am-5pm, Sat 9am-4pm, Sun 10am-4pm.

INTERNET ACCESS
Network Café
Crown Street Mall, Wollongong.
☎ (02) 4228 8686.
Website www.networkcafe.com.au.

LAUNDRY
City Central Laundry
82 Kembla Street, Wollongong.
☎ (02) 4228 6686.

Coming & Going
The easiest way to get in and out of Wollongong is by train. The CityRail network covers the city and its surrounding area and there are frequent trains between Wollongong and Sydney as well as trains further south to Kiama and Nowra. The train from Sydney Central to Wollongong costs $8.80 one-way or $10.80 for an off-peak return.

Buses go to destinations south of Nowra as well as to Canberra and Melbourne. Buses terminate at the bus station on the corner of Campbell and Keira Streets.

New South Wales

New South Wales

Local Transport
The CityRail network serves the metropolitan area including Port Kembla. Buses supplement the suburban rail system although the central area is compact enough to get around on foot.

Accommodation
Keiraleagh House
This is a big old house in the city centre that has loads of character. Facilities include a fully equipped kitchen, a TV lounge and a backyard with barbecue.
60 Kembla Street, Wollongong.
☎ *(02) 4228 6765.*
Dorm bed *$18;* **single room** *$30;* **double/twin room** *$50; includes breakfast.*

Maintenance & cleanliness	★★★
Facilities	★☆
Atmosphere & character	★★★★
Security	★☆
Overall rating	★★☆

Sights
Australia's Industry World
Port Kembla, near Wollongong, is home to one of Australia's highest concentrations of heavy industry. Australia's Industry World consists of a visitors' centre where tours depart for the nearby steel making and port facilities.
Springhill Road, Coniston.
🚉 *Coniston.*
☎ *(02) 4275 7023.*
Website *www.aiw.org.au.*
Admission *$16.*
Tours depart *Wed, Fri 9.30am.*

Illawarra Museum
This small museum has a focus on local history.
11 Market Street, Wollongong.
🚉 *Wollongong.*
☎ *(02) 4228 7770.*
Admission *$2.*
Open *Thu noon-3pm, Sat-Sun 1pm-4pm.*

Nan Tien Buddhist Temple
The Nan Tien Buddhist Temple is the largest in the Southern Hemisphere. The temple has become an integral part of Wollongong's multicultural community with an increasing number of locals adopting Buddhism.

Berkeley Road, Berkeley.
🚌 *34, 43, 67, 69;* 🚉 *Unanderra.*
☎ *(02) 4272 0600.*
Website *www.ozemail.com.au/~nantien/.*
Admission *guided tour $2.20, full day excursion $12.50.*
Open *Tue-Sun 9am-5pm.*

Wollongong City Gallery
This art museum features a small collection of Aboriginal and contemporary art.
Corner Kembla & Burelli Streets, Wollongong.
🚉 *Wollongong.*
☎ *(02) 4228 7500.*
Website *www.wcg.1earth.net.*
Admission *free.*
Open *Tue-Fri 10am-5pm, Sat-Sun noon-4pm.*

Wollongong Science Centre & Planetarium
This science museum north of the city centre has over 120 hands-on exhibits plus a fully-featured planetarium.
Squires Way, Brandon Park, Fairy Meadow.
🚉 *Fairy Meadow.*
☎ *(02) 4286 5000.*
Website *www.uow.edu.au/science_centre.*
Admission *$9.50.*
Open *10am-4pm daily.*

North Coast
The north coast is the most travelled region in New South Wales outside Sydney. Most backpackers travel with either a bus or rail pass from Sydney to Queensland, breaking the journey at various stops along the north coast. Byron Bay is definitely the most popular town with backpackers, although other places like Port Macquarie and Coffs Harbour also have plenty to offer the traveller.

Port Stephens
Heading north from Newcastle, Port Stephens is the first place worth stopping. This small town is a great place for

spotting both dolphins and whales. You can often see dolphins in the harbour, but boat trips are popular particularly between June and October, which is the whale-watching season.

Another big attraction is the sand dunes on Stockton Beach.

Practical Information
Information Centre
Victoria Parade, Nelson Bay.
☎ *(02) 4981 1579*
Website www.portstephens.org.au.
Open Mon-Fri 9am-5pm, Sat-Sun 9am-4pm.

Accommodation
Melaleuca Surfside Backpackers
Melaleuca Surfside is a nice hostel with a relaxed laid-back atmosphere. It is comprised of a main building with a kitchen and lounge, which is linked via a boardwalk to accommodation in wooden cabins.
33 Ecualyptus Drive, One Mile Beach.
☎ *(02) 4981 9422.*
Website www.myportstephens.com/ melaleuca.
Dorm bed $25; double room $70; camping $12.50 per person.
Credit cards MC, Visa.
🚍

Maintenance & cleanliness	★★★
Facilities	★☆
Atmosphere & character	★★★★☆
Security	★
Overall rating	★★☆

Samurai Beach Bungalows
This small hostel consists of cabins set among three acres of bush and there's plenty of wildlife, including koalas, on the hostel's grounds. Facilities include an outdoor kitchen area with barbecues, a volleyball court, a campfire area and a good games room. Accommodation consists of double, twin and family rooms, each with a TV and fridge in the room and nice spacious dormitories. Guests have free use of sand boards, body boards, surfboards and bikes.
Corner Frost Road & Robert Connell Close, Anna Bay.
☎ *(02) 4982 1921.*
Website www.portstephens.org.au/ samurai.

Dorm bed $21 ($20 VIP/YHA); double room $52-69 ($50-65 VIP/ YHA).
Credit cards MC, Visa.
Reception open 8am-10.30pm daily.
🚍

Maintenance & cleanliness	★★★
Facilities	★★☆
Atmosphere & character	★★★★☆
Security	★
Overall rating	★★★

Sights & Activities
Kayaking
Lazy Paddles (☎ 0412 832 220) in Hawks Nest on Port Stephens' northern shore runs sea-kayaking tours on the serene Myall River.

Stockton Beach Sand Dunes
Stockton Beach extends from Port Stephens to Newcastle and is best known for its impressive sand dunes. If you have your own 4WD vehicle you can buy a permit for $5 that allows you to drive on the beach, otherwise you will have to take a tour. Dawsons Scenic Tours (☎ 0425 213 096; website www.portstephensadventure.com.au) operate 4WD tours on the dunes that cost between $20 and $45. A fun alternative is the 4WD quad bike tour that is run by Sand Safaris (☎ (02) 4965 0215; website www.sandsafaris.com.au), these cost $115-125.

Surfing
Anna Bay Surf School (☎ (02) 4981 9919; website www.surfingaustralia.c om) run surfing lessons for $40 ($35 VIP/YHA) and also rent surf gear.

Taree
This town on the Manning River is a down-to-earth place without the touristy feel of other towns on the coast. It has few attractions, but some travellers who stop here take a river cruise.

Practical Information
Manning Valley Visitors Centre
Pacific Highway, Taree North.
☎ *1 800 801 522.*
Website www.retreat-to-nature.com.
Open 9am-5pm daily.

New South Wales

Coming & Going

Taree is on the train line between Sydney and Brisbane and is also served by virtually all buses on this route. The bus station is on the corner of Pacific Highway and Victoria Street.

Port Macquarie

Port Macquarie is a popular holiday destination for Sydneysiders and is popular with backpackers who stop over to take advantage of the cheaper prices on adventure activities compared to destinations further north. Although much of Port Macquarie feels like a featureless Australian suburb, there are some good beaches and it is well situated for exploring nearby lakes and rainforest.

Practical Information
Information Centre
Corner Clarence & Hay Streets, Port Macquarie.
☎ *1800 025 935.*
Website *www.portmacquarieinfo.com.au.*
Open *Mon-Fri 8.30am-5pm, Sat-Sun 9am-4.30pm.*

INTERNET ACCESS
Port Surf Hub
57 Clarence Street, Port Macquarie.
☎ *(02) 6584 4744.*
Open *Sun-Wed 9am-6/7pm, Thu-Sat 9am-7/9pm.*

Accommodation
Lindel Backpackers
This is an old house with a veranda that offers views of the town centre. Facilities include a small kitchen, TV lounge and pool room plus an outdoor area with a barbecue and swimming pool.
2 Hastings River Drive, Port Macquarie.
☎ *(02) 6583 1791.*
Website *www.lindel.com.au.*
Dorm bed *$20-22.*
Credit cards *Diners, MC, Visa.*
Reception open *8am-10pm daily; late check in by prior arrangement.*

Maintenance & cleanliness	★★
Facilities	★★
Atmosphere & character	★★★
Security	★★☆
Overall rating	★★

Ozzie Pozzie Backpackers
This clean and well-maintained hostel is built around a courtyard with hammocks, outdoor furniture and a barbecue. There's also the usual kitchen and TV lounge and guests have free use of bicycles and body boards.
36 Waugh Street, Port Macquarie.
☎ *(02) 6583 8133 or 1800 620 020.*
Dorm bed *$22-25 ($20-23 ISIC/ Nomads/VIP/YHA);* **double room** *$50-60 ($48-55 ISIC/Nomads/VIP/ YHA); includes breakfast.*
Credit cards *MC, Visa.*
Reception open *8am-11am & 3pm-7pm daily.*
☎

Maintenance & cleanliness	★★★★☆
Facilities	★★★☆
Atmosphere & character	★★★
Security	★★
Overall rating	★★★★☆

Beachside Backpackers YHA
This is a small clean hostel with only 30 beds in four and six-bed dormitories.

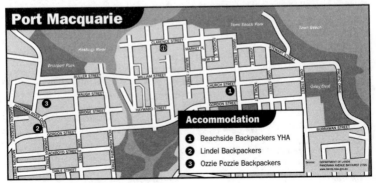

Port Macquarie

Accommodation
1. Beachside Backpackers YHA
2. Lindel Backpackers
3. Ozzie Pozzie Backpackers

Facilities include a kitchen, barbecue area and a lounge room with TV and Internet access.

40 Church Street, Port Macquarie.
☎ *(02) 6583 5512.*
Dorm bed *$25 ($23 YHA);* **twin room** *$60 ($55 YHA).*
Credit cards *MC, Visa.*
Reception open *8am-10pm daily.*

Maintenance & cleanliness	★★★★⯪
Facilities	★★⯪
Atmosphere & character	★★★
Security	★★
Overall rating	★★★⯪

Sights
Billabong Koala Breeding Centre
You can see koalas, kangaroos and wallabies at this small, but popular, wildlife park.

61 Billabong Drive, Port Macquarie.
☎ *(02) 6585 1060.*
Admission *$9.50.*
Open *9am-5pm daily; koala patting 10.30am, 1.30pm, 3.30pm.*

Port Macquarie Historical Museum
This small museum features exhibits on Port Macquarie's convict heritage, including the obligatory display of store dummies in period costume.

22 Clarence Street, Port Macquarie.
☎ *(02) 6583 1108.*
Admission *$4.50.*
Open *Mon-Sat 9.30am-4.30pm, Sun 1pm-4.30pm.*

Timbertown
This open-air museum west of Port Macquarie offers a glimpse of life in the 1900s. It features paddle steamer, stage coach and steam train rides.

Oxley Highway, Wauchope.
☎ *(02) 6585 2322.*
Website *www.timbertown.com.au.*
Admission *free; but charge for individual attractions.*
Open *9.30am-3.30pm daily.*

Port Macquarie Maritime Museum
This museum is much like other maritime museums around Australia and includes the usual collection of model ships and all things nautical. The

museum operates cruises on some of its historic boats.

6 William Street, Port Macquarie.
☎ *(02) 6583 1866.*
Admission *$6; museum tour & one-hour cruise $12.*
Open *Mon-Sat 11am-3pm; 1hr cruise departs Tue, Thu 1pm; 2hr cruise departs Tue-Thu 10.30am.*

Sea Acres Rainforest Centre
This rainforest centre south of the town centre is set among 72 hectares of coastal rainforest and it features a 1.3km boardwalk through the rainforest canopy.

Pacific Drive, Shelly Beach.
☎ *(02) 6582 3355.*
Admission *$9.90.*
Open *9am-4.30pm daily.*

Nambucca Heads
Located mid-way between Brisbane and Sydney, Nambucca Heads offers great beaches, plus plenty of other outdoor experiences including sea kayaking, rainforests and whale watching.

Practical Information
Information Centre
4 Pacific Highway, Nambucca Heads.
☎ *(02) 6568 6954.*
Website *www.nambuccatourism.com.*
Open *9am-5pm daily.*

Coming & Going
Both trains and buses serve Nambucca Heads. Countrylink trains call at the train station on Bowra Street a few kilometres from the town centre while buses stop at the bus station closer to the centre of town near the information centre on Pacific Highway.

Bellingen
Bellingen is an attractive small town situated inland between Nambucca Heads and Coffs Harbour. The town is a good base for exploring the nearby region that includes the Dorrigo National Park. Bellingen has an alternative feel with arts and crafts shops and plenty of cafés and it is one of the loveliest towns between Sydney and Byron Bay.

Coming & Going

Because of its location off the highway, many buses running up and down the east coast don't stop at Bellingen. However there are some buses stopping here that depart from Coffs Harbour, Port Macquarie and Armidale but they don't always run every day.

Accommodation
Bellingen Backpackers YHA

Bellingen Backpackers YHA is a lovely hostel that boasts a laid-back atmosphere that makes it a great place to chill out for a few days. The old wooden building has loads of charm and it features big balconies and verandas with hammocks to laze about in. Facilities include a fully equipped kitchen plus a pool table, a tree house and a campfire area.

2 Short Street, Bellingen.
☎ *(02) 6655 1116.*
Website www.bellingenyha.com.au.
Dorm bed *$25 ($23 YHA);* **double/ twin room** *$58 ($56 YHA);* **camping** *$12 per person.*
Credit cards *MC, Visa.*
Reception open *8am-10am & 5pm-10pm daily.*
☎

Maintenance & cleanliness	★★★★½
Facilities	★★
Atmosphere & character	★★★★★
Security	★
Overall rating	★★★½

Activities
Canoeing

Bellingen Canoe Adventures (☎ *(02) 6655 9955)* operates canoeing trips on the Bellinger River. These start at $14 for a night-time tour and increase to $88 for a full day guided tour with a gourmet lunch.

Coffs Harbour

Coffs Harbour is home to the Big Banana and it is a popular spot with backpackers who come here for adrenaline-producing activities like sky diving and white water rafting. It is one of the cheapest places on the east coast to learn to dive and there are some good beaches here.

Practical Information
Information Centre

Corner Pacific Highway & McLean Street, Coffs Harbour
☎ *(02) 6652 1522.*
Website www.coffscoast.com.au.
Open 9am-5pm daily.

Coming & Going

Coffs Harbour is accessible by both rail and bus. The train station is situated on Angus McLeod Street across from Jetty Beach and buses stop at the coach station near the information centre on the Pacific Highway.

Accommodation
Aussitel Backpackers

Aussitel is a clean, well-maintained hostel. Facilities include a common room with a pool table, TV lounge and Internet access. There's also a swimming pool, table tennis and a barbecue. Guests have free use of canoes, body boards and bicycles.

312 High Street, Coffs Harbour.
☎ *(02) 6651 1871.*
Dorm bed *$24 ($22 VIP);* **double/ twin room** *$60 ($55 VIP).*
Credit cards *MC, Visa.*
Reception open *summer 8am-11am & 1.30pm-9pm daily; winter Sun-Thu 8am-11am & 1.30pm-8pm, Fri-Sat 8am-11am & 1.30pm-9pm.*
☎

Maintenance & cleanliness	★★★★
Facilities	★★★★½
Atmosphere & character	★★★
Security	★★½
Overall rating	★★★★½

Barracuda Backpackers

This clean hostel has a friendly atmosphere. Facilities include a kitchen, TV lounge, Internet access and a swimming pool. The hostel is close to Park Beach Plaza shopping centre and it's about a five-minute walk to the beach.

19 Arthur Street, Coffs Harbour.
☎ *(02) 6651 3514.*
Website www.backpackers.coffs.tv.
Dorm bed *$22 ($20 ISIC/Nomads/ VIP/YHA);* **double/twin room** *$55 ($50 ISIC/Nomads/VIP/YHA).*
Reception open *7.30am-10.30am & 1.30pm-9.30pm daily.*

Maintenance & cleanliness	★★★
Facilities	★★☆
Atmosphere & character	★★★☆
Security	★★
Overall rating	★★★

Coffs Harbour YHA

Coffs Harbour's YHA is a good clean youth hostel with the usual TV lounge, kitchen and Internet access plus a swimming pool and an good open-air games room with pool table and table tennis.

110 Albany Street, Coffs Harbour.
☎ *(02) 6652 6462.*
Dorm bed *$24-26 ($22-24 YHA);*
double room *$57-64 ($55-60 YHA);*
twin room *$54 ($50 YHA).*
Credit cards *MC, Visa.*
Reception open *summer 7am-11pm daily; winter 8am-10pm daily.*

Maintenance & cleanliness	★★★
Facilities	★★☆
Atmosphere & character	★★★☆
Security	★★☆
Overall rating	★★★

Hoey Moey Backpackers

This hostel is a former motel and all rooms have fridges, TVs and en suite bathrooms. The place could be better maintained and it feels old and tired. Facilities are limited to Internet access and a basic kitchen. It's the only hostel in Coffs Harbour that's right on the beach.

Ocean Parade, Coffs Harbour.
☎ *(02) 6651 7966.*
Dorm bed *$22 ($20 VIP/YHA).*
Credit cards *Amex, MC, Visa.*
Reception open *summer 6am-11.30am & 1.30pm-8pm daily; winter 6am-11.30am & 1.30pm-6.30pm daily.*

Maintenance & cleanliness	★★
Facilities	★★
Atmosphere & character	☆
Security	★
Overall rating	★☆

Sights
Big Banana

One of the more famous of Australia's big things, this huge concrete banana is the focal point of a tourist complex that

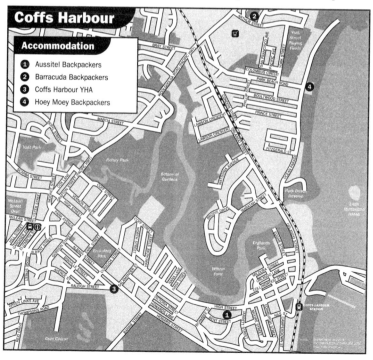

Coffs Harbour

Accommodation

1. Aussitel Backpackers
2. Barracuda Backpackers
3. Coffs Harbour YHA
4. Hoey Moey Backpackers

features monorail tours of a banana plantation.
Pacific Highway, Coffs Harbour.
☎ *(02) 6652 4355.*
Website www.bigbanana.com.
Admission free.
Open 9am-5pm daily.

Coffs Harbour Historical Museum

This small museum focuses on the region's history.
191A High Street, Coffs Harbour.
☎ *(02) 6652 5794.*
Admission $2.
Open Sun-Fri 10am-4pm.

Coffs Harbour Zoo

This small zoo has over 350 animals with an emphasis on Australian wildlife such as kangaroos, koalas and wombats.
1530 Pacific Highway, Moonee (10 minutes north of Coffs Harbour).
☎ *(02) 6656 1330.*
Admission $16.
Open 8.30am-4pm daily.

Muttonbird Island Nature Reserve

Overlooking the harbour and marina, Muttonbird Island is a great retreat and ideal spot for whale watching.

Oceanarium (Pet Porpoise Pool)

This tired-looking marine-themed animal park has performing dolphins and seals as well as native fauna such as cockatoos and kangaroos.
Orlando Street, Coffs Harbour.
☎ *(02) 6652 2164.*
Website www.coffsac.com/petporpoise/.
Admission $17, students $13.
Open 9am-5pm daily, shows at 10.30am & 2.15pm.

Activities
Diving

Coffs Harbour is an increasingly popular place to learn to dive. Diving here is considerably cheaper than in Queensland and the nearby Solitary Islands Marine Park is a top diving spot. Prices start at $185 for a four-day PADI dive course. Dive courses are run by: Divers Depot (☎ *(02) 6652 2033*), Jetty Dive Centre (☎ *(02) 6651 1611; website*

www.jettydive.com.au) and Pacific Blue Dive Centre (☎ *(02) 6652 2759*).

Sea Kayaking

Liquid Assets (☎ *(02) 6658 0850; website www.surfrafting.com*) run good value sea kayaking trips to the Solitary Islands Marine Park that give you the opportunity to see dolphins, turtles and whales. Half-day trips cost $35.

Skydiving

Coffs is a popular skydiving destination. Coffs City Skydivers (☎ *(02) 6651 1167; website www.coffscentral.dnet.tv/ CoffsCitySkyDivers/*) offers tandem skydiving.

Surfing

There is good surfing available around Coffs Harbour. East Coast Surf School (☎ *(02) 6651 5515; website www.east coastsurfschool.com.au*) offers how-to-surf lessons for $40 for two hours on the beach or $160 for a five-day course.

Whale Watching

Up to 4,000 hump back whales migrate through the Coffs Coast each year and the Pacific Explorer (☎ *(02) 6652 7225; website www.pacificexplorer.com*) runs whale watching cruises between June and November.

Whitewater Rafting

There are several companies operating white water rafting trips on rivers between Coffs Harbour and Byron Bay with pickups from Coffs Harbour hostels. The Nymboida River is the closest to Coffs Harbour and is a popular river for rafting. A one-day rafting trip on the Nymboida River costs between $125 and $153. White water rafting companies include: Liquid Assets Adventure Tours (☎ *(02) 6658 0850; website www.surfrafting.com*), Rapid Rafting (☎ *(02) 6652 1741*), Wild Scenic Rivers (☎ *(02) 6651 4575*), Wildwater Adventures (☎ *(02) 6653 3500*) and WOW Rafting (☎ *(02) 6654 4066*).

Ballina

Situated around 30 minutes south of Byron Bay, Ballina has some good beaches and is a useful alternative when Byron Bay is booked out. Generally Ballina is more of a spot to come to make transport connections rather than a destination in its own right. Ballina's attractions include a maritime museum and the Big Prawn.

Practical Information
Information Centre
Las Balsas Plaza, River Street, Ballina. ☎ *(02) 6686 3484.*
Open *Mon-Fri 9am-5pm, Sat-Sun 9am-4pm.*

Coming & Going
Ballina is on the Brisbane to Sydney bus route and also has local buses to nearby towns including Lennox Head, Byron Bay and Mullumbimby. Buses stop at the Big Prawn on the Pacific Highway south of the town centre.

Ballina Airport (☎ *(02) 6686 8385; website www.ncas.com.au/html/ ballinaairport.html)* has several daily flights to Sydney and it is the most northern point that you can fly to with a Rex backpacker pass.

Accommodation
Ballina Travellers Lodge YHA
This youth hostel is comprised of four units within a motel. Everything here is clean and very well maintained and it is nicer than many other motel/hostels. Facilities include the usual kitchen, barbecue area and TV lounge plus a swimming pool. Guests have free use of body boards.
36-38 Tamar Street, Ballina. ☎ *(02) 6686 6737.*
Dorm bed *$22-27.50 ($20-24 YHA);* **double room** *$60-105 ($56-98 YHA).* **Credit cards** *Amex, Diners, MC, Visa.* **Reception open** *7am-10pm daily.*
🚌

Maintenance & cleanliness	★★★★☆
Facilities	★★☆
Atmosphere & character	★★
Security	★☆
Overall rating	★★★

Lennox Head
This small town, between Ballina and Byron Bay is best known for its surf

beaches, which are rated among the world's best.

Coming & Going
BalTrans bus 640 runs between Ballina and Byron Bay stopping en route at Lennox Head. This bus stops in the town centre and also outside Lennox Head Backpackers.

Premier Coaches also stop at Lennox Head, but Greyhound/McCafferty's don't come here.

Accommodation
Lennox Head Backpackers
Lennox Head Backpackers is a clean and well-maintained hostel with a nice courtyard area. Facilities include the usual TV lounge, kitchen and a barbecue area. Bike and surfboard hire is available. It is located on a quiet street only 100 metres from the beach.
2-3 Ross Street, Lennox Head. ☎ *(02) 6687 7636.*
Dorm bed *$25-27 ($24-26 YHA);* **double room** *$52-62 ($50-60 YHA).* **Credit cards** *MC, Visa.* **Reception open** *7am-10pm daily.*

Maintenance & cleanliness	★★★★
Facilities	★★★☆
Atmosphere & character	★★★☆
Security	★★☆
Overall rating	★★★☆

Byron Bay
After Sydney, this small town on the far north coast of New South Wales is the most popular backpacker destination in the state. This laid-back town is populated by a mix of new-age hippies and backpackers and has a fantastic ambience. Apart from the beach and the lighthouse at the eastern-most point on the Australian mainland, Byron Bay doesn't have a lot of attractions, but somehow most travellers find themselves staying much longer than they had originally planned.

Practical Information
INFORMATION & BOOKING CENTRES
Byron Bus & Backpacker Centre
84 Jonson Street, Bryon Bay. ☎ *(02) 6685 5517.*

Open Mon-Fri 7.30am-7pm, Sat-Sun 8am-7pm.

Visitor Information Centre
Stationmaster's Cottage, 80 Jonson Street, Byron Bay.
☎ *(02) 6680 8558.*
Website www.visitbyronbay.com.
Open 9am-5pm daily.

Peter Pan Adventures
87 Jonson Street, Byron Bay
☎ *1800 252 459*
Website www.peterpans.com.
Open 9am-8pm daily.

INTERNET CAFÉS
Byron Bay has loads of Internet cafés including:

Backpackers World
Shop 6, Byron Street, Byron Bay.
☎ *(02) 6685 8858.*
Website www.byron-bay.com/ backpackersworld/.
Open Mon-Fri 9am-8pm, Sat 9.45am-6pm, Sun 11am-5pm.

Global Gossip
84 Jonson Street, Byron Bay.
☎ *(02) 6680 9140.*
Website www.globalgossip.com.au.
Open Mon-Fri 9am-11pm, Sat-Sun 10am-11pm.

Coming & Going
AIR
Byron Bay is located between Ballina and Coolangatta Airports. Ballina Airport has flights to Sydney and regional destinations in NSW while the busier Coolangatta Airport has flights to most parts of Australia as well as some international flights. There are airport buses that connect Byron Bay with both airports.

Airlink (☎ *(02) 6684 3232*) run a shuttle bus between Byron Bay and both Ballina and Coolangata airports.

The Coolangatta/Byron Bay Airporter (☎ *(02) 6680 8726*) picks up from hostels, departing Byron Bay five times daily.

Byron Bay Airbus (☎ *(02) 6681 3355*) picks up from hostels in Byron

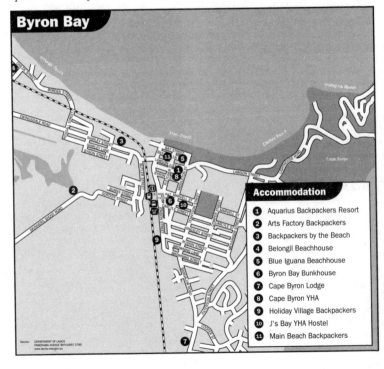

Byron Bay

Accommodation
1. Aquarius Backpackers Resort
2. Arts Factory Backpackers
3. Backpackers by the Beach
4. Belongil Beachhouse
5. Blue Iguana Beachhouse
6. Byron Bay Bunkhouse
7. Cape Byron Lodge
8. Cape Byron YHA
9. Holiday Village Backpackers
10. J's Bay YHA Hostel
11. Main Beach Backpackers

Source: DEPARTMENT OF LANDS
PANORAMA AVENUE BATHURST 2795
www.lands.nsw.gov.au

Bay and connects with flights at Ballina.

TRAIN
Byron Bay is on the Sydney-Brisbane train line with two daily trains in each direction. The train station is situated on Jonson Street right in the centre of town.

BUS
Because Byron Bay is off the main highway some buses don't stop here, but most buses on the Brisbane-Sydney route do. They stop near the information centre on Jonson Street outside the train station.

Brisbane 2 Byron (☎ *1800 626 222; website www.brisbane2byron.com*) operates a minibus service between Brisbane and Byron Bay. The trip takes two hours and costs $28.

There are several companies offering day trips to Nimbin, these trips range from a simple shuttle bus to tours that stop by at a number of local attractions. Because of intense competition, there are some good deals available – check the brochures at your hostel for the best prices.

Local Transport
Byron Bay is small enough to walk around, but there's a shuttle bus (☎ *0411 343 311*) that goes to the lighthouse. It departs central Byron Bay hourly between 9am and 4pm and costs $5 one-way or $9.50 return.

Accommodation
Aquarius Backpackers Resort
This is a high quality hostel with motel-style accommodation, but a better atmosphere than most other motel-style hostels. All rooms have en suite and it features the usual kitchen plus a swimming pool and an excellent outdoor bar with a party atmosphere and good value – mostly barbecue – meals every night.
16 Lawson Street, Byron Bay.
☎ *(02) 6685 7663 or 1 800 028 909.*
Website *www.aquarius-backpack.com.au.*
Dorm bed *$25-28 ($24-27 VIP/YHA); double room $55-75 ($53-73*

VIP/YHA).
Credit cards *MC, Visa.*
Reception open *7am-9.45pm daily; 24 hour check in.*

Maintenance & cleanliness	555
Facilities	★★★★☆
Atmosphere & character	★★★★
Security	★★☆
Overall rating	★★★★☆

Arts Factory Backpackers
The atmosphere at the Arts Factory is very Byron Bay – that is laid back and chilled out with an alternative edge. This is the hostel for you if you're after the ultimate Byron Bay experience. The Arts Factory is a big sprawling complex covering some five acres of sub-tropical gardens and it has an excellent range of facilities that include a big kitchen, Internet access, a quiet reading room, beach volleyball court, swimming pool and a sauna. There is a games room with pool tables, pinball and video games and a kiosk that sells cold drinks. The complex also features a cinema and restaurant. There is plenty to do here including lots of in-house activities such as didgeridoo making plus bike, body board and surfboard rental. There is an eclectic range of accommodation options including canvas huts, a surf shack, tepee, a double-decker bus and camping as well as regular dormitories. The hostel has a quiet location on the edge of town; some people may find it a little inconveniently located but it's only a 15-minute walk and a shuttle bus runs into town 14 times a day.
Skinners Shoot Road, Byron Bay.
☎ *(02) 6685 7709.*
Website *www.artsfactory.com.au.*
Dorm bed *$25-28 ($23-26 VIP/YHA); double/twin room $70-80 ($65-75 VIP/YHA); camping $12 ($10 VIP/YHA) per person.*
Credit cards *MC, Visa.*
Reception open *7am-1pm & 3.30pm-9pm daily.*

Maintenance & cleanliness	★★★
Facilities	★★★★
Atmosphere & character	★★★★★
Security	★★☆
Overall rating	★★★★☆

Backpackers Inn on the Beach

This is a very clean, well-designed place set among sub tropical gardens. The hostel's facilities include a commercial kitchen, a common room with pool table and comfy cane sofas, a café and a very nice outdoor area with a swimming pool, beach volleyball court and a walking track to the beach.
29 Shirley Street, Byron Bay.
☎ *(02) 6685 8231.*
Website www.byron-bay.com/
backpackersinn.
Dorm bed $25 ($24 ISIC/YHA; $23 VIP); double/twin room $32 ($31 ISIC/YHA; $30 VIP).
Credit cards MC, Visa.
Reception open 8am-8pm daily.
🚐

Maintenance & cleanliness	★★★★
Facilities	★★★
Atmosphere & character	★★★★
Security	★★★
Overall rating	★★★☆

Belongil Beachhouse

This is a well-designed hostel set among sub tropical gardens. The common area includes a large kitchen, a TV lounge and a quieter reading area and there is also a café on site. It has a great laid-back atmosphere and it's a 20-minute walk along the beach into town.
Childe Street, Byron Bay.
☎ *(02) 6685 7868.*
Dorm bed $21-26 ($20-25 VIP/ YHA); single room $50 ($49 VIP/ YHA); double room $55-80 ($53-78 VIP/YHA).
Credit cards MC, Visa.
Reception open 8am-7pm daily.
🚐

Maintenance & cleanliness	★★★
Facilities	★★★☆
Atmosphere & character	★★★★☆
Security	★
Overall rating	★★★

Blue Iguana Beachhouse

Byron Bay's smallest hostel has only 12 beds and occupies a charming old beach house in the town centre. The hostel is a bit grubby but the beds are comfy and it has a great friendly atmosphere. Facilities include a cosy little TV lounge and a nice outdoor barbecue area. It has the best location of the Byron Bay hostels.
14 Bay Street, Byron Bay.
☎ *(02) 6685 5298.*
Dorm bed $26-30; double/twin room $60-80.
Reception open 9am-noon & 4pm-9pm daily.

Maintenance & cleanliness	★★★☆
Facilities	★★★
Atmosphere & character	★★★★☆
Security	★★☆
Overall rating	★★★

Byron Bay Bunkhouse

Byron Bay Bunkhouse is a great hostel with a fun atmosphere. It has a big common room and a balcony with lots of places to lounge around plus a games room with pool tables, darts and video games. The atmosphere is friendly and laid back and although it's not quite a party hostel it is still a fun place to stay.
1 Carlyle Street, Byron Bay.
☎ *(02) 6685 8311.*
Website www.byronbay-
bunkhouse.com.au.
Dorm bed $20-22; double room $58-65; includes pancake breakfast.
Credit cards MC, Visa.
Reception open 7.30am-10pm daily.
🚐

Maintenance & cleanliness	★★★☆
Facilities	★★☆
Atmosphere & character	★★★★☆
Security	★★
Overall rating	★★★

Cape Byron Lodge

This is a very good hostel with a great atmosphere. The facilities are well maintained and feature a nice courtyard, landscaped gardens and a common area with a kitchen, a pool table and TV. There's also a swimming pool and guests have free use of bikes and boogie boards. It's not as central as other places in town – the hostel is a good 20-minute walk to the centre of Byron Bay. Apart from the location the other main drawback is that there's nowhere to keep your clothes dry when you take a shower. Overall it's excellent value when compared with other hostels in Byron Bay.

78 Bangalow Road, Byron Bay.
☎ *(02) 6685 6445.*
Website *www.capebyronlodge.com.*
Dorm bed *$13-20;* **double room**
$50-55.
Credit cards *MC, Visa.*
Reception open *9am-2pm & 5pm-9pm.*
🚗

Maintenance & cleanliness	★★★★☆
Facilities	★★★
Atmosphere & character	★★★☆
Security	★☆
Overall rating	★★★☆

Cape Byron YHA

Cape Byron YHA is an excellent hostel and everything is new, clean and well maintained. The hostel is built around a courtyard with a big swimming pool and a barbecue. Facilities include a common room with pool table, video games and Internet access; a big kitchen area and an outdoor area upstairs. Guests have free use of bicycles and body boards.
Corner Byron and Middleton Streets, Byron Bay.
☎ *(02) 6685 8788 or 1800 652 627.*
Dorm bed *$27.50-33.50 ($24-30 YHA);* **double/twin room** *$77-97 ($70-90 YHA).*
Credit cards *MC, Visa.*
Reception open *6.45am-10pm daily.*

Maintenance & cleanliness	★★★★
Facilities	★★★☆
Atmosphere & character	★★★
Security	★★☆
Overall rating	★★★☆

Holiday Village Backpackers

This purpose-built hostel is clean and well maintained. It features a big kitchen, a TV lounge and an outdoor area with a barbecue, swimming pool and volleyball court. Accommodation is in small clean dorms and also in self-contained apartments. The hostel hosts regular barbecues and guests have free use of bikes, boogie boards and surf boards.
116 Jonson Street, Byron Bay.
☎ *(02) 6685 8888.*
Website *www.byronbaybackpackers. com.au.*
Dorm bed *$25 ($24 VIP);* **double room** *$65 ($63 VIP).*

Credit cards *MC, Visa.*
Reception open *6.45am-9.30pm daily.*
🚗

Maintenance & cleanliness	★★★★
Facilities	★★★☆
Atmosphere & character	★★☆
Security	★
Overall rating	★★★☆

J's Bay Hostel YHA

J's Bay YHA is a fairly new purpose-built hostel and everything is new, clean and well maintained. The hostel features a big, well-equipped kitchen with an outdoor dining area with a pool table. There is also a TV lounge and a common room with Internet access and a swimming pool. Guests have free use of bicycles, snorkelling gear and body boards.
7 Carlyle Street, Byron Bay.
☎ *(02) 6685 8853 or 1800 678 195.*
Website *www.jsbay.com.au.*
Dorm bed *$28.50-30.50 ($25-27 YHA);* **double room** *$87-93 ($80-90 YHA).*
Credit cards *MC, Visa.*
Reception open *8am-9pm daily.*
🚗

Maintenance & cleanliness	★★★★★
Facilities	★★★
Atmosphere & character	★★★☆
Security	★★☆
Overall rating	★★★★

Main Beach Backpackers

Main Beach Backpackers is a good clean hostel with a central location. It features a big kitchen, a TV lounge with pool table, a nice outdoor barbecue area, a swimming pool and a large rooftop sundeck.
Corner Fletcher & Lawson Streets, Byron Bay.
☎ *(02) 6685 8695 or 1 800 150 233.*
Dorm bed *$22-25 ($20-23 ISIC/ Nomads/VIP/YHA);* **double room** *$50-90.*
Credit cards *MC, Visa.*
Reception open *8am-9.30pm daily.*
🚗

Maintenance & cleanliness	★★★☆
Facilities	★★★
Atmosphere & character	★★★
Security	★★★☆
Overall rating	★★★☆

Activities
Abseiling, Canyoning & Rock Climbing
The region around Byron Bay offers the opportunity for a multitude of climbing sports. Rockhoppers organise a wide selection of these activities.
Corner Marvel & Jonson Streets, Byron Bay.
☎ *0500 881 881.*
Website www.rockhoppers.com.au.
Cost $119 for abseiling, caving and flying fox.
Departs Mon, Wed, Fri, Sat 9am.

Hang Gliding
Byron Airwaves (☎ *(02) 6629 0354)* and Skylimit (☎ *(02) 6684 3711)* run tandem hang gliding flights and offer hang gliding lessons. Flights are at Cape Byron or Lennox Head and half-hour tandem flights cost $115 to $145.

Sea Kayaking
Sea kayaking puts you in a unique position to discover Byron Bay's marine life, which includes dolphins. Sea-kayaking trips cost around $40 per person.
Byron Bay Sea Kayaks (*Lawson Street, Byron Bay;* ☎ *(02) 6685 4161; website www.byronbayadventureco.com)* and Dolphin Kayaking (*50 Lawson Street, Byron Bay;* ☎ *(02) 6685 8044)* operate sea-kayaking trips.

Surfing
Byron Bay has excellent beginners waves and it's a popular spot to learn to surf. One-day lessons start at $29 and five-day courses cost around $150.
There are loads of surfing schools in Byron Bay including Black Dog Surfing (☎ *(02) 6685 8858)*, Byron Bay Surf School (*87 Jonson Street, Byron Bay;* ☎ *1800 707 274; website www.byronbaysurfschool.com)*, Style Surfing (☎ *(02) 6685 5634)*, Surfing Byron Bay (☎ *0500 853 929; website www.gosurfingbyronbay.com)* and the cheapest, Kool Katz (*4/70 Shirley Street, Bryron Bay;* ☎ *(02) 6685 5169)*.

Lismore
With around 50,000 people, Lismore is the main town in the far north of the state and it's where people from neighbouring towns come to get things done. Lismore is home to a university and has a much more sophisticated air to it than most other regional towns of a similar size – probably due to the alternative/new-age influence of nearby places like Byron Bay and Nimbin.
If you're staying a while in Byron Bay, Nimbin, Lennox Head or Ballina you may find you have to come here for shopping or medical reasons.

Practical Information
Information Centre
Corner Ballina & Molesworth Streets, Lismore.
☎ *(02) 6622 0122.*
Website www.liscity.nsw.gov.au.
Open 9.30am-4pm daily.

INTERNET ACCESS
The Bush Telegraph
50 Magellan Street, Lismore.
☎ *(02) 6621 5324.*

SHOWERS
There are public showers in the transit centre that cost $2.

Coming & Going
Lismore is accessible by both train and bus. The train station is on Union Street with trains to Brisbane, Sydney and Murwillumbah.
Some Brisbane-Sydney buses bypass Lismore so check first if you want to get off here. Most buses, including Kirklands and McCafferty's/Greyhound buses, stop at the Transit Centre at the corner of Magellen and Molesworth Streets.

Accommodation
Lismore Backpackers (Currendina Lodge)
This big old wooden building has the usual kitchen and TV lounge. It has several long-term guests staying here, which compromises security and makes it feel like staying in a doss house.
14 Ewing Street, Lismore.
☎ *(02) 6621 6118.*
Dorm bed $22; double room $47.
Reception open 7am-8pm daily.
☎

Maintenance & cleanliness	★★☆
Facilities	★★☆
Atmosphere & character	★
Security	-
Overall rating	★★☆

Murwillumbah

About 30km from Byron Bay, this small town is well situated to several national parks plus other attractions in the Tweed Valley including Mount Warning.

Practical Information
World Heritage Rainforest & Information Centre
Corner Alma Street & Pacific Highway, Murwillumbah
☎ *(02) 6672 1340.*
Website www.nationalparks.nsw.gov.au.
Open 9am-4.30pm daily.

Coming & Going
Murwillumbah is situated at the end of the Sydney-Murwillumbah train line with one daily train in each direction. There are also frequent buses to Brisbane, Sydney as well as Byron Bay and the Gold Coast that depart from the bus terminal on Murwillumbah Street.

Accommodation
Murwillumbah Hotel
This pub on the main street offers backpackers accommodation in well-maintained rooms above the bar. Although it is very clean, the facilities are limited and the atmosphere is rather sterile.
13 Wharf Street, Murwillumbah.
☎ *(02) 8872 1129.*
Website www.murwillumbahhotel.com.au.
Dorm bed *$15;* **double room** *$50.*
Credit cards *Amex, MC, Visa.*

Maintenance & cleanliness	★★★☆
Facilities	★
Atmosphere & character	★★☆
Security	★★★☆
Overall rating	★★★☆

Riverside YHA Backpackers
This hostel is in an old building with polished floorboards and big solid wooden benches in the fully equipped kitchen. The hostel backs on to the Tweed River and there is decking at the front and rear of the hostel where you can lounge around and take in the great river views. The TV lounge is in a separate building, which separates the TV noise from anyone who wants to get some sleep. A big feature here is the free chocolate chip ice cream that is served at 9pm every night and you get a free trip to Mt Warning if you stay for two nights. The atmosphere is generally quiet but friendly.
1 Tumbulgum Road, Murwillumbah.
☎ *(02) 6672 3763.*
Dorm bed *$25 ($24 YHA);* **double/twin room** *$54 ($52 YHA).*
Credit cards *MC, Visa.*
Reception open *8am-10am & 5pm-10pm daily.*

Maintenance & cleanliness	★★★☆
Facilities	★★☆
Atmosphere & character	★★★★☆
Security	★★☆
Overall rating	★★★★☆

Activities
Mt Warning
Mt Warning is the main reason most travellers visit Murwillumbah. The staff at the YHA hostel know all about climbing the mountain and they may even arrange your transport in time for a pre-sunrise climb. Alternatively, Rockhoppers (☎ *0500 881 881*) organise treks up the mountain with transport from Byron Bay for $59.

Nimbin

This small town has been Australia's hippy heaven ever since the 1973 Aquarius Festival and is now firmly devoted to alternative culture. Nimbin is a popular day-trip from nearby Byron Bay.

Practical Information
LAUNDRY
Village Wash House
Shop 5, 45 Cullen Street, Nimbin.
☎ *(02) 6689 1799.*
Open 8am-6.30pm daily.

Coming & Going
There are several companies offering day trips to Nimbin from Byron Bay.

These trips range from simple shuttle buses to tours that call in at a number of local attractions. Because of intense competition, there are some good deals available – check the brochures at your hostel for the best prices.

A couple of the tours and bus services between Byron Bay and Nimbin include:

Jim's Alternative Tours

Jim's is a popular tour that goes to Nimbin via the Minyon Falls, a country pub and World Heritage rainforest.
☎ *(02) 6685 7720.*
Website *www.byron-bay.com/jimstours/.*
Day trip *$30.*
Departs *Byron Bay 10am, **returns** 6pm.*

Nimbin Shuttle Bus

The Nimbin Shuttle Bus makes a daily return trip between Byron and Nimbin.
☎ *(02) 6680 9189.*
Return trip *$25; **one-way** $14.*
Departs *Byron Bay Mon-Sat 10am; departs Nimbin 4pm.*

Accommodatiom

Granny's Farm

Granny's Farm is a big rural hostel set among 10 acres. There's an outdoor common area with a pool table, fire and a barbecue. Other features include a TV room and a huge kitchen plus two swimming pools. Accommodation is nice and clean and it includes double rooms, big dormitories as well as a dorm in an old train carriage. Camping sites are also available. The hostel organises movie and meal nights at the nearby theatre. It is an overnight stop on the Oz Experience bus.
Cullen Street, Nimbin.
☎ *(02) 6689 1333.*
Dorm bed *$20 ($19 VIP); **double room** $48 ($46 VIP); **camping** $10 (one person), $18 (two people).*
Reception open *8.30am-midnight.*
☎

Maintenance & cleanliness	★★★
Facilities	★★
Atmosphere & character	★★★★☆
Security	★
Overall rating	★★★

Nimbin Hotel & Backpackers

This hostel is located above Nimbin's pub and offers basic but clean accommodation and is undergoing renovation, which should see an improvement in standards.
55 Cullen Street, Nimbin.
☎ *(02) 6689 1246.*
Dorm bed *$15.*
Credit cards *MC, Visa.*
Reception open *Mon-Fri 10.30am-10.30pm, Sat-Sun 10.30am-midnight.*

Maintenance & cleanliness	★★★☆
Facilities	★
Atmosphere & character	★★
Security	★★☆
Overall rating	★★

Nimbin Rox YHA

Nimbin's YHA is a brilliant place that offers very good facilities and a high standard of accommodation, easily making it the best spot to stay in Nimbin. Facilities include a TV lounge, Internet access, and a landscaped garden with a swimming pool and barbecue area. Accommodation is split between a tepee and very nice dorms. It is located out of town near the Rainbow Retreat.
74 Thorburn Street, Nimbin.
☎ *(02) 6689 0022.*
Website *www.nimbinroxhostel.com.*
Dorm bed *$25.50 ($23 YHA); **double/twin room** $55 ($48 YHA).*
Credit cards *Diners, MC, Visa.*
Reception open *8am-11am & 2pm-9pm daily.*
☎ ♿

Maintenance & cleanliness	★★★★☆
Facilities	★★★
Atmosphere & character	★★★★★
Security	★★
Overall rating	★★★★

Rainbow Retreat

This is a chilled out place that captures the spirit of Nimbin. Accommodation is in a bunch of buildings that could be better maintained and there is a café on site. It is a good spot to stay if you're after an authentic Nimbin experience, but probably not such a good choice if Nimbin is a bit too alternative for you.
75 Thornburn Street, Nimbin.
☎ *(02) 6689 1262.*

Dorm bed $15; double room $40; camping $8 per person.
Reception open 8am-8pm daily.

Maintenance & cleanliness	★☆
Facilities	★☆
Atmosphere & character	★★★★
Security	☆
Overall rating	★★

Sights
Nimbin Museum
This unique museum shows things from the hippy perspective. Exhibits include psychedelic art and marijuana paraphernalia.
62 Cullen Street, Nimbin.
☎ *(02) 6689 1123.*
Admission free.
Open 8am-5.30pm daily.

New England
New England is the inland region behind the New South Wales north coast. This is traditionally farming country and is usually bypassed by travellers making their way up the coast, although the more direct route between Queensland and Melbourne or Sydney passes through this area.

Armidale
This small university town is one of the nicer regional towns in New South Wales with some attractive old buildings and more culture than other country towns of a similar size. Armidale is a convenient base if you're exploring nearby national parks.

Practical Information
Information Centre
82 Marsh Street, Armidale.
☎ *1800 627 736.*
Open Mon-Fri 9am-5pm, Sat 9am-4pm, Sun 10am-4pm.

National Parks Visitor Centre
85-87 Faulkner Street, Armidale.
☎ *(02) 6776 0000.*
Website www.nationalparks.nsw.gov.au.
Open Mon-Fri 8.30am-4.30pm.

Coming & Going
Armidale is connected by buses to Brisbane, Sydney and other towns in New England and along the north coast. The bus station is located at the information centre on Marsh Street.

Accommodation
Pembroke Tourist & Leisure Park
This hostel shares premises with a caravan park on the edge of town about 3km from the train station. It is a clean and well-maintained building with a kitchen, TV lounge and a games room with table tennis and pool table. Accommodation is in four 10-bed dormitories. Guests can use caravan park facilities that include tennis courts and a swimming pool.
39 Waterfall Way, Armidale.
☎ *(02) 6772 6470.*
Dorm bed $20; double/twin room $45.
Credit cards Amex, MC, Visa.
Reception open 7.30am-7.30pm daily.
Not yet rated

Glen Innes
With a rich Celtic heritage, Glen Innes is another pleasant stop if you're driving through New England although the town isn't a destination in its own right. The town's main attraction is the Standing Stones that overlook the town from Martins Lookout.

Practical Information
Glen Innes Visitor & Coach Centre
152 Church Street, Glen Innes.
☎ *(02) 6732 2397.*
Open Mon-Fri 9am-5pm, Sat-Sun 9am-3pm.

National Parks Office
68 Church Street, Glen Innes.
☎ *(02) 6732 5133.*
Website www.nationalparks.nsw.gov.au.
Open Mon-Fri 8.30am-4.30pm.

Sights
Land of the Beardies Museum
The region was first settled by a couple of bearded men from whom this

museum takes its name. The museum delves into the town's history with an interesting array of exhibits.
Corner Fergusson Street & West Avenue, Glen Innes.
☎ *(02) 6732 1035.*
Website *www.nnsw. com.au/gleninnes/ beardies01.html.*
Admission *$4.*
Open *Mon-Fri 10am-noon & 2pm-5pm, Sat-Sun 2pm-5pm.*

Standing Stones
Based upon the Ring of Brodgar in Scotland, Glen Innes's Standing Stones are a reflection of the town's Celtic heritage.
Martins Lookout, Watsons Drive, Glen Innes.
Admission *free.*

Scone
Located west of Newcastle, this small town is closer to the Hunter Valley than the other New England towns further to the north and the frequent trains from Newcastle make it accessible enough for a day-trip. Scone is one of the most important towns in New South Wales' horse breeding and racing industry and calls itself 'the horse capital of Australia'.

Practical Information
Information Centre
Corner Kelly & Susan Streets, Scone.
☎ *(02) 6545 2907.*
Website *www.horsecapital.com.au.*
Open *9am-5pm daily.*

Coming & Going
Although it is accessible by bus from Sydney, Newcastle and the Hunter Valley, the train is the best way to visit Scone. Scone lies at the western terminus on the Hunter line on the CityRail network and the frequent trains put it almost within commuting distance of Newcastle.

Accommodation
Scone YHA Hostel
This is a small 26-bed hostel in a converted schoolhouse. It has a small, but fully equipped kitchen and a cosy common room with a fireplace, TV and organ and an outdoor area with a campfire and a barbecue. Accommodation is in small spacious dorms. The hostel is home to many farm animals including horses, chickens and ducks and it has a quiet, friendly and homely atmosphere. The hostel has a quiet rural location among horse studs, 8km from Scone.
1151 Segenhoe Road, Scone.
☎ *(02) 6545 2072.*
Dorm bed *$19;* ***double room*** *$43.*
Reception open *6am-9am & 6pm-10pm daily.*
🚗
Not yet rated

Tamworth
Tamworth is the country music capital of Australia and the home of the annual Tamworth Country Music Festival and the big guitar. This is especially evident during the festival in late January, although at other times Tamworth is just another small regional city.

Practical Information
Information Centre
561 Peel Street, Tamworth.
☎ *(02) 6755 4300.*
Open *Mon-Fri 8.30am-4.30pm, Sat-Sun 9am-3pm.*

Coming & Going
Tamworth has pretty good transport connections including buses to Sydney, Brisbane, Melbourne and towns in the New England and the New South Wales north coast. Buses stop at the bus terminal near the corner of Murray and Peel streets.

Tamworth is also accessible by train with a station at the corner of Brisbane and Marius Streets with Countrylink running one daily train to and from Sydney.

Accommodation
Tamworth YHA
Tamworth YHA is a fairly average hostel with the usual laundry, kitchen and barbecue facilities. Accommodation varies between nice dormitories upstairs and more basic dorms

New South Wales

downstairs. The hostel is in the centre of Tamworth, across the road from the train station.

169 Marius Street, Tamworth.
☎ *(02) 6761 2600.*
Dorm bed *$23.50-25.50 ($20-22 YHA);* **double/twin room** *$53 ($46 YHA).*
Reception open *7am-12.30pm & 4pm-9.30pm daily.*
Not yet rated

Sights
Tamworth Country Centre
This is a tacky collection of country music memorabilia that includes a small wax museum and the big guitar.
New England Highway, South Tamworth.
☎ *(02) 6765 2688.*
Website *www.big.goldenguitar.com.au.*
Admission *$8.*
Open *9am-5pm daily.*

Central West NSW
Central Western New South Wales consists mainly of fairly non-descript rural towns and farming land. You're most likely to pass through this area if you're travelling between Brisbane and Melbourne bypassing Sydney and the coast. If you're taking the bus, it's a 24-hour stretch and you may want to break the journey.

Bathurst
An attractive town west of the Blue Mountains, Bathurst is known throughout Australia as the home of the Mount Panorama racetrack and the annual Bathurst 1000 motor race. When the race isn't being run, the six-kilometre track up Mount Panorama is a public road and virtually everyone with a car who visits Bathurst does a lap of the famous circuit – but it isn't quite the same when you stick to the 60km/h speed limit.

Other attractions in Bathurst are the National Motor Racing Museum and the Sir Joseph Banks Nature Park.

Practical Information
Visitor Information Centre
28 William Street, Bathurst.
☎ *(02) 6332 1444.*
Website *www.bathurst.nsw.gov.au/ tourism.html.*
Open *9am-5pm daily.*

National Parks Visitor Centre
Level 2, 203-209 Russell Street, Bathurst.
☎ *(02) 6332 9488.*
Website *www.nationalparks.nsw. gov.au.*
Open *Mon-Fri 9.30am-4.30pm.*

Coming & Going
Most people visit Bathurst en route to someplace else, although you may want to make the trip out from Sydney for the big race. Bathurst is at the end of the CityRail network and is also served by Countrylink trains with regular services from Sydney. Buses also stop at the train station.

Local Transport
Bathurst has a local bus service comprised of seven routes; all run along Wilson Street and terminate at the Howick Street terminus. Routes 526 and 527 are useful for getting to the National Motor Museum.

Sights
Bathurst & District Historical Museum
This small museum features exhibits on regional history. It is housed in the old courthouse, which is the most impressive of Bathurst's architectural gems.
Russell Street, Bathurst.
🚌 *520, 522, 523, 524, 525, 526, 527.*
☎ *(02) 6332 4755.*
Admission *$2.*
Open *Tue-Wed & Sat-Sun 10am-4pm.*

National Motor Racing Museum
This is worth seeing if you're a motor racing fan and interested in learning more about the sport from an Australian perspective.
Murrays Corner, Mount Panorama.
🚌 *526, 527.*
☎ *(02) 6332 1872.*
Website *www.nmrm.com.au.*

Admission $7.
Open 9am-4.30pm daily.

Cowra

This small country town on the banks of the Lachlan River was the scene of the Cowra Breakout – an escape attempt by Japanese prisoners of war that took place in 1944. Although more than 200 prisoners died during the breakout, the incident has gone a long way in building Australian-Japanese relations and Cowra is now home to Japanese war cemeteries, gardens and a cultural centre.

Practical Information
Cowra Tourism Centre
Corner Boorowa Road and Mid Western Highway, Cowra.
☎ *(02) 6342 4333.*
Open 9am-5pm daily.

Sights
Japanese Gardens & Cultural Centre
Cowra's biggest attraction is the Japanese Gardens and the adjoining cultural centre. It is the setting for many Japanese festivals and public holidays that are celebrated in Cowra.
Scenic Drive, Cowra.
☎ *(02) 6341 2233.*
Admission $7.70.
Open 8.30am-5pm daily.

Cowra Breakout Memorial & Japanese War Cemetery
The memorial is situated at the scene of the Cowra Breakout while the Australian and Japanese War Cemetery lies several kilometres north.
Memorial Corner of Farm Street and Sakura Avenue, Cowra.
Cemetery Doncaster Drive, Cowra.
Admission free.

Mudgee

Although not in the same league as Coonawarra, or the Barossa, Hunter or Yarra Valleys, Mudgee is an important wine producing area that is a nice place to pass through. Some travellers find work here during the harvest.

Practical Information
Mudgee Visitors Centre
84 Market Street, Mudgee.
☎ *(02) 6372 5875.*
Open Mon-Fri 9am-5pm, Sat 9am-3.30pm, Sun 9.30am-2pm.

Orange

This orchard town between Bathurst and Dubbo has a thriving apple and cherry growing industry.

Fruit picking work attracts most travellers to Orange, who come to pick apples during February and March and cherries later in the year around November to December.

Practical Information
Orange Visitors Centre
Byng Street, Orange.
☎ *(02) 6361 5226.*
Open 9am-5pm daily.

Dubbo

A busy town and the main centre of the state's central west, Dubbo is a good place to break your journey. The town has a good range of attractions but the highlight is the excellent Western Plains Zoo.

Practical Information
Dubbo Visitors Centre
Corner Brisbane & Erskine Streets, Dubbo.
☎ *(02) 6884 1422.*
Website www.dubbotourism.com.au.
Open 9am-5pm daily.

Accommodation
Dubbo YHA Hostel
Dubbo's YHA is an old house converted to a hostel. Facilities are old and include a common room with a piano and a log fire. All the rooms open onto a veranda.
87 Brisbane Street, Dubbo.
☎ *(02) 6882 0922.*
Dorm bed $23.50 ($20 YHA);
double/twin room $51 ($44 YHA).
Credit cards MC, Visa.
Reception open 7.30am-10.30pm daily.
Not yet rated

Sights
Dubbo Regional Gallery
Dubbo's art gallery is host to some very good temporary exhibits.
165 Darling Street, Dubbo.
☎ *(02) 6881 4342.*
Admission *free.*
Open *Tue-Sun 11am-4.30pm.*

Old Dubbo Gaol
Dubbo's old prision has been turned into a museum that features animatronic mannequins.
Macquarie Street, Dubbo.
☎ *(02) 6882 8122.*
Admission *$7.*
Open *9am-5pm daily.*

Western Plains Zoo
The Western Plains Zoo is Dubbo's main attraction and it one of Australia's best zoos. There's a good selection of native animals in addition to animals from other continents in open enclosures. There are extensive cycling and walking paths around the zoo. The zoo covers around 300 hectares so renting a bike is probably the best way to see it.
Obley Road, Dubbo.
☎ *(02) 6882 5888.*
Website *www.zoo.nsw.gov.au.*
Admission *$22, students $15.50.*
Open *9am-4pm daily.*

South Coast
Heading south from Wollongong, the New South Wales south coast is made up of pleasant beach resorts and fishing towns. Travelling this route between Melbourne and Sydney is a great alternative to the busy Hume Highway.

Kiama
Kiama is situated 45 minutes south of Wollongong and two hours from Sydney and has more character than most other towns on the south coast. There are good surf beaches here as well as hiking trails in nearby nature reserves.

Kiama's main attraction is the Blowhole, which is a natural formation that, in big seas, spurts water hundreds of metres into the air through two rock caverns.

Practical Information
Information Centre
Blowhole Point Road, Kiama.
☎ *(02) 4232 3322 or 1300 654 262.*
Website *www.kiama.com.au.*
Open *9am-5pm daily.*

Coming & Going
Kiama is on the CityRail network and the train is by far the best way to get here from Wollongong and Sydney although the bus is better for destinations inland and further down the coast.

The train station is on Bong Bong Street and there are frequent trains to Sydney (2 hours) and Wollongong (45 minutes).

Buses also go to Sydney and Wollongong as well as destinations down the coast as far as the Victorian border and onward to Melbourne. Long-distance buses stop at the corner of Collins and Terralong Streets.

Accommodation
Kiama Backpackers Hostel
Kiama Backpackers is a small hostel with basic facilities that include a small kitchen, TV lounge and Internet access. It has a handy location next to the train station.
31 Bong Bong Street, Kiama.
☎ *(02) 4233 1881.*
Dorm bed *$20;* **single room** *$25;* **double/twin room** *$49.*
Reception open *10am-10pm daily.*

Maintenance & cleanliness	★★★
Facilities	★☆
Atmosphere & character	★☆
Security	-
Overall rating	★★

Nowra
Nowra is the biggest city on the NSW coast south of Wollongong. Although a popular destination for Australian tourists, particularly from Canberra, Sydney and Wollongong, it doesn't attract many backpackers who mostly see it as a stop over on the Melbourne-Sydney coastal drive. An increasing

number of backpackers, however, are staying longer in Nowra and using it as a base to explore the surrounding region, which includes the glistening white sand beaches at nearby Jervis Bay as well as the pretty towns of Berry and Kangaroo Valley.

Practical Information
Shoalhaven Visitors Centre
Corner Pleasant Way & Princes Highway, Nowra.
☎ *(02) 4421 0778 or 1800 024 261*
Open *9am-4.30pm daily.*

National Parks Office
55 Graham Street, Nowra.
☎ *(02) 4423 2170.*
Website *www.nationalparks.nsw.gov.au.*
Open *Mon-Fri 8.30am-4.30pm.*

INTERNET ACCESS
Flat Earth Internet Café
Level 1, Nowra Mall, Junction Court, Nowra.
☎ *(02) 4423 7771.*
Open *Mon-Fri 8.30am-5pm daily.*

Coming & Going
Bomaderry is just north of Nowra's centre and is the southern terminus for the CityRail network with frequent trains to Kiama, Wollongong and Sydney. The station is on Railway Street in Bomaderry. There are frequent buses to destinations in both directions along the coast.

Accommodation
M&M's Guesthouse
This big old 1920s house has loads of character and it features a big kitchen, a TV lounge, a games room with a pool table and a nice outdoor barbecue area. It has a nice location on the banks of the Shoalhaven River.
1a Scenic Drive, Nowra.
☎ *(02) 4422 8006.*
Dorm bed *$25;* **single room** *$35.*
Credit cards *MC, Visa.*
Reception open *7am-9.30pm daily.*

Maintenance & cleanliness	★★★★☆
Facilities	★★☆
Atmosphere & character	★★★
Security	★★☆
Overall rating	★★★

Sights and Activities
Nowra Animal Park
This wildlife park on the banks of the Shoalhaven River north of Nowra features a variety of Australian wildlife including koalas, kangaroos, wallabies and wombats.
Rockhill Road, North Nowra.
☎ *(02) 4421 3949.*
Admission *$10.*
Open *9am-5pm daily.*

Rock climbing
The sandstone cliffs around Nowra offer very good rock climbing with some challenging climbs for more advanced climbers, however there isn't so much here for beginners.

Jervis Bay Region (NSW)
Only 20 minutes from Nowra, Jervis Bay is noted as having Australia's whitest sand beaches.

The waters around Jervis Bay are protected as Jervis Bay Marine Park and they are home to dolphins, whales, seals and penguins. The marine park is a popular spot for scuba diving.

Much of the area is national park with the NSW Jervis Bay National Park in NSW and Booderee National Park in Jervis Bay Territory.

Huskisson and Vincentia are the two main towns in the region although many travellers base themselves in Nowra, which is less than 30 minutes away.

Coming & Going
Nowra Coaches (☎ *(02) 4423 5244)* run a bus service linking Nowra and Bomaderry with towns in the Jervis Bay region, including Huskisson and Vincentia. The bus runs four to five times each weekday and two to three times a day on weekends.

Accommodation
Bush n Beach
This small backpackers' bed and breakfast is located close to the beach on the road connecting Huskisson and Vincentia. It moved to a new address in late 2003 so we are not able to provide an up-to-date rating.

16 Elizabeth Drive, Vincentia.
☎ *(02) 4441 6880 or 1800 666 000.*
Website *www.beachnbush.com.au.*
Dorm bed *$25;* **double room** *$60;*
includes breakfast.
Credit cards *MC, Visa.*
☎
Not yet rated

Sights and Activities
Dolphin & Whale Cruises
Dolphin and whale watching is Jervis
Bay's big attraction and cruises depart
from Huskisson.
50 Owen Street, Huskisson.
☎ *(02) 4441 6311 or 1800 246 010.*
Website *www.dolphinwatch.com.au.*
Dolphin watching cruise *$20; departs
10am daily;* **dolphin & bay cruise**
$25; departs 1pm daily; **whale watch-
ing cruise** *$40; Jun-Jul & mid-Sep to
mid-Nov.*

Lady Denman Maritime Museum
This museum features the *Lady
Denman* Ferry and several other his-
toric vessels as well as exhibits on the
heritage of Jervis Bay.
*Corner Dent Street and Woollamia
Road, Huskisson.*
☎ *(02) 4441 5675.*
Website *www.ladydenman.asn.au.*
Admission *$6.*
Open *10am-4pm daily.*

Scuba Diving
Jervis Bay is the best dive destination on
the New South Wales coast and it is well
known for its marine life and crystal-
clear waters. Dive trips can be organised
through companies in Huskisson and it
is also possible to do a PADI dive course
here. Jervis Bay Sea Sports *(47 Owen
Street, Huskisson;* ☎ *(02) 4441 5012;*
website *www.jbseasports.com.au)* and
Pro Dive Jervis Bay *(64 Owen Street,
Huskisson;* ☎ *(02) 4441 5255;* **website**
www.prodivejervisbay.com.au) operate
scuba diving trips and also run PADI dive
courses. A four-day PADI dive course at
Jervis Bay costs between $330 and $385.

Jervis Bay Territory
Jervis Bay was originally earmarked as
Canberra's port with the bay's southern

peninsula administered from Canberra
as a separate territory to New South
Wales. It is now mostly made up of a
military base, an Aboriginal community
and a national park and it is relatively
untouched considering its close proximity to Canberra and Sydney, which are
both only three hours away. It is the
smallest of Australia's mainland states
and territories and has a population of
less than 800 permanent residents.

The main attraction here is Booderee
National Park, which is known for its
wildlife and pristine beaches. Admission to the national park is $10 per car
or $3 if you arrive by bus.

Green Patch is one of the more
popular spots in the national park.
Kangaroos and colourful rainbow
lorikeets frequent this lovely beach.
Further east is Murrays Beach, another
beautiful beach that is a popular swimming spot.

Practical Information
Visitor Centre
Jervis Bay Road, Jervis Bay Territory.
☎ *(02) 4443 0977.*
Open *9am-4pm daily.*

Accommodation
Although many people stay in Nowra
or the towns in the NSW part of Jervis
Bay, some people choose to camp in the
Booderee National Park. The park has
camping areas at Cave Beach and Green
Patch; with another area at Bristol Point
that is reserved for large groups.

The fee for the Green Patch campsite
is $14-17.30 per night. The Cave Beach
campsite costs $8.65-10.75 per night.
These prices are good for a car and up
to five passengers.

The Green Patch camping area can get
crowded during the Christmas school
holidays. Campsites for this busy period
are allocated by ballot, with applications in writing accepted 1-21 August
each year. Ballot application forms can
be downloaded from the park's website
(www.ea.gov.au/parks/booderee/).

Ulladulla
Situated between Nowra and Bateman's
Bay, this small seaside town is a popular

weekend getaway for people from Canberra, Sydney and Wollongong. Most backpackers use Ulladulla as a stop over on the Melbourne-Sydney coastal drive and some people base themselves here to visit Pebbly Beach and Murramarang National Park.

Practical Information
Information Centre
Princes Highway, Ulladulla.
☎ *(02) 4455 1269.*
Open *Mon-Fri 10am-5pm, Sat-Sun 9am-5pm.*

Coming & Going
Premier Motor Services (☎ *13 34 10; website www.premierms.com.au) stop at Ulladulla on their Sydney-Melbourne run. Buses stop outside the Marlin Hotel (southbound) and outside the Traveland travel agency (northbound).

Accommodation
South Coast Backpackers
This is a small hostel in a nice house with polished floors, a fully equipped kitchen, Internet access and a nice outdoor area with hammocks and a barbecue. Guests have free use of bicycles, boogie boards, surfboards and fishing gear.
63 Princes Highway, Ulladulla.
☎ *(02) 4454 0500.*
Website *www.southcoastbackpackers. com.au.*
Dorm bed *$20 ($19 VIP);* **double/ twin room** *$45 ($43 VIP).*
Reception open *8am-8pm daily.*
🚐

Maintenance & cleanliness	★★★★
Facilities	★★★
Atmosphere & character	★★★★
Security	★★
Overall rating	★★★½

Murramrang National Park & Pebbly Beach
For many travellers, Pebbly Beach (in Murramrang National Park) is the highlight of the NSW South Coast.

Located less than 30 minutes north of Batemans Bay, Pebbly Beach consists of a sheltered cove with a beautiful sandy beach that is frequented by abundant wildlife including scores of kangaroos. This is better than any wildlife park as you get to see wild animals rather than kangaroos in an enclosure.

There are some good hiking trails that depart from Pebbly Beach, including one to Durras Mountain (4 hours return), Depot Beach (30 minutes) and the Discovery Trail (45 minutes). Entry to the park is $6 per car.

Accommodation
Most backpackers visit on a day trip from Batemans Bay or Ulladulla, but you can camp at Pebbly Beach. Camping costs $5 per person, in addition to the vehicle entry fee, and must be booked on (02) 4478 6006.

Batemans Bay
Batemans Bay is around 150km east of Canberra and is a popular weekend destination for families from the capital. Although there aren't a lot of things to see or do, the town is one of the nicer holiday destinations on the coast. Many travellers stay in Bateman's Bay and make a day trip to Pebbly Beach and Murramarang National Park, which is only about 30 minutes from here.

Practical Information
Information Centre
Corner Beach Road & Princes Highway (near McDonalds), Batemans Bay.
☎ *(02) 4472 6900.*
Website *www.naturecoast-tourism.com.au.*
Open *9am-5pm daily.*

Coming & Going
There are buses to destinations up and down the coast including services to Sydney and Melbourne. There are also daily buses to Canberra. Buses stop outside the Promenade Plaza.

Accommodation
Beach Road Backpackers Hostel
This house on Beach Road has been converted into a small 16-bed hostel. There is a kitchen and a cosy TV lounge plus an outdoor area with a barbecue. All beds come made up with linen and duvets and towels are also supplied.

The hostel manager organises trips to Pebbly Beach. It has the nicest location of the two hostels in Batemans Bay, as it is across the road from the sea, but it's about 1km from the town centre.
92 Beach Road, Batemans Bay.
☎ *(02) 4472 3644.*
Dorm bed *$23 ($22 VIP);* **double room** *$48 ($45 VIP).*

Maintenance & cleanliness	★★★
Facilities	★★
Atmosphere & character	★★★★
Security	★☆
Overall rating	★★★

Shady Willows YHA
This hostel is located in a caravan park that has facilities that include a barbecue area and swimming pool. The hostel also has a good kitchen, TV lounge and Internet access.
Corner of Old Princes Highway & South Street, Batemans Bay.
☎ *(02) 4472 4972.*
Dorm bed *$25.50-31.50 ($22-28 YHA);* **single room** *$38.50 ($35 YHA);* **double/twin room** *$55-63 ($48-56 YHA).*
Credit cards *MC, Visa.*
Reception open *8am-9pm daily.*

Maintenance & cleanliness	★★★
Facilities	★★★
Atmosphere & character	★★
Security	★
Overall rating	★★☆

Merimbula
Merimbula is a popular spot for holidaymakers from Victoria and Canberra. It has nice beaches that are good for fishing, surfing and swimming.

Whales can be seen off the coast between October and November.

Practical Information
Merimbula Visitor Information Centre
Beach Street, Merimbula.
☎ *(02) 6495 1129.*
Website *www.sapphirecoast.com.au*

National Park Visitor Centre
Corner Sapphire & Merimbula Drives, Merimbula.

☎ *(02) 6495 5000.*
Website *www.nationalparks.nsw.gov.au.*
Open *Mon-Fri 9am-4pm.*

Coming & Going
Rex has daily flights from Merimbula's small airport to Melbourne and Sydney and Merimbula is the nicest stop over for travellers using Rex's backpacker pass to travel between Melbourne and Sydney.

Buses run to Melbourne, Sydney and Canberra and stop at the Ampol service station on the Princes Highway. McCafferty's/ Greyhound buses also stop at the YHA.

Accommodation
Wandarrah Lodge YHA
This is a good purpose-built hostel with a fully equipped kitchen, Internet access and a pool table as well as a small TV lounge. Double rooms come with linen and duvets.
8 Marine Parade, Merimbula.
☎ *(02) 6495 3503.*
Dorm bed *$23.50-30.50 ($22-27 YHA);* **double room** *$55-69 ($48-62 YHA);* **twin room** *$55-65 ($48-58 YHA).*
Credit cards *MC, Visa.*
Reception open *7.30am-10.30am & 4pm-7pm daily.*
☎

Maintenance & cleanliness	★★★★☆
Facilities	★★
Atmosphere & character	★★★
Security	★★
Overall rating	★★★☆

Eden
If you're taking the coastal route between Melbourne and Sydney, Eden is the first town on the New South Wales coast after crossing the Victorian border. It is a quiet holiday resort with several attractions including the Killer Whale Museum, however it is less touristy than places further up the coast.

Practical Information
Eden Gateway Visitor Information Centre
Princes Highway, Eden.
☎ *(02) 6496 1953.*

Open summer 9am-5pm daily; winter Mon-Fri 9am-4pm, Sat-Sun 9am-noon.

Sights
Killer Whale Museum
Eden's top attraction, the Killer Whale Museum has interesting exhibits on Killer Whales and the history of the region's whaling industry.
94 Imlay Street, Eden.
☎ *(02) 6496 2094.*
Admission $5.50.
Open 9.15am-3.45pm daily.

Snowy Mountains
Just six hours drive south of Sydney, the Snowy Mountains includes Australia's highest peak, Mount Kosciuszko.

Settled in the mid-1800s, the area was originally used by cattlemen to feed cattle during long, hot summers. In 1964 the area was declared a National Park and grazing ceased.

The seven ski resorts in the region have more than 50 ski lifts and the official ski season runs from June to October.

Serious adventurers will thrive on challenging treks, rock and mountain climbing, cross country skiing and heart-stopping downhill ski runs. Ski resorts such as Kosciuszko-Thredbo, Perisher Blue, Charlotte's Pass and Mount Selwyn each have their own character and village atmosphere.

If you're coming here for the skiing, the easiest option is to organise a ski package from Canberra or Sydney.

Cooma
Situated midway between Canberra and the Victorian border, Cooma is far enough from the main ski resorts to be an affordable place to base yourself but close enough to the action to enjoy the region.

Practical Information
Information Centre
119 Sharp Street, Cooma.
☎ *(02) 6450 1742.*
Open 9am-5pm daily.

Coming & Going
During the ski season the bus isn't too bad a way to get around, although you really need a car at other times of the year. Mojo Snow (☎ *(02) 8558 8888 or 1300 850 380; website www.mojosnow.com.au*) run coaches between Jindabyne and Sydney, which cost $75 one-way or $140 return. They also have ski and snowboarding package deals that include accommodation, lift tickets and lessons.

Accommodation
Cooma Bunkhouse Backpackers
This motel has small self-contained units for backpackers with dorm beds, TV and a small kitchen. There is a nice courtyard but other facilities are limited.
28 Soho Street, Cooma.
☎ *(02) 6452 2983.*
Website www.bunkhousemotel.com.au.
Dorm bed $20 ($19 VIP); single room $35; double room $45.
Credit cards MC, Visa.
Reception open 6.45am-10.30pm daily.
🚌

Maintenance & cleanliness	★★
Facilities	★
Atmosphere & character	★
Security	★★✫
Overall rating	★★✫

Sights
Snowy Mountains Hydro-Electric Scheme
One of Australia's biggest engineering feats involves 16 large dams on the Snowy River that produce huge amounts of electricity and irrigate large areas of farmland. The scheme's headquarters is located about 3km from the centre of Cooma and includes a visitor centre with information on touring the facilities.
Yulin Avenue, Cooma.
☎ *1800 623 776.*
Website www.snowyhydro.com.au.
Open Mon-Fri 8am-5pm, Sat-Sun 8am-1pm.

Jindabyne
During the ski season this resort town on the shore of Lake Jindabyne is a

cheaper place to stay than Thredbo and there are frequent buses and trains that bring it within commuting distance of the ski slopes.

Outside the ski season, Jindabyne is a popular base for bush walking in Kosciuszko National Park.

Practical Information
Information Centre
Kosciuszko Road, Jindabyne.
☎ *(02) 6450 5600.*
Open *winter 8am-6pm daily; summer 8.30am-5pm daily.*

Accommodation
Snowy Mountain Backpackers
Snowy Mountain Backpackers is a very nice hostel right in the town centre. It doesn't have a lot of facilities but the hostel is very clean and well maintained.
7-8 Gippsland Street, Jindabyne.
☎ *(02) 6456 1500 or 1 800 333 468.*
Website *www.snowybackpackers.com .au.*
Dorm bed *$20-38 ($19-37 VIP);* **double room** *$50-110 ($48-108 VIP).*
Credit cards *MC, Visa.*
Reception open *9am-1pm & 4pm-6pm daily.*

Maintenance & cleanliness	★★★★★
Facilities	★★☆
Atmosphere & character	★★★
Security	★★☆
Overall rating	★★★★☆

Thredbo
Arguably Australia's top ski resort, Thredbo is a party town with 11 ski lifts and plenty of challenging runs. Like any ski resort, it can be a little expensive, so you can always commute in from Jindabyne or even Cooma. Outside the ski season, Thredbo is a useful base for hiking in Mt Kosciuszko.

Practical Information
Information Centre
6 Friday Drive, Thredbo.
☎ *(02) 6459 4198.*
Website *www.thredbo.com.au.*
Open *summer 9am-5pm daily; winter 8am-6pm daily.*

Accommodation
Thredbo YHA Hostel
Thredbo's YHA is a luxury ski lodge with top quality fittings and a warm and cosy atmosphere. It has a common room with a fireplace, plus a TV lounge and a good kitchen.
8 Jack Adams Path, Thredbo.
☎ *(02) 6457 6376.*
Dorm bed *$25.50 ($22 YHA);* **double/ twin room** *$57-65 ($50-58 YHA); prices skyrocket during the ski season.*
Credit cards *MC, Visa.*
Reception open *summer 8.30am-10am & 3pm-8pm daily; winter 7am-10am & 4.30pm-9pm daily.*

Maintenance & cleanliness	★★★★★
Facilities	★★
Atmosphere & character	★★★
Security	★★
Overall rating	★★★★☆

Hume Highway
The Hume Highway is the quickest route between Melbourne and Sydney. Although it is generally a quick boring route although there are a few places of interest along the way such as Gundagai and Albury.

Goulburn
Goulburn was proclaimed a City by Queen Victoria in 1863 and was the first inland city in Australia. It was also the location of the State's last public hanging. Inspired by the region's sheep farming industry, Goulburn's main landmark is an enormous sheep where many of the Melbourne-Sydney buses stop for a meal break.

Practical Information
Information Centre
201 Sloane Street, Goulburn.
☎ *(02) 4823 0492.*
Open *9am-5pm daily.*

Coming & Going
Goulburn is easily accessible by both rail and bus. Melbourne-Sydney buses stop in the edge of town at the Big Merino, while trains stop in the more centrally situated train station on Sloane Street.

Goulburn has Countrylink trains on the Melbourne-Sydney route and is also the southern terminus for CityRail trains that provide a cheaper and more frequent, although slower, rail transport option to Sydney and Newcastle.

Accommodation
Nomads Tattersalls Hotel
From the outside this place looks like a dive but first impressions can be deceiving and it is surprisingly nice inside. The hostel is located above a pub and amenities include a TV lounge and a basic kitchen. The rooms all feature made up beds and lockers. Some of the facilities look a little dated but the hostel is kept clean and it is generally well maintained.
76 Auburn Street, Goulburn.
☎ *(02) 4821 3088.*
Dorm bed $17-20; double/twin room $40.

Maintenance & cleanliness	★★☆
Facilities	★★☆
Atmosphere & character	★★★☆
Security	★★★☆
Overall rating	★★★☆

Gundagai

Gundagai was a popular stopover for early settlers and the town is frequently mentioned in early Australian literature. Australian poet Jack Moses wrote the famous line "and the dog sat on the tuckerbox nine miles from Gundagai" although this was adapted from an earlier poem where "the dog shat on the tuckerbox five miles from Gundagai". The early folk song *Along the Road to Gundagai* is almost as well known among Australians.

The town is best known for the Dog on the Tucker Box monument at Five Mile Creek, 8km north of town, and many people stop here for a bite to eat before continuing on. Gundagai is a nice place with some old historic buildings and there is definitely more to the town than the tacky monument and adjoining souvenir shop.

Practical Information
Gundagai Tourist & Travel Centre
294 Sheridan Street, Gundagai.
☎ *(02) 6944 1341.*

Open Mon-Fri 8am-5pm, Sat-Sun 9am-5pm.

Coming & Going
Buses terminate at the tourist information centre on Sheridan Street.

Accommodation
Blue Heeler Guesthouse
The Blue Heeler is a big old building in the town centre with a big kitchen, TV lounge, games room with table tennis and a big balcony that looks over the main street. It is pretty clean but parts of the hostel need a bit of work.
Sheridan Street, Gundagai.
☎ *(02) 6944 2286.*
Dorm bed $20; double room $30-40; twin room $30.

Maintenance & cleanliness	★★★
Facilities	★
Atmosphere & character	★★★★☆
Security	★★☆
Overall rating	★★★☆

Sights
Gundagai Historical Museum
Gundagai's small museum has an interesting collection of exhibits about pioneer life. These exhibits include an old drover's cart, Phar Lap's saddlecloth and the shirt and jacket worn by Kiley of Kiley's Run (the poem by Banjo Patterson).
Homer Street, Gundagai.
☎ *(02) 6944 1995.*
Admission $3.
Open 9am-3pm daily.

Albury

Sitting on the Murray River just north of the Victorian border, Albury is a major regional centre that is a good base for exploring the surrounding countryside. At Albury the Murray River has been dammed to form Lake Hume, a popular spot for boating, water-skiing, sail boarding and fishing.

Practical Information
Information Centre
Gateway Village, Hume Highway, Albury.
☎ *(02) 6041 3875 or 1800 800 743.*
Open 9am-5pm daily.

Coming & Going

Most Melbourne-Sydney buses and trains pass through Albury. The bus and train station is on Young Street (Hume Highway) near the town centre.

Accommodation
Albury Backpackers

Albury Backpackers has a good atmosphere with a small, but comfy TV lounge, a nice open-air kitchen and fast Internet access. It is definitely the most fun hostel in Albury and it also has the best location. The people who run this hostel also organise canoeing trips on the Murray River.
452 David Street, Albury.
☎ *(02) 6041 1822.*
Dorm bed *$18;* **double room** *$44.*
Reception open *9am-midnight.*
🚌

Maintenance & cleanliness	★★☆
Facilities	★★☆
Atmosphere & character	★★★★★
Security	★
Overall rating	★★★

Albury Motor Village YHA

This hostel is within a caravan park and the standard of the hostel's facilities is quite good. It is very clean and it has a swimming pool as well as a big common area with a kitchen and TV lounge. However it is very quiet with little atmosphere and it is inconveniently located on an ugly stretch of highway about 5km north of the centre of Albury.
372 Wagga Road (Hume Highway), Lavington.
☎ *(02) 6040 2999.*
Dorm bed *$23 ($19.50 YHA);* **double/twin room** *$52 ($45 YHA).*
Credit cards *Amex, Diners, JCB, MC, Visa.*
Reception open *8am-8pm daily.*
🚌

Maintenance & cleanliness	★★★★★
Facilities	★★☆
Atmosphere & character	★☆
Security	★☆
Overall rating	★★★☆

Sights
Albury Botanic Gardens

These four-hectare botanic gardens at the western end of Albury's city centre have an impressive collection of plants and feature a rainforest walk.
Wodonga Place, Albury.
☎ *(02) 6023 8769.*
Website *www.albury.net.au/~accparks.*
Admission *free.*

Albury Regional Museum

This museum features a series of exhibits about local history and culture.
Wodonga Place, Albury.
☎ *(02) 6051 3450.*
Admission *free.*
Open *10.30am-4.30pm daily.*

Riverina

Watered primarily by the Murrumbidgee River, this area produces citrus and stone fruits, vegetables, wines, rice, canola, wheat, sheep, cattle, pistachio nuts, olives and much more. The fertile farmlands have attracted migrants from many nations, creating a surprising and eclectic mix of cuisines and cultures.

Fruit picking work draws most backpackers here. There is work at most times throughout the year, but December to April is the busiest period when work is easiest to find.

Griffith

Griffith was designed by Walter Burley Griffin, the American architect and town planner who also designed Canberra. The town has a large Italian population that ensures plenty of good pizza and pasta joints.

The surrounding region is home to many orchards, vineyards and even rice paddies and many backpackers come here for fruit picking rather than to see the sights.

Practical Information
Information Centre

Corner Banna & Jondaryan Avenues, Griffith.
☎ *(02) 6962 4145.*
Open *9am-5pm daily.*

Coming & Going

The Mobil service station at 121 Banna Avenue serves as Griffith's bus terminal with buses to Adelaide, Canberra, Melbourne and Sydney as well as most other destinations in the Riverina region.

Accommodation
Griffith International Hostel
Griffith International Hostel caters to working travellers and it features a large kitchen, laundry, TV lounge and barbecue.
112 Binya Street, Griffith.
Website www.griffithinternational.com.au.
☎ *(02) 6964 4236.*
***Dorm bed** $20.*
***Reception open** Mon-Fri 10am-11am & 5pm-6pm, Sat-Sun 5pm-6pm.*
Not yet rated.

Hay
This town is home to some interesting museums that showcase the culture of rural Australia and it is one of the more interesting towns in the Riverina region.

Practical Information
Hay Visitor's Centre
Hay's visitor information centre has free showers, which makes it an essential stopover if you're travelling by campervan.
407 Moppett Street, Hay.
☎ *(02) 6993 4045.*
Website www.hay.nsw.gov.au.

Sights
Hay Gaol Museum
This old prison has been converted into a museum with a variety of local history exhibits.
Church Street, Hay.
☎ *(02) 6993 4045.*
***Admission** $2.*
***Open** 9am-5pm daily.*

Hay Prisoner of War & Internment Camp Interpretive Centre
Two old train carriages at Hay's train station contain exhibits about prisoners of war who were held at Hay during World War II.
Hay Train Station, Murray Street, Hay.
☎ *(02) 6993 2112.*

***Admission** $2.*
***Open** Mon-Fri 9am-5pm.*

Shear Outback
Hay's big attraction is this flash new museum dedicated to sheep, sheep shearers and sheep dogs.
Corner Cobb & Sturt Highways, Hay.
☎ *(02) 6993 4000.*
Website www.shearoutback.com.au.
***Admission** $15.*
***Open** 9am-5pm daily.*

Wagga Wagga
New South Wales' largest inland city lies on the Sturt Highway and many travellers pass through here on the way to somewhere else. There's not a lot to draw you to town but it's a good place to take a break if you're driving.

Practical Information
Information Centre
Tarcutta Street, Wagga Wagga.
☎ *(02) 6926 9621.*
Website www.tourismwaggawagga.com.au.
***Open** 9am-5pm daily.*

Coming & Going
Both Wagga's bus and train station are located on Baylis Street although buses better serve the city. Buses run from Wagga Wagga to Adelaide, Canberra, Melbourne, Sydney as well as many regional destinations throughout New South Wales.

Sights
National Art Glass Gallery
Wagga's unique National Art Glass Gallery has two storeys of exhibits of glass artworks.
Baylis Street, Wagga Wagga.
☎ *(02) 6926 9660.*
Website www.waggaartgallery.org.
***Admission** free.*
***Open** Tue-Sat 10am-5pm, Sun noon-4pm.*

Wagga Wagga Art Gallery
Wagga's main art museum has an expansive exhibition space that is host to a programme of temporary exhibits.
Baylis Street, Wagga Wagga.

☎ *(02) 6926 9660.*
Website *www.waggaartgallery.org.*
Admission *free.*
Open *Tue-Sat 10am-5pm, Sun noon-4pm.*

Outback NSW

Although not as wild as the outback regions in other states, the New South Wales outback is more accessible, particularly if you don't have the time to visit South Australia or the Northern Territory.

Bourke

The Australian expression "back of Bourke" means a long way from anywhere and it is generally assumed that this is where the outback starts. Although Bourke is a remote town by anyone's standards, it is the closest bit of outback to Sydney.

The area around Bourke is surprisingly fertile and there is quite a bit of fruit picking work between November and February although there are nicer spots elsewhere in Australia for this sort of work.

Practical Information
Bourke Information Centre
Anson Street, Bourke.
☎ *(02) 6872 2280.*
Open *9am-5pm daily.*

Coming & Going
Most travellers arrive in Bourke either by car or bus. Buses depart from the tourist information centre on Anson Street and run to Dubbo and Sydney.

Accommodation
**Gidgee Guesthouse
(Bourke YHA)**
This youth hostel is located in an historic building that was originally built in 1888 as a bank. It features a shady courtyard with a barbecue and a fountain.
17 Oxley Street, Bourke.
☎ *(02) 6870 7017.*
Dorm bed *$23.50-27.50 ($20-24 YHA);* **double/twin room** *$59-64*

($52-57 YHA).
Credit cards *MC, Visa.*
🚐
Not yet rated

Broken Hill

Broken Hill is the major city in the New South Wales Outback. It is a busy mining town and the original home of Broken Hill Proprietary (BHP), now called BHP Billiton, which started out mining silver here and grew to become Australia's largest company.

Broken Hill is a great opportunity to see what life is like in an outback mining town and it offers the chance to tour the mines. You can also experience some real outback institutions including the Royal Flying Doctor Service and the School of the Air.

Practical Information
**National Parks
Information Centre**
183 Argent Street, Broken Hill.
☎ *(08) 8088 5933.*
Website *www.nationalparks.nsw. gov.au.*
Open *Mon-Fri 8.30am-4.30pm*

Visitor Information Centre
Corner Blende & Bromide Streets, Broken Hill.
☎ *(02) 8087 6077.*
Website *www.murrayoutback.org.au.*
Open *8.30am-5pm daily.*

Coming & Going
Despite its remote location, Broken Hill is easy to get to. If you're driving in the region around the Murray River then Broken Hill is just a three-hour drive north of Mildura. It is also on the train and bus route that connects Adelaide with Sydney.

Its airport handles flights from Adelaide, Melbourne and Sydney but there is no public transport from the airport so you'll have to take a taxi in town.

The train is the best way to get here; the *Indian-Pacific* and *the Ghan* stop here between Adelaide and Sydney. Both these trains are considered Australia's two classic train journeys, particularly if you travel all the way to Perth or Alice Springs. The train station is on Crystal Street in the city centre near the corner of Chloride Street.

Buses stop at the tourist information centre at the corner of Blende and Bromide Streets. Buses go to Adelaide, Dubbo and Mildura. Take a bus to Dubbo to connect with buses to other destinations in New South Wales or Mildura for connections in Victoria.

Accommodation
The Tourist Lodge
This hostel has a good central location and amenities that include a swimming pool. However the quality of facilities leaves a lot to be desired. It appears that everything – furniture, TVs, kitchen appliances, etc. – were either bought second-hand or a long, long time ago. The common areas close at 9pm making it a very dull place to stay.
100 Argent Street, Broken Hill.
☎ *(02) 8088 2086.*

Maintenance & cleanliness	★★☆
Facilities	★★★☆
Atmosphere & character	★★
Security	★★☆
Overall rating	★★

Sights
BHP Mine
The BHP Mine is one of Broken Hill's highlights. Much of the two-hour tour is conducted 130 metres underground and you get to wear a miner's helmet.
☎ *(08) 8088 1604.*
Admission $34, students $30.
Tours Mon-Fri 10.30am, Sat 2pm.

Broken Hill City Art Gallery
Broken Hill has spawned a surprising number of Australia's top artists making this one of the country's best small town art galleries.
Corner Blende & Chloride Streets, Broken Hill.
☎ *(08) 8088 5491.*
Admission $2.
Open Mon-Fri 10am-5pm, Sat 10am-5pm, Sun 1pm-4pm.

Broken Hill Heritage Trail
Broken Hill is much more prosperous than most other outback towns and over the years many grand old buildings have been erected. The Broken Hill Heritage Trail is a walking tour that takes you around the city's most historic buildings. You can either take a guided tour or follow the trail yourself.
Tours Mon, Wed, Fri & Sat 10am.
Tours depart from the information centre.

Line of Lode Visitors Centre
The centre includes a mining museum and a memorial to miners.
South Mine, 260 Eyre Street, Broken Hill.
Website www.lineoflodebrokenhill.org.au.
Admission $5.50.
Open 9am-10pm daily.

Royal Flying Doctor Service
This outback institution provides medical support in isolated communities. Although the RFDS also maintains visitors centres in other outback towns, this one is a working base that was the site of the Flying Doctors TV show. There is a museum on site and a visit includes a one-hour tour of the base.
Broken Hill Airport.
☎ *(08) 8080 1777.*
Website www.flyingdoctor.net/vc-brokenhill.htm.
Admission $5.50.
Open Mon-Fri 9am-5pm, Sat-Sun 11am-4pm.

School of the Air
While the Flying Doctor looks after medical problems in the outback, the School of the Air educates the outback. This unique correspondence school allows visitors to experience what life is like for children in the more remote parts of the outback. It is essential to book ahead through the tourist office.
Lane Street, Broken Hill.
Book ahead through the tourist information centre at ☎ *(08) 8087 6077.*
Admission $3.30.
Tours Mon-Fri 8.20am during school term.

Silverton

Silverton is an easy day-trip from Broken Hill making it an easily accessible yet quintessential outback town. The local pub – the Silverton Hotel – is the main attraction and the classical image of a pub sitting smack-bang in the middle of the desert has made it a popular film set.

Although many travellers spend most of their time in the pub, there is a walking tour around town that passes the more historic buildings and there are also couple of art galleries that are worth visiting.

Coming & Going

Silverton is only a short drive (25km) from Broken Hill and it is best visited by car. Although there is no proper bus service between Broken Hill and Silverton, several companies operate overpriced day tours.

Northern Territory

The Northern Territory covers one-sixth of Australia and is split into two regions: the Top End, which includes the capital Darwin, and Central Australia, home to Ayers Rock and Alice Springs.

The Northern Territory remains Australia's most sparsely populated region and an area rich in Aboriginal culture and natural attractions.

Darwin

Darwin, with its lush vegetation and diverse population, is a surprisingly vibrant city considering its small size. The city's diversity is reflected in the its array of Asian and Western eating places, ranging from upmarket restaurants to budget-priced food stalls at the Mindil Beach Sunset Markets.

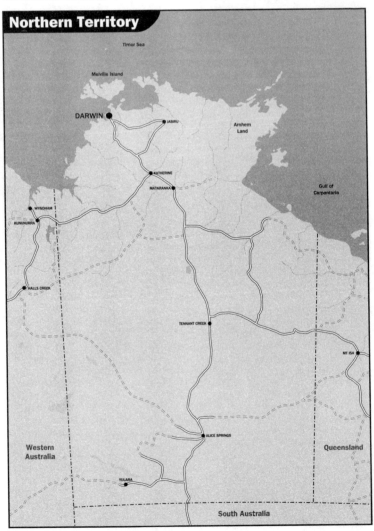

Northern Territory

Timor Sea

Melville Island

DARWIN • JABIRU

Arnhem Land

KATHERINE
MATARANKA

Gulf of Carpentaria

WYNDHAM
KUNUNURRA

HALLS CREEK

TENNANT CREEK

MT ISA

ALICE SPRINGS

Western Australia

Queensland

YULARA

South Australia

Practical Information
INFORMATION CENTRES & USEFUL ADDRESSES
Darwin Visitor Centre
Corner Mitchell & Knuckey Streets, Darwin.
☐ *4, 5, 6, 8, 10.*
☎ *(08) 8936 2499.*
Open *Mon-Fri 9am-5pm, Sat 9am-3pm, Sun 10am-3pm.*

American Express
18 Knuckey Street, Darwin.
☐ *4, 5, 6, 8, 10.*
☎ *(08) 8981 4699.*
Website *www.americanexpress.com.*
Open *Mon-Fri 8am-5pm, Sat 9am-noon.*

INTERNET ACCESS
Didjworld Internet
Harry Chan Arcade, 60 Smith Street, Darwin.
☐ *4, 5, 6, 8, 10.*
☎ *(08) 8981 3510.*
Website *www.didjworld.com.*
Open *Mon-Sat 9am-10pm, Sun 10am-8pm.*

Internet Outpost
5/69 Mitchell Street, Darwin.
☐ *4, 5, 6, 8, 10*
☎ *(08) 8942 3044*
Open *Mon-Thu 9am-11pm, Fri-Sat 9am-10pm.*

Global Gossip
44 Mitchell Street, Darwin.
☐ *4, 5, 6, 8, 10*
☎ *(08) 8942 3044*
Website *www.globalgossip.com.au.*
Open *Mon-Fri 8am-midnight, Sat-Sun 9am-midnight.*

Coming & Going
AIR
Darwin is the closest Australian city to Asia and its airport handles many of the cheapest international flights into and out of Australia, making Darwin a popular gateway.

Darwin International Airport (☎ *(08) 8920 1811; **website** www.darwinairport.com.au*) is 10km northeast of the city centre and is served by the airport shuttle bus that meets most (but not all) flights and drops off at hostels. The one-way fare is $7.50 but many hostels will reimburse the fare if you book a couple of nights accommodation with them.

BUS
McCafferty's/Greyhound coaches terminate at the Transit Centre at 69 Mitchell Street, which is located between the YHA and Chilli's backpackers' hostels.

TRAIN
Starting in February 2004, Great Southern Railway's *Ghan* train service will run from Darwin to Adelaide three times a week. The station is in Berrimah in Darwin's outer suburbs, which is accessible by buses 5 and 8.

HITCHHIKING
The Stuart Highway is the only road out of Darwin, which makes it a fairly easy city to hitchhike from. Take bus 5 or 8 to get out on the Stuart Highway from the city centre.

The Stuart Highway continues south to Alice Springs and Adelaide, while the Victoria Highway to Western Australia branches off near Katherine. The Barkly Highway to Cairns and Townsville joins the Stuart Highway at Three Ways, just north of Tennant Creek. If you were heading to Queensland or Western Australia, it would be helpful to use a destination sign.

Because Darwin is a such long way from anywhere else, you can get some long rides. But you can also get dropped off in some pretty remote places, which means that it's a good idea to bring along plenty of drinking water.

An easier option is to use a web-based ride sharing service such as BUG Ride (*website* *http://australia.bugride.com*), which allows travellers to both offer lifts and search for rides throughout Australia.

Local Transport
Although Darwin is a small city, it has a relatively good bus network. Darwin's buses are supplemented by minibuses, which are a good way to get around the city.

The city centre is small enough to easily walk around.

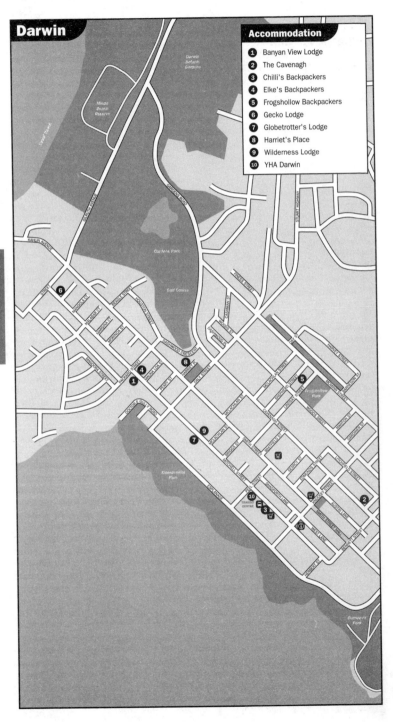

Darwin

Accommodation

1. Banyan View Lodge
2. The Cavenagh
3. Chilli's Backpackers
4. Elke's Backpackers
5. Frogshollow Backpackers
6. Gecko Lodge
7. Globetrotter's Lodge
8. Harriet's Place
9. Wilderness Lodge
10. YHA Darwin

Northern Territory

BUS

Darwinbus (☎ *(08) 8924 7666; website www.nt.gov.au/dtw/public/bustimes/)* operates 14 bus routes, which are a handy way to get around the suburban area. The most useful routes are routes 4 and 10, which run between the city centre and Casuarina Shopping Centre via the Mindil Beach and Parap markets.

Buses run down Mitchell and Cavenagh Streets in the city centre with the city bus interchange on Harry Chan Avenue. During the week, most buses run at half-hourly intervals.

Single fares cost between $1.40 and $2.40. Both daily and weekly Tourcards are available, these cost $5 for a daily ticket and $25 for a seven-day pass. Tourcards allow unlimited travel on Darwinbuses.

MINIBUS

Darwin's minibuses are a bit like a cross between a bus and a taxi. For a flat $2.50 fare, they will take you wherever you want to go in the city centre, which includes Cullen Bay Marina and Stokes Hill Wharf. Once you leave the central area, prices increase substantially. Minibuses depart from a stand near the corner of Knuckey Street and the Smith Street Mall; they wait here until they have several passengers before leaving.

FERRY

The Sea-Cat ferry service (☎ *(08) 8941 1991; website www.seacat.com.au)* runs between Cullen Bay marina and Mandorah. This is the easiest way to get into town if you're staying at the Mandorah Beach Hotel. The return fare is a steep $16, but the weekly pass is better value at $48.

Accommodation
Banyan View Lodge

This large hostel is run by the YWCA and it has an institutional feel to it. Accommodation consists mostly of twin rooms as well as some double and single rooms – there are only a few dorms. It is a quiet place that may suit someone looking for a little privacy but it is not a good option if you're looking for a party.
119 Mitchell Street, Darwin.

☎ *(08) 8981 8644.*
Website www.travel-y.com.
Dorm bed $18; single room $38-43; twin room $48-53.
Credit cards MC, Visa.
Reception open Jan-Jun 8am-4.30pm daily; Jul-Aug 8am-10pm daily; Sep-Dec 8am-4.30pm daily.

Maintenance & cleanliness	★★★
Facilities	★★☆
Atmosphere & character	★
Security	★
Overall rating	★★☆

The Cavenagh

The Cavenagh is a centrally located place centred on a big swimming pool. All rooms have en suite and air conditioning and double rooms also have a fridge and TV. There is also a large bar.
12 Cavenagh Street, Darwin.
☎ *(08) 8941 6383.*
Dorm bed $16-21; double room $52-75.
Credit cards Amex, Diners, MC, Visa.
Reception open 6am-9pm daily; 24-hour check in.

Maintenance & cleanliness	★★★★☆
Facilities	★★
Atmosphere & character	★★★☆
Security	★☆
Overall rating	★★★

Chilli's Backpackers

This hostel has good facilities and everything is nice and clean. There is an excellent kitchen and open-air dining area overlooking Mitchell Street as well as a spa and sundeck with a barbecue. The only real drawback is the lack of a swimming pool. There is also an Internet café next to the reception.
69A Mitchell Street, Darwin.
☎ *(08) 8941 9722 or 1800 351 313.*
Dorm bed $21 ($20 VIP/YHA); double/twin room $50-55 ($48-53 VIP/YHA).
Credit cards MC, Visa.
Reception open 6am-10pm daily.

Maintenance & cleanliness	★★★☆
Facilities	★★
Atmosphere & character	★★★★☆
Security	★★★☆
Overall rating	★★★

Northern Territory

Northern Territory *(side tab)*

Elke's Backpackers

Elke's Backpackers has a laid-back atmosphere with lush tropical gardens and a nice swimming pool. It has all the usual facilities including a TV lounge, Internet access and several kitchens.
112 Mitchell Street, Darwin.
☎ *(08) 8981 8399.*
Website www.elkesbackpackers.com.au.
Dorm bed $22 ($20 VIP/YHA);
single/twin room $54 ($50 VIP/YHA);
double room $56 ($52 VIP/YHA).
Credit cards Amex, Diners, MC, Visa.
Reception open 6am-9pm daily.
🚌

Maintenance & cleanliness	★★★☆
Facilities	★★
Atmosphere & character	★★★★
Security	★
Overall rating	★★★☆

Frogshollow Backpackers

This well-run hostel has good facilities and a nice laid-back atmosphere. This includes a swimming pool and two spa pools set in a lush tropical setting. There is a good kitchen, barbecue area and a large common room.
27 Lindsay Street, Darwin.
☎ *(08) 8941 2600 or 1800 068 686.*
Website www.frogs-hollow.com.au.
Dorm bed $21 ($20 ISIC/VIP/YHA);
double/twin room $50-60 ($48-58 ISIC/VIP/YHA); includes breakfast.
Credit cards MC, Visa.
Reception open 6am-9pm daily.
🚌

Maintenance & cleanliness	★★★★
Facilities	★★★
Atmosphere & character	★★★☆
Security	★★
Overall rating	★★★★☆

Gecko Lodge

This hostel at the northern end of Mitchell Street has an open-air TV lounge, a small kitchen and a swimming pool, but the standard of some facilities such as the bathrooms could be improved.
146 Mitchell Street, Darwin.
☎ *(08) 8981 5569 or 1800 811 250.*
Website www.geckolodge.com.au.
Dorm bed $15-22 ($15-21 VIP/YHA);
double/twin room $55 ($53 VIP/YHA); includes pancake breakfast.

Credit cards MC, Visa.
Reception open 6am-8pm daily; 24-hour check in.

Maintenance & cleanliness	★★
Facilities	★★★☆
Atmosphere & character	★★★★☆
Security	★★
Overall rating	★★★☆

Globetrotter's Lodge

This former motel is built around a swimming pool. Like many other former motels, it doesn't have quite the same level of comfort and atmosphere as other hostels. It has a tiny kitchen, Internet access and a great bar with pool tables and cheap $5 meal deals. Accommodation is comfortable, if a little drab, and all rooms have en suite bathrooms.
97 Mitchell Street, Darwin.
🚌 *4, 5, 6, 8, 10.*
☎ *(08) 8981 5385.*
Website www.globetrotters.com.au.
Dorm bed $22 ($20 VIP); double room $60 ($56 VIP); twin room $58 ($54 VIP); triple room $80 ($74 VIP); include breakfast.
Credit cards MC, Visa.
Reception open 6am-9pm daily.
🚌

Maintenance & cleanliness	★★
Facilities	★★★☆
Atmosphere & character	★★★
Security	★
Overall rating	★★★☆

Harriet's Place

This small hostel caters primarily to backpackers working in Darwin. It is a quiet place with basic facilities including an outdoor TV lounge and a balcony overlooking a park. All rooms have fridges and there are TVs in the double rooms.
4 Harriet Place, Darwin.
☎ *(08) 8981 5694.*
Dorm bed $14-18 ($12-16 VIP/YHA);
double/twin room $48 ($45 VIP/YHA); camping $19-12 ($8-10 VIP/YHA) per person.
Reception open 9am-7pm daily.

Maintenance & cleanliness	★★★
Facilities	★★☆
Atmosphere & character	★★★
Security	★★☆
Overall rating	★★★☆

Mandorah Beach Hotel

The Mandorah Beach Hotel has great value accommodation with a beautiful beachfront setting across the harbour from Darwin. Accommodation is in basic, but spacious, four-bed dorms with en suite bathrooms. It features a large swimming pool, beach volleyball and an area with video games and pool tables. There is also a restaurant with good value meals and a 24-hour bar. It is a very relaxing place to stay. The hostel is best reached by ferry from Cullen Bay in Darwin. The ferry costs $16 return or $48 for a weekly pass.
Mandorah, Cox Peninsula.
🚢 *ferry from Cullen Bay.*
☎ *(08) 8978 5044.*
Dorm bed *$14;* **twin room** *$64-74;* **camping** *$6 per person (unpowered site) or $14 per couple (powered site).*
Credit cards *Diners, MC, Visa.*
🚗

Maintenance & cleanliness	★★★☆
Facilities	★★
Atmosphere & character	★★★
Security	★★☆
Overall rating	★★★

Wilderness Lodge

Wilderness Lodge is a small hostel with a laid-back atmosphere and a nice swimming pool. However there is no TV lounge and the outdoor kitchen is rather limited.
88 Mitchell Street, Darwin.
🚌 *4, 5, 6, 8, 10.*
☎ *(08) 8941 2161 or 1800 068 686.*
Website *www.wildlodge.com.au.*
Dorm bed *$20 ($18 ISIC/VIP/YHA);* **double room** *$52 ($50 ISIC/VIP/ YHA).*
Credit cards *MC, Visa.*
Reception open *6am-9pm daily.*

Maintenance & cleanliness	★★★
Facilities	★★
Atmosphere & character	★★★★☆
Security	★★☆
Overall rating	★★★

YHA Darwin

Darwin's YHA hostel is a top-class hostel with great facilities. Despite its large size (over 300 beds) it has a better atmosphere than many other big city YHA hostels. Everything here is clean and tidy and the fittings are in good condition. The hostel features a big swimming pool and a nice rooftop sundeck as well as a games room with a pool table and a fully equipped kitchen. Security here is very good with lockers in the rooms and mini safes at reception.
69 Mitchell Street, Darwin.
🚌 *4, 5, 6, 8, 10.*
☎ *(08) 8981 3995.*
Dorm bed *$16-20 ($19.50-23.50 YHA);* **single room** *$51-52 ($54.50-55.50 YHA);* **double room** *$51-67 ($58-74 YHA);* **twin room** *$51-52 ($58-59 YHA).*
Credit cards *MC, Visa.*
Reception open *24 hours.*
🚗

Maintenance & cleanliness	★★★★☆
Facilities	★★★☆
Atmosphere & character	★★★
Security	★★★★☆
Overall rating	★★★★☆

Eating & Drinking

Darwin has a good choice of eating and drinking options.

Smith Street Mall in the city centre has plenty of good value food courts, while there are a few fast food places around Knuckey Street.

There are also a couple of bars and restaurants geared towards backpackers that offer very cheap, and sometimes free, food to attract the punters. These include the Vic on Smith Street Mall and the H Club on the corner of Mitchell and Daly Streets. Just ask the staff at your hostel for details about which bars have free food offers.

Bars on Mitchell Street include Rourke's Drift with its popular beer garden, the Shennanigans Irish pub next to the YHA hostel and the H Club. The Lizard Bar in the Top End Hotel has Darwin's best beer garden.

There are two Woolworths supermarkets on Smith Street. One is on the corner of Knuckey Street, and other a couple of blocks northwest on the corner of Peel Street.

There's also a new 24-hour Coles supermarket in the Mitchell Centre next door to Chilli's Backpackers on Mitchell Street.

Sights

Aquascene
Darwin's most unique and fun attraction involves feeding the fish that arrive at each high tide at a small bay in Doctors Gully at the northern end of the city centre. Thousands of milkfish, mullet, catfish and barramundi as well as rays come to be handfed.
28 Doctors Gully Road, Darwin.
🚌 *4, 5, 6, 8, 10.*
Admission *$5.50.*
Open *at high tides, call (08) 8981 7937 for current opening hours.*

Australian Aviation Heritage Centre
This aviation museum features classic old planes including a B-52, Spitfires and Tiger Moths.
557 Stuart Highway, Winnellie.
🚌 *5, 8.*
☎ *(08) 8947 2145.*
Website *www.darwinsairwar.com.au.*
Admission *$11, students $7.50.*
Open *9am-5pm daily; tours: 10am, 2pm, 4pm.*

Australian Pearling Exhibition
The Pearling Exhibition has displays on the history of Australia's pearling industry from hard-hat diving to modern times.
Stokes Hill Wharf, Darwin.
☎ *(08) 8941 2177.*
Admission *$6.60.*
Open *10am-5pm daily.*

Crocodylus Park
This popular wildlife park is home to a variety of Australian wildlife with an emphasis on crocodiles.
815 McMillans Road, Knuckey Lagoon, Berrimah.
🚌 *5, 9.*
☎ *(08) 8922 4500.*
Website *www.wmi.com.au/crocpark/crocpark.html.*
Admission *$25.*
Open *9am-5pm daily; tours and feeding: 10am, noon, 2pm.*

Fannie Bay Gaol
Fannie Bay Gaol is a former prison that has been turned into a museum. It provides an insight into the early Northern Territory penal system.
East Point Road, Fannie Bay.
🚌 *4, 6.*
☎ *(08) 8999 8201.*
Admission *free.*
Open *Mon-Fri 9am-5pm, Sat-Sun 10am-5pm.*

Mindil Beach Sunset Market
This is one of Australia's top markets with an excellent selection of food stalls plus the usual art and craft stalls.
Mindil Beach.
🚌 *4, 6.*
☎ *(08) 8981 3454.*
Website *www.mindilbeachsunsetmarkets.com.au.*
Admission *free.*
Open *Thu (in Dry season) 5pm-10pm, Sun (in Dry season) 4pm-9pm.*

Museum & Art Gallery of the Northern Territory
This is an excellent museum with exhibits focusing on the cultural, social and natural history of the Northern Territory. Some of the better displays include the Aboriginal Art Gallery, exhibits on Cyclone Tracy and a five-metre crocodile named 'Sweetheart'.
Conacher Street, Fannie Bay.
🚌 *4, 6.*
☎ *(08) 8999 8201.*
Admission *free.*
Open *Mon-Fri 9am-5pm, Sat-Sun 10am-5pm.*

Northern Territory Parliament House
Australia's newest parliament house is an imposing modern building at the southern end of Mitchell Street. Guided tours are conducted on Saturdays.
Mitchell Street, Darwin.
☎ *(08) 8946 1434.*
Admission *free.*

Territory Wildlife Park
Run by the NT Parks & Wildlife Commission, this accessible wildlife park features 6km of walking trails as well as an excellent collection of native animals.
Cox Peninsula Road, Berry Springs (45 minutes from Darwin).
☎ *(08) 8988 7200.*

Website *www.territorywildlifepark.
com.au.*
Admission *$18, students $9.*
Open *8.30am-6pm daily (last entry
4pm).*

The Top End

The Top End of Australia juts north-
ward into the Arafura and Timor
Seas. Its magnificent scenery includes
escarpments, gorges and broad wetlands that experience a spectacular
tropical summer season (October to
May), when monsoon rains bring on
a renewal of lush vegetation; and the
cooler dry season (May to September),
when it's the best time to pursue outdoor activities.

The Top End's two big attractions
are Kakadu and Litchfield National
Parks.

Litchfield National Park

Easily accessible from Darwin, Litchfield National Park is a worthwhile
excursion.

Although not as well known as
Kakadu, this compact national park
also features spectacular scenery including gorges and waterfalls. Litchfield
National Park is only 45 minutes from
Darwin and many travellers visit as a
day trip. Because Litchfield is smaller
and closer to Darwin than Kakadu, it
can become more crowded, but it is still
a worthwhile trip.

Because the park is accessible by
sealed roads, it is easy to visit all year
round but most 4WD tracks within the
park are closed during the Wet season
and some swimming spots are closed
after heavy rain.

There are several short hiking trails
in the park, mostly 1-3km long; the
more spectacular trails go to waterfalls,
for which Litchfield is famous.

Litchfield's waterfalls include the
Florence, Tjaynera, Tolmer and Wangi
Falls. These pretty waterfalls are fantastic swimming spots. Many people also
take a dip in the popular Buley Rockhole, but swimming is not permitted in
the Reynolds River.

Coming & Going & Local Transport

Hostels around Darwin can book tours
to Litchfield. One-day tours generally
cost around $100 and visit all the main
sights. Two-day tours are only a little
more expensive (around $135) and
offer a better opportunity to experience
the park.

Accommodation

Most people stay in hostels in Darwin
and visit Litchfield as a day trip,
although camping is possible within
the park. The main camping sites are
located at Buley Rockhole, Walker
Creek, Florence Falls and Wangi Falls.
The Wangi Falls campground is the
most crowded, but has better facilities
than the others. Camping in the park
costs $6.60 per person.

Lower Adelaide River District

The region where the Adelaide River
crosses the Arnhem Highway is popular with travellers stopping en route to
Kakadu and it is also a popular daytrip
from Darwin, which is only 70km away.

The popular river cruises allow you to
see crocodiles in their natural habitat.

Practical Information
Window on the Wetlands Visitor Centre

This excellent information centre has
exhibits about the flora and fauna of
the wetlands in the Top End.
Arnhem Highway.
☎ *(08) 8988 8188.*
Open *7.30am-7.30pm daily.*

Crocodile Cruises

There are several companies that operate
cruises departing from the Windows on
the Wetlands Visitor Centre and from
the Adelaide River Bridge.

These include the Adelaide River
Queen (☎ *(08) 8988 8144; website
www.jumpingcrocodilecruises.com.au)*
and Jumping Crocodile (☎ *(08) 8988
4547; website www.jumpingcrocodile.
com.au).* A 90-minute cruise costs from
$25 to $36.

Mary River National Park (proposed)

Located between Darwin and Kakadu National Park, the proposed Mary River National Park is an excellent spot for crocodile spotting and bird watching.

The highlight of the park is Bird Billabong, which is a fantastic spot for bird watching.

If you're staying at the Mary River Park YHA, they have their own 500-acre park with an excellent Bamboo Walk (4.5km, 2 hours) that takes you past shady native bamboo to a billabong, returning along the river.

There are a number of excursions that you can organise from the YHA that include bird watching tours ($75-125, 3-5 hours) and sunset stargazing and dinner cruises ($60). The cheapest option is the popular river cruises that cost between $28 and $38 and are ideal for spotting crocodiles and birds. It is common to see between 20 and 50 crocodiles if you go on a cruise between April and August (which is the best time of year to visit).

Coming & Going

McCafferty's/Greyhound stop here on their Darwin to Kakadu service.

Accommodation

Annaburro Billabong

Annaburro Billabong offers very basic dormitory accommodation in decrepit old huts. You need to book a whole dorm room, which can be good value if six people are travelling together but it's not so great for single travellers. Guests have free use of canoes but there aren't any other shared facilities. The double rooms are very nice air-conditioned cabins and provide a much higher standard of accommodation than the dorms. The toilet/shower block is surprisingly clean and well maintained.
Arnhem Highway, Annaburro.
☎ *(08) 8978 8971.*
Six-bed dormitory $45-65; ten-bed dormitory $100; double room $60; camping $6 per person.
Reception open 9am-5.30pm daily; later check in by prior arrangement.

Maintenance & cleanliness	★★⯪
Facilities	★
Atmosphere & character	★★⯪
Security	⯪
Overall rating	★★⯪

Mary River Park YHA

This hostel is set on 500 acres and it features hiking trails, a billabong and loads of wildlife including crocodiles and wallabies. Accommodation is in small air-conditioned cabins and there is a larger dormitory that's used mostly for groups. Facilities include a spa, swimming pool, volleyball court, a bar/restaurant and a nice deck with a barbecue. The McCafferty's/Greyhound bus stops outside.
Mary River Crossing, Arnhem Highway, near Mary River National Park.
☎ *(08) 8978 8877 or 1800 788 844.*
Website www.maryriverpark.com.au.
Dorm bed $18-31 ($15-28 YHA); double cabin $99; family cabin $125.
Credit cards MC, Visa.
Reception open 8am-8pm daily.

Maintenance & cleanliness	★★★⯪
Facilities	★★★
Atmosphere & character	★★
Security	★
Overall rating	★★★⯪

Point Stuart Wilderness Lodge

This hostel/camping ground has nice air-conditioned dormitories with en suite plus a good swimming pool and a bar/restaurant. There's also an Aboriginal culture show every night ($5) and they also operate boat cruises on the Mary River ($32.50).
Point Stuart Road off Arnhem Highway, Mary River Wetlands.
☎ *(08) 8936 1311 or 1800 654 604.*
Dorm bed $22; double/twin room $50-140; camping $7-10 per person.
Credit cards Amex, Diners, MC, Visa.
Reception open 7.30am-midnight daily.

Maintenance & cleanliness	★★★★★
Facilities	★★★⯪
Atmosphere & character	★★★⯪
Security	★★⯪
Overall rating	★★★★⯪

Northern Territory

Kakadu National Park

The World Heritage listed Kakadu National Park is regarded by many to be Australia's best national park.

At almost 20,000 square kilometres, Kakadu covers a large area but only a relatively small part of the park can easily be explored in a car.

Many travellers organise tours from Darwin that take in the main attractions in the park, but independent travel is also possible with accommodation and other services available from areas within the park.

Jabiru is the main town serving the park and it has accommodation, shops, a visitor centre and an airport. The East and South Alligator areas are two other accessible parts of Kakadu, each with accommodation and other services.

Kakadu is a very different park in the Wet (Nov-Mar) and Dry (Apr-Oct) seasons. Most backpackers visit in the Dry when it is easier to travel and more comfortable. However Kakadu is much greener in the Wet when it teems with wildflowers and the waterfalls are at their most powerful, but it is harder to get around as some roads are closed – even to 4WD vehicles. A wider variety of boat cruises operate during the Wet and are an enjoyable way to see Kakadu at this time of year.

Tours from Darwin operate throughout the year and they tailor their itinerary to capture the best sights in each season.

Highlights of the park, which are accessible in both the Wet and Dry seasons, include the Mamukala Wetlands, Nourlangie rock art site and Yellow Water.

Entry to the park costs $16.25 per person for up to seven days.

Practical Information
Bowali Visitor Centre
This Bowali Visitor Centre has a café, shop, theatrette and a small museum with exhibits on the park and Aboriginal culture.
Kakadu Highway, Jabiru
☎ *(08) 8938 1120.*
Website www.ea.gov.au/parks/kakadu/.
Admission free.
Open 9am-5pm daily.

Crocodile Warning

Kakadu is a great place to spot crocodiles – unfortunately this also makes swimming in the park's waters dangerous.

Some visitors risk swimming at some beautiful spots such as Gubara, Maguk Gorge, Jim Jim Falls and Twin Falls. However freshwater crocodiles live here and the more dangerous estaurine (or saltwater) crocs sometimes move into these areas.

These areas are surveyed at the opening of each Dry season and information is posted next to crocodile warning signs at each gorge and plunge pool area.

Park rangers recommend that the only safe places to swim are the pools at the hostels and the swimming pool at Jabiru.

Coming & Going & Local Transport
McCafferty's/Greyhound operate buses between Darwin and Kakadu National Park with stops at Jabiru and other areas of interest. The bus service is a little like a mini-tour and is included in some of McCafferty's/Greyhound bus passes.

Other options include a wide range of tours that can be booked from Darwin that include a good selection catering to backpackers. Tour prices range from $250 to more than $600 for a 5-day 4WD safari.

Accommodation
Gagudju Lodge YHA
This hostel is part of a resort complex that also includes a more upmarket lodge as well as caravan and camping areas. Accommodation is in prefabricated units, but they are clean and face onto a nice shady veranda. The kitchen area consists of a small building with mesh walls that has a fridge and two barbecues. There is also a laundry, shop, bar, restaurant and a swimming pool. It is the nicest of Kakadu's hostels.
Cooinda, off Kakadu Highway, Kakadu National Park.
☎ *(08) 8979 0145 or 1800 500 401.*
Website www.gagudjulodgecooinda. com.au.
Dorm bed $30.50 ($27 YHA); double room $70 ($60 YHA); camping $10

one person, $15 two people.
***Credit cards** JCB, MC, Visa.*
***Reception open** 6am-10pm daily.*

Maintenance & cleanliness	★★★★
Facilities	★★
Atmosphere & character	★
Security	★
Overall rating	★★½

Kakadu Ubirr Hostel

This hostel provides basic accommodation. There is a kitchen, a barbecue area and an above-ground swimming pool. There is a shady semi-outdoor lounge between the two accommodation blocks.
Oenpelli Road, Ubirr, East Alligator, Kakadu National Park.
☎ *(08) 8979 2232.*
***Dorm bed** $25 ($22 YHA); **camping** $8-11 per person.*
***Credit cards** MC, Visa.*
***Reception open** 8.30am-5.30pm; check in at the Border Store.*

Maintenance & cleanliness	★★½
Facilities	★
Atmosphere & character	★★½
Security	½
Overall rating	★★

Mary River Roadhouse

This is the best value of the Kakadu hostels and it is just a couple of kilometres from the park's southern entrance. Accommodation is in basic, but clean, pre-fabricated units. Facilities include a swimming pool, bar and shop.
Kakadu Highway, via Pine Creek.
☎ *(08) 8975 4564.*
***Dorm bed** $15; **motel-style double room** $90; **camping** $6.50 per person.*
***Credit cards** MC, Visa.*
***Reception open** 7am-11pm daily.*

Maintenance & cleanliness	★★½
Facilities	★★
Atmosphere & character	★★½
Security	★
Overall rating	★★½

Sights

Jim Jim Falls

This spectacular waterfall stops flowing in the Dry season, which unfortunately is the only time when the falls are accessible by road (4WD only). A scenic flight in the Wet season is the only way to see the falls in their full glory. Flights depart from the Cooinda and Jabiru East airstrips.
103km south of the Bowali Visitor Centre, Jim Jim area, Kakadu National Park.
☎ *(08) 8979 2411.*

Mamukala wetlands

The Mamukala wetlands are a great place to see bird life including thousands of magpie geese that flock here towards the end of the Dry season (Sep-Oct). There is an observation platform and a couple of short walks (1km; 20 mins and 3km; 2 hours) that allow you to see more of the wetlands.
Arnhem Highway, 7km east of South Alligator River.

Nourlangie rock art site

A short (1.5km) walk takes you past the exceptional Nourlangie rock art site and there is also a short climb to the Gunwarddehwardde lookout with views of the surrounding area. Rangers give talks about Aboriginal art and culture here three times a day during the Dry season.
20km south of the Bowali Visitor Centre, Nourlangie area, Kakadu National Park.

Ubirr

At Ubirr a short walk (1¼km; 1 hour) takes you past Aboriginal rock art sites and climbs to a lookout that offers fantastic views that are particularly magnificent at sunset.
East Alligator area, Kakadu National Park.
***Open** Apr-Nov 8.30am-sunset; Dec-Mar 2pm-sunset.*

Warradjan Aboriginal Cultural Centre

The Warradjan Aboriginal Cultural centre features displays on Aboriginal culture and it also includes a small video theatre.
Cooinda, off Kakadu Highway 50km south of Bowali Visitor Centre, Kakadu National Park.

☎ *(08) 8979 0051.*
Admission *free.*
Open *9am-5pm daily.*

Yellow Water

The Yellow Water wetlands are a popular spot to see crocodiles as well as bird life including Jabiru storks. The seasons dictate how you will visit this area. A boardwalk provides a good vantage point for observing wildlife during the early Dry season; later in the Dry (when the water has dried up) there is a walk (1km) across the floodplains to a viewing platform. In the Wet you'll need to take a cruise on the river, although these cruises operate year round.
Cooinda, off Kakadu Highway 50km south of Bowali Visitor Centre, Kakadu National Park.
☎ *(08) 8979 0111.*
Cruises cost *$33-38.*

Katherine

Katherine is the most popular stop on the highway between Darwin and Alice Springs. The town is nothing special, but it's a good place to base yourself if you want to explore the nearby Katherine Gorge.

Practical Information
Information Centre
Corner Katherine Terrace & Lindsay Street, Katherine.
☎ *(08) 8972 2650.*
Open *Mon-Fri 8.30am-5pm.*

Coming & Going

Buses travelling between Alice and Darwin stop at the transit centre on Katherine Terrace near the information centre.

Accommodation
Coco's Didj Backpackers
Coco's is a small 16-bed hostel with an alternative atmosphere. It is in an old house and the hostel won't appeal to everyone but it has an atmosphere that some people really love. It is very popular with artists, musicians, cyclists and Japanese backpackers touring Australia by motorcycle. Coco's also have a small shop that sells Aboriginal art and digeridoos.
21 First Street, Katherine.
☎ *(08) 8971 2889.*
Website *www.21firstst.com.*
Dorm bed *$16;* **camping** *$9 per person.*
🚗

Maintenance & cleanliness	★
Facilities	★½
Atmosphere & character	★★★★
Security	½
Overall rating	★★

Kookaburra Backpackers
Kookaburra Backpackers is made up of air-conditioned self-contained units each with a small kitchen and en suite bathroom. There is an outdoor TV lounge plus a backyard with a big mango tree, a nice swimming pool and a barbecue area.
Corner Lindsay & Third Streets, Katherine.
☎ *(08) 8971 0257 or 1800 808 211.*
Website *www.inspirit.com.au/kookaburra.*

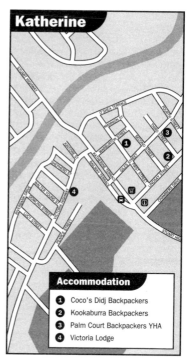

Accommodation
1. Coco's Didj Backpackers
2. Kookaburra Backpackers
3. Palm Court Backpackers YHA
4. Victoria Lodge

Northern Territory

Dorm bed $19 ($17 ISIC/VIP/YHA); double/twin room $50 ($45 ISIC/ VIP/YHA); includes breakfast.
Credit cards MC, Visa.
Reception open 7.30am-7.30pm daily.

🚗

Maintenance & cleanliness	★★★
Facilities	★★
Atmosphere & character	★☆
Security	★★
Overall rating	★★☆

Palm Court Backpackers

Katherine's YHA has helpful staff and a good atmosphere. All rooms have fans, air-conditioning and en suite bathrooms; double rooms have fridges and there are lockers in the dorms. The hostel also has Internet access, a laundry/TV room plus a barbecue area and a swimming pool.
Corner Gilles & Third Streets, Katherine.
☎ *(08) 8972 2722 or 1800 626 722*
Dorm bed $17; double room $48; twin room $46.
Credit cards Amex, Diners, MC, Visa.
Reception open 6.30am-2.30pm & 4.30pm-7pm daily; check in until 8.30pm.

🚗

Maintenance & cleanliness	★★★
Facilities	★★
Atmosphere & character	★★★
Security	★★
Overall rating	★★☆

Victoria Lodge

This is a clean hostel with self-contained units, each with a small kitchen, en suite bathroom and a living area with a TV. There's also a swimming pool and a nice shady barbecue area.
21 Victoria Highway, Katherine.
☎ *(08) 8972 3464 or 1800 808 875.*
Dorm bed $17 ($16 VIP); double room $55 (53 VIP); twin room $50 ($48 VIP).
Credit cards MC, Visa.
Reception open 7.30am-10pm daily.

🚗

Maintenance & cleanliness	★★★☆
Facilities	★★☆
Atmosphere & character	★
Security	★
Overall rating	★★☆

Nitmiluk National Park (Katherine Gorge)

Nitmiluk National Park in the Katherine Gorge area is well known for its system of 13 giant gorges.

The park offers a wide range of hiking trails ranging from walks lasting a couple of hours to challenging 65km overnight hikes. An easier option is a cruise on the Katherine River.

Many of the shorter walks depart from the visitors centre. These include the Butterfly Gorge, Lookout Loop and Windolf walks. The demanding Butterfly Gorge walk (12km; 4½ hours) takes you through a varied landscape and ends at a good swimming spot. The Lookout Loop (3.6km; 2 hours) takes you up the side of the gorge and offers great views of the river. The Windolf walk (8.4km; 3½ hours) features Aboriginal art and also has lovely views.

The most taxing of the overnight hikes is the Jatbula Trail (65km; 5 days). This one-way hike starts at the visitor centre and takes you past rainforests, gorges and waterfalls before finishing at Edith Falls. It is essential to register with the visitors centre if you're walking the Jatbula Trail or any of the other overnight hikes in Nitmiluk.

The park is also a popular spot for canoeing; but it can be tough going at times, as you'll have to carry your canoe over the rocks that separate each gorge. There are several camping areas set aside for canoeists, although registration is required at the visitor centre.

Boat cruises on the Katherine River are popular with many tourists and are the easiest way to see the gorge, but they are touristy and it can feel like you're being rushed. The two-hour trips cost $39.50 and are operated by Nitmiluk Tours (☎ *(08) 8972 1253*), who also organise canoe rental.

May to September is the best time to visit. In the Wet season, parts of the park are subject to flooding and some trails, including the Jatbula Trail, are closed.

Practical Information
Nitmiluk Visitor Centre
Gorge Road, Nitmiluk National Park.
☎ *(08) 8972 3150.*

Open 7am-6pm daily.

Coming & Going

Travel North (☎ *1800 089 103; website www.travelnorth.com.au*) operates a bus service connecting the national park and Katherine. The return fare is $19.

Maintenance & cleanliness	★
Facilities	★½
Atmosphere & character	★★
Security	★
Overall rating	★½

Mataranka & Elsey National Park

This small town is a handy base for exploring the nearby Elsey National Park where the main attractions are the Mataranka Homestead and swimming at the thermal pool.

Elsey National Park is located about 9km from Mataranka. The park features a palm forest and it feels like a bit of an oasis, particularly if you've just arrived from Alice Springs. There is great swimming at the thermal pool, Bitter Springs and also on the Roper River.

Coming & Going

McCafferty's/Greyhound coaches stop at both the town centre and the homestead on their Alice-Darwin run. It sometimes stops for enough time to see the thermal pool, but not for long enough to get wet.

Accommodation
Mataranka Homestead

This hostel offers very basic accommodation in the original homestead that was established in 1916. Accommodation is in mostly small two-bed dorms although there are a couple of larger ones. Facilities include a laundry, limited kitchen facilities and a bar, restaurant and a shop. It is 9km from Mataranka town and right next to Elsey National Park and only 100 metres from the thermal springs.
Homestead Road, Mataranka.
☎ *(08) 8975 4544 or 1800 754 544.*
*Dorm bed $17; **twin room** $36.*
Credit cards Amex, MC, Visa.
Reception open peak season 7am-8pm daily; off-peak season 9am-5pm daily; check in at bar when the reception is closed.

Central Northern Territory

There's not a lot between Alice Springs and Katherine, but there are a few worthwhile detours along the highway.

Tennant Creek

If you're travelling on the Stuart Highway between Alice Springs and Darwin you may want to break your journey at this small mining town, although there isn't really a lot to see here. It's the only town of any size for at least 500km in any direction and is home to facilities such as ATMs, grocery stores and a hospital.

Practical Information
Information Centre

Peko Road, Tennant Creek.
☎ *(08) 8962 3388.*
Website www.tennantcreektourism.com.au.
Open Mon-Fri 9am-5pm, Sat 9am-noon.

Coming & Going

Buses to Alice Springs, Darwin and Townsville stop on Patterson Street in the town centre.

Accommodation
Safari Backpackers

Safari Backpackers is a small clean hostel that offers basic accommodation on a quiet street near the town centre. Common areas are limited to a small kitchen and TV lounge and there's also a TV in each double/twin room.
12 Davidson Street, Tennant Creek.
☎ *(08) 8962 2207.*
*Dorm bed $17 ($14 YHA); **double/ twin room** $40 ($36 YHA).*
Credit cards Amex, Diners, MC, Visa.
Reception open 7am-9pm daily.

Maintenance & cleanliness	★★★
Facilities	★
Atmosphere & character	★☆
Security	★☆
Overall rating	★★

Tourist's Rest Youth Hostel

Tourist's Rest is run down hostel that has a good range of facilities that include a swimming pool and a barbecue area with an outdoor TV lounge. *Corner Windy & Leichhardt Streets, Tennant Creek.*
☎ *(08) 8962 2719*
Website *www.touristrest.com.au.*
Dorm bed *$18 ($17 ISIC/Nomads, $16 VIP/YHA);* **double/twin room** *$40 ($39 ISIC/Nomads, $38 VIP/ YHA); camping $8 per person.*
Credit cards *MC, Visa.*
Reception open *9am-1pm & 4pm-11pm daily.*

Maintenance & cleanliness	★
Facilities	★★
Atmosphere & character	★★
Security	★
Overall rating	★☆

Devils Marbles

This rock formation is located about 100km south of Tennant Creek. There is a short walking track (30 minutes) with signs explaining how the 'marbles' were formed. There isn't enough to keep you busy for very long, but it is definitely worth a stop to break the journey.

Alice Springs

With a population of about 26,000, Alice Springs is much like any other small country town, however it is the only major town in central Australia and is almost 1000km to the nearest town of a similar size.

Alice is a good spot to explore the surrounding area. It lies at the foot of the world's oldest mountain range, the MacDonnell Ranges, and is a popular stopping-off point for travellers on their way to Uluṟu-Kata Tjuṯa National Park.

Attractions and diversions include the Alice Springs Desert Park and several outback institutions such as the School of the Air and the Royal Flying Doctor Service.

Practical Information
Information Centre
Gregory Terrace, Alice Springs.
☎ *(08) 8952 5800.*
Open *Mon-Fri 8.30am-5.30pm, Sat-Sun 9am-4pm.*

Coming & Going
Alice Springs enjoys good transport connections with a busy airport and buses and trains to Adelaide and Darwin.

AIR
Alice Springs Airport (☎ *(08) 8951 1211; website www.aliceairport.com.au),* situated 15km south of town, handles only domestic flights.

Some hostels arrange pick-ups from the airport, particularly if several people book in advance, otherwise the best way into town from the airport is by the airport shuttle bus (☎ *(08) 8953 0310)* that meets most flights, will drop you off at your hostel and costs $10. A taxi will cost about twice this and may work out better value between a few people.

BUS
McCafferty's/Greyhound buses stop on Gregory Terrace, near Railway Terrace and the Coles Complex.

TRAIN
The *Ghan* is one of Australia's great train journeys and it stops in Alice en route between Adelaide and Darwin. The train station is on George Terrace, about a 20-minute walk from the town centre.

Local Transport
Alice Springs has a local bus service, but it runs infrequently making it a difficult way to get around. There are four routes, the east route is handy for Ossies Homestead and the south route runs past Elkes and Toddys hostels. Buses terminate on Railway Terrace

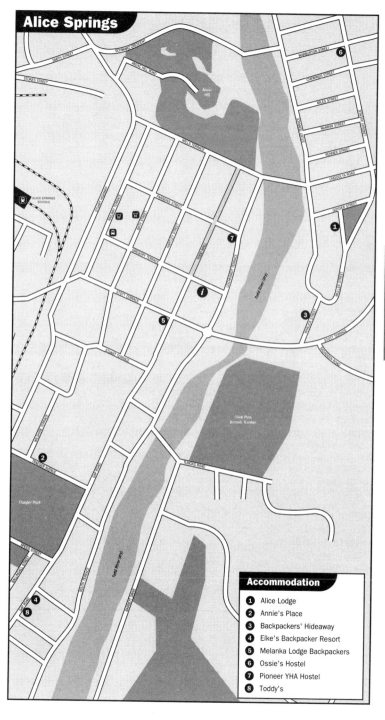

Alice Springs

Northern Territory

Accommodation

1 Alice Lodge
2 Annie's Place
3 Backpackers' Hideaway
4 Elke's Backpacker Resort
5 Melanka Lodge Backpackers
6 Ossie's Hostel
7 Pioneer YHA Hostel
8 Toddy's

near the Coles Complex and fares vary from $1.40 to $2.20.

Many travellers rent a bike or walk around town, although a lot of places are a long walk so it's a good idea to take along a bottle of water.

Accommodation

Alice Lodge Backpackers

Alice Lodge is a small, quiet hostel in a suburban location. Although there is a swimming pool, the hostel's other facilities are fairly basic and are limited to a TV room, Internet access and a small kitchen.

4 Mueller Street, Alice Springs.
☎ *(08) 8952 8855.*
***Dorm bed** $18-20 ($17-19 VIP);*
single room** $38 ($36 VIP); **double/
***twin room** $48 ($46 VIP); includes*
breakfast.
***Credit cards** MC, Visa.*
***Reception open** 7am-12.30pm & 2pm-8pm daily.*

Maintenance & cleanliness	★★★☆
Facilities	★★★☆
Atmosphere & character	★★★
Security	★
Overall rating	★★☆

Annie's Place

Annie's is a nice hostel that is built around a courtyard with a swimming pool. All rooms are air-conditioned with TVs and most have en suite bathrooms. This hostel has Internet access and an excellent bar/restaurant with a great atmosphere and delicious $6 meals.

4 Traeger Avenue, Alice Springs.
☎ *(08) 8952 1545.*
***Dorm bed** $16; **double room** $55;*
includes breakfast.
***Credit cards** MC, Visa.*
***Reception open** 5am-9pm daily.*

Maintenance & cleanliness	★★★★
Facilities	★★
Atmosphere & character	★★★
Security	★★
Overall rating	★★★

Backpackers Hideaway

Backpackers Hideaway is a small quiet hostel with a great atmosphere. It features a big backyard with a spa pool, table tennis and barbecue area and it also has a cosy TV lounge.

6 Khalick Street, Alice Springs.
☎ *(08) 8952 8686.*
***Dorm bed** $15-18 ($14-17 VIP);*
double room** $45 ($43 VIP); **twin
***room** $40 ($39 VIP).*
***Credit cards** MC, Visa.*
***Reception open** 7.30am-7.30pm daily.*

Maintenance & cleanliness	★★★
Facilities	★★
Atmosphere & character	★★★★
Security	★
Overall rating	★★☆

Elke's Backpackers Resort

This former motel features an en suite bathroom, kitchenette and TV in each room, which keeps people from congregating in the common areas. Shared facilities include a swimming pool, barbecue area and a kitchen and a TV lounge with Internet access.

39 Gap Road, Alice Springs.
🚌 *4.*
☎ *(08) 8952 8422 or 1800 633 354.*
***Website** www.elkesbackpackers.com.au.*
***Dorm bed** $18-20 ($16-18 VIP/*
*YHA); **double/twin room** $50-75*
*($45-75 VIP/YHA); **triple room** $56*
($50 VIP/YHA); includes breakfast.
***Credit cards** Amex, Diners, MC, Visa.*
***Reception open** 6am-8pm daily.*

Maintenance & cleanliness	★★★
Facilities	★★★☆
Atmosphere & character	★
Security	★
Overall rating	★★☆

Melanka Backpackers

The largest hostel in town is a big and impersonal place with facilities that include a swimming pool, beach volleyball court plus a tiny kitchen and a TV lounge. The standard of the facilities is pretty low and the emphasis seems to be quantity over quality.

94 Todd Street, Alice Springs.
☎ *(08) 8952 4744 or 1800 815 066.*
***Dorm bed** $20-25 ($19-25 VIP);*
***single/double/twin room** $55 ($53-54 VIP).*
***Credit cards** Amex, Diners, MC, Visa.*
***Reception open** 5am-8pm daily.*

Maintenance & cleanliness	★★
Facilities	★★
Atmosphere & character	★★
Security	★★
Overall rating	★★

Ossie's Homestead

This is a nice small hostel with a swimming pool and a nice barbecue area. There's a small kitchen and a lounge with a pool table and Internet access. It's located about 1½km northwest of the town centre.

Corner Lindsay Avenue & Warburton Street, Alice Springs.

🚌 *2.*

☎ *1800 628 211.*

Website www.ossies.com.au.

Dorm bed *$16-18;* **double/twin room** *$42; includes breakfast.*

Credit cards *MC, Visa.*

Reception open *8am-7.30pm daily.*

Maintenance & cleanliness	★★★☆
Facilities	★★
Atmosphere & character	★★★☆
Security	★★
Overall rating	★★★

Pioneer YHA Hostel

This is a nice hostel with a great location and a good atmosphere – it's the most centrally located hostel in Alice Springs. The hostel is built in an old outdoor cinema with a combination of original buildings and purpose-built accommodation. There is a nice outdoors setting centred on a swimming pool. There's also a good kitchen, TV lounge, pool table and Internet access.

Corner Leichhardt & Parsons Streets, Alice Springs.

☎ *(08) 8952 8855.*

Dorm bed *$22.50-25.50 ($19-22 YHA);* **twin room** *$57-76 ($50-69 YHA).*

Credit cards *JCB, MC, Visa.*

Reception open *7.30am-8.30pm daily.*

Maintenance & cleanliness	★★★★★
Facilities	★★★☆
Atmosphere & character	★★★
Security	★★
Overall rating	★★★☆

Toddy's Backpackers Resort

This former motel has a common room with a TV, pool table and Internet access; a big barbecue area with table tennis and a swimming pool. Kitchen facilities are limited but they do a good barbecue meal each evening for $8.50.

41 Gap Road, Alice Springs.

🚌 *4.*

☎ *(08) 8952 1322 or 1800 806 240.*

Dorm bed *$12-16 ($12.15 Nomads);* **double/twin room** *$46-59 ($44-57 Nomads);* **triple room** *$65 ($62 Nomads); includes breakfast.*

Credit cards *Amex, Diners, JCB, MC, Visa.*

Reception open *6am-8.30pm daily.*

Maintenance & cleanliness	★★☆
Facilities	★★★
Atmosphere & character	★★★
Security	★
Overall rating	★★☆

Sights

Alice Springs Cultural Precinct

The Alice Springs Cultural Precinct has a number of attractions including the Aviation Museum and the Museum of Central Australia.

Corner Memorial Avenue & Larapinta Drive, Alice Springs.

☎ *(08) 8951 1122.*

Admission *$8 for all attractions in the Cultural Precinct.*

Open *10am-5pm daily.*

Alice Springs Desert Park

Run by the NT Parks & Wildlife Commission, the Alice Springs Desert Park portrays the wildlife and plants that thrive in the harsh Central Australian landscape. The park features three different desert habitats with over 400 different types of plants and more than 120 different species of animals. There is also an exhibition centre and an area with rare and endangered nocturnal animals.

Larapinta Drive, 6km from central Alice Springs.

☎ *(08) 8951 8788.*

Website www.alicespringsdesertpark. com.au.

Admission *$18.*

Open *7.30am-6pm daily.*

Anzac Hill

This is the best spot to watch the sun set over Alice Springs. You can get here by

Northern Territory

walking the Lions Walk trail, which is accessible via Wills Terrace.

Central Australian Aviation Museum

Plane spotters will love this museum, which is situated in the original hanger of Connellan Airways in what was the site of Alice Springs' first airport. The museum is home to several historic aircraft including early flying doctor planes and the remains of the *Kookaburra*, which crashed in the Tanami Desert in 1929

Corner Memorial Avenue & Larapinta Drive, Alice Springs.
☎ *(08) 8951 1122.*
Admission *$8, entry fee includes admission to other attractions in the Alice Springs Cultural Precinct.*
Open *10am-5pm.*

Frontier Camel Farm

This camel farm operates a number of popular camel rides and also maintains a small museum with exhibits about all things related to camels.
Ross Highway, Alice Springs.
☎ *(08) 8953 0444.*
Website *www.cameltours.com.au.*
Museum admission *$6; one-hour ride $75-100 including breakfast or dinner.*
Open *9am-5pm.*

Museum of Central Australia

The Museum of South Australia is a good introduction to Alice Springs and the surrounding region and it has an emphasis on Central Australia's natural history.
Corner Memorial Avenue & Larapinta Drive, Alice Springs.
☎ *(08) 8951 1122.*
Admission *$8, entry fee includes admission to other attractions in the Alice Springs Cultural Precinct.*
Open *10am-5pm.*

National Pioneer Women's Hall of Fame

The National Pioneer Women's Hall of Fame is located in the old courthouse and has exhibits on the lives and achievements of pioneer women in central Australia.

27 Hartley Street, Alice Springs.
☎ *(08) 8952 9006.*
Website *www.pioneerwomen.com.au.*
Admission *$2.20.*
Open *10am-5pm daily.*

Old Ghan Museum

This museum about the old *Ghan* railway is a must for railway enthusiasts. It's about 10km out of town.
MacDonnell Siding, Norris Bell Avenue, Alice Springs.
☎ *(08) 8955 5047.*
Admission *$5.50, students $4.50.*
Open *9am-5pm daily.*

Royal Flying Doctor Service

The Alice Springs branch of the RFDS is open to visitors and includes a small museum with informative displays about this outback institution.
8-10 Stuart Terrace, Alice Springs.
☎ *(08) 8952 1129.*
Website *www.flyingdoctor.net/ alicevisit.htm.*
Admission *$5.25.*
Open *Mon-Sat 9am-4pm, Sun 1pm-4pm.*

School of the Air

The Alice Springs branch of the School of the Air has a visitors' centre where you can learn about this unique education programme for students in remote areas.
Head Street, Alice Springs.
☎ *(08) 8951 6834.*
Website *www.assoa.nt.edu.au.*
Admission *$3.50.*
Open *Mon-Sat 8.30am-4.30pm, Sun 1.30pm-4.30pm.*

Telegraph Station

Alice Springs was originally established as a telegraph station in 1871. This 2,000 hectare reserve, 2km north of the centre of Alice Springs, is situated on the site of the original settlement. It features some of the original structures including the old telegraph station, which is open to the public.
Stuart Highway, Alice Springs.
☎ *(08) 8952 3993.*
Admission *reserve free, buildings $6.25.*
Open *reserve 8am-9pm daily, historic buildings 8am-5pm.*

MacDonnell Ranges

The MacDonnell Ranges are the closest important natural feature to Alice Springs and provides a worthwhile detour en route to Uluru. The national park is home to surprising scenery of canyons and rugged gorges.

West MacDonnell National Park

The West MacDonnell National Park is the largest in the MacDonnell Ranges and combines some of the best natural attractions in central Australia.

Simpsons Gap is the closest feature to Alice Springs and worth visiting as a daytrip from Alice even if you don't plan on visiting Uluru. This part of the park is an excellent place to see the black-footed rock wallaby, particularly at dawn or dusk

Going west the next major attraction is Standley Chasm, a breathtakingly narrow canyon that is a big hit with bus tours. Standley Chasm is open 8am-6pm daily and admission is $6.

Ormiston Gorge and Pound is located further towards the western end of the park. There is a waterhole at the southern end of the gorge that is said to be up to 14 metres deep. Hiking the Ormiston Pound Walk (7km, 3 hours) is the best way to see the area; this walk starts at the visitors' centre and takes you through the Pound, returning along Ormiston Gorge via the waterhole. Shorter walks around Ormiston Gorge and Pound include trails to the Waterhole (40 mins return) and Ghost Gum Lookout (30 mins return).

Glen Helen Gorge is nearby and is well worth visiting. The mostly dry Finke River passes through here, but the main feature of the gorge is the waterhole that is a beautiful spot for a swim.

The most challenging hike in the park is the Larapinta Trail. The entire trail is not yet open, but will eventually be a 250km trek from Alice Springs to Mt Sonder. It is expected that most people will hike the trail in smaller sections. Eight of the 13 sections of the trail are open including Alice Springs to Simpsons Gap and Ormiston Gorge to Glen Helen.

Accommodation

West MacDonnell National Park offers a variety of camping sites that range in price from $3.30-6.60 per person. Alternatively the Glen Helen Resort offers dorm accommodation for backpackers.

Glen Helen Resort

This large complex has accommodation ranging from hotel rooms to camping. Backpackers stay in the Stockman's Quarters with accommodation in basic four-bed dormitories. Common areas are limited but the resort has a bar and restaurant.

Namitjira Drive, West MacDonnell Ranges.
☎ *(08) 8956 7489.*
Website *www.melanka.com.au/ melanka_glenhelen/gh_index.html.*
Dorm bed *$20-30;* ***double room*** *$150;* ***camping*** *$10 per person.*
Credit cards *Amex, Diners, MC, Visa.*
🚗

Maintenance & cleanliness	★★⯪
Facilities	★★
Atmosphere & character	★⯪
Security	★⯪
Overall rating	★★

Finke Gorge National Park

This national park, 138km west of Alice Springs, includes the impressive Palm Valley that is home to an abundance of rare flora including the Red Cabbage Palm.

There are several hiking trails in the park. These include the Kalaranga Lookout walk (1.5km, 45 minutes), which is an easy 20-minute climb with spectacular views of the rock amphitheatre encircled by rugged cliffs. Another popular walk is the Mpaara Walk (5km, 2 hours), which introduces the mythology of the Western Arrernte Aboriginal culture.

Kings Canyon

This spectacular natural feature in the Watarrka National Park located between the West MacDonnell and Uluru-Kata Tjuta National Parks. The Canyon is a spectacular spot although it is one of the more expensive destinations in central Australia.

There are two hiking trails in the park. The Canyon Walk (6km; 3-4 hours) is the most rewarding walk and begins with a steep climb to the top of the Canyon, and then follows the Canyon rim around before descending again. The highlight of this walk is the 'Garden of Eden', an enchanting area of lush vegetation and cool waterholes. The Kings Creek Walk (2.6km; one hour) winds along Kings Creek ending at a lookout point.

Accommodation
Kings Canyon YHA

The Kings Canyon Resort has accommodation ranging from deluxe hotel rooms to camping sites and it includes a YHA hostel. It has good facilities that include two swimming pools, tennis courts, three restaurants and two bars. However it is way overpriced and the hostel has no common areas other than the limited kitchen facilities that don't even include a toaster.
Ernest Giles Road, Watarrka National Park.
☎ *(08) 8956 7442 or 1800 817 622.*
Dorm bed $39; double/twin room $98.
Credit cards *Amex, Diners, JCB, MC, Visa.*
Reception open *6.30am-9.30pm daily.*
☎

Maintenance & cleanliness	★★☆
Facilities	★★★
Atmosphere & character	-
Security	★★
Overall rating	★★

Uluru-Kata Tjuta National Park

Within the vast Uluru-Kata Tjuta National Park (*website www.ea.gov.au/parks/uluru/*), 460 kilometres southwest of Alice Springs lay many Aboriginal sacred sites, including Kata Tjuta (the Olgas) and Uluru (Ayers Rock), the world's largest monolith.

This area is of vital significance to the Anangu people (the traditional Aboriginal owners), whose ancestors are thought to have lived in the area for at least 10,000 years and possibly far longer.

Entry to the national park costs $16.25, which allows the visitor to spend three days exploring the park. The park is only open during the following hours: Jan-Feb 5am-9pm, Mar 5.30am-8.30pm, Apr 6am-8pm, May 6am-7.30pm, Jun-Jul 6.30am-7.30pm, Aug 6am-7.30pm, Sep 5.30am-7.30pm, Oct 5am-8pm, Nov 5am-8.30pm, Dec 5am-9pm.

Practical Information
Uluru-Kata Tjuta Cultural Centre
Lasseter Highway, Uluru.
☎ *(08) 8956 3138.*
Open *Jan-Mar 7am-6pm daily; Apr-Oct 7am-5.30pm daily; Nov-Dec 7am-6pm daily.*

Visitors Centre
Yulara Drive, Yulara.
☎ *(08) 8956 7377.*
Open *8.30am-8pm daily.*

Coming & Going

There are several tours operating from Alice Springs that cater to backpackers that generally take in Ayers Rock and the Olgas, visiting the West MacDonnell National Park and either Finke Gorge or Kings Canyon en route. These tours can be booked through most hostels and range in price from around $200 for a simple overnight trip to Ayers Rock and the Olgas to $400 for a 3-day tour that also takes in Kings Canyon. Companies that operate these tours include Mulga's Adventures (☎ *(08) 8952 1545; website www.mulgas.com.au*), Outback Safaris (☎ *1300 306 499*), Sahara Outback Tours (☎ *1800 806 240; website www.saharatours.com.au*), Wayward Bus (☎ *1800 882 823; website www.waywardbus.com.au*) and Wildway (☎ *(08) 8953 7045 or 1300 720 777; **website** www.wildway.com.au*).

Emu Run (☎ *(08) 8953 7057; **website** www.emurun.com.au*) operates day trips from Alice Springs, which cost $175. This is a long day that leaves Alice Springs at 6am and returns at midnight, but it is a good option if your time is limited.

McCafferty's/Greyhound operate a bus service between Alice Springs and Yulara that includes transport to Ayers Rock and the Olgas. This route is included on some of their travel passes.

Driving is the best travel option, this way you can see the main sights in the MacDonnell Ranges on the way here and you can visit Ayers Rock and the Olgas at your own pace rather than when bus or tour schedules allow. There are plenty of car rental companies in Alice Springs and most hostels can organise rental cars for you.

Local Transport

There is a free shuttle bus operated by the Yulara Resort that runs to the main areas in Yulara. There is also a free shuttle between the airport and Yulara that picks up from all accommodation establishments including the hostel and meets all flights.

The best value and most flexible transport option is to drive yourself. Several rental car companies including Avis (☎ *(08) 8956 2266)*, Hertz (☎ *(08) 8956 2244)* and Thrifty (☎ *(08) 8956 2030)* can be booked through the airport or the visitor centre in Yulara.

The next best option is the Uluru Express (☎ *(08) 8956 2152; **website** www.uluruexpress.com.au)* shuttle bus, which operates a shuttle bus between Yulara, Ayers Rock and the Olgas. The first service to Uluru (Ayers Rock) departs Yulara an hour prior to sunrise at the rock and runs every 45 minutes with the last service back leaving Uluru after sunset. Buses leave Yulara for Kata Tjuta (the Olgas) at 6am, 8am, 1.30pm and 3.30pm. The Yulara-Uluru service costs $35-40 return and the Yulara-Kata Tjuta service costs $50-55return. Uluru Express also has a three-day pass, which costs $130 and includes the entrance fee to the national park.

McCafferty's/Greyhound operate coaches from Yulara to the Olgas each morning at 6am ($40), returning to Yulara several hours later and then heading to Ayers Rock at 3pm ($62). These services are a little inflexible, but you do get the chance to see the sun set over Ayers Rock. This service is included on some McCafferty's/Greyhound bus passes.

You can also see Uluru from the back of a Harley. Uluru Motorcycle Tours (☎ *(08) 8956 2019)* charge $125-150 for a trip to Uluru (Ayers Rock), $210-225 to Kata Tjuta (the Olgas) and $345 to visit both Ayers Rock and the Olgas.

Uluru (Ayers Rock)

The world's largest monolith is the main attraction in Uluru-Kata Tjuta National Park. There is a walking trail around the base of the rock and a two-hour climb to the summit, which is not as popular as it used to be, as more people respect the wishes of the local Aboriginal people and choose not to climb.

There is an informative cultural centre located about 1km to the southwest of the rock, which is a good spot to learn more about the Anangu people and to understand their reasons for not climbing Uluru.

If you do decide to climb, you'll be rewarded by spectacular views that encompass Kata Tjuta (the Olgas) and Mount Connor. Although the climb is relatively easy, it can be a dangerous venture and more than 30 people have died attempting it over the past 30 years. Hold on to the chain, wear hiking boots and take along a bottle of drinking water. As a safety precaution, the climbing route is closed during extreme weather conditions.

There are several hiking trails around the base of the rock; these include the 9.4km circuit walk that can take up to four hours. Shorter and easier walks include the Mala Walk (2km; one hour), accessible from the western car park and the Mutitjulu Walk (1km; 45 minutes), accessible from the southern car park.

After travelling so far, some travellers splurge on a scenic flight. Ayers Rock

Helicopters (☎ (08) 8956 2077), Ayers Rock Scenic Flights (☎ (08) 8956 2345) and Professional Helicopter Services (☎ (08) 8956 2003; *website www.phs.com.au*) operate scenic helicopter flights of Ayers Rock ($85-100) or both Ayers Rock and the Olgas ($129-195).

Kata Tju_ta (The Olgas)

Kata Tju_ta, meaning 'many heads', is comprised of 36 rocks and in many ways this rock formation is a more rewarding destination than the more popular Ulu_ru.

There are several hiking trails among the Olgas that include the relatively easy Wu_lpa Gorge Walk (2.6km; one hour) that takes you between Mount Olga and Mount Wu_lpa – two of the more imposing rocks. Another popular hike is the Valley of the Winds Walk (7.5km; three hours), which is a circuit taking in the Karingana and Karu lookouts.

Yulara

The Yulara resort complex is 20 kilometres from Ulu_ru. Apart from accommodation, Yulara offers restaurants, bars and clubs and a giant telescope for night-sky viewing. This is the commercial centre of the national park featuring an airport, shopping centre and it is where virtually everyone stays regardless of their budget.

Accommodation
If you're driving the cheapest option is the free camping at Curtin Springs Roadhouse, about a 45-minute drive from Ayers Rock. Otherwise you have to stay at the overpriced campground or youth hostel in Yulara.

Outback Pioneer Lodge YHA
Outback Pioneer Lodge is a very nice YHA hostel with facilities that include a god bar/restaurant, a big kitchen and a common room with Internet access and a TV lounge. Accommodation is in air-conditioned rooms that include big 20-bed dorms divided by partitions into four-bed units, smaller four-bed dorms and double/twin rooms (both with and without en suite bathrooms). It is a clean place with a high standard of amenities but it is also one of the most expensive hostels in Australia, however it's the cheapest accommodation option if you're not camping.
Ayers Rock Resort, Yulara.
☎ *(08) 8957 7888 or 1300 139 889.*
***Dorm bed** $33.50-40.50 ($30-37 YHA).*
***Credit cards** Amex, Diners, JCB, MC, Visa.*
***Reception open** 24 hours.*
🚐

Maintenance & cleanliness	★★★★★
Facilities	★★☆
Atmosphere & character	★★☆
Security	★★☆
Overall rating	★★★☆

Queensland

Queensland is a popular destination with thousands of backpackers drawn to the Sunshine State by the beaches, islands and the Great Barrier Reef.

Queensland's attractions range from theme parks and surf beaches to Fraser Island, the Great Barrier Reef, and the Daintree Rainforest.

The state also provides more active outdoor holiday pursuits – from white water rafting and whale-watching trips to hiking, paragliding and bungy jumping.

Brisbane

Queensland's largest city sits on the banks of the meandering Brisbane River, close to the waters of Moreton

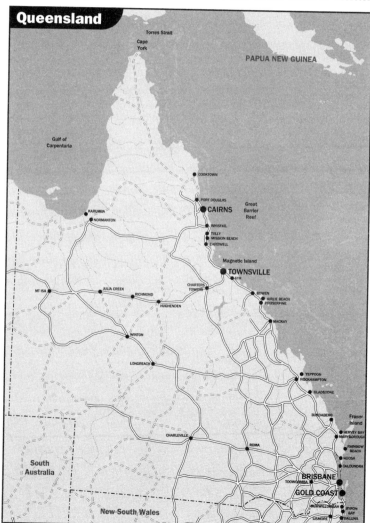

Bay, and is home to about 1.6 million people.

Selected as a convict settlement in 1824, the original town was established near Redcliffe before moving to its current site in 1825. The penal settlement closed in 1839 and the area opened to free settlers in 1842.

Brisbane's attractions include the Queensland Cultural Centre, housing Queensland's Art Gallery, Performing Arts Complex, Museum and State Library. Other draw cards include the South Bank Parklands and Lone Pine Koala Sanctuary.

Practical Information
INFORMATION CENTRES & USEFUL ADDRESSES
American Express
131 Elizabeth Street, Brisbane
🚉 *Central.*
☎ *(07) 3229 2729.*
Website www.americanexpress.com.
Open Mon-Fri 9am-5pm, Sat 9am-noon.

Brisbane Visitor Centre
Queen Street Mall, Brisbane.
🚉 *Central.*
☎ *(07) 3229 5918.*
Open Mon-Thu 9am-6pm, Fri 9am-8pm, Sat 9am-5pm, Sun 9am-4.30pm.

Naturally Queensland Information Centre
This information centre provides information on Queensland's national parks.
160 Ann Street, Brisbane.
🚉 *Central.*
☎ *(07) 3227 8185.*
Website www.env.gov.qld.au.
Open Mon-Fri 8.30am-5pm.

Public Transport Hotline
☎ *131230*

YHA Travel & Resource Centre
George Street, Brisbane.
🚌 *370, 374, 375, 377, 378, 379, 380, 381, 382, 383, 426, 431, 441, 446, 455, 456, 461, 470, 475, 476;*
🚉 *Roma Street.*
Open Mon-Tue 8.30am-6pm, Wed 9am-6pm, Thu-Fri 8.30am-6pm, Sat 9am-3pm.

LAUNDRY
New Farm Launderette
Corner Brunswick & Harcourt Streets, New Farm.
🚉 *Brunswick Street;* 🚌 *190, 191, 193, 194.*

INTERNET CAFÉS
Dialup Cyber Lounge
126 Adelaide Street, Brisbane.
☎ *(07) 3211 9095.*
Website www.dialup.com.au.
Open Mon-Thu 9.30am-7.30pm, Fri 9.30am-8pm, Sat 9.30am-7.30pm, Sun 10am-6pm.

Email Plus
328 Upper Roma Street, Brisbane.
☎ *(07) 3236 0433.*
Open 9am-late.

Global Gossip Brisbane
288 Edward Street, Brisbane.
☎ *(07) 3229 4033.*
Website www.globalgossip.com.au.
Open 8am-midnight daily.

Coming & Going
AIR
Brisbane is well connected by air and it is increasingly affordable to fly in and out of here.

Brisbane's Eagle Farm airport *(website www.brisbaneairport.com.au)* is located about 16km northwest of the city centre and is comprised of two terminals – domestic and international – located 2km apart.

The easiest way to the airport is by the Air Train *(website www.airtrain.com.au).* The Air Train runs to the city centre four times an hour and to the Gold Coast twice an hour. The trip between the airport and the city centre takes 22 minutes and costs $9. Many hostels sell discounted tickets for the Air Train.

Alternatively, Coachtrans *(website www.coachtrans.com.au)* run buses into central Brisbane that cost $9-11 each way.

BUS
McCafferty's/Greyhound and Premier Motor Service buses arrive at the Roma Street Transit Centre. There are

Queensland

daily buses to most destinations with more frequent services on the popular Sydney and Cairns routes.

TRAIN

The Roma Street Transit Centre is also Brisbane's main train station for long-distance travel with daily trains to most major destinations including interstate services and trains on the Brisbane-Cairns line.

HITCHHIKING

Because Brisbane is so close to the Sunshine and Gold Coasts, a lot of traffic heading out of town is local traffic bound for the nearby resort cities. If you're hitching from Brisbane, your best bet is to catch a train beyond either the Gold or Sunshine Coast where you're more likely to catch long-distance traffic.

Heading north, catch a train to Gympie. Both Citytrain and long-distance services should stop here. Once in Gympie, it's just a matter of walking to the northern edge of town and hitching a lift on the Bruce Highway.

Alternatively you can get off the train in either Cooroy or Eumundi, both a little closer to Brisbane (and cheaper to get to). However Cooroy and Eumundi are both located a couple of kilometres off the Bruce Highway, so you'll have a bit of a walk to get to the prime hitching spots.

Heading south from Brisbane, you'll need to get to Bilinga, near Coolangatta on the Gold Coast. You can take either a bus from Brisbane or a train to Robina and a connecting bus.

Once you're on the Gold Coast, you'll need to hop on a local bus heading south to Coolangatta and ask to be let off on the Gold Coast Highway outside Coolangatta Airport. This should place you just before the turn-off for the Tweed Heads Bypass where you can find a safe stretch of road to stick your thumb out.

An easier option is to use a web-based ride sharing service such as BUG Ride *(http://australia.bugride.com)*, this website allows travellers to both offer lifts and search for rides throughout Australia.

Local Transport

Brisbane's transport network is comprised of buses, trains and ferries and is a convenient way to get around town, although the city centre is compact enough to walk around.

TRAIN

Citytrain operates Brisbane's suburban train network that has seven lines and extends as far as Ipswich, Beenleigh and Caboolture. All trains stop at the three main central stations – Roma Street, Central and Brunswick Street.

BUS

Most of Brisbane's local buses terminate at the central Queen Street Bus Station underneath the Queen Street Mall.

Although the train is generally handier for covering longer distances, there are some handy bus routes around the city centre and between various inner-city neighbourhoods. The more useful bus routes include buses 190, 191, 193 and 194, which run between the city centre and the hostels in Fortitude Valley, New Farm and South Brisbane/West End.

There is a free downtown loop bus that runs around the city centre every 10 minutes (Mon-Fri 7am-5.50pm). This is a good way to travel between Central Station, the Botanic Gardens and the Eagle Street Pier.

Fares are calculated on the number of zones crossed and there are five zones. Zone 1 is the city centre.

FERRY

Brisbane has an efficient ferry network and it is a pleasant way to travel to destinations along the river. Ferries are divided between the City Cat that runs a route upriver stopping at a multitude of points along the way and the Crossriver ferries which operate a triangular route between Eagle and Edward Streets in the city centre and Thornton Street in Kangaroo Point. Ferries run about once every 20 minutes.

FARES

Fares on Brisbane's transport network are determined by a zone system with most points of interest located in zone

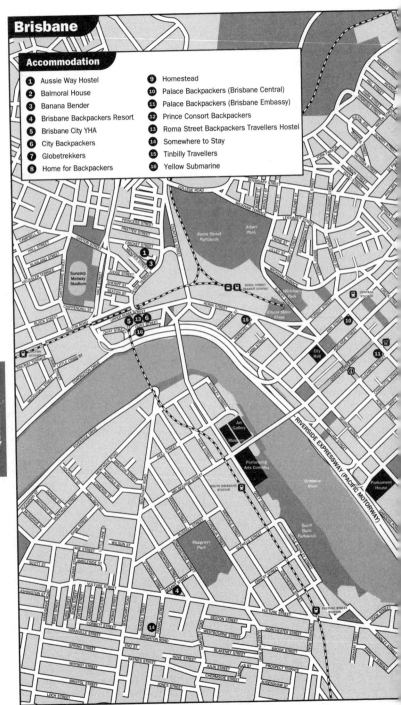

Brisbane

Accommodation

1. Aussie Way Hostel
2. Balmoral House
3. Banana Bender
4. Brisbane Backpackers Resort
5. Brisbane City YHA
6. City Backpackers
7. Globetrekkers
8. Home for Backpackers
9. Homestead
10. Palace Backpackers (Brisbane Central)
11. Palace Backpackers (Brisbane Embassy)
12. Prince Consort Backpackers
13. Roma Street Backpackers Travellers Hostel
14. Somewhere to Stay
15. Tinbilly Travellers
16. Yellow Submarine

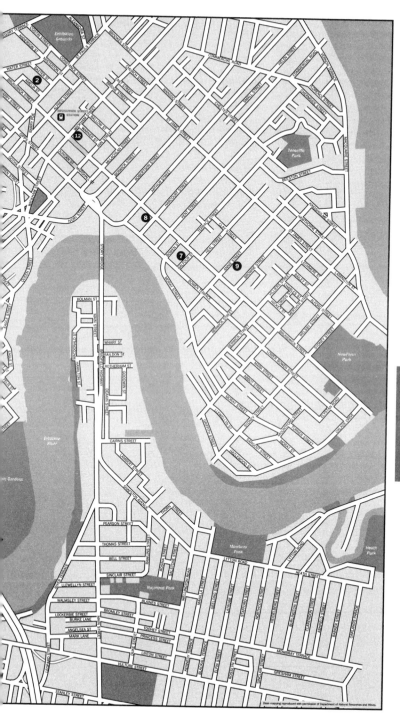

one. A single trip within zone one is $1.80.

Single bus and ferry fares are listed below:

Zones	Fare
1 zone	$1.80
2 zones	$2.60
3 zones	$3.40
All zones	$3.80

There are also a number of multi-trip tickets available for more frequent travellers. The various multiple trip tickets include:

Ten Trip Saver

The Ten Trip Saver ticket allows ten trips on buses and ferries. They are a good idea if you're planning on spending a while in Brisbane. Bus travel with a Ten Trip Saver allows a two-hour transfer on every trip.

Zones	Fare
1 zone	$13.80
2 zones	$20.80
3 zones	$27.20

1-2-3 Ticket

This allows two hours of travel with transfers between buses, ferries and trains. The 1-2-3 Intermodal ticket costs $3.80.

Off-Peak Saver

This allows unlimited travel on buses and ferries between 9am and 3.30pm and after 7pm on weekdays and all day on weekends and public holidays. This ticket costs $4.60 but cannot be purchased on board ferries.

Day Rover (Bus/Ferry)

For $8.40, a Day Rover ticket allows unlimited travel on buses and ferries.

South East Explorer

The South East Explorer is a good deal if you want to venture beyond the Brisbane area and explore other areas in South East Queensland. The South East Explorer pass allows unlimited one-day travel on train, bus and ferry travel as far as Coolangatta on the Gold Coast and Noosa on the Sunshine Coast.

Ticket	Fare	Area covered
Explorer 1	$8.60	Central Brisbane metropolitan area as far north as Petrie and south to Kingston.
Explorer 2	$15.00	Brisbane metropolitan area including Caboolture, Redcliffe and Ormeau.
Explorer 3	$21.60	Brisbane metropolitan area, plus the Sunshine Coast as far north as Noosa, the Gold Coast as far south as Coolangatta and west to Helidon.

Accommodation
Aussie Way Hostel

Aussie Way is a small quiet hostel in an historic home that has a lot of charm. There's a small fully equipped kitchen, pool table, Internet access, swimming pool and a nice balcony overlooking the street. The hostel is located on a quiet residential street close to bars and cafés on nearby Caxton Street and the Transit Centre is a short walk way.

34 Cricket Street, Petrie Terrace.
◙ *350, 352, 355, 379, 380, 381, 384; Roma Street.*
☎ *(07) 3369 0711 or 0800 242 997.*
***Dorm bed** $22 ($21 VIP/YHA);* ***single room** $34 ($33 VIP/YHA);* ***double/ twin room** $50 ($48 VIP/YHA).*
***Credit cards** MC, Visa.*
***Reception open** 7.30am-2pm & 6pm-8pm daily.*

Maintenance & cleanliness	★★★☆
Facilities	★★
Atmosphere & character	★★★★
Security	★★★☆
Overall rating	★★★

Balmoral House

This small hostel has the usual kitchen, TV lounge and Internet access plus a small outdoor area at the rear of the hostel. It is located on a semi-industrial street close to the shops and restaurants of Fortitude Valley and it is within walking distance of the city centre.
33 Amelia Street, Fortitude Valley.

🚌 *31, 310, 315, 320;* 🚉 *Brunswick Street.*
☎ *(07) 3252 1397.*
Dorm bed *$16;* **double room** *$38-46.*
Reception open *7am-11am & 3.30pm-8pm daily.*

Maintenance & cleanliness	★★★
Facilities	★⯪
Atmosphere & character	★
Security	★⯪
Overall rating	★★

Banana Bender Backpackers

Banana Bender is a nice hostel with a good TV lounge, Internet access, bar, barbecue and a deck with nice views. Accommodation is mostly in four-bed dorms. It's located on the corner of Jessie Street and Petrie Terrace, close to the Transit Centre and the bars and cafés on nearby Caxton Street.

118 Petrie Terrace, Petrie Terrace.
🚌 *350, 352, 355, 379, 380, 381, 384;* 🚉 *Roma Street.*
☎ *(07) 3367 1157 or 1800 241 157.*
Website *www.bananabenders.com.*
Dorm bed *$21-23 ($20-22 VIP/YHA);* **double/twin room** *$50 ($48 VIP/YHA).*
Reception open 7am-10pm daily.

Maintenance & cleanliness	★★★⯪
Facilities	★★
Atmosphere & character	★★★★⯪
Security	★★
Overall rating	★★★

Brisbane Backpackers Resort

This big purpose-built hostel has loads of facilities including a swimming pool, sauna, Internet access and a bar/restaurant with pool tables and a big screen TV. The rooms have en suite bathrooms, lockers and the double rooms and small dorms have TVs. It is in South Brisbane, about a 10 to 15-minute walk to Southbank Beach and it is also close to restaurants and cafés in West End. New owners have taken over since we rated this hostel and feedback from other travellers indicates that they have made a big difference.

110 Vulture Street, West End.
🚌 *190,191,193,194.*
☎ *(07) 3844 9956 or 1800 626 452.*
Website *www.brisbanebackpackersresort.com.*

Dorm bed *$19-24 ($18-23 VIP);* **double/twin room** *$59 ($57 VIP).*
Credit cards *Amex, Diners, MC, Visa.*
Reception open *24 hours.*
🚌

Maintenance & cleanliness	★★★
Facilities	★★★★
Atmosphere & character	★★
Security	★★★
Overall rating	★★★

Brisbane City YHA

The Brisbane City YHA is a nice clean complex with accommodation in two buildings – dormitories in the older building and twin, double and triple rooms in the nicer, newer building. The older building has a basic common area with a TV lounge, pool table and a big kitchen. The new building's common areas include a café, Internet access and the reception.

392 Upper Roma Street, Brisbane.
🚌 *470, 475;* 🚉 *Roma Street.*
☎ *(07) 3236 1004.*
Dorm bed *$24.50-26.50 ($21-23 YHA);* **double/twin room** *$57-77 ($50-70 YHA).*
Credit cards *MC, Visa.*
Reception open *5.30am-midnight daily.*
🚌

Maintenance & cleanliness	★★★★
Facilities	★★
Atmosphere & character	★★⯪
Security	★★★
Overall rating	★★★

City Backpackers

This big 300-bed hostel is a clean and well-maintained hostel with good facilities that include a great pub with a pool table and big screen telly plus a swimming pool and a deck with brilliant city views. There's also a TV lounge and a big kitchen. It has a fun atmosphere.

380 Upper Roma Street, Brisbane.
🚌 *470, 475;* 🚉 *Roma Street.*
☎ *(07) 3211 3221 or 1800 062 572.*
Website *www.citybackpackers.com.*
Dorm bed *$17-23 ($16-22 VIP/YHA);* **single room** *$42-55 ($41-54 VIP/YHA);* **double/twin room** *$50-65 ($48-63 VIP/YHA).*
Credit cards *MC, Visa.*

Queensland

Reception open 7am-7pm daily.

Maintenance & cleanliness	★★★★☆
Facilities	★★★
Atmosphere & character	★★★★
Security	★★★★☆
Overall rating	★★★★

Globetrekkers

Globetrekkers is a small quiet hostel with a relaxed and laid back atmosphere. There's a small kitchen and dining room with lockers, a cosy TV lounge, Internet access and a swimming pool. The rooms are clean and spacious with eclectic furnishings. It's located on a quiet leafy street a short walk from the shops on Brunswick Street.
35 Balfour Street, New Farm.
190, 191, 193, 194.
(07) 3358 1251.
Website www.geocities.com/globetrekkersbackpackers/.
Dorm bed $19; double/twin room $44-48.

Maintenance & cleanliness	★★★
Facilities	★★
Atmosphere & character	★★★★☆
Security	★★☆
Overall rating	★★★☆

Home for Backpackers

This small hostel feels like a shared house and it caters mostly to backpackers staying long-term while working in Brisbane. It has a leafy backyard plus the usual kitchen and TV lounge but it is messy and poorly maintained.
515 Brunswick Street, Fortitude Valley.
190, 191, 193, 194; Brunswick Street.
(07) 3254 1984 or 1800 808 941.
Dorm bed $17.
Reception open 10am-10pm daily.

Maintenance & cleanliness	★★
Facilities	★
Atmosphere & character	★★★★
Security	★
Overall rating	★★

Homestead

Homestead is a popular hostel with backpackers working in Brisbane. Facilities include Internet access, a pool table, kitchen and a TV lounge. It's on a residential street near the New Farm Village shops.
57 Annie Street, New Farm.
190, 191, 193, 194.
(07) 3358 3538.
Dorm bed $16-19 ($15-18 VIP/YHA); double/twin room $44 ($42 VIP/YHA).
Credit cards MC, Visa.
Reception open 7am-7pm daily.

Maintenance & cleanliness	★★★
Facilities	★★☆
Atmosphere & character	★★☆
Security	★
Overall rating	★★☆

Moreton Bay Lodge

This clean hostel has the usual kitchen and TV lounge plus accommodation in spacious dorms with new beds. It's located in the harbourside suburb of Manly, which is 30 minutes by train from the city centre.
45 Cambridge Parade, Manly.
Manly.
(07) 3396 3824.
Dorm bed $21-22; double room $75.
Credit cards Amex, Diners, MC, Visa.
Reception open Mon-Fri 8.30am-5.30pm, Sat-Sun 9.30am-5.30pm.

Maintenance & cleanliness	★★★★
Facilities	★★☆
Atmosphere & character	★★☆
Security	★★☆
Overall rating	★★★

Palace Backpackers (Brisbane Central)

Palace Backpackers occupies a heritage building right in the heart of the city centre that is generally clean and well maintained. It's a big hostel with 350 beds and there are good facilities including three laundries, and in-house employment agency, a licensed travel agency, a huge kitchen, big balconies, a rooftop sundeck with a barbecue and great city views and several TV lounges. It is a party hostel with a great bar downstairs that goes off until around 3am, but the accommodation is separated from the bar by the ground floor with the reception and café so the

Queensland

rooms are generally quiet. The rooms facing the street are also double-glazed to keep the noise out.

Corner Ann & Edward Streets, Brisbane. ⚑ *Central.*
☎ *(07) 3211 2433 or 1800 676 340.*
Website *www.palacebackpackers.com.au.*
Dorm bed *$20-23 ($19-22 VIP);* **single room** *$36 ($35 VIP);* **double room** *$48 ($46 VIP);* **twin room** *$52 ($50 VIP).*
Reception open *24 hours.*

Maintenance & cleanliness	★★★☆
Facilities	★★☆
Atmosphere & character	★★★★
Security	★★★☆
Overall rating	★★★☆

Palace Backpackers (Brisbane Embassy)

This is an excellent new hostel right in the heart of the city centre that is very clean with brand new fittings. It features a brilliant kitchen with stainless steel appliances, several rooftop sundecks and two TV lounges, including a brilliant one with surround sound, cinema-style seating and a big screen. It is a quieter place than the other Palace hostel but guests have access to the other hostel's facilities so they can still party up the road.

Corner Edward & Elizabeth Streets, Brisbane.
⚑ *most buses;* ⚑ *Central.*
☎ *(07) 3002 5777 or 1800 676 340.*
Dorm bed *$20-25 ($19-24 VIP);* **double room** *$48 ($46 VIP).*
Credit cards *MC, Visa.*
Reception open *7am-9pm daily.*

Maintenance & cleanliness	★★★★★
Facilities	★★★
Atmosphere & character	★★
Security	★★★★☆
Overall rating	★★★★

Prince Consort Backpackers

This large backpackers hostel is located above the Elephant & Wheelbarrow pub near the Brunswick Street Mall in the Valley. It's an older building with high ceilings and there is a big TV lounge, Internet access and the usual kitchen and laundry. The biggest dorm

has 22 beds but most dorms have either six or eight beds. About half the rooms have air-conditioning.

230 Wickham Street, Fortitude Valley.
⚑ *190, 191, 193, 194;* ⚑ *Brunswick Street.*
☎ *(07) 3257 2252.*
Dorm bed *$16-22 ($15-21 Nomads);* **double room** *$48-52 ($46-50 Nomads);* **triple room** *$66-89 ($63-66 Nomads).*
Credit cards *Amex, Diners, MC, Visa.*
Reception open *8am-10pm daily.*

Maintenance & cleanliness	★★★★☆
Facilities	★★☆
Atmosphere & character	★★★☆
Security	★★★
Overall rating	★★★☆

Roma Street Backpackers Travellers Hostel

This hostel is sandwiched between City Backpackers and the YHA and doesn't look too great from the outside but it is better inside. However it's unlikely that you'll stay here, as the owners are very selective about whom they let in. It's a quiet hostel so don't expect to party here. It is far from the best choice but it's cheap and for some reason it is popular with Asian travellers.

390 Roma Street, Brisbane.
⚑ *470, 475;* ⚑ *Roma Street.*
☎ *(07) 3236 2961.*
Dorm bed *$15;* **single room** *$30;* **twin room** *$40.*
Not yet rated.

Somewhere to Stay

This is a relatively quiet hostel with accommodation in two big old Queenslander-style buildings that have a lot of charm. Facilities include a kitchen, a TV lounge, Internet access, a pool table and an outdoor area with a barbecue and swimming pool. Dormitories have four to six beds and the hostel features balconies with city views.

45 Brighton Road, Highgate Hill.
⚑ *190, 191, 193, 194, 198.*
☎ *(07) 3846 2858 or 1800 812 398.*
Dorm bed *$16-25 ($15-24 Nomads/VIP/YHA);* **single room** *$32-37 ($31-36 Nomads/VIP/YHA).*
Credit cards *Amex, JCB, MC, Visa.*
Reception open *8am-8.30pm daily.*

📷

Maintenance & cleanliness	★★⯪
Facilities	★★★
Atmosphere & character	★★★★
Security	★⯪
Overall rating	★★★

Tinbilly Travellers

Tinbilly is a new hostel that is maintained to a very high standard. All the rooms have air-conditioning and en suites. There is a kitchen, laundry, Internet access and a TV lounge on the first floor and the ground floor has a bar and restaurant. It has a central location across the road from the Roma Street Transit Centre and it's only four blocks from the Queen Street Mall.

462 George Street, Brisbane.
🚌 *370, 374, 375, 377, 378, 379, 380, 381, 382, 383, 426, 431, 441, 446, 455, 456, 461, 470, 475, 476;*
🚉 *Roma Street.*
☎ *1800 446 646.*
Website *www.tinbilly.com.*
Dorm bed *$20-26 ($19-25 VIP);*
double room *$74-84 ($73-84 VIP);*
twin room *$74 ($73 VIP).*
Credit cards *MC, Visa.*
Reception open *24 hours.*

Maintenance & cleanliness	★★★★★
Facilities	★★
Atmosphere & character	★★
Security	★★★★★
Overall rating	★★★⯪

Yellow Submarine

This small hostel has extremely helpful staff and it features a small swimming pool, an outdoor covered common area with barbecue, pool table and TV, Internet access and a small kitchen. It's a popular hostel and bookings are recommended if you're planning to stay here during the busy season.

66 Quay Street, Brisbane.
🚌 *470, 475;* 🚉 *Roma Street.*
☎ *(07) 3211 3424.*
Dorm bed *$20-22;* **double/twin room** *$48.*
Reception open *7am-10pm daily.*

Maintenance & cleanliness	★★★⯪
Facilities	★★★⯪
Atmosphere & character	★★★★⯪
Security	★★⯪
Overall rating	★★★

Eating & Drinking

Brisbane has a good range of budget eateries, including food halls and fast food places in the city centre and good value Chinese restaurants in Fortitude Valley.

Brisbane has a reasonably good pub scene, but most backpackers tend to party at either the Down Under bar under Palace Backpackers, at Rosie's Tavern on Edward Street or the Elephant & Wheelbarrow on the corner of Brunswick and Wickham Streets in Fortitude Valley.

Sights
Alma Park Zoo

As well as Australian animals like kangaroos, koalas, emus, wombats, dingoes, goannas and possums in their natural surroundings, Alma Park Zoo is home to a wide range of exotic animals including monkeys, baboon, red deer, fallow deer, leopards, camels, water buffalo and sun bears.

Alma Road, Kallangur (about 30 minutes north of Brisbane).
🚉 *Dakabin, then courtesy bus (courtesy bus meets the 9.02am departure from Roma Street, 9.08am from Central, 9.10am from Brunswick Street).*
☎ *(07) 3204 6566.*
Website *www.almaparkzoo.com.au.*
Admission *$22.*
Open *9am-5pm daily.*

Australian Woolshed

This animal park has the usual collection of native animals, but the focus is on sheep and sheep dogs.

148 Samford Road, Ferny Hills.
🚉 *Ferny Hills.*
☎ *(07) 3872 1100.*
Website *www.auswoolshed.com.au.*
Admission *$16.50.*
Open *8.30am- 4pm daily.*

Carlton Brewery

The large Carlton Brewery, located in the southern suburbs on the way to the Gold Coast, brews Carlton, Fosters and Victoria Bitter and offers tours that include samples. Bookings essential, but it is difficult to get to without a car.

Corner Mulles Road & Pacific Highway, Yatala.

☎ *(07) 3826 5858.*
Admission $10.
Tours Mon-Fri 10am, noon, 2pm.

Castlemaine Brewery

There are regular tours of the brewery that produces XXXX beer. Each 75-minute tour gives you the chance to learn more about how beer is made, learn a few bits of useless trivia and most importantly taste the finished product. Bookings recommended.
50 Heusser Terrace, Milton.
🚌 *470, 475;* 🚆 *Milton.*
☎ *(07) 3361 7597.*
Website www.xxxx.com.au/Alehouse/.
Admission $18, includes four beers at the end of the tour.
Tours Mon-Tue 10am, 11am, noon, 2pm, 2.30pm, 3.30pm, 4pm, Wed 10am, 11am, noon, 2pm, 2.30pm, 3.30pm, 4pm, 6pm, Thu-Fri 10am, 11am, noon, 2pm, 2.30pm, 3.30pm, 4pm.

City Hall

City Hall is a major landmark in central Brisbane that features a clock tower with an observation deck with good views of the downtown area. The newly opened Museum of Brisbane (MoB) is on the ground floor.
King George Square, Brisbane.
🚆 *Central.*
☎ *(07) 3403 4048.*
Admission free; observation deck $2.
Open Mon-Fri 8am-5pm, Sat-Sun 10am-5pm; observation deck open Mon-Fri 10am-3pm, Sat 10am-2.30pm.

Eagle Street Pier Craft Market

This is a great place if you love poking around markets.
Eagle Street, Brisbane.
🚢 *Eagle Street Pier;* 🚆 *Central.*
☎ *0414 888 041.*
Website www.espcraftmarket.com.au.
Admission free.
Open Sun 8am-4pm.

Lone Pine Koala Sanctuary

Lone Pine is a large wildlife sanctuary with loads of native Australian animals including kangaroos and koalas as well as Tasmanian devils, wombats, dingoes and various reptiles.

Jesmond Road, Fig Tree Pocket.
🚌 *430, 445.*
☎ *(07) 3878 1366.*
Website www.koala.net.
Admission $16, $12.80 (Nomads/VIP/YHA).
Open 8.30am-5pm daily.

Museum of Brisbane (MoB)

The new Museum of Brisbane inside City Hall has exhibits about the city's history and culture.
King George Square, Brisbane.
🚆 *Central.*
☎ *(07) 3403 8888.*
Admission free.
Open 10am-5pm daily.

Parliament House

If you're interested in Queensland state politics, you may want to take advantage of the free tours of Parliament House, which run regularly.
Corner Alice & George Streets, Brisbane.
🚆 *Alice Street.*
☎ *(07) 3406 7111.*
Admission free.
Tours on sitting days, or when Parliament is in session, tours leave at 10.30am and 2.30pm. On non-sitting days tours leave at 9.30am, 10.30am, 11.15am, 2.30pm, 3.15pm and 4.15pm. The tours last 30 minutes. Sunday tours last for 20 minutes and operate between 10am and 2pm.

Queensland Art Gallery

Brisbane's major art gallery has a large collection of Australian artworks.
Queensland Cultural Centre, Melbourne Street, South Brisbane.
🚆 *South Brisbane;* 🚆 *Convention Centre.*
☎ *(07) 3840 7303.*
Website www.qag.qld.gov.au.
Admission free, charge for special exhibits.
Open Mon-Fri 10am-5pm, Sat-Sun 9am-5pm.

Queensland Maritime Museum

The Queensland Maritime Museum is an excellent museum featuring a large range of nautical exhibits. The museum's collection includes several vessels including steam tug *SS Forceful* and

Queensland

frigate *HMAS Diamantina* as well as several smaller boats.
Sidon Street, South Brisbane.
🚉 *South Brisbane;* 🚌 *Convention Centre.*
☎ *(07) 3844 5361.*
Website www.qmma.ecn.net.au.
Admission $6.
Open 9.30am-4.30pm daily.

Queensland Museum

This important museum features a diverse collection of artefacts ranging from dinosaur skeletons to exhibits on local history.
Queensland Cultural Centre, Corner Grey & Melbourne Streets, South Brisbane.
🚉 *South Brisbane;* 🚌 *Convention Centre.*
☎ *(07) 3840 7555.*
Website www.qmuseum.qld.gov.au.
Admission free, charge for special exhibits.
Open 9.30am-5pm daily.

Southbank Beach

Australia's only artificial inland city beach holds three mega litres of water or approximately three Olympic size swimming pools and is surrounded by 4000 cubic metres of sand that comes from Rous Channel in Moreton Bay. It's a great place to chill out on a hot summer day.
South Bank, South Brisbane.
🚉 *South Brisbane;* 🚌 *Convention Centre.*
Admission free.

Moreton Bay

Despite its easy accessibility from Brisbane, Moreton Bay and its islands receive very few visitors. Moreton Bay is home to spectacular marine life and its islands are well worth visiting and are comparable to Fraser Island.

Moreton Island

This sand island, only 35km from Brisbane, is often compared to Fraser Island and offers pretty much the same attractions without the crowds.

You can visit as a day trip from Brisbane, but a longer visit gives you a better experience of the island.

Coming & Going

Moreton Island is best reached by ferry from Lytton to the southeast of Brisbane's city centre or Scarborough on the Redcliffe Peninsula north of Brisbane.

Moreton Island Ferries (☎ *(07) 3895 1000; website www.moretonventure. com.au)* charge $25 return or $130 return for a 4WD with up to three passengers. Their ferries depart from Howard Smith Drive in Lytton (with pick up service from Wynnum North train station) and sail to the Tangalooma Wreck.

The *Combie Trader II* (☎ *(07) 3203 6399; website www.moreton-island.com/how.html)* charges $28 return or $130 return with up to four passengers. This ferry runs between Scarborough and Bulwer.

Another option is the more expensive *Tangalooma Flyer*, a fast ferry that departs Brisbane at Holt Street Wharf, Pinkenba and goes to the Tangalooma Resort. This is popular with day-trippers and return fares are $56.

Local Transport

Because it's a sand island, you'll need a 4WD vehicle to explore Moreton Island, however there is a network of hiking tracks. There are plenty of places in Brisbane to rent a 4WD, and also a number of companies that organise affordable tours to the island.

Moreton Island is a national park and you will have to pay $30.80 for a vehicle access permit, this permit is sometimes included if you're taking a tour.

Companies operating tours of the island include:

Moreton Bay Escapes

This highly recommended company run tours to the island that includes sailing, snorkelling and hiking.
☎ *1300 559355.*
Website www.moretonbayescapes.com .au.
Cost two day tour $219-239, three day tour $269.

Sunrover Expeditions
This tour operator runs day trips from Brisbane as well as longer two and three day camping safaris.
☎ *(07) 3203 4241.*
Website *www.sunrover.com.au.*
Cost *day tour $90-120, two day tour $195-250, three day tour $300.*

Accommodation
There are five campgrounds on the island, which is really the only affordable accommodation option. You'll have to pay camping fees of $4 per person per night.

Sights & Activities
Tangalooma Wild Dolphin Resort
This is one of the few places in the world where visitors can hand feed wild dolphins in their natural environment and every evening, several wild dolphins swim here. The resort's dolphin care programme staff supervises the nightly feedings to ensure the dolphins are protected and not harmed in any way. Daily pelican feeding is another of Tangalooma's natural animal attractions.
Tangalooma Resort, Moreton Island.
☎ *(07) 3268 6333.*
Website *www.tangalooma.com.*

Whale Watching
From June to October every year, you can see humpback whales on their annual northern migration from Antarctica. The whales put on a spectacular show and you can see them from Cape Moreton – the only part of the island that isn't sand – or you can take one of the whale watching trips that are offered by a number of operators; these trips depart from Manly and Scarborough.

St Helena Island
St Helena Island is Queensland's version of Alcatraz. This prison island is interesting although some of the trips are quite touristy with re-enactments of historical events in the same style you would expect from a tacky theatre restaurant.

Both day and night trips are available with ghost tours at night. Day trips cost $69, nighttime ghost tours $79.

A B Sea Cruises (☎ *(07) 3396 3994;* **website** *www.sthelenaisland.com.au)* run the trips from Manly in Brisbane's southeast to St Helena Island. Manly is easily reached by train on the Cleveland line.

North Stradbroke Island
North Stradbroke Island, or Straddie, is the most popular of the islands and is easily accessible from Brisbane. Straddie offers excellent white sand beaches, diving and snorkelling.

Coming & Going
Frequent ferries run to North Stradbroke Island from Cleveland in Brisbane's southeast, which is reached by frequent trains on the Citytrain network or from Redland Bay, which is south from Cleveland.

Islands Transport ferries (☎ *(07) 3829 0008; **website** www.islandstransport.com)* charge $11 return or $88 return for a car with passengers. Their ferries depart from Redland Bay.

Stradbroke Ferries (☎ *(07) 3286 2666; **website** www.stradbroke-island.com.au)* charge $13 return or $88 for a car with passengers. Stradbroke Ferries depart from Toondah Harbour, Middle Street, Cleveland. They have a courtesy bus that picks up from Cleveland train station and Cleveland Mall.

The *Stradbroke Flyer* (☎ *(07) 3286 1964; **website** www.flyer.com.au)* is a fast ferry that charges $12 return. Their ferries depart from Cleveland and they also have a courtesy bus that picks up from Cleveland train station.

Local Transport
There is a reasonable local bus service on the island that meets all ferries. Buses run between Dunwich and Point Lookout with some services also going to Amity. The return fare between Dunwich and Point Lookout is $9.

Accommodation
Stradbroke Island Guesthouse
This good hostel is popular with divers and features a common room with

Queensland

TV, pool table and table tennis plus a kitchen and an outdoor area. The rooms are clean and well maintained. It is 3km from the centre of Point Lookout.
1 Eastcoast Road, Point Lookout.
☎ *(07) 3409 8888.*
Website *www.stradbrokeislandscuba.com.au.*
Dorm bed *$22-25;* **double/twin room** *$50-55.*
Not yet rated

Straddie Hostel
Straddie Hostel is a small hostel with a good atmosphere. Accommodation is in four basic self-contained units, each with their own bathroom and kitchen. The kitchen is in a corner of the dorm, which makes it difficult to cook at night if people are trying to sleep. There's also a good common room with a TV downstairs. This hostel has the better location of Straddie's two hostels.
76 Mooloomba Road, Point Lookout.
☎ *(07) 3409 8679.*
Dorm bed *$18;* **double room** *$42.*
Reception open *9am-12.30pm &*
2.30pm-7.30pm daily.
Not yet rated

Gold Coast
This high-rise tourist strip, an hour's drive south of Brisbane, spans 70 kilometres of Queensland coastline. Most people stay in Surfers Paradise, which is the coast's hub of accommodation, shopping and nightlife. Surfers is one of Australia's main backpacker party destinations but there are some travellers who come here for the beaches and for the theme parks on the Gold Coast hinterland.

Practical Information
Backpackers Information Centre
Transit Centre, corner Beach Road &
Remembrance Drive, Surfers Paradise.
☎ *(07) 5592 2911 or 1800 359 830.*
Open *8am-5.30pm daily.*

Coolangatta Information Centre
4 Wharf Street, Coolangatta.
☎ *(07) 5536 4244 or 1800 674 414.*
Open *Mon-Sat 9am-5pm.*

Gold Coast Tourism Bureau
Cavill Mall, Surfers Paradise.
☎ *(07) 5538 4419.*
Open *Mon-Fri 8.30am-5.30pm, Sat*
9am-5pm, Sun 9am-4pm.

INTERNET ACCESS
Email Centre
51 Orchid Avenue, Surfers Paradise.
🚍 *1, 1A, 2, 3, 10.*
☎ *(07) 5538 7500.*
Open *9am-midnight daily.*

Coming & Going
Many people come the Gold Coast via Brisbane, but the coast also has its own international airport at Coolangatta, plus bus links to destinations on the east coast.

AIR
Although the Gold Coast is close enough to make Brisbane's airport a convenient gateway, Coolangatta airport at the southern end of the coast has frequent flights from most major destinations in Australia.

Surfside buses stop on the Gold Coast Highway outside Coolangatta Airport, and they also operate an airport shuttle service from both Brisbane and Coolangatta Airports with drop-offs to hostels and hotels along the Gold Coast.

If you're travelling from Brisbane Airport, the Airtrain *(website www.airtrain.com.au)* operates twice an hour with a connecting bus to Surfers Paradise. It costs $18 from the airport to Robina station or $35 with a connecting shuttle bus to your hostel. Alternatively, Coachtrans *(website www.coachtrans.com.au)* run buses between Brisbane Airport and the Gold Coast that drop you off at the door of your hostel. The one-way fare is $35.

BUS
McCafferty's/Greyhound buses stop at Coolangatta and Surfers Paradise. In Coolangatta, buses stop at the Coolangatta Transit Centre on the corner of Griffith and Warner Streets. The bus terminal in Surfers Paradise is at the corner of Beach and Cambridge Roads.

TRAIN

A train line runs through the Gold Coast Hinterland with stations at Nerang and Robina. Although it isn't on a main interstate rail line, there are frequent Citytrain services into Brisbane. Surfside operate regular bus services that connect with train services.

Local Transport

There is a good local bus service along the coast that is supplemented by a rail line in the hinterland. Although services are frequent, it can take a while to travel the complete length of the coast.

TRAIN

Citytrain operate a rail line in the hinterland that connects to the Brisbane suburban rail network. The main stations on the Gold Coast are Coomera, Nerang and Robina. There are frequent buses that connect these stations with the coast, these include bus 2 from Robina station to Surfers Paradise and Sea World, bus 20 from Robina station to Coolangatta, bus 22 from Nerang station to Surfers Paradise, buses 1A, 1X, 3, 14 and 16 from Helensvale station to Southport and buses 1A, 1X and 3 from Helensvale station to Surfers Paradise.

BUS

Surfside (☎ *(07) 5571 6555;* ***website*** *www.surfside.com.au)* operate a good bus network along the coast. The main route, which runs the length of the Gold Coast Highway with stops every 300 metres, is the most frequent, although they also operate buses to Southport, the train stations at Nerang and Robina and the theme parks to the north. Bus services on the Gold Coast Highway operate 24 hours a day.

The EZY Pass is a travel pass that offers unlimited bus travel. A one-day pass is $10 while the three-day pass costs $25 and a five-day pass is $35.

Accommodation
COOLANGATTA

Coolangatta is on the New South Wales/Queensland border at the southern end of the Gold Coast. It is more low key than Surfers and has some of Australia's best surfing.

Coolangatta YHA

Coolangatta YHA is a well-run hostel catering to surfers. Accommodation ranges from single and double rooms to four, six and eight-bed dormitories. There's a good range of facilities such as a well-equipped kitchen with a walk-in cool room, a barbecue area, swimming pool and a games room with a pool table, table tennis and piano. Cheap bike hire is also available. This hostel is 3km north of the centre of Coolangatta close to Coolangatta Airport and 20km south of Surfers Paradise.

230 Coolangatta Road, Bilinga.
🚌 *1, 7, 8, 11, 20.*
☎ *(07) 5536 7644.*
Dorm bed *$23-25 ($20-22 YHA);*
double/twin room *$52 ($46 YHA); includes breakfast.*
Credit cards *MC, Visa.*
Reception open *7.30am-9.30pm daily.*
🚗

Maintenance & cleanliness	★★★★
Facilities	★★★
Atmosphere & character	★★★✰
Security	★★✰
Overall rating	★★★✰

SOUTHPORT

Southport is about 5km north of Surfers Paradise. It is the coast's main business centre and is home to the huge Australia Fair shopping centre and it is a good alternative if Surfers feels too touristy for you.

There are frequent buses between Southport and Surfers Paradise.

Aquarius

Aquarius is a good hostel with new facilities including a fully equipped kitchen; a nice big TV lounge with comfy sofas; an outdoor bar with a pool table and barbecue and a spa pool and swimming pool. The hostel operates a free shuttle bus into Surfers.

44 Queen Street, Southport.
🚌 *1, 1A, 3, 5, 9, 10, 14, 15, 18, 18A.*
☎ *(07) 5527 1300 or 1800 229 955.*
Website *www.aquariusbackpack.com.au.*
Dorm bed *$20 ($19 VIP/YHA);*
double room *$45 ($43 VIP/YHA).*
Credit cards *MC, Visa.*
Reception open *7am-7pm daily.*
🚗

Queensland

Queensland

Maintenance & cleanliness	★★★☆
Facilities	★★★☆
Atmosphere & character	★★★☆
Security	★★
Overall rating	★★★☆

Trekkers

This small friendly hostel has a common room with a piano and pool table, a fully equipped kitchen, TV lounge and a nice backyard with a swimming pool. The largest dorm has six beds, all the double/twin rooms have TVs and one of the double rooms has a waterbed. Guests have free use of bicycles, boogie boards and surfboards.

22 White Street, Southport.

▢ *1, 1A, 3, 5, 9, 10, 14, 15, 18, 18A.*

☎ *(07) 5591 5616.*

Dorm bed *$21 ($20 VIP/YHA);*
double/twin room *$50 ($48 VIP/YHA).*

Reception open *7am-noon & 5pm-7.30pm daily.*

Maintenance & cleanliness	★★★★
Facilities	★★★★☆
Atmosphere & character	★★★★★
Security	★★★☆
Overall rating	★★★★

SURFERS PARADISE

Surfers is the hub of the Gold Coast and it's here that you'll find most of the nightlife. It is one of Australia's top party spots and most of the hostels here have a party atmosphere.

Backpackers in Paradise

This former motel is set up better than most other hostels in old motels. It is built around a courtyard with picnic tables and hammocks and there's also a big swimming pool. Other facilities include a games room with pool tables and Internet access, a bar and TV lounge with cinema-style big screen, a small kitchen, plus a shop and café. All rooms have lockers and en suite bathrooms. It has a party atmosphere at night but it's more relaxed during the day.

40 Peninsular Drive, Surfers Paradise.

▢ *1, 1A, 2, 3, 10.*

☎ *(07) 5538 4344 or 1800 268 621.*

Dorm bed *$15-23;* ***double room*** *$50-55;* ***apartment*** *$55-60.*

Credit cards *MC, Visa.*

Reception open *8am-7pm daily.*

Maintenance & cleanliness	★★★
Facilities	★★★
Atmosphere & character	★★★★★☆
Security	★★★☆
Overall rating	★★★★☆

British Arms International YHA

This hostel is in a marina development, but it's not as well maintained as you would expect even though it is relatively clean. It has the usual TV lounge, Internet access and kitchen plus a balcony with views across the marina to Southport. The dorms seem a little crowded (my six-bed dorm had a sign on the door saying "5 beds" so it seems that they squeeze a few extra beds in). It is about half way between Sea World and Surfers Paradise, and is only really handy if you have a car. No alcohol allowed.

Mariner's Cove, 70 Seaworld Drive, Main Beach.

▢ *2, 9.*

☎ *(07) 5571 1776.*

Website *www.britisharms.com.au.*

Dorm bed *$22 ($21 YHA);* ***double rooms*** *$52 ($50 YHA).*

Credit cards *Amex, Diners, JCB, MC, Visa.*

Reception open *8am-9pm daily.*

▢

Maintenance & cleanliness	★★★
Facilities	★★☆
Atmosphere & character	★
Security	★★☆
Overall rating	★★

Cheers Backpackers

Cheers is a good party hostel with a great bar with foosball and pool tables. There's also a barbecue area, swimming pool and spa. Accommodation is mostly in four-bed dorms.

8 Pine Avenue, Surfers Paradise.

▢ *1, 1A, 2, 3, 10.*

☎ *(07) 5531 6539 or 1800 636 539.*

Dorm bed *$22 ($21 VIP/YHA);* ***double room*** *$48-56 ($46-54 VIP/YHA).*

Credit cards *MC, Visa.*

Reception open *7.30am-10.30pm daily.*

Maintenance & cleanliness	★★★★☆
Facilities	★★★☆
Atmosphere & character	★★★★
Security	★★★☆
Overall rating	★★★★☆

Couple O'Days

This small friendly hostel has a laid-back atmosphere. Facilities include a TV lounge with old sofas, Internet access and an outdoor area with a barbecue and swimming pool.

18 Peninsular Drive, Surfers Paradise.
🚌 *1, 1A, 2, 3, 10.*
☎ *(07) 5592 4200.*
Dorm bed *$18;* **double room** *$36.*
Reception open *Mon-Sat 7.30am-8pm, Sun 7.30am-7pm.*

Maintenance & cleanliness	★★
Facilities	★★
Atmosphere & character	★★★
Security	★
Overall rating	★★

Gold Coast International Backpackers Resort

This is an excellent hostel that is clean and well maintained. Most of the rooms are twins and the largest dorm has four beds. All the rooms have TVs and en suite bathrooms. Other facilities include a small kitchen, gym, pool table, Internet access and a bar. There is also a nice outdoor barbecue area. It has a very good location and it is a short walk to most attractions in the centre of Surfers.

28 Hamilton Avenue, Surfers Paradise.
🚌 *1, 1A, 2, 3, 10.*
☎ *(07) 5592 5888.*
Website *www.goldcoastbackpackers.com.au.*
Dorm bed *$20;* **double/twin room** *$50; includes breakfast.*
Credit cards *MC, Visa.*
Reception open *8am-10pm daily.*
🚌

Maintenance & cleanliness	★★★★★
Facilities	★★
Atmosphere & character	★★
Security	★★★
Overall rating	★★★★

Islander Backpackers Resort

This is a huge complex that combines a hotel with backpackers' accommodation. Although backpackers share the complex with the hotel, they have full use of facilities that include a bar, restaurant, swimming pool, spa, tennis court, squash court and sauna. There is also a games room with pool tables and video games as well as Internet access and a kitchen. Dorms are mostly four-share converted hotel rooms and all have en suite bathrooms, fridges, TVs and balconies.

6 Beach Road, Surfers Paradise.
🚌 *1, 1A, 2, 3, 10.*
☎ *(07) 5538 8000.*
Dorm bed *$21 ($20 Nomads);* **double/twin room** *$60 ($58 Nomads).*
Credit cards *Amex, Diners, JCB, MC, Visa.*
Reception open *24 hours.*
🚌

Maintenance & cleanliness	★★★★
Facilities	★★★★★
Atmosphere & character	★★
Security	★★★★
Overall rating	★★★★

Sleeping Inn Surfers

This good hostel has accommodation in self-contained units, each with two to three dormitories; a small kitchen, bathrooms and TV lounge. There's also a poolroom and a swimming pool and spa. They have a big screen where they show movies that you can watch from the pool. Sleeping Inn Surfers is famous for its free pick up service in a stretch limousine.

26 Peninsular Drive, Surfers Paradise.
🚌 *1, 1A, 2, 3, 10.*
☎ *(07) 5592 4455.*
Website *www.sleepinginn.com.au.*
Dorm bed *$21 ($20 ISIC/VIP/YHA);* **double room** *$52-62 ($50-60 ISIC/VIP/YHA).*
Credit cards *Amex, JCB, MC, Visa.*
Reception open *7am-10pm daily.*

Maintenance & cleanliness	★★★
Facilities	★★★
Atmosphere & character	★★★
Security	★★
Overall rating	★★★

Surf n Sun Beachside Backpackers

This hostel has a fun atmosphere with friendly staff plus a swimming pool and a common area with a pool table and a cosy TV lounge. It is a former motel that is a little dated but the owners are renovating the place. It is right on the highway a little north of the centre of

Queensland

Surfers and it is only 30 metres from the beach.

3323 Gold Coast Highway, Surfers Paradise.

☐ *1, 1A, 2, 3, 10.*

☎ *(07) 5592 2363 or 1800 678 194.*

Website *www.surfnsun-goldcoast.com.*

Dorm bed *$22 $21 VIP/YHA);*
double room *$52 ($50 VIP/YHA).*

Credit cards *MC, Visa.*

Reception open *7am-10.30pm daily.*

☐

Maintenance & cleanliness	★★
Facilities	★★★
Atmosphere & character	★★★½
Security	★★½
Overall rating	★★½

Surfers Paradise Backpackers Resort

Surfers Paradise Backpackers Resort is a fun hostel with a good bar. Other facilities include a tennis/volleyball court, a barbecue area, TV lounge, Internet access and kitchen. It is at the southern end of Surfers Paradise about a 15-minute walk to the centre of Surfers and two minutes walk to the beach. The hostel runs a free shuttle bus into town.

2837 Gold Coast Highway, Surfers Paradise.

☐ *1, 1A, 3, 10.*

☎ *(07) 5592 4677 or 1800 282 800.*

Website *www.surfersparadisebackpack ers.com.au.*

Dorm bed *$22-26 ($21-25 VIP/ YHA); **double room** $52 ($50 VIP/ YHA).*

Credit cards *MC, Visa.*

Reception open *7.30am-7pm daily.*

Maintenance & cleanliness	★★★½
Facilities	★★★½
Atmosphere & character	★★★★
Security	★★
Overall rating	★★★½

Eating & Drinking

The Gold Coast is a good place for a cheap meal, there are loads of fast food joints along the coast and Surfers has a good selection of food courts and bars offering bargain meals.

Surfers Paradise is the best value spot on the coast. Many of the Surf Lifesaving Clubs, pubs, bars and nightclubs offer cut-price meals to attract the punters. These deals change all the time although hostel staff always seem to know about the latest special offers.

If you're preparing your own food, head to the Woolworths supermarket in the basement of the Paradise Centre or the Coles in the Chevron Rennaissance Centre to stock up on groceries.

Sights & Activites

The Gold Coast's main attractions are the beaches and the nightlife, however there are plenty of other attractions including a host of amusement parks catering to Australian families. If you don't want to plough through a wad of cash it would be a good idea to stick to the beach or the natural attractions in the hinterland.

If you're planning on visiting several theme parks, you may want to consider a Three Park Super Pass which allows entry to Movie World, Seaworld and Wet 'n' Wild for $153 including a free return visit to the theme park of your choice. All four entries must occur within a 14-day period.

Currumbin Wildlife Sanctuary

Currumbin Sanctuary is an excellent wildlife park at the southern end of the Gold Coast. The park is home to wombats, tree kangaroos, kangaroos, wallabies and Tasmanian devils; although birds are the main attraction.

Gold Coast Highway, Currumbin.

☐ *1, 1A, 7, 8, 11, 20.*

☎ *(07) 5534 1266.*

Website *www.currumbin-sanctuary.org.au.*

Admission *$23.*

Open *8am-5pm.*

Dreamworld

Dreamworld is a big theme park that features the Tower of Terror – the world's tallest and fastest ride. Other features include an IMAX theatre and an animal park.

Dreamworld Parkway, Coomera.

☐ *1A, 1X.*

☎ *(07) 5588 1111 or 1800 073 300.*

Website *www.dreamworld.com.au.*

Admission *$56.*

Open *10am-5pm.*

Fly Coaster

An adrenaline-filled ride where you free fall 36 metres in 13 seconds reaching 125 km/h. Up to three people can fly on the fly coaster at the same time.
Cypress Avenue, Surfers Paradise.
☐ *1, 1A, 2, 3, 10.*
☎ *(07) 5539 0474.*
Website *www.wotson.com.au/ flycoaster/wow.html.*
Single or double fly *$29*, **triple fly** *$25 each.*
Open *10am-10pm daily.*

Lamington National Park

This national park in the Gold Coast hinterland has been classified by UNESCO as a World Heritage area and is home to unique flora and fauna. The park is close enough to the Gold Coast to make an easy day trip from either Coolangatta or Surfers and there is a good choice of both half-day and full-day walks.
Beechmont, via Nerang.
☎ *(07) 5534 1266.*

Movie World

The Warner Bros theme park has a good range of rides and areas themed on Warner Bros movies.
Pacific Highway, Helensvale.
☐ *1A, 1X.*
☎ *(07) 5573 8485.*
Website *www.movieworld.com.au.*
Admission *$58 or $153 for a 3 Park Super Pass.*
Open *9.30am-5.30pm daily.*

Sea World

Home to Australia's only polar bear enclosure, Polar Bear Shores, Sea World offers a range of shows and rides. The interactive marine programme offers visitors a chance to get up close to the park's popular residents, including going behind the scenes with Sea World's marine mammal trainers to meet the dolphins and sea lions, snorkelling and swimming with dolphins and, for the more adventurous, diving with sharks.
Seaworld Drive, The Spit.
☐ *2, 9.*
☎ *(07) 5588 2222.*
Website *www.seaworld.com.au.*

Admission *$58 or $153 for a 3 Park Super Pass.*
Open *10am-5pm daily.*

Wet 'n' Wild

Wet 'n' Wild features loads of water slides and many people find it is the most fun of the theme parks.
Pacific Highway, Oxenford.
☐ *1A, 1X.*
☎ *(07) 5573 2277.*
Website *www.wetnwild.com.au.*
Admission *$36 or $153 for a 3 Park Super Pass.*
Open *10am-5pm daily.*

Sunshine Coast

The Sunshine Coast begins an hour's drive north of Brisbane and extends through the Glasshouse Mountains to the Blackall Ranges.

The region crosses the coast at Caloundra and Bribie Island, and then extends up through the laid-back yet cosmopolitan beach towns of Noosa and on to the Cooloola region, including Gympie and the Cooloola Coast.

Coming & Going

AIR

Sunshine Coast Airport (☎ *(07) 5453 1500)* has flights to most major destinations in Australia making it a viable alternative to Brisbane Airport. The airport is located about 10km north of Maroochydore on the way to Noosa. Airport shuttle buses run to destinations both north and south along the Sunshine Coast. The bus costs $12 to Maroochydore and $15 to Noosa.

Sun-Air Bus Services (☎ *(07) 5478 2811 or 1800 804 340; website www.sunair.com.au)* run bus transfers between Brisbane Airport and the Sunshine Coast, which cost $28-40.

BUS

Some coaches run inland along the Bruce Highway, where it is possible to get off at either Nambour or Cooroy and get a connecting bus from there to the coast. However most coaches also call in at Maroochydore and Noosa. Alternatively buses operated by

Suncoast Pacific (☎ *(07) 5443 1011; website www.suncoastpacific.com.au)* go to destinations along the coast from Brisbane and Hervey Bay.

TRAIN

Frequent trains run between Brisbane and the Sunshine Coast hinterland. Take the train to Cooroy, Eumundi or Nambour and take a connecting bus to Noosa or Maroochydore on the coast.

Local Transport

Sunbus buses run along the coast with connecting services to the main towns in the Hinterland. Tewantin Bus Services, Sunbus and Sunshine Coast Coaches operate most local services.

Caloundra

The southern-most urban area in the Sunshine Coast has some of Australia's best sky diving and it also a handy base for visiting attractions in the southern parts of the Sunshine Coast hinterland, including the popular Australia Zoo.

Practical Information
Caloundra Tourism

7 Caloundra Road, Caloundra.
🚌 *1, 1a, 2, 2a.*
☎ *(07) 5491 9233 or 1800 644 969.*
Website www.caloundratourism.com .au.
Open 9am-5pm daily.

Coming & Going

Sunbus (☎ *(07) 5450 7888; website www.sunbus.com.au)* route 1a connects Caloundra with Landsborough Station, route 1 goes to Nambour station via Maroochydore and routes 2 and 2a go up to coast to Maroochydore via Mooloolaba and Alexandra Headland.

Suncoast Pacific (☎ *(07) 5443 1011; website www.suncoastpacific.com.au)* runs coaches to Brisbane, Hervey Bay and destinations along the Sunshine Coast.

Accommodation
Caloundra City Backpackers

Caloundra City Backpackers is a brilliant new purpose-built hostel that is well equipped with new furnishings throughout. It features two TV rooms; two small, but fully equipped, kitchens and a barbecue area. It is only a one minute walk to the Sunland Shopping Centre and five minutes to the beach.
84 Omrah Avenue, Caloundra.
🚌 *1, 1a, 2, 2a.*
☎ *(07) 5499 7655.*
Dorm bed $17 ($16 VIP); double room $48 ($46 VIP); twin room $40 ($38 VIP).
Credit cards MC, Visa.
Reception open 7am-10pm daily.
🚌 👤

Maintenance & cleanliness	★★★★★
Facilities	★★
Atmosphere & character	★★
Security	★★
Overall rating	★★★★⯪

Sights & Activities
Kayaking

Blue Water Kayak Tours (☎ *(07) 5494 7789; website www.bluewaterkayaktours.com)* run kayaking trips to Pumicestone Passage and Moreton Bay Marine Park that allow you to paddle over to secluded beaches on Bribie Island. Half day tours cost $60 and full day tours are $90.

Queensland Air Museum

This aviation museum at Caloundra Aerodrome features around 40 historic aircraft.
Caloundra Aerodrome, Caloundra.
☎ *(07) 5492 5930.*
Website www.qam.com.au.
Admission $8.
Open 10am-4pm daily.

Sky Diving

Caloundra is a great spot for skydiving and it is one of the very few places where you can have a beach landing. Most people jump from 12,000ft, which gives you 45 seconds of freefall, but you also have the option of a jump from 14,000ft with 60 seconds freefall or the budget option from 6,000ft with only 10 seconds freefall.
Pathfinder Drive, Caloundra Aerodrome, Caloundra.
☎ *0500 522 533.*
Website www.scskydivers.com.
6,000ft tandem skydive $179;

*12000ft tandem skydive $245;
14000ft tandem skydive $300.*

Maroochydore & Mooloolaba

The Sunshine Coast's largest urban area encompasses the towns of Alexandra Heads, Maroochydore and Moolool-aba. There are some great beaches here and although quite built up, it seems laid back compared to the Gold Coast. Maroochydore is the major town in this area with a couple of big shopping centres, but Mooloolaba is the most happening spot on the coast and has plenty of bars, cafés and nightspots.

Practical Information
Mooloolaba Information Centre
Corner First Avenue & Brisbane Road, Mooloolaba.
☎ *(07) 5444 5755.*
*Website www.maroochytourism.com.
Open Mon-Fri 8am-5.30pm, Sat-Sun 8am-5pm.*

Maroochydore Information Centre
Corner Sixth Avenue & Melrose Place, Maroochydore.
☎ *(07) 5479 1566.*
*Website www.maroochytourism.com.
Open Mon-Fri 9am-5pm, Sat-Sun 9am-4pm.*

Sunshine Coast Airport Information Centre
Friendship Drive, Marcoola.
☎ *(07) 5448 9088.*
*Website www.maroochytourism.com.
Open 8.30am-3.45/4pm daily.*

INTERNET ACCESS
Email Central Internet Lounge
19 The Esplanade, Cotton Tree, Maroochydore.
☎ *(07) 5443 5451.*
Open Mon-Sat 10am-5.30pm, Sun 2pm-5.30pm.

Coming & Going
Sunbus (☎ *(07) 5450 7888; website www.sunbus.com.au)* operates local

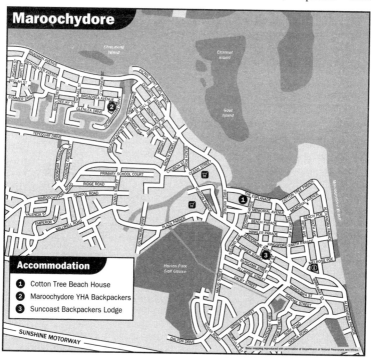

Maroochydore

Accommodation
1. Cotton Tree Beach House
2. Maroochydore YHA Backpackers
3. Suncoast Backpackers Lodge

buses in the Sunshine Coast with excellent connections in the Maroochy area. These include buses 1, 1a and 5x, which run between Maroochydore, Alexandra Headland and Mooloolaba and buses 2 and 1a, which run between Maroochydore and Nambour train station. Buses 1 and 2a head up the coast towards Noosa.

Suncoast Pacific (☎ *(07) 5443 1011;* ***website*** *www.suncoastpacific.com.au)* runs coaches to Brisbane, Hervey Bay and destinations along the Sunshine Coast.

Accommodation
MAROOCHYDORE
Cotton Tree Beach House
Cotton Tree Beach House is a small brightly painted hostel with a great location close to the beach and shops. Facilites include a TV lounge, pool table, kitchen and a barbecue area. Guests have free use of kayaks, surfboards and boogie boards. It has a relaxed laid back atmosphere.
15 The Esplanade, Maroochydore.
☎ *(07) 5443 1755.*
Website *www.cottontreebackpackers. com.*
Dorm bed *$21 ($19 Nomads/VIP/ YHA);* ***single room*** *$38 ($25 Nomads/ VIP/YHA);* ***double room*** *$46 ($42 Nomads/VIP/YHA).*
Reception open *8am-11pm daily.*

Maintenance & cleanliness	★★★½
Facilities	★★★½
Atmosphere & character	★★★★
Security	★★
Overall rating	★★★

Maroochydore YHA Backpackers
The Maroochydore YHA is a good purpose-built hostel. Facilities include a TV lounge, a huge kitchen and dining room with a pool table, Internet access, barbecue and a swimming pool. There's also free use of canoes, boogie boards, surfboards and fishing gear. It's a one-minute walk to the Maroochy River and 1½km to the town centre. A courtesy bus runs to shops and the beach and they operate low cost tours of the Sunshine Coast hinterland.
24 Schirmann Drive, Maroochydore.
☎ *(07) 5443 3151.*

Website *www.yhabackpackers.com.*
Dorm bed *$22 ($20 YHA);* ***double room*** *$50 ($46 YHA).*
Credit cards *Amex, MC, Visa.*
Reception open *7am-8pm daily.*

Maintenance & cleanliness	★★★
Facilities	★★★★½
Atmosphere & character	★★★
Security	★
Overall rating	★★★

Suncoast Backpackers Lodge
Suncoast has a covered courtyard area with a pool table plus the usual kitchen and TV lounge. Guests have free use of bikes, boogie boards and surfboards. It's located on a residential street, one block back from busy Aerodrome Road. There are lots of fast food place nearby and the beach is only 400 metres away.
50 Parker Street, Maroochydore.
☎ *(07) 5443 7544.*
Dorm bed *$19 ($18 VIP/YHA);* ***double room*** *$40 ($38 VIP).*
Credit cards *MC, Visa.*
Reception open *8.30am-1pm & 5pm-8pm daily.*

Maintenance & cleanliness	★★
Facilities	★★★½
Atmosphere & character	★★★
Security	★
Overall rating	★★★½

MOOLOOLABA
Mooloolaba Beach Backpackers
Mooloolaba Beach Backpackers is a very nice hostel with good facilities that include a common area with a café, TV, pool table and Internet access. There's also a nice outdoor area with a barbecue and swimming pool. Accommodation is in small dormitories with new furnishings including real mattresses on the bunks and lockers in all rooms.
75 Brisbane Road, Mooloolaba.
🚌 *2, 2a, 5x.*
☎ *(07) 5444 3399 or 1800 210 120.*
Dorm bed *$21-24 ($20-23 Oz Experience/VIP);* ***double room*** *$52-60 ($50-55 Oz Experience/$51-58 VIP);* ***twin room*** *$52-60 ($48-60 Oz Experience/$50-60 VIP).*
Credit cards *MC, Visa.*
Reception open *7am-10pm daily.*

Maintenance & cleanliness	★★★★⯪
Facilities	★★★⯪
Atmosphere & character	★★⯪
Security	★★⯪
Overall rating	★★★⯪

Sights
Underwater World
The largest aquarium in the southern hemisphere is worth a look. It is home to a wide variety of marine life ranging from crocodiles to colourful tropical fish, turtles and seals. You also have the opportunity to dive with sharks and sting rays.

The Wharf, Parkyn Parade, Mooloolaba.
☎ *2, 2a, 5x.*
☎ *(07) 5444 2255.*
Website www.underwaterworld.com.au.
Admission $22.50; shark dive $95-145.
Open 9am-6pm daily.

Coolum

Located around halfway between Maroochydore and Noosa, Coolum has great beaches backed by Mt Coolum National Park.

A hiking trail (800m, 2hrs return) climbs to the top of 208m Mt Coolum, rewarding the exhausted hiker with stunning 360-degree views.

Practical Information
Visitor Information Centre
Corner David Low Way & Williams Street, Coolum.
☎ *(07) 5446 5910 or 1800 448 833.*
Website www.maroochytourism.com.
Open 9am-5pm daily.

Coming & Going
Sunbus (☎ *(07) 5450 7888; website www.sunbus.com.au*) operates local buses in the Sunshine Coast and route 1 runs between Maroochydore and Noosa via Coolum.

Accommodation
Coolum Beach Budget Accommodation
This place is clean and well maintained but doesn't have much in the way of atmosphere. Not many backpackers stay here and there are only three four-bed dorms – the rest of the rooms are doubles. Shared facilities include a swimming pool, kitchen and barbecue area. It is a quiet place – definitely not a party hostel – there are signs all over the place indicating that alcohol consumption is not encouraged! The hostel is close to shops and the national park and the beach is just 100 metres away.
Corner David Low Way & Ann Street, Coolum Beach.
☎ *(07) 5471 6666.*
Dorm bed $25; double room $44-85.
Credit cards MC, Visa.
Reception open 7.30am-8.30pm daily.

Maintenance & cleanliness	★★★★★
Facilities	★★
Atmosphere & character	⯪
Security	★★⯪
Overall rating	★★★

Noosa

Noosa, at the northern end of the Sunshine Coast, is popular with travellers who come for the small national park and the pristine beaches.

Noosa's suburbs stretch from the ocean and along the Noosa River and comprise several towns. Noosa Heads is the upmarket resort area while Noosa Junction and Noosaville are more affordable residential and commercial areas and Sunshine Beach is more surfer oriented.

The wilderness areas north of the Noosa River are a big contrast from the commercial heart of Noosa.

Practical Information
Noosa Visitor Information Centre
Corner Noosa Drive & Hastings Street, Noosa Heads.
☎ *(07) 5447 4988.*
Website www.tourismnoosa.com.au.
Open 9am-5pm daily.

Great Sandy National Park Information Centre
Moorindil Street, Tewantin.
☎ *(07) 5449 7792.*
Website www.epa.qld.gov.au.
Open 7am-4pm daily.

Queensland

Coming & Going

Sunbus (☎ *(07) 5450 7888; website www.sunbus.com.au)* operates local buses in the Sunshine Coast with excellent connections in the Noosa area. Useful routes are route 1, which goes from Noosa Heads to Maroochydore and Mooloolaba via Coolum; route 12, which goes from Noosa Heads to Cooroy train station and route 12x, which goes from Noosa Heads to Eumundi.

Suncoast Pacific (☎ *(07) 5443 1011; website www.suncoastpacific.com.au)* coaches go to Brisbane, Hervey Bay and destinations along the Sunshine Coast.

Accommodation

Accommodation in Noosa is split between the resort areas of Noosa Heads and Noosaville and the wilderness areas on the north shore and around the Noosa River.

NOOSA HEADS & NOOSAVILLE
Halse Lodge YHA

This is a brilliant hostel in a restored National Trust and Heritage listed Queenslander-style building with loads of character. Common areas include a TV lounge, plus a big lounge room with a pool table and piano. There's also a lovely outdoor sitting area on the veranda. The hostel has a great atmosphere and a bar with good value drinks. Guests have free use of surfboards and boogie boards. This is the best located hostel in Noosa and is just a short stroll to the beach and upmarket Hastings Street.

Corner Noosa Drive & Noosa Parade, Noosa Heads

☒ *1, 10, 10b, 11, 12, 12x.*
☎ *(07) 5447 3377 or 1800 252 567.*
Website *www.halselodge.com.au.*
Dorm bed *$26 ($24 YHA);* ***double/twin room*** *$65 ($55 YHA).*
Credit cards *MC, Visa.*
Reception open *7am-8pm daily.*
🚌

Maintenance & cleanliness	★★★★☆
Facilities	★★★
Atmosphere & character	★★★★★
Security	★☆
Overall rating	★★★★

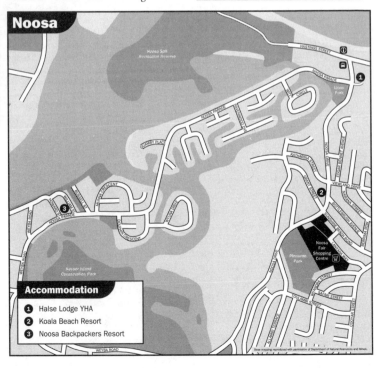

Noosa

Accommodation
1 Halse Lodge YHA
2 Koala Beach Resort
3 Noosa Backpackers Resort

Koala Beach Resort

Koala Beach Resort is Noosa's party hostel and it boasts an excellent bar that features live music every Wednesday. It is a former motel set among tropical gardens and all dormitories have en suite bathrooms. Facilities include a laundry, kitchen, Internet access, beach volleyball court and a swimming pool. It's on a busy road close to the Noosa Fair shopping centre and the shops on Sunshine Beach Road.

44 Noosa Drive, Noosa Heads.
1, 10, 10b, 11.
(07) 5447 3355 or 1800 357 457.
Dorm bed *$22 ($21 VIP);* **double/ twin room** *$55 ($53 VIP).*
Credit cards *MC, Visa.*
Reception open *7.30am-8pm daily.*

Maintenance & cleanliness	★★★
Facilities	★★★
Atmosphere & character	★★★★☆
Security	★☆
Overall rating	★★★

Noosa Backpackers Resort

This is a nice hostel with a great social atmosphere. Facilities include a god kitchen, Internet access and a games room with table tennis and a pool table. There's also an outdoor bar and swimming pool and a café at the entrance. Guests have free use of boogie boards, surfboards and kayaks. The hostel has a quiet location in Noosaville, about a 10-15 minute walk to the local shops.

11 Williams Street, Noosaville.
10, 10b, 12, 12x.
(07) 5449 8151 or 1800 626 673.
Website *www.noosabackpackers.com.*
Dorm bed *$23 ($22 VIP);* **double room** *$50-60 ($48-58 VIP).*
Credit cards *Amex, MC, Visa.*
Reception open *8am-9pm daily.*

Maintenance & cleanliness	★★★
Facilities	★★★★
Atmosphere & character	★★★★
Security	★
Overall rating	★★★★☆

NOOSA RIVER & NORTH SHORE
Gagaju Bush Camp

Gagaju boasts a rustic bush setting on six acres with accommodation in big tents. Facilities include a TV/video room, book exchange, a games room with table tennis, darts and a pool table, a gym, volleyball court and an outdoor kitchen with barbecues. Activities include didgeridoo making workshops and canoe trips and guests have free use of fishing rods. It is in a natural bush setting on the banks of the Noosa River, about 15km from Noosa. There's a good chance of seeing wildlife here.

118 Johns Road, Cooroibah.
(07) 5474 3522.
Website *www.travoholic.com/gagaju.*
Dorm bed *$15;* **double room** *$35;* **camping** *$10.*
Credit cards *MC, Visa.*
Reception open *am-9pm daily.*

Maintenance & cleanliness	★
Facilities	★★
Atmosphere & character	★★★★★
Security	★
Overall rating	★★

Noosa North Shore Retreat

This hostel has nice self-contained units, each with en suite bathroom and a TV lounge. The complex also has a swimming pool, bar/restaurant and a pond with ducks and geese and it is common to see kangaroos hopping around the place. It has a quiet bush setting on Noosa's North Shore that's accessible only by ferry ($4.50 each way if you want to take your own car).

Maximilian Road, Noosa North Shore (via Tewantin).
(07) 5447 1225.
Website *www.noosaretreat.com.au.*
Dorm bed *$20 ($19 VIP);* **double room** *$50 ($48 VIP).*
Credit cards *Amex, MC, Visa.*
Reception open *8am-5pm daily.*

Maintenance & cleanliness	★★★★★
Facilities	★★★☆
Atmosphere & character	★★☆
Security	★★☆
Overall rating	★★★★☆

Sights
Eumundi Markets

This large craft market takes place every Wednesday and Saturday and is

Queensland

one of the best markets in Australia. It is held in Eumundi, which is about 15km west of Noosa. Storeyline Tours (☎ *(07) 5474 1500)* run a shuttle bus from Caloundra, Mooloolaba, Maroochydore, Coolumn and Noosa that costs $12-16.

Noosa National Park

This is a small, but excellent, national park easily accessible from the centre of Noosa Heads. The park has great beaches plus wildlife including koalas.

Sunshine Coast Hinterland

The area inland from the Sunshine Coast is home to natural attractions including the Glasshouse Mountains. Most of the sights in the hinterland are an easy daytrip from Maroochydore, Mooloolaba, Noosa or Brisbane.

Sights
Australia Zoo

Famed as the home of Steve Irwin, television's Crocodile Hunter, Australia Zoo was established in 1973 and is now home to more than 750 animals. The park features giant pythons, some of the world's most venomous snakes, wild birds and native turtles, Murray and Molly, a pair of fierce saltwater crocodiles, and Harriet, a 172-year-old tortoise introduced to Australia from the Galapagos Islands by Charles Darwin. *Glasshouse Mountains Tourist Route, Beerwah.*
Beerwah.
☎ *(07) 5494 1134.*
Website www.crocodilehunter.com.
Admission $23.
Open 8.30am-4pm daily.

Fraser Coast

The World Heritage-listed Fraser Island is the world's largest sand island, stretching for 124 kilometres, offering spectacular beaches, headlands, lakes, creeks and rainforests.

Access to Fraser Island is the main reason people visit the Fraser Coast.

Most backpackers use Hervey Bay as a base but Rainbow Beach is becoming a popular alternative.

Hervey Bay

Hervey Bay is the largest city on the Fraser Coast and it is a good place to organise an excursion to Fraser Island.

It is an ordinary town with no charm and it feels like a string of anonymous suburbs has been plucked from Sydney or Brisbane and dropped beside the sea.

Despite the drawbacks, it is a popular spot with backpackers who pass through here to get to Fraser Island. Although the ferry to Fraser Island is cheaper from Rainbow Beach, Hervey Bay is a better place to organise self-drive trips to the island. Hervey Bay also has a lively backpacker scene with big choice of budget accommodation.

Hervey Bay is a good spot for whale watching with humpback whales visiting Hervey Bay between August and October.

Practical Information
Information Centre

63 Old Maryborough Road, Pialba.
☎ *1800 649 926.*
Website www.herveybaytourism.com.au.
Open Sun-Fri 9am-9pm, Sat 9am-4.30pm.

Marina Kiosk

You can obtain permits for Fraser Island here.
Buccaneer Avenue, Urangan.
☎ *(07) 4128 9800.*
Open 6am-6pm daily.

River Heads Information Kiosk

This small information centre has information on Fraser Island and also sells permits for the island.
River Heads.
☎ *(07) 4125 8473.*
Open 6.15am-11.15am & 2pm-3.30pm daily

Coming & Going

Coaches to Hervey Bay stop at the Bay Central Bus Terminal at the Bay Central Shopping Centre in Pialba.

If you're travelling by train, you'll need to get off in nearby Maryborough and change for a shuttle bus to Hervey Bay. Both the train and bus station in Maryborough are located on Lennox Street.

Local Transport

Hervey Bay is spread out along the bay and it's a long way between different parts of town. This means that those without their own car will need to rent a bike, or rely on public transport and hostel shuttle buses.

Wide Bay Transit (☎ *(07) 4123 1733; website www.widebaytransit.com .au*) run buses in Hervey Bay and they also operate an Intercity service that connects Hervey Bay with Maryborough with buses timed to meet train connections. One-way fares cost $1.30-3.20 or you can buy a day ticket for $6.70. Most buses terminate at the Bay Central shopping centre in Pialba.

Accommodation
Beaches Backpackers

Beaches has good facilities that include a great bar/restaurant, a swimming pool, TV lounge, kitchen and a barbecue area. Accommodation is in cute blue and yellow cabins.

195 Torquay Road, Scarness.
🚌 *18*
☎ *(07) 4124 2727 or 1800 655 501.*
Website www.beaches.com.au.
Dorm bed *$18 ($17 VIP);* **double room** *$45-50 ($45-48 VIP).*
Credit cards *Amex, Diners, MC, Visa.*
Reception open *7am-8pm daily.*
🚌🚪

Maintenance & cleanliness	★★★★✫
Facilities	★★✫
Atmosphere & character	★★★✫
Security	★★✫
Overall rating	★★★✫

Billabong Beach House & Backpackers

This hostel provides clean accommodation in self-contained units, but there isn't much in the way of shared facilities or much of a social atmosphere. It is suited to couples or travellers seeking a quiet alternative to other hostels.

335 Esplanade, Scarness.
🚌 *5, 16.*
☎ *(07) 4124 2877 or 1800 004 655.*
Dorm bed *$20;* **double room** *$40.*
Credit cards *MC, Visa.*
Reception open *7.30am-6.30pm daily.*
🚌

Maintenance & cleanliness	★★★★
Facilities	★✫
Atmosphere & character	-
Security	★
Overall rating	★★

Colonial Log Cabins YHA

This hostel is made up of various cabins; many of them are self-contained units and the facilities inside the units can keep people away from the hostel's main common areas and this detracts from the hostel's overall atmosphere. This is a pity as the common areas are pretty good and include a bar/restaurant, pool table, TV lounge, kitchens, plus a swimming pool and spa and tennis and basketball courts. The whole complex sprawls over 8½ acres and includes 15 separate buildings. It is on a quiet residential street near the boat harbour. Although it's a long walk to the local shops a courtesy bus runs into town throughout the day.

Corner Boat Harbour Drive &Pulgul Street, Urangan.
🚌 *5, 16.*
☎ *(07) 4125 3161 or 1800 818 280.*
Dorm bed *$21 ($19 YHA);* **double room** *$56-88 ($48-88 YHA).*
Credit cards *Amex, MC, Visa.*
Reception open *6.45am-9.30pm daily.*
🚗

Maintenance & cleanliness	★★★★
Facilities	★★★★✫
Atmosphere & character	★★✫
Security	★✫
Overall rating	★★★✫

Country Cottage Backpackers

This is a nice clean hostel with an outback/bush theme. Facilities are not very extensive, but the overall quality is very high. Accommodation is spread over several buildings and the biggest dormitory has six beds.

181 Torquay Road, Scarness.
🚌 *5, 16, 18.*
☎ *(07) 4124 0677.*
Dorm bed *$18;* **double/twin room**

$44; includes breakfast.
Credit cards *MC, Visa.*

Maintenance & cleanliness	★★★★☆
Facilities	★☆
Atmosphere & character	★★★★☆
Security	★
Overall rating	★★★★☆

Fraser Escape Backpackers

This former caravan park has been converted into a backpackers' hostel. There is a variety of accommodation that ranges from nice small cabins to more basic caravans. It has a great bar and the low price makes it a very good value place to stay.

21 Denmans Camp Road, Scarness.
🚌 *18.*
☎ *1800 646 711.*
Dorm bed *$9-15;* ***double room*** *$30;*
camping *$5 per person.*
Credit cards *MC, Visa.*
Reception open *7am-9pm daily.*
🚗

Maintenance & cleanliness	★★★
Facilities	★★
Atmosphere & character	★★☆

Security	★★☆
Overall rating	★★☆

Fraser Roving

Fraser Roving is a good hostel in a former hospital on the Esplanade. This hostel has a swimming pool and spa, a barbecue area, a nice outdoors bar, a big kitchen, a good TV lounge with comfy sofas and cheap fast Internet access. Accommodation is in spacious dorms and the biggest dormitory has eight beds.

412 Esplanade, Torquay.
🚌 *5, 16.*
☎ *(07) 4125 6386 or 1800 989 811.*
Website *www.fraserroving.com.au.*
Dorm bed *$15-18 ($14-17 Nomads/ VIP/YHA);* ***double room*** *$44-60 ($42-58 Nomads/VIP/YHA).*
Credit cards *MC, Visa.*
🚗 ♿

Maintenance & cleanliness	★★★★
Facilities	★★★
Atmosphere & character	★★★
Security	★☆
Overall rating	★★★★☆

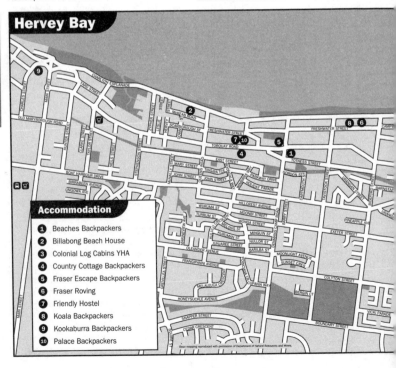

Hervey Bay

Queensland

Accommodation

1. Beaches Backpackers
2. Billabong Beach House
3. Colonial Log Cabins YHA
4. Country Cottage Backpackers
5. Fraser Escape Backpackers
6. Fraser Roving
7. Friendly Hostel
8. Koala Backpackers
9. Kookaburra Backpackers
10. Palace Backpackers

Friendly Hostel

This is a nice small 26-bed hostel with four self-contained units, each with a TV lounge, kitchen and bathroom. There's also a shared deck area with a barbecue where everyone can relax and watch the rainbow lorikeets that sometimes come here to feed. It's a nice place with shiny polished wooden floors and the biggest dorm has only three beds.

182 Torquay Road, Scarness.

🚌 *5, 16, 18.*

☎ *(07) 4124 4107 or 1800 244 107.*

Website *www.thefriendlyhostel.com.*

Dorm bed *$19; **double/twin room** $44.*

Reception open *6.30am-8pm daily.*

Maintenance & cleanliness	★★★★
Facilities	★★
Atmosphere & character	★★★★☆
Security	★
Overall rating	★★★

Koala Backpackers

Koala's is a good hostel with accommodation in self-contained units and regular dormitories (the regular dorms are nicer than the units). Facilities include a TV room, a nice landscaped garden area around the swimming pool and a bar/restaurant that serves up cheap meals. Overall it's a pretty good place to stay with a lively atmosphere.

408 The Esplanade, Scarness.

🚌 *5, 16.*

☎ *(07) 4125 3601 or 1800 354 535.*

Dorm bed *$18-22 ($17-21 VIP);*
double room *$45-55 ($43-53 VIP).*

Credit cards *MC, Visa.*

Reception open *7am-7pm daily.*

🚌

Maintenance & cleanliness	★★★
Facilities	★★☆
Atmosphere & character	★★★★
Security	★
Overall rating	★★★

Kookaburra Backpackers

Kookaburra Backpackers is a nice hostel in an old Queenslander-style building with hardwood floors and lots of character. Breakfast and dinner are provided so there are no cooking facilities other than a barbecue. There's

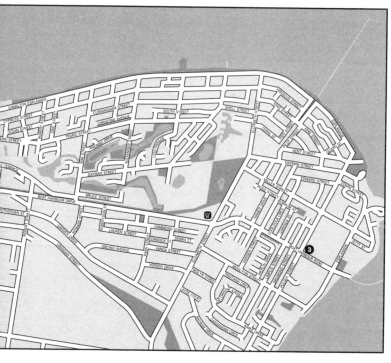

also a TV lounge, Internet access and a small rear deck. Accommodation is in four to six-bed dorms and some rooms have en suite bathrooms.

264 Charles Street, Pialba.
🚌 *5, 13, 14, 16, 18, 20.*
☎ *1800 111 442.*
***Website** www.kookaburrabackpackers. com.*
***Dorm bed** $18;* ***double room** $40; includes breakfast and dinner.*
***Credit cards** MC, Visa.*
***Reception open** 6am-10pm daily.*
🚌

Maintenance & cleanliness	★★★★⯪
Facilities	★★⯪
Atmosphere & character	★★★★
Security	★★⯪
Overall rating	★★★

The Palace Backpackers

This is a clean and well-maintained hostel with accommodation in self-contained units, each with its own bathroom, kitchen and lounge. Although the lounge in each unit can keep travellers from meeting each other, there's also a good TV lounge, another communal kitchen, a pool table and a swimming pool.

184 Torquay Road, Scarness.
🚌 *5, 16, 18.*
☎ *1800 063 168.*
***Dorm bed** $18-19 ($17-18 VIP); double/twin room $44 ($42 VIP).*
***Credit cards** MC, Visa.*
***Reception open** 6am-8.30pm daily.*
🚌

Maintenance & cleanliness	★★★★
Facilities	★★★⯪
Atmosphere & character	★★
Security	★★⯪
Overall rating	★★★

Maryborough

This small city is the closest place to Hervey Bay with a train station and you'll have to stopover here if you're travelling with a rail pass and want to visit Hervey Bay or Fraser Island.

Although Maryborough is a bustling little city, there's not much to keep you in town and most travellers get off the train and get the first bus to Hervey Bay.

Practical Information
Maryborough-Fraser Island Visitor Information Centre

Bruce Highway, Maryborough.
☎ *(07) 4121 4111.*
***Website** www.maryborough.qld.gov.au.*
***Open** Mon-Fri 8.30am-5pm, 10am-4pm daily.*

Coming & Going

Trains and coaches stop at the train station on Lennox Street. The train is met by connecting buses to Hervey Bay.

Rainbow Beach

Located between Hervey Bay and the Sunshine Coast, Rainbow Beach is closer to Fraser Island than Hervey Bay is and it is also a cheaper and more laid back place to plan your trip to the island.

Practical Information
Queensland Parks & Wildlife Service

This small information centre has information about Fraser Island and

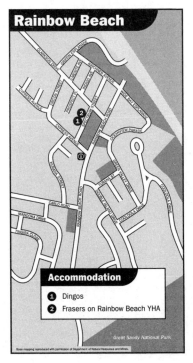

Rainbow Beach

Accommodation
❶ Dingos
❷ Frasers on Rainbow Beach YHA

Great Sandy National Park

Base mapping reproduced with permission of Department of Natural Resources and Mines.

also sells permits for the island.
Rainbow Beach Road, Rainbow Beach.
☎ *(07) 5486 3160*
Open *7am-4pm daily.*

Shell Tourist Centre
This information centre sells the Indi-GePass, which is a cheaper alternative to the national parks permit for Fraser Island.
Rainbow Beach Road, Rainbow Beach.
☎ *(07) 5486 8888.*
Website www.rainbowbeach.info.

Coming & Going
McCafferty's/Greyhound, Premier Motor Services and Suncoast Pacific have daily coaches to Rainbow Beach. Poleys Coaches connect with train services at Gympie.

Accommodation
Dingo's
This purpose-built hostel offers good accommodation with en suite bathrooms in all rooms. There is also a swimming pool, a bar with a pool table, a big screen TV and Internet access.
Spectrum Street, Rainbow Beach.
☎ *1800 111 126.*
Website www.dingosatrainbow.com.
Dorm bed $20.
Credit cards MC, Visa.
Reception open 6am-10pm daily.

Maintenance & cleanliness	★★★★
Facilities	★★★
Atmosphere & character	★★★☆
Security	★★
Overall rating	★★★☆

Fraser's on Rainbow Beach YHA
This is a very nice hostel with a swimming pool, bar with pool table, TV lounge with big screen telly and a big commercial kitchen. There are also hammocks and outdoor seating. Accommodation is in motel-style units with en suite bathrooms.
18 Spectrum Street, Rainbow Beach.
☎ *(07) 5486 8885 or 1800 100 170.*
Dorm bed $22-24 ($20-22 Nomads/VIP/YHA); double room $60 ($58 Nomads/VIP/YHA).
Credit cards MC, Visa.

Maintenance & cleanliness	★★★★☆
Facilities	★★
Atmosphere & character	★★★★
Security	★★☆
Overall rating	★★★☆

Fraser Island
Fraser Island is unique in that it is – at 120km by 15km – the world's largest

Dingos

Dogs are not permitted on Fraser Island and the lack of crossbreeding has resulted in Fraser Island's dingoes being the most pure breed in Australia. These native wild dogs are one of Fraser Islands attractions, however they can also be dangerous.

Because dingoes have many of the same characteristics as regular domestic dogs, many visitors feed them. This has made dingoes become less afraid of people, they have become dependent on handouts and their hunting skills have declined. Dingoes can also become aggressive towards people who do not feed them. In April 2001 a dingo on Fraser Island killed a nine-year-old boy.

The Queensland Parks & Wildlife Service has set a number of guidelines that are designed to protect you and ensure that dingoes retain their hunting skills and do not become too aggresive.
- Never feed dingoes.
- Lock food in strong lockable containers in your car. Dingoes can open iceboxes if they are left on the ground!
- Always stay close to children
- Walk in small groups
- Put rubbish in bins or keep it in your car.
- Keep your tent wide-open so dingoes can see that there is nothing to take.
- Bury fish waste at least 30cm deep in sand below high tide.

Don't leave expensive gear such as hiking boots or sleeping bags in your tent, as dingoes have been known to carry these off.

If you feel threatened by a dingo:
- stand up and face the dingo
- fold your arms and maintain eye contact
- calmly back away

sand bar. Despite being composed entirely of sand, the island boasts verdant rainforests and crystal clear lakes and is home to dingoes, wild horses and an abundance of bird life.

Coming & Going

The central west coast of the island is connected to Hervey Bay by a ferry service. Ferries operate from River Heads (south of Hervey Bay) and Urangan Harbour in Hervey Bay and charge $110 return for a 4WD and four passengers with each additional passenger costing $6.

Ferries from Inskip Point near Rainbow Beach work out cheaper, for example Rainbow Venture (☎ *(07) 5486 3154)* charge $60 return for a 4WD vehicle including passengers.

You will need a vehicle permit if you are taking a vehicle across on the ferry. You can either buy a National Parks permit or the cheaper IndigePass. Both let you take a 4WD onto the island for one month.

The National Parks permits are more widely available and cost $31.85. The national parks permit includes an information pack with a colour guide as well as details on camping and hiking on the island. National parks permits are available from the Marina Kiosk at Urangan boat harbour as well as from the Brisbane, Bundaberg, Maryborough, Rainbow Beach and River Heads offices of the Queensland Parks & Wildlife Service.

The new IndigePass is issued by the Dalungbara, Batchala and Ngulungbara Aboriginal peoples of Fraser Island and does virtually the same thing as the National Parks permit, except it only costs $15. The IndigePass is available from the Shell Tourist Centre in Rainbow Beach and also from outside the national parks office in Rainbow Beach.

Local Transport & Tours

Because it is a sand island, a four-wheel-drive vehicle is essential for

Driving a 4WD Vehicle

There's more to driving a 4WD vehicle than simply putting it in gear and heading off-road. You shouldn't run into too many problems if you follow these guidelines:

- The best time to travel is around low tide. Avoid two hours either side of high tide.
- When arriving on the island or before driving on to the beach, check that your wheel locks are in the right position to engage four-wheel drive.
- Tyre pressure should be adjusted before driving on the island. Generally, tyres should be 25psi. Some areas on Fraser have signs suggesting specific reduced tire pressure to 15 psi to enable driving through soft dry sand.
- The beach is a designated road and the normal "keep to the left" rules apply as well as using indicators for turning. Speed should be kept to below 80km/h on the beach and 35km/h on the inland roads. Police patrol the island and enforce speed limits and breathalyse drivers.
- There are stretches of the beach that are used as aircraft landing/take-off strips. Take note of the signs in designated areas and watch for aircraft.
- Drivers should note the numerous gutters that have been created by the creeks flowing into the sea from the island. Even gutters with small banks – if hit at speed – can overturn a vehicle.
- Drivers should beware the rising tide. Vehicles driven too close to the water can become trapped in wet sand. Drivers of hired vehicles lose their bond immediately if they drive in salt water.
- On "good beach days" the sand is hard-packed and makes for excellent driving conditions. On bad days, the tides may not have been high enough to wash way the ruts from the previous days' traffic – resulting in build-up of sand banks.
- When driving in deep banks of dry sand, keep the car in a low gear, do not change gears, keep the revs high and do not lose momentum.
- Where possible, follow someone else's tracks – choose a set of tracks and stay on them. Do not stop the vehicle in soft sand or in creek beds.

exploring Fraser Island; this explains why it is so expensive to get around the island. Renting your own 4WD (which usually comes complete with camping gear) is the way to go as it gives you much more independence than a tour, although you need to split the cost with a few others to make it affordable.

Most backpackers take advantage of the so-called self-drive tours of the island. These aren't really tours; they're more along the lines of car rental with a few extras thrown in. Generally a bunch of travellers each pay between $135 and $190 per person for a three-day trip and are given a 4WD and a lecture about what to see and the dos and don'ts of driving on Fraser Island. Ferry fares, camping gear and a vehicle permit are usually included in the price but a lot of the companies that organise these trips will charge you an extra $10 for fuel and $15 for insurance. These self-drive 'tours' give you the independence that comes with having your own set of wheels and no tour guide. Most hostels in Hervey Bay or Rainbow Beach can organise self-drive tours.

There are also plenty of companies that offer more conventional guided tours.

Guided and self-drive tours of Fraser Island include:

Aussie Trax

Aussie Trax rent 4WDs and organise self-drive trips to Fraser Island departing from Hervey Bay.
56 Boat Harbour Drive, Pialba.
☎ *(07) 4124 4433.*
Website www.aussietraxfraserisland. com.

Fraser Island Company

Fraser Island Company run two and three day tours departing from Hervey Bay.
☎ *(07) 4125 3933 or 1800 063 933.*
Website www.fraserislandco.com.au.
One-day tour $99-133, two-day tour $185, three-day tour $319.

Fraser Venture Tours

Eurong Beach Resort organises tours around the island with departures from Hervey Bay.

☎ *(07) 4125 4444 or 1800 249 122.*
Website www.fraser-is.com.
One-day tour $99 ($94 VIP), two-day tour $195, three-day tour $250-310.

Koala Adventures

Self-drive tours of the island organised by Koala Backpackers in Hervey Bay. These trips allow more flexibility than a tour and include 4WD rental, national park fees and camping gear although you will have to organise your own food.
408 The Esplanade, Scarness.
🚌 *5, 16.*
☎ *1 800 466 444.*
Website www.koala-backpackers.com.
Three-day trip $135.

Palace Fraser Island Safaris

Self-drive tours of the island organised by Palace Backpackers in Hervey Bay. These trips allow more flexibility than a tour and include 4WD rental, national park fees and camping gear although you will have to organise your own food.
184 Torquay Road, Scarness.
🚌 *5, 16, 18.*
☎ *1800 063 168.*
Three-day trip $135.

Sun Safari Tours

One and two day tours departing from Rainbow Beach. The overnight tour includes accommodation at Eurong Beach Resort.
☎ *(07) 5486 3154.*
One-day tour $75, two-day tour $195.

Wilderness Adventure

Wilderness Adventure operates two and three day tours with dormitory accommodation on the island. Wilderness Adventure tours depart from Hervey Bay.
☎ *(07) 4120 3333 or 1800 072 555.*
Website www.kingfisherbay.com/eco/ pgsix.html.
Two-day tour from $230, three-day tour from $303.

Accommodation

Camping is the main accommodation option on Fraser Island. Most campsites are operated by the national park and require camping permits that are available from shops, both in Hervey Bay, Rainbow Beach and on the island for $4 per person per night.

You can also buy a camping permit with your IndigePass for just $2 per person per night. These are available from the Shell Tourist Centre in Rainbow Beach and also from outside the national parks office in Rainbow Beach.

There are also a couple of resorts on the island that provide accommodation for some of the tour operators.

You should bring 50c coins for coin-operated showers and gas barbecues that are located at camping areas on the island.

Bundaberg Region

The Bundaberg region is the most southerly access point to the Great Barrier Reef. Two pristine coral cays, Lady Elliot and Lady Musgrave Islands, are a short boat trip from the mainland with excursions departing both from Bundaberg and the Town of 1770.

Bundaberg

Bundaberg (Bundy) is famous as the home of Bundaberg Rum – produced in the here since 1889 from sugar cane crops grown in the district.

Bundaberg has an abundance of fruit picking work, which is the main drawcard for most travellers.

Practical Information
Visitor Information Centre
186 Bourbong Street, Bundaberg.
☎ *(07) 4153 9289.*
Website *www.bundaberg.qld.gov.au.*
Open *Mon-Fri 8.30am-4.45pm, Sat-Sun 10am-1pm.*

INTERNET ACCESS
Bundy Email Centre
200 Bourbong Street, Bundaberg.
Open *Mon-Fri 9am-9pm, Sat 10am-5pm, Sun 10am-9pm.*

Cosy Corner Internet Café
Barolin Street, Bundaberg.
Open *Mon-Fri 7am-7.30pm, Sat 9am-5pm, Sun 11am-5pm.*

LAUNDRY
Laundromat
202 Bourbong Street, Bundaberg.
Open *6am-11pm daily.*

Coming & Going
Most travellers arrive by bus but the train is also a popular option. Buses stop at the coach terminal at 66 Targo Street. There are several trains a day from Bundaberg, although they don't run as frequently as buses. The train station is on McLean Street in the town centre.

Accommodation
Bundaberg Backpackers Travellers Lodge
This is a clean hostel with good facilities that include a big kitchen, TV lounge and Internet access. It's the only air-conditioned hostel in town and security is good. No alcohol allowed.
2 Crofton Street, Bundaberg.
☎ *(07) 4152 2080.*
Dorm bed *$20 per night, $120 per week.*
Credit cards *MC, Visa.*
Reception open *8am-noon & 3pm-7pm daily.*

Maintenance & cleanliness	★★★★★
Facilities	★★
Atmosphere & character	★☆
Security	★★☆
Overall rating	★★★

City Centre Backpackers
This is a secure and friendly hostel near the train station with the usual kitchen and TV lounge plus pool tables and a barbecue area. No alcohol allowed.
216 Bourbong Street, Bundaberg.
☎ *(07) 4151 3501.*
Dorm bed *$20-22 per night, $120-122 per week;* **double room** *$43 per night, $258 per week.*
Credit cards *MC, Visa.*
Reception open *5am-10pm daily.*

Maintenance & cleanliness	★★★
Facilities	★★☆
Atmosphere & character	★★★★☆
Security	★★★☆
Overall rating	★★★☆

Federal Backpackers

Federal Backpackers is located above a pub near the train station. It is a big wooden building that is kept clean and it offers a kitchen, TV lounge and balconies.

221 Bourbong Street, Bundaberg.

☎ *(07) 4153 3711.*

Dorm bed *$20-23 per night, $120-122 per week;* **double/twin room** *$46 per night, $258 per week.*

Credit cards *MC, Visa.*

Reception open *Mon-Fri 8am-noon & 2.30pm-7pm, Sat-Sun 9am-noon & 4pm-7pm.*

Maintenance & cleanliness	★★★
Facilities	★★
Atmosphere & character	★★
Security	★★★☆
Overall rating	★★★☆

Grand Backpackers

Grand Backpackers consists of accommodation above a pub. There's a TV lounge, kitchen and a balcony overlooking the Bourbong Street. It's the most centrally located hostel in Bundaberg.

Corner Bourbong & Targo Streets, Bundaberg.

☎ *(07) 4154 1166.*

Dorm bed *$20 per night, $115 per week.*

Reception open *Mon-Sat 8.30am-noon & 3.30pm-7.30pm, Sun 8.30am-noon & 4pm-7.30pm.*

Maintenance & cleanliness	★★★
Facilities	★★
Atmosphere & character	★★★
Security	★★☆
Overall rating	★★★☆

Workers and Dive Hostel

This hostel consists of an old Queenslander-style house and an old block of flats, but accommodation is cheaper and the atmosphere better in the old house. The flats are self-contained each with a bathroom, kitchen and TV. There's a swimming pool and a nice common area under the main house with a pool table, table tennis and Internet access. No alcohol allowed but this restriction is sometimes relaxed on Saturdays.

64 Barolin Street, Bundaberg.

☎ *(07) 4151 6097.*

Dorm bed *$20-21 per night, $120-125 per week.*

Credit cards *MC, Visa.*

Reception open *Mon-Sat 8.30am-noon & 3.30pm-7.30pm, Sun 9am-noon & 4pm-7.30pm.*

Maintenance & cleanliness	★★☆
Facilities	★★★☆
Atmosphere & character	★★
Security	★★☆
Overall rating	★★

Sights
Bundaberg Distillery

Bundaberg Rum is Australia's biggest-selling spirit and Bundaberg's main attraction is the distillery where it is made. Distillery tours include a taste of Bundaberg's biggest export.

Avenue Street, East Bundaberg.

🚌 *4, 5.*

☎ *(07) 4131 2900.*

Website *www.bundabergrum.com.au.*

Admission *$9.90, admission includes one drink.*

Open *Mon-Fri 10am-3pm, Sat-Sun 10am-2pm; tours leave every hour.*

Bundaberg

Accommodation

1. Bundaberg Backpackers Travellers Lodge
2. City Centre Backpackers
3. Federal Backpackers
4. Grand Backpackers
5. Workers & Dive Hostel

Based mapping reproduced with permission of Department of Natural Resources and Mines.

Hinkler House Museum

This museum focuses on the life of Bert Hinkler, a local lad who made the first solo flight between Australia and England.

Young Street, North Bundaberg.
☎ *(07) 4152 0222.*
Admission *$5.*
Open *10am-4pm daily.*

Mon Repos

This beach, 15km from the town centre, is famous for its turtle rookery.
☎ *(07) 4159 1652.*
Turtle rookery season Nov-Mar.

Agnes Water & Town of 1770

Captain James Cook visited this spot in 1770, giving this small coastal settlement its unusual name. Although there's not a lot to see or do here, 1770, or more accurately the nearby town of Agnes Water, has become a popular backpackers' destination no doubt helped by the two excellent hostels.

It is the most northern spot that you can surf in Queensland and it also makes a good base for visiting Lady Musgrave Island.

Practical Information
The Discovery Centre
(Visitor Information Centre)
Shop 12, Endeavour Plaza, Agnes Water.
☎ *(07) 4974 7002.*
Website *www.discover1770.info.*
Open *9am-5pm daily.*

Coming & Going

McCafferty's/Greyhound have coaches to Bundaberg and Gladstone with connections for other McCafferty's services at Fingerboard Road.

Accommodation
1770 Backpackers

This new purpose-built hostel has good quality facilities including a good kitchen with lots of appliances and a nice courtyard. Rooms have en suite bathrooms with big showers. Richard, the owner/manager, has loads of experience in the backpacking industry and

works hard to ensure that the place has a good atmosphere.

6 Captain Cook Drive, Agnes Water.
☎ *1800 121 770.*
Website *www.backpackersqueensland.com.*
Dorm bed *$20;* ***double room*** *$40.*
Credit cards *MC, Visa.*
Reception open *8am-9.30pm daily.*
☎

Maintenance & cleanliness	★★★★★
Facilities	★★
Atmosphere & character	★★★★☆
Security	★
Overall rating	★★★☆

Cool Bananas

This clean purpose-built hostel features a big common area with a TV, Internet access and board games, a good kitchen and a nice barbecue area. Guests have free use of boogie boards and the hostel has a great atmosphere.

2 Springs Road, Agnes Water.
☎ *1800 227 660.*
Dorm bed *$22 ($21 VIP/YHA).*
Credit cards *MC, Visa.*

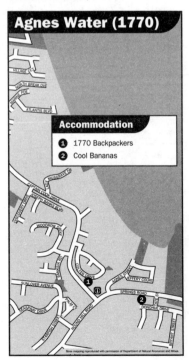

Agnes Water (1770)

Accommodation
1. 1770 Backpackers
2. Cool Bananas

Base mapping reproduced with permission of Department of Natural Resources and Mines

Reception open 7am-2pm & 4pm-10.30pm daily.

Maintenance & cleanliness	★★★★★
Facilities	★★
Atmosphere & character	★★★★☆
Security	★★☆
Overall rating	★★★☆

Sights & Activities

Many travellers visit 1770 and Agnes Water for its easy access to Lady Musgrave Island (see following section), but there are also amphibious LARC trips and cruises to Pancake Creek and Fitzroy Reef Lagoon on the Great Barrier Reef.

Amphibious LARC Trips

1770 Environmental Tours (☎ *(07) 4974 9422; website www.1770holidays.com*) have a couple of pink amphibious vehicles that they use to run day tours to Eurimbula National Park, Bustard Head Lightstation and Middle Island. Day tours cost $95 and the shorter sunset cruises are $25.

Reef Trips

The Reef Jet (☎ *1800 177 011; website www.1770holidays.com*) run trips to the relatively accessible Pancake Creek and Fitzroy Reef Lagoon. Both reefs offer excellent snorkelling. Trips to Fitzroy Reef Lagoon go every day except Wednesdays and Pancake Creek day trips run on Wednesdays and when weather conditions prevent travel to the outer reef.

Lady Musgrave Island

Lady Musgrave Island is one of the closest coral cays to Brisbane. It boasts a unique deep-water lagoon with brilliant snorkelling and diving opportunities. It is part of Capricornia Cays National Park.

Coming & Going

Lady Musgrave Island is accessible from both 1770 or Bundaberg with 1770 being the closest town to the island. Because 1770 is closer, daytrips from here allow you to spend longer on the reef.

From 1770 you can go to Lady Musgrave Island onboard MV Spirit of 1770 (☎ *(07) 4974 9077; website www.1770reefcruises.com),* which takes 85 minutes and costs $125 for a day cruise. LM Cruises (☎ *(07) 4159 4519 or 1800 072 110; website www.lmcruises. com.au)* run trips from 1770 and Bundaberg, they charge $128 for day trips from 1770 and $135 from Bundaberg. The ferry costs considerably more if you plan on returning on a different day.

Accommodation

Camping is the only accommodation option on the island. There are no services on the island so you'll need to bring everything you need with you, including water.

Camping permits are available from the Queensland Parks & Wildlife Service *(website www.epa.qld.gov.au)* for $4 per night.

Ferry transfers are considerably more expensive if you plan on spending several nights on the island.

Capricorn Coast

The Capricorn Coast region, straddling the Tropic of Capricorn, is where Tropical Queensland begins. Dramatic mountain ranges, gorges scoring deep into the earth, images of outback desert and dead flat plains stretching to the horizon are the hallmarks of this region.

Most backpackers shoot through en route between Hervey Bay and Airlie Beach and those that stop over here come to visit the Keppel Islands.

Gladstone

Gladstone is an industrial city that is home to the country's largest aluminium smelter and cement operation and Queensland's biggest power station. Despite the city's industrial importance, it is a pleasant place off the main tourist trail.

Some people come here for the ferry connections to nearby Heron Island although this isn't popular with backpackers.

Queensland

Practical Information
Information Centre
Marina Ferry Terminal, Gladstone.
☎ *(07) 4972 9922.*
Open *8.30am-5pm daily.*

Queensland Parks & Wildlife Service
Floor 3, Centrepoint Building, 136 Goondoon Street, Gladstone.
☎ *(07) 4971 6500.*
Website *www.epa.qld.gov.au.*

Coming & Going
Gladstone is located off the Bruce Highway and may be bypassed by some buses. Those buses that do pass here stop on Dawson Highway near the intersection with Glenlyon Road.

The train station is located in the city centre near the intersection of Tank and Toolooa Streets and is on the main rail line between Brisbane and Rockhampton.

Accommodation
Gladstone Backpackers
This is a small hostel that could do with a little maintenance work, but it is clean. It has a kitchen, a cosy TV lounge and guests have free use of bicycles. No alcohol allowed.
12 Rollo Street, Gladstone.
☎ *(07) 4972 5744.*
Dorm bed *$22 ($20.50 VIP);* **double room** *$48 ($45 VIP);* **twin room** *$44 ($41 VIP).*

Maintenance & cleanliness	★★
Facilities	★★★☆
Atmosphere & character	★★☆
Security	★★
Overall rating	★★

Sights & Activities
Gladstone Regional Art Gallery & Museum
This museum has displays on local history and a collection of artwork significant to the Central Queensland region.
Corner Bramston & Goondoon Streets, Gladstone.
☎ *(07) 4970 1242.*
Website *www.gragm.qld.gov.au.*
Admission *free.*
Open *Mon-Fri 10am-5pm, Sat 10am-4pm.*

Industry Tours
Informative tours of Gladstone's industrial plants take place on a regular basis. These tours can be very interesting if you've always wanted to know how aluminium, cement or petroleum is produced. Group sizes are generally small and you have a good opportunity to see behind the scenes. Bookings are essential and must be made through the information centre at the marina.
☎ *(07) 4972 9000.*
Admission *free.*
Tours *Monday Queensland Alumina Limited refinery; Wednesday Gladstone Port Authority; Thursday Southern Pacific Petroleum & Comalco Alumina Refinery; Friday Boyne Smelter & Queensland Cement Limited.*

Rockhampton
Rocky is the major city on the central Queensland coast and likes to call itself the beef capital of Australia. Although there isn't really a lot to do here, many travellers stop here to visit nearby Great Keppel Island.

Practical Information
Information Centre
208 Quay Street, Rockhampton.
☎ *(07) 4922 5339 or 1800 805 865.*
Open *Mon-Fri 8.30am-4.30pm, Sat-Sun 9am-4pm.*

INTERNET ACCESS
Cybernet
12 William Street, Rockhampton.
☎ *(07) 4927 3633.*
Website *www.cybernet.com.au.*
Open *Mon-Fri 10am-5.30pm daily.*

Coming & Going
Most buses going up the coast will stop at Rockhampton. McCafferty's/Greyhound buses stop at the terminal at the corner of Brown and Linnet Streets near Queen Elizabeth Drive in North Rockhampton and Premier coaches stop at their terminal on George Street (Bruce Highway), between Archer and Fitzroy Streets.

Rockhampton's train station is located at the end of Murray Street, southeast of the town centre.

Local Transport

Rockhampton's bus service (☎ (07) 4936 1002; *website* www.sunbus.com.au) consists of nine routes connecting the city centre with outlying suburbs. It is handy for getting to the youth hostel and Shopping Fair. One-way fares range from $1.35 to $4.25.

Accommodation
Ascot Backpackers

This hostel is comprised of rooms above a pub. It is a quiet place with a laid back atmosphere. Facilities include a TV lounge, Internet access and a small kitchen. The showers and toilets are brand new, but otherwise this place feels a little dated.

117 Musgrave Street, Rockhampton.
☎ *(07) 4922 4719.*
Website www.ascothotel.com.au.
Dorm bed *$18 ($17 VIP/YHA).*

Credit cards *Amex, Diners, MC, Visa.*
Reception open *7am-late.*

Maintenance & cleanliness	★★★
Facilities	★★½
Atmosphere & character	★★★
Security	★★
Overall rating	★★★½

Downtown Backpackers (Oxford Hotel)

This is a clean and tidy hostel above a pub in central Rockhampton. Facilities include a common room with a TV and Internet access and a basic kitchen. Accommodation is in small dormitories and the biggest dorm has four beds. It's the most centrally located hostel in Rocky.

Corner Denham &East Streets, Rockhampton.
🚌 *1, 3, 3A, 4A, 6, 10, 11.*
☎ *(07) 4922 1837.*

Jellyfish Warning

Marine Stingers, or Box Jellyfish, are among Australia's deadliest creatures. Swimmers who come into contact with the tentacles of these jellyfish have been known to die within five minutes and often become unconscious before they can leave the water.

Box jellyfish are found in tropical waters between Gladstone in Queensland and Broome in Western Australia, but are not normally found on the Great Barrier Reef. The box jellyfish season is variable, although it is generally between November and March in southern areas and October to April in Far North Queensland and the Northern Territory. They are sometimes found a couple of weeks beyond the official close of the season.

Box jellyfish are also known as sea wasps and can weigh up to six kilograms and have a body 25-30cm in diameter with up to 60 tentacles, which can stretch for up to two metres.

It is best to ask locals first before swimming. Some beaches have jellyfish nets or stinger-resistant enclosures – if you're at a beach that has one of these, always swim inside the enclosure. These enclosures will keep out box jellyfish but not Irukandji, which can still get through. If no one else is swimming on the beach, there's probably a very good reason.

Some people wear a lycra suit, similar to a thin wetsuit, to protect themselves from stingers although there is no guaranteed way to avoid stingers other than sticking to swimming pools.

If you, or someone you're swimming with, are stung you should flood the stung area with vinegar (never use alcohol) for about half a minute and then seek immediate medical help. Mouth-to-mouth resuscitation may also be necessary. Many beaches in infected areas have vinegar on hand, but it's still a good idea to bring a big bottle of vinegar with you.

Although box jellyfish are found mostly in shallow water and not normally on the Great Barrier Reef, there are other jellyfish to watch out for including Irukandji. These small creatures have a body only around two centimetres in diameter and are usually found in deeper water making them a greater threat to divers. Every summer around 60 people are hospitalised from Irukandji stings. Although the sting is not as painful as other jellyfish, about 30 minutes after being stung the victim develops a series of symptoms including severe back and abdominal pain, nausea and vomiting, sweating and agitation.

Another potentially deadly jellyfish in Australian waters is the Portuguese man o war, or bluebottle. Vinegar is not recommended for bluebottle stings, although no deaths from these have been reported in Australia.

Dorm bed $16.50.
Reception open 8.30am-10/11pm daily.

Maintenance & cleanliness	★★★
Facilities	★
Atmosphere & character	★★
Security	★★☆
Overall rating	★★

Rockhampton Youth Hostel YHA

This is a clean hostel and facilities include a kitchen, TV lounge, Internet access and an outdoor area with barbecues. It is in a quiet street in North Rockhampton.

60 MacFarlane Street, North Rockhampton.
🚌 *1, 3, 3A, 4A, 6, 10.*
☎ *(07) 4927 5288.*
Dorm bed $21.50-22.50 ($18-19 YHA); double/twin room $49-59 ($42-52 YHA).
Credit cards MC, Visa.
Reception open 7am-11.30am & 3.30pm-9.30pm daily.
🚌

Maintenance & cleanliness	★★★★☆
Facilities	★★
Atmosphere & character	★★
Security	★★
Overall rating	★★★☆

Eating & Drinking

Rockhampton is Australia's beef capital and there are plenty of pubs and restaurants that serve succulent cuts of prime beef. The pub downstairs from Ascot Backpackers *(117 Musgrave Street, Rockhampton;* ☎ *(07) 4922 4719)* may not have the ambience of a fine restaurant but the stone grilled steaks are the tastiest around.

Sights

Botanic Gardens & Zoo

The gardens are nice and there's also a free zoo, with mostly native animals.
Spencer Street, South Rockhampton.
🚌 *4A.*
☎ *(07) 4922 1654.*
Admission free.
Open 6am-6pm daily.

Dreamtime Cultural Centre

This interesting cultural centre focuses on the traditions of Aboriginal and Torres Strait Islanders. There are also displays on bush tucker and boomerang and didgeridoo demonstrations.
Corner Bruce Highway & Yeppoon Road, Parkhurst.
🚌 *10.*
☎ *(07) 4936 1655.*
Website www.dreamtimecentre.com.au.
Admission $12.75.
Open Mon-Fri 10am-2.30pm; regular tours from 10.30am.

Emu Park & Yeppoon

These two towns on the Capricorn Coast are an alternative to Rockhampton as gateways to Great Keppel Island. Both towns have a relaxed feel and backpackers accommodation.

Practical Information

Capricorn Coast Visitor Information Centre

Fig Tree Creek Roundabout, Yeppoon.
☎ *(07) 4939 4888.*
Website www.capricorncoast.com.au.
Open 9am-5pm daily.

Coming & Going

Young's Coaches (☎ *(07) 4922 3813)* run regular buses from Rockhampton to Emu Park and Yeppoon. Route 20 goes from Rockhampton to Emu Park via Yeppoon and route 29 runs between Rocky and Emu Park.

Accommodation

Emu Park Beach House

This quiet and laid-back hostel offers basic accommodation in dorms, double rooms and self-contained units. It needs a bit of maintenance work, but it does have a big kitchen and a pleasant dining/living area as well as Internet access and a climbing wall. The hostel is on the main road about 1km from the centre of Emu Park. A local bus service runs to Rockhampton and Yeppoon and the hostel provides free pickups from Rockhampton.

88 Pattison Street, Emu Park.
🚌 *20, 29.*
☎ *(07) 4939 6111 or 1800 333 349*
Dorm bed $18.
🚌

Maintenance & cleanliness	★★☆
Facilities	★★☆

Atmosphere & character	★★★☆
Security	☆
Overall rating	★★

Yeppoon Backpackers

This big old wooden building features a common room with a piano, TV and pool table plus a big backyard with a barbecue and swimming pool. It has a good location close to the town centre. *30-32 Queen Street, Yeppoon.* ☎ *(07) 4939 8080 or 1800 636 828.* **Dorm bed** *$20 ($19 VIP/YHA);* **double room** *$42 ($40 VIP/YHA).* **Credit cards** *MC, Visa.* **Reception open** *7am-11.30pm daily.* 🚌

Maintenance & cleanliness	★★☆
Facilities	★★☆
Atmosphere & character	★★★★☆
Security	★★
Overall rating	★★☆

Great Keppel Island

This is one of the most accessible islands on the east coast. It has a couple of hiking tracks, water sports, some good beaches and affordable accommodation. It's a great deal for backpackers who want a resort holiday at backpackers' prices.

Coming & Going

Great Keppel Island is located 17km off the coast from Rosslyn Bay, which is near Yeppoon – about a 40-minute drive north of Rockhampton. The YHA hostel in Rockhampton runs a bus to meet the ferry. If you're not staying at the YHA, you'll need to take the Young's (☎ *(07) 4922 3813)* bus from Rockhampton to Rosslyn Bay, which costs $7.50 for the trip with buses departing from the corner of Bolsover & Denham Streets in Rockhampton.

The return ferry trip between Rosslyn Bay and Great Keppel Island costs $32. Two companies operate ferries: the Freedom Flyer (☎ *(07) 4933 6244)* departs from Keppel Bay Marina, while the Great Keppel Tourist Services (☎ *(07) 4933 6744)* ferry leaves from the Great Keppel Island Transit Centre.

It's worth checking the package deals offered by the hostels in Rockhampton

and Yeppoon before you book your transport to the island. There are often good deals that include both transport and accommodation on Great Keppel Island.

Accommodation

Great Keppel Island Backpackers

This friendly hostel is in a nice bush setting with lots of hammocks and accommodation in small two and four-bed dorms and nice double/twin tents. There's a good kitchen, a barbecue area and a small shop. You can organise canoe trips and snorkelling from here. *Great Keppel Island.* ☎ *(07) 4939 8655 or 1800 180 235.* **Website** *www.gkiholidayvillage.com.au.* **Dorm bed** *$27;* **single room or tent** *$40;* **double/twin room or tent** *$60.* **Reception open** *8.30am-6.30pm daily.*

Maintenance & cleanliness	★★★★☆
Facilities	★★☆
Atmosphere & character	★★★★☆
Security	★★☆
Overall rating	★★★☆

YHA Backpackers Village

Great Keppel Island's YHA is set among tropical gardens and it features a big kitchen, TV lounge and barbecue areas. *Great Keppel Island.* ☎ *(07) 4927 5288 or (07) 4933 6416* **Dorm bed** *$23.50-31.50 ($20-28 YHA);* **single room** *$33.50 ($30 YHA);* **double/twin room** *$53-82 ($46-75 YHA).* **Credit cards** *MC, Visa.* **Reception open** *7.30am-5pm daily.*

Maintenance & cleanliness	★★★
Facilities	★★
Atmosphere & character	★★★
Security	★
Overall rating	★★☆

Whitsunday Coast

The Whitsundays is a group of 74 tropical islands that is an extremely popular spot for yacht charters. The main towns in this region are Mackay and Proserpine, although most backpackers head straight for Airlie Beach.

Mackay

This sugar-processing city mid-way up the Queensland coast doesn't hold a lot to interest the traveller, but you may want to stop here to break your journey if you're driving up the coast. Mackay is also a good base for exploring the Eungella National Park, about an hour inland.

Practical Information
Mackay Visitors' Centre
320 Nebo Road, South Mackay.
☎ *(07) 4952 2677 or 1300 130 001.*
Website www.mackayregion.com.
Open Mon-Fri 8.30am-5pm, Sat-Sun 9am-4pm.

63 Sydney Street, Mackay.
☎ *(07) 4951 4803.*
Website www.mackayregion.com.
Open Mon-Fri 8.30am-5pm, Sat-Sun 9am-4pm.

Queensland National Parks & Wildlife Service
2 Wood Street, Mackay.
☎ *(07) 4944 7800.*
Open Mon-Fri 8.30am-5pm.

Coming & Going
Coaches stop at the bus terminal on Milton Street, between Gordon and Victoria Streets. The airport and train station are located about 4km south of the town centre.

Local Transport
Mackay Transit (☎ *(07) 4957 3330; website www.mackaytransit.com.au)* runs local buses but services are infrequent on some routes and they don't go anywhere other than the outlying suburbs. Buses only operate Monday to Friday.

Accommodation
Larrikin Lodge
This is a quiet hostel with a homely atmosphere. It has clean dormitories; a small kitchen and a TV lounge with Internet access and a nice backyard area with a barbecue. The hostel organises tours to the nearby Eungella National Park.
32 Peel Street, Mackay.
☎ *(07) 4951 3728.*

Dorm bed $21 ($18 YHA); twin room $48 ($42 YHA).
Credit cards MC, Visa.
Reception open 7am-2pm & 5pm-9pm daily.
☎

Maintenance & cleanliness	★★★
Facilities	★★☆
Atmosphere & character	★★★★
Security	★★
Overall rating	★★★☆

Sights
Artspace Mackay
Mackay's art gallery is host to a selection of temporary art exhibitions.
Gordon Street, Mackay.
☎ *(07) 4968 4444 (Mon-Fri); (07) 4957 1775 (Sat-Sun).*
Admission free.
Open Tue-Sun 10am-5pm.

Eungella National Park

Eungella National Park is about an hour inland from Mackay. It is home to Australia's largest stretch of subtropical rainforest. The park's highlight is the impressive Finch Hatton Gorge.

At Broken River there is a viewing deck that is an excellent place for spotting platypus. Dusk and dawn are the best times to catch a glimpse of a platypus and it helps if you are both quiet and patient.

Eungella National Park is difficult to reach without a car but there are tours to the park that operate from Mackay, which include the excellent Jungle Johno Tours (☎ *(07) 4941 3728)* that are geared to backpackers. Jungle Johno has half-day tours for $58 ($53 YHA) and full day tours for $75 ($68 YHA) that take in the park's main attractions including Finch Hatton Gorge and Broken River and give you the opportunity to see Eungella's unique array of wildlife.

Proserpine

Proserpine is a busy town serving the region's sugar cane farms and it stands in sharp contrast to energetic Airlie Beach.

There's no backpackers' accommodation here, but it is the main transport hub of the Whitsunday region with and many backpackers pass through here en route to Airlie Beach and the Whitsunday Islands.

Coming & Going

Proserpine enjoys good transport connections with a busy regional airport, train station and frequent coaches up and down the coast.

McCafferty's/Greyhound and Premier Coaches pass through here en route to Airlie Beach and Whitsunday Transit (☎ *(07) 4946 1800; website www.whitsundaytransit.com.au)* provide good connections between Proserpine and Airlie Beach with many services timed to meet airline and train connections.

Proserpine's Whitsunday Coast Airport is 12km south of Proserpine and is served by both Qantas and Virgin Blue. Whitsunday Transit's buses meet every flight but it is essential to book ahead for the airport bus transfer.

Whitsunday Transit also has transfers between Proserpine train station and Airlie Beach.

Airlie Beach

Beautiful Airlie Beach is a relaxed tropical town with great hostels and it is one of the most popular backpacker destinations between Brisbane and Cairns. There's not a lot to see here but there are plenty of things to do such as skydiving and scuba diving as well as sailing trips around the 74 islands of the Whitsundays chain.

The eight million dollar lagoon by the waterfront is a bit like a cross between a beach and a huge swimming pool and is yet another reason to stay an extra day.

Practical Information
Marine Parks Authority Information Centre
Corner Mandalay Street & Shute Harbour Road, Airlie Beach.
☎ *(07) 4946 7022.*
Open *Mon-Fri 9am-5pm, Sat 9am-1pm.*

INTERNET ACCESS
Airliebeach.com Internet Centre
259 Shute Harbour Road, Airlie Beach.

☎ *(07) 4946 5299 or 1800 677 119.*
Open *7.30am-8pm daily.*

Beaches
356 Shute Harbour Road, Airlie Beach.
☎ *(07) 4946 6244.*
Open *7am-8pm daily.*

Copy Connection
The Esplanade, Airlie Beach.
☎ *(07) 4948 0091.*
Open *Mon-Fri 9am-5pm.*

LAUNDRY
Al's Laundry
Shute Harbour Road, Airlie Beach.
☎ *(07) 4945 1739.*
Open *6am-10pm daily.*

Julee's Beach Plaza Laundromat
The Esplanade, Airlie Beach.
☎ *(07) 4946 4977.*

LOCKERS
The Locker Room
Shute Harbour Road, Airlie Beach.
Open *24 hours.*

Coming & Going

Most buses running between Brisbane and Cairns stop in Airlie Beach dropping off on Shute Harbour Road in the centre of town.

The nearest airport and train station is at Proserpine and there are regular buses that run between Proserpine and Shute Harbour stopping at Airlie Beach. The bus fare from Proserpine Airport to Airlie Beach is $14.50 one-way. There's another airport at nearby Hamilton Island.

Ferries operated by Blue Ferries (☎ *(07) 4946 5111)* run between Shute Harbour and Hamilton Island, Long Island and South Molle Island. The ferry to Hamilton Island costs $29 each way or $44 for a day return.

Local Transport

Airlie Beach is small enough to walk around but Whitsunday Transit (☎ *(07) 4946 1800; website www.whitsundaytransit.com.au)* operates a local bus service that connects it to the neighbouring towns of Cannonvale and Shute Harbour. Buses run

Queensland

about every half hour and cost $1.85 one-way ($3.40 return) between Airlie Beach and the shopping centre in Cannonvale. A better deal is the $8 all day ticket that includes unlimited travel on all Whitsunday Transit services including buses to Proserpine.

Accommodation
Airlie Waterfront Backpackers
Airlie Waterfront is a quiet hostel with mostly double and twin rooms and a few small dorms. It has all the usual facilities and there are great views from the balcony.
6 The Esplanade, Airlie Beach.
☎ *(07) 4948 1300 or 1800 089 000*
Website www.airliebackpackers.com.au.
Dorm bed *$18-25;* **double/twin room** *$55.*
Credit cards *MC, Visa.*
Reception open *7am-8pm daily.*

Maintenance & cleanliness	★★★★
Facilities	★★
Atmosphere & character	★★★
Security	★☆
Overall rating	★★★

Backpackers by the Bay
Backpackers by the Bay is a very nice hostel with excellent facilities. Accommodation is good with small four-share dormitories, some of which are air-conditioned. Shared facilities include a kitchen, a common room with a pool table and Internet access and an outdoor area with a swimming pool, barbecue and fantastic views. It is 400 metres out of town on the road to Shute Harbour.
12 Hermitage Drive, Airlie Beach.
☎ *(07) 4946 7267 or 1 800 646 994.*
Website www.backpackersbythebay.com.
Dorm bed *$22 ($21 VIP/YHA);* **double/twin room** *$52 ($50 VIP/YHA).*
Credit cards *MC, Visa.*
Reception open *7am-7.30pm daily.*

Maintenance & cleanliness	★★★★★
Facilities	★★★★
Atmosphere & character	★★★★★
Security	★★☆
Overall rating	★★★★☆

Beaches
This former motel has self-contained units, each with four to five single beds (not bunks), plus a fridge, TV and en suite bathroom. There's also a kitchen, TV lounge, Internet café and a good bar. The central location on Shute Harbour Road in the centre of town makes it a good place to stay if you want to party but the noise from the bar makes it not so great if you want an early night. Although Beaches has a great bar, the hostel's atmosphere isn't so great if you don't want to drink there and the TVs in the dorms keep travellers from meeting each other.
356-362 Shute Harbour Road, Airlie Beach.
☎ *(07) 4946 6244 or 1800 636 630*
Website www.beaches.com.au.
Dorm bed *$22 ($21 VIP);* **double/twin room** *$50 ($45 VIP).*
Credit cards *MC, Visa.*
Reception open *7am-8pm daily.*

Maintenance & cleanliness	★★★☆
Facilities	★★★☆
Atmosphere & character	★★★☆
Security	★★☆
Overall rating	★★★

Bush Village Backpackers Resort
This is a quiet hostel with good facilities that include a swimming pool, spa, pool table, TV lounge, Internet access and a big backyard with kangaroos and wallabies that are part of a rehabilitation programme. Accommodation is in self-contained units, each with a TV, kitchen and en suite bathroom. The cabins are in the process of being renovated – the renovated cabins are of a very high standard, but those awaiting renovation look a little tired.
2 St Martins Road, Cannonvale.
☎ *(07) 4946 6177 or 1800 809 256.*
Dorm bed *$21;* **double room** *$70; includes breakfast.*
Credit cards *MC, Visa.*
Reception open *7.30am-9pm daily.*

Maintenance & cleanliness	★★★★
Facilities	★★★★☆
Atmosphere & character	★★★
Security	★
Overall rating	★★★★☆

Queensland

Club Habitat YHA

This youth hostel is a former motel and all rooms have their own balcony and en suite bathroom. There's also a TV lounge, a big kitchen and a swimming pool but the communal areas close at 10pm. There's good security with lockers in the rooms.

394 Shute Harbour Road, Airlie Beach.
☎ *(07) 4946 6312 or 1800 247 251.*
Dorm bed *$22.50 ($19 YHA);*
double/twin room *$54 ($47 YHA).*
Credit cards *MC, Visa.*
Reception open *7am-7pm daily.*
☎

Maintenance & cleanliness	★★★
Facilities	★★
Atmosphere & character	★★
Security	★★☆
Overall rating	★★★☆

Club Whitsunday Backpacker Hostel

This hostel consists of self-contained units, each with a TV, fridge and bathroom but the courtyard is the only common area.

346 Shute Harbour Road, Airlie Beach.
☎ *(07) 4948 1511 or 1800 678 755.*
Dorm bed *$21;* **double room** *$50; includes breakfast.*
Credit cards *MC, Visa.*
Reception open *7am-9pm daily.*

Maintenance & cleanliness	★★★☆
Facilities	★
Atmosphere & character	★
Security	★
Overall rating	★★☆

Koala

Koala's occupies a huge 17-hectare site in the centre of town. It features two swimming pools, a beach volleyball court and bar. Accommodation is in self-contained units, each with TV and en suite bathroom.

Shute Harbour Road, Airlie Beach.
☎ *(07) 4946 6001 or 1800 800 421.*
Website *www.koala-backpackers.com.*
Bed in a large dorm *$16;* **bed in a small dorm** *$22 ($21 VIP);* **double/ twin room** *$60 ($58 VIP);* **camping** *$10 per person.*
Credit cards *MC, Visa.*
Reception open *7am-8.30pm daily.*

Maintenance & cleanliness	★★★
Facilities	★★☆
Atmosphere & character	★★
Security	★★☆
Overall rating	★★★☆

Magnums

Magnums is a party hostel with good facilities and accommodation in air-conditioned cabins set among tropical gardens. The main feature of this place is the bar/nightclub, which is one of the most happening spots in Airlie Beach. Other amenities include a small kitchen, Internet access, pool tables and a beach volleyball court. Although the bar is loud till the early hours, most accommodation (except for the cheapest dorms) is set back far enough to ensure a good night sleep. Overall Magnums is a good mix of quality facilities, value and fun.

Shute Harbour Road, Airlie Beach.
☎ *(07) 4946 6266 or 1 800 624 634.*
Dorm bed *$13-16;* **double room** *$42;*
camping *$15 per tent, $17 per van.*
Credit cards *Amex, MC, Visa.*
Reception open *6am-10pm daily.*

Maintenance & cleanliness	★★★★☆
Facilities	★★★
Atmosphere & character	★★★★☆
Security	★★
Overall rating	★★★★

Reef O

This resort-style hostel is a great value place to stay with good facilities, but some cabins could be a little better maintained. Accommodation consists of self-contained units, each with en suite bathrooms, which are set among tropical gardens. There is a nice swimming pool, beach volleyball court, a small convenience store/Internet café, a barbecue area, ATM and a great bar/ restaurant. It is located in Cannonvale, a couple of kilometres outside Airlie Beach and there are frequent shuttle buses into town.

147 Shute Harbour Road, Cannonvale.
☎ *(07) 4946 6137 or 1800 800 795.*
Website *www.reeforesort.com.*
Dorm bed *$12-18;* **double/twin room** *$55;* **family room** *(sleeps 6) $82.50.*
Credit cards *MC, Visa.*
Reception open *24 hours.*

Queensland

Maintenance & cleanliness	★★
Facilities	★★★★☆
Atmosphere & character	★★★★☆
Security	★★
Overall rating	★★★

Eating & Drinking

Airlie Beach has plenty of places for a cheap snack and a few more upscale restaurants but the big emphasis here is on partying all night. It all happens on Shute Harbour Road with Beaches, Magnums and Morocco's fuelling Airlie's reputation as the hottest backpacker party zone south of Cairns. Many of the bars run theme nights such as foam parties.

The closest real supermarket is in Cannonvale, a couple of kilometres outside Airlie Beach.

Whitsunday Islands

The Whitsunday Island group offers myriad opportunities for sailing, snorkelling or just cruising around the islands.

The islands are renowned for their lovely beaches, particularly the world famous Whitehaven Beach on Whitsunday Island. The 6km long Whitehaven Beach is the most popular with day-trippers but somehow that doesn't spoil its allure. Make sure you do the 650-metre walk to the lookout at Hill Inlet.

Many of the islands including Daydream, Hamilton, Hayman and South Molle have upmarket resorts. Although you may feel out of place here, the island resorts provide pockets of civilisation among the wilderness.

Coming & Going
FERRIES

Ferries are one of the cheaper options and ideal if you just want to visit one or two of the more popular islands such as Hamilton Island, Long Island or South Molle Island. However you won't get the true Whitsunday experience.

Blue Ferries

Blue Ferries, aka FantaSea, is the main ferry operator in the Whitsundays with frequent shuttle services from Shute Harbour to Daydream Island, Hamilton Island, Long Island, South Molle Island and Whitehaven Beach on Whitsunday Island.
☎ *(07) 4946 5111.*
Website www.fantasea.com.au.

SAILING

Many backpackers opt for a sailing package, which allows you to see a variety of islands and for many people it is the only chance they will ever have of sailing a yacht.

Airlie Beach has a huge range of yachts ranging from modern catamarans and racing maxi yacht to historic tall ships and encompassing everything in between. Two-night sailing excursions cost $300-600 depending on the boat and the type of onboard accommodation provided.

With the exception of day trips on large boats with licensed bars, you can bring your own alcohol but most of the sailing boats prohibit glass, which means you can't enjoy a nice wine aboard the yacht (just beer and cask wine).

You will also need to pay the Great Barrier Reef Marine Park levy and administration charge of $27, which most sailing companies do not include in their prices.

Most sailing trips have two to three crew and eight to 20 passengers.

Aussie Adventure Sailing

This company has a great selection of classic yachts including a tall ship and several timber ketches.
***Departs** Abel Point Marina.*
☎ *1800 359 554.*
Website www.aussiesailing.com.au.
Cost $305 2 days/2 nights; $380-410 3 days/3 nights.

Koala Sail Adventures

Koala has several boats including a large luxury catamaran and a couple of maxi racing yachts. Their catamaran trip includes accommodation on South Molle Island resort, although the big modern boat is perhaps not the sailing experience that most people imagine. The maxi yachts include *Anaconda II*,

the world's largest fibreglass maxi yacht, and *The Card*, a world class racing yacht that has competed in the Whitbread Around the World yacht race.
Departs *Shute Harbour.*
☎ *1800 466 444.*
Cost *catamaran trip with accommodation on South Molle Island $285; maxi racing yacht $390.*

Oz Sail
Oz Sail has a good selection of yachts that are small enough to really get a feel for sailing. They are good value for money and are a more authentic sailing experience than some of the huge catamarans that some other companies sail.
Departs *Abel Point Marina.*
☎ *(07) 4948 1388 or 1800 102 030.*
Website *www.ozsail.com.au.*
Cost *$349-389 3 days/2 nights; $389-425 3 days/3 nights.*

ProSail
ProSail offers day sailing trips on a fast catamaran and multi-day trips on more conventional cruising and racing yachts.
☎ *(07) 4946 5433 or 1800 810 116.*
Website *www.prosail.com.au.*
Cost *$99 day trip; $429-439 3 days/2 nights; $469 3 days/3 nights.*

Ragamuffin
Ragamuffin is legendary among yacht racing circles as one of the most successful boats in the famous Sydney to Hobart yacht race. This 24 metre racing yacht now makes one-day sailing trips that either feature snorkelling at Blue Pearl Bay on Hayman Island or a picnic lunch at Whitehaven Beach on Whitsunday Island.
Departs *Shute Harbour.*
☎ *(07) 4946 7777 or 1800 454 777.*
Website *www.maxiaction.com.au.*
Cost *$99.*

Team Sail
Team Sail has several large cruising and racing yachts and operates three day/two night sailing trips around the Whitsundays.
☎ *(07) 4948 2202 or 1800 100 666.*
Website *www.teamsailoz.com.*
Cost *$299-369 3 days/2 nights.*

Tongarra Cruises
Tongarra is a spacious catamaran that runs flexible two night sailing trips around the Whitsundays.
Departs *Abel Point Marina.*
☎ *(07) 4946 6952.*
Website *www.tongarra.com.*
Cost *$269 3 days/2 nights.*

DAY TRIPS
If your time is limited and you don't mind missing out on the authentic sailing experience, then a launch day trip is a good option for exploring the islands. You may feel like a tourist on these trips but you can pack a lot into one day and most of the trips offer excellent snorkelling opportunities.

FantaSea
FantaSea's day trip on a luxury catamaran visits Whitehaven Beach on Whitsunday Island and also visits the uninhabited Bali Hai Island for snorkelling and coral viewing aboard the Yellow Sub.
Departs *Shute Harbour.*
☎ *(07) 4946 6900.*
Cost *$89.*

The Kookaburra
The *Kookaburra* is a large launch that makes a day trip, which includes stops at Hill Inlet and Whitehaven Beach on Whitsunday Island with opportunities for snorkelling on coral reefs.
Departs *from Abel Point Marina.*
☎ *(07) 4946 5299.*
Cost *$90; includes buffet lunch.*

Mantaray
Mantaray makes a day trip to Whitehaven Beach and Mantaray Bay on Hook Island allowing around two hours snorkelling time at Mantaray Bay.
Departs *from Abel Point Marina.*
☎ *(07) 4946 4321 or 1800 816 365.*
Cost *$90; includes lunch.*

Ocean Rafting
Ocean Raftings's day trip is on a large high-speed inflatable raft that visits Hook and Whitsunday Islands and includes a guided national park walk and snorkelling on the reef.

Queensland

Departs *Coral Sea Resort, Airlie Beach.*
☎ *(07) 4946 6848.*
Cost *$73.*

ReefJet

ReefJet's island day trip visits Hook Island, Hayman Island and Whitehaven Beach on Whitsunday Island. They also make a trip to the outer Great Barrier Reef, which gives you up to five hours snorkelling on the reef.
Departs *Airlie Beach.*
☎ *(07) 4946 5366.*
Website *www.reefjet.com.au.*
Cost *island day trip $90; outer reef day trip $120.*

Whitehaven Xpress

Whitehaven Xpress visits Mantaray Bay on Hook Island and includes a barbecue lunch at Whitehaven Beach on Whitsunday Island.
Departs *Abel Point Marina.*
☎ *(07) 4946 7172.*
Cost *$90.*

Whitsunday Island Adventure Cruises

Whitsunday Island Adventure Cruises visits Whitehaven Beach, Hook Island and Long Island and includes admission to the underwater observatory on Hook Island.
Departs *Shute Harbour.*
☎ *(07) 4946 5255.*
Cost *$69.*

Accommodation

Apart from pricey resorts or sleeping on a yacht, camping is the main accommodation option in the islands. The Queensland Parks & Wildlife Service runs 21 campgrounds on the islands, but you'll need to buy a camping permit from the Marine Parks Authority office in Airlie Beach (see Practical Information listing under Airlie Beach). Camping permits cost $3.85 per night.

Bowen

Bowen is a small seaside town that has some nice beaches. It is a good spot for fruit picking work and – because of the nearby beaches – it is a good alternative to working in Bundaberg.

Practical Information
Bowen Visitor Information Centre

Bruce Highway, Mt Gordon.
☎ *(07) 4786 4222.*
Website *www.bowentourism.com.au.*
Open *8.30am-5pm daily.*

Coming & Going

McCafferty's/Greyhound buses stop at 40 Williams Street in Bowen's town centre. Bowen is also on the main Brisbane-Cairns train line with the station a couple of kilometres south of the town centre.

Accommodation
Bowen Backpackers

Bowen Backpackers is a new purpose-built hostel that features the usual kitchen and TV lounge. It is a nice place that is better than the average workers' hostel.
Corner Dalrymple & Herbert Streets, Bowen.
☎ *(07) 4786 3433.*
Website *www.users.bigpond.com/ bowenbackpackers.*
Dorm bed *$19.50 per night, $125 per week;* **double room** *$47 per night, $296 per week.*
Credit cards *MC, Visa.*
Open *Apr-Nov;* **reception open** *7.30am-11am & 3.30pm-6.30pm daily.*
☎

Maintenance & cleanliness	★★★★☆
Facilities	★★
Atmosphere & character	★★★★
Security	★
Overall rating	★★★☆

Ayr

This busy farming town in the Burdekin region between Bowen and Townsville doesn't offer many attractions other than fruit picking work, which both hostels can help organise.

Practical Information
Burdekin Visitor Information Centre

Plantation Park, Bruce Highway, Ayr.
☎ *(07) 4783 5988.*
Website *www.burdekintourism.com.au.*
Open *10am-4pm daily.*

Coming & Going

McCafferty's/Greyhound coaches stop at Rotary Park on Graham Street. Trains on the Brisbane-Cairns line stop at the new train station on Railway Street.

Accommodation

Ayr Backpackers

Ayr Backpackers is a clean workers' hostel that consists of a couple of restored Queenslander-style buildings. This hostel's facilities include several kitchens and TV lounges plus a volleyball court, swimming pool and barbecue. It is on a quiet street near the Coles supermarket.

54 Wilmington Street, Ayr.
☎ *(07) 4783 5837.*
Dorm bed *$100 per week.*
Reception open *5am-7pm daily.*

Maintenance & cleanliness	★★★
Facilities	★★☆
Atmosphere & character	★★★★☆
Security	★
Overall rating	★★★

Danny's Backpackers

Danny's Backpackers is a large working hostel with facilities that include a big kitchen, two TV lounges (one inside and one outside), a swimming pool, beach volleyball court and a bar. It has a good location right on the main street.

139 Queen Street, Ayr.
☎ *(07) 4783 6430.*
Dorm bed *$17.50 per night, $100 per week.*

Maintenance & cleanliness	★★☆
Facilities	★★★
Atmosphere & character	★★★
Security	★
Overall rating	★★☆

North Queensland

North Queensland between the Whitsunday Islands and Cairns ranges from the city lights of Townsville to laidback beach communities like Cardwell and Mission Beach.

Magnetic Island, 8km from Townsville is one of Australia's most popular backpacker island destinations.

Townsville

Townsville is a relaxed, tropical, coastal city at the base of red granite Castle Hill. It is a relatively large city with little tourism compared with Cairns, and it provides access to the Great Barrier Reef and Magnetic Island. Although the city isn't packed with tourists there are plenty of attractions such as Reef HQ and the Museum of Tropical Queensland.

Flinders Mall is the heart of the city centre and provides a blend of modern architecture and older buildings and you'll find pubs and outdoor cafés across Ross Creek in South Townsville, where most of the hostels are also situated. The beachfront park on the Strand is a popular spot for locals on weekends.

Practical Information

Townsville Tourist Information Centre

Flinders Mall, Townsville.
☎ *(07) 4721 3660.*
Open *Mon-Fri 9am-5pm, Sat-Sun 9am-1pm.*

Marine & National Park Information Centre

Reef HQ, 2/68 Flinders Street, Townsville.
☎ *(07) 4721 2399.*
Open *Mon-Sat 9am-5pm, Sun 9am-1pm.*

INTERNET ACCESS

The Internet Den

265 Flinders Mall, Townsville
☎ *(07) 4721 4500.*
Website *www.internetden.com.au.*
Open *9am-9pm daily.*

MB Travel Internet Café

This 24-hour Internet café operates by a vending machine that dispenses cards with a username and password, but the cards sometimes do not work and you have to see the travel agent (open 9am-7pm daily) to get one that works.

Transit Centre, Townsville.
Open *24 hours.*

Queensland

Coming & Going
AIR
Townville's airport, located 5km north of the city centre, handles regular flights to Brisbane and Cairns although it doesn't get the same amount of traffic that Cairns gets.

The airport is connected to the centre of town by a shuttle bus (☎ *(07) 4775 5544)* that meets all flights. The one-way fare between Townsville Airport and central Townsville is $7.

BUS
Townsville is an important hub with many travellers stopping here to transfer between the coastal Brisbane-Cairns route and the inland route between Townsville and the Northern Territory. Coaches arrive at the Transit Centre on Palmer Street in South Townsville. There are several good hostels within close proximity of the Transit Centre.

TRAIN
Trains stop at the new station on Charters Towers Road, which has train departures to Brisbane and Cairns and trains running through the outback to Mount Isa.

Local Transport
Sunbus (☎ *(07) 4725 8482; **website** www.sunbus.com.au*) operates Townsville's local bus service with most routes converging near Flinders Street Mall.

Accommodation
Adventurers Resort
This big hostel has good facilities that include a rooftop swimming pool with nice views, barbecue areas, a shop with Internet access plus a huge kitchen and TV lounge. This hostel has improved a lot since new management took over last year, but it still lacks atmosphere. The institutional design and vast common room do nothing for the ambience.
75 Palmer Street, South Townsville.
☎ *(07) 4721 1522.*
***Dorm bed** $20 ($18 ISIC/VIP/YHA);* ***single room** $32 ($29 ISIC/VIP/ YHA);* ***double room** $42-48 ($38-42*

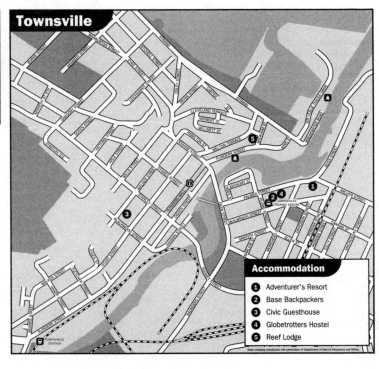

Townsville

Accommodation
1. Adventurer's Resort
2. Base Backpackers
3. Civic Guesthouse
4. Globetrotters Hostel
5. Reef Lodge

Base mapping reproduced with permission of Department of Natural Resources and Mines.

Queensland

ISIC/VIP/YHA); **twin room** *$42 ($38 ISIC/VIP/YHA).*
Credit cards *MC, Visa.*
Reception open *8am-9pm daily.*

Maintenance & cleanliness	★★★★⯨
Facilities	★★★★⯨
Atmosphere & character	★
Security	★★⯨
Overall rating	★★★

Base Backpackers

This excellent hostel is a clean place with brand new furnishings including real mattresses. Facilities include a small kitchen, TV lounge with big screen TV, a pool table, bar and a nice outdoor terrace with a spa and great views. The bunks are very low, which is great if you're on top but a bit cramped if you're on the bottom bunk. The location above the Transit Centre is handy if you're travelling by bus.
Transit Centre, Palmer Street, South Townsville.
☎ *(07) 4721 2322 or 1800 628 836*
Website *www.basebackpackers.com.*
Dorm bed *$20;* ***double/twin room*** *$50-65.*
Credit cards *Amex, Diners, MC, Visa.*
Reception open *24 hours.*

Maintenance & cleanliness	★★★★★
Facilities	★★★★⯨
Atmosphere & character	★★
Security	★★★
Overall rating	★★★★

Civic Guesthouse

This small hostel has a nice atmosphere and facilities that include a TV lounge, several kitchens and nice barbecue areas.

Although clean, some aspects of the hostel feel a little dated and the kitchen facilities could be improved.
262 Walker Street, Townsville.
☎ *(07) 4771 5381.*
Website *www.backpackersinn.com.au.*
Dorm bed *$20 ($19 VIP);* ***single room*** *$39-42 ($38-42 VIP);* ***double room*** *$42 ($40-58 VIP).*
Credit cards *MC, Visa.*
Reception open *Mon-Fri 8am-8pm, Sat-Sun 8am-1pm & 5pm-8pm.*

Maintenance & cleanliness	★★★⯨
Facilities	★★★⯨
Atmosphere & character	★★★⯨
Security	★★⯨
Overall rating	★★⯨

Globetrotters Hostel

Globetrotters is a small, peaceful and quiet hostel with a good atmosphere. It has good dorm rooms plus a kitchen, TV lounge, barbecue area and a swimming pool.
45 Palmer Street, South Townsville.
☎ *(07) 4771 3242.*
Dorm bed *$20 ($19 VIP/YHA);* ***double/twin room*** *$46 ($44 VIP/YHA).*
Credit cards *MC, Visa.*
Reception open *8am-7.30pm daily.*

Maintenance & cleanliness	★★★
Facilities	★★★⯨
Atmosphere & character	★★★★⯨
Security	★★
Overall rating	★★★

Reef Lodge

Reef Lodge is an old building in the heart of Townsville. Most rooms at this hostel are newly renovated with air-conditioning and fridges. There are several TVs, a nice barbecue area and an Internet café at the front of the building.
4 Wickham Street, Townsville.
☎ *(07) 4721 1112.*
Website *www.reeflodge.com.au.*
Dorm bed *$15-17;* ***double/twin room*** *$38-49.*
Credit cards *Amex, Diners, JCB, MC, Visa.*
Reception open *7.30am-10pm daily.*

Maintenance & cleanliness	★★★
Facilities	★★
Atmosphere & character	★★★
Security	★★
Overall rating	★★⯨

Sights

Billabong Sanctuary

This wildlife sanctuary is located about 20 minutes south of town and features a selection of native animals including kangaroos, wombats and snakes.
Bruce Highway, 17km south of town.
☎ *(07) 4778 8344.*
Website *www.billabongsanctuary.com.au.*

Queensland

Admission $23 ($21 ISIC/VIP/YHA).
Open 8am-5pm daily.

Castle Hill
The lookout at the summit of Castle Hill offers great views of Townsville. Some hostels operate trips up here although it is more rewarding to hike up the steep trail to the top.
Walking track from Hillside Crescent, Townsville.

Maritime Museum
Townsville's Maritime Museum features exhibits on the city's port and its maritime history. It is near the Transit Centre in South Townsville.
42-68 Palmer Street, South Townsville.
☎ *(07) 4721 5251.*
Admission $4.
Open Mon-Fri 10am-4pm, Sat-Sun noon-4pm.

Museum of Tropical Queensland
The Museum of Tropical Queensland is an excellent new museum, which is situated next door to Reef HQ and focuses on the history and nature of North Queensland.
70-102 Flinders Street, Townsville.
☎ *(07) 4726 0606.*
Website www.mtq.qld.gov.au.
Admission $9.
Open 9am-5pm daily, last entry 4pm.

ReefHQ
ReefHQ includes a huge aquarium as well as a theatre and informative displays about the Reef.
2-68 Flinders Street, Townsville.
☎ *(07) 4750 0800.*
Website www.reefhq.org.au.
Admission $19.50.
Open 9.30am-5pm daily.

Markets
The Strand Night craft market on Townsville's beach features entertainment and food.
Strand Park, Townsville.
Open First Friday May-Dec 5pm-9.30pm.

The Flinders Mall Cotters Market claims to be North Queensland's largest arts and craft market.

Flinders Mall, Townsville.
Open Sun 8am-1pm.

Yongala Wreck
This 90-metre passenger ship sank in 1911 and is now one of Australia's top dive sites. Several dive companies including Blue Angel Adventure Diving (☎ *(07) 4723 0630 or 1800 330 191;* *website www.mvblueangel.com)* and the Dive Shack at Geoff's Place on Magnetic Island (☎ *(07) 4778 5577 or 1800 285 577)* operate dive trips out to the SS Yongala.

Magnetic Island
Only 8km from Townsville, Magnetic Island is one of the most accessible islands in Australia and the abundance of good cheap accommodation ensures that it is also the most popular island for backpackers.

There are some good hiking trails on Magnetic Island and it is also a good spot to see wild koalas. Much of the island is national park, although the southeast coast is quite residential with many people commuting to work in Townsville.

Coming & Going
Sunferries and Magnetic Island Car & Passenger Ferries both operate a ferry service between Townsville and Magnetic Island.

Sunferries (☎ *(07) 4771 3855;* *website www.sunferries.com.au)* is the cheaper of the two ferry companies and generally costs $19.90 return but there are sometimes deals available through hostels in Townsville that may work out cheaper. Sunferries have two terminals in Townsville, one on Flinders Street East in the city centre and one on Sir Leslie Thiess Drive on the Breakwater; Sunferries terminate at Nelly Bay on Magnetic Island and run the fastest boats but they're restricted to passengers only.

Magnetic Island Car & Passenger Ferry (☎ *(07) 4772 5422)* is more expensive and slower but are the only boats that take cars. They depart from the terminal on Ross Street in South Townsville, directly across the river from Sunferries' Breakwater terminal. They sail to Nelly Bay on Magnetic Island.

Local Transport

Moke rental is a popular way to get around the island although there is also a bus service that is a much cheaper option.

Magnetic Island Buses (☎ (07) 4778 5130) run a route between Picnic Bay and Horseshoe Bay. Buses run at least once an hour and one-way fares range from $1.90 to $4.30. A daily pass costs $11.80 for a daily pass and a two-day pass is $13.20. The bigger hostels on Magnetic Island also run their own shuttle buses between the hostel and Picnic Bay.

Accommodation
Arkie's Backpacker Resort

Arkies is a large resort-style place with a swimming pool, beach volleyball court and Internet access, but the kitchen here is tiny considering the size of the hostel. All rooms are air-conditioned

with en suite bathrooms. Although Arkies has a party atmosphere, the ambience here could still be much better. There are TVs in some smaller dorms, which tends to keep people inside their rooms.

7 Marine Parade, Arcadia, Magnetic Island.

☎ *(07) 4778 5177 or 1800 663 666.*
Website *www.magnetic-island.com.au/ arc-rsrt.htm.*
Bed in a 10-bed dorm *$15 one night, $20 two nights, $29 3 nights, $35 4 nights, $40 5 nights;* ***bed in a six-bed dorm*** *$15;* ***bed in a four-bed dorm*** *$20;* ***double room*** *$49-50.*
Credit cards *MC, Visa.*
Reception open *8am-8.30pm daily.*

Maintenance & cleanliness	★★
Facilities	★★★
Atmosphere & character	★★½
Security	★
Overall rating	★★½

Base Backpackers

When we visited this hostel it was just about to close for extensive renovations

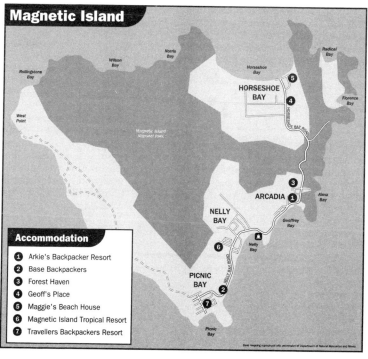

Magnetic Island

Accommodation
1. Arkie's Backpacker Resort
2. Base Backpackers
3. Forest Haven
4. Geoff's Place
5. Maggie's Beach House
6. Magnetic Island Tropical Resort
7. Travellers Backpackers Resort

before reopening in February 2004, so we are not able to give a rating. Formerly known as Coconuts, Base Backpackers has a resort setting comprised of cabins set among palm trees and the facilities include a dive school, restaurant, bar, Internet access and a swimming pool. It has a relaxed and laid-back atmosphere during the day and a party atmosphere at night – the hostel has live bands and full moon parties. It has the best location on the island with absolute beach frontage and a coral reef with good snorkelling just 20 metres from the hostel. You can walk to the shops in both Nelly and Picnic Bays from the hostel. There is a shuttle bus to the ferry terminal.

Not yet rated

Forest Haven

Forest Haven is a small quiet hostel suited to travellers looking for a quieter alternative to the island's party hostels. It features a swimming pool and barbecue but the kitchen is tiny.
11 Cook Road, Arcadia, Magnetic Island.
☎ *(07) 4778 5153.*
***Dorm bed** $15; **double/twin room** $40; **self-contained unit** $70.*
***Credit cards** MC, Visa.*
***Reception open** 8am-6pm daily.*

Maintenance & cleanliness	★★
Facilities	★★☆
Atmosphere & character	★★
Security	★
Overall rating	★★

Geoff's Place

This resort-style hostel complex has accommodation in chalets/cabins and camping sites set among the bush. Facilities include a swimming pool and a good bar with pool tables and Internet access.
40 Horseshoe Bay Road, Horseshoe Bay, Magnetic Island.
☎ *(07) 4778 5577 or 1800 285 577.*
***Website** www.geoffsplace.com.au.*
***Dorm bed** $18-20; **double/twin room** $46-58; **camping** $10 per person.*
***Credit cards** MC, Visa.*
***Reception open** 8am-late (around 10-11pm) daily.*

Maintenance & cleanliness	★★☆
Facilities	★★★★☆
Atmosphere & character	★★★★★☆

Security	★★☆
Overall rating	★★★

Maggie's Beach House

Maggie's is a new purpose-built hostel with excellent facilities including a bar/restaurant, Internet access, kitchen and lounge areas. Accommodation is pretty good – all rooms are air-conditioned, many have en suite bathrooms and some of the dorms have balconies with sea views. The hostel is at Horseshoe Bay at the northern end of the island, directly across the road from the beach and close to a good pub.
Pacific Drive, Horseshoe Bay, Magnetic Island.
☎ *(07) 4778 5144.*
***Website** www.maggiesbeachhouse.com.au.*
***Dorm bed** $21 ($20 Nomads/VIP); **double room** $59-75 ($58-74 Nomads/VIP); **twin room** $52 ($51 Nomads/VIP).*
***Credit cards** MC, Visa.*
***Reception open** 8am-7pm daily.*

Maintenance & cleanliness	★★★★★
Facilities	★★★☆
Atmosphere & character	★★★
Security	★★
Overall rating	★★★★☆

Magnetic Island Tropical Resort

This resort offers a mix of upmarket accommodation along with around 30 backpacker beds. Accommodation is in A-frame cabins with en suite and decking at the front. Shared facilities include a kitchen, volleyball court, swimming pool, spa, a bar and restaurant. It is quieter than most other hostels on the island and you get the opportunity to hand-feed rainbow lorikeets twice a day.
56 Yates Street, Nelly Bay, Magnetic Island.
☎ *(07) 4778 5955.*
***Dorm bed** $20 ($19 Nomads); **double/twin room** $65-99.*
***Credit cards** MC, Visa.*
***Reception open** 8am-6pm daily.*
🚌

Maintenance & cleanliness	★★★★
Facilities	★★★★☆
Atmosphere & character	★★★★☆
Security	★
Overall rating	★★★★☆

Travellers Backpackers Resort

Accommodation here consists of air-conditioned motel-style units with en suite. There is also a shared kitchen, TV lounge, Internet access plus a basketball court, volleyball court and a 15-metre swimming pool. The place has a good bar/bistro with pool tables and the shops and beach are also close by.

1 The Esplanade, Picnic Bay, Magnetic Island.
☎ *(07) 4778 5166 or 1800 000 290.*
Website *www.travellers-on-maggie.com.*
Dorm bed *$8-20; **double/twin room** $50.*
Credit cards *MC, Visa.*
Reception open *8am-midnight.*

Maintenance & cleanliness	★★☆
Facilities	★★★☆
Atmosphere & character	★★
Security	★★
Overall rating	★★☆

Cardwell

Cardwell is an idyllic beachfront town between Townsville and Mission Beach surrounded by farmland making it a good spot to stop for fruit picking work. Most of the travellers who don't come to pick fruit come here to visit Hinchinbrook Island.

Practical Information
Reef & Rainforest Centre
142 Victoria Street, Cardwell.
☎ *(07) 4066 8601.*
Website *www.gspeak.com.au/cardwell/.*
Open *8am-4.30pm daily.*

Coming & Going
Buses to Cairns and Townsville stop at the Seaview Café on Victoria Street (Bruce Highway).

Ferries between Cardwell and Hinchinbrook Island are operated by Hinchinbrook Ferries (☎ *(07) 4066 8270 or 1800 682 702; website www. hinchinbrookferries.com.au).* A day return fare costs $85 and they can drop you off at Ramsay Bay at the northern end of the Thorsborne Trail for $59. Transport between the other end of the trail and the mainland costs $46 and is operated by Hinchinbrook Wilderness Safaris (☎ *(07) 4777 8307).*

Accommodation
Cardwell Backpackers Hostel
This hostel caters primarily to travellers on a working holiday and the management can help find work on farms in the area. There are good facilities that include a swimming pool, trampoline, pool table, TV lounge, Internet access, kitchen, a barbecue area and a bar. Guests have free use of bicycles and fishing gear and the atmosphere is pretty good.

178 Bowen Street, Cardwell.
☎ *(07) 4066 8014.*
Dorm bed *$15.40-16.50.*
Reception open *9am-midnight daily.*

Maintenance & cleanliness	★★★
Facilities	★★★★☆
Atmosphere & character	★★★★☆
Security	☆
Overall rating	★★★

Cardwell Beach Backpackers
Cardwell Beach Backpackers occupies a former motel inside the Sunrise Village Motel & Van Park. It has clean accommodation with en suite bathrooms but there aren't a lot of shared facilities

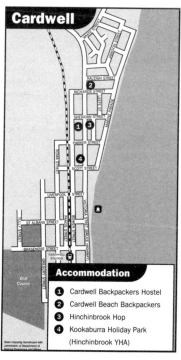

Cardwell

Accommodation
1. Cardwell Backpackers Hostel
2. Cardwell Beach Backpackers
3. Hinchinbrook Hop
4. Kookaburra Holiday Park (Hinchinbrook YHA)

Base mapping reproduced with permission of Department of Natural Resources and Mines

Queensland

other than the swimming pool in the adjoining caravan park.
212-220 Victoria Street, Cardwell.
☎ *(07) 4066 8800 or 1800 886 033.*
Dorm bed *$15.*
Credit cards *MC, Visa.*
🚗

Maintenance & cleanliness	★★★
Facilities	★★
Atmosphere & character	☆
Security	★
Overall rating	★★

Hinchinbrook Hop

Hinchinbrook Hop is a small hostel with accommodation in cute little rooms. Guests have use of caravan park facilities that include a swimming pool and barbecue area.
186 Victoria Street, Cardwell.
☎ *(07) 4066 8671.*
Dorm bed *$14.*
Credit cards *MC, Visa.*
Reception open *6am-9pm daily.*

Maintenance & cleanliness	★★★
Facilities	★★☆
Atmosphere & character	★★☆
Security	★
Overall rating	★★

Kookaburra Holiday Park (Hinchinbrook YHA)

This is a nice youth hostel in a caravan park that caters to short-term guests rather than workers. Dormitories are air-conditioned and facilities include a kitchen, Internet access and a swimming pool. Guests have free use of bicycles and sports equipment. It is a good spot to organise trips to Hinchinbrook Island.
175 Victoria Street, Cardwell.
☎ *(07) 4066 8648.*
Website *www.kookaburraholidaypark. com.au.*
Dorm bed *$19 ($18 YHA);* **single room** *$35;* **double/twin room** *$40.*
Credit cards *Amex, MC, Visa.*
Reception open *8am-6pm daily; late check in by prior arrangement.*
🚗

Maintenance & cleanliness	★★★★☆
Facilities	★★★
Atmosphere & character	★★☆
Security	★
Overall rating	★★★

Sights
Historic Cardwell Post Office & Telegraph Station

Cardwell's old post office has been restored and reopened as a museum. The museum features exhibits on local history with displays on the construction of the telegraph and the road and rail lines.
53 Victoria Street, Cardwell.
☎ *(07) 4066 2412.*
Admission *free.*
Open *Tue-Thu 10am-1pm, Sat 9am-noon.*

Hinchinbrook Island

Hinchinbrook Island is Australia's largest island national park and it is home to a diverse natural habitat that encompasses mountains, rainforest and the Great Barrier Reef World Heritage Area.

The Thorsborne Trail is the highlight of the island but there are also shorter hiking trails that are ideal if you're just visiting for the day.

Coming & Going

Ferries between Cardwell and Hinchinbrook Island are operated by Hinchinbrook Ferries (☎ *(07) 4066 8270 or 1800 682 702;* **website** *www.hinchinb rookferries.com.au*). A day return fare costs $85 and they can drop you off at Ramsay Bay at the northern end of the Thorsborne Trail for $59.

Transport between the mainland and the George Point end of the trail costs $46 and is operated by Hinchinbrook Wilderness Safaris (☎ *(07) 4777 8307*).

Hiking

Hinchinbrook Island has some great hiking trails and the highlight is the brilliant Thorsborne Trail.

THE THORSBORNE TRAIL

This 32km trail is a fairly difficult track, recommended for experienced hikers. Permits are required to hike the trail and it's best to apply in advance as only a maximum of 40 people are permitted on the trail at any time. Most hikers take at least four days and three nights to complete the trail. Permits are available from the Rainforest and Reef Centre in Cardwell.

You can hike the trail in either direction but the north to south direction is described below:

Ramsay Bay to Little Ramsay Bay
(6.5km, 4½hrs)
The ferry from Cardwell drops you at Ramsay Bay and the trail starts out by following the beach southward and then going through tall forest and mangrove swamps to Nina Bay where there is a campsite with toilets. From Nina Bay the trail follows the headland to Boulder Bay, where green sea turtles can often be seen and then heads over a ridge to the campsite at Little Ramsay Bay.

Little Ramsay Bay to Zoe Bay
(10.5km, 6hrs)
The trail follows the coast past Little Ramsay Bay to Banksia Bay and then heads inland through open forest and rainforest. Parts of this section of the track towards the Zoe Bay campsite pass swampy areas and involve several creek crossings.

Zoe Bay to Mulligan Falls
(7.5km, 4½hrs)
After leaving Zoe Bay the trail follows South Zoe Creek and passes Zoe Falls. It then goes inland and crosses Diamantina Creek shortly before arriving at Mulligan Falls campsite.

Mulligan Falls to George Point
(7.5km, 2½hrs)
The final leg of the track starts in rainforest but is mostly a beach walk along Mulligan Bay.

Mission Beach

Around mid-way between Townsville and Cairns, Mission Beach is fast becoming another hot backpacking destination in the same mould as Airlie Beach. This beautiful beach stretches for 14km and has a great laid back feel and is the perfect spot to kick back and relax for a week or so.

Like many other beachfront towns, there aren't a lot of attractions, although it is close to the Tully River and hostels in town can book you on a white water rafting trip on the Tully. The Mission Beach region is also home to some great rainforest and is one of the few places where you stand a good chance of seeing the endangered cassowary in the wild.

Mission Beach is also the gateway to nearby Dunk Island, which is only 10 minutes away by ferry and close enough to kayak to.

Practical Information
Wet Tropics Visitor Information Centre
Porter Promenade, Mission Beach.
☎ *(07) 4068 7099.*
Website *www.missionbch.com.*
Open *9am-5.30pm daily.*

Coming & Going
McCafferty's/Greyhound coaches stop at Island Coast Travel in the centre of Mission Beach. Premier stops at the Mission Beach Resort in Wongaling Beach. The closest train station is in Tully.

Local Transport
For a small town Mission Beach is spread out over a wide area and it is necessary to either drive or catch a bus to get from one end to the other. Mission Beach Bus Service (☎ *(07) 4068 7400)* operates a route between Bingil Bay and South Mission Beach. The fare varies from $1.50 to $6.

Accommodation
Beach Shack
The Beach Shack is a big house across the road from the beach and it is a good place to stay with extensive facilities and a great atmosphere. It features spacious dorms, two with en suite spa baths; a big TV lounge with surround-sound TV; a fully equipped kitchen; an outdoor pool room/balcony with sea views and a nice outdoor area with barbecue and a swimming pool. Guests have free use of bicycles, fishing and snorkel gear. Free apple crumble and ice cream is served every second night.
86 Porter Promenade, Mission Beach.
☎ *(07) 4068 7783 or 1800 333 115.*

Dorm bed $18; double room $45; twin room $40.
Credit cards MC, Visa.
Reception open 7am-9pm daily.

Maintenance & cleanliness	★★★★✩
Facilities	★★★★
Atmosphere & character	★★★★★
Security	-
Overall rating	★★★★

Bingil Bay Backpackers Resort

This is a former motel that features a bar/bistro with live music and a pool table and also a swimming pool with fantastic ocean views. There is also a TV lounge and very basic kitchen facilities. All rooms have en suite bathrooms.

The Esplanade, via Cutten Street, Bingil Bay.
☎ *(07) 4068 7208.*
Dorm bed $20; double room $50-65.
Reception open 8am-6pm daily.

Maintenance & cleanliness	★★★✩
Facilities	★★★
Atmosphere & character	★★★
Security	★
Overall rating	★★★✩

Mission Beach Backpackers Lodge

Mission Beach Backpackers Lodge has an outdoor area with a swimming pool, volleyball court and barbecues and there is also the usual kitchen, TV lounge and fast satellite Internet access.

28 Wongaling Beach Road, Wongaling Beach.
☎ *(07) 4068 8317.*
Dorm bed $18 ($17 VIP/YHA); double room $38-46 ($36-44 VIP/YHA).
Credit cards MC, Visa.
Reception open 7.30am-7pm daily.

Maintenance & cleanliness	★★★✩
Facilities	★★★
Atmosphere & character	★★★
Security	✩
Overall rating	★★★✩

Mission Beach Resort

The Mission Beach Resort has a large range of accommodation including an area set aside for backpackers. The backpackers' area is set around a very nice swimming pool in a resort-style setting, but the TVs in the rooms detract from the atmosphere. There is a small kitchen, a bar/restaurant with a $12.95 buffet deal and Internet access.

Wongaling Beach Road, Wongaling Beach.
☎ *(07) 4068 8288.*
Dorm bed $19; double room $70.
Credit cards Amex, Diners, MC, Visa.
Reception open 7am-9pm daily.

Maintenance & cleanliness	★★★★
Facilities	★★★
Atmosphere & character	★
Security	★
Overall rating	★★★

Mission Beach Retreat

This is a small hostel that is clean and well maintained. Facilities include an open-air kitchen and TV lounge, Internet access and a swimming pool. It is the most centrally located of the Mission Beach hostel.

49 Porters Promenade, Mission Beach.
☎ *(07) 4088 6229 or 1800 001 056.*
Dorm bed $19 ($18 YHA); double room $40; twin room $37-39.
Reception open 7.30am-noon & 4.30pm-7pm daily.

Maintenance & cleanliness	★★★
Facilities	★★★✩
Atmosphere & character	★★★✩
Security	★★✩
Overall rating	★★★✩

Sanctuary Retreat

This is a quiet place set among 50 acres of rainforest. Accommodation is in elevated cabins with screen walls, verandas and ceiling fans. It is a romantic option for couples that want to experience the rainforest and wildlife, which includes goannas and cassowaries. Facilities include Internet access, a kitchen, swimming pool and a bar that serves meals. It is in rainforest, about a 10-minute drive from the centre of Mission Beach. You can't drive all the way to the retreat, instead you have to park your car 600 metres away and hike through the rainforest or call to be picked up by 4WD.

Holts Road, Bingil Bay.

☎ *(07) 4088 6064 or 1800 777 012.*
Website www.sanctuaryatmission.com.
Bed in a two-bed dorm $29.50;
double room $60-135; twin room $59.
Credit cards Amex, Diners, MC, Visa.
Reception open 8am-9pm daily.
☎

Maintenance & cleanliness	★★★★★
Facilities	★★★
Atmosphere & character	★★★★☆
Security	★
Overall rating	★★★★

Scotty's

Scotty's is a nice hostel centred on a swimming pool with lots of palm trees, hammocks and sun lounges. Facilities include an open-air kitchen, a TV lounge and Internet access. Some rooms could be a little nicer and the biggest dorms have 16 beds. The hostel has a laid back atmosphere around the pool and a party atmosphere in the bar, which has good value meals. Guests get two free drinks every night.
167 Reid Road, Wongaling Beach.
☎ *(07) 4068 8676 or 1800 665 567.*
Website www.scottysbeachhouse.com.au.
Dorm bed $18-22 ($17-21 ISIC/VIP);
double room $38-52 ($36-50 ISIC/VIP).
Credit cards MC, Visa.
Reception open 7.30am-7pm daily; 24 hour check in.
☎

Maintenance & cleanliness	★★☆
Facilities	★★☆
Atmosphere & character	★★★★★
Security	-
Overall rating	★★★

The Treehouse

The Treehouse is in a nice rainforest setting and it boasts a great laid-back atmosphere. The common areas are open to fresh breezes and there's a nice balcony overlooking the swimming pool. There are nice quiet areas with hammocks, sun lounges and comfy chairs to relax in. Facilities include a kitchen and a laundry with table tennis, but there's no TV. Some people may not feel comfortable using the communal showers.
Frizelle Road, Bingil Bay.
☎ *(07) 4068 7137.*

Dorm bed $20; double room $50;
camping $12 per person.
Credit cards Amex, Diners, MC, Visa.
Reception open 7am-8.30pm daily.
☎

Maintenance & cleanliness	★★☆
Facilities	★★★
Atmosphere & character	★★★★★
Security	-
Overall rating	★★★

Activities
HIKING

There are some good hiking trails around Mission Beach, including the Licuala Walking Track.

Licuala Walking Track

This popular 7.8km walk through the Tam O'Shanter State Forest gives you the opportunity to see the rare cassowary.

REEF TRIPS

A couple of companies run day trips to the Great Barrier Reef. The cheaper Thunder Cruises (☎ *(07) 4086 6007)*, charges $65 and gives you around five hours on the reef and Quick Cat Cruises (☎ *(07) 4068 7289)* cost $88 and give you around 3½ hours on the reef. Both companies include lunch, reef tax and pick up from hostels in the Mission Beach area.

SKYDIVING

The beach landing on either Dunk Island or Mission Beach makes this a popular spot for skydiving.

Jump the Beach
☎ *1800 638 005.*
Website www.jumpthebeach.com.
8000ft tandem skydive $215;
10000ft tandem skydive $263;
12000ft tandem skydive $311;
14000ft tandem skydive $359; plus compulsory Australian Parachute Federation Student License $25.

Paul's Parachuting
☎ *1800 005 006.*
Website www.paulsparachuting.com.au.
8000ft tandem skydive $209;
10000ft tandem skydive $258;
12000ft tandem skydive $307;

14000ft tandem skydive $356; plus compulsory Australian Parachute Federation Student License $25.

WHITE WATER RAFTING
The nearby Tully River has some of Australia's best rafting. See the Tully section (on pages 192-3) for more information.

Dunk Island

Dunk Island is easily accessible from Mission Beach. It is a typical tropical island with beautiful white sand beaches and well worth the excursion. The island is home to a National and Marine Park, although the eastern end of the island has a big resort. There are some good walking tracks including the Island Circuit (9.2km, 3hrs return) and Coconut Beach walk (6km, 2km return).

A Great Barrier Reef Marine Park tax ($4.50) is payable by all visitors to Dunk Island.

Coming & Going
Two companies operate ferries between Mission Beach and Dunk Island.

Dunk Island Ferry & Cruises (☎ *(07) 4068 7211; website www.dunkferry.com.au*) departs from Clump Point Jetty north of the centre of Mission Beach. They charge $29 return including free snorkelling.

Dunk Island Express Water Taxi (☎ *(07) 4068 8310*) departs from Point Banfield Parade, Wongaling Beach near Scotty's hostel. They charge $22 for a day return.

Coral Sea Kayaking (☎ *(07) 4068 9154; website www.coralseakayaking.com*) is by far the most fun way to get to the island. The $93 trip involves paddling out to the island and includes lunch and snorkelling gear.

Tully

People come to Tully for two things – work and white water rafting – although many travellers who come for the rafting are just passing through on day trips from Mission Beach and Cairns. No one comes here for the weather, as Tully is the wettest spot in Australia with an average annual rainfall of around four metres.

Work is available year round, mostly on banana farms.

Practical Information
Visitor Information Centre
Bruce Highway, Tully.
☎ *(07) 4068 2288.*
Open *Mon-Fri 8.30am-4.30pm, Sat-Sun 9.30am-2.30pm.*

Coming & Going
Tully is on the main train and coach route linking Brisbane and Cairns. Trains stop at the station on the Bruce Highway north of the Visitor Information Centre and buses stop in Banyan Park, near the Big Gumboot.

Accommodation
Banana Barracks and Rafters
Banana Barracks is popular with working travellers and it has extensive facilities compared to most other hostels that cater to workers. Most dorms have eight beds and include lockers and en suite.

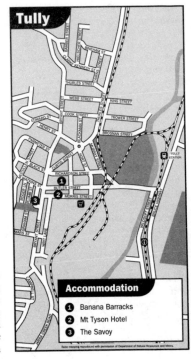

Accommodation
1. Banana Barracks
2. Mt Tyson Hotel
3. The Savoy

Facilities include a good kitchen, an outdoor barbecue area, Internet access, a volleyball court and a swimming pool. The hostel is home to Rafters Bar, which is the Tully base for R'n'R Rafting and is an excellent bar with pool tables, a beer garden and bistro.
50 Butler Street, Tully.
☎ *(07) 4068 0455.*
Dorm bed *$18 per night, $100 per week;* **double/twin room** *$36 per night, $200 per week.*
Credit cards *Amex, Diners, MC, Visa.*
Reception open *Mon-Sat 8am-6pm, Sun 8am-noon & 3pm-8pm.*

🚗

Maintenance & cleanliness	★★★
Facilities	★★★
Atmosphere & character	★★☆
Security	★★☆
Overall rating	★★★

Mount Tyson Hotel
There's very basic accommodation in four-share dormitories above this pub on Tully's main street, but not much atmosphere or shared facilities.
23 Butler Street, Tully.
☎ *(07) 4068 1088.*
Dorm bed *$15 per night, $80 per week.*
Reception open *Mon-Sat 10am-10pm, Sun 10am-7pm.*

Maintenance & cleanliness	★
Facilities	★★☆
Atmosphere & character	★★☆
Security	★★☆
Overall rating	★★☆

The Savoy Backpackers
This is a small, quiet and clean hostel with around 30 beds. It features a fully equipped kitchen, a nice swimming pool, Internet access, TV room and a pool table. Like other hostels in Tully, it caters almost exclusively to backpackers working around Tully.
4 Plumb Street, Tully.
☎ *(07) 4068 2400.*
Dorm bed *$17-18 per night, $95-100 per week.*
Credit cards *MC, Visa.*

Maintenance & cleanliness	★★☆
Facilities	★★
Atmosphere & character	★★
Security	★★
Overall rating	★★☆

Sights & Activities
Tully Sugar
The Tully Sugar Mill runs tours during the crushing season (Jun-Nov).
Book at the visitor information on the Bruce Highway.
☎ *(07) 4068 2288.*
Admission *$9.90.*

RAFTING
Tully is handy to the Tully River which is the country's best one day rafting experience and also the most popular rafting destination for backpackers. Two companies – R'n'R Rafting and Raging Thunder – offer rafting on the Tully River with transfers from as far a field as Port Douglas, however both Tully and Mission Beach are the cheapest spots to organise your rafting from.

Raging Thunder
☎ *(07) 4030 7990.*
Website *www.ragingthunder.com.au.*
One day trip *$145 + $20 park fee.*

R'n'R Rafting
☎ *1800 079 039.*
Website *www.raft.com.au.*
One day trip *$135 + $20 park fee.*

Innisfail
This sugar cane growing town is the last spot worth stopping on the way to Cairns. It is a handy base for whitewater rafting and fishing although it is also possible to find work on nearby farms.

Practical Information
INTERNET ACCESS
Flexi Cyber Café
38 Rankin Street, Innisfail.
☎ *(07) 4061 6250.*
Open *Mon 9am-6pm, Tue 9am-7pm, Wed 9am-6pm, Thu 9am-7pm, Fri 9am-6pm, Sat 10am-2pm.*

Coming & Going
Both buses and trains travelling between Cairns and Townsville stop at Innisfail. The train station is west of the town centre on Station Street. Buses stop closer to the town centre on Edith Street.

Accommodation
Codge Lodge

This is a nice old building with loads of character. It has large front and rear verandas, several kitchens, a TV lounge and a big swimming pool. Some accommodation is in the building next door, which is also clean but isn't as well maintained as the main building.
63 Rankin Street, Innisfail.
☎ *(07) 4061 8055.*
Dorm bed *$18 per night, $105 per week.*

Maintenance & cleanliness	★★★★☆
Facilities	★★★☆
Atmosphere & character	★★★★★
Security	★★☆
Overall rating	★★★★☆

Innisfail Backpackers Retreat

This clean hostel has good facilities that include a TV lounge, Internet access, pool table, a small kitchen and a swimming pool.
73 Rankin Street, Innisfail.
☎ *(07) 4061 2284.*
Dorm bed *$15 per night, $100 per week.*
🚐

Maintenance & cleanliness	★★★★☆
Facilities	★★
Atmosphere & character	★★★★☆
Security	-
Overall rating	★★★

Innisfail Budget Backpackers Hostel

This workers' hostel has a good atmosphere and facilities that include a TV lounge, Internet access, a pool table and two kitchens. The manager guarantees work and he will only take guests when work is available.
125 Edith Street, Innisfail.
☎ *(07) 4061 7833.*
Dorm bed *$18 per night, $105 per week.*
Reception open *Mon-Fri 6.30am-8am & 9.30am-noon, Sat-Sun 9.30am-noon.*

Maintenance & cleanliness	★★☆
Facilities	★★☆
Atmosphere & character	★★★
Security	★★☆
Overall rating	★★

Walkabout Motel & Backpackers

This hostel has a big kitchen and a common room with a pool table and TV. The accommodation is in converted motel units that each have a TV, fridge and air-conditioning.
20-24 McGowen Drive, Innisfail.
☎ *(07) 4061 2311.*
Dorm bed *$15 per night, $90 per week.*
Credit cards *Amex, Diners, MC, Visa.*
🚐

Maintenance & cleanliness	★★★☆
Facilities	★★
Atmosphere & character	★★☆
Security	★
Overall rating	★★

Sights
Johnstone River Crocodile Farm

This crocodile-breeding farm has over 1500 crocodiles as well as native animals including emus, kangaroos, wallabies and even two cassowaries.
Flying Fish Point Road, Innisfail.
☎ *(07) 4061 1121.*
Website *www.crocfarm.com.*
Admission *$16.*
Open *8.30am-4.30pm daily; tours begin 9.30am.*

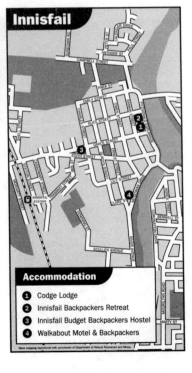

Innisfail

	Accommodation
①	Codge Lodge
②	Innisfail Backpackers Retreat
③	Innisfail Budget Backpackers Hostel
④	Walkabout Motel & Backpackers

Base mapping reproduced with permission of Department of Natural Resources and Mines.

Queensland

Sugar Industry Museum

The Australian Sugar Industry Museum gives you the facts about the history of the industry and how the fields of cane are processed into sugar.
Bruce Highway, Mourilyan.
☎ *(07) 4063 2656.*
Website www.sugarmuseum.org.au.
Admission $6.
Open Jan-Apr Mon-Fri 9am-5pm, Sat 9am-3pm, Sun 9am-noon; May-Oct Mon-Sat 9am-5pm, Sun 9am-3pm; Nov-Dec Mon-Fri 9am-5pm, Sat 9am-3pm, Sun 9am-noon.

Cairns

Cairns is a hugely popular backpackers' destination with over 40 hostels in the city and a great backpacker-oriented nightlife scene. Although it's a very touristy city, Cairns also has a relaxed and laid-back ambience and it is a fun place to visit.

Many travellers are disappointed with Cairns as there are no worthwhile attractions in the city centre and the closest beaches are in the northern suburbs, but there is now a big new lagoon on the Esplanade.

Cairns is a fantastic base for exploring the surrounding area and it is within easy reach of the World Heritage-listed Great Barrier Reef, rainforest and the vast wilderness of Cape York Peninsula.

Practical Information
INFORMATION CENTRES & USEFUL ADDRESSES
Cairns Visitor Centre
51 The Esplanade, Cairns.
☎ *(07) 4051 3588.*
Website www.tnq.org.au.
Open 8.30am-6.30pm daily.

Queensland Parks & Wildlife Centre
10 McLeod Street, Cairns.
☎ *(07) 4046 6600.*
Open Mon-Fri 8.30am-5pm.

INTERNET ACCESS
Global Gossip
125 Abbott Street, Cairns.
☎ *(07) 4031 6411.*

Website www.globalgossip.com.au.
Open 8.30am-11pm daily.

Travellers Contact Point
13 Shields Street, Cairns.
☎ *(07) 4041 4677.*
Website www.travellers.com.au.
Open 7am-midnight daily.

Coming & Going

Cairns is reasonably well connected to all forms of transport. There's a busy international airport as well as regular train, bus and ferry connections.

AIR
Cairns International Airport (☎ *(07) 4052 9744)* is located about 6km north of the city centre on Captain Cook Highway and handles frequent flights within Australia and is increasingly becoming a popular international gateway with flights from Asia and Papua New Guinea.

Many backpackers either arrive or depart Cairns by air and flights between Cairns and Alice Springs, Darwin and Sydney are often bundled with backpacker bus package deals.

Buses between the airport and the centre of Cairns run frequently and cost $4.50 although many hostels also provide a free shuttle service. Alternatively there's an Airport Shuttle (☎ *(07) 4048 8355)* that costs $8 between the city centre and the airport. A taxi between the airport and the city centre costs around $14 for up to four passengers.

BUS
The bus terminal is located at Trinity Wharf.

Coral Coaches (☎ *(07) 4031 7577)* have buses to Port Douglas, Cape Tribulation and Cooktown. McCafferty's/Greyhound coaches go to the Northern Territory. Both McCafferty's/Greyhound and Premier have buses going south to Sydney and Melbourne.

TRAIN
The train station is located between Bunda and McLeod Streets, next to the Cairns Central shopping centre. There are five trains a week down the

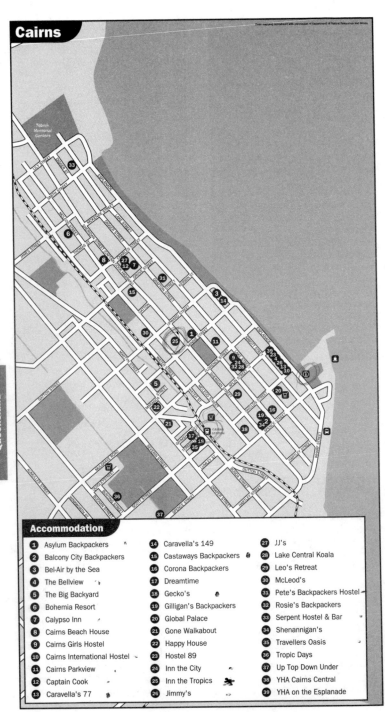

Cairns

Accommodation

1. Asylum Backpackers
2. Balcony City Backpackers
3. Bel-Air by the Sea
4. The Bellview
5. The Big Backyard
6. Bohemia Resort
7. Calypso Inn
8. Cairns Beach House
9. Cairns Girls Hostel
10. Cairns International Hostel
11. Cairns Parkview
12. Captain Cook
13. Caravella's 77
14. Caravella's 149
15. Castaways Backpackers
16. Corona Backpackers
17. Dreamtime
18. Gecko's
19. Gilligan's Backpackers
20. Global Palace
21. Gone Walkabout
22. Happy House
23. Hostel 89
24. Inn the City
25. Inn the Tropics
26. Jimmy's
27. JJ's
28. Lake Central Koala
29. Leo's Retreat
30. McLeod's
31. Pete's Backpackers Hostel
32. Rosie's Backpackers
33. Serpent Hostel & Bar
34. Shenannigan's
35. Travellers Oasis
36. Tropic Days
37. Up Top Down Under
38. YHA Cairns Central
39. YHA on the Esplanade

coast to Brisbane as well as daily trains to Kuranda.

FERRY

Quicksilver (☎ *(07) 4099 5500)* operate a daily ferry to Port Douglas that departs from the Marlin Jetty at the Pier Marketplace at 8am. The 1½-hour trip costs $24 one-way or $36 return.

HITCHHIKING

It's not too difficult finding a good hitching spot for a lift out of Cairns and there are usually plenty of other backpackers driving in and out of town that may give you a ride. It is easier, however, to put a notice up in the hostels around town asking for a lift or to use a web-based ride sharing service.

The Bruce Highway runs south from Cairns and the Captain Cook Highway heads north. Take bus 1, 1A or 1Z up the Captain Cook Highway for rides north to Port Douglas and Cape Tribulation or bus 1B south to the Bruce Highway for a lift down the coast.

BUG Ride *(website* http://australia. bugride.com) is BUG's own web-based ride sharing service; it allows travellers to both offer lifts and search for rides throughout Australia.

Local Transport

Local buses run by Sunbus (☎ *(07) 4057 7411; website* www.sunbus.com.au) operate from the Lake Street Transit Centre in City Place with many routes operating 24-hours. Fares start at $1.55 but longer trips can cost as much as $8.80. There are also three different all-day tickets that cost between $5.80 and $9.40 depending on the distance that you want to cover.

Accommodation
Asylum Backpackers

Asylum Cairns (formerly Tracks Hostel) offers basic facilities and it feels a little worn around the edges, but the management are making improvements to the place. In addition to the basic TV lounge and kitchen, there is a swimming pool and free Internet access. The main feature is the management, who go out of their way to look after guests and create a great party atmosphere.

They run a brilliant $10 pub-crawl on Monday nights that include a t-shirt, pizza and five drinks.
149 Grafton Street, Cairns.
☎ *(07) 4031 1474 or 1800 065 464.*
Website www.asylumbackpackers.com.
Dorm bed *$15;* ***single room*** *$30;*
double room *$38.*
Credit cards *Amex, Diners, MC, Visa.*
Reception open *6.30am-midnight; 24-hour check in.*
🚌

Maintenance & cleanliness	★★☆
Facilities	★★☆
Atmosphere & character	★★★★★
Security	★★☆
Overall rating	★★★☆

Balcony City Backpackers

This small hostel offers basic accommodation and the quality of the furnishings could be better. It is a friendly place with a nice balcony with pool tables, a TV lounge and a small kitchen.
42 Spence Street, Cairns.
🚌 *1, 1A, 1C, 1D, 1E, 1G, 1H, 1X, 7.*
☎ *(07) 4041 0866.*
Dorm bed *$15;* ***double/twin room*** *$40; includes dinner at the Piranha Bar.*
Reception open *Mon-Sat 9am-noon & 2pm-6pm, Sun 9am-noon.*

Maintenance & cleanliness	★
Facilities	★
Atmosphere & character	★★
Security	★★
Overall rating	★★☆

Bel-Air by the Sea

Accommodation here is pretty basic. The common areas are nice and include an open area underneath one of the hostel buildings with a pool table and TV lounge and an outdoor area with a swimming pool, barbecue, picnic tables and a spa. There are several kitchens dotted throughout the hostel. Bel-Air is situated at the quieter end of the Esplanade, within walking distance to the centre of Cairns.
155-157 The Esplanade, Cairns.
🚌 *5, 5A, 6, 6A.*
☎ *(07) 4031 4790.*
Website www.cairns.net.au/~haka/.
Dorm bed *$5-20;* ***double room*** *$36.*
Credit cards *MC, Visa.*

Reception open 7am-9pm daily.

Maintenance & cleanliness	★⯪
Facilities	★★
Atmosphere & character	★★
Security	★★
Overall rating	★★

The Bellview

This secure motel/hostel has good amenities including a TV lounge, kitchen and a swimming pool. It is a clean place but some furnishings are a little dated. All dorm rooms have an en suite bathroom plus a fridge and air-conditioning and there are also motel-style double rooms. The Bellview is a quiet hostel – look elsewhere if you want to party.

85-87 The Esplanade, Cairns.
🚌 *5, 5A, 6, 6A.*
☎ *(07) 4051 4377.*
Dorm bed $20; single room $35; double/twin room $45-59.
Credit cards MC, Visa.
Reception open 6am-10pm daily; 24 hour check in.

Maintenance & cleanliness	★★★
Facilities	★★
Atmosphere & character	★
Security	★★⯪
Overall rating	★★⯪

The Big Backyard

The Big Backyard is a clean and well-maintained hostel with a good atmosphere. The hostel consists of three renovated Queenslander-style houses, all with their own kitchen and bathrooms. Some rooms are air-conditioned while others are fan cooled. There's a laundry, drink machines, a cable TV lounge, free Internet access, a swimming pool and beach volleyball court.

34 Martyn Street, Cairns.
☎ *(07) 4031 3133 or 1800 025 070.*
Website www.backyard.com.au.
Dorm bed $15-18; double room $30-36; includes dinner at the Woolshed.
Credit cards MC, Visa.
Reception open 7am-noon & 4pm-8pm daily.

Maintenance & cleanliness	★★★
Facilities	★★⯪
Atmosphere & character	★★★⯪
Security	★★
Overall rating	★★★

Bohemia Resort

This is an excellent purpose-built hostel with great facilities that include a good bar and a nice outdoor area with a swimming pool and pool table. There's also the usual kitchen, TV lounge and Internet access. Everything is very clean and it is one of the best hostels in Cairns, but it is further from the centre than most.

231 McLeod Street, Cairns.
🚌 *5, 5A, 6, 6A.*
☎ *(07) 4041 7290 or 1800 155 353.*
Website www.bohemiaresort.com.au.
Dorm bed $22; double/twin room $52-62.
Credit cards MC, Visa.
Reception open 7.30am-8pm daily; late check in by prior arrangement.
🚲🔒

Maintenance & cleanliness	★★★★★
Facilities	★★★★⯪
Atmosphere & character	★★★
Security	★★
Overall rating	★★★★

Calypso Inn

Calypso Inn is a fun hostel to stay at and it has a great atmosphere. Accommodation is in five separate houses each with its own kitchen and the hostel is clean and freshly painted. Facilities include fast ADSL Internet access, wake up calls, a nice outdoor area with a swimming pool and a pool table and an excellent bar with $7 all-you-can-eat meals.

5-9 Digger Street, Cairns.
☎ *(07) 4031 0910 or 1800 815 628.*
Website www.calypsobackpackers.com.au.
Dorm bed $21 ($20 VIP); single room $33 ($32 VIP); double/twin room $46 ($44 VIP).
Credit cards Amex, Diners, MC, Visa.
Reception open 7am-10pm daily.
🚲

Maintenance & cleanliness	★★★⯪
Facilities	★★★
Atmosphere & character	★★★★★
Security	★
Overall rating	★★★★⯪

Cairns Beach House

Cairns Beach House is a former motel on a busy road on the city's fringe.

Accommodation is in air-conditioned three-bed dormitories with en suite bathrooms. Hostel facilities include a small TV lounge and kitchen, Internet access, a salt-water swimming pool and a bar/restaurant where free meals are served each evening.

239 Sheridan Street, Cairns.
🚌 *1B, 1C, 1C, 1E, 1G, 1H, 1X, 7.*
☎ *(07) 4041 4116 or 1800 229 228.*
Website *www.cairnsbeachhouse.com. au.*
Dorm bed *$16-18;* **double room** *$40-42; includes dinner.*
Credit cards *Amex, Diners, JCB, MC, Visa.*
Reception open *7.30am-9.30pm daily.*
🚗

Maintenance & cleanliness	★★★
Facilities	★★★
Atmosphere & character	★★
Security	★★½
Overall rating	★★★½

Cairns Girls Hostel

This is a female-only hostel in the centre of Cairns. Facilities include two kitchens, two TV lounges, Internet access and a laundry. There are new fridges but most other furnishings are old. The décor is dated but it is kept clean. The dorms consist mostly of single beds.

147 Lake Street, Cairns.
☎ *(07) 4051 2016.*
Website *www.cairnsgirlshostel.com.au.*
Dorm bed *$16;* **twin room** *$36.*
Reception open *7.30am-9pm daily.*

Maintenance & cleanliness	★★★★½
Facilities	★★½
Atmosphere & character	★★
Security	★★½
Overall rating	★★

Cairns International Hostel

Cairns International Hostel is a good hostel with an excellent location on the Esplanade across the road from the lagoon. It is a large place that appears deceptively small from the reception area. Facilities include a kitchen, Internet access, a games area with a pool table and TV and a nice rooftop sundeck.

67 The Esplanade, Cairns.
🚌 *5, 5A, 6, 6A.*
☎ *(07) 4031 1545.*
Website *www.internationalhostel.*

com.au
Dorm bed *$19-22 ($18-21 VIP);* **single room** *$33 ($32 VIP);* **double room** *$48 ($46 VIP);* **twin room** *$46 ($44 VIP).*
Credit cards *MC, Visa.*
Reception open *7am-10pm daily.*

Maintenance & cleanliness	★★★
Facilities	★★½
Atmosphere & character	★★★
Security	★★½
Overall rating	★★★

Cairns Parkview

This poorly maintained hostel offers very basic accommodation. There are several kitchens, a laundry, Internet access, a TV room and a tropical garden area with a barbecue, picnic tables and a swimming pool.

174 Grafton Street, Cairns.
☎ *(07) 4051 3700 or 1800 652 215.*
Dorm bed *$17 ($15 VIP/YHA);* **single room** *$31 ($30 VIP/YHA);* **double/ twin room** *$38 ($36 VIP/YHA).*
Credit cards *MC, Visa.*
Reception open *7am-8.30pm.*

Maintenance & cleanliness	★
Facilities	★★
Atmosphere & character	★★
Security	★★½
Overall rating	★★½

Captain Cook Backpackers' Hostel

Captain Cook is a former motel that has very good facilities but the standard of accommodation is nothing special. Facilities include a tennis court, beach volleyball court, two swimming pools, a TV lounge, Internet access, a small kitchen and two bars. Guests get a free meal at the main bar, which has a good party atmosphere.

204 Sheridan Street, Cairns.
🚌 *1B, 1C, 1D, 1E, 1G, 1H, 1X, 7.*
☎ *(07) 4051 6811 or 1800 243 512.*
Website *www.backpacker-cairns.com.*
Dorm bed *$18-20 ($17-19 VIP);* **single room** *$25 ($24 VIP);* **double/ twin room** *$40-60 ($38-58 VIP); includes dinner.*
Credit cards *MC, Visa.*
Reception open *Mon-Fri 6.30am-8.30pm, Sat-Sun 6.30am-noon & 3pm-8.30pm.*

Queensland

Maintenance & cleanliness	★★☆
Facilities	★★★★☆
Atmosphere & character	★★★★
Security	★☆
Overall rating	★★★

Caravella's 77

Caravella's 77 offers clean accommodation with the usual facilities including a basic kitchen, Internet access and an outdoor TV lounge with pool tables and a swimming pool.
77 The Esplanade, Cairns.
🚌 *5, 5A, 6, 6A.*
☎ *(07) 4051 2159 or 1800 112 159.*
Website *www.caravella.com.au.*
Dorm bed *$21 ($20 VIP);* **single room** *$32 ($30 VIP);* **double/twin room** *$47-57 ($45-55 VIP).*
Credit cards *MC, Visa.*
Reception open *7.30am-10pm daily.*

Maintenance & cleanliness	★★★★
Facilities	★★★☆
Atmosphere & character	★★★☆
Security	★★
Overall rating	★★★

Caravella's 149

This hostel has clean but basic accommodation with several small kitchens and a big outdoor area with a swimming pool, pool table and plenty of picnic tables. All the rooms have fridges and air-conditioning and some have nice sea views.
149 The Esplanade, Cairns.
🚌 *5, 5A, 6, 6A.*
☎ *(07) 4031 5680.*
Website *www.caravella.com.au.*
Dorm bed *$17-20 ($16-19 VIP);* **double room** *$47-60 ($45-58 VIP).*
Credit cards *MC, Visa.*
Reception open *7.30am-10.30pm daily.*

Maintenance & cleanliness	★★★
Facilities	★★
Atmosphere & character	★★★☆
Security	★★
Overall rating	★★★☆

Castaways Backpackers

Castaways features accommodation in small dorms with single beds (no bunks). It also has the usual kitchen and TV lounge plus a swimming pool. Guests have free use of bicycles and free

Internet access.
207 Sheridan Street, Cairns.
🚌 *1B, 1C, 1D, 1E, 1G, 1H, 1X, 7.*
☎ *(07) 4051 1238 or 1800 351 115.*
Website *www.castawaysbackpackers.com.au.*
Dorm bed *$18 ($17 Nomads/VIP/YHA);* **single room** *$32 ($31 Nomads/VIP/YHA);* **double/twin room** *$40 ($38 Nomads/VIP/YHA); includes dinner at the Woolshed.*
Credit cards *MC, Visa.*
Reception open *7.30am-8pm.*

Maintenance & cleanliness	★★★
Facilities	★★★☆
Atmosphere & character	★★☆
Security	★
Overall rating	★★★☆

Corona Backpackers

This cheap centrally located hostel has limited facilities and accommodation in small three and four-bed dorms. There aren't many common areas to meet other travellers, which means this hostel doesn't have such a great atmosphere.
72 Grafton Street, Cairns.
☎ *(07) 4041 5288.*
Dorm bed *$14; includes dinner at the Woolshed.*

Maintenance & cleanliness	★★★☆
Facilities	★
Atmosphere & character	★
Security	★★
Overall rating	★★

Dreamtime

This hostel is in a beautiful old building in a tropical setting and it has loads of atmosphere. Inside there's a small kitchen and laundry. There's a swimming pool, spa and barbecue outside. The largest dorms have four beds and linen and towels are supplied. It is on a quiet street close to the train station and Cairns Central shopping centre.
4 Terminus Street, Cairns.
☎ *(07) 4031 6753.*
Website *www.dreamtimetravel.com.au/dt/.*
Dorm bed *$20;* **double/twin room** *$45.*
Credit cards *MC, Visa.*
Reception open *7.30am-noon & 4pm-8pm daily.*

Maintenance & cleanliness	★★★★★
Facilities	★★✫
Atmosphere & character	★★★★★
Security	★✫
Overall rating	★★★★

Gecko's

Gecko's is a good hostel with nice, spacious dorms with single beds (no bunks). Five of the double/twin rooms are air-conditioned and all the other rooms have fans. Other features include a nice kitchen, Internet access, a barbecue and a nice swimming pool set in tropical gardens.

187 Bunda Street, Cairns.
☎ *(07) 4031 1344 or 1800 011 344.*
Website www.geckosbackpackers.com.au.
Dorm bed *$19;* **single room** *$28;*
double room *$42-45.*
Credit cards *MC, Visa.*
Reception open *7am-noon & 4pm-8pm daily.*

Maintenance & cleanliness	★★★★★
Facilities	★★✫
Atmosphere & character	★★★★
Security	★★
Overall rating	★★★★

Gilligan's Backpackers

This brand new backpackers' hostel only opened in November 2003 and we were not able to see the finished hostel when we were reviewing the Cairns' hostels so it is not rated. It is a big flash 500-bed hostel in the city centre that features a bar, swimming pool, volleyball court and half-size soccer field.

57-89 Grafton Street, Cairns.
☎ *(07) 4041 6566.*
Website www.gilligansbackpackers.com.au.
Dorm bed *$24;* **double/twin room** *$68.*

Not yet rated

Global Palace

Global Palace is an excellent purpose-built hostel. Facilities include a fully equipped kitchen, an open-air common area with a pool table and a balcony overlooking the street. There's another common room with table tennis, another pool table and a big screen TV. There's also a rooftop swimming pool.

City Place, Corner Lake & Sheilds Streets, Cairns.
🚌 *all buses.*
☎ *(07) 4031 7921 or 1800 819 024.*
Dorm bed *$21-23 ($20-22 VIP);* **double room** *$52 ($50 VIP);* **twin room** *$50 ($48 VIP); includes dinner at PJ O'Brien's.*
Credit cards *MC, Visa.*
Reception open *7am-10pm daily.*

Maintenance & cleanliness	★★★★★
Facilities	★★★★✫
Atmosphere & character	★★★
Security	★★
Overall rating	★★★★

Gone Walkabout

This is a small quiet hostel with an outdoor area featuring a small swimming pool and barbecue. Other facilities include two kitchens and air-conditioning in all the rooms.

274 Draper Street, Cairns.
☎ *(07) 4051 6160.*
Dorm bed *$18;* **double/twin room** *$38.*
Credit cards *MC, Visa.*
Reception open *7am-1pm & 4pm-8pm daily.*

Maintenance & cleanliness	★★★★✫
Facilities	★★
Atmosphere & character	★★★★
Security	★★
Overall rating	★★★

Happy House

This is a good hostel catering to travellers on a working holiday with the average guest staying three months. The hostel features a nice TV lounge, a spa and laundry. Accommodation is in seven self-contained flats. Most rooms have a maximum of two people and some are air-conditioned. It's a popular hostel with couples staying long term in Cairns.

23 Maranoa Street, Cairns.
🚌 *1, 1A, 1C, 1D, 1E, 1G, 1H, 1X.*
☎ *(07) 4031 5898.*
Dorm bed *$105 per week;* **double room** *$210 per week.*

Maintenance & cleanliness	★★★
Facilities	★★✫
Atmosphere & character	★★★
Security	★
Overall rating	★★★✫

Queensland

Hostel 89

This hostel features clean bathrooms and quality dorms, each with a sink and air-conditioning. Facilities include two kitchens, a TV lounge and swimming pool. It has a great location on the Esplanade opposite the lagoon.

89 The Esplanade, Cairns.
☎ *(07) 4031 7477.*
Website *www.jimmys.com.au.*
Dorm bed *$22;* **double/twin room** *$48.*
Credit cards *Amex, Diners, JCB, MC, Visa.*
Reception open *7am-10pm daily.*

Maintenance & cleanliness	★★★★
Facilities	★★
Atmosphere & character	★★
Security	★★
Overall rating	★★★

Inn the City

Inn the City is located behind A1 Car Rentals on Lake Street in the centre of Cairns. It is a nice place with a secluded saltwater swimming pool, a volleyball court and barbecue area. There are several TV lounges and also a TV in each room.

141 Lake Street, Cairns.
☎ *(07) 4031 1326.*
Website *www.inn-the-city.com.*
Dorm bed *$18-22;* **single room** *$48;* **double room** *$48-78.*
Credit cards *Amex, Diners, JCB, MC, Visa.*
Reception open *7am-7pm daily.*

Maintenance & cleanliness	★★★
Facilities	★★★
Atmosphere & character	★★★
Security	★★★
Overall rating	★★★

Inn the Tropics

Inn the Tropics is a clean hostel with the usual kitchen, laundry and TV lounge. It has a nice outdoor area with a barbecue and a good swimming pool.

141 Sheridan Street, Cairns.
🚌 *1B, 1C, 1D, 1E, 1G, 1H, 1X, 7.*
☎ *(07) 4031 1088 or 1800 807 055.*
Website *www.innthetropics.com.*
Dorm bed *$18;* **single room** *$33-44;* **double/twin room** *$44-55.*
Credit cards *Amex, Diners, JCB, MC, Visa.*

Reception open *24 hours.*

Maintenance & cleanliness	★★★
Facilities	★★
Atmosphere & character	★★½
Security	★★★½
Overall rating	★★★½

Jimmy's

This quiet, clean hostel on the Esplanade features an outdoor lounge area with a barbecue and swimming pool. All the female dorms and most male dorms have en suite bathrooms and all rooms have coin-operated air-conditioning. There isn't much of a communal atmosphere and this isn't helped by the fact that most rooms have TVs.

83 The Esplanade, Cairns.
🚌 *5, 5A, 6, 6A.*
☎ *(07) 4031 4411.*
Website *www.jimmys.com.au.*
Dorm bed *$20-22;* **single room** *$40;* **double room** *$48-58;* **twin room** *$48.*
Credit cards *Amex, Diners, JCB, MC, Visa.*
Reception open *7am-10pm daily.*

Maintenance & cleanliness	★★★
Facilities	★★
Atmosphere & character	★
Security	★★
Overall rating	★★

JJ's

This hostel has a swimming pool, TV lounge, pool table, table tennis and a small kitchen. It's not as nice or as well maintained as most other hostels.

11-13 Charles Street, Cairns.
🚌 *5, 5A, 6, 6A.*
☎ *1800 666 336.*
Dorm bed *$16;* **double room** *$34.*
Credit cards *MC, Visa.*
Reception open *7am-noon & 4.30pm-7.30pm daily.*
🚌

Maintenance & cleanliness	★★½
Facilities	★★½
Atmosphere & character	★★★½
Security	★★½
Overall rating	★★

Lake Central Koala Beach Resort

Unlike Koala's other hostels, the Lake Central Koala Beach Resort is more of a motel than a hostel. There are no common areas, but each four-bed

Queensland

dorm has a TV and en suite bathroom. Compared with other hostels in town, this place has very little atmosphere or character and it's about a lively as a retirement home after 9pm on a Tuesday night.

137-139 Lake Street, Cairns.
☎ *(07) 4051 4933 or 1800 066 514.*
Website www.koalaresort.com.au.
Dorm bed *$25 ($24 VIP);* **double room** *$60-88 ($58-88 VIP).*
Credit cards *Amex, Diners, MC, Visa.*
Reception open *7am-10.30pm daily.*

Maintenance & cleanliness	★★★★★
Facilities	★★★½
Atmosphere & character	-
Security	★½
Overall rating	★★★

Leo's Retreat

Leo's has a lot of atmosphere and great big balconies. The accommodation is split between three buildings – one of them air-conditioned and the other two fan-cooled. There are mostly twin and double rooms and the largest dormitory has only four beds. The furnishings are old and facilities include a kitchen with lockers, Internet access and a backyard area with a swimming pool.

100 Sheridan Street, Cairns.
☎ *(07) 4051 1264 or 1800 080 809.*
Dorm bed *$16-19 ($15-18 VIP/YHA);* **double room** *$40-54 ($38-52 VIP/YHA); includes breakfast & dinner at PJ O'Brien's.*
Credit cards *MC, Visa.*
Reception open *7am-10pm daily.*

Maintenance & cleanliness	★★
Facilities	★★
Atmosphere & character	★★★
Security	★★
Overall rating	★★

McLeod's Backpackers' Hostel

This small hostel is slowly being renovated and some areas like the kitchen, common room and some downstairs areas are quite nice, but other parts of the hostel still need a bit of work. Facilities include a swimming pool plus the usual TV lounge and a small kitchen.

77 McLeod Street, Cairns.
☎ *(07) 4051 8883.*
Dorm bed *$16-17.*

Reception open *7am-7pm daily.*

Maintenance & cleanliness	★★★½
Facilities	★★
Atmosphere & character	★★★½
Security	★½
Overall rating	★★★½

Pete's Backpackers Resort

Pete's boasts Cairns' best hostel swimming pool and a big backyard with an outdoor TV lounge with a big screen telly. Accommodation is in three old Queenslander-style houses with new furnishings.

242-248 Grafton Street, Cairns.
☎ *(07) 4051 9166 or 1800 681 889.*
Website www.petescairns.com.au.
Dorm bed *$20 ($19 VIP);* **single room** *$25 ($24 VIP);* **double room** *$45 ($43 VIP);* **twin room** *$44 ($42 VIP); includes dinner at the Woolshed.*
Credit cards *Amex, Diners, MC, Visa.*
Reception open *7am-noon & 3.30pm-8pm daily.*

Maintenance & cleanliness	★★★★
Facilities	★★★
Atmosphere & character	★★★
Security	★★½
Overall rating	★★★★½

Rosie's Backpackers

This hostel is a former block of flats that has been converted to a backpackers' hostel. Accommodation is fairly basic and consists of units of two rooms and a bathroom. There's also Internet access, an outdoor TV lounge and a nice swimming pool.

136 Grafton Street, Cairns.
☎ *(07) 4041 0267 or (07) 4041 0249.*
Dorm bed *$18;* **double room** *$40-50; includes dinner at the Woolshed.*
Credit cards *MC, Visa.*
Reception open *7am-8pm dialy.*

Maintenance & cleanliness	★★★
Facilities	★★
Atmosphere & character	★★★
Security	★★
Overall rating	★★★½

Serpent Hostel & Bar

This big flash purpose-built hostel has all the mod cons including a bar, swimming pool, beach volleyball court, pool tables, a fully equipped kitchen and several TV rooms scattered throughout the hostel. Everything here is brand new and very clean. It's a long walk from the city centre but there is a courtesy bus into town every hour.

341 Lake Street, Cairns.

▣ *1B, 1C, 1D, 1E, 1G, 1H, 1X, 7.*

☎ *(07) 4040 7777.*

Website *www.serpenthostel.com.*

Dorm bed *$20 ($19 Nomads);* **single room** *$45 ($44 Nomads);* **double/ twin room** *$52-62 ($50-60 Nomads); includes dinner.*

Credit cards *MC, Visa.*

Reception open *7am-11.30pm daily; 24 hour check in.*

▣

Maintenance & cleanliness	★★★★★
Facilities	★★★★☆
Atmosphere & character	★★★★☆
Security	★★★★☆
Overall rating	★★★★☆

Shenannigans

Shenannigans offers very basic accommodation above a pub. Facilities are limited, but there's a nice balcony and it has a very central location.

Corner Spence & Sheridan Streets, Cairns.

▣ *1, 1A, 1C, 1D, 1E, 1G, 1H, 1X, 7.*

☎ *(07) 4051 2490.*

Website *www.shenanigans.com.au.*

Dorm bed *$16;* **double room** *$38-55.*

Credit cards *MC, Visa.*

Reception open *9am-6pm daily.*

Maintenance & cleanliness	★★☆
Facilities	★★☆
Atmosphere & character	★★
Security	★★☆
Overall rating	★★☆

Travellers' Oasis

This is a very nice hostel comprised of three renovated 'Queenslanders' set in lush tropical gardens with a swimming pool, outdoor seating and a barbecue. Accommodation is in clean rooms, some of which are air-conditioned. There are no bunk beds and all beds come with linen and towels. It's a quiet hostel with a relaxed atmosphere and no TV.

8 Scott Street, Cairns.

☎ *(07) 4052 1377 or 1800 621 353.*

Website *www.travoasis.com.au.*

Dorm bed *$20;* **single room** *$30;* **double/twin room** *$44.*

Credit cards *MC, Visa.*

Reception open *7am-noon & 4pm-8pm daily.*

♿

Maintenance & cleanliness	★★★★★
Facilities	★★★☆
Atmosphere & character	★★★★★☆
Security	★★☆
Overall rating	★★★★

Tropic Days

Tropic Days is a lovely hostel set in a beautiful old Queenslander-style building that has been restored with polished hardwood floors. Accommodation is in small dorms with single beds (not bunks), most dorms have three beds and the biggest has four beds. It has a nice backyard with hammocks, a barbecue and a swimming pool. There's also a TV lounge, a quiet lounge with no TV and a couple of fully equipped kitchens. Although quiet, this hostel has a great atmosphere. It's located in a quiet residential street, about a 20-minute walk from the city centre. The hostel runs a courtesy bus so you don't always have to walk.

26-28 Bunting Street, Cairns.

▣ *1, 1A, 1C, 1D, 1E, 1G, 1H, 1X, 7.*

☎ *(07) 4041 1521.*

Website *www.tropicdays.com.au.*

Dorm bed *$20;* **double/twin room** *$45;* **camping** *$11 per person; includes dinner at the Woolshed.*

Credit cards *MC, Visa.*

Maintenance & cleanliness	★★★★★
Facilities	★★★☆
Atmosphere & character	★★★★★
Security	★★☆
Overall rating	★★★★

Up Top Down Under

This hostel's appearance from the street isn't much but once you get inside you'll discover that it is quite a nice complex with a pool table, kitchen, barbecue, several TV lounges, Internet access and a nice swimming pool.

164-170 Spence Street, Cairns.

▣ *7.*

☎ *(07) 4051 3636 or 1800 243 944.*

Website *www.uptopdownunder.com.au.*

*Dorm bed $18 ($17 ISIC/VIP/YHA);
single room $34 ($33 ISIC/VIP/
YHA); double/twin room $40 ($38
ISIC/VIP/YHA); includes dinner at the
Woolshed.*
Credit cards Amex, JCB, MC, Visa.
Reception open 7.30am-8pm.

Maintenance & cleanliness	★★★
Facilities	★★★½
Atmosphere & character	★★★½
Security	★★½
Overall rating	★★★½

Utopia Cairns
Backpackers Resort

This former motel is built around a
courtyard with a swimming pool, palm
trees and sun lounges. Accommodation
is in three, four and six-share rooms, all
with air-conditioning, en suite bathrooms, fridge and telephone. Utopia is
the least central of all Cairns' hostels.
It is on a service road of the busy Bruce
Highway on the edge of town, 7km (10
minutes by bus) from the city centre, but
the hostel runs a courtesy bus runs into
town every hour.
702 Bruce Highway, Woree.
🚌 *1, 1A, 1C, 1D, 1E, 1G, 1H, 1X.*
☎ *(07) 4054 4444.*
*Dorm bed $18 ($17 Nomads/VIP);
double room $42 ($40 Nomads/VIP);
includes breakfast.*
Credit cards MC, Visa.
*Reception open 7am-11am & 3pm-
9pm daily.*

Maintenance & cleanliness	★★★
Facilities	★★★
Atmosphere & character	★★★½
Security	★
Overall rating	★★★

YHA Cairns Central

This hostel, opposite Cairns Central
shopping centre, has been recently
remodelled. It features a swimming
pool, two spa pools, a TV lounge with
big screen TV and surround sound plus
a kitchen and a games area with pool
table and foosball. The newer section
features en suite bathrooms but rooms
in the older section have shared bathrooms.
20-24 McLeod Street, Cairns.

🚌 *1, 1A, 1C, 1D, 1E, 1H, 1X.*
☎ *(07) 4051 0772.*
*Dorm bed $24.50-26.50 ($21-23
YHA); double/twin room $57-65
($50-58 YHA).*
Credit cards MC, Visa.
Reception open 6.30am-11pm daily.

Maintenance & cleanliness	★★★★★
Facilities	★★★
Atmosphere & character	★★★
Security	★★★★
Overall rating	★★★★

YHA on the Esplanade

This youth hostel offers basic, but clean
accommodation in air-conditioned
rooms. Facilities are limited to the
usual kitchen, laundry and TV room.
This hostel has a great location right on
the Esplanade in the centre of Cairns.
93 The Esplanade, Cairns.
🚌 *5, 5A, 6, 6A.*
☎ *(07) 4031 1919.*
*Dorm bed $22.50 ($20 YHA);
double/twin room $49 ($44 YHA).*
Credit cards MC, Visa.
Reception open 7am-10.30pm daily.

Maintenance & cleanliness	★★★
Facilities	★★½
Atmosphere & character	★★½
Security	★★★½
Overall rating	★★★½

Eating & Drinking

Cairns is a good spot for cheap eats and
it has pretty good nightlife for a small
city. There is a thriving backpacker
scene here with a bunch of bars and
pubs catering to the backpacker market
that operate shuttle buses with pick up
service from local hostels.

The four main backpacker bars are
PJ O'Brien's *(87 Lake Street, Cairns;*
☎ *(07) 4031 5333)*, Shenannigans
*(Corner Spence & Sheridan Streets,
Cairns;* ☎ *(07) 4051 2490; website
www.shenannigans.com.au)*, Sports Bar
(33 Spence Street, Cairns; ☎ *(07) 4041
2533)* and the Woolshed *(24 Shields
Street, Cairns;* ☎ *(07) 4031 6304;
website www.thewoolshed.com.au)*. The
Woolshed is the biggest and most popular of these four places and many hostels
give out vouchers for free meals here.
Some hostels also hand out vouchers for
free meals at the Sports Bar, which gets

a mixed crowd of both backpackers and locals. PJ O'Brien's and Shenannigans are both Irish pubs, PJ O'Brien's is the more popular of the two and guests at the Global Palace get free meal vouchers here.

There are also several hostels with their own bars, including Calypso, Captain Cook, Cairns Beach House, Serpents and Utopia. The Zanzibar, at Calypso Backpackers, is the best of the hostel bars and it features $7 all-you-can-eat meals.

Good value fast food is easy to find with several food courts around the city including one near the night market on the Esplanade as well as one in the Cairns Central shopping centre.

The Woolworths supermarket on Abbot Street and the Bi-Lo and Coles Supermarkets in the Cairns Central shopping centre are the places to go if you're preparing your own food.

Sights

Cairns' city centre doesn't have very much in the way of sights and most travellers use it mainly as a base for exploring the Great Barrier Reef and the surrounding region.

Cairns Museum

This is a small museum with exhibits on local history.
Corner Lake & Shields Streets, Cairns.
🚌 *all buses.*
☎ *(07) 4051 5582.*
Website *www.cairnsmuseum.org.au.*
Admission *$4.*
Open *Mon-Sat 10am-3pm.*

Cairns Regional Art Gallery

This central gallery has exhibitions of works by local artists and it also hosts a programme of temporary exhibits.
Corner Abbot & Shields Streets, Cairns.
☎ *(07) 4031 6865.*
Website *www.cairnsregionalgallery. com.au.*
Admission *$4.*
Open *Mon-Sat 10am-5pm, Sun 1pm-5pm.*

Flecker Botanic Gardens

Cairns' botanic gardens feature a variety of tropical plants and a board-walk through wetlands. There is also a rainforest boardwalk across the road in Centenary Lakes.
Collins Avenue, Edge Hill.
🚌 *7.*
☎ *(07) 4044 3398.*
Admission *free.*
Open *Mon-Sat 7.30am-5.30pm, Sat-Sun 8.30am-5.30pm.*

Reef Teach

The Reef Teach slide show and lecture provides an entertaining and educational insight into the reef. It is highly recommended if you plan on diving or snorkelling on the Great Barrier Reef
14 Spence Street, Cairns.
☎ *(07) 4031 7794.*
Website *www.reefteach.com.au.*
Admission *$13.*
Show *Mon-Sat 6.15pm.*

Royal Flying Doctor Service

Cairns is the Royal Flying Doctors Service regional office for northern Queensland and like most other branches of the RFDS, there is a visitors' centre with a small museum about the service.
1 Junction Street, Edge Hill.
🚌 *5A, 6, 6A, 7.*
☎ *(07) 4053 5687.*
Website *www.flyingdoctorqueensland. com.*
Admission *$5.50.*
Open *Mon-Sat 9am-4.30pm; tours depart every half-hour.*

Tanks Arts Centre

This arts centre is housed among three oil tanks and features excellent exhibitions of local art and also a market is held here on the last Sunday of each month during the Dry Season (June-November).
46 Collins Avenue, Edge Hill.
🚌 *7.*
☎ *(07) 4032 2349.*
Website *www.cityofcairns.qld.gov.au/ council/services/tanks_art_centre.html.*
Open *Mon-Fri 11am-4pm.*

Tjapukai Aboriginal Dance Theatre

The Tjapukai Aboriginal Cultural Park at the base of Skyrail is home to the

Tjapukai Aboriginal Dance Theatre and there are also exhibits on Aboriginal culture.
Captain Cook Highway, Smithfield.
🚌 *1B, 1C, 1E, 1G, 1X, 2, 2A.*
☎ *(07) 4042 9999.*
Website *www.tjapukai.com.au.*
Admission *$29.*
Open *9am-5pm daily.*

Undersea World
This small aquarium near the Pier Marketplace offers the opportunity to swim with sharks.
Pier Marketplace, Cairns.
🚌 *5, 5A, 6, 6A.*
☎ *(07) 4041 1777.*
Website *www.iig.com.au/underseaworld/.*
Admission *$12.50, $85 to swim with the sharks.*
Open *8am-8pm daily, shark diving 3.30pm-8pm, shark feeding 10am, noon, 1.30pm, 3pm.*

Wild World
This wildlife park on Cairns' northern beaches is home to tropical Australian wildlife including scrub pythons, Boyd's rainforest dragons and various parrots. The park also features cane toad races and it is one of the few wildlife parks that give you the opportunity to hold a koala.
Captain Cook Highway, Palm Cove.
🚌 *1B, 1X.*
☎ *(07) 40455 3669.*
Website *www.wildworld.com.au.*
Admission *$24.*
Open *8.30am-5pm.*

Activities
While there may not be too much to see in Cairns, there's certainly plenty to do. Activities include bungy jumping, white water rafting and scuba and sky diving.

BUNGY JUMPING
AJ Hackett runs a popular bungy site north of Cairns with a 44-metre jump.
MacGregor Road, Smithfield.
☎ *(07) 4057 7188 or 1800 622 888.*
Website *www.ajhackett.com.au.*
Cost *jump $109; unlimited jumps $139; jump & Minjin Jungle Swing combo $138; unlimited jump, lunch &*

Minjin Jungle Swing combo $168.
Open *10am-5pm daily.*

DIVE COURSES
There are several companies that offer scuba dive courses that include several dives on the reef. These courses give you your PADI certification, which is essential for diving on the reef.

Most dive schools run several different courses but the open water courses are the most popular; these courses combine theory and pool dives with a couple of dives on the Great Barrier Reef. Open water PADI courses generally run over four to five days, the cheaper courses involve daily trips out to the reef and the more expensive course include accommodation aboard a boat on the reef.

You can still dive without PADI certification, but this will involve doing an introductory dive as part of a day trip to the reef. An introductory dive is a good way to find out whether diving is for you.

Cairns Dive Centre
121 Abbott Street, Cairns.
☎ *(07) 4051 0294 or 1800 642 591.*
Website *www.cairnsdive.com.au.*
Open water course *$297-550; open water & advanced course $726.*

Deep Sea Divers Den
319 Draper Street, Cairns.
☎ *(07) 4046 7333.*
Website *www.divers-den.com.*
Open water course *$300-550; open water & advanced course $730.*

Down Under Dive
287 Draper Street, Cairns.
☎ *(07) 4052 8300 or 1800 079 099.*
Website *www.downunderdive.com.au.*
Open water dive course *$290-550; open water & advanced course $730.*

Pro Dive
116 Spence Street, Cairns.
☎ *(07) 4031 5255.*
Website *www.prodive-cairns.com.au.*
Open water course *$325-650.*

Tusa Dive
Corner Shield Street & Esplanade, Cairns.

Queensland

☎ *(07) 4031 1028.*
Website www.tusadive.com.
Open water dive course $325-572

REEF TRIPS

Cairns has excellent access to the Great Barrier Reef and there's a huge range of trips available that offer both diving and snorkelling. Most reef trips depart from Marlin Marina.

Cairns Dive Centre

121 Abbott Street, Cairns.
☎ *(07) 4051 0294 or 1800 642 591.*
Website www.cairnsdive.com.au.
Snorkelling day trip $75; diving day trip $120 (includes two dives).

Compass Cruises

100 Abbott Street, Cairns.
☎ *(07) 4051 5777 or 1 800 GO REEF.*
Website www.reeftrip.com.
Snorkelling day trip $60.

Deep Sea Divers Den

319 Draper Street, Cairns.
☎ *(07) 4046 7333.*
Website www.divers-den.com.
Snorkelling day trip $75; introductory dive day trip $120-175; certified dive day trip $125-150.

Down Under Dive

287 Draper Street, Cairns.
☎ *(07) 4052 8300 or 1800 079 099.*
Website www.downunderdive.com.au.
Snorkelling day trip $75-95; introductory dive day trip $99-185; certified dive day trip $99-165.

Ecstasea

☎ *(07) 4041 3055*
Website www.reef-sea-charters.com.au
Snorkelling day trip $95.

Passions of Paradise

☎ *(07) 4041 1600.*
Website www.passions.com.au.
Snorkelling day trip $89.

Tusa Dive

Corner Shield Street & Esplanade, Cairns.
☎ *(07) 4031 1028.*
Website www.tusadive.com.
Snorkelling day trip $115; certified dive day trip $180.

JUNGLE SWING

AJ Hackett's bungy jump site is also home to the Minjin Jungle Swing. This involves being strapped into a harness suspended by stainless steel cables and swinging from 40 metres at 100km/h.
MacGregor Road, Smithfield.
☎ *(07) 4057 7188 or 1800 622 888.*
Website www.ajhackett.com.au.
Solo swing $70; twin swing $59 (per person); triple swing $39 (per person); bungy jump & Minjin Jungle Swing combo $138.
Open 10am-5pm daily.

SKYDIVING

Cairns is a popular skydiving destination and two companies offer tandem jumps.

Paul's Parachuting

☎ *1800 005 006.*
Website www.paulsparachuting.com.au.
8000ft tandem skydive $235; 10000ft tandem skydive $284; 12000ft tandem skydive $333; 14000ft tandem skydive $382; plus compulsory Australian Parachute Federation Student License $25.

Skydive Cairns

☎ *(07) 4031 5466 or 1800 444 568.*
Website www.skydivecairns.com.au.
8000ft tandem skydive $235; 10000ft tandem skydive $283; 12000ft tandem skydive $331; 14000ft tandem skydive $379; plus compulsory Australian Parachute Federation Student License $25.

WHITEWATER RAFTING

Cairns is a good base for rafting the Barron, Johnstone, Russell and Tully Rivers.

The Barron River (grade 3 rapids) is only a 20-minute drive north of Cairns, the Russell River (grades 3-4 rapids) is an hour south of Cairns and the Tully River (grades 3-4 rapids) – Australia's best one-day rafting trip – is over 1½ hour south of Cairns. If you're planning to visit Mission Beach or Tully is it cheaper to raft the Tully River from there.

The remote Johnstone River features World Heritage rainforest but it is only accessible by helicopter and it's a very expensive multi-day camping trip.

All rafting trips include transport from Cairns but require payment of an additional rafting levy (tax). The trips may be slightly cheaper if you drive to the rafting destination.

Foaming Fury
Foaming Fury runs half-day rafting trips on the Barron River and full day trips on the Russell River.
19-21 Barry Street, Cairns.
☎ *(07) 4031 3460 or 1800 801 540.*
Website *www.foamingfury.com.au.*
Barron River half-day trip *$81 plus $6 rafting levy;* ***Russell River full-day trip*** *$125 plus $10 rafting levy.*

Raging Thunder
☎ *(07) 4030 7990.*
Website *www.ragingthunder.com.au.*
Barron River half-day trip *$88 plus $20 rafting levy;* ***Tully River full-day trip*** *$145 plus $20 rafting levy.*

R'n'R White Water Rafting
R'n'R runs half-day trips on the Barron River and full-day trips on the Tully River. They also run multi-day adventures on the Johnstone River.
Corner Shields & Abbott Streets, Cairns.
☎ *(07) 4041 2272.*
Website *www.raft.com.au.*
Barron River half-day trip *$88 plus $20 rafting levy;* ***Tully River full-day trip*** *$145 plus $20 rafting levy;* ***Johnstone River*** *$630 (2-days)-$1200 (4-days) plus $17 rafting levy.*

Around Cairns
From Cairns, boats travel daily to Green Island, Fitzroy Island and the outer reef where visitors can peer through a diving mask or a glass-bottomed boat at numerous species of coral and marine life.

A short distance northwest of Cairns is Kuranda, a village in the rainforest, which makes a great daytrip. Inland from Kuranda is farming country and the Atherton tablelands.

Most travellers head north from Cairns to Cape Tribulation and the Daintree rainforest and stop at Port Douglas. Cooktown is as far north as most independent travellers go, as roads north of here require 4WD vehicles.

Green Island
This tiny coral cay, just 26km off the coast of Cairns, is a popular spot with day-trippers. The island is a national park and there is very good snorkelling.

It is best visited as a day-trip as accommodation on the island is expensive. Part of the resort has facilities for day-trippers.

Coming & Going
Great Adventures (☎ *(07) 4044 9944 or 1800 079 080; **website** www.greatadventures.com.au)* ferry passengers between Cairns and Green Island. Prices start at $50 return but full day trips cost $98 including lunch and use of resort facilities.

Fitzroy Island
Fitzroy Island is larger than Green Island. It is also a national park that offers good snorkelling. There are also a couple of hiking trails on the island and also some good beaches.

It is about the same distance from Cairns as Green Island but it is less crowded, cheaper to get to and a more popular destination for backpackers.

A $5 national park fee is payable by visitors to the island.

Coming & Going
Sunlover Cruises (☎ *(07) 4050 1333 or 1800 810 512; **website** www.sunlover.com.au)* operates ferry services to the island. A return trip costs $39.

Activities
Dive Courses
Several Cairns-based dive courses operate from here (see page 207 for more information).

Sea Kayaking
Raging Thunder runs daytrips to Fitzroy Island, which include the ferry

trip over and sea kayaking to the more remote parts of the island.
☎ *(07) 4030 7900.*
Website www.ragingthunder.com.au.
Cost $115 plus $10 land management fee.

Kuranda

A short distance northwest of Cairns is Kuranda, a village in the rainforest full of craft shops, galleries and restaurants. Kuranda is a popular daytrip from Cairns, partly because of the cool climate and relaxed feel of the town but more so because the cable car and train rides there offer breathtaking views.

Coming & Going
BUS
The cheapest option is the bus, which costs only $2-4. White Car Coaches (☎ *(07) 4091 1855)* operate a regular service from Cairns to Atherton, stopping at Kuranda along the way.

CABLE CAR
If you've slept in and missed the train, you can always take the Skyrail cable car (☎ *(07) 4038 1555; website www.skyrail.com.au)* – the world's longest gondola cableway that runs to Kuranda above the rainforest for 7½km from Smithfield, north of Cairns. It is possible to get off at points along the way to explore the rainforest.

The Skyrail Rainforest Cableway operates from 8am-5pm daily. As you would expect, this is an expensive transport option at $34 for a one-way, $49 return or $67 returning by train.

TRAIN
The train is the nicest way to travel from Cairns to Kuranda. The Kuranda Scenic Railway (☎ *(07) 4031 3636)* operates the historic train and the ride is so popular that many people rate the train trip higher than Kuranda itself, although others find the endless commentary a little irritating. Trains leave Cairns at 8.30am (daily) and 9.30am (Sun-Fri), returning at 2pm (Sun-Fri) and 3.30pm (daily). The train isn't cheap at $34 for a one-way ticket or $48 return.

Accommodation
Kuranda Backpackers Hostel
Kuranda Backpackers Hostel is comprised of two old Queenslander-style buildings in a relaxing setting near the train station. Facilities include a pool table, table tennis, a TV lounge, kitchen, a swimming pool and a spacious back yard. Accommodation is in big dorms crammed with rickety old metal bunk beds.
6 Arara Street, Kuranda.
☎ *(07) 4093 7355.*
Website www.kurandabackpackershos tel.com.
Dorm bed $18; single room $37; double/twin room $42.
Credit cards MC, Visa.
Reception open 9am-noon & 2.30pm-6.30pm daily.

Maintenance & cleanliness	★⯪
Facilities	★★
Atmosphere & character	★★⯪
Security	★
Overall rating	★★

Sights
Birdworld
This large aviary is home to Australia's largest collection of free flying birds representing almost 80 species.
Heritage Markets, Therwine Street, Kuranda.
☎ *(07) 4093 9188.*
Website www.birdworldkuranda.com.
Admission $12; $30 for a ticket that also allows admission to the Butterfly Sanctuary and Koala Gardens.
Open 9am-4pm daily.

Butterfly Sanctuary
Just like Birdworld, but with butterflies. There are regular guided tours that depart every 10-15 minutes.
8 Rob Vievers Drive, Kuranda.
☎ *(07) 4093 7575.*
Admission $13; $30 for a ticket that also allows admission to the Birdworld and Koala Gardens.
Open 10am-4pm daily.

Kuranda Koala Gardens
Just like the Butterfly Sanctuary, but with koalas.
Rob Vievers Drive, Kuranda.
☎ *(07) 4093 9953.*

Admission $13, an additional $13 if you want to hold a koala; $30 for a ticket that also allows admission to the Birdworld and the Butterfly Sanctuary.
Open 9am-4pm daily.

Kuranda Markets

The most popular attraction in Kuranda is the Kuranda Markets, which feature arts and crafts as well as clothing stalls.
Corner Therwine & Thooree Streets, Kuranda.
Admission free.
Open 8.30am-3pm daily, but it's best to visit Wed-Sun when the original markets are also open.

Atherton Tablelands

The Atherton Tablelands plateau is about an hour inland from Cairns. It offers a cooler climate and very different scenery to what you would find on the coast and features waterfalls, some great hiking trails and the opportunity to see wildlife including platypus and tree kangaroos.

The major towns on the tablelands include Mareeba, Atherton and Yungaburra.

Coming & Going

White Car Coaches (☎ *(07) 4091 1855)* operate a regular bus service from Cairns to Atherton.

There are also several tours that operate from Cairns that are a good option for travellers without a car; these include Bandicoot Bike Tours, On the Wallaby and Uncle Brian's. Bandicoot Bike Tours (☎ *(07) 4041 0100)* operates cycling tours on quiet back roads in the Tablelands with day trips costing $109. On the Wallaby (☎ *(07) 4091 3552; website www.onthewallaby.com)* run excellent tours including a one-day canoe tour ($80), one-day waterfalls tour ($80) or an overnight tour ($150) with accommodation at their hostel in Yungaburra. Uncle Brian's (☎ *(07) 4050 0615; website www.unclebrian.com.au)* have fun day tours for $85. All three tours get you to the waterfalls and give you the opportunity to see wildlife.

Accommodation
Atherton Travellers Lodge

Atherton Travellers' Lodge is a clean and well-maintained hostel catering to the working backpacker. Rooms open on to a balcony and all beds come with real mattresses and linen. Facilities include a TV lounge, free Internet access, a brilliant kitchen and a dining room with a pool table and log fire.
37 Alice Street, Atherton.
☎ *(07) 4091 3552.*
Dorm bed $18; double room $42.
Credit cards MC, Visa.
Reception open 7am-9pm daily.

Maintenance & cleanliness	★★★★★
Facilities	★★★☆
Atmosphere & character	★★★★
Security	★★☆
Overall rating	★★★★

On the Wallaby

On the Wallaby is a friendly hostel with a great atmosphere. It's a small hostel with a maximum of only 30 guests and everything is clean and well maintained. The kitchen is well equipped and there are also barbecues available. They organise platypus spotting, canoe trips and nocturnal wildlife walks.
34 Eacham Road, Yungaburra.
☎ *(07) 4050 0650.*
Website www.onthewallaby.com.
Dorm bed $20; double/twin room $45.
Credit cards MC, Visa.
Reception open 8am-1pm & 4pm-8pm daily.

Maintenance & cleanliness	★★★★★
Facilities	★★
Atmosphere & character	★★★★★
Security	-
Overall rating	★★★☆

Port Douglas

Port Douglas, about an hour's drive north of Cairns, is a laid back resort town. Although Port Douglas has developed into an upmarket resort, there are also some brilliant budget accommodation options, plus access to the reef and rainforest making it a quieter and more sophisticated alternative to Cairns.

Queensland

Coming & Going

Buses run between Port Douglas and Cairns, Cairns Airport, Cape Tribulation, Cooktown, Mossman and Weipa. Buses depart from the end of Dixie Street.

Local Transport

Coral Reef Coaches (☎ (07) 4098 2600) operate the local bus service that runs between Rainforest Habitat and the town centre. Fares are $3.50.

There is also a steam train that runs between the marina and the Radisson Resort, but it's hardly a route that many backpackers will be taking.

Accommodation

Dougies Backpackers

This is a nice resort-style place set among tropical gardens that boasts excellent facilities, which include a fully equipped kitchen, a couple of pool tables, an outdoor TV lounge, Internet access, a bar with a pool table, foosball and a swimming pool. All accommodation is air-conditioned, double rooms have fridges and TV and dorms have lockers.

111 Davidson Street, Port Douglas.
☎ *(07) 4099 6200 or 1800 996 200.*
Website *www.dougies.com.au.*
Dorm bed *$23 ($22 Nomads/VIP/YHA);* ***double/twin room*** *$65;* ***camping*** *$11 (one person), $20 (two people).*
Credit cards *MC, Visa.*
Reception open *7.30am-midnight daily.*
🚐

Maintenance & cleanliness	★★★★
Facilities	★★★✫
Atmosphere & character	★★★★✫
Security	★★
Overall rating	★★★★

Parrotfish Lodge

Parrotfish Lodge is a brilliant new purpose-built hostel with great facilities that include a bar, Internet access, pool tables and a clean kitchen. It also features a swimming pool surrounded by decking. Accommodation and facilities are of a high standard. Dorms have ex-Olympic Village bunk beds and all rooms have lockers, air-conditioning and en suites.

37-39 Warner Street, Port Douglas.
☎ *(07) 4099 5011 or 1800 995 011.*
Website *www.parrotfishlodge.com.*
Dorm bed *$23-26 ($21-25 VIP);*
double/twin room *$75-85 ($73-83 VIP).*
Credit cards *Amex, Diners, MC, Visa.*
Reception open *7am-9pm daily.*
🚐

Maintenance & cleanliness	★★★★★
Facilities	★★★
Atmosphere & character	★★★★
Security	★★✫
Overall rating	★★★★

Port o'Call YHA Lodge

This clean hostel has good facilities that include a swimming pool, restaurant, kitchen and Internet access. Accommodation consists of double rooms and four-bed dorms with en suite bathrooms and a larger bunkhouse with shared bathrooms.

7 Craven Close, Port Douglas.
☎ *(07) 4099 5422 or 1800 892 800.*
Website *www.portocall.com.au.*
Dorm bed *$21-25 ($20-23.50 YHA);*

Port Douglas

Accommodation

1. Dougie's Backpackers
2. Parrotfish Lodge
3. Port O'Call YHA

Base mapping reproduced with permission of Department of National Resources and Mines.

double room $89-99.
Credit cards MC, Visa.
Reception open 7.30am-7.30pm daily.
🚗

Maintenance & cleanliness	★★★★★
Facilities	★★★
Atmosphere & character	★★
Security	★
Overall rating	★★★⯪

Sights
Port Douglas Court House Museum
This small museum in Port Douglas's old courthouse has exhibits on local history.
Wharf Street, Port Douglas.
☎ (07) 4099 4635.
Admission free.
Open 10am-1pm daily.

Rainforest Habitat
Rainforest Habitat is an enclosed animal park in a rainforest setting, featuring 1600 animals and 180 different species.
Corner Port Douglas Road & Captain Cook Highway, Port Douglas.
☎ (07) 4099 3235.
Website www.rainforesthabitat.com.au.
Admission $24.
Open 8am-4.30pm daily.

Activities
DIVE COURSES
There are several Port Douglas-based companies that can teach you to dive. These include:

Quicksilver Dive
Marina Mirage, Port Douglas.
☎ (07) 4099 5050.
Website www.quicksilver-cruises.com.
Open water dive course $535.

Tech Dive Acadamy
1/18 Macrossan Street, Port Douglas.
☎ (07) 4099 6880.
Website www.tech-dive-academy.com.
Open water dive course $675.

REEF TRIPS
Several companies run trips to the outer Barrier Reef from Port Douglas, including:

Quicksilver Cruises
Marina Mirage, Port Douglas.
☎ (07) 4087 2100.
Website www.quicksilver-cruises.com.
Snorkelling day trip $120-174;
introductory dive trip $194-236;
certified dive day trip $184-219.

Wavelength
2/38 Wharf Street, Port Douglas.
☎ (07) 4099 5031.
Website www.wavelength-reef.com.au.
Snorkelling day trip $135.

Wonga Beach
This is the last town before the Daintree River and it's a good spot if you want to relax, explore the surrounding area or spot crocodiles on the Daintree River. It is a good alternative to Cairns and many of the activities that can be booked through Cairns or Port Douglas can also be booked from here.

Accommodation
Daintree Palms Beach Resort
This resort caters mainly to families so it isn't the place for you if you don't like loads of kids running around. It boasts a beautiful tropical setting by the beach with lots of palm trees. The complex includes a restaurant, nightclub, swimming pool, volleyball and tennis courts and a good bar. The largest dorm has 12 beds but the others are four-bed dorms.
17 Oasis Drive, Wonga Beach.
☎ (07) 4098 7871.
Website www.daintreepalms.com.
Dorm bed $20; *double room* $70.
Credit cards MC, Visa.
Reception open 8am-8pm daily.
🚗

Maintenance & cleanliness	★★★★★
Facilities	★★★
Atmosphere & character	★★⯪
Security	★
Overall rating	★★★⯪

Activities
Daintree River Cruises
A number of companies operate crocodile spotting cruises along the Daintree River. Cruises cost $15-28 and depart throughout the day. Cruise boat opera-

tors include Bruce Belcher's Daintree River Cruise (☎ *(07) 4098 7717)*, Daintree River Cruise Centre (☎ *(07) 4098 6115)*, Electric Boat Cruises (☎ *1800 686103)* and Nice n Easy Cruises (☎ *(07) 4098 7456)*.

Cape Tribulation

Cape Trib is as far north as most travellers venture on the East Coast before heading inland or back south. The scenery here is fantastic with spectacular World Heritage rainforest and pristine beaches.

Activities here involve crocodile spotting, sea kayaking and horse riding through the rainforest and along the beach. There are several excellent hiking trails around Cape Trib including guided rainforest walks where you can see the area's nocturnal wildlife.

There are no banks at Cape Tribulation although you can withdraw money by EFTPOS if you have an Australian bank account.

Coming & Going

Coral Coaches (☎ *(07) 4031 7577)* operate buses from Cairns and Port Douglas which stop at all the hostels, except Koala, and continue north to Cooktown.

If you are driving you will need to take the car ferry across the Daintree River, which costs $12 one-way or $20 return.

Accommodation
Cape Tribulation Beach House

This is a quiet hostel with a laid back atmosphere. It doubles as a resort for non-backpackers and it has an upmarket feel. The hostel is comprised of cabins set among the rainforest – most cabins have their own veranda out front but the cheaper dormitory cabins features a covered courtyard between the two rooms. There is a kitchen and an outdoor dining area with a barbecue and also a bar/restaurant, swimming pool and Internet access.
MS 2041, Cape Tribulation.
☎ *(07) 4098 0030.*
Dorm bed *$25-32;* **double room** *$70-125.*

Credit cards Amex, Diners, MC, Visa.
Reception open 7.30am-7.30pm daily.
☎

Maintenance & cleanliness	★★★★
Facilities	★★★
Atmosphere & character	★★★★☆
Security	★
Overall rating	★★★★☆

Club Daintree Koala Beach Resort

This Koala hostel has a lovely rainforest setting next to the beach at Cape Kimberley just north of the Daintree River en route to Cape Tribulation. It features a bar/restaurant with pool tables, a barbecue area and a swimming pool. Accommodation is in air-conditioned cabins with a veranda. There are also small dorms in permanently erected tents. It is located down a 5km unsealed road.
Cape Kimberley Road, Cape Kimberley.
☎ *(07) 4090 7500 or 1800 466 444.*
Dorm bed *$16-22 ($15-21 VIP);*
double room *$77-99 ($75-97 VIP);*
camping *$10-13 ($9-12 VIP).*
Credit cards MC, Visa.
Reception open 7am-9pm daily.
☎

Maintenance & cleanliness	★★★★☆
Facilities	★★★☆
Atmosphere & character	★★★★
Security	★★☆
Overall rating	★★★★☆

Crocodylus Village

This eco-retreat is set amongst the World Heritage-listed Daintree Rainforest. It's a quiet hostel best suited to those who want to experience the rainforest, with accommodation in cabins with tarpaulin walls, which are a bit like a cross between a tent and a cabin. Some dormitories are very large with around 20 beds. Facilities include a fully equipped kitchen, swimming pool and a bar/café with outdoor seating under a canvas canopy. Crocodylus is located about 30km south of the Cape, 3.5km from the beach at Cow Bay and 14km north from the Daintree River ferry.
Buchanan Creek Road, Cow Bay.
☎ *(07) 4098 9166.*
Dorm bed *$20 ($18 YHA);* **double cabin** *$75 ($65 YHA).*

Credit cards MC, Visa.
Reception open 5.30am-midnight.

Maintenance & cleanliness	★★★⯪
Facilities	★★⯪
Atmosphere & character	★★★★⯪
Security	⯪
Overall rating	★★★

PK's Jungle Village

PK's Jungle Village is a resort-style place that is built among lush tropical rainforest. Accommodation is comprised of log cabins, each with two eight-bed dorms. There is a big outdoor camp kitchen and dining room, a volley ball court, swimming pool and a good bar and restaurant with pool tables and Internet access.
PMB 5, Cape Tribulation Road, Cape Tribulation.
☎ *(07) 4098 0040.*
Dorm bed $25 ($24 VIP); *double room* $75-98 ($73-96 VIP); *camping* $12 ($11 VIP) per person.
Credit cards MC, Visa.
Reception open 7.30am-7.30pm daily.

Maintenance & cleanliness	★★⯪
Facilities	★★⯪
Atmosphere & character	★★★★⯪
Security	★★⯪
Overall rating	★★★

Cooktown

Unless you've got a 4WD, Cooktown is about as far north as you can get in Queensland. Captain Cook first visited the area when his ship, the Endeavour, ran aground in 1770 and the town's heyday was during the gold rush of the 1870s when thousands of miners briefly moved into town. Nowadays Cooktown is a sleepy, but fascinating town with a frontier feel to it and is close to the reef, rainforest and beautiful beaches.

Coming & Going

Coral Coaches run from Cairns every day except Mondays. The buses take the scenic Bloomfield Track through the Daintree Rainforest calling in at Cape Tribulation and Port Douglas. This route is recommended for 4WD vehicles only as it involves several river crossings. There is an alternate inland route if you're driving a regular car.

Accommodation

Pam's Place

Pam's Place is a nice hostel with a good atmosphere. It is set among tropical gardens and features a salt water swimming pool, a bar with a pool table and TV, Internet access and a fully equipped kitchen.
Corner Charlotte & Boundary Streets, Cooktown.
☎ *(07) 4069 5166.*
Dorm bed $19-20 ($18-19 YHA); *single room* $36 ($35 YHA); *double/ twin room* $47 ($45 YHA).
Credit cards MC, Visa.
Reception open 7am-11pm daily.

Maintenance & cleanliness	★★★★
Facilities	★★★
Atmosphere & character	★★★★
Security	★★
Overall rating	★★★★⯪

Sights

James Cook Museum

This museum contains artefacts relating to Captain James Cook including the original anchor and one of the cannons from the *Endeavour*. It also has exhibits on local history.
Corner Furneaux & Helen Streets, Cooktown.
☎ *(07) 4069 5386.*
Admission $7.
Open 9.30am-4pm daily.

Outback Queensland

This is an expansive landscape extending north from the New South Wales-Queensland border to the Burke and Wills Junction on the edge of the Gulf Country, a distance of some 1,600 kilometres.

Charters Towers

Although Charters Towers is located less than two hours inland from Townsville and it is not really the true outback, this town is the gateway to the outback and you'll pass through here if you're travelling between Townsville and the Northern Territory.

Gold was discovered here in 1871 making it Queensland's second largest city for a brief period. In its heyday in the 1880s, Charters Towers was home to Australia's first stock market. Although it's now only a shadow of its former self, the wealth generated by the gold rush is evident in the city's grand architecture.

Practical Information
Visitor Information Centre
74 Mosman Street, Charters Towers.
☎ *(07) 4752 0314.*
Website *www.charterstowers.qld.gov.au*
Open *Mon-Fri 8.30am-5pm.*

Coming & Going
Charters Towers lies on the bus and train routes between Townsville and Mt Isa. Trains only pass through here twice a week in each direction. Buses are much a much frequent alternative with daily coaches on the Townsville-Tennant Creek run.

The train station is located on Enterprise Road on the eastern edge of town while buses stop at the corner of Church and Gill Streets in the town centre.

Accommodation
York Street B&B
York Street B&B consists of a lovely old Queenslander-style house, but backpacker rooms are in the old building out the back. Accommodation is in small dorms with TVs in the rooms. It is a clean place but the bathroom and kitchen facilities are very basic. There is also a swimming pool.
58 York Street, Charters Towers.
☎ *(07) 4787 1028.*
Dorm bed *$17;* **double/twin room** *$45.*
Credit cards *Amex, Diners, JCB, MC, Visa.*
🚗

Maintenance & cleanliness	★★✬
Facilities	★★
Atmosphere & character	★★✬
Security	★
Overall rating	★★✬

Hughenden
This small town is a pleasant enough place to stop on the long drive between Townsville and Mt Isa. A lot of dinosaur fossils have been found in the region between here and Mt Isa and a Muttaburrasauras skeleton is on display at the dinosaur centre behind the information centre.

Practical Information
Visitor Information Centre
Gray Street, Hughenden.
☎ *(07) 4741 1021.*
Website *www.outback.sunzine.net.*
Open *9am-5pm daily.*

Accommodation
Grand Hotel Backpackers
This old pub has backpackers' accommodation upstairs. It's an old wooden building with lots of character and it also shows plenty of wear and tear although it is kept clean. It has a small TV lounge and a balcony looking over the dinosaur in the main street.
Corner Gray & Stansfield Streets, Hughenden.
☎ *(07) 4741 1588.*
Dorm bed *$15;* **single room** *$25;* **double room** *$35.*
Credit cards *MC, Visa.*
🚗

Maintenance & cleanliness	★★
Facilities	★★✬
Atmosphere & character	★★★
Security	★
Overall rating	★★

Richmond
Lying in the heart of Queensland's dinosaur country, Richmond is a good rest stop with an excellent marine fossil museum.

Practical Information
Visitor Information Centre
93 Goldwing Street, Richmond.
☎ *(07) 4741 3429.*
Open *8.30am-4.45pm daily.*

Accommodation
Richmond Van Park
This caravan park has backpackers' accommodation in prefabricated units

that feature two-bed dorms with made-up beds. It is a clean and well-maintained place but it is not set up in a manner that is conducive to meeting other travellers so it doesn't score well for atmosphere. Facilities are limited to a small kitchen.
109 Goldwing Street, Richmond.
☎ *(07) 4741 3772.*
Dorm bed $20; double/twin room *$40; camping $11-14 per site.*
Credit cards *MC, Visa.*

Maintenance & cleanliness	★★★½
Facilities	★★½
Atmosphere & character	★
Security	★
Overall rating	★★

Sights
Richmond Marine Fossil Museum (Kronosaurus Korner)
This excellent little museum has some of the world's best palaeontology artefacts including the Richmond Pliosaur, which many believe to be the best vertebrate fossil found in Australia. Another highlight is a 100 million year old dinosaur with its fossilised skin still intact.
93 Goldwing Street, Richmond.
☎ *(07) 4741 3429.*
Admission *$9.*
Open *8.30am-4.45pm daily.*

Mount Isa

Miles from anywhere, Mount Isa is the biggest town on the long road between Townsville and the Northern Territory. It is a busy mining town producing copper, lead, silver and zinc and doesn't hold much to entice the traveller to stay. Most backpackers stop for fuel and food and leave as soon as they can.

Practical Information
Visitor Information Centre
Centenary Park, Marion Street, Mt Isa.
☎ *(07) 4749 1555.*
Website *www.riversleigh.qld.gov.au.*
Open *Mon-Fri 9am-4.30pm, Sat-Sun 9am-noon.*

Coming & Going
Mount Isa is on the Barkly Highway, which connects Townsville with the

Northern Territory and it lies at the terminus of the train line from Townsville.

Campbell's and McCafferty's/Greyhound buses arrive at 29 Barkly Highway. The train station is located on Station Street in Miles End.

Accommodation
Traveller's Haven
This hostel has a dated feel with cracked lino floors, old curtains and creaky bunk beds. Although facilities are minimal, it does have a swimming pool in addition to the usual TV lounge, kitchen and Internet access.
Corner Pamela & Spence Streets, Mt Isa.
☎ *(07) 4743 0313.*
Dorm bed $20; single room $32; *double/twin room $46.*
Credit cards *MC, Visa.*
Reception open *6.30am-12.30pm & 5pm-7pm daily.*

Maintenance & cleanliness	★★½
Facilities	★★★½
Atmosphere & character	★
Security	★
Overall rating	★★½

Sights
Frank Aston Museum
This is an interesting museum with displays on local history, mining and Aboriginal culture.
Shackleton Street, Mount Isa.
☎ *(07) 4743 0610.*
Admission *$6.*
Open *9am-4pm daily.*

MIM Mine
The mine is Mount Isa's major attraction and the reason for the city's existence. Surface tours run six days a week. The underground tours stopped running in 2002, but are set to recommence at the Riversleigh Centre by mid-2003. It's a good idea to book ahead through the Riversleigh Centre if you want to visit the mine.
☎ *(07) 4749 1555 or 1300 659 660.*
Tours cost *$19.80.*
Tours depart *Mon-Sat 11am.*

Riversleigh Fossil Centre
The museum focuses on the world heritage Riversleigh fossil sites just north

of Mount Isa and features a huge replica fossil studded limestone outcrop, a simulated tropical rainforest recreating the Miocene period of 25 million years ago and many other displays.
Marian Street, Mt Isa.
☎ *(07) 4749 1555.*
Website www.riversleigh.qld.gov.au.
Admission $9.50.
Open Mon-Fri 9am-4.30pm, Sat-Sun 9am-noon.

Longreach

This small outback town is considered the major town in central Queensland and it has an impressive range of attractions considering its diminutive population.

Longreach was the original home of Queensland and Northern Territory Aerial Service (now known as Qantas), and the company was headquartered here until 1930.

Practical Information
Visitor Information Centre
Corner Duck & Eagle Streets, Longreach.
☎ *(07) 4658 3555.*
Open Mon-Fri 9am-5pm, Sat-Sun 9am-1pm.

Coming & Going
McCafferty's/Greyhound buses connect Longreach to Brisbane, Mt Isa and Rockhampton and stop at 115A Eagle Street.

The train station on Landsborough Highway serves the twice-weekly *Spirit of the Outback* service to Rockhampton.

Accommodation
Royal Hotel
Cheap accommodation in dormitories above a pub on the main street of town.
111 Eagle Street, Longreach.
☎ *(07) 4658 2118.*
***Dorm bed** $12; **single room** $23-35; **double room** $35-70.*
***Reception open** Sun-Thu 10am-11pm, Fri-Sat 10am-2am.*
Not yet rated

Sights
Qantas Founders Outback Museum
Aviation buffs and plane spotters will love this museum at Longreach Airport, which is home to the original Qantas hangar as well as a replica of the first Qantas aircraft.
Hudson Fysh Drive, Longreach Airport.
☎ *(07) 4658 3737.*
Website www.qfom.com.au.
Admission $15; 747 tour $10.
Open 9am-5pm daily.

Stockman's Hall of Fame
Outback Queensland's biggest and best attraction is an outstanding museum dedicated to the pioneers of the early outback. It is well worth the visit - some people even go as far as saying that this museum alone is worth the trip to Longreach.
Landsborough Highway, Longreach.
☎ *(07) 4658 2166.*
Website www.outbackheritage.com.au.
Admission $20, students $10.
Open 9am-5pm daily.

South Australia

South Australia is known for its food, wine and festivals but the great beaches and awesome stretches of Outback are the main drawcard for backpackers.

South Australia differs from other Australian states in several respects. It was colonised by free settlers without the use of convicts. Many early settlers were religious non-conformists and South Australia has led Australia in social and political reform. It was first to grant votes to women, first to appoint an Aboriginal governor and first to appoint a woman governor.

Known as the wine state, South Australia produces more than 70 per cent of Australia's wine, which rivals the world's best. There are more than 50 wineries in the Barossa Valley alone and many visitors make a day trip to

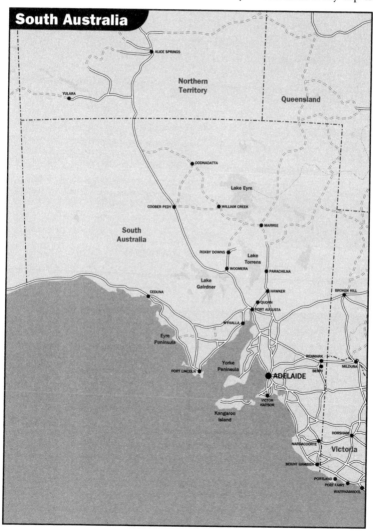

South Australia

the Barossa to take advantage of the free tastings offered by many of the wineries.

Adelaide

Unlike most other big Australian cities, Adelaide was designed and built to a master plan that has been largely adhered to. In the 1830s, city founder Colonel William Light created a pleasant city by surrounding Adelaide with 850 hectares of parkland and providing plenty of gardens, open space and wide roads.

Adelaide also has some of Australia's best city beaches as well as some brilliant pubs. Overall it is an enjoyable, yet seldom visited city that is worth spending the time to get to know.

Practical Information
INFORMATION CENTRES & USEFUL ADDRESSES
Adelaide Greeters
Local volunteers give free three to four-hour orientations of their city, answering any questions that you may have. Advance bookings are essential.
☎ *(08) 8267 5840.*
Website www.adelaidegreeters.asn.au.
Open 9am-5pm daily.

American Express
Shop 32 City Centre Arcade, Rundle Mall, Adelaide.
🚌 *99B Bee Line, 99C City Loop, 140-146, 151-155, T155, 171, 172, 173-179, 191-199, 201, 203, 210-218, T218, 231, 233, 235-237, T240, 241-248, 263-266, 280-282, 286, 287, 291, 292, 296, 297, T500, T530, 711-725, T721, T726, 727F;* 🚉 *Adelaide.*
☎ *(08) 9271 8255.*
Website www.americanexpress.com.
Open Mon-Fri 9am-5pm, Sat 9am-noon.

South Australian Information Centre
18 King William Street, Adelaide.
🚌 *99B Bee Line, 99C City Loop, 140-146, 151-155, T155, 171, 172, 173-179, 191-199, 201, 203, 210-218, T218, 231, 233, 235-237, T240, 241-248,*
263-266, 280-282, 286, 287, 291, 292, 296, 297, T500, T530, 711-725, T721, T726, 727F; 🚉 *Adelaide.*
☎ *(08) 8303 2201 or 1300 655 276.*
Website www.southaustralia.com.
Open Mon-Fri 8.30am-5pm, Sat-Sun 9am-2pm

Glenelg Information Centre
Moseley Square, Glenelg.
🚌 *260, 266, 340, 345;* 🚉 *Glenelg.*
☎ *(08) 8294 5833.*
Open Mon-Fri 9am-5pm, Sat-Sun 10am-3pm.

Port Adelaide Visitor Centre
66 Commercial Road, Port Adelaide.
🚌 *118, 118N, 151, 152, 153, T225, 301, 307, 312, 333, 333B, 334, 336B, 340, 345;* 🚉 *Port Adelaide.*
☎ *(08) 8447 4788.*
Open 9am-5pm daily.

Flinders Ranges & Outback SA Information Centre
142 Gawler Place, Adelaide.
🚌 *99B Bee Line, 171, 172, 191-199, 210-218, T218, 231-233, 235-237, 263-266, 296, 297, T500, T530.*
☎ *1 800 633 060.*
Open Mon-Fri 9am-5.30pm, Sat-Sun 10am-4pm.

YHA Office
135 Waymouth Street, Adelaide.
🚌 *99C City Loop, 102, 105, 106, 111-118, 122-125, 130-137, 161-168, T163, 274-278, 505-508, 540-546, 550-552, 576-577, 820-821, 830F-843F.*
☎ *(08) 8414 3000.*
Website www.yha.com.au.
Open Mon-Fri 9am-6pm, Sat 10am-1pm.

INTERNET ACCESS
Subbie's Internet Café
299 Hindley Street, Adelaide.
🚌 *99C City Loop, 102-106, 111-118, 122-125, 151-T151, 272, 273, 286, 287.*
Open 24 hours.

Talking Cents
53 Hindley Street, Adelaide.
☎ *(08) 8212 1266.*

Open Mon-Thu 8am-9pm, Fri-Sat 8am-10pm.

Coming & Going

Adelaide is well connected by road and rail to the rest of the country and most travellers heading to the outback will pass through the city.

AIR

Adelaide Airport is centrally located between the city centre and West Beach. The airport has frequent flights to most domestic destinations including Alice Springs, Melbourne, Perth and Sydney and also handles some international flights.

Many hostels in Adelaide offer free pick up from the airport but it is best to phone ahead to book first. The next cheapest option is the regular city bus routes 276 and 278 that stop on Sir Donald Bradman Drive about a 15-minute walk from the terminal buildings. If you don't fancy the walk, the Skylink airport shuttle bus (☎ *(08) 8332 2644; website www.skylinkadelaide.com)* costs $9 and runs between the airport terminals and the city centre with a stop at the Keswick Rail Terminal. The airport bus only runs into town until 9.45pm, if your flight arrives later than this you'll need to take a taxi into town, which will cost $12-15.

BUS

The Central Bus Station is situated on Franklin Street and is close to several backpackers hostels. Premier Stateliner and several other smaller companies run to destinations within South Australia, Firefly has buses to Melbourne and Sydney and McCafferty's/Greyhound go everywhere including the long-haul across the outback to Darwin via Coober Pedy and Alice Springs and also the marathon 35 hour journey to Perth. There are quite a few travel agencies around the bus station who sell discount tickets and travel passes.

TRAIN

Train service is pretty good out of Adelaide with trains to Alice Springs, Broken Hill, Melbourne, Perth and Sydney. Trains terminate at the Keswick Interstate Rail Terminal about 2km southwest of the city centre.

Both the *Ghan* to Alice Springs and Darwin and the *Indian Pacific* to Perth are rated as Australia's top train journeys. Although you're really just looking at desert for hours on end, it is a much more comfortable option than the bus. The train is usually more expensive than travelling by bus, however the discounts offered by flashing your VIP or YHA card make this a travel option worth considering. Check the budget travel agents around Franklin Street for the best deal.

HITCHHIKING

Hitching out of Adelaide is fairly average although you can sometimes get lucky with long rides, especially if you're heading north or west.

If you're heading to Melbourne it is best to wait for a lift on Mount Barker Road before it joins the South Eastern Freeway. Take bus 100, 146, 161, 163, 163F, 164, 164F, 165, 166, 830F, 832, 840F, 841F and 842F and get off at Mount Barker Road in Urrbrae. The area on Mount Barker Road to the east of the intersection of Cross, Glen Osmond and Portrush Roads is a good spot to try your luck. Use a sign because this road gets a bit of local traffic to the Adelaide Hills.

Main North Road between Elizabeth and Gawler is your best bet for lifts to the fruit picking spots on the Murray River as well as rides to Broken Hill and Sydney. Take the train to Munno Para or Kudla station and walk about five minutes to Main North Road to wait for a lift. This road gets a bit of local traffic to the Barossa Valley and splits into two roads shortly after the turn off for Gawler so you'll need to use a sign indicating either your destination or the road you want to travel along. The Barrier Highway (route 32) goes to Sydney via Broken Hill. While the Sturt Highway (route 20) goes via the fruit picking areas near the Murray and Murrumbidgee Rivers and joins up with the Hume Highway near Wagga Wagga where you can continue on to Sydney.

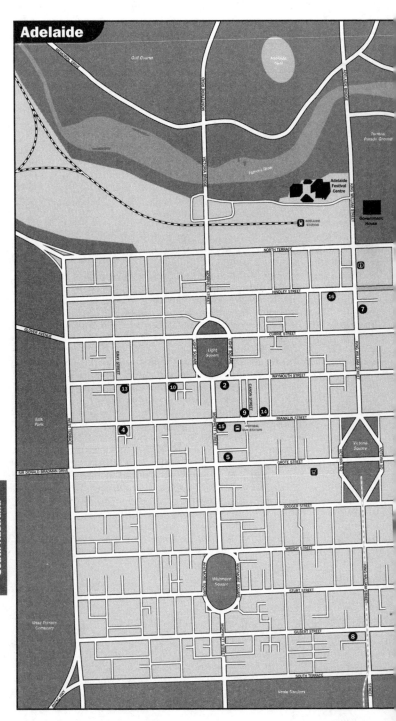

Adelaide

South Australia

Accommodation

1. Adelaide Backpackers Inn
2. Adelaide City YHA
3. Adelaide Travellers Inn
4. Annie's Place (Adel. City BPers)
5. Backpack Australia
6. Backpack Oz
7. Blue Galah
8. Brecon Inn
9. Canon Street Backpackers
10. Cumberland Arms Hotel
11. East Park Lodge
12. The Guesthouse
13. My Place
14. Raglan's Backpackers
15. Sunnys Backpackers Hostel
16. Tattersalls Adel. City BPers

South Australia

You may be lucky enough to get some really long lifts if you're heading north towards Coober Pedy, Alice Springs and Darwin or west towards Perth. You'll need to get a lift north along the Princes Highway towards Port Augusta. At Port Augusta the road will split into two, the Eyre Highway (route 1) to Perth and the Stuart Highway (route 87) north to Alice Springs and Darwin. To leave Adelaide in this direction, you'll need to get a northbound lift on the Princes Highway (route 1), also known as Port Wakefield Road. Take buses 222 or 224 past the intersection where the road splits into Main North Road (route 20) and Port Wakefield Road (route 1), bus 222 terminates at this intersection and bus 224 continues along Port Wakefield Road. Get off the bus on Port Wakefield Road and find a safe place to wait for a lift.

Be careful not to confuse the Sturt and Stuart Highways if you're hitching with a sign showing the name of the road you want to travel on.

An easier option is BUG Ride (*website http://australia.bugride.com*), BUG's own web-based ride sharing service, which allows travellers to offer lifts and search for rides throughout Australia.

Local Transport

Adelaide has a good public transport network comprising trains, trams and buses. It is an affordable way to get around particularly if you buy a day pass or take advantage of the two free bus services in the city centre.

The different modes of transport use the same ticketing system that is organised by Adelaide Metro (☎ *(08) 8210 1000; website www.adelaidemetro.com. au*) who also run an extremely helpful information centre on King William Street near the corner with Currie Street. The Adelaide Metro information centre sells travel passes and has route maps and timetables for all train and bus routes. Pop in to pick up a free copy of The Metro Guide, this handy booklet explains the whole system and has maps of all bus routes. This is especially handy as the bus and train routes are superimposed upon a map showing all the streets in the metropolitan area

– it's good enough to use as a street directory.

TRAM

Adelaide has only one tram route, but it's a handy option for travellers as it connects the city centre with the beach at Glenelg. The tram runs from the city terminus on Victoria Square.

TRAIN

The suburban train network is the quickest way to get out to the suburbs. It is a good way to get between the train station on North Terrace and the Keswick interstate train station. It is also the best way to get between the city centre and historic Port Adelaide.

BUS

Like most cities, the bus routes fill the gaps where there are no trains or trams. The bus is a good way to get to some beaches, while there are also routes to the good hitchhiking spots and a service to McLaren Vale.

Buses are also a good way of getting around in the city centre. With a day pass you should be able to hop on any bus to get a lift around the city although there are also two free bus services for those without a day pass. The free Beeline bus (route 99B) runs a circuit between the tram terminus on Victoria Square and the train station on North Terrace and the free City Loop bus (route 99C) runs around the city centre calling at the Central Bus Station, Victoria Square, Hindmarsh Square, North Terrace and Light Square.

Adelaide's unique O-Bahn is the world's longest guided bus way. Basically these are just regular buses in the city centre (they stop on Grenfell Street between King William and Pulteney Streets) that join a guided track outside the city centre. O-Bahn services run about every five minutes, and are a quick way to get between the city centre and the suburban shopping centre/bus interchange at Tea Tree Plaza.

FARES AND TICKETS

The same fare structure applies on buses, trams and trains, and metrotickets are valid on all three modes of transport with the exception of the airport bus and some buses to outlying areas.

There are three main types of tickets: Singletrip, Daytrip and Multitrip.

A Singletrip ticket is your best option if you're planning on making only one journey during a day or if you're making your return trip within two hours. You're better off with a Daytrip ticket if you are making a return journey on the same day. There are a couple of different Singletrip tickets available depending on the distance you are travelling and whether you are travelling during a peak or off-peak period. Generally a Zone ticket means that you can go anywhere in Adelaide, transferring between buses, trains and the tram taking up to two hours to complete your trip. A two-section ticket is a little cheaper but is restricted to shorter trips of around three kilometres.

Most travellers find the Daytrip ticket the best value. It allows unlimited travel on the tram, trains and buses during an entire day. Daytrip tickets cost $6.20.

Multitrip tickets are a good idea if you're planning on staying in Adelaide for a few days. These tickets are good for ten trips.

You are required to validate your ticket each time you board a bus, tram or train.

All tickets are available at train stations, post offices and convenience stores although only Daytrip and Singletrip tickets can be bought on board buses and trams.

Ticket	Zone	Time	Cost
Singletrip	Zone	All times	$3.30
Singletrip	Zone	Interpeak	$2
Singletrip	2-section	All times	$1.90
Singletrip	2-section	Interpeak	$1.40
Multitrip	Zone	All times	$21.60
Multitrip	Zone	Interpeak	$12.10
Multitrip	2-section	All times	$11.80
Multitrip	2 section	All times	$9

Accommodation
Adelaide Backpackers Inn

This hostel needs a bit of work, but it has helpful management and lots of freebies including free apple pie and ice cream every night. Most dorm beds are in the older, main building and most double/twin rooms are in the slightly nicer building across the road.

112 Carrington Street, Adelaide.
🚌 *161-166, 191-199, 182, 201, 203;* 🚌.
☎ *(08) 8223 6635 or 1800 247 725.*
Dorm bed *$23 ($22 VIP/YHA);* **single room** *$45 ($44 VIP/YHA);* **double room** *$57 ($55 VIP/YHA);* **twin room** *$52 ($50 VIP/YHA).*
Credit cards *MC, Visa.*
Reception open *6am-8pm daily.*

Maintenance & cleanliness	★★
Facilities	★★
Atmosphere & character	★★★½
Security	★★
Overall rating	★★

Adelaide Central YHA

Adelaide Central YHA is a big new hostel with excellent amenities that include a large kitchen, several TV lounges and Internet access. The main drawback is the mattresses that have a waterproof covering that makes them horrible to sleep on and very noisy whenever anyone rolls over in their sleep. Security here is excellent with keycard access and lockers in all the rooms. This hostel has a nice location overlooking Light Square and it is also close to the bus terminal.

135 Waymouth Street, Adelaide.
🚌 *99C City Loop, 102, 105, 106, 111-118, 122-125, 130-137, 161-168, T163, 274-278, 505-508, 540-546, 550-552, 576-577, 820-821, 830F-843F.*
☎ *(08) 8414 3010.*
Dorm bed *$25 ($20 YHA);* **double room** *$67-82 ($57-72 YHA);* **twin room** *$67 ($57 YHA).*
Credit cards *MC, Visa.*
Reception open *24 hours.*
🚌 *$6 per day.*

Maintenance & cleanliness	★★★★★
Facilities	★★
Atmosphere & character	★★★½
Security	★★★★★
Overall rating	★★★★½

Adelaide Travellers Inn

This is a basic hostel that's a little run down but otherwise it's a good value bed for the night. It is a popular hostel with Japanese travellers and amenities include a small kitchen, TV lounge, Internet access and a backyard barbecue area.

118 Carrington Street, Adelaide.
■ *161-166, 191-199, 182, 201, 203;* ▣.
☎ *(08) 8224 0753.*
Website *www.adelaidebackpackers.com.au.*
Dorm bed *$16-20.*
Credit cards *MC, Visa.*
Reception open *6am-9pm daily.*

Maintenance & cleanliness	★★☆
Facilities	★
Atmosphere & character	★★★☆
Security	★★☆
Overall rating	★★☆

Annie's Place
(Adelaide City Backpackers)

This hostel is located in a 137-year-old historic building with plenty of old world charm. It features a nice outdoor courtyard and facilities include a bar and a fully equipped kitchen. There's no TV lounge, but there are TVs in the rooms. Good value $5 meals are served here each evening.

239 Franklin Street, Adelaide.
■ *167, 168, 231-233, 235-237, 253.*
☎ *(08) 8212 2668.*
Website *www.anniesplace.com.au.*
Dorm bed *$20;* **double room** *$55; includes breakfast.*
Credit cards *MC, Visa.*
Reception open *8am-9pm.*

Maintenance & cleanliness	★★★
Facilities	★★★☆
Atmosphere & character	★★★★★☆
Security	★★☆
Overall rating	★★★

Backpack Australia

This small friendly hostel has a bar plus a small kitchen and a TV lounge. It is the only hostel in Adelaide with a rooftop terrace, which offers great city views, but some furnishings are a little old. The staff are very helpful and they serve pancakes for breakfast.

128 Grote Street, Adelaide.
■ *99C City Loop, 210-218, 231-237, 253, 296, 297.*
☎ *(08) 8231 0639 or 1800 804 133.*
Dorm bed *$20-26;* **single room** *$30; camping on roof* *$12 per person; includes breakfast.*
Credit cards *MC, Visa.*
Reception open *6am-1pm & 4pm-8.30pm daily.*

Maintenance & cleanliness	★★
Facilities	★★★☆
Atmosphere & character	★★★★☆
Security	★
Overall rating	★★★☆

Backpack Oz

This clean hostel has good facilities that include a nice big TV lounge, a pool table, Internet access and a good kitchen.

144 Wakefield Street, Adelaide.
■ *99C City Loop, 161-166, 171, 172, 173, 179, 191-199, 231-233, 235-237.*
☎ *(08) 8223 3551 or 1800 633 307.*
Website *www.backpackoz.com.au.*
Dorm bed *$20-22;* **single room** *$49;* **double room** *$55;* **twin room** *$57;* **triple room** *$75; includes breakfast.*
Credit cards *MC, Visa.*
Reception open *6am-10pm daily.*

Maintenance & cleanliness	★★★★★☆
Facilities	★★★
Atmosphere & character	★★★★☆
Security	★★☆
Overall rating	★★★★☆

Blue Galah

The Blue Galah is a centrally located hostel that boasts a balcony with a pool table plus a TV lounge and a fully equipped kitchen. It is clean and features good bunk beds and individual bedside lamps.

1st floor, 62 King William Street, Adelaide.
■ *99B Bee Line, 99C City Loop, 140-146, 151-155, T155, 171, 172, 173-179, 191-199, 201, 203, 210-218, T218, 231, 233, 235-237, T240, 241-248, 263-266, 280-282, 286, 287, 291, 292, 296, 297, T500, T530, 711-725, T721, T726, 727F;* ▣ *Adelaide.*
☎ *(08) 8231 9295 or 1800 555 322.*
Website *www.bluegalah.com.au.*
Dorm bed *$23 ($22 ISIC/VIP/YHA);* **single room** *$55 ($54 ISIC/VIP/YHA);* **twin room** *$66 ($64 ISIC/VIP/YHA); includes breakfast.*
Credit cards *MC, Visa.*

Maintenance & cleanliness	★★★★★
Facilities	★★
Atmosphere & character	★★★☆
Security	★★★☆
Overall rating	★★★☆

Brecon Inn

The Brecon Inn is the nicest of Adelaide's three Nomads hostels. It is a clean hostel with good quality amenities that include a good TV lounge with Internet access, however the kitchen is very small.

11-13 Gilbert Street, Adelaide.
204, 207-209; South Terrace.
(08) 8211 8985 or 1800 990 009.
Website *www.breconinn.com.au.*
Dorm bed *$20.*
Reception open *Mon-Fri 6am-noon & 1pm-6pm, Sat-Sun 6am-1pm.*

Maintenance & cleanliness	★★★★★
Facilities	★★
Atmosphere & character	★☆
Security	★★★
Overall rating	★★★☆

Canon Street Backpackers

This hostel is built in a converted warehouse and it features a brilliant bar, plus a TV lounge, a big kitchen and a games room with ping-pong and pool tables. Free apple pie and cream is served every evening.

11 Canon Street, Adelaide.
99C City Loop, 830F-843F.
(08) 8410 1218 or 1800 804 133.
Dorm bed *$20 ($19 VIP);* **double room** *$55 ($52 VIP); includes breakfast.*
Credit cards *MC, Visa.*
Reception open *Mon-Fri 6am-8.30pm, Sat-Sun 6am-1pm & 5pm-8.30pm.*

Maintenance & cleanliness	★★★★
Facilities	★★★☆
Atmosphere & character	★★★★
Security	★★
Overall rating	★★★☆

Cumberland Arms Hotel

The focus of the Cumberland Arms Hotel is the nightclub downstairs, which belts out dance tunes till the wee hours of the morning making it a fun place to stay if you want to party but not so great if you're looking for a place to sleep.

205 Waymouth Street, Adelaide.
99C City Loop, 111-118, 130-137, 167, 168, 274-278, 830F-843F.
Dorm bed *$20;* **single room** *$30;* **double room** *$40.*
Reception open *Mon-Fri 9am-late, Sat-Sun 9am-11am & 6pm-late.*

Maintenance & cleanliness	★★★☆
Facilities	★
Atmosphere & character	★★★☆
Security	★★
Overall rating	★★

East Park Lodge

The hostel is housed in a large building with large verandas along the front of the building. It has a nice courtyard and it is the only hostel in Adelaide with a swimming pool. There are the usual facilities that include a large kitchen, a spacious dining room, a TV lounge with pool table, Internet access, clean bathrooms and nice beds. It's on a quiet residential area at the eastern end of Angas Street and it's close to restaurants on Hutt Street and a relatively short walk into the centre of town.

341 Angas Street, Adelaide.
171-179, 820, 821, 830F, 840F-843F.
(08) 8223 1228.
Website *www.eastparklodge.com.au.*
Dorm bed *$23-26 ($21-24 VIP);* **single room** *$33 ($31 VIP);* **double/ twin room** *$65 ($61 VIP);* **family room** *$96-104 ($90-96 VIP); includes breakfast.*
Credit cards *MC, Visa.*
Reception open *7am-8pm daily.*

Maintenance & cleanliness	★★★☆
Facilities	★★★☆
Atmosphere & character	★★★★☆
Security	★★★☆
Overall rating	★★★

The Guesthouse

This clean hostel has limited, but top quality, facilities. It is a quiet place that acts as an overflow for Backpack Oz and it caters mostly to couples.

Check in at Backpack Oz, 144 Wakefield Street, Adelaide.
99C City Loop, 161-166, 171, 172, 173, 179, 191-199, 231-233, 235-237.
(08) 8223 3551 or 1800 633 307.
Website *www.backpackoz.com.au.*

South Australia

Dorm bed $22; single room $55; double room $60; twin room $65; includes breakfast.
Credit cards MC, Visa.
Reception open 6am-10pm daily.

Maintenance & cleanliness	★★★★★
Facilities	★☆
Atmosphere & character	★
Security	★☆
Overall rating	★★★

My Place

My Place is a nice clean hostel that features a comfy TV lounge, a good kitchen, a sauna and a balcony with a barbecue.
257 Waymouth Street, Adelaide.
☎ *111-118, 130-137, 167, 168, 274-278.*
☎ *(08) 8221 5299.*
Website www.adelaidehostel.com.au.
Dorm bed $21 ($20 VIP); includes breakfast.
Credit cards MC, Visa.
Reception open 8am-9pm daily.
🚌

Maintenance & cleanliness	★★★★☆
Facilities	★★
Atmosphere & character	★★★
Security	★★
Overall rating	★★★★☆

Raglan's Backpackers

Raglan's is a clean hostel above a pub near the bus station. The bar has a big screen telly and pool table as well as a tour-booking desk, but the accommodation upstairs has more basic facilities.
2 Franklin Street, Adelaide.
🚌 *99C City Loop, 830F-843F.*
☎ *(0) 8231 4703.*
Dorm bed $18-23; twin room $50; includes breakfast.
Credit cards MC, Visa.
Reception open 7.30am-9pm daily.

Maintenance & cleanliness	★★★☆
Facilities	★★
Atmosphere & character	★★☆
Security	★☆
Overall rating	★★★☆

Sunny's Backpackers Hostel

This small hostel is in an old building next to the bus station. It has the usual facilities such as a kitchen, TV lounge and Internet access and there's a nice sunny area out the front. There's a travel agent on site and the manager is very helpful.
139 Franklin Street, Adelaide.
☎ *(08) 8231 2430 or 1800 SUNNYS.*
Dorm bed $22 ($20 ISE/ISIC/Nomads/VIP/YHA).
Credit cards Amex, Diners, JCB, MC, Visa.
Reception open 6am-8pm daily.

Maintenance & cleanliness	★★
Facilities	★★☆
Atmosphere & character	★★★★☆
Security	★★☆
Overall rating	★★

Tattersalls Adelaide City Backpackers

This hostel has a brilliant central location and a big balcony overlooking Hindley Street. It offers fairly basic amenities, which include a kitchen, TV lounge and Internet access.
17 Hindley Street, Adelaide.
🚌 *99B Bee Line, 99C City Loop, 140-146, 151-155, T155, 171, 172, 173-179, 191-199, 201, 203, 210-218, T218, 231, 233, 235-237, T240, 241-248, 263-266, 280-282, 286, 287, 291, 292, 296, 297, T500, T530, 711-725, T721, T726, 727F;* 🚆 *Adelaide.*
☎ *(08) 8231 3225 or 1800 133 355.*
Dorm bed $20-22 ($18-20 ISIC/Nomads/VIP/YHA); double room $50 ($46 ISIC/Nomads/VIP/YHA); includes breakfast.
Credit cards MC, Visa.
Reception open 8.30am-12.30pm & 5pm-8pm daily.

Maintenance & cleanliness	★★★☆
Facilities	★★☆
Atmosphere & character	★★
Security	★★
Overall rating	★★

Eating & Drinking

Eating out in Adelaide is outstanding with a huge range of affordable options and a couple of streets full of restaurants, pubs and cafés. Adelaide even has its own budget-priced culinary speciality – the pie floater.

You can't leave Adelaide without trying this delicious meat pie floating in pea soup and topped with tomato sauce. It tastes much better than it

South Australia

sounds! You can try a pie floater from the pie carts located either outside the train station on North Terrace or outside the post office near the corner of Franklin and King William Streets. This is a good option for a late-night feed, generally pie carts open from the afternoon through to the wee hours of the morning.

In the city centre, Gouger Street, Hutt Street and Rundle Street are the main restaurant strips with a good selection of fast food and take away places squeezed among the more upmarket restaurants. Melbourne Street in North Adelaide is another good street for eating out. If you're in Glenelg, then Jetty Road is the local restaurant strip.

If you're preparing your own food, the Coles supermarket on Grote Street near Victoria Square is your best option in the city centre.

Sights
Adelaide Botanic Gardens
Adelaide's city centre is completely surrounded by parkland including the beautiful Botanic Gardens at the north east of the city. The gardens make a great picnic spot and also feature a huge conservatory that recreates a tropical rainforest.
Botanic Road, Adelaide.
☎ *(08) 8222 9311.*
Admission *free, conservatory $3.40.*
Open *Mon-Fri 8am-dusk, Sat-Sun 9am-dusk; conservatory 10am-5pm daily.*

Adelaide Gaol
Every Australian City has a prison turned into a museum and Adelaide is no exception. The gaol was operated as a prision as recently as 1988 and was the scene of 49 hangings.
18 Gaol Road, Thebarton.
🚌 *111, 112, 113, 115, 118, 151, 152, 153, 155, 286, 187.*
☎ *(08) 8231 4062.*
Admission *$7.*
Open *11am-3.30pm daily.*

Adelaide Zoo
Adelaide's zoo is home to around 1500 animals including an excellent South-East Asian Rainforest exhibit.

Frome Road, Adelaide.
🚌 *272, 273.*
☎ *(08) 8267 3255.*
Admission *$15.*
Open *9.30am-5pm daily.*

Art Gallery of South Australia
The Art Gallery of South Australia has a good collection of Australian and European paintings, although it is not quite up there with the galleries in Canberra or Melbourne.
North Terrace, Adelaide.
🚌 *99C City Loop, 140-146, 173-179, 241-248, T240, 280-282, 291, 292, T500;* 🚊 *Adelaide.*
☎ *(08) 8207 7000.*
Admission *free, charge for special exhibitions.*
Open *10am-5pm daily.*

The Bradman Collection
This exhibition features a collection of cricketing memorabilia dating from 1929 to 1977. Sir Donald Bradman donated most of the collection to the State Library.
State Library of South Australia, Corner Kintore Avenue & North Terrace, Adelaide.
🚌 *99C City Loop, 140-146, 173-179, 241-248, T240, 280-282, 291, 292, T500;* 🚊 *Adelaide.*
☎ *(08) 8207 7595 or 1800 182 013.*
Admission *free.*
Open *Mon-Thu 9.30am-6pm, Fri 9.30am-8pm, Sat-Sun noon-5pm; tours Sun 2pm.*

Festival Centre
Adelaide's answer to the Sydney Opera House is the Festival Centre, which is the city's major landmark and occupies a lovely riverside setting.
North Terrace, Adelaide.
🚌 *99C City Loop, 140-146, 173-179, 241-248, T240, 280-282, 291, 292, T500;* 🚊 *Adelaide.*

Maritime Museum
Adelaide's Maritime Museum features several old ships and a lighthouse as well as the usual nautical exhibits.
126 Lipson Street, Port Adelaide.
🚌 *151, 152, 153;* 🚊 *Port Adelaide.*
☎ *(08) 8207 6255.*

Admission $8.50.
Open 10am-5pm daily.

Migration Museum

This is a fascinating museum about people who have migrated and settled in South Australia.
82 Kintore Avenue, Adelaide.
🚌 *99C City Loop, 140-146, 173-179, 241-248, T240, 280-282, 291, 292, T500;* 🚆 *Adelaide.*
☎ *(08) 8207 7580.*
Admission by donation.
Open Mon-Fri 10am-5pm, Sat-Sun 1pm-5pm.

Museum of South Australia

Adelaide's big museum features all the usual exhibits – rocks, Aboriginal artefacts, an Egyptian mummy and a whale skeleton.
North Terrace, Adelaide.
🚌 *99C City Loop, 140-146, 173-179, 241-248, T240, 280-282, 291, 292, T500.*
☎ *(08) 8207 7500.*
Admission free.
Open 10am-5pm daily.

Tandanya-National Aboriginal Cultural Institute

This is an interesting museum that provides a good introduction to Aboriginal culture. Every day at noon there is either a didgeridoo demonstration or a Torres Strait Islander dance demonstration.
253 East Terrace, Adelaide.
🚌 *99C City Loop, 122-125, 130-137, 820-821, 830F, 840F-843F.*
☎ *(08) 8224 3200.*
Admission $4.
Open 10am-5pm daily.

Adelaide Hills

Only around half an hour from central Adelaide, the Adelaide Hills is a pleasant area full of quaint towns with antique and craft shops, country pubs and day-trippers from Adelaide. It is a nice spot to visit particularly as a detour if you're coming to or from the city, and also as an extension to a day-trip in the Barossa Valley.

Practical Information
Adelaide Hills Visitor Information Centre
41 Main Street, Hahndorf.
☎ *(08) 8388 1185*
Website www.visitadelaidehills.com.au.
Open Mon-Fri 9am-5pm, Sat-Sun 10am-4pm.

Accommodation
Geoff and Hazels
Geoff and Hazel's is an excellent place that caters to backpacking couples. It features three double rooms, a cosy lounge and kitchen facilities. Outside the hostel there are hammocks to laze around in and each room has its own balcony. It is about 20-30 minutes from the centre of Adelaide and there is a supermarket, pub and cinema just down the road.
19 Kingsland Road, Aldgate.
🚌 *163F, T163, 165, 166.*
☎ *(08) 8339 8360.*
Website www.geoffandhazels.com.au.
Double room $50.
🚍

Maintenance & cleanliness	★★★★★
Facilities	★☆
Atmosphere & character	★★★★★
Security	★
Overall rating	★★★☆

Birdwood

This small town is best known for its excellent car museum. If you're not into cars, it's still a nice spot to stop for a drink or two.

Sights
National Motor Museum
This museum provides a good overview of Australian motoring history with over 300 cars, motorcycles and commercial vehicles. The National Motor Museum also features relics from South Australia's colonial past and interpretive exhibits in the recently opened Holden Pavillion of Australian Motoring.
Shannon Street, Birdwood.
☎ *(08) 8568 5006.*
Website www.history.sa.gov.au/ birdwood.htm.
Admission $9, students $7.
Open 9am-5pm daily.

Hahndorf

Probably the most popular destination in the Adelaide Hills, Hahndorf is an easy exit off the South Eastern Freeway if you're driving between Adelaide and Melbourne. The town was settled by German immigrants in 1839 and retains a strong German heritage with German themed pubs and Mettwurst shops.

Sights
The Cedars
The home of Hahndorf painter, Hans Heysen has been restored featuring the artist's studio. You can only visit by taking a guided tour of the house.
Heysen Road, Hahndorf.
☐ *164, 164F, 165, 166, 840,F, 843F.*
☎ *(08) 8388 7277.*
Admission *$8, students $6.*
Tours *Sun-Fri 11am, 1pm, 3pm.*

Hahndorf Academy
The largest regional art gallery in South Australia is noted for its exhibits of work by former Hahndorf resident Hans Heysen and also includes a museum that reveals the contribution that German migrants have made to South Australia while explaining what life was like for the region's first German settlers.
Main Street, Hahndorf.
☐ *164, 164F, 165, 166, 840,F, 843F.*
☎ *(08) 8388 7250.*
Admission *free.*
Open *Mon-Sat 10am-5pm, Sun noon-5pm.*

Barossa Valley

The Barossa is one of Australia's major wine-producing areas with 45 wineries producing about a quarter of Australia's total vintage.

The valley is easy to explore: just 30km long by 14 km wide. The centre of the Barossa is the area bounded by the valley's three main towns, Angaston, Nurioopta and Tanunda; although it extends further south towards Lyndoch.

Tanunda is the cultural heart of the Barossa and it is perhaps the most centrally located of the towns in the Barossa and is home to some good pubs and camping grounds. Most of the Barossa is situated within easy cycling distance from Tanunda.

North of Tanunda, Nurioopta is the more modern commercial centre of the valley while Angaston, 6km east of Nurioopta, retains a more historic ambience.

Practical Information
Barossa Visitor Information Centre
66 Murray Street, Tanunda.
☎ *1800 812 662.*
Website *www.barossa-region.org.*
Open *Mon-Fri 9am-5pm, Sat-Sun 10am-4pm.*

Coming & Going
The Barossa Valley is close enough to Adelaide to make an easy day-trip. If you're driving follow the Sturt Highway and take the Nurioopta turn-off. However a car won't be much use if you want to indulge in wine tasting when you get there and you may decide to travel to the Barossa by bus or to take a day tour.

Barossa Adelaide Passenger Service (☎ *(08) 8564 3022)* operates an infrequent bus service connecting Angaston, Lyndoch, Nurioopta and Tanunda with Adelaide. The bus departs from the central bus station at Franklin Street in Adelaide. A one-way ticket costs around $11.90 between Adelaide and Tanunda.

Alternatively, you may choose to take a tour starting in Adelaide. There is a good choice of day tours as well as a few that allow you to stay over at a hostel in the Barossa and rejoin the return leg a day or two later.

Oz Experience buses visit the Barossa Valley on their Adelaide to Alice Springs route.

Another option is the day tour offered by Groovy Grape Getaways (☎ *1800 66 11 77; website www.groovygrape.com.au).* For $65 Groovy Grape's trips take in a few wineries and include a barbecue lunch. Tours run seven days a week and depart Glenelg at 7.15am with pickups in Adelaide City at 7.45am.

Local Transport

Although driving is usually the best way to get around rural areas like the Barossa, it's not a good idea since you're not going to appreciate it without stopping for a drink or three – especially since the local police are extremely vigilant when it comes to drink driving.

A better idea is to rent a bicycle from the Bunkhaus hostel near Nuriootpa or the bicycle rental companies in Tanunda. The valley is small enough to make cycling the most enjoyable way to get around.

Accommodation

Barossa Bunkhaus Travellers Hostel

This small long-established hostel is set among vineyards and it's a good choice if you want to spend longer in the Barossa than a day trip. The hostel has a quiet laid-back atmosphere and everything is clean and well maintained. Facilities include a fully equipped kitchen, TV lounge, swimming pool and bicycle rental. It has an idyllic setting among vines about 2km south of Nuriootpa. *Corner Barossa Valley Way & Nuraip Road, Nuriootpa.*
☎ *(08) 8562 2260.*
Dorm bed *$17.*

Maintenance & cleanliness	★★★	
Facilities	★	
Atmosphere & character	★★★	
Security	★	
Overall rating	★★☆	

Eating & Drinking

Sampling the region's wine is the main reason to visit the Barossa. The best way to do this is to rent a bicycle and cycle from one winery to the next, stopping for a picnic lunch en route. You can pick up picnic supplies at the supermarkets at any of the towns in the valley and many of the wineries have picnic areas where you can enjoy their wine.

If you prefer beer to wine, both Angaston and Tanunda have excellent pubs.

Sights

Although the main attraction in the Barossa Valley is sampling wine at the many wineries, the valley also holds a few other attractions.

Mengler Hill Lookout

Although it's not a huge must-see attraction, this lookout, located east of Tanunda offers excellent views of the Barossa Valley. It's a pretty steep hill and a hard ride if you're cycling so you really need your own car to get here although many of the day tours also visit this lookout.
Mengler Hill Road, near Tanunda.
Admission *free.*

Norm's Coolies

For something completely different you can watch a performance by trained sheepdogs.
Breezy Gully Farm, Gomersal Road, near Tanunda.
☎ *(08) 8563 2198.*
Admission *$8.*
Performances *Mon, Wed, Sat 2pm.*

Fleurieu Peninsula

Situated less than an hour south of Adelaide, the Fleurieu Peninsula encompasses the McLaren Vale vineyards and the seaside resort towns of Cape Jervis and Victor Harbor.

The Fleurieu Peninsula makes either a pleasant detour or a day-trip from Adelaide.

Cape Jervis

Most travellers see Cape Jervis as the departure point for the ferry to Kangaroo Island although the small town is also a popular weekend destination for people from Adelaide.

Coming & Going

Cape Jervis is connected to Adelaide by an infrequent bus. There are only two daily coach services between Adelaide and Cape Jervis. They depart Adelaide at 6.45am and 3.45pm and return from Cape Jervis at 9.40am and 8.30pm. This is run by Sealink (☎ *13 13 01; website www.sealink.com.au*)

and it connects with Sealink's ferry to Kangaroo Island. See the Kangaroo Island section on page 234 for more information about the ferry between Cape Jervis and Penneshaw.

Accommodation
Cape Jervis Station
Cape Jervis Station offers a wide range of accommodation ranging from 4½ star luxury to backpackers' cabins. Backpackers stay in the Shearer's Quarters, which is a two room stone building with a veranda and a small kitchen. Shared facilities include a pool table, table tennis, croquet, badminton, tennis courts and a golf driving range. It's about 3km from the town centre.
Main Road, Cape Jervis.
☎ *(08) 8598 0288.*
Website www.capejervisstation.com.au.
Dorm bed $20.
Not yet rated

McLaren Vale
After the Barossa Valley and Coona-warra, this is one of South Australia's main wine producing regions. There are more than 45 wineries in McLaren Vale including Andrew Garret Wines, Hardy's and Wirra Wirra. It is a good place to stop over en route from Adelaide to either Victor Harbor or Kangaroo Island.

Practical Information
McLaren Vale and Fleurieu Visitor Information Centre
Main Road, McLaren Vale.
☎ *(08) 8323 9944.*
Open 10am-5pm daily.

Coming & Going & Local Transport
With only three daily buses to McLaren Vale from Adelaide and infrequent transportation within the region, driving is the easiest way to get around, but whoever is driving will have to keep off the booze since the police often operate random breath tests in wine tasting regions.

Coming from Adelaide, follow Main South Road until you see signs to McLaren Vale.

Victor Harbor
Victor Harbor is a popular weekend destination for people from Adelaide. It is a nice town with plenty of old colonial architecture and good pubs and fish and chip shops. The main attraction here is whale and penguin watching although there are plenty of other attractions ranging from camel rides on the beach to vintage horse-drawn tram rides across the causeway to Granite Island.

Practical Information
Victor Harbor Visitor Information Centre
Causeway, Esplanade, Victor Harbor.
☎ *(08) 8552 5738.*
Open 9am-5pm daily.

Coming & Going
Premier Stateliner (☎ *(08) 8415 5555)* runs two daily coach services between Adelaide's central bus station and Victor Harbor.

Steam trains run between Victor Harbor, Port Elliot and Goolwa every Sunday.

Accommodation
Arnella by the Sea YHA
This historic youth hostel is in an old hotel dating from 1851. Amenities include a fully equipped kitchen and a courtyard area with a barbecue. It is in Port Elliot, which is 4km from Victor Harbor.
28 North Terrace, Port Elliot.
☎ *(08) 8554 3611 or 1800 066 297.*
Dorm bed $23.50 ($20 YHA); single room $33.50 ($30 YHA); double/twin room $57 ($50 YHA).
Credit cards MC, Visa.
Reception open Jan- Apr 8am-8pm daily; May-Sep 8am-6pm daily; Oct-Dec 8am-8pm daily.
🚗
Not yet rated

Grosvenor Hotel
The Grosvenor Hotel features backpackers' accommodation above a pub. It is a beautiful old building with balconies overlooking the main street and the place is well maintained, but the facilities are fairly basic and

comprise a TV lounge and fridge, but no kitchen.

40 Ocean Street, Victor Harbor.
☎ *(08) 8552 1011*
Dorm bed *$25;* **double room** *$60.*
Reception open *8am-5pm daily.*
Not yet rated

Sights
Granite Island & Penguin Watching
The main attraction here is the penguin watching every night although the island is also a nice excursion during the day as well. Access is by either a horse-drawn tram ($5 return) or a short walk across the causeway.
Granite Island, Victor Harbor.
☎ *(08) 8552 7555.*
Guided penguin spotting walks *$10.*
Penguin spotting walks depart from the island side of the causeway every night at dusk.

South Australian Whale Centre
This is the place to come to find out all about marine mammals and get further information on whale watching.
2 Railway Terrace, Victor Harbor.
☎ *(08) 8552 5644.*
Website *www.webmedia.com.au/whales/.*
Admission *$6*
Open *11am-4.30pm daily.*

Kangaroo Island

Kangaroo Island, Australia's third-largest island, 16km from the mainland, is a haven for native flora and fauna and is renowned for its unspoilt natural environment. Animals and birds on the island are abundant. Flinders Chase National Park, at the island's western end, is one of the state's most important national parks. In a day trip you've got a good opportunity of seeing kangaroos, wallabies, emus, goannas, echidna and koalas in their natural surroundings and you can see sea lions on the beaches.

Kangaroo Island is a wilderness refuge with a fascinating past. It was discovered in 1802 by English sea captain Matthew Flinders, who never travelled without his cat, Trim. Flinders and Trim found Kangaroo Island uninhabited, but stone tools since discovered indicate people lived there about 10,000 years ago. The fate of the original inhabitants remains a mystery.

The main towns on the island are American River, Kingscote and Penneshaw.

Coming & Going
Kangaroo Island is easily accessible by air and sea, but it is an expensive island to get to. It is 30 minutes by air from Adelaide and ferries sail there from Cape Jervis on the Fleurieu Peninsula.

Rex (☎ *13 17 13; website www.rex.com.au)* flies between Adelaide and Kangaroo Island three times a day. One-way fares start at $55. Flights arrive at Kingscote Airport near Cygnet River, about 14km from Kingscote.

Kangaroo Island Sealink (☎ *13 13 01; website www.sealink.com.au)* operates several ferries per day between Cape Jervis and Penneshaw on Kangaroo Island. The return fare is $64 per person and $138 for a car.

Campwild Adventures (☎ *1800 444 321; website www.campwild.com.au),* operate three-day 4WD adventures. They charge $370 ($340 ISIC/VIP/YHA) for an all-inclusive package departing from Adelaide.

Local Transport
KI Coach Service, operated by Sealink (☎ *13 13 01; website www.sealink.com.au),* links Penneshaw, American River and Kingscote, the three main towns on Kangaroo Island. Unfortunately there are only two services a day, but they do connect with the ferry. The return fare between Penneshaw and Kingscote is $22.

Renting a car is the best way to explore the island, particularly since the main attractions are away from the towns. Although expensive for a single traveller, renting a car becomes more affordable when the cost is split between several people. Rental car companies on Kangaroo Island include Budget (☎ *(08) 8553 3133)* and Wheels Over Kangaroo Island (☎ *(08) 8553 3030 or 1800 750 850;* **website** *www.kangaro oislandholidays.com).*

Kingscote

Kangaroo Island's largest town and South Australia's oldest European settlement is a small town of only 1500 people. Kingscote is the main centre on the island and you'll need to come here if you need an ATM or supermarket.

Practical Information
National Parks & Wildlife Office
39 Dauncey Street, Kingscote.
☎ *(08) 8553 2381.*
Open *Mon-Fri 9am-5pm.*

Accommodation
Kangaroo Island Centre Backpackers
This small hostel is a house in the centre of Kingscote. Facilities are fairly basic and you have to check in at the service station up the road.
19 Murray Street, Kingscote.
☎ *(08) 8553 2787.*
Dorm bed *$20;* **double/twin room** *$50.*
Not yet rated

Penneshaw

You'll arrive here if you take the ferry from Cape Jervis. The main attraction in Penneshaw is the penguin colony where you can watch the little penguins waddle to shore every night at dusk.

Practical Information
Kangaroo Island Gateway Visitor Information Centre
Howard Drive, Penneshaw.
☎ *(08) 8553 1185.*
Open *Mon-Fri 9am-5pm, Sat-Sun 10am-4pm.*

Accommodation
Penguin Walk YHA
This is the best of the Kangaroo Island hostels, although the facilities are nothing special. The hostel is a former motel and amenities include the usual TV room, kitchen and laundry. It is close to the ferry terminal and the penguin viewing area.

33 Middle Terrace, Penneshaw.
☎ *(08) 8553 1344.*
Dorm bed *$26.50 ($23 YHA).*
Credit cards *MC, Visa.*
Reception open *Mon-Fri 9am-5pm, Sat-Sun 9am-noon.*
🚌
Not yet rated

Penneshaw Youth Hostel
This hostel is fairly basic and offers the usual kitchen and TV lounge and a small courtyard. It is close to shops and restaurants as well as the ferry terminal.
43 North Terrace, Penneshaw.
☎ *(08) 8553 1284.*
Website *www.penneshawyh.com.*
Dorm bed *$20 ($19 VIP);* **double room** *$50 ($48 VIP);* **twin room** *$44 ($42 VIP).*
Reception open *7.30am-12.30pm & 5pm-7.30pm daily.*
Not yet rated

Flinders Chase National Park

Wildlife watching is the main reason to visit Kangaroo Island, and Flinders Chase National Park is where you have the best chance of seeing it. The park is situated at the western end of the island with Rocky River as its small commercial centre. The national park is home to echidnas, kangaroos, koalas, pelicans, platypus and wallabies.

Entry to the park is $7 per person.

The park management organise a number of tours that include beach, cave and light station tours. A 12-month Kangaroo Island Parks Pass is available for $42 and allows access to the park in addition to tours of Seal Bay Beach, Kelly Hill Show Cave and Cape Borda and Cape Willoughby Light stations. An Island Parks Caving Pass is also available for $42, which gives you all the benefits of the Island Parks Pass plus an adventure caving tour.

Practical Information
Flinders Chase Visitor Centre
Rocky River, Flinders Chase National Park.

☎ *(08) 8559 7235.*
*Website www.parks.sa.gov.au/
flinderschase*
Open 9am-5pm daily.

Accommodation

Camping is the most popular accommodation option within the national park, but there is also budget accommodation in the Postmans Hut for $20 per night. Contact the National Parks & Wildlife office in Kingscote on (08) 8553 2381 for bookings.

Eyre Peninsula

The Eyre Peninsula has some great surf beaches and good fishing and is a pleasant detour en route between Adelaide and Perth, and when you're driving to the west coast an extra 300km shouldn't make too much difference.

Although rarely visited by backpackers, this region on the edge of the Nullarbor Plain has a lot to offer the travellers including spectacular white sand dunes, wildlife as well as whale watching and exceptional fishing.

Ceduna

Ceduna is the last real town before the long boring drive across the Nullarbor Plain to Western Australia. There's not a lot to do in town, although the surrounding area is spectacular and Ceduna makes an excellent base for exploring this region.

Practical Information
Ceduna Gateway Tourist Centre
58 Poynton Street, Ceduna.
☎ *(08) 8625 2780 or 1800 639 413.*
*Open Mon-Fri 9am-5.30pm, Sat-Sun
9am-5pm.*

Accommodation
Greenacres Backpackers
Greenacres provides basic backpackers' accommodation. Facilities are limited to a tiny kitchen and a TV lounge. The biggest dorm has four beds and guests have free use of bicycles.
12 Kuhlman Street, Ceduna.
☎ *(08) 8625 3811.*

Dorm bed $16.50; double room $33.

Maintenance & cleanliness	★★☆
Facilities	★★
Atmosphere & character	★★
Security	★★☆
Overall rating	★★

Sights
Astrid Oysters
Land-based tours show you how an oyster farm operates. The tour lasts around 30 minutes and includes oyster tasting.
*Government Road, Denial Bay (about
10km from Ceduna).*
☎ *(08) 8625 3554.*
Cost $5.50.
Tours Mon-Fri 3pm.

Old Schoolhouse Museum
This small museum has exhibits on the region's early settlers and also displays about the Maralinga nuclear test site.
*Corner Murat & Park Terraces,
Ceduna.*
*Open Mon-Tue 10am-noon, Wed-
Thu 10am-noon & 2pm-4pm, Fri-Sat
10am-noon.*

Thevenard Fish Processors
This fish processing factory in Thevenard (3km from Ceduna) operates tours where you can see the local seafood catch being processed. Bookings essential.
303 Bergmann Drive, Thevenard.
☎ *(08) 8625 3111.*
Cost $5.50.
Tours Mon, Wed, Fri 10am.

Port Lincoln

Port Lincoln is a busy fishing port on Boston Bay, the world's second-largest natural harbour.

Although commercial fishing is the main industry with a big tuna exporting business, Port Lincoln is also a popular destination for amateur anglers from Adelaide.

Practical Information
Visitor Information Centre
3 Adelaide Place, Port Lincoln.
☎ *(08) 8683 3544 or 1800 629 911.*
Website www.visitportlincoln.net.
Open 9am-5pm daily.

South Australia

INTERNET ACCESS
Zorro's Computer Services
22 Edinburgh Street, Port Lincoln.
☎ *(08) 8682 1700.*
Open *Mon-Fri 10am-6pm, Sat 10am-3pm.*

Sights
Axel Stenross Maritime Museum
This maritime museum is in the boat building workshop established by the Finnish boat builder, Axel Stenross. It features nautical exhibits with an emphasis on windjammer sailing boats.
97 Lincoln Highway, Port Lincoln.
☎ *(08) 8682 2963.*
Admission *$4.*
Open *Tue, Thu, Sun 1pm-5pm.*

Mill Cottage Museum
This small museum has exhibits on Port Lincoln's history.
Flinders Park, 20 Flinders Highway, Port Lincoln.
☎ *(08) 8682 4650.*
Admission *$4.*
Open *Mon, Wed, Sat 2pm-4.30pm.*

Whyalla
South Australia's second-largest city is an industrial town that is not really worth the detour. Whyalla's main attraction is the BHP Steelworks, which dominates the town.

Practical Information
Whyalla Visitor Information Centre
Lincoln Highway, Whyalla.
☎ *(08) 8645 7900 or 1800 088 589.*
Open *Mon-Fri 9am-5pm, Sat 9am-4pm, Sun 120am-4pm.*

Sights
BHP Whyalla Steelworks
BHP Whyalla Steelworks is the city's largest employer and visitors can take tours of the steel-making plant. This is Australia's only regular steelworks tour. Tours depart from the Tourist Information Centre on Lincoln Highway.
☎ *(08) 8645 7900.*
Admission *$16.*
Tours *Mon, Wed, Fri 1.30pm.*

Whyalla Maritime Museum
This maritime museum features the HMAS Whyalla, Australia's largest permanently landlocked ship, which was the first ship to be built at the Whyalla shipyards. The museum has exhibits of the city's ship building industry and the WWII warships that were constructed here.
Lincoln Highway, Whyalla.
☎ *(08) 8645 7900.*
Admission *$6.60*
Open *10am-4pm daily; ship tours 11am, noon, 1pm, 2pm & 3pm.*

Riverland
South Australia's Riverland region doesn't offer as many attractions as the area around the Murray across the border in Victoria, but it is a popular spot for many travellers who come here to pick up fruit picking work.

Berri
Many travellers come to Berri for fruit picking work. The town doesn't have a lot of attractions but it is home to one of Australia's best worker's hostels. The main crops here are grapes and oranges and the town is home to a large fruit juice factory and Australia's largest winery, which produces the cheap cask wine that is so popular with many backpackers.

Practical Information
Berri Library & Information Centre
Kay Avenue, Berri.
☎ *(08) 8595 2666.*
Open *Mon-Wed 8am-6pm, Thu 8am-8pm, Fri 8am-6pm, Sat 9am-noon.*

Berri Visitor Information Centre
Riverview Drive, Berri.
☎ *(08) 8582 1922.*
Open *Mon-Fri 9am-5.30pm, Sat-Sun 10am-4pm.*

Coming & Going
Premier Stateliner (☎ *(08) 8415 5555; website www.premierstateliner.com.au*) coaches stop at Berri on their Adelaide-Renmark run; they run two daily

coaches on weekdays and one coach on Saturdays and Sundays. Because Berri is on the Sturt Highway, which runs between Adelaide and Sydney, McCafferty's/Greyhound also operate daily coaches that stop here (but they also run an Adelaide-Sydney service via Broken Hill, which doesn't stop in Berri). Coaches stop outside the Visitor Information Centre on Riverview Drive.

Accommodation
Berri Backpackers
This brilliant hostel is one of Australia's best workers' hostels. It is an old house with loads of character and the hostel is set on a large block of land with plenty of room for a large array of facilities that include a sauna, beach volleyball court, tennis court, soccer pitch, swimming pool and several tree houses to chill out in. There is also the usual TV lounge and kitchen plus a great games room with a pool table, table tennis and a piano. Guests have free use of bicycles and cars.
Old Sturt Highway, Berri.
☎ *(08) 8582 3144.*
Dorm bed *$20.*
Reception open *8am-10pm daily.*
🚌

Maintenance & cleanliness	★★★
Facilities	★★★★★
Atmosphere & character	★★★★☆
Security	★
Overall rating	★★★★

Renmark
The oldest town in the Riverland region has a lovely riverfront and it is one of the more interesting places in the area. The town is a popular spot for cruises and houseboat rentals and is home to the PS Industry, a wood-fired paddle steamer that operates cruises on the river on the first Sunday of each month.

There is no backpackers' accommodation in Renmark.

Practical Information
Renmark Paringa Visitor Information Centre
84 Murray Avenue, Renmark.
☎ *(08) 8586 6704.*

Open *Mon-Fri 9am-5pm, Sat 9am-4pm, Sun 10am-4pm.*

Loxton
This charming garden town has more character than other towns in the region and some travellers use Loxton as a base for fruit picking work. The Loxton Historical Village, a small open-air museum, is the main tourist attraction here.

Practical Information
Loxton Visitor Information & Arts Centre
Bookpurnong Terrace, Loxton.
☎ *(08) 8584 7919.*
Open *Mon-Fri 9am-5pm, Sat 9am-12.30pm, Sun 1pm-4pm*

Coming & Going
Premier Stateliner (☎ *(08) 8415 5555; website www.premierstateliner.com.au)* run a coach service between Adelaide and Loxton every day except Saturday.

Accommodation
Harvest Trail Lodge
This is a clean and well-maintained hostel that features two kitchens, Internet access, a TV lounge and a big balcony with a barbecue. All the rooms have air-conditioning, a fridge and a TV.
Kokoda Terrace, Loxton.
☎ *(08) 8584 5646.*
Website *www.harvesttrail.com.*
Dorm bed *$18.50-26.40.*
Credit cards *MC, Visa.*
Reception open *10am-10pm daily.*

Maintenance & cleanliness	★★★★☆
Facilities	★★
Atmosphere & character	★★☆
Security	★★☆
Overall rating	★★★☆

Sights
Loxton Historical Village
This small open-air museum is a historical village with a main street that features more than 30 buildings. The Historical Village has been created to portray life here during the early 20th century.
Riverfront Road, Loxton.

☎ *(08) 8584 7194.*
Admission $5.

Kingston-on-Murray

This tiny town looks run down and it doesn't offer much for visitors, however there is a large vineyard and wetlands conservation complex several kilometres outside town that is worth a visit.

Accommodation
Nomads on Murray

This is a basic workers' hostel with a nice common area with a pool table and TV. Other facilities include the usual kitchen and laundry. The dormitories have lovely river views. It is 3km from the centre of Kingston-on-Murray and a 10-minute drive to Barmera.
Sturt Highway, Kingston-on-Murray.
☎ *(08) 8583 0211 or 1800 665 166.*
Dorm bed $17-20; double room $42.
Credit cards *MC, Visa.*
☎

Maintenance & cleanliness	★★☆
Facilities	★★☆
Atmosphere & character	★★★★☆
Security	★
Overall rating	★★★

Limestone Coast

Most people speed through this region while travelling between Adelaide and Melbourne, perhaps stopping for no more than a quick bite. If you're driving along the coastal route between Adelaide and the South Australia/Victoria border you'll pass by the Coorong National Park that is noted for its bird life, particularly pelicans. Closer the to border at the extreme South-East of the state, you'll find Mt Gambier, a pleasant regional city known for its crater lakes.

Coorong National Park

This large national park on the coast around mid-way between Adelaide and the Victorian border is known for its lagoons, sand dunes and bird life.

Practical Information
National Park Office

34 Princes Highway, Meningie.
☎ *(08) 8575 1200.*
Website *www.environment.sa.gov.au/ parks/coorong/.*
Open *Mon, Wed, Fri 9am-5pm.*

Coming & Going

Access to the Coorong National Park is via several points on Princes Highway that include Jack's Point, Policeman's Point and Salt Creek. Access from the Princes Highway is normally to bird watching observation points although there is also some access to campgrounds.

Alternatively you can organise tours from Meningie, which is the closest major town. If you're come here for fishing, then Meningie is the best access point for the park. It is also possible to visit the Coorong National Park by taking a cruise from Goolwa on the Fleurieu Peninsula.

Accommodation

There are several camping grounds within the national park. Visit the national parks office on Main Street in Meningie for detailed information and to organise camping permits ($6.50 per car). Camping permits are also available from the Shell service station in Salt Creek.

Mount Gambier

Located in South Australia's southeast corner, Mount Gambier is a major regional centre that is worth a look. The main attractions are the two crater lakes, Blue Lake and Valley Lake, which are both located on an extinct volcano overlooking the city.

Mount Gambier is also a good spot to base yourself while exploring the Coonawarra wine region, which is located about 30km north of town.

Practical Information
Lady Nelson Visitor Information Centre

Jubilee Highway East, Mount Gambier.
☎ *1800 087 187.*
Open *9am-5pm daily.*

South Australia

Accommodation
The Jail

The Jail is a unique hostel in an old prison, which features tall stone walls topped with razor wire, a big exercise yard and accommodation in former cells. It has a bar/restaurant with a pool table and lots of atmosphere.

25 Margaret Street, Mount Gambier.
☎ *(08) 8723 0032.*
***Dorm bed** $24 ($22 YHA); **single room** $32 ($30 YHA); **double/twin room** $52 ($48 YHA).*
***Credit cards** MC, Visa.*
***Reception open** 9am-2pm & 4.30pm-10pm daily.*
🚐

Maintenance & cleanliness	★★★
Facilities	★★☆
Atmosphere & character	★★★★
Security	★★☆
Overall rating	★★★☆

Naracoorte Caves National Park

South Australia's only World Heritage area is comprised of several caves that feature fragile stalactite and stalagmite formations. The caves have earned their World Heritage listing because of the extensive collection of fossils that have been unearthed here.

Fossils found in the caves provide a unique glimpse into the past and the Wonambi Fossil Centre inside the park has an excellent display featuring animatronic depictions of the extinct marsupial megafauna that lived here around 200,000 years ago.

One of the caves is home to a colony of the rare Southern Bentwing Bat and infrared video cameras have been set up that allow you to view the bat from the Bat Cave Teleview Centre.

There are various tours of the different caves, each with its own unique features.

An hour-long tour takes you to a large fossil deposit in the Victorian Fossil Cave where you get to experience the cave's World Heritage values.

Alexandra and Cathedral Caves offers a beautiful glimpse of cave decorations.

Tickets for the Alexandra Cave and Wonambi Fossil Centre also include entrance to Wet Cave, which features a self-guided walk that is ideal if you want to explore the cave at your own pace.

With the exception of adventure caving trips (see below) and the Cathedral Cave tour ($12), cave tours cost $10 for one tour, $18 for two tours, $22 for three tours and $28 for four tours.

Most of the cave tours are fairly tame, focusing mostly on the caves' natural history but there are also some excellent value adventure caving tours that operate in Stick-Tomato, Blackberry and Fox Caves. Adventure caving trips cost $22.

Coming & Going

Naracoorte Caves National Park is 10km south of Naracoorte and it is difficult to reach without your own transport.

Oz Experience stops here, but if you're travelling by regular bus you'll need to take a taxi from Naracoorte.

Accommodation

The closest hostel to the national park is Naracoorte Backpackers in Naracoorte, but it is also an easy trip from the Jail YHA in Mt Gambier, a one-hour drive south of here.

There is also a camping site at the park that is well equipped and features a free laundry.

Naracoorte Backpackers Hostel

This small hostel caters mostly to backpackers working around Naracoorte. It provides basic accommodation with limited facilities that include two kitchens, a TV lounge and a games room with a pool table. Although it's little old, the manager does a good job organising work and he runs bus trips on the weekends.

4 Jones Street, Naracoorte.
☎ *(08) 8762 3835.*
***Dorm bed** $20 per night, $130 per week.*

Maintenance & cleanliness	★★☆
Facilities	★★★☆
Atmosphere & character	★★★★
Security	★★☆
Overall rating	★★★☆

Port Augusta

If you're travelling west or north from Adelaide, you'll pass through Port Augusta. This industrial city lies at a crossroads between Adelaide, Alice Springs and Perth and is the last large town before the outback.

Port Augusta doesn't have a lot to offer the traveller, apart from a convenient place to stock up on supplies before heading into the outback.

The town doesn't have a very good reputation with Adelaide residents, however its attractions are surprisingly interesting and worth visiting if you have time to spare. In general the town's sights reflect Port Augusta's position as gateway to the outback and the Flinders Ranges.

Practical Information
Port Augusta Tourist Information Centre
Wadlata Outback Centre, 41 Flinders Terrace, Port Augusta.
☎ *(08) 8641 0793 or 1800 633 060.*
Website *www.flinders.outback.on.net.*
Open *Mon-Fri 9am-5pm, Sat-Sun 10am-4pm.*

Accommodation
Blue Fox Lodge
The better of Port Augusta's two hostels is a small place that sleeps only 20 people. It is a nice house with solid bunk beds, a bar, barbecue area, a small kitchen and a TV lounge.
Corner Trent Road & National Highway One, Port Augusta.
☎ *(08) 8641 2960.*
Website *www.bluefoxlodge.com.*
Dorm bed *$19 ($16 VIP/YHA).*
Reception open *9am-10pm daily.*

Maintenance & cleanliness	★★★★
Facilities	★★
Atmosphere & character	★★★★½
Security	★★½
Overall rating	★★★★½

Port Augusta International Backpackers Hostel
This cheap hostel is a bit rough around the edges and has basic facilities including a TV lounge and a small kitchen.

17 Trent Road, Port Augusta.
☎ *(08) 8641 1063.*
Dorm bed *$11.*
Reception open *noon-9pm daily.*

Maintenance & cleanliness	★★½
Facilities	★
Atmosphere & character	★★★
Security	★★½
Overall rating	★★½

Sights
Arid Lands Botanic Gardens
This unique park north of the town centre showcases a range of plant-life that thrives in desert conditions. The Arid Lands Botanic Gardens also includes a research centre and fascinating information centre.
Stuart Highway, Port Augusta.
☎ *(08) 8641 1049.*
Admission *free.*
Open *Mon-Fri 9am-5pm, Sat-Sun 10am-4pm.*

Homestead Park Pioneer Museum
This old pioneer homestead has been restored and features period furnishings and loads of old farm machinery. Most travellers would probably give this a miss although there are enough old gadgets to keep enthusiasts busy for hours.
Elsie Street, Port Augusta.
☎ *(08) 8642 2035.*
Admission *$2.50.*
Open *9am-noon & 1pm-4pm daily.*

School of the Air
Children living in remote outback areas learn through this correspondence school that is noted for running classes over the airwaves.
59 Power Crescent, Port Augusta.
☎ *(08) 8642 2077.*
Admission *$2.50.*
Tours depart *Mon-Fri 10am except school holidays.*

Wadlata Outback Centre
An interesting attraction depicting Outback culture with displays on early exploration, geology and Aboriginal culture.
41 Flinders Terrace, Port Augusta.
☎ *(08) 8642 4511.*

Admission $8.25
Open *Mon-Fri 9am-5.30pm, Sat-Sun 10am-4pm.*

Flinders Ranges

This remote mountain range, which encompasses Wilpena Pound and the Flinders Ranges National Park, is one of South Australia's best attractions. The Flinders Ranges start south of Port Augusta, although the big attraction is Wilpena Pound and the Flinders Ranges National Park in the north-central Flinders Ranges. Some of the towns between Port Augusta and Wilpena Pound are worth visiting on the way to the national park.

Coming & Going & Local Transport

Although most express buses bypass the Flinders Ranges, backpacker buses such as Adventure Tours, Groovy Grape, Oz Experience, and the Wayward Bus go via this region on their routes connecting Adelaide with Alice Springs. Even if you are travelling on an express bus pass, it's possible to pick up a connecting Premier Stateliner bus from Adelaide or Port Augusta as far as Wilpena Pound.

The guys at Andu Lodge ((08) 8648 6655 or 1800 639933; *website www. headingbush.com)* in Quorn are experts on the Flinders Ranges and run tours departing from the lodge in Quorn. A two-night tour is $199 while a three-night tour costs a little more at $275.

Quorn

Quorn is a quaint town with some interesting old buildings.

The unique heritage streetscapes have been a backdrop for many Australian films during the 1970s and 1980s including *Gallipoli*, the *Shiralee* and the *Sundowners*.

It was once an important railway town used to service the *Old Ghan* Railway before the route was discontinued in 1980 in favour of the less flood-prone route that more closely follows the Stuart Highway.

This is the first town after the turn-off for Wilpena Pound and is worth a stop.

Practical Information
Flinders Rangers Visitor Information Centre
3 Seventh Street, Quorn.
 (08) 8648 6419.
Open *9am-5pm daily.*

Accommodation
Andu Lodge Backpackers
Andu Lodge is a small friendly hostel with fairly basic facilities that include a kitchen, laundry and a TV lounge. The staff are very helpful and knowledgeable about the surrounding region and they operate tours to the Flinders Ranges.
12 First Street, Quorn
 (08) 8648 6655 or 1800 639 933.
Dorm bed $23.50 ($20 YHA); single room $33.50 ($30 YHA); double/ twin room $57 ($50 YHA); includes breakfast.
Credit cards MC, Visa.
Reception open 7.30am-9pm daily.

Maintenance & cleanliness	★★⯨
Facilities	★★
Atmosphere & character	★★★★
Security	★
Overall rating	★★⯨

Eating & Drinking
There are four pubs in Quorn, although the Transcontinental, aka the Tranny, is by far the most popular with excellent meals at bargain prices.

Sights
Warren Gorge
This small scenic reserve makes a nice daytrip from Quorn or a detour en route between Quorn and Flinders Ranges National Park.

The gorge itself is around 300 metres long and 100 metres deep and is one of several small gorges in the area.

The main reason to visit is to spot the endangered Yellow Footed Rock Wallaby. You can spot the wallaby from your car as you drive around the reserve, but you'll have better luck if you walk around, as they're easier to find if you are quiet.

Warren Gorge is around a 20-minute drive north of Quorn and there are no entry fees to the reserve. Free camping is available in the reserve.

The Dutchmans Stern
This hill, northwest of Quorn, has a popular hiking trail (10.5km, five hours) that goes up to the ridge offering views to Port Augusta and Wilpena Pound. It is accessible by bicycle from Quorn, making it a popular excursion for travellers staying at the Andu Lodge.

Pichi Richi Railway
Enthusiasts have restored part of the *Old Ghan* railway and now operate a number of steam trains between Quorn and Port Augusta.
☎ *(08) 8658 1109.*
Website www.prr.org.au.
Fares single $34, return $29-85.
Trains run most days Apr-Oct Sat-Mon.

Hawker
Heading north, Hawker is the last real town before the national park so you'll need to stop here to buy groceries, fuel, get money from the ATM and buy some snacks for the trip north. There's not much else to do in town, although some people use the town as a base and there are several places where you can organise trips to the national park including scenic flights and camel trekking.

Practical Information
Hawker Visitor Information Centre
Hawker Motors, Corner Cradock & Wilpena Roads, Hawker.
☎ *(08) 8648 4022.*
Open 8.30am-5.30pm daily.

National Parks & Wildlife Service
60 Elder Street, Hawker.
☎ *(08) 8648 4244.*

Wilpena Pound & Flinders Ranges National Park
The Flinders Ranges National Park is home to some of the most spectacular

scenery in the outback and it is one of South Australia's most visited national parks. The national park has an extensive network of walking tracks which range from short ten-minute walks to more challenging hikes lasting for several days.

Wilpena Pound is the main centre within the national park and is home to the information centre, camping grounds, motel and general store. Many of the walking tracks within the park originate here. Wilpena Pound is a spectacular natural basin ringed by steep cliffs with some rewarding hiking trails. Perhaps the most popular short hike is the two-hour walk to Wangara Lookout that offers dramatic views. Popular longer walks include Edowie Gorge and St Mary's Peak, each of these is a very long day hike although the two walks can be combined into a longer two or three day trek.

The region is also home to fascinating Aboriginal rock paintings. Ask at the information centre about hiking trails that include rock art. If you're travelling on Adventure Tours or Oz Experience you'll stop at the Yourambulla Caves that contain some of the area's best rock paintings.

If you're going on any walks in the park, remember to take plenty of water, particularly in summer. A litre for every couple of hours is essential.

Admission to the national park costs $6.50 per day for a car or $4 if you're arriving by bus. Alternatively you can buy a four week parks pass for $21 that allows you to visit all South Australian national parks except desert parks and parks on Kangaroo Island.

Practical Information
Wilpena Pound Visitor Information Centre
National Park entrance, Wilpena Pound.
☎ *(08) 8648 0048.*
Website www.wilpenapound.com.au.
Open 8am-6pm daily.

Coming & Going
If you're not driving or travelling on one of the backpackers' buses, then your only transport option is the Premier Stateliner (☎ *(08) 8415 5555;*

website www.premierstateliner.com.au) bus from Adelaide via Port Augusta. This service departs Adelaide on Wednesday and Friday mornings with an additional service from Port Augusta on Sundays. The return service departs Wilpena Pound on Thursdays, Fridays and Sundays.

Accommodation

Unless you want to stay at the over-priced motel, camping is the only accommodation within the national park. If you don't have one already, your best bet is to buy a tent at one of the camping stores in Adelaide, or possibly in Port Augusta.

Camping in the park costs $11 per car or $4 per person per night.

Parachilna

With a permanent population of only six, this tiny town just north of Flinders Ranges National Park can be a surprisingly lively place. You'll stop here for the night if you're travelling on the Oz Experience bus on their route between Adelaide and Alice Springs.

Parachilna revolves around the bar at the Prairie Hotel, which is renowned for its native cuisine which features plenty of emu and kangaroo served up with bush tomatoes. There are several unique excursions that can be arranged from the hotel.

Accommodation
Parachilna Overflow

The Parachilna Overflow is the cluster of air-conditioned prefabricated units behind the Prairie Hotel. Although barren, the rooms are clean and comfortable with made up beds. Common areas include a swimming pool and barbecue area. There is also a nice common room that is reserved for Adventure Tours and Oz Experience customers, which has a modern kitchen, pool table and Internet access.

Corner High Street & West Terrace, Parachilna.
☎ *(08) 8648 4814.*
Website *www.prairiehotel.com.au.*
Dorm bed *$25;* **double room** *$60.*
Credit cards *Amex, Diners, MC, Visa.*

Maintenance & cleanliness	★★★☆
Facilities	★★
Atmosphere & character	★★★☆
Security	★
Overall rating	★★★☆

Outback South Australia

South Australia is Australia's driest state and this is most evident when travelling in the Outback. For most travellers, the Outback is the vast expanse of red sand that you see from the bus window en route to destinations north and west of Port Augusta. In most cases the only places you'll stop are the lonely roadhouses on the highway, although Coober Pedy on the Stuart Highway between Adelaide and Alice Springs is a popular and unique stop over.

If you're travelling on one of the backpackers' buses, you may take the Oodnadatta Track between Flinders Ranges and Coober Pedy.

The Oodnadatta Track

The 615km Oodnadatta Track is a convenient shortcut between the Flinders Ranges and Central Australia. It also gives you a more genuine outback experience than sticking to the highway.

The track runs from Marree, 1½ hours north of Parachilna, to Marla, on the Stuart Highway between Coober Pedy and Alice Springs. Many travellers, and several of the backpacker buses, take the track as far as William Creek and then continue on William Creek Road to Coober Pedy.

The Oodnadatta Track follows the path of the old Ghan railway and also passes by the 5,300km-long dog fence and the southern edge of Lake Eyre. Some of the small outback communities on the track provide a glimpse of Australia that few tourists ever have the chance to experience. The main towns on the track are Marla, William Creek and Oodnadatta.

Marree is the starting point for both the Oodnadatta and Birdsville Tracks.

Normally a sleepy town of around 80 people, it comes alive in July when it hosts the annual Camel Cup. If possible it is worth planning your trip around this event since it is not everyday that you get the opportunity to attend a camel race.

William Creek is Australia's smallest town with a population of only 12, but it is located on the world's largest cattle property. At 32,500 square km, Anna Creek Station is about the same size as Belgium. Scenic flights over Lake Eyre depart from here.

If you continue north along the track, you'll come to Oodnadatta; an uninspiring place that was the birthplace of the Royal Flying Doctor Service. There are a few interesting sites here including a small museum.

Despite popular misconceptions, a 4WD vehicle is not necessary to tackle the track and many people head up this way in a regular car, especially during dry weather. However it is an unsealed road so you are prohibited from taking rental cars on it.

Accommodation
MARREE
Marree Drover's Rest Tourist Park

This caravan park has air-conditioned cabins, although not much in the way of other facilities.

Corner Oodnadatta & Birdsville Tracks, Marree.
☎ *(08) 8675 8371.*
***Dorm bed** $15.*

WILLIAM CREEK
William Creek Hotel

The backpackers' accommodation at the William Creek Hotel consists of pre-fabricated units with old beds. There aren't any communal facilities other than the pub, which is where most people staying here spend all their time.

Oodnadatta Track, William Creek.
☎ *(08) 8670 7880.*
***Dorm bed** $14-19; **camping** $3.40 per person or $10 per car.*
***Credit cards** Amex, MC, Visa.*

Maintenance & cleanliness	★★☆
Facilities	☆

Atmosphere & character	★★☆
Security	★★☆
Overall rating	★★☆

OODNADATTA
Pink Roadhouse

The Pink Roadhouse offers very basic accommodation in an old shack behind their shop. Everything here is old and worn and facilities are limited, however it's cheap and the people who work here are a mine of information about travelling along the track.

Oodnadatta Track, Oodnadatta.
☎ *(08) 8670 7822.*
***Dorm bed** $10; **double room** $48; **camping** $9.50 for the first person then $5 per each extra person.*
***Credit cards** Amex, MC, Visa.*

Maintenance & cleanliness	☆
Facilities	★
Atmosphere & character	★
Security	★
Overall rating	★

Woomera

This modern town between Port Augusta and Coober Pedy is an interesting place with an intriguing history. The location of Woomera was top secret for many years and visiting the town was prohibited until 1982.

Woomera was established in 1947 as missile testing site for the British government and over 4,000 missiles were launched from the expansive Woomera Prohibited Area over the following 30 years. Some of the rockets and missiles tested at Woomera are on display at the Woomera Missile Park in the town centre.

Although originally a British base, Woomera has played host to a number of military and aerospace organisations including ELDO (European Launcher Development Organisation), NASA and the United States Air Force.

In its heyday Woomera had a population of 6,800 but this has dropped to the 600 that live here today. The town's former importance has left it well endowed with an excellent infrastructure that is the envy of other towns of a similar size.

Practical Information
Woomera Heritage & Visitor Centre
Dewrang Avenue, Woomera.
☎ *(08) 8673 7799.*
Website www.woomerasa.com.au.
Open 9am-5pm daily.

Accommodation
Woomera Travellers Village
The large Woomera Travellers Village has all the charm of an army barracks. However the size of the complex means that it is very likely that you'll have a whole room to yourself. Each of the backpackers' rooms has two single beds plus a fridge and hand basin. The furnishings are old and it could be better maintained.
Old Pimba Road, Woomera.
☎ *(08) 8673 7800.*
Website www.woomera.com.
Dorm bed $22-25; double room $55-66; camping $9 per person.
Reception open 8am-7pm daily.
🚌

Maintenance & cleanliness	★★
Facilities	★★☆
Atmosphere & character	-
Security	★
Overall rating	★★☆

Sights
Woomera Heritage Centre
This small museum has fascinating exhibits about previously classified aspects of Woomera's history.
Dewrang Street, Woomera.
☎ *(08) 8673 7042.*
Admission $3.
Open 9am-5pm daily.

Coober Pedy

This outback opal-mining town is unique in that much of it is built underground. Many of Coober Pedy's homes and other facilities such as churches and a backpackers hostel have been built underground to escape the summer heat, which sometimes reaches 50° C.

Coober Pedy is the source of 80% of the world's opals. If you want to buy opals you may get a better deal here than in the big cities, although the shops here do a roaring business with passing tourist coaches so it would be best to avoid the busy times if you want to save money.

There are more than a million abandoned mine shafts around Coober Pedy so in the interests of your safety it is a good idea to avoid wandering around the outskirts of town alone.

The town's unique setting has been used as the film-set for several movies including *Priscilla Queen of the Desert* and *Mad Max III.*

Practical Information
Visitor Information Centre
Hutchison Street, Coober Pedy.
☎ *(08) 8672 5298 or 1800 637 076.*
Open Mon-Fri 9am-5pm.

Accommodation
All the hostels in Coober Pedy have at least some accommodation underground. An underground hostel is basically a series of caves and there are not always doors to the rooms, for this reason there may not be the same level

Coober Pedy

Accommodation
❶ Bedrock Backpackers
❷ Radeka's Backpackers Inn

of security or privacy that you would find in a more conventional hostel.

Bedrock Backpackers

Bedrock Backpackers is a clean but basic underground hostel with a TV room and a tiny kitchen. Toilets and showers are outside next to the spaceship in the car park. Check in next door at the Opal Cave.
Hutchison Street, Coober Pedy.
☎ *(08) 8672 5028.*
Website www.opalcavecooberpedy.com.
Dorm bed $17.
Credit cards Amex, Diners, JCB, MC, Visa.
🚌

Maintenance & cleanliness	★★☆
Facilities	★
Atmosphere & character	★★★
Security	★
Overall rating	★★

Radeka's Backpackers Inn

Radeka's is the longest running backpackers hostel in Coober Pedy. Facilities include a pool table, a bar and Internet access and an above ground common area with a laundry, and a big kitchen and a TV lounge. Accommodation is underground. Radeka's has the best facilities and atmosphere of the Coober Pedy hostels.
Corner Hutchison & Oliver Streets, Coober Pedy.
☎ *(08) 8672 5223 or 1800 633 891.*
Dorm bed $22 ($21 VIP/YHA); double room $52 ($50 VIP/YHA).
Reception open summer 7.30am-10pm daily; winter 7.30am-9pm daily.
Credit cards Amex, MC, Visa.
🚌

Maintenance & cleanliness	★★★☆
Facilities	★★☆
Atmosphere & character	★★★☆
Security	-
Overall rating	★★★☆

Riba's Underground Camping

Riba's is a unique accommodation option with a choice of above and underground camping. There are no dorms, you just pitch your tent underground. Facilities include a cosy underground TV room and an outdoors kitchen area. It is on William Creek Road about 5km south of the town centre. Because Riba's isn't a hostel, it has no star rating.
William Creek Road, Coober Pedy.
☎ *(08) 8672 5614.*
Camping $15 for two people above ground, $9 per person underground.

Tasmania

Australia's island state provides a totally different experience from the mainland. Forget any notions of arid Outback – Tasmania is a land of rugged mountains, rolling green hills and raging rivers.

Tasmania is one of the world's most picturesque islands. About 20 per cent of Tasmania has been designated World Heritage area and another 10 per cent is national park or reserve.

There's more to Tasmania than the great outdoors, the island state has a fascinating convict past and it is one of the first areas in Australia to be settled by Europeans. Although small, the main cities have a more established feel than elsewhere in Australia. The former penal colony at Port Arthur on the Tasman Peninsula is the state's most popular tourist attraction and perhaps your best opportunity to gain an understanding of what life was like during the convict days.

Coming & Going

Most travellers visit Tasmania via Melbourne, which is the departure point for most flights and ferries. Flying is generally the cheapest and quickest option, however you'll need to take the ferry if you want to take your car over.

AIR

Although there are some flights to other destinations, the majority of flights to Tassie depart from Melbourne.

Qantas flys into Burnie, Devonport, Hobart and Launceston; Rex flies from Melbourne to Burnie and Devonport and Virgin Blue fly to Hobart and Launceston.

Many travellers book one-way tickets and fly into one city and out from another.

FERRY

The *Spirit of Tasmania* (☎ *1800 634 906; website www.spiritoftasmania.com.*

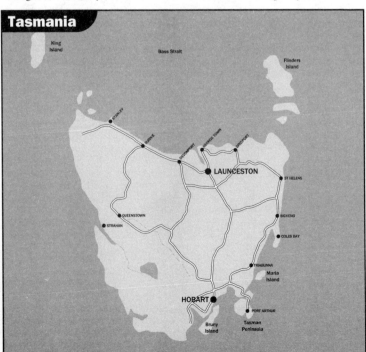

au) sails to Devonport from both Melbourne and Sydney.

The *Spirit of Tasmania I* and *II* depart Melbourne and Devonport at 9pm everyday, arriving at around 7am. Fares on the *Spirit of Tasmania* are $112-140 one-way per person for a cruise seat.

A new ship, the *Spirit of Tasmania III*, will sail between Sydney and Devonport from January 2004. It will sail from Berth 7 at Darling Harbour in Sydney and the journey to Devonport will take 20½-hours. Fares on this trip are $230-304 one-way per person including hostel-style accommodation and meals.

On both routes you can take a car across for free in the off-peak season, but you need to pay an additional $55 between 10 December and 30 January.

It is a good idea to book well ahead as ferries can fill up fast, particularly during long weekends and school holidays.

Local Transport

Tasmania is cut-off from mainland Australia meaning that transport networks have developed separately to the rest of the country. For instance, apart from tourist railways, there are no regular passenger train services and McCafferty's/Greyhound do not serve the state.

Many travellers choose to rent a car to explore Tassie and this gives you the most freedom, however there is good bus network that offers some good value travel passes.

BUS

TassieLink/Tigerline (☎ *1300 653 633; website www.tigerline.com.au)* and Redline (☎ *(03) 6336 1446 or 1300 360 000; website www.tasredline.com)* are Tasmania's two main coach operators with scheduled services to most major destinations within the state. They also offer several travel passes that are good value, particularly for solo travellers who may not be able to justify the cost of car rental.

Both companies meet the Devonport ferry and run services to Cradle Mountain-Lake St Clair National Park, but TassieLink has the more extensive route network.

Redline Tassie Pass

This pass allows unlimited travel on Redlines coaches within the timeframe indicated on the pass.

Pass	Cost
7 day pass	$135
10 day pass	$160
14 day pass	$185
21 day pass	$219

TassieLink Explorer Bus Pass

This pass allows unlimited travel on TassieLink buses within a network that covers most major destinations within Tasmania including the Tasman Peninsula. It even gets you off-the-beaten-track to destinations such as national parks and World Heritage areas.

Pass	Cost
7 days travel in a 10 day period	$160
10 days travel in a 15 day period	$190
14 days travel in a 20 day period	$220
21 days travel in a 30 day period	$260

Adventure Tours
Hop-On Hop-Off Bus

Adventure Tours (☎ *1300 654 604; website www.adventuretours.com.au)* operate a hop-on hop-off backpackers bus around Tasmania that follows an anti-clockwise circular route visiting virtually every point of interest on the island.

Because it makes overnight stops, you should allow a minimum of 10 days to complete the journey. The travel pass costs $325 and is valid for up to two months of travel. You can only travel once on each sector.

TOURS

There are several companies that operate tours aimed at the backpacker market. You may want to consider these if you want to see a lot and your time is limited although they don't have the flexibility that comes with independent travel. The following companies offer tours of Tasmania:

Adventure Tours

Adventure Tours (☎ *1300 654 604; website www.adventuretours.com.au)* operate several excellent tours. Three-day tours cost $355-365 and the longer six and seven-day tours cost $690-710. They also run a hop-on hop-off bus.

Bottom Bits Bus

Bottom Bits Bus (☎ *1800 777 103; website www.bottombitsbus.com)* offers three-day tours of either the east or west coast for $325 ($310 ISIC/VIP/YHA). They also run day tours from Hobart to Freycinet National Park, the Huon Valley, Mount Field National Park and Port Arthur; these day tours cost $89 ($85 ISIC/VIP/YHA).

Under Down Under

Under Down Under (☎ *(03) 6369 5555 or 1800 064 726; website www. underdownunder.com.au)* operate a good selection of tours that range from two to seven days.

DRIVING

Car rental is by far the most popular transport option in Tasmania. It's the most flexible way to get around as you're not tied to bus routes or time-tables and it is relatively affordable, particularly if the cost is split among several travellers.

National Parks

Tasmania's wilderness is one of its main attractions with thousands of travellers visiting its national parks each year. Entry fees for Tasmanian national parks are $10 per day for a car and up to eight passengers or $3.50 per person travelling by bike or public transport.

Most travellers find the Holiday Pass much better value – this allows you to visit national parks throughout the state for up to two months. The Holiday Pass costs $33 for a car and up to eight passengers or $13.20 per person travelling by bike or public transport.

National Park Passes can be bought at park entry booths, tourist information centres and national park visitor centres.

Hobart National Park Visitor Centre

134 Macquarie Street, Hobart.
☎ *(03) 6233 6191.*
Open *Mon-Fri 9am-5pm.*

Launceston National Park Visitor Centre

Prospect Offices, Bass Highway, South Launceston.
☎ *(03) 6336 5312.*
Open *Mon-Fri 9am-5pm.*

Hobart

Tasmania's largest city is perfectly situated at the mouth of the Derwent River with a compact centre and suburbs clinging to the hillside overlooking the wide estuary. The city is well located as a base for exploring the surrounding countryside making it ideal for excursions to the Huon Valley, Port Arthur on the Tasman Peninsula, and nearby towns like Richmond and New Norfolk.

It is the second oldest state capital and it has retained its old colonial architecture more so than any other large Australian city. Battery Point and the downtown area, particularly around Salamanca Place, is full of renovated sandstone buildings which have been converted into pubs, cafés and restaurants which give the city a vibrant air despite the general slow pace of the city. Held here each Saturday, Salamanca Market is a great place to hang around and soak up the atmosphere.

Although Tasmania's main appeal is its wilderness, Hobart does have a few worthwhile sights. There are some interesting museums and it is also possible to take a guided tour of the Cadbury chocolate factory and the Cascade brewery, both of which offer tasting.

Practical Information
INFORMATION CENTRES & USEFUL ADDRESSES
American Express

74A Liverpool Street, Hobart.
☎ *(03) 6234 3711.*
Website *www.americanexpress.com.*
Open *Mon-Fri 9am-5pm.*

Hobart Information Centre

20 Davey Street, Hobart.
☎ *(03) 6230 8233.*
Open *Mon-Fri 8.30am-5.15pm, Sat-Sun 8am-4pm.*

INTERNET ACCESS
Access on Macquarie
157 Macquarie Street, Hobart.
☎ *(03) 6231 6848.*
Open *10am-dusk daily.*

The Pelican Loft
35A Elizabeth Street, Hobart.
☎ *(03) 6234 2225.*
Open *summer Mon-Fri 9am-9pm, Sat 10.30am-6pm; winter Mon-Fri 9am-6pm, Sat 10.30am-4pm.*

LAUNDROMAT
Machine Laundry Café
12 Salamanca Square, Hobart.
☎ *(03) 6224 9922.*
Open *Mon-Sat 8am-4.30pm, Sun 8.30am-4.30pm.*

Coming & Going
AIR
Hobart Airport (☎ *(03) 6216 1600; website www.hobartairpt.com.au)* is on the A3 highway about 17km east of the city centre. The Airporter bus service (☎ *0419 382240)* runs regularly between the airport and central Hobart and they can drop you off at your hostel. The 15-minute trip costs $9.20.

BUS
Bus travel is the most common form of public transport within Tasmania, and Hobart is well connected to other destinations within the state. Redline bus services terminate at the Transit Centre at 199 Collins Street. The TassieLink and Tigerline coach terminal is at 64 Brisbane Street.

HITCHHIKING
Tasmania is Australia's best state for hitching and Hobart is a great city to hitch from.

The Midland Highway (route 1) is the main road through the middle of Tasmania and the quickest route to Devonport and Launceston. The Murchison Highway (route A10) runs from Hobart to Burnie on the north coast via Queenstown. Either of these roads is a good bet if you're heading to the north coast, although the Midland Highway

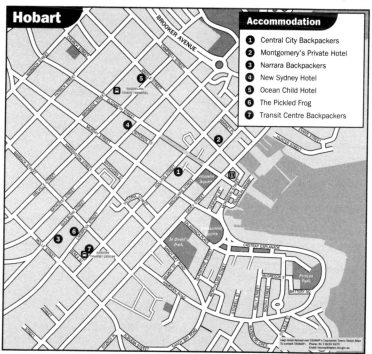

Hobart

Accommodation
1. Central City Backpackers
2. Montgomery's Private Hotel
3. Narrara Backpackers
4. New Sydney Hotel
5. Ocean Child Hotel
6. The Pickled Frog
7. Transit Centre Backpackers

Tasmania

will be a much quicker run. The best hitching spot to catch traffic bound for both these roads is the patch of road just north of Claremont in Hobart's northern suburbs. Use a sign as the spot has traffic bound for both highways. Local buses run from the centre of Hobart to Claremont.

The Tasman Highway (route A3) runs from Hobart up the east coast. If you're heading in this direction, take a bus to Cambridge (near the airport) and try your luck there.

An easier option is to use a web-based ride sharing service such as BUG Ride (*website http://australia.bugride.com*), this allows travellers to both offer lifts and search for rides throughout Australia.

Local Transport

Hobart Metro (☎ *13 22 01; website www.metrotas.com.au*) runs buses within the Hobart area with most buses terminating near the main post office on Elizabeth Street and also in Macquarie Street and Franklin Square in the city centre.

Single tickets start at $1.40 and go up to $3.20 depending on the route. Off-peak multi-trip tickets are available for $3.60.

Accommodation
Adelphi Court YHA

This hostel consists of an old building with a reception and common room and another building with accommodation. There's a shady courtyard between the two buildings. Shared facilities include a big common room with table tennis, pool table and a TV. There's also a kitchen and barbecue area. It is inconveniently located in the suburbs about 2½km north of the city centre.
17 Stoke Street, New Town.
🚌 *15, 16, 17, 25-42, 100, 105-128.*
☎ *(03) 6228 4829.*
Dorm bed *$23.50-25.50 ($20-22 YHA);* **single room** *$59.50-74.50 ($56-71 YHA);* **double room** *$63-78 ($56-71 YHA);* **twin room** *$63-69 ($56-62 YHA).*
Credit cards *MC, Visa.*
Reception open *1 Jan-15 Mar 7.30am-10.30am & 4pm-9pm daily; 15 Mar-15*

Dec 8am-10am & 4pm-7pm daily; 16-31 Dec 7.30am-10.30am & 4pm-9pm daily.
🖥

Maintenance & cleanliness	★★★
Facilities	★★
Atmosphere & character	★★☆
Security	★
Overall rating	★★☆

Allports Hostel

This is a big place comprising an old building with a newer extension at the back. The quality of accommodation and other facilities is very good, particularly in the newer part of the building. It has a TV lounge, a fully equipped kitchen, Internet access and a recreation area with table tennis and a pool table.
432 Elizabeth Street, North Hobart.
🚌 *100, 110.*
☎ *(03) 6231 5464.*
Website *www.tassie.net.au/~allports.*
Dorm bed *$20;* **single room** *$35;* **double room** *$50-60.*
Credit cards *MC, Visa.*
Reception open *7am-11pm daily.*
🖥 ♿

Maintenance & cleanliness	★★★★☆
Facilities	★★
Atmosphere & character	★★★★☆
Security	★★☆
Overall rating	★★★★☆

Central City Backpackers

Central City Backpackers is a large hostel with a brilliant central location. It has a fully equipped kitchen and a common room with a TV and fireplace.
138 Collins Street, Hobart.
☎ *(03) 6224 2404 or 1800 811 507.*
Website *www.centralbackpackers.com .au.*
Dorm bed *$18-22 ($17-21 VIP);* **single room** *$36 ($35 VIP);* **double/ twin room** *$48 ($46 VIP).*
Reception open *8am-9pm daily.*

Maintenance & cleanliness	★★★
Facilities	★★☆
Atmosphere & character	★★★
Security	★★★☆
Overall rating	★★★☆

Montgomery's Private Hotel

This centrally located hostel is very clean and everything is brand new.

There is a small fully equipped kitchen and a small TV lounge with Internet access. The largest dorm has 12 beds, but most are either six or eight-bed dorms. The bunk beds have individual reading lights. The double and twin rooms are very nice and some of them have en suite bathrooms, TVs, fridges and telephones.

9 Argyle Street, Hobart.
☎ *(03) 6231 2660.*
Dorm bed *$25 ($22 YHA);* **single room** *$65-89;* **double/twin room** *$65-89.*
Credit cards *MC, Visa.*
Reception open *8.30am-9pm daily.*

Maintenance & cleanliness	★★★★★
Facilities	★☆
Atmosphere & character	★★★☆
Security	★★★
Overall rating	★★★★☆

Narrara Backpackers

Narrara Backpackers is a very nice hostel that is clean and well maintained. It features several lounge areas with TVs plus free Internet access. It has the best atmosphere of Hobart's hostels.

88 Goulburn Street, Hobart.
☎ *(03) 6231 3191.*
Dorm bed *$19;* **single room** *$44;* **double/twin room** *$48.*
Reception open *7am-10pm daily.*
🚗

Maintenance & cleanliness	★★★★☆
Facilities	★☆
Atmosphere & character	★★★★★
Security	★★
Overall rating	★★★★☆

New Sydney Hotel

This small hostel is above a pub in the city centre. It has basic accommodation in small dorms. Facilities include a small kitchen and TV lounge. The furnishings are old and it could be better maintained.

87 Bathurst Street, Hobart.
☎ *(03) 6234 4516.*
Dorm bed *$18.*
Credit cards *Amex, MC, Visa.*
Reception open *Mon noon-10pm, Tue noon-midnight, Wed-Fri 11.30am-midnight, Sat 1pm-midnight, Sun 4pm-9pm.*

Maintenance & cleanliness	★★
Facilities	★☆
Atmosphere & character	★★★☆
Security	★★
Overall rating	★★

Ocean Child Hotel

This hostel is small and friendly. It is a clean place but the amenities are very dated. It is situated across the road from the fire station so you could have an early wake up call. The pub downstairs is really nice – like your local at home.

86 Argyle Street, Hobart.
☎ *(03) 6234 6730.*
Dorm bed *$18.*
Reception open *11am-late daily.*

Maintenance & cleanliness	★★★
Facilities	★☆
Atmosphere & character	★★★
Security	★★
Overall rating	★★☆

The Pickled Frog

The Pickled Frog is converted from an old pub. It has a big common area with a pool table and TV, a big kitchen and Internet access.

281 Liverpool Street, Hobart.
☎ *(03) 6234 7977.*
Website *www.thepickledfrog.com.*
Dorm bed *$19-22 ($18-21 ISIC/VIP/YHA);* **single room** *$30 ($27 ISIC/VIP/YHA);* **double/twin room** *$48 ($44 ISIC/VIP/YHA).*
Credit cards *MC, Visa.*
Reception open *7.30am-11pm daily.*

Maintenance & cleanliness	★★
Facilities	★☆
Atmosphere & character	★★★★
Security	★★
Overall rating	★★☆

Transit Centre Backpackers

This is a clean hostel, above the Redline coach terminal, but the facilities could be a little newer. It has a big common room with a pool table, kitchen and a TV lounge. Accommodation is in six to ten-bed dorms.

First floor, Redline Transit Centre, 199 Collins Street, Hobart.
☎ *(03) 6231 2400.*
Website *www.salamanca.com.au/backpackers.*
Dorm bed *$19.*

Tasmania

Credit cards MC, Visa.
Reception open 8am-11pm daily.

Maintenance & cleanliness	★★★
Facilities	★★
Atmosphere & character	★★
Security	★
Overall rating	★★☆

Waterfront Cottage

Waterfront Cottage is a very nice hostel that is located in an old building behind a motel in Hobart's suburbs. The building features hardwood floors and a balcony overlooking the swimming pool. All the dorms have a fridge, sink and microwave and linen is supplied. There's plenty of parking but the inconvenient location restricts it to people travelling by car.
153 Risdon Road, New Town.
☎ *(03) 6228 4748.*
Website www.waterfrontnewtownbay.com.
Dorm bed $20.
Credit cards MC, Visa.
Reception open 8am-8.30pm daily.
🚗

Maintenance & cleanliness	★★★★☆
Facilities	★★
Atmosphere & character	★★★☆
Security	★★
Overall rating	★★★

Eating & Drinking

Tasmania has a reputation for excellent food, but it's noted mainly for quality ingredients like salmon and King Island creams and cheeses rather than its restaurants. From a budget traveller's perspective, the best value meals are the fish and chip shops around Constitution and Victoria Docks.

There are plenty of places to drink around Salamanca Place, nice cafés and some brilliant pubs.

On Saturdays go to Salamanca Market for both the fast food stalls and fresh fruit and picnic food. When the market isn't open your best bet is to head to the Woolworths supermarket on Campbell Street in the city centre.

Sights
Antarctic Adventure

An interesting museum featuring exhibits about Antarctica. It's a hands-on interactive museum, which makes it popular with kids and it features exhibits such as a virtual blizzard. There is also a planetarium in the complex.
2 Salamanca Square, Hobart.
☎ *(03) 6220 8220 & 6223 8383.*
Website www.antarctic.com.au.
Admission $22.50.
Open 10am-5pm daily.

Cadbury Chocolate Factory

This is an extremely popular factory tour where you can see Cadbury chocolate being produced and you also get the chance to sample the finished product. Tours are popular and it's essential to phone to make a booking.
Cadbury Road, Claremont.
🚌 *37, 38, 39.*
☎ *(03) 6249 0333 or 1800 627 367.*
Website www.cadbury.com.au/magicaltours/claremont.php.
Admission $12.50.
Tours Mon-Fri from 8.30am, bookings essential.

Cascade Brewery

The factory tour of Australia's oldest brewery is very popular with backpackers. Like all good brewery tours, there's free beer awaiting you at the end. Tours are popular and it's essential to phone to make a booking.
Cascade Road, South Hobart.
🚌 *43, 44, 46, 49.*
☎ *(03) 6221 8300.*
Admission $11 ($7.50 students).
Tours Mon-Fri 9.30am & 1pm.

Female Factory Historic Site

This former prison is the female equivalent to Port Arthur and female convicts were kept here between 1828 and 1877.
16 Degraves Street, South Hobart.
🚌 *43, 44, 46, 49.*
☎ *(03) 6223 1559.*
Website www.femalefactory.com.au.
Admission $9.
Tours Mon-Fri 9.30am & 2pm, Sat-Sun 9.30am.

Maritime Museum

Interesting museum exploring Tasmania's maritime past with exhibits on whaling and shipwrecks.

Corner Argyle & Davey Streets, Hobart.
☎ (03) 6223 5082.
Website www.maritimetas.org.
Open 9am-5pm daily.
Admission $6.

Mercury Print Museum
Housed in one of Tasmania's oldest buildings, this museum focuses on newspaper publishing and the history of printing.
89 Macquarie Street, Hobart.
☎ (03) 6230 0736.
Website www.themercury.com.au/nie/ingle/menu.html.
Admission $1-2 donation.
Open Mon-Fri 10am-1pm & 1.30pm-4pm.

Mt Wellington
If you have a car an excursion to the summit of Mt Wellington is a must. The views of the city from here are spectacular and on a clear day you can see half of Tasmania.

Mt Wellington Shuttle Bus Service (☎ 0417 341 804) leaves the city centre for Mt Wellington daily at 9.30am, noon & 2.30pm.

Alternatively Island Cycle Tours (☎ 1300 880 334; website www.island cycletours.com) run trips to the summit of Mt Wellington with a downhill mountain bike ride back to Hobart. The trip takes around three hours and costs $48.

Tasmanian Museum & Art Gallery
This museum and gallery exhibits modern Australian art and artefacts depicting Tasmania's convict history.
40 Macquarie Street, Hobart.
☎ (03) 6235 0777.
Website www.tmag.tas.gov.au.
Admission free.
Open 10am-5pm daily.

Tasmanian Transport Museum
Railway enthusiasts will love this museum that focuses on trains but also features bus, tram and steam technology exhibits. Train trips are run at the museum twice monthly, on the first and third Sunday.
Anfield Street, Glenorchy.
☎ X1.

☎ (03) 6272 7721.
Website www.railtasmania.com/ttms/.
Admission $5/$6 on the first & third Sunday of each month.
Open Sat, Sun & public holidays 1pm-4.30pm, 11am-4.30pm on first & third Sun.

Around Hobart
Tasmania's capital is well positioned for excursions into the surrounding countryside. Nearby attractions include picturesque small towns like New Norfolk and Richmond.

Huon Valley
This region, around an hour southwest of Hobart, is a popular spot with backpackers who come here for fruit picking work between Nov and May.

Huonville is the main town in the Huon Valley, but Geeveston at the southwestern end of the valley is a good base for visiting the Tahune Forest Reserve.

Practical Information
INFORMATION CENTRES
Geeveston Forest & Heritage Centre
Church Street, Geeveston.
☎ (03) 6297 1836.
Website www.forestandheritagecentre.com.au.
Open 9am-5pm daily.

Huonville Visitor Information Centre
Esplanade, Huonville.
☎ (03) 6264 1838.
Website www.huonjet.com/trips/viscentre1.html.
Open 9am-5pm daily.

National Parks Shop
24 Main Road, Huonville.
☎ (03) 6264 8460.
Open Mon-Fri 9am-4.30pm.

INTERNET ACCESS
Geeveston Online Access Centre
School Road, Geeveston.
☎ (03) 6297 0074.

Tasmania

Open *Mon 10am-5pm, Tue noon-6pm, Wed 10am-5pm, Thu noon-6pm, Fri 10am-5pm.*

Huonville Online Access Centre
23 Wilmot Road, Huonville.
☎ *(03) 6264 3441.*
Open *Mon-Fri 10am-5pm, Sat-Sun 10am-1pm.*

Accommodation
Geeveston Forest House
Geeveston Forest House is a small hostel providing very basic accommodation in an old house. It is a cosy place, but many of the fittings and furnishings are old. Facilities include a small kitchen and TV room.
24 Arve Road, Geeveston.
☎ *(03) 6297 1102.*
Dorm bed *$17.*
Website *www.tassie.net.au/~ldillon/.*
🚐

Maintenance & cleanliness	★
Facilities	★
Atmosphere & character	★★★★
Security	★
Overall rating	★⯪

Huon Valley Backpackers
This Nomads hostel caters to both tourists and fruit pickers. The main hostel building is clean and well maintained and it features a common area with a kitchen, TV lounge, a dining area and Internet access. There is decking at the rear of the hostel with lovely views of the Huon Valley.
4 Sandhill Road, Cradoc.
☎ *(03) 6295 1551.*
Dorm bed *$20.*
Credit cards *MC, Visa.*
🚐♿

Maintenance & cleanliness	★★★⯪
Facilities	★★
Atmosphere & character	★★★★
Security	★
Overall rating	★★★

Sights & Activities
Jet Boating
The Huon Jet boat operates jet boat rides from the outside the Huonville Visitor Information Centre, which take you for a 35 to 40-minute spin on the Huon River.

☎ *(03) 6264 1838.*
Website *www.huonjet.com.*
Cost *$52.*
Open *9am-5pm daily.*

Wooden Boat Centre
The Wooden Boat Centre in the small town of Franklin has interesting displays where you can learn about the history of boat building and water transport.
Main Road, Franklin.
☎ *(03) 6266 3586.*
Website *www.woodenboatschool.com.*
Admission *$4.50.*
Open *10am-5pm daily.*

Tahune Forest Reserve
The Tahune Forest Reserve is a popular destination because of the impressive Tahune Forest Air Walk and it is an easy day trip from Hobart.

Coming & Going
Tahune is about a 70-minute drive south from Hobart. Take the Huon Highway (A6) south to Geeveston before turning off the main road towards the Tahune Forest Reserve.

Sights & Activities
Tahune Forest Air Walk
The Air Walk is 570 metres long and allows visitors to see the forest from an unusual perspective among the treetops at a height of between 25 and 45 metres above ground level.
Tahune Forest Reserve, via Geeveston.
☎ *(03) 6297 0068.*
Website *www.forestrytas.com.au/ forestrytas/pages/tahune_air_walk.htm.*
Admission *$9.*
Open *9am-5pm daily.*

Dover & Far South Tasmania
Dover is the most southern town in Tasmania and it makes a good base for exploring the island's far south. Attractions here include sea kayaking and tours of glowworm caves. This region also provides access to the South West National Park.

Practical Information
INTERNET ACCESS
Dover Online Access Centre
"The Old School", Main Road, Dover.
☎ *(03) 6298 1552.*
Open *Mon-Sat 11am-3pm.*

Coming & Going
During summer, TassieLink/ Tigerline (☎ *1300 300 520; website www.tigerline.com.au)* run two buses a day from Hobart.

Accommodation
Far South Wilderness Lodge & Backpackers
Australia's southern-most backpackers' hostel is made up of log cabins on 35 acres of native bush on the waterfront. It has a big common room with a fireplace and TV and also has a bar and a big dining room with a commercial kitchen.
247 Narrows Road, Strathblane.
☎ *(03) 6298 1922.*
Website *www.farsouthwilderness.com .au.*
Dorm bed *$20.*
Credit cards *MC, Visa.*
Reception open *8am-11am & 4pm-8pm daily.*
🚗

Maintenance & cleanliness	★★★★☆
Facilities	★★☆
Atmosphere & character	★★★★☆
Security	★
Overall rating	★★★☆

Activities
CAVING
There are several caves in Tasmania's far south.

Glow Worm Adventure Caving
Southern Wilderness Eco Adventure Tours (SWEAT) run excellent adventure caving trips to a glowworm cave in the South West World Heritage area.
Trips depart from Far South Wilderness Lodge & Backpackers, 247 Narrows Road, Strathblane.
☎ *(03) 6297 6368*
Website *www.tasglow-wormadventure.com.au.*
Half day tour *$65.*
Tours depart *1pm, 6pm daily.*

Hastings Caves & Thermal Springs
The Hastings Caves are a popular tourist spot south of Dover. It is more tourist-oriented than the Glow Worm Adventure Caving trip (see above) and there are several tour options that range from a short 45-minute guided tour to eco adventure tours that last up to six hours.
☎ *(03) 6298 3209.*
45-minute guided tour *$16; eco adventure cave tour $89-159.*

New Norfolk
This historic town northwest of Hobart is in the centre of hop-growing country. It is a pleasant place with plenty of buildings from the 19th century, however the main attraction is the Oast House with it's hop museum. There's also a Museum of Trout Fishing and jet boat rides on the Derwent River.

Richmond
Richmond is another small town with plenty of buildings dating from convict times.

It is a popular destination for day-trippers from Hobart with the predictable collection of cafés, craft shops and guesthouses. The main attractions here include Australia's oldest Catholic Church, Australia's oldest bridge and the nearby river where you can feed the ducks. Richmond Goal is the most authentic reminder of the town's convict history.

Coming & Going
The Richmond Tourist Bus (☎ *0408 341 804)* runs twice each day between Hobart and Richmond.

Sights
Richmond Gaol
Australia's oldest existing colonial gaol is well preserved and offers the only surviving example of female solitary confinement cells in Tasmania as well as an extensive collection of convict relics.
37 Bathurst Street, Richmond.
☎ *(03) 6260 2127.*

Tasmania

Admission $4.50.
Open 9am-5pm daily.

Port Arthur & the Tasman Peninsula

The notorious convict settlement at Port Arthur is Tasmania's biggest tourist attraction and one of the most educational attractions in the state. Elsewhere on the peninsula are the natural rock formations on the rugged coast and the Tasmanian Devil Park at Taranna midway between Eaglehawk Neck and Port Arthur.

There are other attractions outside the Port Arthur Historic Site that are worth visiting if you've got your own car. You may want to take the turn-off near Eaglehawk Neck and take a look at the natural attractions on the peninsula's rugged coast, which include Devils Kitchen, Tasman Arch, Tasman Blowhole and Tessellated Pavement. A short walk on the Tasman Trail will take you to Waterfall Bluff; if you continue on this trail you will end up at Fortescue Bay.

Practical Information
Port Arthur Visitor Information Centre
Port Arthur Historic Site, Port Arthur.
☎ *(03) 6251 2371.*
Open 8.30am-dusk.

Coming & Going
TassieLink/Tigerline (☎ *1300 300 520; website www.tigerline.com.au)* run a daily service between Hobart and Port Arthur. The one-way fare is $18.50.

Accommodation
Eaglehawk Neck Backpackers
This small hostel has a total of nine beds in two buildings, one with lovely sea views. It is a clean place but the amenities are old and dated.
94 Old Jetty Road, Eaglehawk Neck.
☎ *(03) 6250 3248.*
Dorm bed $18.
Reception open 8am-8pm daily.
🚌

Maintenance & cleanliness	★★
Facilities	★✰
Atmosphere & character	★★★
Security	★
Overall rating	★★

Port Arthur Caravan & Cabin Park
This hostel consists of a bunkhouse in a caravan park about 3km from Port Arthur village. It has a quiet natural bush setting with extensive barbecue areas. Accommodation is in clean spacious dorms with three-tier bunk beds with plastic mattresses.
Garden Point, Port Arthur.
☎ *(03) 6250 2340.*
Dorm bed $15.
Credit cards MC, Visa.
Reception open 8am-8pm daily.
🚌

Maintenance & cleanliness	★★★★✰
Facilities	★
Atmosphere & character	★
Security	★
Overall rating	★★

Roseview YHA
This small hostel is in a cute old house right in the centre of Port Arthur village, making it the best located of the Tasman Peninsula hostels. The furnishings are old and facilities are limited to a small TV room and kitchen and the bathrooms are in a separate building.
Champ Street, Port Arthur.
☎ *(03) 6250 2311.*
Dorm bed $22.50 ($19 YHA);
double/twin room $49 ($42 YHA).
Credit cards MC, Visa.
Reception open 8.30am –10am &
5pm-8pm daily.
🚌

Maintenance & cleanliness	★★
Facilities	★★
Atmosphere & character	★★★★
Security	-
Overall rating	★★★✰

Sights
Tasman National Park
Tasman National Park is easily accessible from Port Arthur. The park's rugged coastline is home to caves and natural features including Devil's Kitchen, Tasman's Arch and Tasman Blowhole. Seals, penguins, dolphins and whales are among the wildlife that can be seen at the park.

Taranna Field Centre, 5801 Arthur Highway, Taranna.
☎ *(03) 6250 3497.*
Website *www.parks.tas.gov.au/ natparks/tasman/.*
Admission *$3.50 per person, $10 for a car and up to eight passengers.*

Tasmanian Devil Park
This wildlife park features Tasmanian Devils plus other animals such as kangaroos, wallabies and eagles.
Arthur Highway, Taranna.
☎ *(03) 6250 3230.*
Admission *$19.*
Open *9am-5.30pm daily; devil feeding 10am, 11am, 1.30pm, 5pm daily; kangaroo & wallaby feeding 2.30pm daily; outdoor bird presentation 11.15am, 3.30pm daily.*

Historic Ghost Tour
This a popular walking tour that recounts spooky stories about convict ghosts.
Tours depart *from the Port Arthur Visitor's Centre.*
☎ *(03) 6251 2371.*
Admission *$14.*

Port Arthur Historic Park
This is a must-see attraction that gives you an excellent impression of Australia's convict history. The Port Arthur Historic Park covers a large area and includes ruins of the prison settlement with several restored buildings. Admission to the site includes a guided tour and a cruise around the harbour.
Port Arthur Historic Site, Port Arthur.
☎ *1800 659 101.*
Website *www.portarthur.org.au.*
Admission *day entry $22; day & night entry $33.20.*
Open *8.30am-dusk daily, most buildings close at 5pm.*

East Coast
Moving north from Hobart along the Tasman Highway takes you through many small pleasant seaside towns as well as Freycinet National Park's renowned hiking trail to Wine Glass Bay. The sunny east coast is a popular

route for those who are either driving or cycling and it's a preferable route to the Midland Highway.

Triabunna & Maria Island National Park
Maria Island, 15km offshore from Triabunna, is a former penal settlement that has been protected as a national park. The park is also known for its wildlife and many endangered species have been introduced to the island in a bid to build their numbers in a car-free environment.

There are some good hiking trails on the island. The Fossil Cliffs walk (2 hours) and Painted Cliffs walk (2½ hours) are popular with day trippers and the challenging Bishop and Clerk walk (4 hours) offers breathtaking ocean views. The ruins of the penal settlement at Darlington, where the ferry arrives, is also worth exploring.

There are no shops on the island so you'll need to stock up on supplies in Triabunna. A lot of travellers use Triabunna as a base for exploring the island and many stay overnight at the hostel here before catching the ferry to the island.

Practical Information
Triabunna Visitor Information Centre
Esplanade, Triabunna.
☎ *(03) 6257 4772.*
Open *10am-4pm daily.*

Coming & Going
TassieLink/Tigerline (☎ 1300 300 520; **website** *www.tigerline.com.au*) stop at Triabunna on their Hobart-Swansea service. Buses stop outside the Shell service station.

The Cruise Company (☎ 0427 100 104; **website** *www.thecruisecompany. com.au*) runs a ferry to Maria Island, which departs Triabunna daily at 9.30am. The ferry trip costs $25.

Accommodation
Camping and hostel accommodation is available on the island. Camping at Darlington on Maria Island costs

$4.40 per person and there are free campsites at Encampment Grove and French's Farm, both campsites are a three to four hour hike from Darlington. Hostel-style accommodation on the island is in the old penitentiary.

Old Penitentiary

The Parks & Wildlife Service runs the Old Penitentiary in Darlington as very basic dormitory accommodation. There are nine rooms, each with six bunk beds. Facilities are limited to a wood-fired heater that can also be used for cooking, plus a barbecue area and an amenities block with hot showers.
Darlington, Maria Island
☎ *(03) 6257 1420.*
Dorm bed *$8.80.*
Not yet rated

Many travellers stay in Triabunna, and occasionally Little Swanport, before coming out to the island. The following accommodation is available in Little Swanport and Triabunna.

Gumleaves

Gumleaves is a sprawling complex on 400 acres with a wide variety of facilities including mini golf, tennis, basketball and volleyball courts, a lake and even a deer park. Not many backpackers stay here and it seems to be geared mostly towards groups. It is in a peaceful setting, down an unsealed road about 25km north of Triabunna.
Swanston Road, Little Swanport.
☎ *(03) 6244 8147.*
Website *www.gumleaves.com.au.*
Dorm bed *$25;* **camping** *$8 per person.*
Credit cards *MC, Visa.*

Maintenance & cleanliness	★★★★
Facilities	★★★
Atmosphere & character	★★✩
Security	★★✩
Overall rating	★★★

Udda Backpackers

This small hostel is clean but it has old furnishings. Facilities include a good common room and a small shop at reception. The managers are very helpful and know a lot about the local area and they can organise trips to Maria Island.

12 Spencer Street, Triabunna.
☎ *(03) 6257 3439.*
Dorm bed *$17;* **single room** *$20;* **twin room** *$38.*
Reception open *8am-10am & 5pm-9pm daily.*

Maintenance & cleanliness	★★★
Facilities	★★✩
Atmosphere & character	★★★★★
Security	-
Overall rating	★★★✩

Swansea

Overlooking Great Oyster Bay, this historic seaside resort is a pleasant spot to break your journey. There isn't a lot to do here although there is an interesting bark mill and a small museum. You can sometimes see dolphins in the bay.

Coming & Going

TassieLink/Tigerline (☎ 1300 300 520; **website** *www.tigerline.com.au*) run bus services between Hobart and Swansea.

Sights
Black Wattle Bark Mill & Museum

Australia's only bark crusher was once used to make leather tan from black wattle bark. The adjoining museum details the town's history.
96 Tasman Highway, Swansea.
☎ *(03) 6257 8382.*
Admission *$5.50.*
Open *9am-5pm daily.*

Bicheno

This small town is a popular stop on the east coast. It is conveniently situated as an ideal base for exploring both the Douglas Apsley and Freycinet National Parks.

Penguin spotting tours are the main attraction in Bicheno.

Practical Information
INTERNET ACCESS
Bicheno Online Access Centre

The Oval, Burgess Street, Bicheno.
☎ *(03) 6375 1892.*
Open *Tue 10am-1pm, Thu 9am-noon, Fri-Sat 10am-2pm.*

Accommodation
Bicheno Backpackers Hostel
Bicheno Backpackers is a nice small hostel with solid bunk beds; each with lockers and the bottom bunks have curtains for a bit of privacy. There's a good common area with a TV and a small kitchen and also a free washing machine.
11 Morrison Street, Bicheno.
☎ *(03) 6375 1651.*
Dorm bed *$18.*
Reception open *8am-8pm daily.*
🚍

Maintenance & cleanliness	★★★★⯪
Facilities	★⯪
Atmosphere & character	★★★★
Security	★⯪
Overall rating	★★★⯪

Seaview Accommodation Centre
This is a well-equipped hostel but it caters mostly to church and school groups rather than independent travellers. Facilities include a small kitchen, a big recreation room with table tennis and a pool table and a sun deck with nice sea views.
29 Banksia Street, Bicheno.
☎ *(03) 6375 1247.*
Website *www.users.bigpond.com/ seaview_accom/.*
Dorm bed *$15; double/twin room $35; family room $55-65.*
Credit cards *MC, Visa.*
🚍

Maintenance & cleanliness	★★★★⯪
Facilities	★★
Atmosphere & character	★
Security	★
Overall rating	★★★

Sights & Activities
Penguin Tours
Bicheno Penguin Tours *(*☎ *(03) 6375 1333)* is a unique experience where you are taken in a small group to see little penguins waddle in from the sea at dusk. It's highly recommended as it is a much more intimate experience than penguin viewing centres in Victoria or New Zealand and the number of penguins is relatively high, particularly between July and November. Penguin tours cost $16, but are $14 if you book through Bicheno Backpackers.

Coles Bay & Freycinet National Park
Coles Bay is the gateway to Freycinet National Park *(*☎ *(03) 6257 0107; website www.parks.tas.gov.au/natparks/ freycinet/),* and is the perfect place to rest after hiking in the park.

The most popular hiking trail in Freycinet National Park is the one-hour walk to the Wine Glass Bay lookout although many backpackers prefer the longer route which continues on to Wine Glass Bay and Hazards Beach.

Practical Information
National Park Information Centre
park entrance, Freycinet National Park.
☎ *(03) 6256 7000.*
Open *9am-6pm daily.*

Accommodation
Coles Bay YHA
This rustic hostel has basic facilities including a fridge, stove, heating, cold water showers and a pit toilet. However it has an idyllic location overlooking a secluded cove, which ensures that it is often full and bookings are essential. In fact it is so popular in summer that a ballot system applies for bookings between 15 December and 15 February. To apply for the ballot you must register with YHA Tasmania on (03) 6234 9617 before mid-September to register for accommodation the following summer. During this period you can only book an entire five-bed room, but dorm beds are available throughout the rest of the year.
Parsons Cove Drive, Freycinet National Park.
☎ *(03) 6234 9617.*
Five-bed dorm *$45-50 (15 Dec-15 Feb);* **dorm bed** *$10 (rest of year).*
🚍

Maintenance & cleanliness	★★⯪
Facilities	⯪
Atmosphere & character	★★★
Security	★
Overall rating	★★

Iluka Holiday Centre YHA
This youth hostel is part of a larger accommodation complex that also includes more upmarket cabins. The

hostel is clean and well maintained but the facilities in the common areas are a little dated. There's a TV room, table tennis and a big kitchen with a log fire.

The Esplanade, Coles Bay.
☎ *(03) 6257 0115.*
Dorm bed $22 ($18.50 YHA); single room $53.50 ($50 YHA); double/ twin room $59 ($52 YHA).
Credit cards *MC, Visa.*
Reception open *8am-6pm daily.*
🚗

Maintenance & cleanliness	★★✫
Facilities	★✫
Atmosphere & character	★★
Security	★
Overall rating	★★

Douglas Apsley National Park

Being one of Tasmania's less popular national parks means that you don't have to share the wilderness with too many other people. Douglas Apsley National Park is mostly dry eucalypt forest, however it also harbours pockets of rainforest and there are plenty of hiking trails and spots for a swim.

The easiest hike is the 10-minute walk to the Apsley Waterhole from the southern car park.

This is a relatively new park with very basic facilities. There is free camping in the park including a campground at the Apsley Waterhole. There is no fresh water in the park so stock up on supplies before you get here.

St Helens

St Helens is both the most northerly and the largest town on the east coast. There isn't really a lot to do here apart from surfing and you'll probably just stop long enough to visit the supermarket and get cash from the ATM.

Practical Information
Visitor Information Centre
59 Cecilia Street, St Helens.
☎ *(03) 6376 1744.*
Open *Mon-Fri 9am-5pm, Sat 9am-noon, Sun 10am-2pm.*

INTERNET ACCESS
St Helens Online Access Centre
State Library Building, 61 Cecilia Street, St Helens.
☎ *(03) 6376 1116.*
Open *Mon-Fri 9am-5pm, Sat-Sun 10am-noon.*

Coming & Going
TassieLink/Tigerline (☎ *1300 300 520;* **website** *www.tigerline.com.au)* run bus services between Hobart and St Helens and Redline (☎ *1300 3600 000;* **website** *www.tasredline.com)* have a service to Launceston.

Accommodation
Pelican Sands Backpackers
Pelican Sands Backpackers is part of a motel complex. It consists of a small common room with a kitchen and TV and three dormitories, each with en suite. It is in Scamander, a seaside village about 20km south of St Helens.
157 Scamander Avenue, Scamander.
☎ *(03) 6372 5231.*
Website *www.pelicansandsscamander. com.au.*
Dorm bed $21.
Credit cards *Amex, Diners, JCB, MC, Visa.*
Reception open *8am-8pm daily.*
🚗

Maintenance & cleanliness	★★★
Facilities	★✫
Atmosphere & character	★★
Security	★
Overall rating	★★

St Helens YHA
St Helens youth hostel is in a house on a quiet street near the town centre. The house is outdated and facilities include the usual TV lounge, kitchen and barbecue area.
5 Cameron Street, St Helens.
☎ *(03) 6376 1661.*
Dorm bed $20.50 ($17 YHA); double room $45 ($38 YHA).
Reception open *8am-10am & 5pm-8pm daily.*

Maintenance & cleanliness	★★★
Facilities	★★
Atmosphere & character	★★✫
Security	★
Overall rating	★★✫

Launceston

Tasmania's second largest city is also one of Australia's oldest.

This pleasant city is built on the banks of the Tamar River and boasts some outstanding natural attractions; particularly the awesome Cataract Gorge, which is only 15 minutes walk from the city centre.

Practical Information
Gateway Tasmania Information Centre

Corner Paterson & St John Streets, Launceston.
☎ *(03) 6336 3133*
Website www.gatewaytas.com.au.
Open Mon-Fri 9am-5.30pm, Sat 9am-3pm, Sun 9am-noon.

Launceston National Park Visitor Centre

Prospect Offices, Bass Highway, South Launceston.
☎ *(03) 6336 5312.*
Open Mon-Fri 9am-5pm.

INTERNET ACCESS
Cyber King Internet Lounge

113 George Street, Launceston.
☎ *0417 393 540.*

Launceston Online Access Centre

State Library, Civic Square, Launceston.
☎ *(03) 6334 9559.*
Open Mon-Wed 9am-6pm, Thu-Fri 9am-7pm, Sat 9am-12.30pm.

Coming & Going
AIR

Launceston's small airport is 20km south of the city centre and has frequent flights to Melbourne and Sydney. Qantas and Virgin Blue both fly into here.

The airport shuttle bus (☎ *0500 512 009*) connects with all flights and will pick up and drop off at hostels. The one-way fare is $10.

BUS

Buses operate to destinations throughout Tasmania. TassieLink (☎ *1300 300 520; website www.tigerline.com.au*) coaches arrive and depart from the ter-

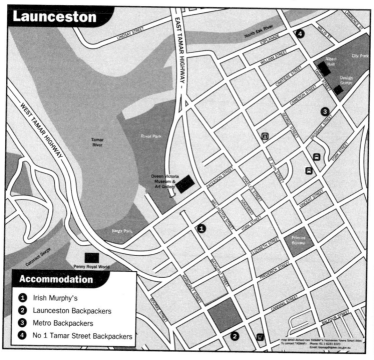

Launceston

Accommodation

1. Irish Murphy's
2. Launceston Backpackers
3. Metro Backpackers
4. No 1 Tamar Street Backpackers

Tasmania

minal at 101 George Street in the city centre. The Redline (☎ *1300 360 000; website www.tasredline.com*) coach terminal is at 18 Charles Street.

Local Transport
Launceston has a fairly comprehensive bus network with one-way fares ranging from $1.40-3.20. An off-peak multi-trip ticket costs $3.60. The main drawback is that buses stop running at around 7pm, but most things in Launceston are centrally located and it's unlikely that you'll need to use the bus.

Accommodation
Irish Murphy's
This hostel consists of accommodation above an Irish pub in the city centre. Facilities are limited to a small kitchen and a TV lounge. The dorms are nice and clean with solid wooden bunk beds.
211 Brisbane Street, Launceston.
☎ *(03) 6331 4440.*
Dorm bed *$17;* **double room** *$34.*
Credit cards *Amex, JCB, MC, Visa.*
Reception open *Sun-Wed noon-midnight, Thu-Sat noon-2am.*

Maintenance & cleanliness	★★★★
Facilities	★★☆
Atmosphere & character	★★★
Security	★★
Overall rating	★★★

Launceston Backpackers
This hostel is in a lovely building that is clean and well maintained. It features a big TV lounge, a huge kitchen and a common room with a piano. It is in a quiet location across the road from a park and a short walk from most attractions in the city centre and a 15-minute walk to the gorge.
103 Canning Street, Launceston.
☎ *(03) 6334 2327.*
Website *www.launcestonbackpackers. com.au.*
Dorm bed *$17;* **single room** *$38;* **double room** *$40;* **twin room** *$38.*
Credit cards *MC, Visa.*
Reception open *8am-10am & 4pm-9pm daily.*

Maintenance & cleanliness	★★★★☆
Facilities	★★☆
Atmosphere & character	★★★★
Security	★★
Overall rating	★★★★☆

Launceston City Youth Hostel
This big hostel is a couple of kilometres south of the city centre. It has an institutional feel similar to some outdated European youth hostels. In this instance it caters mostly to groups and families and not so many independent travellers stay here. Facilities include a big kitchen, a TV lounge and table tennis.
36 Thistle Street, Launceston.
🛏 *24.*
☎ *(03) 6344 9779.*
Dorm bed *$15;* **single room** *$20.*
Credit cards *MC, Visa.*
Reception open *8am-10.30pm daily.*

Maintenance & cleanliness	★★★☆
Facilities	★
Atmosphere & character	-
Security	★★
Overall rating	★★☆

Metro Backpackers
This is a great hostel in the heart of the city centre. It is clean and well maintained and it features a good kitchen and TV lounge, Internet access and a nice sundeck with a barbecue.
16 Brisbane Street, Launceston.
☎ *(03) 6334 4505.*
Website *www.backpackersmetro.com.au.*
Dorm bed *$23 ($20 YHA);* **double room** *$55-65 ($50-60 YHA);* **twin room** *$55 ($50 YHA).*
Credit cards *MC, Visa.*
Reception open *7.45am-9.45pm daily.*

Maintenance & cleanliness	★★★★★
Facilities	★★★☆
Atmosphere & character	★★★★
Security	★★★☆
Overall rating	★★★★

The Mowbray Backpackers
The Mowbray Hotel is a suburban pub with backpackers' accommodation upstairs. It is clean and well maintained but facilities are limited to a barren TV lounge and a very small kitchen. It is about four minutes by bus to the city centre.

254 Invermay Road, Mowbray.
🚌 *10, 12, 13, 14, 17, 18, 19.*
☎ *(03) 6326 1633.*
Dorm bed $23; double room $55.
Credit cards *Amex, MC, Visa.*
Reception open *10am-late.*
🚗

Maintenance & cleanliness	★★★★
Facilities	★☆
Atmosphere & character	★☆
Security	★☆
Overall rating	★★★☆

No 1 Tamar Street Backpackers
This small hostel features a small balcony overlooking the Esk River plus a small common room with a TV and Internet access and very limited kitchen facilities.
1 Tamar Street, Launceston.
🚌 *(03) 6331 1938.*
Dorm bed $20.
Credit cards *MC, Visa.*
Reception open *10am-10pm daily.*

Maintenance & cleanliness	★★★
Facilities	★
Atmosphere & character	★★★
Security	★☆
Overall rating	★★★☆

Eating & Drinking
Launceston is a pretty good place for eating out, particularly when you consider the city's small size. The pubs serve up some good quality meals and there is the usual selection of fast food places.

If you're preparing your own food, the cheapest option is the Coles supermarket at 198 Charles Street or the Woolworths supermarket at 128 Wellington Street.

Sights
Cataract Gorge
Launceston's major attraction is the spectacular Cataract Gorge. The gorge is about a 15-minute walk from the centre of Launceston and there are several lovely walks within the Cataract Gorge Reserve.

The reserve is also home to the Duck Reach Power Station, which was the first hydroelectric power station in the Southern Hemisphere when it was constructed in 1895.

Queen Victoria Museum, Art Galley & Planetarium
Launceston's most important museum has two branches – at Royal Park and at Inveresk. The Royal Park museum is home to the planetarium, a Chinese temple, decorative arts and an exhibit of metals in Tasmania. The Inveresk museum has an art gallery plus exhibits on migration and railways.
Corner Cameron & Wellington Streets, Launceston.
☎ *(03) 6323 3777.*
Website *www.qvmag.tased.edu.au.*
Admission *museum free; planetarium $5.*
Open *museum 10am-5pm daily; planetarium Tue-Fri 3pm, Sat 2pm & 3pm.*

Around Launceston
The area around Launceston includes the ports of George Town and Bridport. These places can be visited either as a day trip or en route to the east coast.

Bridport
This small seaside town is a relaxing spot to spend a day or two, although there isn't a lot to do here.

Practical Information
INTERNET ACCESS
Bridport Online Access Centre
Behind the library, Main Street, Bridport.
☎ *(03) 6356 0258.*
Open *Mon 10am-noon & 1pm-4pm, Tue 10am-noon, Wed 10am-noon & 2pm-5pm, Thu 10am-noon, Fri 10am-noon & 1pm-4pm, Sat 10am-noon.*

Coming & Going
Stan's Coach Service (☎ *(03) 6356 1662*) runs a twice-daily service to Scottsdale, where it connects with the Redline bus to Launceston.

If you want to visit Flinders Island in Bass Strait, the ferry run by Southern Shipping (☎ *(03) 6356 1753*) departs from here. The return fare is $79.

Tasmania

Accommodation

Bridport has an excellent hostel but if you're driving you may want to take advantage of the free camping site at Northeast Park on Ringarooma Road (A3) in Scottsdale, about a 20-minute drive south of Bridport. Maximum stay seven days.

Bridport Seaside Lodge

This is a beautiful purpose-built hostel with exposed beams, polished Tasmanisn oak floors and huge windows to take in the sea views. Facilities include a nice common room and kitchen.
47 Main Street, Bridport.
☎ *(03) 6356 1585.*
***Website** www.bridportseasidelodge.com.*
***Dorm bed** $19.50-22.50 ($16-19 YHA);* ***double/twin room** $45-54 ($38-47 YHA).*
***Credit cards** MC, Visa.*
***Reception open** 8am-9pm daily.*
🚗

Maintenance & cleanliness	★★★★
Facilities	★★★☆
Atmosphere & character	★★★★
Security	★
Overall rating	★★★★☆

George Town

Australia's third oldest settlement doesn't really have a lot to show for all its years of history, but it is a pleasant enough town to spend a night.

Practical Information
Visitor Information Centre
Main Road, George Town.
☎ *(03) 6382 1700.*
***Open** 9am-5pm daily.*

INTERNET ACCESS
George Town Online Access Centre
Macquarie Street, George Town.
☎ *(03) 6382 1356.*
***Open** Mon-Fri 9am-1pm, Sat-Sun 1pm-8pm.*

Coming & Going
Redline (☎ *1300 360 000; website www.tasredline.com)* have several buses each day between Launceston and George Town.

Accommodation
Traveller's Lodge YHA

This lovely small hostel is in a restored 1890s building that has loads of character. Facilities include a cosy TV room, a piano and an outdoor area with a barbecue. Accommodation is in three-tier bunks, but the ceilings are high so it isn't as cramped as you may expect.
4 Elizabeth Street, George Town.
☎ *(03) 6382 3261.*
***Dorm bed** $21.50 ($18 YHA).*
***Reception open** 9am-11am & 2pm-9.30pm daily.*

Maintenance & cleanliness	★★★★
Facilities	★★
Atmosphere & character	★★★★☆
Security	★★☆
Overall rating	★★★★☆

Sights
Low Head Historic Precinct

The Low Head Historic Precinct is home to Australia's third oldest light station, several historic buildings and a maritime museum. One of the highlights is *Windeward Bound*, a majestic tall ship that sails five days a week (Wed-Sun). Low Head is several kilometres north of George Town.
West Tamar Highway, Low Head.
☎ *1800 008 343.*
***Website** www.lhhp.com.au.*
***Sailing trip** $55.*

Great Western Tiers

This scenic region south of Devonport is best known for the caves at Mole Creek.

Deloraine

About midway between Devonport and Launceston, Deloraine is a good base for exploring the Great Western Tiers region.

Practical Information
Great Western Tiers Visitor Centre
98-100 Emu Bay Road, Deloraine.
☎ *(03) 6362 3471.*
***Open** 9am-5pm daily.*

INTERNET ACCESS
Deloraine Online Access Centre
West Parade, Deloraine.
☎ *(03) 6362 3537.*
Open *Mon-Tue 10am-4pm, Wed 10am-7pm, Thu 10am-4pm, Fri 10am-7pm, Sun 1pm-4pm.*

Accommodation
There are two hostels in Deloraine, but if you're driving you may want to stop at Westbury, 15km west of Deloraine, where there's free camping at the rear of Andy's Hot Bread shop.

Highview Lodge YHA
Highview Lodge is a small youth hostel on a residential street with great views of town. It's in an old building that is cluttered but well maintained, but the dorms have old bunk beds with thin mattresses.
8 Blake Street, Deloraine.
☎ *(03) 6362 2996.*
Dorm bed *$21.50 ($18 YHA);*
double/twin room *$47 ($40 YHA).*
Reception open *8am-10am & 5pm-10pm daily.*

Maintenance & cleanliness	★★★
Facilities	★☆
Atmosphere & character	★★★
Security	★☆
Overall rating	★★☆

Modern Backpackers
Modern Backpackers is a basic hostel with a small kitchen/common area with a TV. It doesn't have much character, but it is clean and it has more comfortable beds than the YHA hostel.
24 Old Bass Highway, Deloraine.
☎ *(03) 6362 2250.*
Dorm bed *$18.*
☎

Maintenance & cleanliness	★★★
Facilities	★
Atmosphere & character	★★☆
Security	-
Overall rating	★★

Sights
Deloraine Museum & Yarns Artwork in Silk
Deloraine Museum has displays on local history. The museum is accompanied by Yarns Artwork in Silk, which is a series of four large silk panels, each depicting the Great Western Tiers in a different season.
98-100 Emu Bay Road, Deloraine.
☎ *(03) 6362 3471.*
Open *9am-5pm daily.*

Mole Creek Karst National Park
Around midway between Deloraine and Cradle Mountain, Mole Creek Karst National Park is noted for its spectacular caves.

There are over 200 caves but the two main ones are Marakoopa and King Solomons Caves, which are located 11km apart. The Parks & Wildlife department operate tours of both these caves.

King Solomons Cave
King Solomons Cave is much smaller than Marakoopa and it has lavish decorative stalagmites and stalactite formations.
☎ *(03) 6363 5182.*
Admission *$11.*
Tours *10.30am, 11.30am, 12.30pm, 2.30pm, 4pm daily.*

Marakoopa Cave
Marakoopa Cave is best known for its glow-worms, boasting Australia's largest glow-worm display.
☎ *(03) 6363 5182.*
Admission *$11.*
Tours *10am, 11.15pm, 1pm, 2.30pm, 4pm daily.*

Devonport
Devonport will be your first taste of Tasmania if you're arriving from Melbourne on the *Spirit of Tasmania*.

This industrial city doesn't really have a lot to offer and isn't typical of the rest of the state but it has a developed infrastructure and it's a good place to organise the rest of your trip. It's close proximity to Cradle Mountain and the Overland Track also means that you get plenty of handy tips from people who have just done the trek.

Tasmania

Practical Information
Visitor Information Centre
92 Formby Road, Devonport.
☎ *(03) 6424 4466.;*
Open *7.30am-5pm daily.*

INTERNET ACCESS
Devonport Online Access Centre
21 Oldaker Street, Devonport.
☎ *(03) 6424 9413.*
Open *Mon-Tue 9.30am-5.30pm, Wed 9.30am-6.30pm, Thu-Fri 9.30am-5.30pm, Sat 9.30am-3.30pm.*

Coming & Going
Devonport is a busy transport hub that has buses, ferries and an airport with flights to Melbourne.

AIR
Both Rex and Qantas fly between Devonport and Melbourne. Devonport's small airport is only 6km outside town. A shuttle bus (☎ *(03) 6424 1431)* runs to the airport twice a day from the tourist information centre on Formby Road. The fare is $10 per person so it is

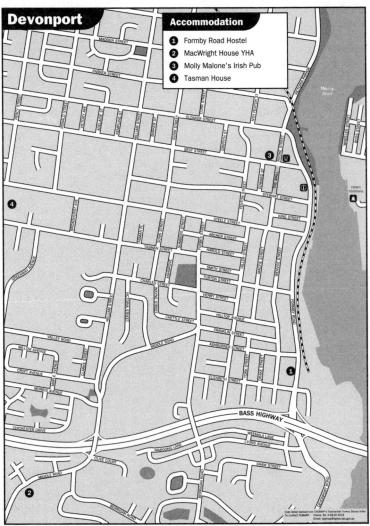

Devonport

Accommodation
1. Formby Road Hostel
2. MacWright House YHA
3. Molly Malone's Irish Pub
4. Tasman House

cheaper to catch a taxi ($15) if there are two or more of you.

BUS
Buses run between Devonport and most destinations in Tasmania. The bus station is at the corner of Best and Edward Streets.

FERRY
The Spirit of Tasmania ferry arrives at the ferry terminal in East Devonport. Ferries depart Devonport at 9pm every day.

Local Transport
Merseylink (☎ *1300 367 590; website www.merseylink.com.au*) operates a local bus service with six routes running Mon-Sat. Many backpackers find they need to use the bus, particularly if they're staying at the Tasman House or YHA hostels, which are a long way from the centre.

The most useful bus service is route 40, which runs between Latrobe and the city centre via the Formby Road, Tasman House and MacWright House YHA hostels. Buses 20 and 25 also go to the Tasman House hostel.

Fares are $1.40-2.30 for a single journey or $3.60 for a Day Rover ticket that is good for unlimited bus travel between 9am and 4pm.

Accommodation
Formby Road Hostel
This hostel is housed in a big old Federation-style mansion. The building has a lot of character and there are new furnishings in the common rooms.
16 Formby Road, Devonport.
🚌 *40.*
☎ *(03) 6423 6563.*
***Dorm bed** $16;* ***double room** $38-48.*

Maintenance & cleanliness	★★★
Facilities	★✫
Atmosphere & character	★★★★
Security	★✫
Overall rating	★★✫

MacWright House YHA
MacWright House is an old wooden house several kilometres from the city centre. Facilities are very basic and include a small kitchen and a TV lounge with old ratty chairs. The hostel

is clean but it is poorly maintained and it has a depressing atmosphere.
115 Middle Road, Devonport.
🚌 *40.*
☎ *(03) 6424 5696.*
***Dorm bed** $16.50 ($13 YHA);* ***single room** $22.50 ($19 YHA).*
***Reception open** 7am-10pm daily.*
🚌

Maintenance & cleanliness	★✫
Facilities	★
Atmosphere & character	★✫
Security	★
Overall rating	★✫

Molly Malone's Irish Pub
This Irish pub in the city centre has clean accommodation in small dorms. Facilities are limited to a small kitchen and TV lounge. It is the most centrally located of Devonport's hostels.
34 Best Street, Devonport.
🚌 *40.*
☎ *(03) 6424 1898.*
***Dorm bed** $15.*
***Credit cards** Amex, Diners, MC, Visa.*
***Reception open** Mon-Sat 10am-late, Sun noon-10pm.*

Maintenance & cleanliness	★★★
Facilities	★★
Atmosphere & character	★★★✫
Security	★★✫
Overall rating	★★★✫

Tasman House
This big hostel is set on 11 acres and can sleep up to 102 guests. It has an institutional feel and the amenities are dated, but it is a cheap place to stay. Facilities include a big common room with table tennis, a pool table, Internet access and a TV.
114 Tasman Street, Devonport.
🚌 *20, 25, 40.*
☎ *(03) 6423 2335.*
***Website** www.tasmanhouse.com.*
***Dorm bed** $12;* ***double room** $30-38;* ***twin room** $28.*
***Credit cards** MC, Visa.*
***Reception open** 8am-10pm daily.*
🚌

Maintenance & cleanliness	★★✫
Facilities	★★
Atmosphere & character	✫
Security	★
Overall rating	★★✫

Tasmania

Sights
Penguin Viewing
Every evening at sunset during the nesting season (Oct-Mar) you can watch little penguins return to their burrows from the specially constructed viewing platforms.
Lillico Beach, Devonport.

Tiagarra Aboriginal Cultural Centre
Tiagarra is an interesting museum and cultural centre exploring Tasmania's Aboriginal history. It is north of the centre at Devonport Bluff.
Off Bluff Road, Mersey Bluff.
☎ *(03) 6424 8250.*
Admission $3.80.
Open 9am-5pm daily.

North-West Coast
By Tasmanian standards, the northwest coast is densely populated with a string of medium sized towns stretching from Devonport to Stanley. There isn't really a lot to see or do here, but it's a nice coastal drive.

Burnie
The region's major town is of little interest to most travellers but you may have to pass through town to make transport connections.

Practical Information
Visitor Information Centre
Little Alexander Street, Burnie.
☎ *(03) 6434 6111.*
Open 8am-5pm daily.

Internet Access
Burnie Online Access Centre
2 Spring Street, Burnie.
☎ *(03) 6431 9469.*
Open Mon-Wed 9am-5pm, Fri 9am-8pm, Sat 9.30am-12.30pm.

Sights
Pioneer Village Museum
The Pioneer Village Museum features an indoor recreation of a street scene from the late 19th century.
Civic Centre Plaza, Little Alexander Street, Burnie.
☎ *(03) 6430 5746.*
Website www.tased.edu.au/tasonline/pivilmus/.
Admission $4.50.
Open Mon-Fri 9am-5pm, Sat-Sun 1.30pm-4.30pm.

Wynyard
With flights from Melbourne, this small town is a gateway to Tasmania for some travellers.

There are some nice coastal walks starting in town including the popular and easy 3km walk to Fossil Bluff.

Practical Information
Visitor Information Centre
Corner Goldie & Hogg Streets, Wynyard.
☎ *(03) 6442 4143.*
Open 9am-5pm daily.

INTERNET ACCESS
Wynyard Online Access Centre
21 Saunders Street, Wynyard.
☎ *(03) 6442 4499.*
Open Mon-Thu 10am-5pm, Fri 10am-4pm, Sat 7pm-9pm.

Coming & Going
Wynyard-Burnie Airport is less than a kilometre from the centre of town so you can just walk into town. Rex and Qantas fly here from Melbourne.

There are buses to other destinations on the northwest coast, with services between Burnie and Wynyard the most frequent. You may need to make transport connections at Burnie or Devonport for destinations further afield.

Accommodation
Beach Retreat Tourist Park
This caravan park by the beach has backpackers' accommodation in clean cabins. It is a good place if you want a little privacy as everyone gets their own room unless they're travelling with someone else. Shared facilities include a kitchen and TV lounge.
30 Old Bass Highway, Wynyard.
☎ *(03) 6442 1998.*
Dorm bed $20; double/twin room $35.

Credit cards MC, Visa.
Reception open 8am-9pm daily.
🚌

Maintenance & cleanliness	★★★⯨
Facilities	★⯨
Atmosphere & character	★⯨
Security	★
Overall rating	★★⯨

Stanley

This small town is built around the base of a volcanic rock formation known as The Nut. Most visitors either take the chairlift or climb to the top of The Nut for a rewarding view of the town and surrounding countryside.

Practical Information
Visitor Information Centre
45 Main Road, Stanley.
☎ *(03) 6458 1330.*
Open Mon-Fri 9am-5pm, Sat-Sun noon-4pm.

Accommodation
Stanley YHA Backpackers Hostel
This small YHA hostel is an old house on the grounds of a caravan park. Facilities include a small kitchen and at tiny TV room. Accommodation is mostly in twin rooms.
Wharf Road, Stanley.
☎ *(03) 6458 1266.*
Website www.stanleycabinpark.com.au.
Dorm bed $21.50 ($18 YHA); double room $47 ($40 YHA).
Credit cards MC, Visa.
Reception open 8am-8pm daily.
🚌

Maintenance & cleanliness	★★★
Facilities	★⯨
Atmosphere & character	★★⯨
Security	★⯨
Overall rating	★★⯨

Western & Central Tasmania

The wild west coast and central region of Tasmania is the state's most popular area for hiking and home to most of Tasmania's better known national parks including a large chunk of Tasmania that has been classified as a World Heritage Area.

Strahan

The nicest town in western Tasmania is situated on Macquarie Harbour. It started out as a transport hub for the penal colony at nearby Sarah Island but later became a major port for the timber and mining industries. Nowadays Strahan is a popular base for travellers exploring the Franklin-Gordon Wild Rivers National Park.

Practical Information
INFORMATION CENTRES
Strahan Visitors Centre
The Esplanade, Strahan.
☎ *(03) 6471 7622.*
Open Jan-Feb 10am-9pm daily; Mar-Dec 10am-8pm daily.

Parks & Wildlife Office
The Esplanade, Strahan.
☎ *(03) 6471 7122.*
Open Mon-Fri 9am-noon & 1pm-5pm.

INTERNET ACCESS
Strahan Online Access Centre
The Esplanade, Strahan.
☎ *(03) 6471 7788.*
Open Mon-Tue 1pm-5pm, Wed 10am-1pm, Thu 2pm-5pm daily.

Accommodation
Strahan Hostel
This hostel has a bush setting and it is comprised of several buildings. It has a couple of kitchens, a TV lounge and a sheltered outdoors area with picnic tables.
Harvey Street, Strahan.
☎ *(03) 6471 7255 or 1800 444 442.*
Dorm bed $20; single room $25; double room $50; twin room $40.
Credit cards MC, Visa.
Reception open 8am-8pm daily.
🚌

Maintenance & cleanliness	★★★⯨
Facilities	★
Atmosphere & character	★★★★⯨
Security	★
Overall rating	★★

Tasmania

Activities
Macquarie Harbour
World Heritage Cruises operate cruises on the harbour that include Sarah Island.
☎ *(03) 6471 7174.*
***Website** www.worldheritagecruises. com.au.*
***Full-day cruise** $60-65.*

Queenstown

This mining town has a unique Wild West ambience with a few interesting old buildings. The surrounding region has a barren landscape that makes it such a contrast to the rest of Tasmania; this was caused by a combination of mining and extensive deforestation that has created a landscape almost devoid of trees or other vegetation.

Accommodation
Mountain View Holiday Lodge
This place provides accommodation in en suite rooms that include four single beds, fridge, TV and a kettle. There is also a basic kitchen with an old oven that looks like it has come straight from a museum.
1 Penghana Road, Queenstown.
☎ *(03) 6471 1163.*
***Dorm bed** $15.*
***Reception open** 8am-9pm daily.*
☎

Maintenance & cleanliness	★☆
Facilities	★☆
Atmosphere & character	★☆
Security	★
Overall rating	★☆

Sights
Abt Wilderness Railway
This restored steam railway runs through pristine wilderness between Queenstown and Strahan crossing 40 bridges and climbing a 1:16 gradient.
Driffield Street, Queenstown.
☎ *(03) 6471 1700.*
***One-way fare** $65.*

Galley Museum
The Eric Thomas Galley Museum documents the history of life in Queenstown through photographic exhibits.
Driffield Street, Queenstown.

☎ *(03) 6471 1483.*
***Admission** $4.*
***Open** Jan-Mar Mon-Fri 9.30am-6pm, Sat-Sun 12.30pm-6pm; Apr-Sep Mon-Fri 10am-5pm, Sat-Sun 1pm-5pm; Oct-Dec Mon-Fri 9.30am-6pm, Sat-Sun 12.30pm-6pm.*

Cradle Mountain-Lake St Clair National Park

Tasmania's most popular national park attracts visitors from around the world. The best way to explore the park is by hiking the Overland Track – a five-day hike from Cradle Mountain to Lake St Clair – however there are many other shorter walks that are also rewarding.

The park is broken into two parts: Lake St Clair, accessible from the south and Cradle Mountain, accessible from Devonport or Launceston in the north. Most visitors to the park visit Cradle Mountain at the northern end of the national park.

Practical Information
Cradle Mountain Visitors Centre
Cradle Mountain, Cradle Mountain-Lake St Clair National Park.
☎ *(03) 6492 1133.*
***Open** 8am-5.30pm daily.*

Lake St Clair Visitors Centre
Lake St Clair, Cradle Mountain-Lake St Clair National Park
☎ *(03) 6289 1172.*
***Open** 8am-5pm daily.*

Coming & Going & Local Transport
The park is one of Tasmania's biggest attractions and it is well served by public transport. TassieLink (☎ *1300 653 633; **website** www.tigerline.com.au)* operate a bus service to Devonport and Launceston with daily departures between December and April and services on Tuesdays, Thursdays and Saturdays during the rest of the year.

Maxwell's Coach Service (☎ *(03) 6492 1431)* operates a local bus service that runs between Dove Lake, the campground and the visitor information centre.

Accommodation
Cradle Mountain Tourist Park

This good hostel has clean bunkrooms with an individual reading light for each bed. There is also a fully equipped kitchen with a wood heater and dining room plus a barbecue and laundry facilities. There's a small shop and Internet access at the reception, but the reception and accommodation are 500 metres apart. It is 2km from the national park entrance.

Cradle Mountain Road, Cradle Mountain

☎ *(03) 6492 1395.*

Dorm bed *$22 ($20 YHA).*

Credit cards *MC, Visa.*

Reception open *Jan-May 8am-7pm, Jun-Oct 8am-6pm, Nov-Dec 8am-7pm.*

🚗

Maintenance & cleanliness	★★★★
Facilities	★½
Atmosphere & character	★★½
Security	★
Overall rating	★★½

Hiking
DAY HIKES IN CRADLE MOUNTAIN

There are plenty of day hikes originating at both the northern and southern parts of the national park. These range from easy ten-minute walks to more strenuous treks up Cradle Mountain. The Dove Lake Loop Track (2 hours) is the most popular and is a good introduction to the park. The information centre sells a detailed map of these hiking trails for $4.

DAY HIKES IN LAKE ST CLAIR

There's also a good range of hiking trails in the southern – Lake St Clair – part of the park. These include the Watersmeet walk (1 hour), which is noted for its wildflowers that bloom in springtime. It is possible to continue on along the Platypus Bay track and the Woodland Naturewalk (1½ hours).

THE OVERLAND TRACK

One of Australia's most popular hiking trails is the 80km Overland Track that runs between Cradle Mountain and Lake St Clair. The track is well maintained with eight huts along the route, however it is a very popular trek and the huts are often full, making it essential to bring along a tent and a warm sleeping bag. Public transport is available with pick-ups at either end of the track from both Hobart and Launceston. It is also possible to stay at luxury accommodation en route with hot showers and fully catered meals, but this option is guaranteed to blow your budget.

Franklin-Gordon Wild Rivers National Park

This huge national park in southwest Tasmania has been classified as a World Heritage Area. Much of the Franklin-Gordon Wild Rivers National Park is pure wilderness with virtually no roads and very few hiking trails, making it a difficult place to explore. However there are several short walks that originate from various points along the Lyell Highway (A10) that are very accessible.

Frenchmans Cap track (46km, 4-5 days) is no stroll in the park, this epic hiking trail is one of the most arduous in Australia and it is recommended that you practice on several other overnight hikes before attempting this one. A detailed map and hiking guide is available from Service Tasmania shops (☎ *1300 135 513; website www.service tasmania.tas.gov.au)* for $9.

It is possible to raft the Franklin River, which rates among the world's best white water rafting trips. However rafting the Franklin is very expensive activity with rafting trips costing over a thousand dollars. Rafting here is no ordinary day-trip, and rafting expeditions on the Franklin River can last anywhere from five to eleven days and the price does include the seaplane back to Strahan.

South West National Park

Tasmania's largest national park is in the midst of a World Heritage Area.

It's a very difficult national park to visit if you want to attempt the more difficult hiking trails. Often the only

Tasmania

way in is by light plane and many hikers arrange for their food supplies to be airdropped in. The park's isolation makes it a reasonably expensive place to visit.

There are several short walks in South West National Park that are relatively accessible. These shorter walks include the highly recommended Creepy Crawly Nature Trail (2.5km, 20 mins).

More challenging day walks include the Eliza Plateau walk (5-6 hours) and the Lake Judd walk (8 hours). These two walks should only be attempted by experienced hikers.

Overnight walks in the South West National Park include the Mount Anne Circuit, Port Davey Track, South Coast Track and the Western Arthurs Traverse.

Victoria

Victoria is a small state that provides dramatic contrasts in a compact area. It is slightly smaller than the United Kingdom and all destinations within it are no more than a day's drive from Melbourne.

Melbourne

With lovely parks and gardens, Melbourne stands on the banks of the Yarra River and the shores of Port Phillip Bay. The city is Australia's second largest and home to around 3½ million people.

It is Australia's major events capital – home to such international sporting events as the Australian Formula One Grand Prix, the Australian Tennis Open and the Melbourne Cup horse race.

Melbourne is a city of diverse and vibrant neighbourhoods. Each of these areas has its own character and personality and combined they make up the cultural patchwork that is Melbourne. Venture away from the skyscrapers of the central city and explore the quirky nature of areas like Toorak Road and Chapel Street in South Yarra, which offer the city's best shopping, dining and people watching or Lygon Street, Carlton, which is Melbourne's slice of Italy, with pizza and pasta restaurants galore or perhaps enjoy authentic and cheap Vietnamese cuisine in one of the many restaurants on Victoria Street, Richmond, which is known as Melbourne's Little Siagon.

The beachfront neighbourhood of St Kilda is best known for its cake shops and backpacker scene. It has two distinct faces: the 24-hour nightlife of Fitzroy Street and the café and delicatessens of Acland Street. St Kilda's landmark is Luna Park with its laughing face and roller coaster rides. St Kilda Beach also features a weekend craft market.

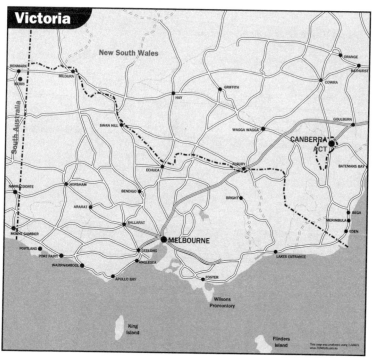

Brunswick Street, Fitzroy, reflects the alternative side of Melbourne. The streets buzz with activity and are crammed with alternative lifestyle shops, second-hand clothing and funky restaurants.

Information
INFORMATION CENTRES & USEFUL ADDRESSES
American Express
233 Collins Street, Melbourne.
🚌 *1, 3, 5, 6, 8, 11, 12, 16, 22, 25, 19, 42, 57, 59, 64, 67, 68, 72, 109;* 🚆 *Flinders Street.*
☎ *(03) 9633 6333.*
Website www.americanexpress.com.
Open Mon-Fri 9am-5pm, Sat 9am-noon.

Melbourne Tourist Information Centre
Federation Square, Corner Flinders Street & St Kilda Road, Melbourne.
🚌 *1, 3, 5, 6, 8, 11, 12, 16, 22, 25, 42, 64, 67, 72, 109;* 🚆 *Flinders Street.*
☎ *(03) 9658 9658.*
Website www.visitvictoria.com.
Open 9am-6pm daily.

Natural Resources & Environment Information Centre
8 Nicholson Street, East Melbourne.
🚌 *86, 96; Q Parliament.*
☎ *(03) 9412 4745.*
Open Mon-Fri 8am-8pm.

EMBASSIES & CONSULATES
British Consulate
17th Floor, 90 Collins Street, Melbourne.
Website www.uk.emb.gov.au.
🚌 *11, 12, 42, 109;* 🚆 *Parliament.*
☎ *(03) 9652 1600.*
Open Mon-Fri 9am-4.30pm.

Canadian Consulate
Level 50, 101 Collins Street, Melbourne.
🚌 *313, 315, 316, 605;* 🚆 *11, 12, 31, 42, 109, 112;* 🚆 *Flinders Street, Parliament.*
☎ *(03) 9653 9674.*
Website www.canada.org.au.
Open Mon-Fri 8.30am-5.15pm.

New Zealand Consulate
Suite 2 North, Level 3, 350 Collins Street, Melbourne.
🚌 *11, 12, 19, 31, 42, 57, 59, 68, 109, 112;* 🚆 *Flinders Street.*
☎ *(03) 9642 1279.*
Website www.nzembassy.com/australia.
Open Mon-Fri 9am-12.30pm & 1.30pm-5pm.

USA Consulate
6th Floor, 553 St Kilda Road, Melbourne.
🚌 *3, 5, 6, 16, 64, 67.*
☎ *(03) 8526 5900.*
Website http://usembassy-australia.state.gov/melbourne/.
Open Mon-Fri 9am-noon.

INTERNET ACCESS
Backpackers World
Hotel Bakpak, 167 Franklin Street, Melbourne.
🚌 *220, 232;* 🚆 *19, 57, 59, 68;* 🚆 *Melbourne Central.*
☎ *(03) 9329 1990.*
Open Mon-Fri 8.30am-7pm, Sat 9am-6pm, Sun 10am-6pm.

Cyberia Internet Lounge
19 Carlisle Street, St Kilda.
🚌 *246, 600, 623, 922, 923; T 3, 16, 69, 79.*
☎ *(03) 9534 6221.*
Website http://members.ozemail.com.au/~cyberia2/.
Open 10am-8pm daily.

Global Gossip
440 Elizabeth Street, Melbourne.
🚌 *19, 57, 59, 68;* 🚆 *Melbourne Central.*
☎ *(03) 9663 0511.*
Website www.globalgossip.com.au.
Open Mon-Fri 8am-midnight, Sat-Sun 9am-midnight.

Internet Café St Kilda
9 Grey Street, St Kilda.
🚌 *600, 922, 923;* 🚆 *16, 96.*
☎ *(03) 9525 3748.*
Open Mon-Thu 8.30am-10.30pm, Fri-Sun 9.30am-10pm.

Satellite Café
476 Elizabeth Street, Melbourne.
🚌 *19, 57, 59, 68;* 🚆 *Melbourne Central.*
☎ *(03) 9639 0099.*
Open 9am-midnight daily.

Coming & Going

AIR

Melbourne is served by Tullamarine International Airport (☎ (03) 9297 1600; **website** *www.melair.com.au*), 21km north of the city centre. This airport handles all international flights and most domestic flights, although Essendon and Moorabbin airports are used by some of the lesser-known airlines that fly to Tasmania.

The Tullamarine Freeway and Citylink tollway lead from the airport to the northern fringes of the city centre, hitchhikers can try their luck at the traffic lights just before the freeway entrance at the airport.

Skybus (☎ (03) 9335 2811; **website** *www.skybus.com.au*) runs frequent airport bus services to the Spencer Street coach terminal in the city centre. The Skybus runs 24 hours with services every 15 minutes during the day and it costs $13 one-way. Between 7am and 6pm Skybus provide a complimentary shuttle service between the Spencer Street and Franklin Street coach terminals and to backpackers hostels in the city centre.

A taxi from the airport to the city centre costs between $40 and $45.

BUS

Melbourne has two bus terminals.

The Spencer Street Coach Terminal is situated next to the Spencer Street train station and handles Firefly and V/line buses.

The Franklin Street Coach Terminal is a few streets north of Melbourne Central Station on Franklin Street, near RMIT University and is the terminus for McCafferty's/Greyhound buses.

TRAIN

All long-distance train services terminate at Spencer Street Station at the western edge of the city centre.

FERRY

The *Spirit of Tasmania* leaves Station Pier in Port Melbourne every night at 9pm for Devonport, Tasmania. Tram 111 runs between Station Pier and the city centre.

HITCHHIKING

It is pretty easy to get a lift out of Melbourne as just a few roads carry the majority of traffic heading out of the city.

For lifts to Sydney, take a train to Upfield and walk to the Hume Highway. This is a great hitching spot – virtually all traffic heading to Sydney and Canberra passes this point.

If you're heading to Adelaide, Ballarat or the Grampians, take a train to Deer Park, then walk up Station Road to the Western Highway and try your luck there.

An easier option is BUG Ride (**website** *http://australia.bugride.com*), BUG's own web-based ride sharing service, which allows travellers to both offer lifts and search for rides throughout Australia.

Local Transport

Melbourne's public transport system is operated by several companies and is collectively known as Metlink (**website** *www.metlinkmelbourne.com.au*) and is comprised of buses, trams and trains.

BUS

Buses go everywhere that isn't covered by trams or trains, although it is unlikely that you'll need to travel by bus.

TRAM

Most travellers find trams the most useful way to get around the city. They slowly rattle down the major streets and cover most of the inner city neighbourhoods. Trams are particularly useful for travelling between the city centre, South Melbourne and St Kilda.

The best deal is the free City Circle tram, which runs a circular route around the city centre along Flinders, La Trobe, Spencer and Spring Streets.

TRAIN

Trains are a good way to get to the outer suburbs. The five stations on the underground city loop serve as the core of Melbourne's extensive suburban train network of 232 stations. Taking a train is a handy way to get out to the choice hitchhiking spots on the

Victoria

Melbourne

Accommodation

1. All Nations
2. Bev & Mick's Backpackers
3. Carlton College Hostel
4. Carlton Hotel
5. City Scene Backpackers
6. Elephant Backpackers
7. Elizabeth Hostel
8. Exford Hotel
9. Flinders Station Backpackers
10. The Friendly Backpacker
11. Global Backpackers
12. The Greenhouse Backpacker
13. Hotel Bakpak
14. Melbourne Connection
15. Melbourne International Backpackers
16. Nomads Market Inn
17. The Nunnery
18. Queensberry Hill YHA
19. Toad Hall

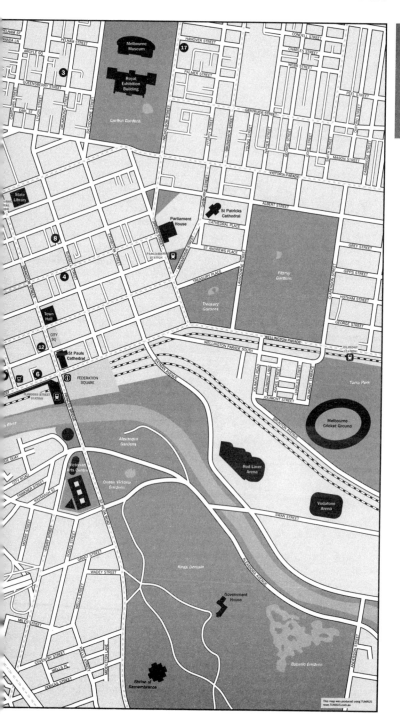

edge of town, for catching the Phillip Island ferry at Stony Point, for visiting friends or going to job interviews in the suburbs.

FARES
The Metcard ticketing system allows you to transfer between these three modes of transport within a two-hour, daily, weekly or monthly period. The Melbourne area is divided into three fare zones, with virtually everything of interest located within Zone One.

Two-hour tickets are valid for two hours from the next full hour. For instance a ticket purchased or validated at 10.55am expires at 1pm, but if you wait 10 minutes and validate your ticket at 11.05am it will not expire until 2pm. Two-hour tickets are valid until 2am the next morning if validated after 6pm.

Only a limited range of tickets is available from buses, trams and at the machines at some of the smaller train stations. The full range of tickets is available from major train stations and many convenience stores. Note that some ticket machines only accept coins.

Refer to the following table for ticket prices:

Zones	2 hour	Daily	Weekly
One	$3	$5.80	$25
Two	$2.20	$4	$17.20
Three	$2.20	$4	$17.20
One & Two	$5	$9.40	$42.60
Two & Three	$4	$7.80	$34.70
All Zones	$7	$12.30	$52

The two-hour and daily tickets are cheaper if you buy a multi-trip ticket that bundles either 10 two-hour tickets or five daily tickets. This is often the best ticket option if you're staying a while in Melbourne, but don't need to use public transport every day. Prices for these tickets are as follows:

Zones	10 x 2 hour	5 x Daily
One	$26	$26
Two	$18	$18
Three	$18	$18
One & Two	$44	$44
Two & Three	$36	$36
All Zones	$58.50	$58.50

Another option is the City Saver ticket, which is good for a single trip within the city centre and some inner city neighbourhoods. This ticket costs $2.20 or $19 for 10 City Saver tickets.

DRIVING
Because you will be sharing the road with trams, Melbourne is one of Australia's more challenging cities to drive in.

Whenever a tram stops at a tram stop you must also come to a complete stop and wait until the tram leaves the tram stop before you start moving again, so people can alight safely. This is not necessary at many of the tram stops in the city centre which have a barrier called a Safety Zone or when you are travelling in the opposite direction to the tram.

If you're driving in the rain, avoid braking on tram tracks. They can be very slippery.

Hook Turns
A hook turn is a bizarre driving rule unique to Melbourne. In certain intersections in the city centre (where there is a sign indicating Right Turn from Left Lane), a right-hand-turn must be made from the left-hand-side of the road. Although this sounds confusing, it actually makes a lot of sense as hook turns prevent trams from being held up in traffic.

Instead of turning right from the right lane, you should get into the left lane and cross three-quarters of the intersection and then stop, indicating to turn right, until you have a green light in the direction you are turning. Only when you have a green light should you complete the hook turn.

Citylink
Citylink, Melbourne's new tollway, is a quick way to get in and out of the city. The tollway runs from Tullamarine Freeway at Bell Street to the Westgate Freeway and also from the city centre to the Monash Freeway at Toorak Road. The electronic payment system ensures that there are no queues at tollbooths and is a convenient system for residents, but for visitors to Melbourne it is much less convenient. Residents using

Citylink affix an electronic device to their windscreen called an eTag, which automatically debits the toll from their account. If you're just visiting Melbourne, it is inconvenient and expensive to buy an eTag and it a better idea to buy a 24-hour or weekend Citylink pass for $9.40 that allows you to use Citylink for either a 24-hour period during weekdays or all weekend. Passes are available from Citylink offices, Post Offices and from machines inside most Shell service stations around Melbourne. You have until the following morning after driving on Citylink to pay for your Citylink pass. Passes can also be ordered by calling 13 26 29 or online at www.transurban.com.au. There are heavy fines if you do not pay.

There are alternate routes if you want to avoid the tolls. Going to the airport from the city centre, you can avoid Citylink by getting on the West Gate Freeway at Power Street or Kings Way and heading west and then taking the Western Ring Road north to the Tullamarine Freeway. If you're heading to Gippsland, Phillip Island or the south-eastern suburbs, you can get to the Monash Freeway via Toorak Road.

Accommodation
CITY CENTRE & NORTH MELBOURNE
The city centre is close to all the action and is handy for transport connections to other parts of Melbourne. A lot of Melbourne's hostels are clustered around Queen Victoria Market, which includes a few north of Victoria Street in North Melbourne.

All Nations
This is an older building and it looks run-down from the outside, but it's not too bad inside. The All Nations has a good atmosphere and good facilities that include a small kitchen, a chill out room with Internet access, and a TV lounge. It has over 200 beds on three levels and dormitories have four, six and eight beds. It is on the corner of Flinders and Spencer Streets – not the nicest part of town, but handy to most attractions and close to the nightclubs on King Street.

2 Spencer Street, Melbourne.
🚌 *232, 238;* 🚊 *City Circle, 12, 48, 70, 75, 96, 109, 112;* 🚉 *Spencer Street.*
☎ *(03) 9620 1022 or 1800 222 238.*
Website *www.allnations.com.au.*
Dorm bed *$16-20;* ***double/twin room*** *$55; includes breakfast.*
Credit cards *MC, Visa.*
Reception open *24 hours.*

Maintenance & cleanliness	★★☆
Facilities	★★☆
Atmosphere & character	★★★
Security	★★★
Overall rating	★★☆

Bev & Mick's Backpackers
This small friendly hostel above a pub is a great place for backpackers working in Melbourne. It's an old building with Baltic pine floors, a great late night bar and a warm welcome.
312 Victoria Street, Melbourne.
🚌 *546;* 🚊 *55, 57.*
☎ *(03) 9329 7156.*
Dorm bed *$15 per night; $80 per week.*

Maintenance & cleanliness	★★☆
Facilities	★★☆
Atmosphere & character	★★★★★
Security	★★☆
Overall rating	★★★

Chapman Gardens YHA
This youth hostel has fewer facilities than the larger YHA closer to the city centre, but it is a clean and well-maintained hostel. It has two kitchens and a nice outdoors area with a gazebo and barbecue. It is on a quiet residential street, north of the city centre near Royal Park.
76 Chapman Street, North Melbourne.
🚌 *402, 479;* 🚊 *55, 57, 59, 68.*
☎ *(03) 9328 3595.*
Dorm bed *$28.50 ($25 YHA);* ***single room*** *$53.50 ($50 YHA);* ***double room*** *$65 ($58 YHA);* ***twin room*** *$61 ($54 YHA).*
Credit cards *MC, Visa.*
Reception open *7.30am-12.30pm & 2pm-10pm daily.*
🚭

Maintenance & cleanliness	★★★★
Facilities	★★
Atmosphere & character	★★
Security	★★★★
Overall rating	★★★

Carlton Hotel

This hostel is above a dodgy 24-hour pub and it offers basic accommodation in small three-bed dormitories that include a sink and wardrobe. Double/twin rooms also have a fridge and TV. It is centrally located, but the bar downstairs is full of shady characters.
197 Bourke Street, Melbourne.
☒ *250, 251, 253, 350, 479;* ☒ *1, 3, 5, 6, 8, 16, 22, 64, 67, 72, 86, 96.*
☎ *(03) 9650 2734.*
Website *www.carltonhotel.com.au.*
Dorm bed *$25;* **double/twin room** *$55.*
Credit cards *Amex, Diners, MC, Visa.*
Reception open *24 hours.*

Maintenance & cleanliness	★★
Facilities	★
Atmosphere & character	★☆
Security	★★☆
Overall rating	★★☆

City Scene Backpackers

This is a good small hostel with mostly four-bed dorms. It has a small kitchen with new appliances, a cosy TV lounge and a nice courtyard. There are TVs and fridges in the double/twin rooms.
361 Queensberry Street, North Melbourne.
☒ *546;* ☒ *55.*
☎ *(03) 9348 9525.*
Dorm bed *$15-21;* **double room** *$45-55;* **twin room** *$40-50.*
Credit cards *MC, Visa.*
Reception open *7.30am-11am & 5.30pm-7pm daily.*

Maintenance & cleanliness	★★★
Facilities	★★☆
Atmosphere & character	★★★★☆
Security	★★
Overall rating	★★★☆

Elephant Backpackers

Elephant Backpackers is a clean hostel with good quality facilities. It features new bunk beds with real mattresses, and a downstairs common area with a TV lounge, kitchen and Internet access. The main drawback is that the rooms don't have ceilings – the walls are just partitions and you can hear people several rooms away.
250 Flinders Street, Melbourne.
☒ *235, 237, 238, 253, 350, 479;*
☒ *City Circle, 1, 3, 5, 6, 8, 16, 19, 22, 48, 57, 59, 64, 67, 68, 70, 72, 75;*
☒ *Flinders Street.*
☎ *(03) 9654 2616.*
Website *www.elephantbackpackers.citysearch.com.au.*
Dorm bed *$20;* **single room** *$35;* **twin room** *$50.*
Reception open *7am-11pm daily.*

Maintenance & cleanliness	★★★★★
Facilities	★☆
Atmosphere & character	★★★
Security	★★★
Overall rating	★★★★☆

Elizabeth Hostel

A year ago this was the worst hostel in Melbourne, but it has now been thoroughly renovated. It is now a very clean hostel with good quality fittings, but facilities are limited and it has a sterile atmosphere.
Level 1, 490-494 Elizabeth Street, Melbourne.
☒ *19, 57, 59, 68;* ☒ *Melbourne Central.*
☎ *(03) 9663 1685.*
Website *www.elizabethhostel.com.au.*
Dorm bed *$17-25;* **single room** *$55;* **double/twin room** *$65.*
Credit cards *MC, Visa.*
Reception open *8am-10pm daily.*

Maintenance & cleanliness	★★★★★
Facilities	★★☆
Atmosphere & character	★★☆
Security	★★★☆
Overall rating	★★★

Exford Hotel

This is a nice hostel with a good atmosphere, above a pub in Chinatown. The hostel has plenty of common areas including a TV lounge and a good kitchen. Accommodation is very good and it has excellent security with key card access and lockers in all rooms.
199 Russell Street, Melbourne.
☒ *200, 201, 203, 207, 250, 241;*
☒ *1, 3, 5, 6, 8, 16, 22, 64, 67, 72, 86, 96.*
☎ *(03) 9663 2697.*
Website *www.exfordhotel.com.au.*
Dorm bed *$20-24 ($19-23 VIP);* **double/twin room** *$58 ($56 VIP).*
Credit cards *MC, Visa.*
Reception open *24 hours.*

Maintenance & cleanliness	★★★
Facilities	★★
Atmosphere & character	★★★★☆
Security	★★★★☆
Overall rating	★★★

Flinders Station Backpackers

This is a big centrally located hostel with 11 floors. The common areas on the third floor include TV lounges, Internet access, a pool table and a big kitchen. There isn't a lot of atmosphere but the brilliant location compensates for this.

35 Elizabeth Street, Melbourne.
☎ *235, 237, 253, 350;* ☎ *City Circle, 11, 12, 19, 31, 42, 48, 57, 59, 68, 70, 75, 109, 112;* ☎ *Flinders Street.*
☎ *(03) 9620 5100.*
Website *www.flindersbackpackers. com.au.*
Dorm bed *$20 ($19 VIP);* **double room** *$58-74 ($56-72 VIP);* **twin room** *$58 ($56 VIP).*
Credit cards *MC, Visa.*
Reception open *24 hours.*

Maintenance & cleanliness	★★★
Facilities	★★
Atmosphere & character	★★☆
Security	★★★★★
Overall rating	★★★

The Friendly Backpacker

The Friendly Backpacker is an excellent hostel that is spotlessly clean and has top class facilities. The hostel has a well-equipped kitchen and a large dining room with a pool table downstairs, while the upper levels have several lounges and quiet reading areas.

197 King Street, Melbourne.
☎ *216, 219, 684;* ☎ *55, 70, 86, 96;*
☎ *Spencer Street.*
☎ *(03) 9670 1111 or 1800 671 115.*
Website *www.friendlygroup.com.au.*
Dorm bed *$25;* **double room** *$80; includes breakfast.*
Credit cards *MC, Visa.*
Reception open *7.30am-11pm daily; late check in by prior arrangement.*

Maintenance & cleanliness	★★★★☆
Facilities	★★☆
Atmosphere & character	★★★★☆
Security	★★★★☆
Overall rating	★★★★☆

Global Backpackers

Global Backpackers has a very friendly relaxed atmosphere. The rooms are small and clean, but dated. It's above a lively pub and opposite the fantastic buzzing Queen Victoria Market.

238 Victoria Street, Melbourne.
☎ *(03) 9328 3728.*
Dorm bed *$21.*

Maintenance & cleanliness	★★★
Facilities	★★★
Atmosphere & character	★★★
Security	★★
Overall rating	★★★

The Greenhouse Backpacker

This hostel is clean and well maintained. It features a rooftop garden, a huge laundry, a fully equipped kitchen, TV lounge and pool tables. There are also lots of quiet sitting areas and free Internet access. The accommodation is excellent and features lots of little touches such as individual reading lights by the beds. The largest dorm has only six beds and the hostel is fully air-conditioned.

228 Flinders Lane, Melbourne.
☎ *235, 237, 238, 253, 350;* ☎ *City Circle, 1, 3, 5, 6, 8, 11, 12, 16, 19, 22, 31, 42, 48, 57, 59, 64, 67, 68, 70, 72, 75, 109, 112;* ☎ *Flinders Street.*
☎ *(03) 9639 6400 or 1800 249 207.*
Website *www.friendlygroup.com.au.*
Dorm bed *$27;* **double room** *$78; includes breakfast.*
Credit cards *MC, Visa.*
Reception open *24 hours.*

Maintenance & cleanliness	★★★★★
Facilities	★★★★☆
Atmosphere & character	★★★★☆
Security	★★★★☆
Overall rating	★★★★☆

Hotel Bakpak

This is a huge 650-bed hostel that has a good atmosphere and a good range of facilities including an excellent basement bar with pool tables, a cinema-style TV lounge with a huge projection screen and a rooftop barbecue area with great city views. The ground floor features a café, employment agency, travel agency and Internet Café.

167 Franklin Street, Melbourne.
☎ *220, 232; T 19, 57, 59, 68;*

Melbourne Central.
☎ *(03) 9329 7525.*
Website www.bakpak.com/franklin/.
Dorm bed $22-25; single room $55;
double room $60.
Credit cards MC, Visa.
Reception open 24 hours.

Maintenance & cleanliness	★★★☆
Facilities	★★★☆
Atmosphere & character	★★★☆
Security	★★★★★
Overall rating	★★★☆

Melbourne Connection

This newly renovated hostel is an excellent place with great facilities that include a TV room, fully-equipped kitchen and Internet access.
205 King Street, Melbourne.
216, 219, 684; *55, 70, 86, 96;*
Spencer Street.
☎ *(03) 9642 4464.*
Website www.melbourneconnection.
com.
Dorm bed $21-25; double/twin room $70.
Credit cards MC, Visa.
Reception open 8am-12.30pm & 1pm-9pm daily; 24-hour check in.

Maintenance & cleanliness	★★★★★
Facilities	★★☆
Atmosphere & character	★★★
Security	★★★★☆
Overall rating	★★★★☆

Melbourne International Backpackers

This is a big, clean 380-bed hostel right in the heart of the city centre near the Melbourne Central shopping centre and the Queen Victoria Market. It's at the corner of Elizabeth and Franklin Streets, with the entrance on Franklin Street. Common areas include a big dining/TV room with a courtyard and a big kitchen. Accommodation consists of new furnishings and the security is excellent with key card access and lockers in the rooms.
450 Elizabeth Street, Melbourne.
19, 57, 59, 68; *Melbourne Central.*
☎ *(03) 9662 4066.*
Dorm bed $20 ($19 VIP).
Credit cards MC, Visa.

Reception open 24 hours.

Maintenance & cleanliness	★★★★
Facilities	★★☆
Atmosphere & character	★★☆
Security	★★★★★
Overall rating	★★★

Queensberry Hill YHA

Queensberry Hill YHA is a large well-maintained hostel with a good range of facilities, which include a café/bar, a pool table, Internet access and several small TV lounges. Accommodation is very nice with real mattresses, individual bedside lamps and lovely double rooms with a standard similar to a top hotel. It is in a quiet location opposite a church on a leafy street in North Melbourne. It's about a 15-minute walk into the city centre and local shops on Errol Street are a five-minute walk from the hostel.
78 Howard Street, North Melbourne.
402, 546; *55, 57.*
☎ *(03) 9329 8599.*
Dorm bed $28.50-30.50 ($25-27 YHA); single room $65.50-77.50 ($62-74 YHA); double/twin room $79-91 ($72-84 YHA).
Credit cards MC, Visa.
Reception open 7am-10.30pm daily.

Maintenance & cleanliness	★★★★★
Facilities	★★★★☆
Atmosphere & character	★★☆
Security	★★★★★
Overall rating	★★★★

Toad Hall

Toad Hall is a nice small hostel that appeals to couples and more mature backpackers. There are two TV lounges including a brilliant basement TV room with thick bluestone walls. Other amenities include a clean kitchen and a nice courtyard with a barbecue.
441 Elizabeth Street, Melbourne.
19, 57, 59, 68; *Melbourne Central.*
☎ *(03) 9600 9010.*
Website www.toadhall-hotel.com.au.
Dorm bed $25; single room $60; double room $70-90; twin room $60.
Credit cards MC, Visa.
Reception open 7am-10pm daily.
$10 per day.

Maintenance & cleanliness	★★★★☆
Facilities	★☆
Atmosphere & character	★★★★
Security	★★☆
Overall rating	★★★☆

FITZROY & CARLTON

The neighbourhoods north east of the city centre boast lovely Victorian terrace houses and the ambience ranges from the alternative feel of Brunswick Street in Fitzroy to the Italian restaurants that line Lygon Street in Carlton. The main attractions here include Melbourne Museum and the Royal Exhibition Buildings in Carlton Gardens.

Carlton College Hostel

This hostel is housed in a row of terrace houses. Facilities include a TV lounge, Internet access and several kitchens. It has a great location in a quiet street in Carlton, within a short walk to most attractions in the city centre. It is very convenient to the Melbourne Museum and the Royal Exhibition Buildings as well as great Italian restaurants on nearby Lygon Street.
97 Drummond Street, Carlton.
⊟ *200, 201, 203, 207, 250, 251, 253, 402.*
☎ *(03) 9664 0664 or 1800 066 551.*
Website *www.carltoncollege.com.au.*
Dorm bed *$15-20;* ***double room*** *$48; includes breakfast.*
Credit cards *Amex, MC, Visa.*
Reception open *8am-noon & 4pm-8pm daily.*

Maintenance & cleanliness	★★★☆
Facilities	★★☆
Atmosphere & character	★★★
Security	★★☆
Overall rating	★★★☆

The Nunnery

The Nunnery consists of four grand old Victorian terrace houses that were once used as a nunnery. It has a fun atmosphere and all the usual facilities such as a kitchen, TV lounge, Internet access and a laundry.
116 Nicholson Street, Fitzroy.
⊟ *96.*
☎ *(03) 9419 8637 or 1800 032 635.*
Website *www.bakpakgroup.com/nunnery.*

Dorm bed *$23-27 ($22-26 VIP);* ***single room*** *$60-75 ($59-74 VIP);* ***double room*** *$80-110 ($78-108 VIP);* ***twin room*** *$70-110 ($68-108 VIP); includes breakfast.*
Credit cards *MC, Visa.*
Reception open *8am-8pm daily; check in till 1am.*

Maintenance & cleanliness	★★★
Facilities	★★
Atmosphere & character	★★★★★
Security	★★☆
Overall rating	★★★

ST KILDA

This bohemian seaside suburb is popular with backpackers and has plenty of good value hostels. The area has a good beach, great pubs and cafés and a busy weekend market.

Coffee Palace

This is a big hostel with a good atmosphere but limited facilities. Amenities include the usual kitchen, a dining area with a pool table and a rooftop barbecue area. It could be better maintained.
24 Grey Street, St Kilda.
⊟ *600;* ⊟ *12, 16, 96.*
☎ *(03) 9534 5283 or 1800 654 098.*
Website *www.coffeepalace.com.au.*
Dorm bed *$17-25 ($16-24 VIP);* ***double/twin room*** *$65 ($63 VIP); includes pancake breakfast.*
Credit cards *MC, Visa.*
Reception open *24 hours.*

Maintenance & cleanliness	★★☆
Facilities	★★☆
Atmosphere & character	★★★★
Security	★★★☆
Overall rating	★★

Jackson's Manor

Jackson's Manor is a quiet backpackers' hostel in an historic building that has a lot of charm. The hostel has the usual kitchen, Internet access and a TV lounge.
53 Jackson Street, St Kilda.
⊟ *600;* ⊟ *12, 16, 96.*
☎ *903) 9534 1877.*
Website *www.jacksonsmanor.com.au.*
Dorm bed *$19-22;* ***double/twin room*** *$50.*

Victoria

Maintenance & cleanliness	★★★★☆
Facilities	★★☆
Atmosphere & character	★★★
Security	★★★☆
Overall rating	★★★

Maintenance & cleanliness	★★★★
Facilities	★★
Atmosphere & character	★★★★★
Security	★★
Overall rating	★★★★☆

Olembia

Olembia is classier and more upmarket than the other St Kilda hostels and it is a good choice if you want to stay in St Kilda but prefer something quieter. It appeals to couples and older backpackers. Olembia's facilities include a fully equipped kitchen and a nice lounge room with lots of magazines (but no TV). Most dorms only have three beds.

96 Barkly Street, St Kilda.
🚌 *246;* 🚊 *3, 67, 79.*
☎ *(03) 9537 1412.*
Website *www.olembia.com.au.*
Dorm bed *$25;* ***single room*** *$46;*
double/twin room *$78.*
Credit cards *MC, Visa.*
Reception open *8am-1pm & 5pm-7pm daily.*
🚌

Oslo Hotel

The Oslo Hotel is a basic hostel with lower standards than the other places in St Kilda. It has brand new bathrooms and a nice TV lounge and Internet room near the reception, but the rest of the hostel has a drab old fashioned feel with old second-hand furnishings.

38 Grey Street, St Kilda.
🚌 *600;* 🚊 *12, 16, 96.*
☎ *(03) 9525 4498 or 1800 501 752.*
Dorm bed *$20-24;* ***double/twin room*** *$55.*
Credit cards *MC, Visa.*
Reception open *summer 7am-11pm daily; winter 9am-11pm daily.*

Maintenance & cleanliness	★★
Facilities	★★
Atmosphere & character	★★☆
Security	★★
Overall rating	★★

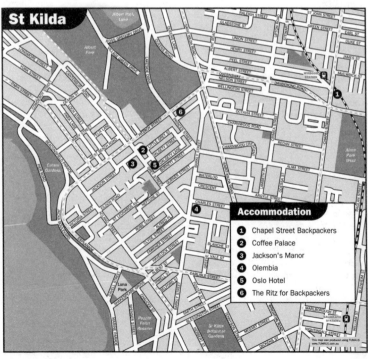

St Kilda

Accommodation

1. Chapel Street Backpackers
2. Coffee Palace
3. Jackson's Manor
4. Olembia
5. Oslo Hotel
6. The Ritz for Backpackers

The Ritz for Backpackers

The hostel above the Elephant and Wheelbarrow pub has a good atmosphere, but it could be better maintained. Facilities include a common room with a pool table and foosball. There's also a TV lounge, Internet access and a kitchen.

169 Fitzroy Street, St Kilda.
🚌 *600;* 🚋 *16, 96.*
☎ *(03) 9525 3501.*
Website *www.backpackerscentre.com.*
Dorm bed *$20-25;* **double room** *$60.*
Credit cards *Amex, Diners, MC, Visa.*
Reception open *24 hours.*

Maintenance & cleanliness	★★
Facilities	★★
Atmosphere & character	★★★★
Security	★★★
Overall rating	★★½

SOUTH MELBOURNE

The area between St Kilda and the city centre is a nice place to stay with easy access to beaches and the city centre.

Gunn Island Hotel

This hostel is above a nice pub and facilities are limited to a small kitchen and a TV lounge. It is in a nice neighbourhood close to shops and the beach.

102 Canterbury Road, Middle Park.
🚌 *96.*
☎ *(03) 9690 1882.*
Website *www.gunnisland.com.au.*
Dorm bed *$22;* **single room** *$41.50;* **double/twin room** *$58;* **triple room** *$68; includes breakfast.*
Credit cards *Amex, MC, Visa.*
Reception open *8.30am-around midnight daily.*

Maintenance & cleanliness	★★★½
Facilities	★★
Atmosphere & character	★★★
Security	★★½
Overall rating	★★★½

Nomads Market Inn

This is a good hostel with a TV lounge, Internet access, a small kitchen and a bar. There's also a small courtyard with a barbecue. It's on the corner of Cecil and Market Streets, across the road from the bustling South Melbourne Market.

115 Cecil Street, South Melbourne.
🚌 *253;* 🚋 *12, 96, 112.*
☎ *(03) 9690 2220.*
Website *www.marketinn.com.au.*
Dorm bed *$19-23;* **double/twin room** *$8; includes breakfast.*
Credit cards *MC, Visa.*
Reception open *6.30am-2pm & 5pm-10pm daily; late check in by prior arrangement.*

Maintenance & cleanliness	★★★
Facilities	★★★½
Atmosphere & character	★★★★
Security	★★★
Overall rating	★★★

SOUTH YARRA & PRAHRAN

Chapel Street, which runs through South Yarra and Prahran is one of Melbourne's best shopping streets, and this area also has good pubs and nightlife. There are several good hostels in this area, mostly around Prahran and in Windsor at the southern (cheaper) end of Chapel Street.

Chapel Street Backpackers

This small hostel is very clean and well maintained with facilities that include a small kitchen, TV lounge, Internet access and a nice courtyard. Accommodation is of a high standard and most rooms have en suite bathrooms.

22 Chapel Street, Windsor.
🚌 *5, 64, 78, 79;* 🚆 *Windsor.*
☎ *(03) 9533 6855.*
Website *www.cdbackpackers.com.au.*
Dorm bed *$25-26 ($24-25 Nomads);* **double room** *$75 ($73 Nomads);* **twin room** *$58-65 ($56-63 Nomads).*
Credit cards *Amex, MC, Visa.*
Reception open *7am-midnight.*

Maintenance & cleanliness	★★★★½
Facilities	★★½
Atmosphere & character	★★★★½
Security	★★★★
Overall rating	★★★★

College Lawn Hotel

This is a hostel above a very nice pub. It has minimal kitchen facilities (just a fridge and microwave) and there's no real common area apart from the pub downstairs.

36 Greville Street, Prahran.
🚌 *246;* 🚋 *6;* 🚆 *Prahran.*
☎ *(03) 9510 6057.*

Website *www.collegelawnhotel.com.au.*
Dorm bed *$15 per night, $100 per*
week; *single room* *$30 per night, $160*
per week; *double room* *$50 per night,*
$250 per week.
Credit cards *MC, Visa.*
Reception open *9am-11pm daily.*

Maintenance & cleanliness	★★★
Facilities	★
Atmosphere & character	★★
Security	★★☆
Overall rating	★★

Lord's Lodge

Lord's Lodge is an old 1870s mansion
with loads of character. It has a small
kitchen and a lounge room with a log
fire, TV and Internet access. Double/
twin rooms are in bungalows in the
small backyard and there's a nice barbecue area in the front yard. It is on
busy Punt Road near the corner of
Greville Street and it's a short walk to
St Kilda Road and everything in the
Prahran/South Yarra area.
204 Punt Road, Prahran.
□ *246;* □ *6;* □ *Prahran.*
☎ *(03) 9510 5658.*
Website *www.lordslodge.com.au.*
Dorm bed *$20-24;* *single room* *$45;*
double/twin room *$62.*
Credit cards *MC, Visa.*
Reception open *Mon-Sat 8am-noon*
& 5pm-6pm; Sun 8am-noon.

Maintenance & cleanliness	★★☆
Facilities	★★
Atmosphere & character	★★★★☆
Security	★★★★☆
Overall rating	★★★

Eating & Drinking

Melbourne is possibly the best Australian city for eating out with a good
selection of restaurants – many of them
falling within a backpackers' budget.

Much of Melbourne's culinary scene
can be attributed to the city's rich
ethnic heritage with different immigrants introducing their cuisine. Melbourne's Italian restaurant strip is on
Lygon Street in Carlton, while Greek
restaurants are clustered along Lons-
dale Street in the city centre and Chinese restaurants are a couple of blocks
south on Little Bourke Street. Victoria
Street in Richmond is the best spot for

Vietnamese food and definitely worth
the trip. Bring your own bottle of wine
for a good night out on the town.

If you're preparing your own food,
then head to the Queen Victoria
Market near the corner of Elizabeth
Street and Victoria Parade. This is one
of the world's largest markets and is
particularly good value for meat as well
as fruit and vegetables.

The most centrally located supermarket is the Coles Express on Elizabeth
Street near Flinders Street Station. If
you're staying at one of the hostels in
St Kilda, then you'll find both a Coles
and a Safeway supermarket on Acland
Street. If you're staying at one of the
hostels in the Windsor/Prahran/South
Yarra area, there are two 24-hour
supermarkets (a Coles and a Safeway)
near the corner of Chapel Street and
Commercial Road in Prahran.

Melbourne has great nightlife with
some good inner city pubs and clubs.
A few of the big nightclubs have
regular backpacker nights that are
excellent value. Tuesday is the main
backpacker night with the Hard Rock
Café (*1 Bourke Street, Melbourne*) serving cheap drinks 7.30pm-11.30pm and
Inflation (*60 King Street, Melbourne;*
website *www.inflation.com.au*) giving
away free beer for two hours.

Sights
THE CITY CENTRE

The central business district bounded
by Flinders, La Trobe, Spencer and
Spring Streets is generally called The
City and is where you'll find most of
Melbourne's attractions.

Australian/Chinese Museum

This great little museum is in the heart
of Chinatown and traces the history
of Melbourne's Chinese community,
from the gold rushes of the 1850s to the
present day. The museum is also home
to Dai Loong, one of the world's largest
Chinese dragons.
22 Cohen Place, Melbourne.
□ *23, 24, 30, 34, 86, 96, City Circle;*
□ *Parliament.*
☎ *(03) 9662 2888.*
Admission *$6.50.*
Open *10am-5pm daily.*

Federation Square

Opened in 2002, this complex includes part of the National Gallery of Victoria as well as restaurants, cafés, pubs and shops. One of the main features of the buildings in Federation Square is the striking design that utilises sandstone, zinc and glass. The square also features open areas including courtyards and a large central plaza.

Corner Swanston & Flinders Streets, Melbourne.

🚌 *235, 237, 238, 253, 350, 479, 605;*
🚊 *1, 3, 5, 6, 8, 16, 22, 25, 64, 67, 72, City Circle;* 🚆 *Flinders Street.*

Website www.federationsquare.com.au.

Flinders Street Station

This is the hub of Melbourne's suburban rail network and for many years has been Melbourne's major landmark. The clocks on the corner of this ornate station have been the favourite meeting place for generations of Melburnians.

Corner Swanston & Flinders Streets, Melbourne.

🚊 *1, 3, 5, 6, 8, 16, 22, 25, 64, 67, 72, City Circle;* 🚆 *Flinders Street.*

Immigration Museum

This fascinating museum recalls the journeys of thousands of immigrants and their contribution to Australia.

Old Customs House, Corner Flinders & William Streets, Melbourne.

🚊 *48, 55, 70, 75, City Circle;*
🚆 *Flinders Street, Spencer Street.*
☎ *(03) 9927 2700.*

Website http://immigration.museum. vic.gov.au.

Admission $6, ground floor free.
Open 10am-5pm daily.

Melbourne Aquarium

Melbourne's impressive new aquarium is home to a variety of Marine Life and features transparent tunnels allowing you to be surrounded by fish in the 2.2 million-litre Oceanarium.

Corner Flinders & King Streets, Melbourne.

🚊 *48, 70, 75, City Circle.*
☎ *(03) 9620 0999.*

Website www.melbourneaquarium. com.au.

Admission $22.

Open Jan 9.30am-9pm daily, Feb-Dec 9.30am-6pm daily.

Museum of Melbourne

Recently relocated to a spot behind the Royal Exhibition Buildings, Australia's largest museum contains some excellent exhibits with a good selection on local and natural history. The museum contains a lot of new exhibits and is divided along different themes with Australian history, Aboriginal and Pacific Island culture, science and natural history. The complex also houses an IMAX theatre as well as ICE (Immersion Cinema Experience).

Carlton Gardens, Nicholson Street, Carlton.

🚊 *250, 251, 253, 402;* 🚊 *86, 96.*
☎ *13 11 02.*

Website http://melbourne.museum.vic. gov.au.

Admission $15.
Open 10am-5pm daily.

NGV – Ian Potter Centre

The National Gallery of Victoria's Ian Potter Centre houses an excellent collection of Australian art ranging from Aboriginal art through to colonial and contemporary art.

Federation Square, Corner Flinders & Swanston Streets, Melbourne.

🚌 *235, 237, 238, 253, 350, 479, 605;*
🚊 *1, 3, 5, 6, 8, 16, 22, 25, 64, 67, 72, City Circle;* 🚆 *Flinders Street.*
☎ *(03) 9208 0222.*

Website www.ngv.vic.gov.au.
Admission free.
Open Mon-Thu 10am-5pm, Fri 10am-9pm, Sat-Sun 10am-6pm.

Old Melbourne Gaol

Built in 1841, this prison has a history of 104 hangings including that of the infamous Ned Kelly in 1880. Displays include Kelly's armour, his guns and his death mask.

Russell Street, Melbourne.

🚌 *200, 201, 203, 207, 479;* 🚊 *23, 24, 30, 34, City Circle;* 🚆 *Melbourne Central.*
☎ *(03) 9663 7228.*

Website www.nattrust.com.au.
Admission $12.50.
Open 9.30am-5pm daily.

Old Treasury

The former state treasury building has been converted into a museum focusing on the story of gold and its role in the development of Victoria.

Spring Street, Melbourne.

🚌 *11, 12, 31, 42, 109, City Circle;*
🚉 *Parliament.*
☎ *(03) 9561 2233.*
Website *www.oldtreasurymuseum. org.au.*
Admission *$8.50.*
Open *Mon-Fri 9am-5pm, Sat-Sun 10am-4pm.*

Parliament House

This imposing building served as the home of Australia's parliament from 1901 till 1927 after which time it has been home to the Victorian state parliament. There are guided tours when parliament is not sitting, and you may sit in on parliament when it is in session.

Spring Street, Melbourne.

🚌 *86, 96, City Circle;* 🚉 *Parliament.*
☎ *(03) 9651 8568.*
Website *www.parliament.vic.gov.au.*
Admission *free.*
Tours *10am, 11am, 12noon, 2pm, 3pm & 3.45pm when parliament is in recess.*

Queen Victoria Market

With more than 1100 stalls, the Victoria Market is one of the world's largest. It is a great place to stock up on fresh food at bargain prices, and there is a huge flea market on weekends.

513 Elizabeth Street, Melbourne.

🚌 *220, 232, 546;* 🚋 *19, 55, 57, 59, 68;* 🚉 *Melbourne Central.*
☎ *(03) 9320 5822.*
Website *www.qvm.com.au.*
Admission *free.*
Open *Tue & Thu 6am-2pm, Fri 6am-6pm, Sat 6am-3pm, Sun 9am-4pm.*

Rialto Towers

The taller of the two Rialto Towers is Melbourne's tallest building and the tallest office building in the southern hemisphere. There are great views from the observation deck at the top. The best time to visit is just before sunset so you can see the city during the day and night.

525 Collins Street, Melbourne.

🚌 *11, 12, 31, 42, 48, 55, 70, 75, 109, City Circle;* 🚉 *Spencer Street.*
☎ *(03) 9629 8222.*
Website *www.rialtoobservationdeck. com.au.*
Admission *$11.80, $9 students.*
Open *Sun-Thu 10am-10pm, Fri-Sat 10am-11pm.*

Royal Exhibition Buildings

Built in 1879 for the International Exhibition of 1880, this exhibition centre is an architectural masterpiece; the concrete dome over the main hall was modelled on Brunelleschi's cathedral in Florence. The exterior is much more impressive than the interior, partially because of its setting within the Carlton Gardens.

Rathdowne, Victoria & Nicholson Streets, Carlton.

🚌 *250, 251, 253, 402;* 🚋 *86, 96.*

SOUTHBANK & SOUTH MELBOURNE

Central Melbourne is expanding across the river into South Melbourne and the heart of all this development is known as Southbank. This new development is growing into a neighbourhood of new inner city apartments, theatres, cafés, restaurants and a casino.

Southbank is home to the Victorian Arts Centre, the Melbourne Exhibition Centre, the huge Crown Casino complex and Southbank Promenade – a pedestrian mall along the river bank which has many sidewalk cafés spilling out from the new shopping complex. It can get quite busy here on weekends and during lunchtime on weekdays when the place is full of office workers.

Performing Arts Museum

Situated in the Melbourne Concert Hall, the Performing Arts Museum hosts a variety of exhibitions involving everything from rock music to circus and opera.

100 St Kilda Road, Southbank.

🚌 *216, 219, 220;* 🚋 *3, 5, 6, 8, 16, 25, 64, 67, 72;* 🚉 *Flinders Street.*
☎ *(03) 9681 8000.*
Admission *free.*
Open *Mon-Sat 9am-11pm, Sun 10am-5pm.*

Polly Woodside Maritime Museum

The *Polly Woodside* was built in Belfast in 1885, and has now been totally restored. This old iron hulled sailing ship is the focal point of this maritime museum located opposite the World Trade Centre.

Lorimer Street East, Southbank.
🚆 *236;* 🚌 *96, 110, 112;* 🚉 *Spencer Street.*
☎ *(03) 9699 9760.*
Website www.nattrust.com.au.
Admission $10.
Open 10am-4pm daily.

Shrine of Remembrance

If you look south down the middle of Swanston Street, you'll be looking directly at the Shrine of Remembrance, which was built as a memorial for those who died in the First World War and now stands as a memorial for all the wars in which Australia has played a part. There's a great view of the city from the top.

Kings Domain (off St Kilda Road), Melbourne.
🚌 *216, 219, 220;* 🚋 *3, 5, 6, 8, 16, 25, 64, 67, 72.*
☎ *(03) 9654 8415.*
Admission by donation.
Open 10am-5pm daily.

Victorian Arts Centre

The Victorian Arts Centre encompasses: the Melbourne Concert Hall, State Theatre, Playhouse Theatre, Studio Theatre, Westpac Gallery, National Gallery of Victoria, Performing Arts Museum, the Australian Ballet Centre and the Victorian College of the Arts. This extensive collection of facilities for both the visual and performing arts makes it one of the best arts centres in the world. While not as visually stimulating, the Arts Centre's theatres have a greater capacity than the Sydney Opera House. The 115-metre spire on the main theatre building is illuminated at night.

100 St Kilda Road, Southbank.
🚌 *216, 219, 220;* 🚋 *3, 5, 6, 8, 16, 25, 64, 67, 72;* 🚉 *Flinders Street.*
☎ *(03) 9281 8000.*
Admission $10.
Tours Mon-Sat noon & 2.30pm.

OTHER AREAS

Australian Gallery of Sport & Olympic Museum at the MCG

This museum covers Australia's involvement in a wide range of sporting events, with emphasis on Australian Rules Football, cricket and the Olympic Games. The museum is housed in the Melbourne Cricket Ground (MCG), which frequently holds capacity crowds of around 110,000 while hosting cricket matches during the summer and Australian Rules Football in the winter. The MCG was the main venue for the 1956 Olympic Games. A must for sports enthusiasts.

Melbourne Cricket Ground, Jolimont Street, East Melbourne.
🚌 *605;* 🚋 *48, 70, 75;* 🚉 *Jolimont.*
☎ *(03) 9657 8879.*
Website www.mcg.org.au/Redesign/tours.htm.
Admission $11-17.50.
Open 9.30am-4.30pm daily; tours 10am & 3pm non-event days.

Carlton Brewhouse

This is one of the world's busiest breweries producing over 1½ million bottles of beer daily and is the home of Fosters Lager and Victoria Bitter. The brewery offers tours that conclude with a free tasting.

Corner Nelson & South Audley Streets, Abbotsford.
🚌 *42, 109.*
☎ *(03) 9420 6800.*
Admission $15.
Tours Mon-Fri 10am & 2pm, bookings essential.

Luna Park

A huge laughing face greets visitors to this small amusement park at St Kilda Beach. Rides include the Scenic Railway (the world's oldest continuously operating roller coaster) as well as a Ferris wheel and several newer "jaw dropping, eye ball popping, lose your lunch super thrill rides" like the Enterprise, Metropolis and the Pharaoh's Curse.

Lower Esplanade, St Kilda.
🚌 *246, 600, 606, 623, 646;* 🚋 *16, 69, 79, 96.*
☎ *1300 888 272.*

Website www.lunapark.com.au.
Admission free, rides $7, unlimited ride ticket $33.95.
Open 1 Jan-27 Apr Fri 7pm-11pm, Sat 11am-11pm, Sun 11am-6pm; 28 Apr-19 Sep Sat-Sun 11am-6pm; 20 Sep-31 Dec Fri 7pm-11pm, Sat 11am-11pm, Sun 11am-6pm.

RAAF Museum
This museum features more than 20 aircraft and exhibits about the Royal Australian Air Force. It is in Point Cook, about 25km southwest of the city centre on the road towards Geelong.
RAAF Base Williams, Point Cook Road, Point Cook.
🚌 *Aircraft, then 7km by taxi.*
☎ *(03) 9256 1300.*
Website www.raafmuseum.com.au.
Admission free.
Open Tue-Fri 10am-3pm, Sat-Sun 10am-5pm.

Ramsay Street
Neighbours fans may want to visit the street where the TV show is filmed. Ramsay Street is actually Pin Oak Court in Vermont South, about a 30 to 40-minute drive into the suburbs.
Pin Oak Court, Vermont South.
🚉 *Glen Waverley or Nunawading, then*
🚌 *888 or 889.*

If you don't have a car you may want to take one of the tours run by the Backpacker King that includes gossip about the show. The tours are highly recommended, take around three hours and run twice daily.
Pick-up from 58 Franklin Street, Melbourne; Flinders Street, Melbourne & corner Jackson & Grey Streets, St Kilda.
☎ *(03) 9534 4755 for bookings.*
Website www.neighbourstour.com.
Cost $25.

The Backpacker King also organises *Neighbours* trivia nights where you get to meet the stars of the show.
Elephant & Wheelbarrow, 169 Fitzroy Street, St Kilda.
🚌 *246, 600, 606, 623, 646;* 🚊 *16, 69, 79, 96.*
☎ *(03) 9534 4755 for bookings.*

Website www.backpackerking.com.au.
Admission $35.
Every Monday night.

Scienceworks
Part of the Museum of Victoria, this museum of science and technology is full of hands-on interactive exhibits. Although it was designed for children, it's a lot of fun for everyone.
2 Booker Street, Spotswood.
🚉 *Spotswood;* 🚌 *Scienceworks.*
☎ *(03) 9392 4800.*
Website http://scienceworks.museum.vic.gov.au.
Admission $6; $12 including Planetarium.
Open 10am-4.30pm daily.

ST KILDA BEACH
This is a great place to catch some rays, or if you're feeling more energetic, go for a swim or rent a bike or a pair of inline skates to cruise the bike path which runs along the beachfront. On Sundays, check out the street market on the Esplanade.
🚌 *246, 600, 606, 623, 646;* 🚊 *16, 69, 79, 96.*

Around Melbourne

There are many attractions within a short drive of Melbourne. In a day, you can visit the Bellarine or Mornington peninsulas with their ocean and bay beaches on either side of Melbourne. Other day trips that you can make from Melbourne include seeing the little penguins at Phillip Island or exploring the Yarra Valley wineries.

Geelong

Victoria's second city is a thriving commercial and industrial centre and major port, but for most travellers, Geelong is just a place to pass through en route to Torquay and the Great Ocean Road.

It has a pleasant waterfront area but its main attractions are the Wool Museum and the Ford Discovery Centre.

Practical Information
INFORMATION CENTRES
Geelong & Great Ocean Road Visitor Information Centre
Stead Park, Princes Highway, Corio.
☎ *(03) 5275 5797 or 1800 620 888.*
Open 9am-5pm daily.

Geelong Visitor Information Centre
National Wool Museum, corner Moorabool & Brougham Streets, Geelong.
☎ *(03) 5222 2900 or 1800 620 888.*
Open 9am-5pm daily.

INTERNET ACCESS
G Net Café
119 Moorabool Street, Geelong.
☎ *(03) 5223 2727.*
Website www.g-netcafe.com.
Open 10am-11pm daily.

Coming & Going
Most people pass through Geelong when driving between Melbourne and the Great Ocean Road.

If you're travelling by public transport, the V/line train service from Melbourne is the easiest way to get here. Trains run hourly from Spencer Street station in Melbourne and take just over an hour. The one-way fare is $14 to $20.

Gull (☎ *(03) 5222 4966; website www.gull.com.au)* run buses to Melbourne airport picking up at 45 McKillop Street and Geelong train station. The one-way fare is $25.

Local Transport
The Geelong Transit System is comprised of buses run by Benders Busways (☎ *(03) 5278 5955; website www.kefford.com.au/keff_benders.html)* and McHarry's (☎ *(03) 5223 2111; website www.mcharrys.com.au).*

The $1.60 fare allows you to travel on any Geelong Transit System bus for two to three hours.

Accommodation
Irish Murphys
This Irish pub has rooms upstairs with backpackers' accommodation. It's a clean, but basic place with a small kitchen and TV lounge.

30 Aberdeen Street, Geelong.
🚌 *35, 36.*
☎ *(03) 5222 2900.*
Website www.irishmurphys.com.au.
Dorm bed $19.
Credit cards Amex, Diners, MC, Visa.

Maintenance & cleanliness	★★★
Facilities	★★☆
Atmosphere & character	★★★
Security	★
Overall rating	★★☆

Sights
Ford Discovery Centre
Thousands of Ford cars roll off the production line in Geelong and the Ford Discovery Centre by the waterfront illustrates the history of Ford cars in Australia. It has displays on the production and design process and also features a collection of cars ranging from the Model T to the latest models.
Corner Brougham & Gheringhap Streets, Geelong.
☎ *(03) 5227 8700.*
Website www.forddiscovery.com.au.
Admission $7.
Open Wed-Mon 10am-5pm daily.

National Wool Museum
Geelong's big attraction is this well designed museum that depicts the history of Australia's wool industry. It also demonstrates the process of shearing, spinning and knitting.
Corner Brougham & Moorabool Streets, Geelong.
☎ *(03) 5227 0701.*
Admission $7.30.
Open 9.30am-5pm daily.

Queenscliff & the Bellarine Peninsula
The Bellarine Peninsula near Geelong has a couple of surf beaches on its southern coastline as well as the historic resort town of Queenscliff.

Queenscliff became a fashionable resort in the 19th century when many grand old hotels were built and nowadays it retains an upmarket feel that separates it from coastal resort towns elsewhere in Australia.

Practical Information
Information Centre
55 Hesse Street, Queenscliff.
☎ (03) 5258 4843.
Open 9am-5pm daily.

Coming & Going
The Bellarine Peninsula is well connected by public transport from Geelong. McHarry's (☎ (03) 5223 2111; *website* www.mcharrys.com.au) run buses from Geelong.

Peninsula Searoad Transport (☎ (03) 5258 3244; *website* www.searoad. com.au) run ferries every hour (7am - 6pm) between Queenscliff and Sorrento on the Mornington Peninsula. The journey takes around half an hour and one-way fares are $8 for a foot passenger or $46 for a car with two passengers.

Accommodation
Queenscliff Inn YHA
The Queenscliff Inn is a quiet place, but unlike many other quiet hostels it has loads of atmosphere. It's set in a historic building with lots of charm and it has a classy upmarket ambience. Accommodation is in large, spacious rooms, but some beds are a little squeaky. Facilities include a small kitchen and a drawing room with board games and a selection of magazines, books and newspapers.
59 Hesse Street, Queenscliff.
☎ (03) 5258 3737.
Dorm bed $25 ($21.50 YHA); *single room* $48.50 ($45 YHA); *double/ twin room* $58 ($51 YHA).
Credit cards MC, Visa.
Reception open 8am-10am & 5pm-10pm daily.

Maintenance & cleanliness	★★★☆
Facilities	★★☆
Atmosphere & character	★★★★☆
Security	★★☆
Overall rating	★★★

Sights
Fort Queenscliff
This coastal fortress was constructed in 1882 as part of an elaborate defence network around the Port Phillip Bay heads. Guided tours of the facility take around an hour and allow you to see the fort's lighthouse and military instalments.

Fort Queenscliff, Queenscliff.
☎ (03) 5258 1488.
Admission $5.
Tours Sat-Sun 1pm, 3pm.

Marine Discovery Centre
The Marine Discovery Centre runs a programme of events throughout summer including beachcombing and snorkelling with seals.
Weeroona Parade, Queenscliff.
☎ (03) 5258 3344.
Website www.nre.vic.gov.au/mafri/ discovery.

Dandenong Ranges
The Dandenong Ranges lie at the eastern edge of Melbourne's suburban sprawl. Not to be confused with the industrial suburb of the same name, the Dandenongs is a region of natural bush land and a favourite picnic spot for Melburnians.

At the summit of Mount Dandenong is a scenic lookout which many locals claim has the best view of the city, but it is over-rated and not worth the effort – there's a view of the eastern suburbs, but central Melbourne is too far away and often shrouded in smog.

A much better idea is to take a ride on *Puffing Billy*. This is an old steam train that runs from Belgrave to Gembrook through the most scenic parts of the Dandenongs, although it is expensive for a return trip.

Coming & Going
Take the train to Belgrave station, then transfer to bus 688, 694 or 698, which will take you along Mount Dandenong Tourist Road, past the area's main attractions. Belgrave station is also the terminus for the *Puffing Billy* steam railway.

Sights
Puffing Billy Railway
Puffing Billy is a century-old steam train, run by volunteer train enthusiasts, that still runs between Belgrave and Gembrook on its original track. The train takes you through scenic countryside and the trip is a lot of fun. There are between three and six trains a

day, although not all of them continue all the way to Gembrook.

Trains depart from Belgrave station, which is at the end of the Belgrave line on Melbourne's suburban rail network. ☎ *(03) 9754 6800.*
Website www.puffingbilly.com.au.
Fares Belgrave-Emerald $17 one-way, $28.50 return; Belgrave-Gembrook $25 one-way, $39 return.

Yarra Valley

Over the Dandenong Ranges is the Yarra Valley, which is one of Australia's best wine producing regions. If you're in the area pop into some of the wineries to sample the locally produced wines, some of the best include: Fergusson, St Hubert, Domaine Chandon and Yarra Ridge.

Wandin, Silvan and Healesville supply Melbourne with many of its vegetables and there is often work available picking vegetables. Ask around at the market gardens or check the employment listings at the Lilydale Centrelink office.

Sights & Activities
Healesville Sanctuary
This wildlife sanctuary is a good spot for seeing kangaroos, koalas and other native animals.
Badger Creek Road, Healesville.
🚌 *685, 686.*
☎ *(03) 5957 2800.*
Website www.zoo.org.au.
Admission $17.50, students $13.
Open 9am-5pm daily.

Wine tasting
Wine tasting is the main reason most backpackers visit the Yarra Valley. Without your own car and a driver who isn't drinking it can be difficult to get around unless you take a tour. Backpacker Winery Tours run winery tours that visit Domaine Chandon, Eyton on Yarra, St Hubert's and Yarra Ridge with pick-ups from hostels in Melbourne.
☎ *(03) 9877 8333.*
Website www.backpackerwinerytours. com.au.
Tour $79 including lunch.
Tours depart 9am-10am daily.

Hanging Rock

This rock formation, 70km north of Melbourne via the Calder Highway, has been made famous by Joan Lindsay's novel Picnic at Hanging Rock that Peter Weir later made into a film.

The rock is a popular picnic spot and lots of fun for novice rock climbers, with plenty of crevices to explore and panoramic views from the pinnacles.

The Hanging Rock Recreation Reserve is home to native wildlife such as wallabies, kookaburras and koalas that are usually easy to find sitting high in the gum trees.

On New Year's Day and Australia Day (26 Jan), the Hanging Rock horse races are held at the racecourse within the reserve.

Phillip Island

Less than a two-hour drive from Melbourne, Phillip Island has some fantastic surf beaches and an abundance of wildlife; including koalas, kangaroos, wallabies, seals and the little penguins for which Phillip Island is famous.

Practical Information
Visitor Information Centre
Phillip Island Road, Newhaven, Phillip Island.
☎ *(03) 5956 7447 or 1300 366 422.*
Open 9am-5pm daily.

Coming & Going
If you're not driving, there are a few transport options between Melbourne and the island.

Inter Island Ferries (☎ *(03) 9585 5730; website www.interislandferries. com.au)* sail several times a day between Cowes on Phillip Island and Stony Point on the Mornington Peninsula. The one-way fare is $9, but you also need to take a train from Melbourne to Stony Point (change trains at Frankston), which costs an additional $7.

A popular option is the Duck Truck tour that is run by the Amaroo Park YHA in Cowes. Their one-day tour is $70 and they also have a package deal that includes transport to and from Melbourne, up to three nights accommodation at the Amaroo Park youth hostel and entry to the Penguin Parade, Churchill Island and the Koala Conservation Centre. The package costs $136.

V/line run a bus service between Melbourne and Cowes although this service only runs a once a day. The V/line bus departs from Spencer Street Station and the return fare costs $22.60-32.20.

There are also several companies that run tours departing from Melbourne. One of the longest established is Autopia Tours (☎ *1800 000 507; website www.autopiatours.com.au*) who runs a popular day trip costing $70 including admission fees to a wildlife park and the Penguin Parade. Wildlife Tours (☎ *(03) 9534 8868; website www.wildlifetours.com.au*) also run day trips from Melbourne, which cost $75 ($69 ISIC/Nomads/VIP/YHA).

Accommodation
Amaroo Park YHA Hostel
Amaroo Park YHA is a small complex of buildings in a pleasant garden setting. The main building has a big kitchen, Internet access, a bar and a games room with a pool table.
97 Church Street, Cowes, Phillip Island.
☎ *(03) 5952 2548.*
Dorm bed *$23-24.50 ($19.50-21 YHA); single room $36.50 ($33 YHA); double/twin room $57 ($50 YHA).*
Credit cards *MC, Visa.*
Reception open *8am-10am & 5pm-10pm daily.*
🚗

Maintenance & cleanliness	★★★
Facilities	★★★
Atmosphere & character	★★★★☆
Security	★☆
Overall rating	★★★

Sights
The Giant Worm
Normally this is the sort of tacky tourist attraction you would go out of your way to avoid; but there is nothing like this anywhere on earth and its uniqueness is a compelling reason to visit. The world's largest earthworms, some of which grow to around three metres in length, are native to this part of Victoria. The Giant Worm has displays of live worms and a huge walk-through display of a worm's anatomy. The complex also includes a wildlife park with kangaroos, wombats and Tasmanian devils. The Giant Worm is located on the way to the island and is difficult to reach without a car, but it's an easy detour if you're driving to Phillip Island.
Bass Highway, Bass.
☎ *(03) 5678 2222.*
Admission *$11.90.*
Open *8.30am-6.30pm.*

Koala Conservation Centre
This is a wildlife park dedicated to koalas where you can walk along a boardwalk in the treetops and see koalas up close.
Phillip Island Road, Sunset Strip.
☎ *(03) 5956 8300.*
Website *www.penguins.org.au.*
Admission *$6.*

The Nobbies
At the south-western tip of the island are a group of rocks called the Nobbies, which are home to a colony of seals that can viewed through coin operated binoculars at the Nobbies kiosk.
Ventnor Road, The Nobbies.

Penguin Parade
Every night at sunset, little penguins emerge from the sea and make their way across the beach to their home amongst the sand dunes. It's best to come here during the summer when there are more penguins; during winter it can be bitterly cold with winds coming up from Antarctica and very few penguins making the trip to their nesting ground. The Phillip Island Penguin Parade is Australia's second-largest tourist attraction; a huge grandstand has been built to accommodate the hundreds of spectators, and the beach is floodlit detracting from what would otherwise be an amazing natural attraction. There is also an information centre on the site with displays and a short film about penguins.
Ventnor Road, Summerland Beach.
☎ *(03) 5956 8691.*
Website *www.penguins.org.au.*
Admission *$15.*
Open *10am-11pm daily; arrive 1hr before sunset for penguin parade.*

Surf Beaches

Phillip Island has excellent surf beaches along its southern coast. These include Cat Bay, Smiths Beach and Cape Woolamai Surf Beach at the southeastern point of the island.

Great Ocean Road

The Great Ocean Road is the most scenic route from Melbourne to Adelaide. It hugs the coastline from Torquay to Peterborough with a brief diversion through the Otway Ranges and connects with the Princes Highway near Warrnambool, which continues onwards toward Adelaide.

Although the entire Great Ocean Road is a scenic drive, the most breathtaking scenery along this route is found around Port Campbell. This includes some spectacular rock formations such as London Bridge and the Twelve Apostles.

Local Transport

If you don't have your own car, V/line (☎ *13 22 32; website www.vlinepassen ger.com.au*) has a bus service along the Great Ocean Road, and several companies operate tours along this route.

Autopia Tours (☎ *1800 000 507; website www.autopiatours.com.au*) run day tours from Melbourne that cost $65, and three-day trips that cost $155 and they also include the Great Ocean Road on their popular Adelaide-Melbourne tour.

Otway Discovery (☎ *(03) 9654 5432*) run a daytrip from Melbourne that visits various spots along the Great Ocean Road, including Bells Beach and the 12 Apolstles. This trip costs $65.

The Wayward Bus (☎ *1800 882 823; website www.waywardbus.com.au*) operates a three-day tour between Melbourne and Adelaide taking in the Great Ocean Road en route.

Wildlife Tours (☎ *(03) 9534 8868; website www.wildlifetours.com.au*) run day trips from Melbourne that go to the 12 Apostles and most other

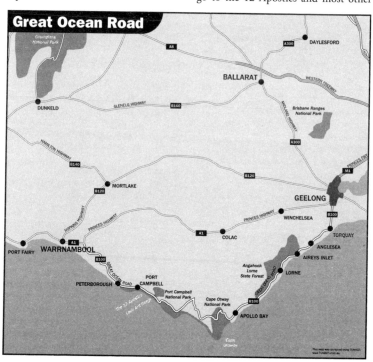

attractions along the road; these tours cost $75 ($69 ISIC/Nomads/VIP/YHA). Wildlife Tours also include the Great Ocean Road on their Adelaide-Melbourne trip.

Oz Experience (☎ *1300 300 028; website www.ozexperience.com)* also includes the Great Ocean Road on their Melbourne to Adelaide route.

Torquay

Torquay is the surfing capital of Australia and marks the beginning of the Great Ocean Road. The main surf beaches are Bells Beach, Jan Juc, Point Danger, Point Impossible and Torquay Surf Beach.

Each year at Easter, Bells Beach hosts an international surfing championship.

Practical Information
Torquay Road Visitor Information Centre
Surf City Plaza, Beach Road, Torquay.
☎ *(03) 5261 4219.*
Open *9am-5pm daily.*

Accommodation
Bells Beach Lodge
This is a good hostel with a handy location and a great laid-back surf atmosphere. It is a clean hostel with good facilities that include Internet access, a kitchen and a TV lounge. Outside there is a beach volleyball court.
51-53 Surf Coast Highway, Torquay
☎ *(03) 5261 7070.*
Website *www.bellsbeachlodge.com.au.*
Dorm bed *$19-23;* **double room** *$45-60.*
Credit cards *MC, Visa.*
Reception open *8am-2pm & 5pm-10pm daily.*

Maintenance & cleanliness	★★★
Facilities	★★
Atmosphere & character	★★★★☆
Security	★★★☆
Overall rating	★★★

Sights
Surfworld
This brilliant museum about surfing and beach culture delves into everything from physics to surf history.

Surf City Plaza, Beach Road, Torquay.
☎ *(03) 5261 4606.*
Website *www.surfworld.org.au.*
Admission *$7.50.*
Open *9am-5pm daily.*

Torquay to Lorne

The Great Ocean Road starts just outside of Torquay, and passes through several small towns including Anglesea and Aireys Inlet. Fairhaven beach near Aireys Inlet has a good surfing beach.

Accommodation
Anglesea Backpackers
This is a clean and well-maintained hostel. It's a small place with minimal facilities but there is the standard kitchen, laundry and TV lounge.
40 Noble Street, Anglesea.
☎ *(03) 5263 2664.*
Dorm bed *$20-23;* **double room** *$60-70.*

Maintenance & cleanliness	★★★★
Facilities	★★☆
Atmosphere & character	★★★★☆
Security	★
Overall rating	★★★

Lorne

Lorne is one of the more upmarket resort towns on the Great Ocean Road. Although there isn't really much to see in Lorne, it has a beautiful setting with a very nice beach and some good hiking trails in the surrounding area.

Practical Information
Lorne Visitor Information Centre
144 Mountjoy Parade, Lorne.
☎ *(03) 5289 1152.*
Open *9am-5pm daily.*

Accommodation
Erskine River Backpackers
This is a lovely hostel with a good atmosphere and big shady verandas. The place is clean and well equipped with nice bathrooms as well as the usual facilities such as a TV lounge, kitchen and a games room. Some rooms have en suite bathrooms.
6 Mountjoy Parade, Lorne.

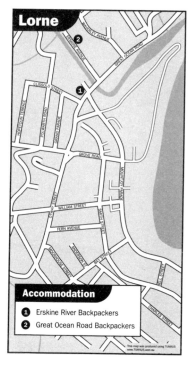

Lorne

Accommodation
1. Erskine River Backpackers
2. Great Ocean Road Backpackers

This map was produced using TUMAUS.
www.TUMAUS.com.au

Apollo Bay

Situated near the Otway National Park, this is another beachside town on the Great Ocean Road with a scenic location.

Practical Information
Great Ocean Road Visitor Information Centre
Great Ocean Road, Apollo Bay
☎ *(03) 5237 6529*
Open *9am-5pm daily.*

Accommodation
Apollo Bay Backpackers
Apollo Bay Backpackers is a small cosy hostel in a house a few streets back from the Great Ocean Road. Facilities include a TV lounge, Internet access, kitchen and a nice outdoor area with a barbecue.
47 Montrose Street, Apollo Bay.
☎ *(03) 5237 7360.*
Dorm bed *$20; double/twin room $50; includes breakfast.*
Reception open *5pm-9pm daily.*

Maintenance & cleanliness	★★★
Facilities	★☆
Atmosphere & character	★★★★☆
Security	★
Overall rating	★★☆

Surfside Backpackers
Surfside Backpackers is a small hostel with a homely atmosphere, but the bulding is a little old and the facilities aren't perfect. Facilities include a kitchen plus a games room with Internet access, but no TV. There are verandas around the hostel and an outdoor barbecue area overlooking the ocean. The fantastic ocean views make this the top choice in Apollo Bay.
Corner Great Ocean Road & Gambier Street, Apollo Bay.
☎ *(03) 5237 7263 or 1800 357 263.*
Dorm bed *$18-22; double room $45-60.*
Credit cards *MC, Visa.*
Reception open *8am-10pm daily.*

Maintenance & cleanliness	★★☆
Facilities	★★☆
Atmosphere & character	★★★★
Security	★
Overall rating	★★☆

☎ *(03) 5289 1496.*
Dorm bed *$25; double room $60.*

Maintenance & cleanliness	★★★☆
Facilities	★☆
Atmosphere & character	★★★★☆
Security	★
Overall rating	★★★

Great Ocean Road Backpackers
This is a well-maintained hostel in a beautiful bush setting that is home to wild birds and possums. There are clean bathrooms, a kitchen and dining room and nice outdoor areas including a balcony and deck.
10 Erskine Avenue, Lorne.
☎ *(03) 5289 1809.*
Dorm bed *$23.50 ($20 YHA); double/twin room $60 ($50 YHA).*
Credit cards *MC, Visa.*
Reception open *8am-9pm daily.*

Maintenance & cleanliness	★★★☆
Facilities	★★☆
Atmosphere & character	★★★★
Security	★
Overall rating	★★★

Victoria

Otway Ranges

After Apollo Bay, the Great Ocean Road turns inland and crosses the Otway Ranges. This is an area of untouched rainforest with huge towering gum trees and shady ferns. There are hiking trails and campsites in the Otway National Park.

Sights & Activities
Otway Fly
The Otway Fly is the longest and highest tree top canopy walk of its kind. It allows you to walk for 600 metres, 25 metres above the ground through the treetops. There is also a 47-metre-high lookout tower with sweeping views.
Phillips Track, Beech Forest.
☎ *(03) 5235 9200 or 1800 300 477.*
Website *www.otwayfly.com.*
Admission *$11.*
Open *1 Jan-30 Jun 9am-7pm daily;*
1 Jul-24 Dec Mon-Sat 9am-5pm, Sun 9am-6pm daily.

Port Campbell & Port Campbell National Park

From the Otway Ranges to Peterborough, much of the area between the road and the ocean is protected as a national park. Port Campbell National Park is the site of the most spectacular scenery on the Great Ocean Road.

If you're driving take the time to check out all the scenic spots; particularly the Twelve Apostles, the Bay of Islands, Loch Ard Gorge and London Bridge.

Practical Information
Port Campbell Visitor Information Centre
26 Morris Street, Port Campbell.
☎ *(03) 5598 6053.*
Open *9am-5pm daily.*

Accommodation
Ocean House Backpackers
This is a nice small hostel opposite the seashore. It is an old house with hardwood floors and new furnishings and it features a veranda overlooking the sea.

It is managed by the Port Campbell National Park Cabin and Camping Park, near the tourist information centre, and you can go there to check in when the hostel is unattended.
32 Cairns Street, Port Campbell.
☎ *(03) 5598 6223.*
Dorm bed *$20.*

Maintenance & cleanliness	★★★½
Facilities	★½
Atmosphere & character	★★★
Security	★
Overall rating	★★½

Port Campbell YHA Hostel
This is a nice hostel, which has a proper reception and good quality facilities. There is a large fully equipped kitchen, Internet access, and a barbecue area.
18 Tregea Street, Port Campbell.
☎ *(03) 5598 6305.*
Dorm bed *$22.50 ($19 YHA);*
double/twin room *$55-69 ($48-62 YHA).*
Credit cards *MC, Visa.*
Reception open *8am-10am & 5pm-10pm daily.*

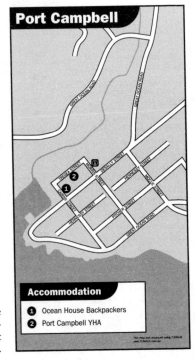

Port Campbell

Accommodation
1. Ocean House Backpackers
2. Port Campbell YHA

Maintenance & cleanliness	★★★★
Facilities	★★
Atmosphere & character	★★★★
Security	★★
Overall rating	★★★

Warrnambool

Warrnambool is a major provincial city at the western extremity of the Great Ocean Road, and is best known for the whales that are regularly seen off the coast.

The southern right whale can be seen from May till October; the best viewing spot is at Logan's Beach where a viewing platform has been constructed.

Practical Information
Warrnambool Visitor Information Centre
600 Raglan Parade, Warrnambool.
☎ *(03) 5564 7837.*
***Open** 9am-5pm daily.*

Coming & Going
Warrnambool has a regular rail service to Geelong and Melbourne and buses to points along the coast as well as Adelaide, Ballarat and Melbourne. The train station is located on Merri Street while buses depart from Raglan Parade.

Accommodation
Backpackers Barn (Victoria Hotel)
This is a basic hostel above the Victoria Hotel in the city centre. It is a little rough around the edges, but it is relatively clean. Facilities consist of a basic kitchen and a lounge room with a piano and TV.
90 Lava Street, Warrnambool.
☎ *(03) 5562 2073.*
***Dorm bed** $20.*

Maintenance & cleanliness	★★
Facilities	★★
Atmosphere & character	★★
Security	★
Overall rating	★★

The Stuffed Backpacker
This is a clean and centrally located hostel in an old building in the town centre and some of the amenities could be a little better maintained. There is a pool table and a TV room and a balcony overlooking the street. Guests get free apple pie and ice cream every night.
52 Kepler Street, Warrnambool.
☎ *(03) 5562 2459.*
***Dorm bed** $20 ($19 VIP/YHA);*
***double room** $45 ($43 VIP/YHA).*
***Credit cards** MC, Visa.*
***Reception open** Mon-Sat 9am-11pm, Sun 11am-10pm.*

Maintenance & cleanliness	★★
Facilities	★★
Atmosphere & character	★★★★
Security	★★
Overall rating	★★

Warrnambool Beach Backpackers
Everything at this hostel is new and well maintained. There is a good range of facilities including the usual kitchen, laundry, Internet access and clean bathrooms as well as nice extras like a bar and free use of mountain bikes. Warrrnambool Beach Backpackers is a little less conveniently located compared to the other hostels in town, however it's close to the beach and there is a free pick up service from the train station. This hostel organises trips to see the penguins every night during summer.
17 Stanley Street, Warrnambool.
☎ *(03) 5562 4874.*
***Dorm bed** $20; **double room** $60.*
***Reception open** 7.30am-10pm daily.*

Maintenance & cleanliness	★★★★★
Facilities	★★★
Atmosphere & character	★★★★
Security	★
Overall rating	★★★★

Sights
Flagstaff Hill Maritime Museum
Flagstaff Hill Maritime Museum comprises a recreated village, restored ships and an exhibition of artefacts recovered from southwest Victoria's many shipwrecks.
Merri Street. Warrnambool.
☎ *(03) 5564 7841.*
***Website** www.flagstaffhill.info.*
***Admission** $12.*
***Open** 9am-5pm daily.*

Port Fairy

This historic township is home to around 50 buildings classified by the National Trust and has a great atmosphere; particularly during the annual Port Fairy Folk Festival held on the Labour Day long weekend in March.

Practical Information
Port Fairy Visitor Information Centre
Railway Place, Bank Street, Port Fairy.
☎ *(03) 5568 2682.*
Open *9am-5pm daily.*

Accommodation
Eumeralla Backpackers
This is a nice hostel in a 150-year-old schoolhouse. It is a beautiful building with hardwood floors and loads of charm. It has a kitchen, TV lounge and a nice barbecue area. It's in the tiny village of Yambuk, 18km west of Port Fairy.
High Street, Yambuk (18km west of Port Fairy).
☎ *(03) 5568 4204.*

Maintenance & cleanliness	★★★★
Facilities	★★
Atmosphere & character	★★★★★
Security	★
Overall rating	★★★

Port Fairy Youth Hostel
This historic building was originally built by one of the town's founders. It has a large kitchen, a cosy TV lounge with a pool table and Internet access and a courtyard barbecue area.
8 Cox Street, Port Fairy.
☎ *(03) 5568 2468.*
Dorm bed *$22.50 ($19 YHA);* **single room** *$40.50 ($37 YHA);* **double/twin room** *$55 ($48 YHA).*
Credit cards *MC, Visa.*
Reception open *8am-10am & 5pm-10pm daily.*

Maintenance & cleanliness	★★★
Facilities	★★
Atmosphere & character	★★★★★
Security	★★
Overall rating	★★★

Portland

Victoria's oldest town was once a busy whaling port but it's now an indus-trial city that is dominated by a big aluminium smelter. Travellers that are interested in Australian maritime history will no doubt find the place interesting although many travellers bypass Portland altogether.

Practical Information
Tourist Information Centre
Lee Breakwater Road, Portland.
☎ *(03) 5523 2671.*
Website *www.maritimediscovery.com.*
Open *9am-5pm daily.*

Accommodation
Bellevue Backpackers
This is a dreadful place that is overpriced considering the location and facilities. The hostel consists of two caravans with very basic facilities and little in the way of privacy. The bathroom is an outhouse. It has an inconvenient location a five-minute drive from the town centre. The beach is a five-minute walk away, but nothing else in within walking distance.
Sheoke Road, Portland.
☎ *(03) 5523 4038.*
Dorm bed *$20;* **double room** *$40.*

Maintenance & cleanliness	★
Facilities	★
Atmosphere & character	★
Security	★
Overall rating	★

Portland Backpackers Inn
This small hostel is in an old house near the town centre. It is a bit shabby but there's a nice courtyard with a barbecue.
14 Gawler Street, Portland.
☎ *(03) 5523 6390.*
Dorm bed *$15.*

Maintenance & cleanliness	★★
Facilities	★
Atmosphere & character	★★★★
Security	★
Overall rating	★★

Sights
Maritime Discovery Centre
This excellent maritime museum has a number of interesting exhibits focusing on local shipwrecks. It also features a huge skeleton of a sperm whale.

Lee Breakwater Road, Portland.
☎ *(03) 55232671 or 1800 035567.*
Website *www.maritimediscovery.com.*
Admission *$8, students $5.50.*
Open *9am-5pm daily.*

Portland Aluminium
This huge aluminium smelter is set among parkland to the southeast of the city centre earning it the title "smelter in the park".
Quarry Road, Portland.
☎ *(03) 5523 2671.*
Admission *free.*
Tours *Mon, Wed, Fri 10am, 1pm.*

Goldfields
Victoria was in the midst of gold fever in the mid-1800s and prospectors rushed to the Victorian goldfields. The Goldfields region is home to old gold mining towns and their grand buildings that were financed by the prosperity that gold brought to the area.

Ballarat
In 1851 gold was discovered in Ballarat and within a few years there were thousands of miners trying their luck on the Ballarat goldfields. The city grew on the wealth of the gold rushes and Ballarat is now Victoria's second largest inland city.

Practical Information
Visitor Information Centre
39 Sturt Street, Ballarat
☎ *(03) 5332 2694.*
Website *www.ballarat.com.*
Open *9am-5pm daily.*

Coming & Going
Ballarat has good transport connections with Melbourne. Both trains and buses depart from the train station on Lydiard Street North.

Local Transport
Ballarat's local bus service has half-hourly departures to most parts of the city with most routes converging near Bridge Street Mall. A two-hour ticket costs $1.55.

Accommodation
Irish Murphys
This small eight-bed hostel is above an Irish pub in the centre of Ballarat. There is a small kitchen and the bathrooms are very clean. It has the best location of Ballarat's hostels.
36 Sturt Street, Ballarat.
☎ *(03) 5331 4091.*
Website *www.irishmurphys.com.au.*
Dorm bed *$16-19.*
Not yet rated

Sovereign Hill YHA Lodge
This is a very nice hostel done in gold rush period architecture overlooking the Soveriegn Hill outdoor museum, about 3km south of the city centre. Facilities are very good and include a big, clean kitchen and landscaped garden barbecue areas. The atmosphere is not as lively as most other hostels.
Magpie Street, Ballarat.
☎ *(03) 5333 3409.*
Dorm bed *$22.50 ($19 YHA);* ***single room*** *$31.50 ($28 YHA);* ***twin room*** *$55-62 ($48-44 YHA).*
Credit cards *MC, Visa.*
Reception open *Sun-Mon 7am-10.30pm, Tue-Sat 24 hours.*
🚗
Not yet rated

Sights
If you visit most of Ballarat's attractions it may be cheaper for you to buy a Ballarat Welcome Pass ($33.50), which allows two days unlimited entry to Sovereign Hill and the Gold Museum plus entry to the Eureka Stockade Centre and the Ballarat Fine Art Gallery.

Ballarat Fine Art Gallery
Australia's first provincial art gallery has an impressive collection of early Australian art including collections from the Colonial and Heidelberg Schools. The main exhibit is the original Eureka flag, which was raised during the Eureka Stockade in 1854 and has been displayed here since 1895.
40 Lydiard Street North, Ballarat.
☎ *(03) 5331 5622.*
Website *www.balgal.com.*
Admission *$5, students $2.*
Open *10.30am-5pm daily.*

Eureka Stockade Centre

This museum sits on the site of the Eureka Stockade, which is the closest Australia has come to having a civil war. In 1854 around 800 miners rebelled against the oppressive taxes and police brutality imposed by the British colonial government. On 3 December 1854 government troopers attacked the stockade. The resulting battle lasted only 20 minutes and left 30 miners and five troopers dead.
Stawell Street South, Ballarat.
🚌 *8.*
☎ *(03) 5333 1854.*
Website www.sovereignhill.com.au/ stockade/.
Admission $8, student $6.
Open 9am-5pm daily.

Sovereign Hill

This 1850s gold mining township is Ballarat's main attraction. It is an excellent living history exhibit featuring staff in period costume, and is the best attraction of its kind in Australia. The Sovereign Hill complex incorporates an excellent Gold Museum, which covers Ballarat's history with an emphasis on the impact of the gold rush.
Bradshaw Street, Ballarat.
☎ *(03) 5331 1944.*
🚌 *2, 9, 10.*
Website www.sovereignhill.com.au.
Admission $27.
Open 10am-5pm daily.

Bendigo

This important provincial city was a major gold mining centre in the 1850s. The city's mineral wealth has resulted in excellent Victorian architecture in the downtown area along Pall Mall.

Practical Information
Visitor Information Centre
51-67 Pall Mall, Bendigo.
☎ *(03) 5444 4445*
Website www.bendigotourism.com.
Open 9am-5pm daily.

INTERNET ACCESS
Bendigo Web Central
36 High Street, Bendigo.
☎ *(03) 5442 6411.*

Website www.bwc.com.au/cafe/.
Open Mon-Fri 9am-8pm, Sat 10am-5pm.

Coming & Going

Bendigo is 2½ hours north of Melbourne with regular bus and train connections. Both buses and trains use the station located on Railway Plaza at the southern end of Mitchell Street.

Local Transport

Christian's Bus Company *(website www.christiansbus.com.au/bendigo.html)* operates a network of 13 bus routes in the Bendigo area. It costs $1.50 for two hours of unlimited travel in the Bendigo area.

Accommodation
Buzza's Bendigo Backpackers YHA

This hostel is set in an old house and features a TV lounge, Internet access, air-conditioning and a well-equipped kitchen. There's also a nice outdoor barbecue area. It is the most centrally located hostel in Bendigo.
33 Creek Street South, Bendigo.
☎ *(03) 5443 7680.*
Dorm bed $21.50 ($18 YHA); double/twin room $53 $46 YHA).
Credit cards MC, Visa.
Reception open 8am-10am & 5pm-10pm daily.

Maintenance & cleanliness	★★★
Facilities	★★
Atmosphere & character	★★★
Security	★★
Overall rating	★★☆

Nomads Ironbark Bush Cabins

This hostel is part of a horse riding complex. There's a big emphasis on horses and there are also hiking trails nearby. Accommodation consists of self-contained cabins with TV, clock radio, fridge and an en suite bathroom. Facilities include a bar, a barbecue area, courtesy bus and something you won't find at any other hostel – a giant waterslide. It's in a quiet rural setting, around a five to 10-minute drive north of the centre of Bendigo.
Watson Street, Bendigo.
☎ *(03) 5448 3344.*

Website *www.bwc.com.au/ironbark.*
Dorm bed *$20;* **double room** *$55.*
Reception open *summer 8.30am-*
5.30pm daily; winter 9am-5pm daily.

Maintenance & cleanliness	★★★★
Facilities	★★★★☆
Atmosphere & character	★☆
Security	★
Overall rating	★★★

Sights
If you plan extensive sightseeing in Bendigo, the Welcome Stranger Pass ($51) may save you money by combining the entry fees of six attractions. The pass includes entry to the Underground Mine Tour and the Vintage Tram Tour at Central Deborah Goldmine as well as entry to the Golden Dragon Museum, Living Wings & Things, Bendigo Art Gallery and the Discovery Science & Technology Centre.

Bendigo Art Gallery
Bendigo's art gallery dates from 1887 and features a collection of local and national art.
42 View Street, Bendigo.
☎ *(03) 5443 4991.*
Admission *free.*
Open *10am-5pm.*

Bendigo Joss House
This temple was built in the 1860s by Chinese miners.
Emu Point, Finn Street, North Bendigo.
☎ *(03) 5442 1685.*
Admission *$3.*
Open *10am-5pm daily.*

Bendigo Tramways
Bendigo's talking trams run from the Central Deborah Goldmine along Pall Mall to the Bendigo Joss House stopping at major attractions along the way. They are known as talking trams because of the commentary explaining Bendigo's attractions. They operate hourly on weekends and school holidays.
Terminus Violet Street, Bendigo.
☎ *(03) 5443 8070.*
Website *www.bendigotramways.com.*
Fare *$12.90; $26.50 combined ticket with Central Deborah Goldmine.*

Trams run 10am-4pm with departures every hour.

Central Deborah Goldmine
Bendigo's last goldmine closed in 1954 and was re-opened for tourists in 1972. The Central Deborah Goldmine has been restored both above and below ground and is a great insight into how gold is mined.
76 Violet Street, Bendigo.
☎ *(03) 5443 8322.*
Website *www.central-deborah.com.*
Admission *$16.50 including underground tour; $26.50 combined ticket with talking tram.*
Open *9.30am-5pm daily.*

Golden Dragon Museum
This museum, run by the Bendigo Chinese Association, has exhibits on Chinese culture in Bendigo from the 1850s to the present day. Exhibits include Sun Loong, the world's longest imperial dragon at more than 100 metres.
5-13 Bridge Street, Bendigo.
☎ *(03) 5441 5044.*
Admission *$7.*
Open *9.30am-5pm daily.*

Daylesford-Hepburn Springs

These two former gold mining townships now comprise Australia's spa capital. Hepburn Springs is the main centre for mineral springs and is home to the historic spa building. Five kilometres away, Daylesford, the larger of the two townships, is the home to an unusually large number of grand old buildings considering the town's small size. The two townships are surrounded by Hepburn Regional Park that has many hiking trails to mineral springs and disused gold mines. The twin towns make a good stop if you're driving between Ballarat and Bendigo.

Practical Information
Daylesford Visitor Information Centre
98 Vincent Street, Daylesford.
☎ *(03) 5321 6123.*
Open *9am-5pm daily.*

Accommodation
Wildwood YHA
Wildwood YHA is a small hostel with lots of charm. Facilities include a small kitchen and a comfortable TV lounge with a well-stocked bookshelf. Some things could be a little better maintained and the linen on the beds is old and mismatched. It's on the main road about mid-way between the centre of Daylesford and the spa at Hepburn Springs.
42 Main Road, Hepburn Springs.
☎ *(03) 5348 4435.*
Dorm bed *$23.50 ($20 YHA); single room $35.50 ($42 YHA); double room $55-67 ($48-60 YHA); twin room $55 ($48 YHA).*
Credit cards *MC, Visa.*
Not yet rated

Grampians (Gariwerd) National Park

The Grampians is a rugged area popular with rock climbers and hikers. There is a multitude of hiking trails leading to various mountains, lakes, canyons and rock formations.

This is a great spot for seeing native wildlife in their natural habitat. Kangaroos and koalas are plentiful and the park is covered with colourful wildflowers between August and November.

The Grampians National Park is known as Gariwerd to the local Aboriginal people and is a place of great cultural significance with more than 100 documented rock art sites.

Halls Gap is a small town near the Wonderland Range area of the park, which is a popular base for visitors to the Grampians.

Practical Information
Brambuk National Park & Cultural Centre
This national park information centre also features excellent displays about Aboriginal culture.
Dunkeld Road, Halls Gap.
☎ *(03) 5356 4381.*
Open *9am-5pm daily.*

Halls Gap Visitor Information Centre
Grampians Road, Halls Gap.
☎ *(03) 5356 4616 or 1800 065 599.*
Website *www.visitgrampians.com.au.*
Open *9am-5pm daily.*

Coming & Going
The Grampians are difficult to explore properly without your own transport, but there is a daily V/line bus between Halls Gap and Melbourne.

Accommodation
Brambuck Backpackers
Brambuck Backpackers is a very nice hostel with good facilities including a large well-equipped kitchen and a large deck with a barbecue at the front of the hostel. Accommodation is in clean rooms with en suite bathrooms. It's opposite the Brambuk Cultural Centre, about 3km from the centre of Halls Gap.
Dunkeld Road, Halls Gap.
☎ *(03) 5356 4250.*
Dorm bed *$22; double room $55.*
Credit cards *MC, Visa.*
Reception open *8.30am-1pm & 5pm-8pm daily.*
🖦

Maintenance & cleanliness	★★★⯪
Facilities	★★
Atmosphere & character	★★★
Security	★★⯪
Overall rating	★★★

Grampians YHA Eco-Hostel
The Halls Gap YHA is a new purpose-built hostel that is well equipped with new facilities. There are two lounge areas, Internet access and a huge kitchen as well as excellent security with lockers in all dormitories. There's also an herb garden and fresh eggs each day.
Corner Buckler Street & Grampians Road, Halls Gap.
☎ *(03) 5356 4544.*
Dorm bed *$25.50 ($22 YHA); single room $53.50 ($50 YHA); double/twin room $62 ($55 YHA).*
Credit cards *MC, Visa.*
Reception open *8am-10am & 5pm-10pm daily.*
🖦♿

Maintenance & cleanliness	★★★★★
Facilities	★★½
Atmosphere & character	★★★★½
Security	★★★
Overall rating	★★★★

Tim's Place

The hostel is a small house with extra buildings out the back for accommodation. The main house is an old building but it is kept clean and there are only 20 beds so it has a nice friendly atmosphere. Facilities include Internet access, a volleyball court, free use of mountain bikes, free vegies from the garden and free tea and coffee. Tim, the manager, organises golf (including golf club hire) for $15 everyday for guests and also a backpacker golf day every Wednesday when people staying at other hostels can come along.

Grampians Road, Halls Gap.
☎ *(03) 5356 4288.*
Website *www.timsplace.com.au.*
Dorm bed *$23;* **single room** *$30-40;* **double/twin room** *$52; includes breakfast.*
🚗

Maintenance & cleanliness	★★★
Facilities	★★½
Atmosphere & character	★★★★½
Security	★
Overall rating	★★★

Sights & Activities
Brambuk Cultural Centre

This is an excellent place to learn and experience the culture of the Koori communities of southwest Victoria. You can arrange tours of the rock art sites from here.

Dunkeld Road, Halls Gap.
☎ *(03) 5356 4452.*
Admission *free.*
Open *9am-5pm daily.*

Rock Climbing & Abseiling

The Grampians Mountain Adventure Company (☎ *0427 747 047;* **website** *www.grampiansadventure.com.au*) runs rock climbing and abseiling trips in the Grampians National Park. Prices start at $60 for an introductory half-day rock climb and abseil. A full day rock climbing and abseiling excursion costs $110.

Zumstein

This camping & picnic area is a good spot for viewing kangaroos and it's very popular with people driving around the park.

Mt Victory Road, Grampians National Park.

Hiking

There are some excellent hiking trails around the Grampians. These include popular short walks in the Wonderland Range area near Halls Gap as well as longer overnight hikes.

Beehive Falls *(2.8km, 1-1½hrs)*

This easy walk follows a stream to Beehive Falls. It departs from Beehive Falls car park on Roses Gap Road.

Boronia Peak Trail *(6.6km, 2-3hrs)*

You can start this trail from either Brambuk Backpackers or Tim's Place. It is a challenging hike to Boronia Peak, where there are nice views of Wonderland Range.

MacKenzie Falls

This is one of the most popular short walks and it can get very crowded at busy times. It is a steep, but short and relatively easy, walk.

Mt Rosea Loop *(12km, 4-5hrs)*

This difficult half-day hike starts and finishes at Rosea campground on Mt Victory Road. It offers stunning views from the summit of Mt Rosea.

Wonderland Loop *(9.6km, 5hrs)*

This is a popular half-day walk that starts and finishes in Halls Gap. It offers brilliant views and visits many of the park's main attractions including Grand Canyon, the Pinnacle, Splitters Falls and Venus Baths. It is a good option if you've only got a day to see the park and it is a relatively easy walk for novice hikers.

Murray River

The Murray is one of Australia's longest and most important rivers. It meanders 2,600km from the Snowy Mountains to Encounter Bay in South Australia. The river forms much of the NSW/ Victorian border and it was once a busy transport route with paddle steamers plying their trade up and down the river.

The area around the Murray is fertile fruit farming country and many backpackers are attracted here by fruit picking work around Echuca and Mildura.

Echuca

In its heyday, Echuca was Australia's largest inland port. Nowadays the historic port area has been restored along with a fleet for paddle steamers. Echuca's heritage makes it the nicest town on the Murray and it is worth visiting if you're in the area.

Although not as popular a fruit picking destination as Mildura, many backpackers come here to pick fruit.

Practical Information
Visitor Information Centre
2 Heygarth Street, Echuca.
☎ *(03) 5480 7555.*
Website www.echucamoama.com.
Open 9am-5pm daily.

Coming & Going
Coaches stop outside the tourist information centre and run to Adelaide, Melbourne and Sydney and to destinations along the Murray including Albury, Mildura and Swan Hill.

Accommodation
Echuca Gardens YHA Hostel
Echuca Gardens YHA has lots of character, which makes it a top accommodation choice. There are the usual facilities such as a kitchen, TV lounge and Internet access. Some accommodation is in caravans. It is on a quiet residential street about 1½km from the town centre.
103 Mitchell Street, Echuca.
☎ *(03) 5480 6522.*
Dorm bed $23.50 ($20 YHA); double room $52 ($45 YHA).
Credit cards MC, Visa.
Reception open 8am-10am & 5pm-10pm daily.

Maintenance & cleanliness	★★★
Facilities	★★☆
Atmosphere & character	★★★★
Security	★★☆
Overall rating	★★★½

Nomads Oasis Backpackers
This is a big clean place with good facilities that include a laundry, a small kitchen, a TV lounge and a nice courtyard with a barbecue. The hostel is geared toward travellers picking fruit on nearby farms and the management organise work and transport to farms. It's not a party hostel as alcohol is not permitted, but they give you a free drinks voucher when you check in.
410-424 High Street, Echuca.
☎ *(03) 5480 7866.*
Dorm bed $23 first night, then $19 per night ($22 first night, then $18 per night Nomads); double room $46.
Credit cards Amex, MC, Visa.
Reception open 8am-6pm daily.

Maintenance & cleanliness	★★★☆
Facilities	★★
Atmosphere & character	★★
Security	★★
Overall rating	★★★½

Sights
Most of Echuca's attractions are centred on the river and the historic port. It's free to wander around the historic streets near the port and several companies, including the Port of Echuca, operate paddle steamer cruises on the Murray.

Historic Port of Echuca
Echuca's historic port features a huge red gum wharf with a multitude of paddle steamers including *PS Adelaide*, the world's oldest wooden hulled paddle steamer; *PS Pevensey*, which starred in the mini-series *All the Rivers Run* and *PS Alexander Arbuthnot*, the last paddle steamer built during the Murray River's heyday. Apart from the boats, which make regular cruises, the historic port is home to numerous heritage buildings, many that can be seen for free before going through the entrance gates, although you need to pay to see the boats, the Wharf Shed Museum and the wharf.

52 Murray Esplanade, Echuca.
☎ (03) 5482 4248.
Website www.portofechuca.org.au.
Admission $10.50, $22 including a
one-hour cruise.
Open 9am-5pm daily.

National Holden Motor Museum
This collection of restored Holden cars
includes some rare models, but it's only
really of interest to enthusiasts.
7-11 Warren Street, Echuca.
☎ (03) 5480 2033.
Admission $6.
Open 9am-5pm daily.

Pride of the Murray & PS Emmylou
Other paddle steamers include the
PS Emmylou and Pride of the Murray,
which run several cruises each day.
57 Murray Esplanade, Echuca.
☎ (03) 5482 5244.
Website www.emmylou.com.au.
One hour cruise $16.50.
Cruises depart 9.45am, 11am,
12.15pm, 1.30pm, 2.45pm & 4pm.

Swan Hill

Swan Hill is the main town between
Echuca and Mildura. There's not much
choice of budget accommodation and
not many backpackers stay overnight
here. However you will want to break
your journey here if you're driving
alongside the river.

Practical Information
Swan Hill Visitor
Information Centre
306 Campbell Street, Swan Hill.
☎ (03) 5032 3033 or 1800 625 373.
Website www.swanhillonline.com.
Open 9am-5pm daily.

Accommodation
Pioneer Settlement Lodge
The Pioneer Settlement Lodge is geared
mostly to school groups and not many
backpackers stay here. There are two
self-contained buildings, each with a
kitchen and dormitories. There is also
a barbecue area. It is a relaxing place
to stay on the odd occasion when there
are no school groups staying here, and
there is not a lot of atmosphere.

Horseshoe Road, Swan Hill.
☎ (03) 5032 1093, bookings essential.
Dorm bed $17.50 first night, then $11
per night.
Credit cards MC, Visa.
Reception open 9am-5pm daily.
🚌

Maintenance & cleanliness	★★★
Facilities	★
Atmosphere & character	★
Security	★
Overall rating	★★

Sights
Swan Hill Pioneer Settlement
Australia's first open-air museum is also
Swan Hill's leading attraction. This
recreated pioneer village showcases
life on the Murray between 1830 and
1930. The Pioneer Settlement features
heritage streetscapes and cruises on the
Murray aboard the PS Pyap.
Horseshoe Bend, Swan Hill.
☎ (03) 5032 1093.
Website www.pioneersettlement.com
.au.
Admission $16.
Open Tue-Sun 10am-5pm.

Mildura

Lying at the heart of the Sunraysia district, Mildura boasts Victoria's best climate. The sunny climate coupled with
irrigation from the Murray makes this
one of the best fruit growing, and fruit
picking, areas in the Murray region.

Mildura is located at the northwest-
ern corner of Victoria and it is one of
the state's most remote cities. It is closer
to Broken Hill than to Melbourne.

Practical Informaton
Mildura Visitors Information
& Booking Centre
The Alfred Deakin Centre, 180-190
Deakin Avenue, Mildura.
☎ (03) 5018 8380.
Website www.visitmildura.com.au.
Open Mon-Fri 9am-5.30pm, Sat-Sun
9am-5pm.

INTERNET ACCESS
Mildura Library
The Alfred Deakin Centre, 180-190
Deakin Avenue, Mildura.

☎ *(03) 5023 5011.*
Website www.mildura.vic.gov.au/ library/.
Open Mon 1pm-5pm, Tue-Fri 10am-7pm, Sat 10am-2pm, Sun 1pm-5pm.

Retro
28 Langtree Avenue, Mildura.
☎ *(03) 5021 3822.*
Open Mon-Sat 9am-2.30pm & 6pm-10.30pm.

SHOWERS
Many caravan parks will let you use their shower facilities for a small fee. Alternatively there are public showers in the Fire Station Arcade *(87 Langtree Avenue, Mildura; open 8.30am-6pm daily).*

Coming & Going
Although Mildura is remote, by Victorian standards, it is well connected with a surprisingly busy airport plus the usual coaches and trains.

Mildura's airport is southwest of the city centre and has several flights a day to Adelaide, Melbourne and Sydney. Both Rex and Qantas fly here.

The train station on Seventh Street is the main transport terminal with both coaches and trains departing from here. There are regular trains to Melbourne plus coaches to Adelaide, Broken Hill, Sydney and also to other destinations along the Murray.

Local Transport
Sunraysia Bus Lines (☎ *(03) 5023 0274)* operate local buses with services as far afield as Merbein and Red Cliffs. The Red Cliffs buses, routes 100 and 200, are handy if you're staying at the hostels in Sunnycliffs and Red Cliffs. Travellers staying closer to the centre of Mildura will find the bus an easy way to get into the city centre and the Centre Plaza shopping centre.

Accommodation
Juicy Grape Backpackers
This small workers' hostel has a great atmosphere. Facilities include a TV lounge and Internet access and there is

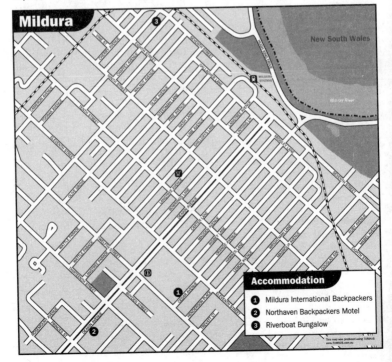

Accommodation
1. Mildura International Backpackers
2. Northaven Backpackers Motel
3. Riverboat Bungalow

a "party shed" with foosball table, pool table and table tennis. Accommodation is in crowded dorms. A rural location among grapevines, about a 15 minute drive south of Mildura.

Calder Highway, Sunnycliffs.

☒ *100, 200.*

☎ *(03) 5024 2905.*

***Dorm bed** $20 per night, $120 per week.*

🚌

Maintenance & cleanliness	★★
Facilities	★★⯪
Atmosphere & character	★★★★★⯪
Security	★
Overall rating	★★★⯪

Mildura International Backpackers

This hostel is in an older building with mediocre facilities that include a TV lounge, a small kitchen, pool table and a big backyard with lots of parking. Like other hostels in Mildura, it is primarily a workers' hostel.

5 Cedar Avenue, Mildura.

☎ *(03) 5021 0133.*

***Dorm bed** $20 per night, $120 per week.*

***Reception open** 6.30pm-8pm.*

🚌

Maintenance & cleanliness	★★
Facilities	★★⯪
Atmosphere & character	★★★
Security	★★⯪
Overall rating	★★

Northaven Backpackers Motel

This backpackers' hostel is part of a motel complex and guests have use of motel facilities that include a swimming pool. It's on busy Deakin Avenue about mid-way between the city centre and the tourist information centre.

138 Deakin Avenue, Mildura.

☎ *(03) 5023 4499.*

***Dorm bed** $120 per week.*

***Reception open** Mon-Fri 8am-6pm.*

Maintenance & cleanliness	★★★⯪
Facilities	★★⯪
Atmosphere & character	-
Security	★
Overall rating	★★⯪

Riverboat Bungalow

The Riverboat Bungalow is a big old house with an eclectic range of fur-

nishings. Facilities include a kitchen, TV lounge and a backyard with a pool table and barbecue area. There is also accommodation in an annex around the corner, which has similar facilities and also boasts a swimming pool. This hostel has a good atmosphere and it is a good spot to stay.

27 Chaffey Avenue, Mildura

☎ *(03) 5021 5315.*

***Dorm bed** $20 ($19 VIP) per night, $120 per week; **double room** $44 ($42 VIP).*

***Reception open** Mon-Sat 9am-noon and 6pm-8pm, Sun 6pm-8pm.*

Maintenance & cleanliness	★★★
Facilities	★★⯪
Atmosphere & character	★★★★★⯪
Security	★
Overall rating	★★★

Red Cliffs Backpackers

This small hostel has a laid back atmosphere that some travellers like, but it is also dirty and it could do with much better facilities. Amenities include free Internet access, a free weekly barbecue, a TV lounge, a front yard with a barbecue and a nice courtyard with palm trees. Furnishings are old and mismatched. Guests working on nearby farms have free use of cars to get to work.

63 Indi Avenue, Red Cliffs.

☒ *100, 200.*

☎ *(03) 5024 2905.*

***Dorm bed** $110 per week.*

Maintenance & cleanliness	⯪
Facilities	★★
Atmosphere & character	★★★★⯪
Security	★
Overall rating	★★⯪

Work

Most work in Mildura involves picking grapes as well as stone fruits like apricots and peaches. The grape-picking season runs from mid-February to late March and the stone fruit harvest is between late November and early April.

All backpackers' hostels in Mildura can organise fruit picking work.

Harvest Labour Office

The Harvest Labour Office co-ordinates work on farms around Mildura.

It's a good idea to contact them to check the availability of work before coming up to Mildura.
Corner 10th Street & Deakin Avenue, Mildura.
⊞ *100, 400, 500.*
☎ *(03) 5022 1797.*
Website www.madec.edu.au/harvest.html.
Open Mon-Fri 7am-7pm.

Sights

Mildura is primarily a working city without a lot of attractions but there are several small museums that may be of interest to some people.
Mildura's sights include:

Mildura Arts Centre

This museum complex, west of the city centre, features the historic Rio Vista house, a regional art gallery, a theatre and a sculpture park. The art gallery features works by local artists and also hosts works by Sir William Orpen, Sir Frank Brangwyn and Edgar Degas.
199 Cureton Avenue, Mildura.
⊞ *400, 500.*
☎ *(03) 5018 8330.*
Admission $3.
Open 10am-5pm daily.

RAAF Air Museum

Located at the airport, the Mildura RAAF museum features early fighter aircraft and displays about Australia's air force.
Mildura Airport.
☎ *(03) 5022 7691.*
Admission $5.
Open Tue, Fri, Sun 10am-4pm.

High Country

The Victorian High Country was once the stamping ground of the infamous Ned Kelly and fictional characters like the Man From Snowy River.

Heading east from Melbourne, the High Country is the region past the Yarra Valley and over the Great Dividing Range. In winter this area is a popular ski destination with both downhill and cross-country resorts. In summer, snow gives way to horse riding and hiking trails among the twisted snow gums and cool running streams.

Beechworth

This prosperous gold town of the 1880s is a lovely place with tree-lined streets and many relics of the gold rush. It is set amongst the rolling countryside of the Ovens Valley.

Practical Information
Beechworth Visitor Information Centre
Old Shire Hall, Ford Street, Beechworth.
☎ *(03) 5728 3233 or 1300 366 321.*
Website www.beechworth.com.
Open 9am-5pm daily.

Sights
Burke Museum
An excellent museum with exhibits on the gold rush and the exploits of the notorious Kelly gang.
Loch Street, Beechworth.
☎ *(03) 5728 1420.*
Website www.beechworth.com/burkemus/.
Admission $5.50.
Open 9am-5pm daily.

Bright

This small alpine town is conveniently located within a short distance of many of Victoria's ski areas including Falls Creek and Mount Hotham. Bright can get very busy during the ski season, however it is much quieter during summer when it makes an ideal base for hiking in the surrounding countryside.

Practical Information
Bright Visitors Centre
119 Gavan Street, Bright.
☎ *(03) 5755 2275 or 1800 500 117.*
Open 8.30am-5pm daily.

Accommodation
Bright Hikers Backpackers Hostel
This is a clean and well-maintained hostel across the road from the post office. It has a big balcony, with a barbecue, overlooking the main street. The hostel's facilities include Inter-

net access, a TV lounge and a fully equipped kitchen.
2nd floor, 2 Ireland Street, Bright.
☎ *(03) 5750 1244.*
***Dorm bed** $19 ($18 VIP/YHA);*
***double room** $42 ($40 VIP/YHA).*
***Credit cards** Amex, Diners, JCB, MC, Visa.*
***Reception open** 10am-9pm daily.*

Maintenance & cleanliness	★★★★☆
Facilities	★★
Atmosphere & character	★★★
Security	★★☆
Overall rating	★★★★☆

Mansfield

Mansfield is a convenient base for skiing at Mt Buller and it makes a good base for exploring the High Country during the summer.

Practical Information
Mansfield Visitor Information Centre
167 Maroondah Highway, Mansfield.
☎ *(03) 5775 7000 or 1800 039 049.*
***Website** www.mansfield-mtbuller.com.au.*
***Open** Jan to mid-Jun 9am-5pm daily; mid-Jun to Sep 8am-9pm daily; Sep-Dec 9am-5pm.*

Accommodation
Mansfield Backpackers Inn
This is a very clean hostel with the usual facilities such as a kitchen and TV lounge. Although the range of facilities is limited the standard of accommodation is very high.
112-116 High Street, Mansfield.
☎ *(03) 5775 1800.*
***Dorm bed** $23; **single room** $60; **double room** $66-85.*
***Credit cards** MC, Visa.*
🚌

Maintenance & cleanliness	★★★★☆
Facilities	★★☆
Atmosphere & character	★★
Security	★★☆
Overall rating	★★★

Activities
Camel Treks
High Country Camel Treks organise a variety of camel treks around the surrounding countryside ranging from

a simple 10-minute ride to overnight alpine treks lasting up to 4½ days.
Rifle Butts Road, 7km north of Mansfield.
☎ *(03) 5775 1591.*
***Cost** 15 minutes $10; 1 hour $35; 3 hours $60; full day $135.*

Horse Riding
Horse riding is a great way to experience the High Country. Stoneys Trail Rides operate horse-riding treks ranging from two hours to 18 days.
☎ *(03) 5775 2212.*
***Website** www.stoneys.com.au.*
***Cost** 1hr $25; 2hrs $45-50; 3hrs $65-75; full day $180.*

White Water Rafting
Adrenaline White Water operates white water rafting trips on the nearby King and Snowy Rivers and the Mitta Mitta Gorge.
RMB9656 Upper King River Road, Cheshunt.
☎ *(03) 5729 8288.*
***Website** www.whitewaterrafting.com .au.*
***Cost** one day $155-185; two days $270-295*

Gippsland

This region in eastern Victoria includes a beautiful coastline that features the solitude of Ninety Mile Beach, the inland waterways of Lakes Entrance and the Gippsland Lakes and the rugged coastline of Wilsons Promontory National Park.

Foster

This small town is the closest real town to Wilsons Promontory National Park, which is 30km south of here. Many travellers stay here before and after visiting the park and some people visit as a day trip from Foster.

Practical Information
Visitor Information Centre
Stockyard Gallery, Main Street, Foster.
☎ *(03) 5682 1125.*
***Open** Thu-Sun 10am-4pm.*

Victoria

Accommodation
Foster Backpackers
This small hostel has accommodation in a small brick bunkhouse and a mud brick cottage with a lovely courtyard. It is a quiet hostel with a high standard of accommodation, but facilities are limited and there is no access to shared facilities between 9am and 5pm. It is on a quiet residential street, just a short walk through a park into the town centre.

17 Pioneer Street, Forster.
☎ *(03) 5682 2614.*
Dorm bed *$20.*
Reception open *8am-9am & 5pm-9pm.*
🚗

Maintenance & cleanliness	★★★★½
Facilities	★
Atmosphere & character	★★★
Security	★
Overall rating	★★½

Wilsons Promontory National Park

Wilsons Promontory is a large national park at the southern most point of the Australian mainland. It is an excellent place to tackle some rewarding hiking trails.

Tidal River has the best infrastructure in the park with a big campsite, service station, post office, café and during busy periods, an outdoor cinema.

Practical Information
Tidal River Information Centre
Wilsons Promontory Road, Tidal River, Wilsons Promontory National Park.
☎ *(03) 5680 9555.*
Open *Nov-Easter Sat-Thu 8am-7.30pm, Fri 8am-9.30pm; Easter-Oct 8am-5pm daily.*

Coming & Going
It is easiest to visit Wilsons Prom in your own car. If you are relying on public transport you will need to catch a V/line bus from Melbourne to Foster, and then hitchhike or get a lift with someone staying at Forster Backpackers.

Accommodation
The closest backpackers accommodation to the park is in nearby Foster, but there are plenty of campsites scattered throughout the park with the main one at Tidal River.

Camping at Tidal River costs $19 for up to three people in summer and $15.50 at other times of the year. Demand is high during Christmas and Easter holidays and long weekends when you will need to book well in advance by a ballot system. Contact the information centre at Tidal River for more information.

Hiking
Wilsons Prom has over 100km of hiking trails, which range from short nature walks to demanding overnight hikes.

SHORT WALKS
Short walks include Lilly Pilly Gully Nature Walk (5km, 2hrs), which takes you through eucalyptus and paperbark forest and Miller's Landing Nature Walk (5km, 1½hr), which goes to mangrove swamp at Corner Inlet.

Mount Oberon Nature Walk (7km, 2-3hrs) is a popular early morning walk to the summit of Mount Oberon, which is a great spot to watch the sunrise.

One of the most popular short walks is the Squeaky Bay Nature Walk (5km, 1½hr), which takes you past sand dunes and tea-tree scrub to the dazzling Squeaky Beach.

DAY WALKS
There are several longer day walks in the park including Oberon Bay Track (12.5km, 5hrs), which passes Norman Bay Beach and follows the coast to Oberon Bay; Sealers Cove Track (20.5km, 5-6hrs), which goes to Sealers Cove on the other side of the Peninsula and Tongue Point Track (5.5km, 2½hrs), which goes past two lookouts offering spectacular coastal views.

Bairnsdale

Bairnsdale doesn't have a lot to offer apart from being the largest town near the Gippsland Lakes. Bairnsdale makes a good base for exploring the lakes and it is big enough to have good supermarkets and camping supplies stores.

Practical Information
Bairnsdale Visitor Information Centre
240 Main Street, Bairnsdale.
Website www.lakesandwilderness. com.au.
☎ *(03) 5152 3444 or 1800 637 060.*
Open 9am-5pm daily.

Lakes Entrance

This small resort town is the most popular destination in the Gippsland Lakes and can get very busy in the middle of summer. Lakes Entrance has a fantastic location on the lakes within easy access to ocean beaches.

Practical Information
Lakes Entrance Visitor Information Centre
Corner Marine Parade & Esplanade, Lakes Entrance.
☎ *(03) 5155 1966 or 1800 637 060.*
Website www.lakesandwilderness. com.au.
Open 9am-5pm daily.

Coming & Going
Premier Motor Service and V/line buses depart from the Esplanade near the post office.

Accommodation
Lakes Main Caravan Park & Hostel
Accommodation is in a couple of new cabins in a run down caravan park. The backpackers' accommodation is OK, but the rest of the park isn't too good.
7 Willis Street, Lakes Entrance.
☎ *(03) 5155 2365.*
Dorm bed *$14.30-24.20.*
Credit cards *MC, Visa.*
Reception open *8am-8.30pm daily.*
🚌

Maintenance & cleanliness	★★★☆
Facilities	★☆
Atmosphere & character	★
Security	★
Overall rating	★★

Riviera Backpackers YHA Hostel
This former motel has the usual TV lounge, kitchen and Internet access plus a swimming pool and a spa.
669 Esplanade, Lakes Entrance.
☎ *(03) 5155 2444.*
Dorm bed *$21 ($17.50 YHA);* **single room** *$33.50 ($30 YHA);* **double/ twin room** *$45-57 ($38-55 YHA).*
Credit cards *Amex, Diners, JCB, MC, Visa.*
Reception open *8am-10pm daily.*
🚌

Maintenance & cleanliness	★★★☆
Facilities	★★☆
Atmosphere & character	★★
Security	★★☆
Overall rating	★★★

Western Australia

Australia's biggest state covers a third of the country, and is larger than the whole of Western Europe and nearly four times the size of Texas.

Perth

Perth, on the Swan River, flanked by the Indian Ocean and the Darling Range, has plenty of city attractions: museums, art galleries, a very popular zoo, theatres, Kings Park overlooking the city and entertainment in the restaurant and nightlife neighbourhood of Northbridge.

Perth's port of Fremantle, boasts a convict-built police station, courthouse and prison. During the 1980s, the port took on new glamour when it became

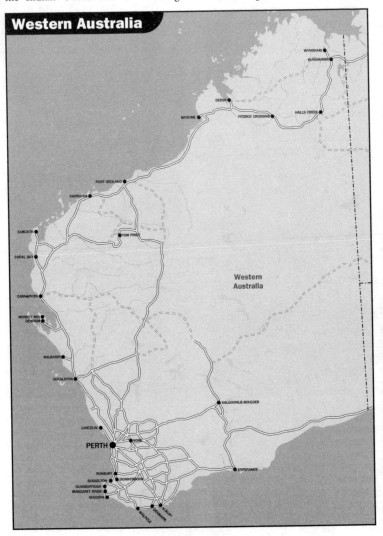

Western Australia

WYNDHAM
KUNUNURRA
DERBY
BROOME
FITZROY CROSSING
HALLS CREEK
PORT HEDLAND
KARRATHA
EXMOUTH
TOM PRICE
CORAL BAY
CARNARVON
MONKEY MIA
DENHAM
Western Australia
KALBARRI
GERALDTON
KALGOORLIE-BOULDER
LANCELIN
PERTH
YORK
ESPERANCE
BUNBURY
BUSSELTON
DONNYBROOK
DUNSBOROUGH
MARGARET RIVER
AUGUSTA
WALPOLE
ALBANY
DENMARK

the centre for the America's Cup regatta. Nowadays, the sea air, weekend markets and outdoor cafés draw the crowds from elsewhere in Perth, particularly at the weekends.

Practical Information
INFORMATION CENTRES & USEFUL ADDRESSES
American Express
645 Hay Street, Perth
🚇 *Perth.*
☎ *(08) 9221 0777.*
Website *www.americanexpress.com.*
Open *Mon-Fri 9am-5pm, Sat 9am-noon.*

Department of Conservation & Land Management (CALM)
47 Henry Street, Fremantle.
🚇 *Fremantle.*
☎ *(08) 9430 8600.*
Website *www.calm.wa.gov.au.*
Open *Mon-Fri 8am-5pm.*

Fremantle Tourist Office
Corner High & William Streets, Kings Square, Fremantle.
🚌 *Orange CAT;* 🚇 *Fremantle.*
☎ *(08) 9431 7878.*
Open *Mon-Fri 9am-5pm, Sat 10am-3pm, Sun noon-3pm.*

Perth Tourist Office
Level 2, Carillion Arcade, Perth.
🚇 *Perth.*
☎ *(08) 9229 2238.*
Open *Mon-Fri 9am-5.30pm, Sat 9am-5pm, Sun noon-4pm.*

Western Australia Tourist Commission
Corner Wellington Street & Forrest Place, Perth.
🚇 *Perth.*
☎ *1300 361 351.*
Website *www.westernaustralia.net.*
Open *Mon-Thu 8.30am-6pm, Fri 8.30am-7pm, Sat 8.30am-12.30pm.*

TransPerth InfoLine
For public transport information.
☎ *13 62 13.*
Website *www.transperth.wa.gov.au.*
Open *Mon-Fri 6.30am-10pm, Sat-Sun 7am-10pm.*

EMBASSIES & CONSULATES
British Consulate
Level 26, Allendale Square, 77 St Georges Terrace, Perth.
☎ *(08) 9224 4700.*
Website *www.uk.emb.gov.au.*
Open *Mon-Fri 9am-5pm.*

USA Consulate
13th floor, 16 St Georges Terrace, Perth.
☎ *(08) 9202 1224.*
Open *Mon-Fri 8am-11am.*

INTERNET ACCESS
Grand Central
379 Wellington Street, Perth.
🚇 *Perth.*
☎ *(08) 9421 1123.*
Open *8am-8pm daily.*

Indigo Netcafé & Lodge
256 West Coast Highway, Scarborough.
🚌 *381, 410, 411.*
☎ *(08) 9245 3388.*
Open *Mon-Sat 8am-9pm, Sun 8am-8pm.*

net.CHAT Fremantle
Shop 14, Wesley Way Arcade, Market Street, Fremantle.
🚌 *Orange CAT, 98,99, 126, 135, 136, 138, 141, 144, 145, 510, 920;* 🚇 *Fremantle.*
☎ *(08) 9433 2011.*
Website *www.netchat.com.au.*
Open *Mon-Sat 8am-11pm, Sun 10am-10pm.*

Traveller's Club
499 Wellington Street, Perth.
☎ *(08) 9226 0660.*
Open *Mon-Fri 9am-8pm, Sat 9am-7pm, Sun 10am-6pm.*

Coming & Going
Perth is a long way from anywhere and most interstate visitors fly here, however there are also regular buses and train connections with the east coast.

AIR
Because of the distance between Perth and the other big cities, flying is the most popular way to get here. Most backpackers fly in on either Qantas or Virgin Blue.

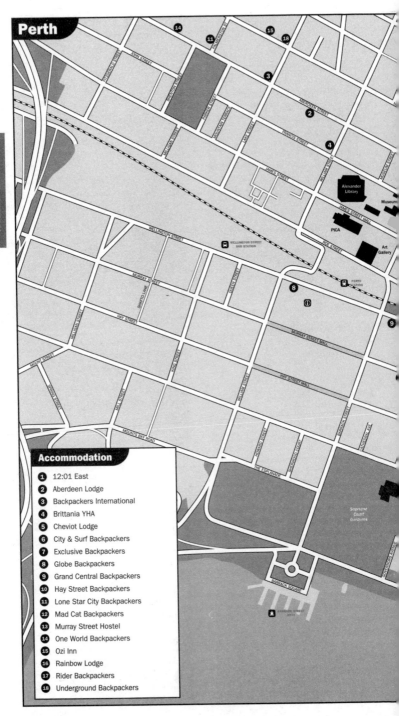

Western Australia

Perth

Accommodation

1. 12:01 East
2. Aberdeen Lodge
3. Backpackers International
4. Brittania YHA
5. Cheviot Lodge
6. City & Surf Backpackers
7. Exclusive Backpackers
8. Globe Backpackers
9. Grand Central Backpackers
10. Hay Street Backpackers
11. Lone Star City Backpackers
12. Mad Cat Backpackers
13. Murray Street Hostel
14. One World Backpackers
15. Ozi Inn
16. Rainbow Lodge
17. Rider Backpackers
18. Underground Backpackers

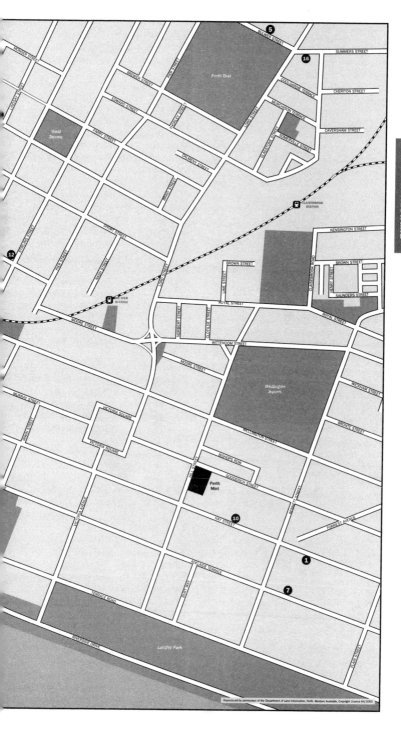

Perth Airport (☎ *(08) 9478 8888; website www.perthairport.net.au)* is 12km northeast of the city centre. The international and domestic terminals are located several kilometres apart and locals often talk about them as if they're separate airports. The domestic terminal is served by local bus routes 37 and 39 as well as the more expensive Airport City Shuttle and Fremantle Airport Shuttle, which also serve the international terminal.

The Airport City Shuttle (☎ *1300 666 806)* is the quickest option into the city centre and charges $13 from the international terminal or $11 from the domestic terminal.

Jandakot Airport, south of the city centre handles some regional flights including flights to Rottnest Island.

BUS

Perth has three bus terminals. Transwa (☎ *1300662205; website www.transwa. wa.gov.au)* buses to destinations in the state's south depart from the East Perth Terminal train station. McCafferty's/Greyhound and Integrity coaches depart from the bus station at 554 Wellington Street near Perth train station. Southwest Coachlines operate buses to the southwest including Bunbury, Busselton and Margaret River. Southwest buses depart from the City Busport on Mounts Bay Road.

TRAIN

The East Perth Terminal is the terminus for long distance trains. Transwa (☎ *1300 662 205; website www.transwa.wa.gov.au)* has trains to Bunbury and Kalgoorlie and Great Southern Railway operate the Indian-Pacific to Sydney with stops at Kalgoorlie, Adelaide and Broken Hill. The East Perth Terminal is part of Transperth's suburban train network with frequent trains to the city centre and Fremantle.

HITCHHIKING

Because local buses in Perth run a long way from the centre, it's pretty easy to get to some prime hitchhiking spots.

If you're heading to Bunbury and the Margaret River region, take a local bus heading to Mandurah and get off at Golden Bay or Singleton.

If you want a lift to Albany or Esperance take a train to Armadale and then walk to the Albany Highway (route 30).

The Great Eastern Highway (route 94) runs from Perth to Kalgoorlie and across the Nullarbor Plain to Adelaide. Take a train to Midland and then a bus to Mundaring and wait for a lift on the highway just outside town. Use a sign as the road splits soon after Mundaring.

The Brand Highway (route 1) heads north up the west coast to Exmouth, Broome and eventually to Darwin. Take a train to Midland, and then it's a long walk to the better hitching spots on the Brand Highway.

An easier option is to use a web-based ride sharing service such as BUG Ride (*website http://australia.bugride.com)*, this allows travellers to both offer lifts and search for rides throughout Australia.

Local Transport

Transperth (☎ *13 62 13; website www. transperth.wa.gov.au)* operates Perth's public transport network, which is comprised of buses, ferries and trains. It is a good value way to get around the city and there's even free transport in the central area.

BUS

Buses form the backbone of Perth's transport system and it is inevitable that you'll ride them at some point or another, particularly if you want to get to the beaches.

Buses are free within the central area, although with regular buses it can be difficult to know which rides are free and which ones you have to pay for. Fortunately there are a couple of frequent bus routes confined to the free central area that are extremely popular with travellers. The Central Area Transit (CAT) buses run three routes – the Red CAT runs an east-west route in the city centre, the Yellow CAT goes between the city centre and East Perth and the more useful Blue CAT connects the hostels in Northbridge with the city centre. The only problem is that the

Western Australia

CAT buses stop running shortly after 6pm. There is also an Orange CAT, which runs a loop around Fremantle.

Perth's bus network covers a large area with buses running as far a field as Rockingham and Mandurah.

TRAIN
Perth's rail network consists of four lines. The most useful is the Fremantle line, which runs from the city centre to Fremantle via Cottesloe. Trains run approximately every half hour.

City West, Perth, McIver and Claisebrook stations lie within the Free Transit Zone.

FERRY
Perth has a limited ferry service between Barrack Street Jetty in the city centre and Coode Street and Mends Street Jetties in South Perth. The Barrack Street Jetty to Mends Street Jetty ferry is a popular route for travellers visiting Perth Zoo. Ferries run around every 20 minutes.

FARES
Perth's public transport network is great value, especially considering that there is free transport in the central Free Transit Zone. Even travel outside this zone is good value.

Like many other public transport networks, Perth is divided into different fare zones. Most attractions are in zones one and two; although the transport network extends as far as zone eight. A Perth to Fremantle train trip requires a two-zone ticket, as does a trip between the city centre and the domestic airport terminal.

A one-zone fare is $2 and a two-zone fare is $3.

If you're planning on using a lot of public transport you may want to invest in a DayRider ticket that allows unlimited travel on Transperth buses, trains and ferries from 9am on weekdays and all day on weekends and public holidays. A DayRider costs $7.50.

Accommodation
BEACHES
Perth has some brilliant beaches and despite the suburban location, they

are a great place to stay; particularly if you're visiting Perth during summer.

Nomads Indigo Lodge
This hostel is a good choice if you want to stay near the beach. It features a barbecue area as well as surfboard, guitar and bike hire. Other facilities, however, are very basic including the kitchen and the small lounge area. There's also an Internet café on site. It's a good choice if you want to be close to the beach, which is across the road.
256 West Coast Highway, Scarborough.
⊟ *381, 400, 410, 411.*
☎ *(08) 9245 3388.*
Website *www.indigonet.com.au.*
Dorm bed *$23-25 ($20 Nomads/ VIP/YHA);* **single room** *$36-39 ($33 Nomads/VIP/YHA);* **double room** *$59-60 ($54 Nomads/VIP/YHA);* **twin room** *$51-55 ($48 Nomads/VIP/ YHA).*
Reception open *Mon-Thu 8am-pm, Fri-Sun 8am-7pm.*

Maintenance & cleanliness	★★☆
Facilities	★☆
Atmosphere & character	★★★
Security	★☆
Overall rating	★★☆

Ocean Beach Backpackers
This is the best of Perth's beach hostels and everything is brand new and very clean. There is a café downstairs and the hostel is built around a courtyard, which creates a great atmosphere. There is a nice lounge area and a fully equipped kitchen. Accommodation is good with en suite bathrooms, lockers and fridges in the rooms and many rooms with ocean views. It's on North Cottesloe Beach, about halfway between the city centre and Fremantle.
1 Eric Street, Cottesloe.
⊟ *71, 72, 75, 381;* ⊟ *Grant Street.*
☎ *(08) 9384 5111.*
Website *www.obh.com.au/backpackers.*
Dorm bed *$21-24 ($20-23 VIP);* **single room** *$60 ($59 VIP);* **double/ twin room** *$63 ($61 VIP).*
Credit cards *MC, Visa.*
Reception open *7am-11pm daily; 24 hour check in.*

Maintenance & cleanliness	★★★★
Facilities	★★☆
Atmosphere & character	★★★★
Security	★★★
Overall rating	★★★★☆

Sunset Coast Backpackers

This laid-back beach house is popular with surfers. It provides basic accommodation with below average facilities. It's on the corner of Abbett Street and Scarborough Beach Road, about a 10-minute walk to the beach.

119 Scarborough Beach Road, Scarborough.
🚌 *400, 408.*
☎ *(08) 9245 1161.*
Dorm bed *$14-18; includes breakfast.*
Reception open *Sun-Thu 8am-11am & 3.30pm-7.30pm, Fri-Sat 8am-10.30am & 3.30pm-7.30pm.*
🚗

Maintenance & cleanliness	★★☆
Facilities	★★☆
Atmosphere & character	★★★★☆
Security	★★☆
Overall rating	★★

Western Beach House

Western Beach House has a friendly laid-back atmosphere that makes it the best of the Scarborough hostels. It is a clean hostel with good facilities that include a fully equipped kitchen, TV lounge, Internet access and a barbecue area.

6 Westborough Street, Scarborough.
☎ *(08) 9245 1624.*
Dorm bed *$19;* **double room** *$44-54.*
Credit cards *MC, Visa.*
🚗

Maintenance & cleanliness	★★★★
Facilities	★★
Atmosphere & character	★★★★★☆
Security	★★
Overall rating	★★★★☆

CITY CENTRE & NORTHBRIDGE

The city centre is right in the centre of the action and has excellent transport connections to the rest of the Perth area. Northbridge is a quieter area just north of the central business district and is home to Perth's nightlife scene with plenty of bars, pubs, restaurants and cafés.

12:01 East

This hostel provides basic accommodation but has an excellent common room, called "the Cave", which has a TV, pool table and table tennis.

195 Hay Street, Perth.
🚌 *Red CAT, 24, 25, 27, 105, 111, 158.*
☎ *(08) 9221 1666.*
Dorm bed *$15-18;* **single room** *$32;* **double room** *$48;* **twin room** *$38.*
Credit cards *MC, Visa.*
Reception open *Mon-Sat 8.30am-noon & 3pm-8pm, Sun 8.30am-11am & 4pm-7.30pm.*

Maintenance & cleanliness	★★★☆
Facilities	★★
Atmosphere & character	★★★★
Security	★★
Overall rating	★★★☆

Aberdeen Lodge

This small hostel has a good atmosphere but the furnishings are old and worn and it could be better maintained. Its best feature is the garden area at the front, which is a great spot to sit and relax.

79-81 Aberdeen Street, Northbridge.
🚌 *Blue CAT.*
☎ *(08) 9227 6137.*
Dorm bed *$15;* **single room** *$30;* **double room** *$38.*
Reception open *Mon-Fri 9am-noon & 4.30pm-6.30pm, Sat-Sun 9.15am-noon & 5pm-7pm.*

Maintenance & cleanliness	★★
Facilities	★
Atmosphere & character	★★★★
Security	★★★
Overall rating	★★★☆

Backpackers International

Backpackers International has one of the best locations of the Northbridge hostels, near the corner of Aberdeen and Lake Streets. It provides basic accommodation with a big TV lounge, a kitchen and a balcony with a barbecue.

110 Aberdeen Street, Northbridge.
🚌 *Blue CAT.*
☎ *(08) 9227 9977.*
Dorm bed *$11.50-15.*
Credit cards *MC, Visa.*
Reception open *9am-8pm daily.*
🚗 *$2 per day.*

Maintenance & cleanliness	★★
Facilities	★⯪
Atmosphere & character	★★★
Security	★⯪
Overall rating	★★

Billabong Backpackers Resort

This is a big modern place with good facilities, but it does have a bit of an institutional feel. Facilities are very extensive and include a gym; games area with table tennis, foosball and a pool table; several TV lounges; an ATM and book exchange. All rooms have en suite and balconies. It's a popular place with international students, particularly those studying at the EF language school next door.

381 Beaufort Street, Northbridge.

🚌 *21, 22, 66, 67, 68, 69.*

☎ *(08) 9328 7720.*

Website *www.billabongresort.com.au.*

Dorm bed *$19-21 ($18-20 Nomads;* ***single/double/twin room*** *$60 ($55 Nomads); includes breakfast.*

Credit cards *MC, Visa.*

Reception open *24 hours.*

🚗

Maintenance & cleanliness	★★★★
Facilities	★★★★★
Atmosphere & character	★★★★⯪
Security	★★
Overall rating	★★★★

Britannia International YHA

Britannia International YHA is a big youth hostel that occupies an older building in the heart of Northbridge. It has a big kitchen, a TV lounge, Internet access and a nice courtyard with barbecues.

253 William Street, Northbridge.

🚌 *Blue CAT, 15-22, 38, 41-44, 48, 55, 60, 66, -69, 401.*

☎ *(08) 9427 5155.*

Dorm bed *$22.50 ($19-22 YHA);* ***single room*** *$38.50 ($35 YHA);* ***double/twin room*** *$56-66 ($49-59 YHA).*

Credit cards *MC, Visa.*

Reception open *24 hours.*

Maintenance & cleanliness	★★★⯪
Facilities	★★
Atmosphere & character	★★
Security	★★★★⯪
Overall rating	★★★⯪

Cheviot Lodge

This big old house has facilities that include the usual kitchen, TV lounge and Internet access.

30 Bulwer Street, East Perth.

🚉 *Claisebrook.*

☎ *(08) 9227 6817.*

Website *www.cheviotlodge.com.*

Dorm bed *$16-18;* ***double room*** *$44;* ***twin room*** *$40.*

Reception open *8am-noon & 5pm-8pm daily.*

🚗

Maintenance & cleanliness	★★
Facilities	★
Atmosphere & character	★★⯪
Security	★★⯪
Overall rating	★★⯪

Club Red Backpackers

Club Red consists of two old houses converted to a backpackers hostel. It's nothing flash but the party atmosphere is legendary. Facilities include a TV room, a small kitchen and a bar with a pool table.

494 Newcastle Street, West Perth.

🚌 *15.*

☎ *(08) 9227 9969 or 1800 679 969.*

Website *www.redbackpackers.com.au.*

Dorm bed *$18 ($17 VIP) per night, $110 ($99 VIP) per week;* ***double/twin room*** *$48 per night, $288 per week.*

Credit cards *MC, Visa.*

Reception open 8am-midnight daily.

Maintenance & cleanliness	★★
Facilities	★★★⯪
Atmosphere & character	★★★★★
Security	★
Overall rating	★★★⯪

City & Surf Backpackers

City & Surf is a small hostel with rooms opening onto a central courtyard. Facilities include a kitchen and TV room. It's located on a quiet leafy street north of Newcastle Street in Northbridge.

41 Money Street, Northbridge.

🚌 *Blue CAT, 15, 38, 41-44, 48, 55.*

☎ *(08) 9227 1234.*

Dorm bed *$18;* ***double room*** *$48.*

Credit cards *MC, Visa.*

Reception open *8am-10.30am & 3.30pm-4pm & 6pm-7.30pm daily.*

🚗

Maintenance & cleanliness	★★☆
Facilities	★☆
Atmosphere & character	★★☆
Security	★☆
Overall rating	★★

Coolibah Lodge

This hostel has good facilities including a leafy outdoor courtyard with a barbecue, plus two kitchens, two TV lounges and Internet access. It's located at the northern end of Northbridge but still close to bars and cafés and less than a 10-minute walk into the city centre.

194 Brisbane Street, Northbridge.
🚌 *16, 17, 18, 19, 20, 21, 22, 60, 66, 67, 68, 69.*
☎ *(08) 9328 9958 or 1800 280 000.*
Website *www.coolibahlodge.com.au.*
Dorm bed *$18 ($17 VIP);* ***single room*** *$36 ($35 VIP);* ***double room*** *$50-52 ($48-50 VIP).*
Credit cards *MC, Visa.*
Reception open *8am-midnight.*

Maintenance & cleanliness	★★★
Facilities	★★
Atmosphere & character	★★★★
Security	★★
Overall rating	★★★

Exclusive Backpackers

This is a nice hostel with a kitchen and TV lounge on the ground floor and accommodation upstairs. Single and double rooms have TVs.

158 Adelaide Terrace, Perth.
🚌 *Red CAT.*
☎ *(08) 9221 9991.*
Website *www.exclusivebackpackers.com.*
Dorm bed *$16.50;* ***single room*** *$38;* ***double room*** *$48-49.50.*
Credit cards *MC, Visa.*
Reception open *8am-11pm daily.*

Maintenance & cleanliness	★★★★☆
Facilities	★★
Atmosphere & character	★★★☆
Security	★★
Overall rating	★★★

Globe Backpackers

This big central hostel has several kitchens and TV lounges plus Internet access. It is a very secure hostel but the overall standard of facilities could be improved.

501 Wellington Street, Perth.
🚌 *Blue CAT, Red CAT, Yellow CAT, 8, 10, 12, 28, 81, 84, 85, 91, 92, 95;*
🚆 *Perth.*
☎ *(08) 9321 4080 or 1800 737 378.*
Dorm bed *$15-20;* ***single room*** *$36;* ***double/twin room*** *$50; includes breakfast.*
Credit cards *MC, Visa.*

Maintenance & cleanliness	★★★☆
Facilities	★★☆
Atmosphere & character	★★☆
Security	★★★★☆
Overall rating	★★

Governor Robinson's

Governor Robinson's is an excellent hostel is in a beautiful old building with stained glass and polished hardwood floors. It is a quiet place with loads of character. Facilities include a huge laundry, Internet access, two nice courtyards and a small, but clean and fully equipped kitchen.

7 Robinson Avenue, Northbridge.
🚌 *16, 17, 18, 19, 20, 21, 22, 60, 66, 67, 68, 69, 401.*
☎ *(08) 9328 3200.*
Website *www.govrobinsons.com.au.*
Dorm bed *$20;* ***double/twin room*** *$55-65.*
Credit cards *MC, Visa.*
Reception open *9am-8pm daily.*

Maintenance & cleanliness	★★★★★
Facilities	★★
Atmosphere & character	★★★★★
Security	★★★☆
Overall rating	★★★★

Grand Central Backpackers

Facilities at Grand Central Backpackers are fairly standard and include an Internet café with cheap rates and a big kitchen.

379 Wellington Street, Perth.
🚌 *Blue CAT, Red CAT, Yellow CAT, 8, 10, 12, 28, 81, 84, 85, 91, 92, 95;*
🚆 *Perth.*
☎ *(08) 9421 1123.*
Dorm bed *$18;* ***single room*** *$36;* ***double room*** *$50-56;* ***twin room*** *$46.*
Credit cards *MC, Visa.*
Reception open *Mon-Fri 8am-8pm, Sat-Sun 8am-8pm.*

Maintenance & cleanliness	★★★
Facilities	★
Atmosphere & character	★★★
Security	★★
Overall rating	★★⯪

Hay Street Backpackers

This is a good hostel with an outdoor area that includes a barbecue and swimming pool. Other facilities include a laundry, TV room, air-conditioning and Internet access.

226 Hay Street, Perth.

☐ *Red CAT; 24, 25, 27, 105, 111, 158.*

☎ *(08) 9221 9880.*

Dorm bed *$20;* **single room** *$35;* **double room** *$48-58.*

Credit cards *MC, Visa.*

Reception open *8.30am-6pm daily.*

Maintenance & cleanliness	★★★★⯪
Facilities	★★
Atmosphere & character	★★⯪
Security	★★
Overall rating	★★★

Lone Star City Backpackers

This is a very basic hostel in an old run down house. It has a TV lounge, limited kitchen facilities and a small backyard.

17-21 Palmerston Street, Northbridge.

☐ *Blue CAT, 15.*

☎ *(08) 9328 6667 or 1800 247 444.*

Dorm bed *$16 ($14 VIP).*

Credit cards *MC, Visa.*

Reception open *Mon 7.30am-12.30pm & 4pm-7pm, Tue 7.30am-12.30pm, Wed 7.30am-12.30pm & 4pm-7pm, Thu 7.30am-12.30pm, Fri 7.30am-8.30pm, Sat 7.30am-12.30pm, Sun 7.30am-12.30pm & 4pm-7pm.*

Maintenance & cleanliness	★★⯪
Facilities	★★⯪
Atmosphere & character	★★★
Security	★★⯪
Overall rating	★★

Mad Cat City Backpackers

This is a cheap friendly hostel in an older building. It is a bit rough around the edges, but it has a good atmosphere. It features a big common room with a TV, foosball, plus a pool table and another TV lounge upstairs that is used mainly for videos. The kitchen is equipped with a mismatch of old rusting ovens.

55-63 Stirling Street, Northbridge.

☐ *Blue CAT, 15-22, 38, 41-44, 48, 55, 60, 66-69, 401.*

☎ *(08) 9228 4966.*

Website *www.madcatbackpackers.com.au.*

Dorm bed *$12-14 ($11-13 ISIC/VIP/YHA);* **double room** *$40 ($38 ISIC/VIP/YHA).*

Credit cards *MC, Visa.*

Reception open *9am-10pm daily.*

Maintenance & cleanliness	★★
Facilities	★★
Atmosphere & character	★★★
Security	★★⯪
Overall rating	★★⯪

Murray Street Hostel

This centrally located hostel is a little run down and it offers basic facilities that include a TV lounge, Internet access and a small kitchen. It is popular with Asian travellers.

119 Murray Street, Perth.

☐ *Blue CAT, Red CAT;* ☐ *Perth.*

☎ *(08) 9325 7627.*

Website *www.murrayst.com.*

Dorm bed *$16.50 ($15 VIP/YHA);* **single room** *$38 ($35 VIP/YHA);* **double room** *$43 ($40 VIP/YHA);* **twin room** *$38 ($34 VIP/YHA); prices subject to seasonal variations.*

Reception open *8am-10pm.*

Maintenance & cleanliness	★★⯪
Facilities	★★⯪
Atmosphere & character	★
Security	★★⯪
Overall rating	★★⯪

One World Backpackers

This small hostel is a lovely restored house with a warm and relaxed atmosphere. It is a quiet place with a brilliant kitchen, Internet access and a nice TV lounge.

162 Aberdeen Street, Northbridge.

☐ *Blue CAT, 15.*

☎ *(08) 9228 8206 or 1800 188 100.*

Website *www.oneworldbackpackers.com.au.*

Dorm bed *$19-26 ($18-25 Nomads/VIP/YHA);* **single room** *$51-60 ($50-59 Nomads/VIP/YHA);* **double room** *$56-66 ($55-65 Nomads/VIP/YHA).*

Credit cards *MC, Visa.*

Reception open *7am-2pm & 4pm-*

9.30pm daily; late check in by prior arrangement.

Maintenance & cleanliness	★★★★★
Facilities	★★
Atmosphere & character	★★★★★
Security	★★
Overall rating	★★★★

Ozi Inn

Ozi Inn is a basic hostel with minimal facilities, which include a kitchen, TV lounge and Internet access. It could be better maintained, but a lot of travellers like the atmosphere.

282 Newcastle Street, Northbridge.
Blue CAT, 15.
(08) 9328 1222.
Dorm bed *$14-17;* **double room** *$45-50.*

Maintenance & cleanliness	★★☆
Facilities	★★
Atmosphere & character	★★☆
Security	★☆
Overall rating	★★☆

Rainbow Lodge

Rainbow Lodge is a colourful hostel with fairly basic facilities that include two kitchens, a laundry, Internet access and a games room with a pool table and table tennis.

133 Summers Street, East Perth.
6, 38, 41, 42, 43, 44, 48, 55;
Claisebrook, East Perth.
(08) 9227 1818.
Website *www.rainbowlodge.com.au.*
Dorm bed *$15;* **double/twin room** *$48; includes breakfast.*
Reception open *8am-8pm daily.*

Maintenance & cleanliness	★★☆
Facilities	★★
Atmosphere & character	★★★★☆
Security	★☆
Overall rating	★★★☆

Rider Backpackers

This is a grungy, run-down place with a relaxed, chilled-out vibe. Facilities are very basic.

158-160 Newcastle Street, Northbridge; check in at Lone Star City Backpackers (17-21 Palmerston Street, Northbridge).
Blue CAT, 15, 38, 41, 42, 43, 44, 48, 55.
(08) 9328 6667.
Dorm bed *$14 per night, $82 per week.*

Maintenance & cleanliness	★
Facilities	★
Atmosphere & character	★★
Security	★
Overall rating	★☆

Shiralee Backpackers

The Shiralee is a nice clean hostel in an old Federation-style house. Accommodation consists of small dormitories; the largest dorm has only six beds. Facilities are on par with other hostels and include the standard kitchen, laundry and TV lounge as well as air-conditioning. There is also a small garden with a barbecue. It's on a residential street in Northbridge, about a 10-minute walk north of the city centre.

107 Brisbane Street, Northbridge.
16, 19, 60, 401.
(08) 9227 7448.
Website *www.shiralee.com.au.*
Dorm bed *$19 ($18 VIP);* **double/twin room** *$52 ($50 VIP).*
Credit cards *MC, Visa.*
Reception open *Mon-Fri 8am-8pm, Sat-Sun 8am-noon & 4pm-8pm.*

Maintenance & cleanliness	★★★★☆
Facilities	★★
Atmosphere & character	★★★
Security	★★
Overall rating	★★★

Spinner's Backpackers

Spinner's is a fairly average backpackers' hostel as far as facilities are concerned but the staff are friendly and helpful and the hostel has a good atmosphere. Facilities include a big kitchen, a TV room with pool table and a barbecue area outside.

342 Newcastle Street, Northbridge.
Blue CAT, 15.
(08) 9328 9468.
Website *www.ic-net.com.au/~spinners.*
Dorm bed *$17; twin room $46.*
Reception open *8.30am-9pm daily.*

Maintenance & cleanliness	★★★
Facilities	★★
Atmosphere & character	★★★
Security	★★★
Overall rating	★★★

Underground Backpackers

This is a good hostel with great facilities that include a TV lounge with big screen telly, Internet access, an ATM, a big kitchen, a bar and a swimming pool.
268 Newcastle Street, Northbridge.
🚌 *Blue CAT, 15.*
☎ *(08) 9228 3755.*
Dorm bed *$19-22;* **single/double/ twin room** *$58-62; includes breakfast.*
Credit cards *MC, Visa.*
Reception open *24 hours.*
♿

Maintenance & cleanliness	★★★⯨
Facilities	★★★
Atmosphere & character	★★★
Security	★★★⯨
Overall rating	★★★⯨

Witch's Hat

The Witch's Hat is one of Perth's best hostels. It is in a beautiful old building that has been tastefully decorated and includes polished floorboards and a nice outdoor area with picnic tables and a barbecue. The hostel has a big clean kitchen and a lounge with a TV and Internet access.
148 Palmerston Street, Northbridge.
🚌 *17, 18, 19, 20, 401.*
☎ *(08) 9228 4228 or 1800 818 358.*
Website *www.witchs-hat.com.*
Dorm bed *$22 ($21 VIP);* **single/ twin room** *$53 ($52 VIP);* **double room** *$62 ($61 VIP).*
Credit cards *MC, Visa.*
Reception open *8am-2pm & 5pm-8pm daily.*
🚌

Maintenance & cleanliness	★★★★★
Facilities	★★
Atmosphere & character	★★★★★
Security	★⯨
Overall rating	★★★★

FREMANTLE

Perth's port is a lively seaside suburb with lots to see and do including several museums, a busy market and some very good pubs. Fremantle has ferries to Rottnest Island and a frequent train service into the city centre.

Backpackers Inn Freo YHA Hostel

Fremantle's YHA is a converted warehouse, which is a nice place with a good range of facilities including pool tables, a TV lounge, kitchen, a sunny courtyard and lots of quiet spots to sit and relax.
11 Pakenham Street, Fremantle.
🚌 *Orange CAT;* 🚌 *Fremantle.*
☎ *(08) 9431 7065.*
Dorm bed *$21.50 ($18 YHA);* **single room** *$33.50 ($30 YHA);* **double/ twin room** *$55 ($48 YHA).*
Credit cards *MC, Visa.*
Reception open *7am-10pm daily.*

Maintenance & cleanliness	★★★★⯨
Facilities	★★
Atmosphere & character	★★★⯨
Security	★★
Overall rating	★★★⯨

Cheviot Marina Backpackers

This hostel is in an older building in one of Fremantle's less attractive areas. It has a couple of kitchens and TV lounges and a pool table, Internet access and a nice outdoor barbecue area with a fish pond. It has more double rooms than many other hostels.
4 Beach Street, Fremantle.
🚌 *Orange CAT;* 🚌 *Fremantle.*
☎ *(08) 9433 2055 or 1800 255 644.*
Dorm bed *$16 ($15 VIP/YHA);* **single room** *$30-35 ($28-33 VIP/YHA);* **double room** *$45-50 ($40-45 VIP/ YHA).*
Credit cards *MC, Visa.*
Reception open *24 hours.*

Maintenance & cleanliness	★★★
Facilities	★⯨
Atmosphere & character	★★
Security	★★⯨
Overall rating	★★⯨

Old Firestation Backpackers

This hostel is popular with backpackers on a working holiday. The place has loads of atmosphere, free Internet access and a big common room with TV and pool table. There is also a women's only area with its own common area. Guests get cut price meals at the restaurant next door.
18 Philimore Street, Fremantle.
🚌 *Orange CAT;* 🚌 *Fremantle.*
☎ *(08) 9430 5454.*
Website *www.old-firestation.net.*
Dorm bed *$17 per night, $105 per week;* **double/twin room** *$44 per night, $250 per week.*

Western Australia

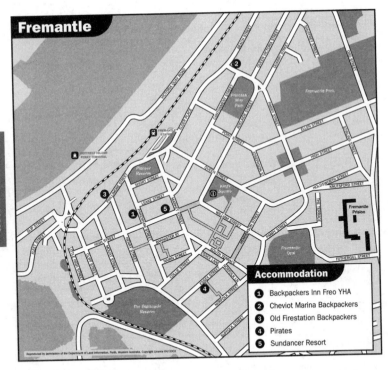

Fremantle

Accommodation

1. Backpackers Inn Freo YHA
2. Cheviot Marina Backpackers
3. Old Firestation Backpackers
4. Pirates
5. Sundancer Resort

Credit cards Amex, Diners, JCB, MC, Visa.
Reception open Mon-Sat 8am-6pm, Sun 9am-6pm.

Maintenance & cleanliness	★★★
Facilities	★★☆
Atmosphere & character	★★★★☆
Security	★★☆
Overall rating	★★★

Pirates

Pirates is a good small hostel right in the centre of Fremantle. It has a nice courtyard with a barbecue as well as the usual TV lounge and kitchen.
11 Essex Street, Fremantle.
🚌 *Orange CAT;* 🚆 *Fremantle.*
☎ *(08) 9335 6635.*
Dorm bed $18 ($17 VIP); double room $50 ($48 VIP).
Reception open 8am-8pm daily.

Maintenance & cleanliness	★★★
Facilities	★★☆
Atmosphere & character	★★★★
Security	★★
Overall rating	★★★☆

Sundancer Resort

This is a brilliant hostel with a great atmosphere. It has a fully-equipped kitchen, a big dining room, a TV lounge, several pool tables and a backyard with a spa and barbecue.
80 High Street, Fremantle.
🚌 *Orange CAT;* 🚆 *Fremantle.*
☎ *(08) 9336 6080 or 1800 061 144.*
Website www.sundancer-resort.com.au.
Dorm bed $16-20 ($16-19 Nomads); single room $40; double room $50-65 ($45-60 Nomads).
Credit cards Amex, JCB, MC, Visa.
Reception open 7am-11pm daily; 24 hour check in.

Maintenance & cleanliness	★★★★
Facilities	★★★
Atmosphere & character	★★★★★
Security	★★★☆
Overall rating	★★★★

OTHER AREAS
Perth Hills YHA

This small YHA hostel is in a natural bush setting 40km from the city centre

and it's a good alternative for travellers who don't want to stay in the city. It is a basic hostel with outside toilets (with creepy crawlies) and the beds have awful plastic mattresses, but the atmosphere is great and there are often kangaroos hopping around. Facilities include a small kitchen and a TV lounge with a wood fire. There's a pub, lake and outdoor cinema nearby, but the closest shops are 4km away.
Mundaring Weir Road, Mundaring.
🚌 *Midland, then* 🚌 *318.*
☎ *(08) 9295 1809.*
Dorm bed *$22.50 ($19 YHA);* ***single room*** *$36.50 ($33 YHA);* ***twin room*** *$51 ($44 YHA).*
Reception open *8am-10am & 5pm-9pm daily.*
🚌

Maintenance & cleanliness	★★★☆
Facilities	★★☆
Atmosphere & character	★★★★★☆
Security	★
Overall rating	★★★☆

Eating & Drinking

Perth isn't the greatest place to eat out in Australia, but there are plenty of good cheap dining options including food courts and fast food places in both Fremantle and central Perth. There are a few pubs and clubs that have special deals for backpackers. Ask the staff at your hostel for the low-down on the drinking scene.

Sights
CITY CENTRE & NORTHBRIDGE
Art Gallery of Western Australia
Australian and international art is shown at the state's most important art museum.
Perth Cultural Centre, James Street, Northbridge.
🚌 *Blue CAT;* 🚌 *Perth.*
☎ *(08) 9492 6622.*
Website *www.artgallery.wa.gov.au.*
Admission *free, charge for some temporary exhibits.*
Open *10am-5pm daily.*

Kings Park
This large city park consists mostly of native bush and is an escape from the city with popular picnic areas and bike paths. There are good views of the city centre from the higher points in the park.
🚌 *15, 18.*

Parliament House
You can take a free tour of the Western Australian state parliament building that offers a crash course in Australian politics.
Harvest Terrace, Perth.
🚌 *Red CAT.*
☎ *(08) 9222 7429.*
Admission *free.*
Tours *Mon, Thu 10.30am.*

Perth Institute of Contemporary Arts (PICA)
The Perth Institute of Contemporary Arts features exhibits of avant garde and contemporary visual and performing arts.
51 James Street, Northbridge.
🚌 *Blue CAT;* 🚌 *Perth.*
☎ *(08) 9227 6144.*
Website *www.pica.org.au.*
Admission *Gallery free, charge for performances.*
Open *Tue-Sun 11am-8pm.*

Perth Mint
This impressive building on Hay Street offers a unique insight into how money is made.
310 Hay Street.
🚌 *Red CAT.*
☎ *(08) 9421 7223 or 1800 098 817.*
Website *www.perthmint.com.au.*
Admission *$6.60.*
Open *Mon-Fri 9am-4pm, Sat-Sun 9am-1pm; gold pours Mon-Fri 10am, 11am, noon, 1pm, 2pm, 3pm, Sat-Sun 10am, 11am, noon.*

Scitech Discovery Centre
This hands-on science museum features over 160 interactive exhibits. However, like many science museums, it is geared mostly toward kids.
Corner Railway Parade & Sutherland Street, West Perth.
🚌 *City West.*
☎ *(08) 9481 5789.*
Website *www.scitech.org.au.*
Admission *$12.*
Open *10am-5pm daily.*

Swan Bells

This impressive 82.5 metre copper and glass tower in Barrack Square is one of the world's largest musical instruments. It houses a set of 18 bells, which includes 12 bells from St Martin-in-the-Fields in Trafalgar Square, London that date from before the 14th century. The tower features galleries where you can see the bell ringers in action as well as observation decks that boast stunning city views.
Barrack Square, Riverside Drive, Perth.
🚌 *Blue CAT;* 🚢 *Barrack Street Jetty.*
☎ *(08) 9218 8183.*
Website www.swanbells.com.au.
Admission $6, students $5.
Open 10am-5pm daily; bell ringing Mon-Fri 11.30am-12.30pm, Sat-Sun noon-2pm.

Western Australian Cricket Museum

This museum at the WACA Ground is a must for cricket fans.
Nelson Crescent, East Perth.
🚌 *Red CAT, Yellow CAT.*
☎ *(08) 9265 7222.*
Admission $5, tour $10.
Open Mon-Fri except match days 10am-3pm; tours Tue-Thu 10am & 1pm.

Western Australian Museum

Western Australia's largest museum features exhibits on natural history including a good selection of stuffed animals and a whale skeleton.
Francis Street, Perth.
🚌 *Blue CAT;* 🚉 *Perth.*
☎ *(08) 9427 2700.*
Website www.museum.wa.gov.au.
Admission free, charge for special exhibits.
Open 9.30am-4.50pm daily.

FREMANTLE

This seaside suburb has long been Perth's port and recently was host to Australia's unsuccessful America's Cup defence. The area has a hip yet laid-back ambience and is worth at least a day-trip from Perth.

Fremantle Markets

This old market hall has been around since 1897 and is now home to one of Fremantle's most popular attractions with over 150 stalls ranging from fruit and veggies to art and craft.
Corner Henderson Street & South Terrace, Fremantle.
🚌 *Orange CAT;* 🚉 *Fremantle.*
☎ *(08) 9335 2515.*
Admission free.
Open Fri 9am-9pm, Sat 9am-5pm, Sun 10am-5pm.

Fremantle Prison

The Fremantle Prison was built with convict labour in the 19th century and was operated as a prison until as recently as 1991. It has now been opened to the public and has frequent guided tours.
1 The Terrace, Fremantle.
🚌 *Orange CAT;* 🚉 *Fremantle.*
☎ *(08) 9336 9200.*
Website www.fremantleprison.com.au.
Admission $14.30.
Open 10am-5pm daily; tours depart every half hour.

Maritime Museum

The new maritime museum on Victoria Quay features an excellent collection of exhibits including a 90-metre-long submarine.
Forrest Landing, Victoria Quay, Fremantle.
🚌 *Orange CAT;* 🚉 *Fremantle.*
☎ *(08) 9335 8921.*
Website www.mm.wa.gov.au.
Admission $10 museum, $8 submarine.
Open 9.30am-5pm daily.

Shipwreck Museum

The old maritime museum on Cliff Street houses a collection of exhibits focusing on shipwrecks.
Cliff Street, Fremantle.
🚌 *Orange CAT;* 🚉 *Fremantle.*
☎ *(08) 9431 8444.*
Admission free.
Open 9.30am-5pm daily.

OTHER AREAS
AQWA

AQWA is home to a large variety of marine life and it features several areas that recreate various marine environments including Australia's largest walk-through aquarium.

91 Southside Drive, Hillarys Boat Harbour.

🚌 *Warwick, then* 🚌 *423.*

☎ *(08) 9447 7500.*

Website www.aqwa.com.au.

Admission $22.

Open 10am-5pm daily.

Perth Zoo

Perth's zoo is home to over 2000 animals representing 280 different species. It has the usual collection of African and native animals and also makes a good picnic spot.

20 Labouchere Road, South Perth.

🚌 *35;* ⛴ *Mends Street Jetty.*

☎ *(08) 9474 3551.*

Website www.perthzoo.wa.gov.au.

Admission $15.

Open 9am-5pm daily.

Rottnest Island

Rottnest Island is known for the island's unique animal, the quokka. Early Dutch explorers originally thought the quokka, which are a marsupial similar to a small wallaby, to be rats and named the island "Rat's Nest".

The island is located 18km offshore and is only 11km long. The eastern coast is built up around the small township of Thompson Bay where most of the shops, restaurants and accommodation are situated.

Practical Information

Visitors Information Centre

Colebach Avenue, Thompson Bay.

☎ *(08) 9372 9752.*

Website www.rottnest.wa.gov.au.

Open 8am-5pm daily.

Coming & Going

There are several ferry companies that ply the waters between Rottnest Island and the mainland.

Boat Torque Cruises *(*☎ *(08) 9430 5844; website www.boattorque.com.au)* operate a ferry service from Fremantle. Day return tickets are $45 ($40 VIP/YHA).

Oceanic Cruises *(*☎ *(08) 9325 1191; website www.oceaniccruises.com.au)* depart from Barrack Street Jetty in Perth and East Street Jetty in Fremantle. Day return fares are $60 ($55 VIP/YHA) from Perth and $45 ($40 VIP/YHA) from Fremantle. Oceanic Cruises have a backpacker package that includes ferry travel and accommodation at the Kingston Barracks YHA, this package costs $71 ($63 YHA) from Fremantle and $81 ($73 YHA) from Perth.

Rottnest Express *(*☎ *(08) 9335 6406; website www.rottnestexpress.com.au)* departs from Victoria Quay in Fremantle. Day return tickets cost $45 ($40 VIP/YHA).

Local Transport

Rottnest Island is surprisingly well served by public transport but cycling is the most popular way to get around.

Bayseeker operate an hourly bus service around the island. A day ticket is $7 but the last bus stops running around 4.30pm. There is also a free bus service that runs every half hour between the youth hostel, Thompson Bay and Geordie Bay.

There is even a train between Thompson Bay and Oliver Hill but this is a more expensive tourist service charging $15.40 for the two-hour return trip.

Accommodation

Kingstown Barracks Youth Hostel

This is an institutional youth hostel that is popular with school groups, but it's the only affordable accommodation on the island. Facilities are basic and include the standard laundry, kitchen and Internet access. It is about a 2-minute walk from the ferry terminal.

Kingstown, Rottnest Island.

☎ *(08) 9372 9780.*

Dorm bed $24.30 ($20.80 YHA); double/twin room $55.80 ($48.80 YHA).

Credit cards MC, Visa.

Reception open 8am-5pm daily.

Not yet rated

Avon Valley

This picturesque region east of Perth is one of Western Australia's first inland regions to be settled. It has some quaint little towns that make a nice daytrip from Perth, which is just a one-hour drive away.

The most visited towns in the valley are Toodyay and York, which are both full of character.

Toodyay

This charming town was settled in the late 1830s by farmers searching for cows that had strayed from their farms in the Swan Valley.

Practical Information
Toodyay Visitor Centre
7 Piesse Street, Toodyay.
☎ *(08) 9574 2435.*
Website *www.gidgenet.com.au/toodyay/.*
Open *Mon-Sat 9am-5pm, Sun 10am-5pm.*

Sights
Connors Mill Museum
This three-storey working flour mill uses 19th century steam-powered machinery.
Stirling Terrace, Toodyay.
☎ *(08) 9574 2435.*
Admission *$2.50.*
Open *Mon-Sat 9am-5pm, Sun 10am-5pm.*

Old Newcastle Gaol
This old prison has a collection of old handcuffs, guns and photographs and exhibits on the outlaws who where once locked up here.
Clinton Street, Toodyay.
☎ *(08) 9574 2435.*
Admission *$2.*
Open *Mon-Fri 10am-3pm, Sat-Sun 10am-4pm.*

York

Western Australia's first inland settlement has a lot more historic charm than your average Australian country town. It has some charming old buildings and a couple of small museums.

Practical Information
York Tourist Bureau
81 Avon Terrace, York.
☎ *(08) 9641 1301.*
Open *9am-5pm daily.*

Accommodation
Kookaburra Dream
Kookaburra Dream is a lovely hostel in a restored 1890s-style building in the historic town centre. It is a clean hostel with a great atmosphere and it features a nice backyard with a barbecue area, plus a cosy TV lounge with a fireplace and brand new bathrooms.
152 Avon Terrace, York.
☎ *(08) 9641 2936.*
Website *www.yorkbackpackerswa.com.*
Dorm bed *$21.50;* **double/twin room** *$47; includes breakfast.*
Credit cards *MC, Visa.*
Reception open *9am-9pm daily.*
🚌 ♿

Maintenance & cleanliness	★★★★
Facilities	★★
Atmosphere & character	★★★★★
Security	★
Overall rating	★★★☆

Sights & Activities
Ballooning
Windward Adventures (☎ *(08) 9621 2000; website www.windwardballooning.com)* run balloon flights over the Avon Valley.

Residency Museum
This small museum has displays on local history.
Brook Street, York.
☎ *(08) 9641 1751.*
Admission *$3.50.*
Open *Tue-Thu 1pm-3pm, Sat-Sun 11am-3.30pm.*

York Motor Museum
The York Motor Museum has a collection of vintage and classic cars dating back to 1886.
116 Avon Terrace, York.
☎ *(08) 9641 1288.*
Admission *$7.50.*
Open *9.30am-3pm daily.*

Southwest WA

The first stop south of the Perth area is Bunbury, the principal city of the southwest. After visiting Bunbury most travellers move onward to the Margaret River region, which lies between Cape

Naturaliste and Cape Leeuwin. The land here is honeycombed with limestone caves, some of which are open to the public. The Yallingup Caves near Dunsborough, are particularly impressive.

Western Australia's southwest offers magnificent forests of tall native trees including four species of rare eucalypts that grow in a small area there and nowhere else on earth.

Bunbury

Situated about two hours south of Perth, Bunbury is Western Australia's second largest city. Although it is a reasonably large town with plenty to keep you busy, its main attraction is the dolphins at Koombana Beach. Every day several dolphins swim up to shore and you can watch them in much the same way as at Monkey Mia.

Bunbury also makes a convenient base for exploring the nearby Wellington National Park.

Practical Information
Visitor Information Centre
Corner Carmody Place & Haley Street, Bunbury.
☎ *(08) 9721 7922.*
Open Mon-Sat 9am-5pm, Sun 9.30am-4.30pm.

Coming & Going
Bunbury's size and proximity to Perth ensures that it is easy to get to.

It lies at the southern extremity of Western Australia's rail network with a couple of daily train services to and from Perth. The train station is 3km north of town in Wollaston, and local buses meet with the train to take you into the town centre. One-way fares for the *Australind* train from Perth are $21.70.

Buses terminate at the tourist information centre.

Local Transport
Bunbury has quite a good local bus network. The most useful bus is the one between the train station and the city centre, which is free when you present your train ticket.

Accommodation
Wander Inn
This hostel is in an old house near the city centre. It has a pool table, TV lounge, Internet access and guests have free use of body boards.
16 Clifton Street, Bunbury.
☎ *(08) 9721 3242.*
***Dorm bed** $22-25 ($20-23 VIP/ YHA);* ***double room** $56 ($50 VIP/ YHA).*
***Credit cards** MC, Visa.*
***Reception open** 8am-1pm & 5pm-9pm daily.*
🚗

Maintenance & cleanliness	★★★☆
Facilities	★★☆
Atmosphere & character	★★★★☆
Security	★
Overall rating	★★★☆

Sights
Big Swamp Wildlife Park
Big Swamp Wildlife Park has the usual collection of native wildlife including kangaroos and birds.
Prince Phillip Drive, Bunbury.
☎ *(08) 9721 8380.*
***Admission** $5.*
***Open** 10am-5pm daily.*

Dolphin Discovery Centre
The Dolphin Discovery Centre features interactive exhibits and a small theatre although the best thing is that you can wade in the water and let the dolphins swim around you.
Koombana Drive, Bunbury.
☎ *(08) 9791 3088.*
***Admission** $2.*
***Open** 8am-5pm daily.*

Donnybrook

Most backpackers visiting Donnybrook come between November and June for fruit picking work on the orchards that surround the town.

Practical Information
Donnybrook Visitor Information Centre
Old Railway Station, South West Highway, Donnybrook.
☎ *(08) 9731 1720.*
***Open** 10am-4pm daily.*

Western Australia

Accommodation
Brook Lodge

Brook Lodge is a very good workers hostel with all the usual facilities such as a kitchen, TV lounge and Internet access. The buildings and some facilities are a little old but it is a clean and well-run hostel with a great atmosphere.
3 Bridge Street, Donnybrook.
☎ *(08) 9731 1520.*
Website www.brooklodge.com.au.
Dorm bed *$17 per night, $100 per week;* **double room** *$40 per night, $220 per week.*
Reception open *Mon-Fri 9am-10.30am & 3.30pm-7pm, Sat-Sun 10am-11am & 1pm-5.30pm.*
▭

Maintenance & cleanliness	★★★⯨
Facilities	★★★
Atmosphere & character	★★★★★
Security	★
Overall rating	★★★⯨

Busselton

Busselton is a popular resort for families from Perth. It boasts good snorkelling from the 2km-long jetty.

Practical Information
Visitor Information Centre

38 Peel Terrace, Busselton.
☎ *(08) 9752 1288.*
Website www.downsouth.com.au.
Open *Mon-Fri 8.30am-5pm, Sat 9am-4pm, Sun 10am-3pm.*

Accommodation
Busselton Backpackers

Busselton Backpackers is a small friendly hostel in an old house near McDonald's. It has a good atmosphere but the furnishings are old and mismatched.
14 Peel Terrace, Busselton.
☎ *(08) 9754 2763.*
Website www.bsnbpk.com.
Dorm bed *$15-20;* **double room** *$30-45.*
Reception open *8am-1pm & 5pm-late.*

Maintenance & cleanliness	★★⯨
Facilities	★⯨
Atmosphere & character	★★★★
Security	★
Overall rating	★★⯨

Sights
Busselton Jetty

This is the longest wooden jetty in the southern hemisphere, with train rides taking you out to the end of the 2km jetty. There is good snorkelling off the jetty. There is also a small museum and an underwater observatory on the jetty.
Busselton Jetty, Busselton.
☎ *(08) 9754 3689.*
Admission *$2.50; train ride $7.50; underwater observatory $12.50.*
Open *Jan-Apr 8am-6pm daily; May-Nov 9am-5pm daily; Dec 8am-6pm daily.*

Dunsborough

Dunsborough is popular with divers who come here to dive the Swan shipwreck. Many travellers visit between September and December when it is a popular spot for whale watching. It is also a good base for surfing at Yallingup and exploring the Margaret River wine region.

Practical Information
Dunsborough Yallingup Tourist Bureau

Dunsborough Park Shopping Centre, Seymour Boulevard, Dunsborough.
☎ *(08) 9755 3299.*
Open *Mon-Fri 9am-5pm, Sat 9am-4pm, Sun 9.30am-4pm.*

Accommodation
Dunsborough Inn

This is an upmarket hostel that also doubles as a motel. It is very clean and facilities are excellent and include a large kitchen and a games room with table tennis and a TV.
50 Dunn Bay Road, Dunsborough.
☎ *(08) 9756 7277 or 1800 819 883.*
Dorm bed *$22.50-25;* **double room** *$45.*
Credit cards *Amex, Diners, MC, Visa.*
Reception open *7.30am-7pm daily.*
▭

Maintenance & cleanliness	★★★★★
Facilities	★★
Atmosphere & character	★★⯨
Security	★
Overall rating	★★★

Dunsborough Lodge
Dunsborough Lodge is a clean hostel in a relatively new building. It has a fully equipped kitchen and a lounge area with a pool table. However it has a sterile atmosphere.
13 Dunn Bay Road, Dunsborough.
☎ *(08) 9756 8866.*
Dorm bed** $17.60-19.80;* ***double room *$44-75.90;* ***twin room*** *$60.50-75.90.*
Credit cards *MC, Visa.*
🚗

Maintenance & cleanliness	★★★★★
Facilities	★☆
Atmosphere & character	★☆
Security	★★☆
Overall rating	★★★

Three Pines YHA Resort
This is a brilliant hostel with absolute beach frontage, 3km from the centre of Dunsborough. Facilities include a fully equipped kitchen, TV lounge, pool table and Internet access.
201-205 Geographe Bay Road, Quindalup, Dunsborough.
☎ *(08) 9755 3107.*
Dorm bed** $23.50 ($20 YHA);* ***single room *$33.50 ($30 YHA);* ***double/ twin room*** *$57 ($50 YHA).*
Credit cards *MC, Visa.*
***Reception open** 8am-11am & 5pm-9pm daily.*
🚗

Maintenance & cleanliness	★★★★☆
Facilities	★★☆
Atmosphere & character	★★★★★
Security	★☆
Overall rating	★★★★

Activities
Diving
The Swan shipwreck is the major attraction for divers to Dunsborough. There are several dive companies in town that organise trips to the wreck and who offer PADI dive courses. These include Bay Dive & Adventures *(26 Dunn Bay Road, Dunsborough;* ☎ *(08) 9756 8577)* and Cape Dive *(*☎ *(08) 9756 8778; **website** www.capedive.com).*

Surfing
Dunsborough is close to the excellent surf beaches at Yallingup, about 10km

from town. Yallingup Surf School *(*☎ *(08) 9755 2755)* can teach you to surf from $30 for one lesson or $80 for a three-day course.

Sights
Cape Naturaliste Lighthouse
This lighthouse, 13km from Dunsborough, features a small maritime museum and walking trails around the surrounding coastline.
Cape Naturaliste, 13km from Dunsborough.
☎ *(08) 9755 3955.*
***Admission** $7.*
***Open** 9.30am-4pm daily; tours depart every 30-45 minutes.*

Ngilgi Caves
This beautiful cave was discovered in 1899 and was the first cave in Western Australia to be open to the paying public. There are regular tours of the cave that last around 45-60 minutes.
Caves Road, Yallingup.
☎ *(08) 9755 2152.*
***Admission** $15.*
***Open** 9.30am-3.30pm daily.*

Quindalup Fauna Park
This fauna park has the usual assortment of Australian wildlife including kangaroos, wallabies, quokka, wombats and dingoes. It also features a butterfly enclosure and a natural light marine aquarium.
Corner Caves & Quindalup Siding Roads, Quindalup.
☎ *(08) 9755 3933.*
***Admission** $8.50.*
***Open** 9.30am-5pm daily.*

Margaret River
Margaret River is one of the most popular destinations in Western Australia's southwest. It has a perfect location with easy access of forests and beaches and lies at the heart of the state's top wine-growing and gourmet dining region.

Practical Information
Margaret River Visitor Information Centre
Corner Bussell Highway & Tunnbridge Street, Margaret River.

☎ *(08) 9757 2911.*
Website www.margaretriver.com.
Open 9am-5pm daily.

Coming & Going
There are daily buses to Perth although it is best to have a car to explore the area around Margaret River. Buses stop outside the tourist information centre.

Accommodation
Inne Town Backpackers
This is the most centrally located hostel in Margaret River. It is a small place in an older building that sleeps around 40 people. Facilities include an outdoor area with a pool table, barbecue and spit, plus a TV lounge with a fireplace and a nice sunny deck. It has a friendly laid-back atmosphere.
93 Bussell Highway, Margaret River.
☎ *(08) 9757 3698 or 1800 244 115.*
Dorm bed *$19;* **double room** *$50.*
Reception open *8am-11am & 3pm-9pm daily.*

Maintenance & cleanliness	★★☆
Facilities	★★
Atmosphere & character	★★★★
Security	★
Overall rating	★★☆

Margaret River Lodge YHA
Margaret River Lodge is the biggest hostel in town and there's a good atmosphere and plenty of facilities. The place has everything including a vegetable garden, pool table, swimming pool and a barbecue area. It's about a five-minute walk into the centre of town.
220 Railway Terrace, Margaret River.
☎ *(08) 9757 9532.*
Website www.mrlodge.com.au.
Dorm bed *$22.50-30.50 ($19-27 YHA);* **single room** *$43 ($39.50 YHA);* **double room** *$70 ($63 YHA);* **twin room** *$60 ($53 YHA).*
Credit cards *MC, Visa.*
Reception open *8.30am-11am & 2pm-7.30pm daily.*

Maintenance & cleanliness	★★★★
Facilities	★★★
Atmosphere & character	★★★★☆
Security	★
Overall rating	★★★★☆

Smiffy's Margaret River Retreat
Smiffy's caters mostly to school groups, but it is a good alternative is the other hostels in Margaret Rivers are booked up. It is a clean and well-maintained hostel, but the dormitories are larger than usual.
343 Bussell Highway, Forrest Grove.
☎ *(08) 9757 7419.*
Dorm bed *$25.*
Credit cards *Amex, MC, Visa.*

Maintenance & cleanliness	★★★☆
Facilities	★★☆
Atmosphere & character	★
Security	★
Overall rating	★★

Surf Point Resort
Surf Point Resort is a luxury hostel that also doubles as a resort. Everything here is new and sparkling clean. It features a huge, well equipped kitchen plus a nice barbecue area. It is well located if you want to be near the beach, which is only 300 metres away, but it's 10km from Margaret River town.
Reidle Drive, Gnaralbup Beach, Margaret River.
☎ *(08) 9757 1777 or 1800 071 777.*
Website www.surfpoint.com.au.
Dorm bed *$22-24;* **double room** *$60-89.*
Credit cards *MC, Visa.*
Reception open *8am-12.30pm & 4pm-7.30pm daily.*

Maintenance & cleanliness	★★★★★
Facilities	★★☆
Atmosphere & character	★★★★☆
Security	★
Overall rating	★★★★

Augusta

Augusta is near Cape Leeuwin at the southern extremity of the Margaret River region. It is close to some good beaches and can also be used as a base for exploring the Margaret River wine region.

Practical Information
Augusta Visitor Centre
75 Blackwood Avenue, Augusta.
☎ *(08) 9758 0166.*

Open Mon-Fri 9am-5pm, Sat-Sun 9am-1pm.

Accommodation
Baywatch Manor Resort YHA
This is a very clean hostel with top quality fittings. It has been rated as Australia's top YHA hostel for six years and it has a big fully equipped kitchen, TV lounge and Internet access.
88 Blackwood Avenue, Augusta.
☎ *(08) 9758 1290.*
Website www.baywatchmanor.com.au.
Dorm bed $23.50 ($20 YHA); double/twin room $57 ($50 YHA).
Credit cards MC, Visa.
Reception open 7.30am-10pm daily.

Maintenance & cleanliness	★★★★★
Facilities	★★✫
Atmosphere & character	★★✫
Security	★★★
Overall rating	★★★★✫

Leeuwin House
This small hostel is a very clean and well-maintained place with shiny polished floorboards. It has made up beds with real mattresses but there isn't much atmosphere.
Blackwood Avenue, Augusta.
☎ *(08) 9758 1944.*
Website www.augusta-resorts.com.au.
Dorm bed $18-22; double room $46-54; twin room $44-52.
Credit cards Amex, Diners, JCB, MC, Visa.
Reception open 7.30am-7.30pm daily.

Maintenance & cleanliness	★★★★★
Facilities	★
Atmosphere & character	★★
Security	★★
Overall rating	★★★

Pemberton

This small timber town in the heart of tall timber country makes an excellent base for exploring the surrounding area. It is close to both the Beedelup and Warren National Parks, which have some rewarding hiking trails.

Most of Pemberton's attractions are out of town so it is essential to have your own car.

Practical Information
Visitor Information Centre
Brockman Street, Pemberton.
☎ *(08) 9776 1133.*
Open 9am-5pm daily.

Department of Conservation & Land Management (CALM)
Kennedy Street, Pemberton.
☎ *(08) 9776 1207.*
Website www.calm.wa.gov.au.
Open Mon-Fri 8am-5pm.

Accommodation
Pemberton Backpackers YHA
Pemberton Backpackers YHA is a centrally located youth hostel in an old building dating from the 1920s. It is clean and features the usual amenities such as a TV lounge and a small kitchen.
7 Brockman Street, Pemberton.
☎ *(08) 9776 1105.*
Dorm bed $19 ($17 YHA); double room $53 ($49 YHA); twin room $42 ($38 YHA).
Credit cards MC, Visa.
Reception open 8am-8.30pm daily.

Maintenance & cleanliness	★★★
Facilities	★★
Atmosphere & character	★★★★
Security	★
Overall rating	★★★

Pemberton Forest Stay
Pemberton Forest Stay consists of self-contained cottages set on 17 acres of bush land. It is a relaxing spot with a beach volleyball court and a barbecue hut that serves as a communal kitchen. There's also an enclosure with five kangaroos. It is located 9km outside Pemberton.
Stirling Road, Pemberton.
☎ *(08) 9776 1153.*
Dorm bed $17; single room $25; double/twin room $45.
Credit cards MC, Visa.
Reception open 8am-8pm daily.

Maintenance & cleanliness	★★✫
Facilities	★★
Atmosphere & character	★★✫
Security	★
Overall rating	★★✫

Sights
Gloucester Tree
This is the biggest attraction in Pemberton. The staircase built around the tree allows you to climb 61 metres above the forest. The view is great and it is a fantastic experience.
Burma Road, Pemberton.

Dave Evans Bicentennial Tree
Although it is a bit further from Pemberton, at more than 70 metres this tree is even taller.
Warren National Park, 10km south of Pemberton.

Walpole & Walpole-Nornalup National Park

This is another popular destination on the tall trees route. Walpole is on the south coast on the way between Pemberton and Denmark, with the Walpole-Nornalup National Park located 14km out of town.

The park is famous for its tree top walk where you can walk 40m above the forest floor.

Practical Information
Walpole-Nornalup Visitors Centre
South Coast Highway, Walpole
☎ *(08) 9840 1111*
Open *Mon-Fri 9am-5pm, Sat-Sun 9am-4pm.*

Accommodation
Tingle All Over YHA
This is an older, more established hostel with a more lived in feel than Walpole Backpackers. The décor looks a bit tired, but it is clean and the rooms have made up beds.
Corner Inlet & Nockolds Streets, Walpole.
☎ *(08) 9840 1041.*
Dorm bed *$23.50 ($20 YHA);* **single room** *$39.50 ($36 YHA);* **double/twin room** *$57 ($50 YHA).*
Credit cards *MC, Visa.*
Reception open *8am-10am & 2pm-10pm daily.*

Maintenance & cleanliness	★★☆
Facilities	★☆
Atmosphere & character	★★
Security	★
Overall rating	★★

Walpole Backpackers
Walpole Backpackers is a clean hostel with a fully equipped kitchen and a big backyard with a barbecue. It has a good atmosphere and the manager is very knowledgeable about things to see and do in the region.
Pier Street, Walpole.
☎ *(08) 9840 1244.*
Website *www.walpolebackpackers.com.*
Dorm bed *$22 ($20 VIP, $21 YHA);* **single room** *$40 ($37 VIP, $38 YHA);* **double/twin room** *$$54-64 ($50-60 VIP, $52-62 YHA).*
Credit cards *MC, Visa.*
Reception open *9am-12.30pm & 3.30pm-9pm daily.*

Maintenance & cleanliness	★★★☆
Facilities	★★☆
Atmosphere & character	★★★★
Security	★★
Overall rating	★★★

Sights
Valley of the Giants Tree Top Walk
The Tree Top Walk offers a unique perspective where you can look 40 metres down from up among the trees. This is the main reason most people visit the national park.
Walpole-Nornalup National Park.
☎ *(08) 9840 8263.*
Website *www.calm.wa.gov.au/tourism/valley_of_the_giants.html.*
Admission *$6.*
Open *9am-5pm daily.*

South Coast

The South Coast of Western Australia is home to Albany, the state's oldest city, the seaside city of Esperance and a wild untouched coastline.

If you're driving across the country when you get to Norseman, you have the choice of heading to Perth via Kalgoorlie or south via Esperance, Albany and the southwest. Take the southern route – sure you'll miss out on a unique outback mining town, but you'll gain by experiencing the wild southern coast before heading up to Perth through the forested southwest corner of Western Australia.

Albany

Established in 1826, two years before Perth, Albany was the first city in Western Australia to be settled by Europeans. The city has some beautiful old buildings dating from colonial times and has a spectacular location within close range of dense forests and stunning beaches. Once a major centre for the whaling industry, whale watching is now one of Albany's big attractions.

Practical Information
Visitors Information Centre
Old Railway Station, Proudlove Parade, Albany.
☎ *(08) 9841 1088.*
Website *www.albanytourist.com.au.*
Open *9am-5pm daily.*

Coming & Going
If you're not driving, the bus is the best way to get into town even though the services are fairly infrequent. Buses arrive at the information centre in the old train station on Lower Stirling Terrace. Buses run from here to Esperance and Perth via Bunbury, Margaret River and other destinations in the southwest.

Local Transport
Loves Bus Service runs local buses around town. There are a couple of handy routes although Albany is small enough to walk around.

Accommodation
Albany Backpackers
This hostel is in a big old building, which is painted inside with lots of colourful murals. It is clean and facilities include a big kitchen, TV lounge, pool table and Internet access. There's also a small barbecue area. The management do a lot for their guests and offer freebies like free coffee and cake and cheap cooked dinners.
Corner Stirling Terrace & Spencer Street, Albany.

☎ *(08) 9842 5255.*
Website *www.albanybackpackers.com .au.*
Dorm bed *$23 ($20 ISIC/Nomads/ VIP/YHA);* **single room** *$40 ($36 ISIC/Nomads/VIP/YHA);* **double/ twin room** *$58 ($55 ISIC/Nomads/ VIP/YHA).*
Credit cards *MC, Visa.*
Reception open *8am-9pm daily.*

Maintenance & cleanliness	★★★★
Facilities	★★☆
Atmosphere & character	★★★★
Security	★★
Overall rating	★★★★☆

Bayview YHA Hostel
Bayview Backpackers YHA is a comfortable hostel on a quiet street near the city centre. It is clean with the usual kitchen, TV lounge, Internet access and barbecue facilities.
49 Duke Street, Albany.
☎ *(08) 9842 3388.*
Dorm bed *$23.50 ($20 YHA);* **double/twin room** *$57 ($50 YHA); includes breakfast.*
Credit cards *MC, Visa.*
Reception open *8am-11am & 3pm-9pm daily.*

Maintenance & cleanliness	★★★☆
Facilities	★★
Atmosphere & character	★★★☆
Security	★
Overall rating	★★★

Blue Water Accommodation
This hostel is in the old London Hotel and it has a small kitchen and a cosy TV lounge, but the overall standard isn't as high as the other two hostels in Albany.
160 Stirling Terrace, Albany.
☎ *(08) 9841 6599.*
Website *www.bluewaterwa.com.au.*
Dorm bed *$17;* **double room** *$50-55.*
Credit cards *MC, Visa.*
Reception open *8am-noon & 2pm-9pm daily.*

Maintenance & cleanliness	★★☆
Facilities	★
Atmosphere & character	★★
Security	★
Overall rating	★★☆

Sights
Whaleworld
Albany was home to Australia's last whaling station, which ceased business as recently as 1978. It has now been turned into the country's largest whaling museum. There are two guided tours a day that show you things that aren't on display in the museum.
Frenchmans Bay Road, Albany.
☎ *(08) 9844 4021.*
Website www.whaleworld.org
Admission $15.
Open 8.30am-6pm daily.

Whale Watching
Southern Ocean Charters (☎ *0409 107 180*) run whale-watching trips between May and October.

Denmark
Denmark doesn't have a lot of attractions, although it is a pleasant place to stop over for the night.

Practical Information
Denmark Visitor Centre
Corner Bent & Strickland Streets, Denmark.
☎ *(08) 9848 2055.*
Website www.denmarkvisitorcentre.com.au.
Open 9am-5pm daily.

Accommodation
Blue Wren Backpackers
The Blue Wren is a clean centrally located hostel with good facilities that include a fully equipped kitchen with an espresso machine plus a cosy TV lounge and a barbecue.
17 Prince Street, Denmark.
☎ *(08) 9848 3300.*
Website http://bluewren.batcave.net.
Dorm bed $22.50 ($19 YHA); double room $61 ($54 YHA); twin room $55 ($48 YHA); includes breakfast.
Reception open 8am-10am & 4pm-8pm daily.

Maintenance & cleanliness	★★★★☆
Facilities	★★
Atmosphere & character	★★★★
Security	★
Overall rating	★★★☆

Mt Barker & Porongurup National Park
Not far to the north of Albany is Mt Barker, a small town in the midst of a wine producing area. Not only does Mt Barker offer wine tasting, but it is also an ideal base for exploring the nearby Porongurup National Park.

Dating more than a billion years, the nearby Porongurups are said to be the oldest hills in the world. The national park features a lush forest of tall karri and colourful wildflowers. There are also some interesting rock formations and walking trails in the park.

Practical Information
Mount Barker Tourist Bureau
Unit 6, Lot 622, Albany Highway, Mount Barker.
☎ *(08) 9851 1163.*
Open Mon-Fri 9am-5pm, Sat 9am-3pm, Sun 10am-3pm.

Accommodation
Chill Out Backpackers
Staying at this tiny hostel is like staying over at someone's house. There is a maximum of only 10 people and the biggest shared room has only two beds. The hostel is a new A-frame house with first class facilities including a spa bath. It's one of Australia's best small hostels.
79 Hassell Street, Mount Barker.
☎ *(08) 9851 2798.*
Dorm bed $20-22; single room $25; double room $50.

Maintenance & cleanliness	★★★★★
Facilities	★★
Atmosphere & character	★★★★
Security	★
Overall rating	★★★☆

Esperance
Esperance is remote. It is more than 700km from Perth, 500km from Albany and a four-hour drive from Kalgoorlie. Given it's location it is surprising that Esperance would be such a popular tourist destination but then maybe it's the beautiful beaches and top

diving sites and the fact in Australia's largest state, a 700km drive isn't considered all that long.

Practical Information
Visitor Information Centre
Corner Dempster & Kemp Streets, Esperance.
☎ *(08) 9071 2330.*
Open *Mon-Sat 9am-5pm, Sun 10am-4.30pm.*

Coming & Going
Although the bus service is infrequent it is the best way to get in and out of Esperance. Buses to Albany, Kalgoorlie and Perth stop at the bus station at the corner of Dempster and Kemp Streets.

Accommodation
Blue Waters Lodge YHA
Esperance's YHA hostel is in a big building that shows its age. There's a big common room with a fireplace, TV and pool table and also a nice backyard barbecue area. It has friendly staff and a nice location near the seafront.
299 Goldfields Road, Esperance.
☎ *(08) 9071 1040.*
Dorm bed *$21.50 ($18 YHA);* **single room** *$33.50 ($30 YHA);* **double/twin room** *$55 ($48 YHA).*
Credit cards *MC, Visa.*
Reception open *8am-10am & 5pm-10pm daily.*

🚗	
Maintenance & cleanliness	★★
Facilities	★★
Atmosphere & character	★★★
Security	★
Overall rating	★★

Esperance Backpackers
Esperance Backpackers is a small clean hostel with a nice TV lounge with a fireplace and Internet access. There's also a kitchen and a barbecue area out the back. This hostel organises fishing trips.
14 Emily Street, Esperance.
☎ *(08) 9071 4724.*
Dorm bed *$20 ($18 Nomads/VIP/YHA);* **double room** *$48 ($45 Nomads/VIP/YHA).*
Credit cards *MC, Visa.*
Reception open *7.30am-11am & 4pm-9pm daily.*

🚗	
Maintenance & cleanliness	★★★★
Facilities	★★
Atmosphere & character	★★★
Security	★★
Overall rating	★★★

Esperance Guest House
This small clean hostel was undergoing renovation when we visited and it has nice rooms, but the areas that weren't yet renovated were a bit rough around the edges. It has a friendly management and guests have free use of bicycles.
23 Daphne Street, Esperance.
☎ *(08) 9071 3396.*
Dorm bed *$25;* **double room** *$45-60;* **twin room** *$50; includes breakfast.*
Reception open *8am-10pm daily.*

🚗	
Maintenance & cleanliness	★★★
Facilities	★★★
Atmosphere & character	★★★
Security	★★
Overall rating	★★★

Kalgoorlie
The gold mining town of Kalgoorlie once drew fortune seekers from around the globe to the Golden Mile, the world's richest square mile of gold-bearing earth. Kalgoorlie-Boulder is still a thriving mining town and the first sizable town you come to if you're driving across the Nullarbor.

Kal is an interesting place if you haven't been to an outback mining town before and there are a few grand old buildings along Hannan Street. There are also some good pubs, although there are also some that are worth avoiding.

Despite the rough and ready image there is plenty to see in Kalgoorlie and it is well worth stopping here, particularly if you're just spent the last 30 hours on the bus from Adelaide. The city's attractions are mostly related to the mining industry and include Hannans North Historic Mining Reserve and the impressive super pit, but Kalgoorlie doesn't have as much to offer as some other outback mining towns such as Broken Hill.

Practical Information
Visitor Information Centre
250 Hannan Street, Kalgoorlie.
☎ *(08) 9021 1966.*
***Open** 9am-5pm daily.*

Coming & Going
Kalgoorlie has plenty of transport options with frequent connections to both Adelaide and Perth.

AIR
There are direct flights to Adelaide and Perth but flying here is not as popular as it once was. The airport is about five minutes from the centre of town and the two hostels should pick you up if you have made a reservation.

BUS
McCafferty's/Greyhound run a daily service to Adelaide and Perth; Gold-fields Express also runs buses to Perth. Transwa buses go between Kalgoorlie and Esperance. Buses stop outside the tourist information centre on St Barbara's Square near the corner of Cassidy and Hannan Streets.

TRAIN
Kalgoorlie is well served by rail services. The *Indian-Pacific* is one of Australia's greatest rail journeys running between Perth and Sydney with a stop in Kalgoorlie. If you don't have a Great Southern Rail pass, Transwa's daily *Prospector* service to Perth is a cheaper alternative at $59.50 one-way. The train station is on Forrest Street opposite the intersection with Wilson Street.

Local Transport
There is a local bus service that runs between Boulder and Kalgoorlie; this is generally the best way to get around if you don't have access to a car.

Accommodation
Both Kalgoorlie's hostels are situated in the heart of the red light district and are a short walk to supermarkets and the town centre.

Golddust Backpackers Hostel
Everything is clean and well maintained at Kalgoorlie's best hostel. Amenities include several TV lounges, a games room with a pool table and Internet access, a swimming pool and a barbecue area. Guests have free use of bicycles.
192 Hay Street, Kalgoorlie.
☎ *(08) 9091 3737.*
***Dorm bed** $18 ($17 ISIC/Nomads/ VIP/YHA);* ***double/twin room** $45 ($40 ISIC/Nomads/VIP/YHA).*
***Credit cards** MC, Visa.*
***Reception open** Mon-Fri 8am-late, Sat-Sun 9am-late.*
🚗

Maintenance & cleanliness	★★★★½
Facilities	★★★★½
Atmosphere & character	★★★★½
Security	★★½
Overall rating	★★★★

Kalgoorlie Backpackers YHA
Kal's YHA is a little rough around the edges but it has good facilities including a swimming pool plus the usual kitchen and TV lounge.
166 Hay Street, Kalgoorlie.
☎ *(08) 9091 1482.*
***Website** www.kalgoorliebackpackers. info.*
***Dorm bed** $20 ($18 YHA);* ***single room** $30 ($28 YHA);* ***double/twin room** $50 ($46 YHA).*
***Credit cards** MC, Visa.*
***Reception open** 5pm-9pm daily.*
🚗

Maintenance & cleanliness	★★½
Facilities	★★★½
Atmosphere & character	★★★½
Security	★★½
Overall rating	★★

Sights
Mining Hall of Fame
This excellent museum focuses on all aspects of mining encompassing geology, the history of mining and its impact on Kalgoorlie, and modern-day mining techniques. The Mining Hall of Fame sits on an original mine that commenced in 1893 when miners used only a pick and shovel. Gold panning and gold pouring demonstrations take place throughout the day as do underground tours of the mine.
Goldfields Highway, Kalgoorlie.
☎ *(08) 9091 4074.*
***Website** www.mininghall.com.*

Admission $20.
Open 9am-4.30pm; gold panning 9.30am, 1pm, 4.10pm; gold pouring demonstrations 11am, 1.30pm, 3pm; underground tours 10am, noon, 2pm, 3.20pm.

Museum of the Goldfields
This museum provides a good introduction to the city's history and life during the height of the gold rush.
17 Hannan Street, Kalgoorlie.
☎ *(08) 9021 8533.*
Admission by gold coin ($1 or $2).
Open 10am-4.30pm daily.

Super Pit
The biggest hole in the Southern Hemisphere is worth a look. The massive Super Pit open cut mine can be seen from the lookout in Outram Street in Fimiston near Boulder or from the Golden Mile Loopline. Alternatively you can take a 20-minute scenic flight over the Pit, which also lets you see Kal from a different perspective.
Super Pit Lookout, Outram Street, Fimiston; Golden Mile Loopline, Corner Burt & Hamilton Streets, Boulder.
Admission free for the lookout, $12 for a ride on the Golden Mile Loopline, around $30 for a 20-minute scenic flight.

Batavia Coast
Heading north from Perth, the Batavia Coast is basically the first day of driving and includes Nambung National Park, better known for the Pinnacles Desert as well as Geraldton and Kalbarri.

Cervantes & Nanbung National Park
Nanbung National Park is best known for the spectacular Pinnacles Desert and its proximity to Perth makes it a very popular day-trip. The main features of the Pinnacles Desert are the limestone columns, some of which stand up to four metres tall.

If you have a car you can take the scenic drive that takes you past the more impressive areas. If you don't have access to a car, a number of companies run day-trips here from Perth and Happyday Tours (☎ *(08) 9652 7244)* meets the bus at Cervantes, which is the closest town to the national park. It is here that you'll find accommodation, food and other services.

Accommodation
Pinnacles Beach Backpackers
This is a brilliant purpose-built hostel. Everything is brand new and the facilities include a cosy lounge, fully equipped kitchen, laundry and very clean bathrooms.
91 Seville Street, Cervantes.
☎ *(08) 9652 7377 or 1800 245 232.*
Website www.wn.com.au/ pbbackpackers/.
Dorm bed $20; double room $55-80.
🚗 ♿

Maintenance & cleanliness	★★★★★
Facilities	★★☆
Atmosphere & character	★★★★☆
Security	★★☆
Overall rating	★★★★☆

Geraldton
The state's third largest city is a busy cray fishing and mining town that doesn't go out of its way to appeal to tourists.

It is a pleasant place with enough attractions to keep you occupied for a day and it is a good spot to stay the night if you're driving up the coast. Geraldton is also a popular windsurfing destination and a departure point for trips to the Houtman Abrolhos Islands.

Practical Information
Visitor Information Centre
Corner Bayly Street & Chapman Road, Geraldton.
☎ *(08) 9921 3999.*
Website www.geraldtontourist.com.au.
Open Mon-Fri 8.30am-5pm, Sat 9am-4.30pm, Sun 9.30am-4.30pm

Coming & Going
McCafferty's/Greyhound and Integrity Coachlines all run regular buses between Geraldton and Perth and also north to Exmouth and Broome.

Coaches terminate at the tourist information centre in front of Batavia Backpackers.

Local Transport

Although central Geraldton is small enough to walk around, there is a good network of local bus routes that are a cheap and easy way to get around town.

Fares are $1.80 for 90 minutes of travel anywhere on the system or $2.50 for an all-day ticket.

Route 800, the City Clipper, is a circular route that takes in most of the city centre. Route 800 is a free service, as are any buses that run between Northgate Shopping Centre and Anzac Terrace.

Accommodation

Batavia Backpackers

This hostel is clean and provides all the basic facilities. It is in a beautiful heritage building that was originally a hospital and now also houses the visitor information centre.
Corner Chapman Road & Bayly Street, Geraldton.
☎ *(08) 9964 3001.*
***Dorm bed** $17 ($16 VIP/YHA);*
***double room** $40 ($38 VIP/YHA).*
Not yet rated

Foreshore Backpackers YHA

This hostel is in an old building in the town centre. The standard of the amenities isn't the best and the furnishings are old and nothing seems to match.
172 Marine Terrace, Geraldton.
☎ *(08) 9921 3275.*
***Dorm bed** $21.50 ($18 YHA); **single room** $30.50 ($27 YHA); **double/ twin room** $49 ($42 YHA).*
***Credit cards** MC, Visa.*
***Reception open** 8am-9pm daily.*
Not yet rated

Freemasons' Hotel

The "Freo" consists of accommodation above a pub in the centre of town. Shared facilities include a small TV room with a microwave and kettle. The pub downstairs has live music on Thursday, Friday and Saturday nights and it can get noisy.
79 Marine Terrace, Geraldton.

☎ *(08) 9964 3457.*
***Dorm bed** $20; **double/twin room** $40-65.*
***Reception open** Mon-Sat 11am-midnight, Sun 11am-10pm.*
Not yet rated

Sights

Museum of Western Australia

The Geraldton branch of the Museum of Western Australia has exhibits about local history and wildlife with an excellent shipwreck gallery and a cinema that shows an interesting film about the shipwreck and mutiny of the *Batavia*.
Marine Terrace, Geraldton.
☎ *(08) 9921 5080.*
***Admission** by donation.*
***Open** 10am-4pm daily.*

St Francis Xavier Cathedral

Although nothing special by European standards, this cathedral is particularly impressive for a small Australian town. It was designed by Monsignor Hawes and it is regarded as one of the best historic churches in the country.
Corner Cathedral Avenue & Maitland Street, Geraldton.
***Admission** free.*
***Tours** Mon 10am, Fri 2pm.*

Sydney Memorial

Located on Mount Scott near the city centre, the HMAS Sydney Memorial features a dome sculptured from 645 silver gulls, each one representing one of the crew that lost their lives when the navy ship sank in 1941.

Kalbarri & Kalbarri National Park

Two Dutch sailors involved in the *Batavia* mutiny on the nearby Houtman Abrolhos Islands were marooned near Kalbarri, making them Australia's earliest European residents. Kalbarri doesn't make a big deal of its history and instead is just a pleasant beach town that is a handy base for exploring nearby Kalbarri National Park.

During spring, Kalbarri is a popular spot for whale watching and dolphin spotting.

The national park features 80km of gorges and there are some very good hiking trails ranging from the easy Z Bend hike (500m) that goes to a rock lookout with views to the Murchison River. Longer walks include the Coastal Trail (8km, 3-5 hours) that takes in coastal views from the cliff tops between Eagle Gorge and Natural Bridge.

Visitors should be very cautious while hiking in the gorge areas and park rangers recommend that you undertake the longer walks in groups of at least five.

Practical Information
Kalbarri Tourist Bureau
Grey Street, Kalbarri.
☎ *(08) 9937 1104 or 1800 639 468.*
Website www.kalbarriwa.info.
Open 9am-5pm daily

Department of Conservation & Land Management (CALM)
Ajana Kalbarri Road, Kalbarri.
☎ *(08) 9937 1140.*
Website www.calm.wa.gov.au.
Open Mon-Fri 8am-5pm.

Coming & Going
Buses terminate outside the tourist information centre on Grey Street. Both McCafferty's/Greyhound and Transwa operate buses between Kalbarri and Perth, while McCafferty's/Greyhound buses also head north to Carnarvon.

Accommodation
Kalbarri Backpackers
This is a clean hostel with Internet access, a fully equipped kitchen and a TV lounge. Outside there's a nice shady barbecue area and a swimming pool.
52 Mortimer Street, Kalbarri.
☎ *(08) 9937 1430.*
Dorm bed $19 ($18 YHA); double/ twin room $46 ($44 YHA).
Credit cards MC, Visa.
Reception open 8.30am-8pm daily.
Not yet rated

Central Coast
The central Western Australian coast includes Monkey Mia at Shark Bay,

which is famous for its dolphins, and Coral Bay and Exmouth with their easy access to excellent diving and snorkelling on the Ningaloo Reef.

If you're driving up the coast, this region basically covers the second day of driving after leaving Perth.

Shark Bay & Monkey Mia
Shark Bay is actually a couple of bays encompassed by two narrow peninsulas. The main attraction here is the tiny settlement of Monkey Mia that is famed for its dolphin visits.

The main town in the region is Denham, on the western side of the Peron Peninsula. Denham is really the main centre for travellers visiting Monkey Mia, 25km away on the other side of the peninsula. Denham is where you'll find most accommodation as well as a supermarket, bakery and a couple of restaurants.

Monkey Mia's main attraction is the dolphins that visit the beach every morning between 8am and 10am. What makes Monkey Mia special is that the dolphins here are especially tame.

Shark Bay is also known for its dugongs. Around 10,000, or around 10% of the world's dugong population, are estimated to live in Shark Bay.

Facilities at Monkey Mia are fairly basic although it is possible to stay here as the Monkey Mia Dolphin Resort has backpacker accommodation. There's also a small general store but it's expensive and you're better off bringing your food in from Denham.

Practical Information
Visitor Information Centre
71 Knight Terrace, Denham.
☎ *(08) 9948 1253.*
Open 9am-6pm daily.

Department of Conservation & Land Management (CALM)
67 Knight Terrace, Denham.
☎ *(08) 9948 1208.*
Website www.calm.wa.gov.au.
Open Mon-Fri 8am-5pm.

Coming & Going

McCafferty's/Greyhound's Perth-Broome-Darwin service stops at the Overlander Roadhouse 150km from Monkey Mia where a shuttle bus runs to Denham and Monkey Mia.

Virtually all backpacker buses heading up the coast call into Monkey Mia.

Local Transport

There is a limited bus service between Denham and Monkey Mia that leaves Denham at 8am giving you time to play with the dolphins with a return service around midday. The youth hostel in Denham also runs a shuttle bus for their guests.

Accommodation

Bay Lodge YHA

This is a fantastic hostel in a former motel with self-contained units. It's very clean with a swimming pool and free transfers to see the dolphins at Monkey Mia.

95 Knight Terrace, Denham.
☎ *(08) 9948 1278.*
***Dorm bed** $23.50 ($20 YHA);* ***single room** $53.50-68.50 ($50-65 YHA);* ***double/twin room** $57-72 ($50-65 YHA).*
***Credit cards** MC, Visa.*
***Reception open** 8am-10pm daily.*
Not yet rated

Monkey Mia Dolphin Resort YHA

The Monkey Mia Dolphin Resort is very close to the beach and offers basic accommodation in big tents that sleep 8-10 people.

Monkey Mia Road, Monkey Mia.
☎ *(08) 9948 1320.*
***Website** www.monkeymia.com.au.*
***Dorm bed** $22 ($18.50 YHA);* ***single room** $37.50 ($34 YHA);* ***double/twin room** $55 ($48 YHA).*
***Credit cards** MC, Visa.*
***Reception open** 7am-8pm daily.*
Not yet rated

Carnarvon

Carnarvon is a busy regional centre that serves the surrounding farming areas. The town also has a fishing industry. There isn't a lot to see or do here although it's worth a stop for an hour or so if you're driving along the coast.

Backpackers who do stop off here are attracted by the availability of work on banana plantations during the winter.

Practical Information

Visitors Information Centre

11 Robinson Street, Carnarvon.
☎ *(08) 9941 1146.*
***Open** Mon-Fri 8.30am-5pm, Sat 8am-noon.*

Coming & Going

Carnarvon has daily buses to Perth, Exmouth and Broome, they stop at the Civic Centre.

Accommodation

Carnarvon Backpackers

This hostel caters mostly to travellers staying here for work. The place is set in two old houses and it has a good games area and barbecue area.

97-99 Olivia Terrace, Carnarvon.
☎ *(08) 9941 1095.*
***Dorm bed** $18-20;* ***double room** $47.*
Not yet rated

Coral Bay

Just 1½ hour south of Exmouth, Coral Bay is a fantastic spot for snorkelling. The Ningaloo Reef at Coral Bay is very close to the shore and it is possible to swim out from the beach.

The small town is also a good spot to see whalesharks. These 18-metre-long fish are the world's largest. They arrive on the reef in April, but you must travel out past the reef with a licenced operator to snorkel with them.

Each year between October and February, around 200 reef sharks visit an area 1km from the main beach at Coral Bay.

Coming & Going

McCafferty's/Greyhound's Perth-Exmouth service stops at the Ningaloo Club in Coral Bay, but this service doesn't run every day.

You can also visit Coral Bay via Exmouth. Exmouth Bus Charters (☎ *(08) 9949 4623)* operates a bus service for $30 one-way or $50 return, but services are sometimes cancelled if there is not sufficient demand.

Accommodation
Coral Bay Backpackers

Coral Bay Backpackers is part of the Ningaloo Reef Resort/Coral Bay Hotel complex and guests have full use of resort facilities including the bar, games room and swimming pool. Accommodation is in small dorms. It is the closest hostel to the beach and there is a nice view of the bay.
Robinson Street, Coral Bay.
☎ *(08) 9942 5934.*
Dorm bed *$16.50.*
Reception open *7.30am-midnight daily.*
Not yet rated

Ningaloo Club

This modern hostel has excellent facilities that include a swimming pool, café, TV lounge with pool table, Internet access and a barbecue area.
46 Robinson Street, Coral Bay.
☎ *(08) 9948 5100.*
Website *www.ningalooclub.com.*
Dorm bed *$18-22;* **double room** *$60-85;* **twin room** *$60-65.*
Credit cards *MC, Visa.*
Not yet rated

Exmouth

Exmouth is the main destination on the west coast between Monkey Mia and Broome. The main attraction here is the excellent diving afforded by easy access to the Ningaloo Reef. It is also a great place to see whales, turtles and whalesharks.

There are several places where you can do a dive course. Expect to pay around $250 for a four-day PADI course.

Practical Information
Visitor Information Centre
Murat Road, Exmouth.
☎ *(08) 9949 1176.*
Open *8.30am-5pm daily.*

Department of Conservartion & Land Management (CALM)
Nimitz Street, Exmouth.
☎ *(08) 9949 1676.*

Website *www.calm.wa.gov.au.*
Open *Mon-Fri 8am-5pm.*

Coming & Going

There are several McCafferty's/Greyhound buses a week between Perth and Exmouth. On days when there isn't a direct bus, you need to get off at the Girala turn-off where a minibus will be waiting to take you into Exmouth. Coaches depart from the tourist office on Murat Road.

Accommodation
Excape Backpackers

Excape Backpackers is part of the Potshot Hotel complex and it features a good bar and swimming pool but the big blue building with the accommodation doesn't have a great deal of character.
Corner Payne Street & Murat Road, Exmouth.
☎ *1800 655 156.*
Dorm bed *$19;* **twin room** *$55.*
Reception open 8am-6pm daily.
Not yet rated

Marina Beach Retreat

This is a very nice resort-style place with dormitories in raised tent-like cabins with a balcony at the front and doubles in safari tents. The hostel features an observation deck for whale watching plus a swimming pool, bar and TV lounge. It is 4km south of the town centre, which is a 25-minute walk along the beach. The beachside setting makes it a more relaxing place to stay compared with the other hostels in town.
50 Market Street, Exmouth.
☎ *(08) 9949 1500.*
Website *www.ningaloochase.com.au.*
Dorm bed *$22-24;* **double room** *$44-165.*
Not yet rated

Petes Exmouth Backpackers YHA

This is part of the Exmouth Cape Tourist Village and accommodation is in air-conditioned portacabins. Shared facilities include a swimming pool and an outdoor kitchen area with barbecues.
Corner Truscott Crescent & Murat Road, Exmouth.

☎ *(08) 9949 1101 or 1800 621 101.*
***Dorm bed** $20;* ***single room** $28;*
***double/twin room** $48.*
***Credit cards** MC, Visa.*
***Reception open** 7am-7pm daily.*
Not yet rated

Winston's Backpackers

Winston's is part of the Ningaloo Caravan Park. It is a clean place that features a swimming pool and a barbecue area. It's located across the road from the tourist information centre.
Murat Road, Exmouth.
☎ *(08) 9949 2377.*
***Dorm bed** $19.50;* ***double room** $60.*

Ningaloo Marine Park & Cape Range National Park

Although smaller and not as well known as the Great Barrier Reef in Queensland, the Ningaloo Reef is much closer to the shore and offers much the same attraction for divers.

The Marine Park stretches for 250km and includes 250 different species of coral and over 500 different types of fish. Diving here is fantastic, and the easy access to the reef makes snorkelling a cheaper and very popular alternative.

Lakeside is the closest snorkelling spot to Exmouth, but Turquoise Bay isn't much further and it is a lot more popular. There are strong currents at Turquoise Bay that you need to swim through to get to the reef so inexperienced swimmers should avoid snorkelling alone.

Cape Range National Park adjoins the marine park and offers an abundance of flora and fauna as well as impressive gorges. The northern entrance to the national park is 40km from Exmouth and most people base themselves in Exmouth and visit as a day trip.

Entry to the park is $9 for a car and eight passengers or $3.40 per person if you arrive by bus.

Coming & Going

It's best to drive here yourself, particularly if you have a 4WD as this will open up more of the park for you to explore.

If you just want to visit for a day's snorkelling at Turquoise Bay, then you can go on one of the trips that are sometimes organised by the hostels around Exmouth or you can take the Ningaloo Reef Bus (☎ *1800 999 941*). The bus operates every day Nov-Mar, but only on Mon, Tue, Fri & Sat during Apr-Oct. A day return from Exmouth to Turquoise Bay costs $20. The bus departs Exmouth at 8.50am and returns from Turquoise Bay at 2.45pm.

The Easyrider bus also makes an excursion to Turquoise Bay and it is well worth the trip if you're travelling this way.

Pilbara

The Pilbara region is often associated with mining towns and is seldom visited by travellers. The main highway passes through the coastal region that includes the towns set up to service the mining region further inland and many travellers who are driving up the coast make a detour inland to see the incredible gorges at Karijini National Park.

Karratha

Karratha is a modern regional centre and home to the state's largest shopping centre north of Perth. Apart from the excellent infrastructure of shops, accommodation and fuel, there's not a lot to make you want to linger in town.

Practical Information
Visitor Information Centre
Karratha Road, Karratha.
☎ *(08) 9144 4600.*
***Open** Mon-Fri 8am-5.30pm, Sat-Sun 9am-4pm.*

Accommodation
Karratha Backpackers

There is a good atmosphere in this hostel, but the two-storey building is not too flash and the facilities are rather basic.
110 Wellard Way, Karratha.
☎ *(08) 9144 4904.*

Western Australia

Dorm bed $20; double/twin room $50.
Not yet rated

Port Hedland

Port Hedland is a busy port that serves the mining operations inland. It is really just an industrial city with little to interest the traveller apart from food, shops and fuel.

The city is nothing much to look at during the day, but at night the whole place lights up like a Christmas tree. There are a couple of minor attractions here but most travellers that choose to stop over here do so to organise a tour or transport 300km inland to the spectacular Karijini National Park.

Whale watching trips depart from Port Hedland between July and October and you can observe Flatback turtles at beaches in the Port Hedland area between October and March.

Practical Information
Visitor Information Centre
13 Wedge Street, Port Hedland.
☎ *(08) 9173 1711.*
Open 8.30am-5pm daily.

Accommodation
Dingo Oasis Backpackers
This place offers quality accommodation and it has a good range of amenities. There is also a separate annex with accommodation for travellers on the Easyrider bus. The best thing about this hostel is the waterfront location – Port Hedland almost looks pretty when you stare out at the lights on the ships at sea from a hammock under a palm tree at Dingo's.
59 Kingsmill Street, Port Hedland.
☎ *(08) 9173 1000.*
Website www.dingotrek.com.au/ accom.html.
Dorm bed $20; double room $50.
Not yet rated

Sights
Dalgety House Museum
This museum has exhibits and audio-visual displays on the city's history.
Corner Anderson & Wedge Streets, Port Hedland.

Admission $3.
Open 10am-3pm daily.

Shipping Observation Lookout
Port Hedland is a major port with big ships coming into port to load up with iron ore and salt. The lookout in Town Park offers an excellent vantage point to watch the shipping activity.
Town Park, Wedge Street, Port Hedland.

Tom Price

Tom Price, like nearby Paraburdoo, is a company town built by Hamersley Iron to house people working on the iron ore mines.

It has a good infrastructure for a small remote place with a good supermarket and even an airport with daily flights to Perth.

Most travellers use Tom Price as a base for exploring the spectacular Karijini National Park, which is 30 minutes outside town.

Practical Information
Tom Price Tourist Bureau
Central Road, Tom Price.
☎ *(08) 9188 1112.*
Website www.tompricewa.com.au.
Open Jan-Apr Mon-Fri 8.30am-2.30pm, Sat 9am-noon; May-Sep Mon-Fri 8.30am-5.30pm, Sat-Sun 9am-noon; Oct-Dec Mon-Fri 8.30am-2.30pm, Sat 9am-noon.

Accommodation
Tom Price Tourist Park
The backpackers' accommodation at this caravan park was set up to cater for backpackers on the Easyrider bus. Accommodation is in prefabricated units that are clean with new furnishings. Other amenities include an outdoor kitchen area and a swimming pool. It is 8km from the town centre.
Mt Nameless Road, Tom Price.
☎ *(08) 9189 1515.*
Dorm bed $20.
Credit cards MC, Visa.

Maintenance & cleanliness	★★☆
Facilities	★☆
Atmosphere & character	★
Security	★
Overall rating	★★

Karijini National Park

Karijini is becoming one of Western Australia's top attractions and a growing number of travellers are making the detour inland to visit the park.

The national park is best known for its gorges, which include waterfalls and several beautiful secluded swimming spots.

Practical Information
National Park Visitors Centre
The national park visitors' centre features excellent exhibits about the park. *Banjima Drive, Karijini National Park.* ☎ *(08) 9189 8121.* **Open** *9am-4pm daily.*

Coming & Going
Tom Price is the closest town to the park and it is a handy place to base yourself, particularly if you're driving.

McCafferty's/Greyhound travels via the coastal route and Port Hedland is the closest spot to Karijini that they stop. From Port Hedland, you can either rent a car or take one of the excellent tours offered by Dingo's Desert Trek Adventures *(59 Kingsmill Street, Port Hedland;* ☎ *(08) 9173 1000; website www.dingotrek.com.au).*

The Easyrider bus stops at Tom Price and also goes right into the national park on its Exmouth-Broome route. Travellers on Easyrider can either spend half a day in the park or stay in Tom Price and rent a car or book a tour of the park from there.

Hiking
The two main spots in Karijini are Dales Gorge and Junction Pool where the Joffre, Hancock, Red and Weano Gorges converge.

Dales Gorge is the most accessible and also the safer of the two spots and it can easily be visited in half a day.

There are a number of hiking trails in Dales Gorge that include the easy Gorge Rim walk (2km, 2 hours) which offers breathtaking views into the gorge; the Fortescue Falls walk (800m, 1 hour) descends the gorge to Fortescue Falls and the swimming spot at Fern Pool. There is also a walking trail to another swimming spot at Circular

Pool (800m, 2 hours) at the other end of the gorge. You can spot a lot of wildlife including goannas and lizards on the Dales Gorge hike (1½km, 3 hours) that runs along the base of the gorge between Circular Pool and Fortescue Falls, this is one of the most popular hiking trails in the park since it takes in two lovely swimming spots.

The area around the Joffre, Hancock, Knox, Red and Weano Gorges has more challenging hiking trails.

Easier short walks in this area include the Joffre Lookout walk (100m, 10 minutes), which offers views of the waterfalls in the Joffre Gorge. The walk to the Oxer and Junction Pool Lookouts (800m, 30 minutes) departs from the Weano carpark and offers spectacular views into the gorge. Another good short walk goes to Knox Lookout (300m, 15 minutes) and is best in the early morning and late afternoon.

Longer walks in this area include Knox Gorge (2km, 3 hours), Joffre Falls (3km, 3 hours), Handrail Pool (970m, 1½ hours) and Hancock Gorge (1½km, 3 hours).

If you enjoy hiking, there is enough in the park to keep you busy for several days.

Accommodation
Many travellers stay in Tom Price, but you can also camp in the national park for $10 per night. The camping sites in the national park are located near Dales, Joffre and Weano Gorges.

Kimberley Region

The Kimberley in Western Australia's far north is a dramatic area of waterfalls, gorges, beaches and rainforest. Despite its remoteness, the Kimberley is growing in popularity as a destination.

Broome
Relaxed Broome serves as the southern gateway to the Kimberley region.

An old pearling port, Broome once supplied eighty per cent of the world's mother-of-pearl shell. Late last century, its fleet of pearling luggers topped 400.

Travellers who visit in March/April or August/September may be lucky enough to see a natural phenomenon called "The Staircase of the Moon", an illusion caused by the full moon reflecting on mud flats at extreme low tide. It can be seen from the Roebuck Bay side of Broome during the king tides in those months. Other attractions include Cable Beach, 5km from the town centre.

The centre of Broome is known as Chinatown, even though there is nothing Chinese about it.

Practical Information
Visitor Information Centre
Corner Bagot Street & Broome Road, Broome.
☎ *(08) 9192 2222.*
Open Mon-Fri 8am-5pm, Sat-Sun 9am-1pm.

Coming & Going
Broome is the biggest destination on the west coast between Perth and Darwin and boasts an international airport as well as frequent buses to Perth and Darwin.

AIR
Because of the long distances on the west coast, many travellers fly from Broome to Perth making the trip here relatively painless. The airport is conveniently situated near the town centre with the terminal on McPherson Road about a five to ten minute walk from three of Broome's backpackers' hostels.

BUS
McCafferty's/Greyhound coaches stop outside the tourist information centre at the corner of Bagot Street and Broome Road. Coaches run stop in Broome en route between Darwin and Perth.

Local Transport
Broome's local bus service consists of an hourly bus between the town centre and Cable Beach. The town bus serves most of Broome's hostels and major attractions. You'll need to take a taxi if you miss the last bus, which leaves as early as 6.10pm. Fares are $2.70 one-way, $12 for a five-ride ticket and $22 for a 10-ride ticket.

Accommodation
Broome's Last Resort YHA
This hostel has a great laid-back tropical atmosphere. There is a swimming pool and bar with a pool table. It also has all the usual hostel amenities including a kitchen and TV room and the dorms are air-conditioned. This hostel has a handy location and it's less than five minutes walk from the airport, the town centre and the bus station.
2 Bagot Street, Broome.
☎ *(08) 9193 5000 or 1800 801 918.*
Dorm bed $24.50 ($21 YHA);
double/twin room $71 ($64 YHA).
Credit cards MC, Visa.
Reception open 6.30am-8pm daily.
🚗

Maintenance & cleanliness	★★★
Facilities	★★☆
Atmosphere & character	★★★★
Security	★
Overall rating	★★★

Broome

Accommodation
1. Broome's Last Resort YHA
2. Kimberley Klub
3. Roebuck Bay Backpackers

Reproduced by permission of the Department of Land Information, Perth, Western Australia. Copyright Licence 04/2003

Cable Beach Backpackers

This hostel has a great laid-back atmosphere and a good range of facilities. There is a swimming pool and basketball as well as a bar with a pool table. Other facilities include the usual kitchen and barbecue. The hostel caters to travellers who come to Broome for the beach and they offer surfboard and body board hire in addition to the usual bike hire. It's the closest hostel to Cable Beach, but the beach is still a five-minute walk away. There's also a shuttle bus to the town centre and the town bus stops nearby.

12 Sanctuary Road, Cable Beach, Broome.
🚌 *Town Bus.*
☎ *(08) 9193 5511 or 1800 655 011.*
Website *www.cablebeachbackpackers. com.*
Dorm bed *$19-22 ($18-21 VIP/ YHA);* ***double/twin room*** *$62 ($60 VIP/YHA).*
Reception open *6.30am-1pm & 4.30pm-10pm daily.*
🚌

Maintenance & cleanliness	★★★
Facilities	★★★
Atmosphere & character	★★★★★
Security	★★
Overall rating	★★★☆

Kimberley Klub

The Kimberley Klub is an excellent hostel. It is purpose-built in a tropical resort style and very tastefully decorated. It is set in a lush garden setting with lots of tropical plants and it features a swimming pool and beach volleyball court. All the usual hostel facilities are here as well, including a big kitchen and a TV room with a pool table. There is a bar that is a great place to hang out. Some people may find the Kimberley Klub a little too commercialised, and they certainly try to make a buck from everything. The air-conditioning is coin-operated, happy hour doesn't save you much and you have to pay for the book exchange. Although not right in the centre of things, Kimberley Klub is still fairly central at about a five-minute walk from the airport terminal, the Broome Boulevard shopping centre and the town centre.

62 Frederick Street, Broome.
☎ *(08) 9192 3233.*
Website *www.kimberleyklub.com.*
Dorm bed *$21-25 ($20-24 Nomads/ VIP/YHA);* ***double/twin room*** *$45- 75 ($43-73 Nomads/VIP/YHA).*
Reception open *6.30am-8pm daily.*
🚌

Maintenance & cleanliness	★★★★
Facilities	★★★★☆
Atmosphere & character	★★★★
Security	★★★☆
Overall rating	★★★★

Roebuck Bay Backpackers

Although Roey Backpackers has the same range of facilities as other hostels in Broome, the quality isn't of the same standard. It has the usual kitchen, TV lounge, barbecue and a swimming pool. It is part of the Roebuck Hotel complex in town centre.

Napier Terrace, Chinatown, Broome
☎ *(08) 9192 1183.*
Dorm bed *$15-18;* ***double room*** *$65.*
Reception open *7am-4pm & 5pm-8pm daily.*

Maintenance & cleanliness	★★☆
Facilities	★★★☆
Atmosphere & character	★★★☆
Security	★
Overall rating	★★

Sights

Broome Bird Observatory

The Broome Bird Observatory is a top destination for birdwatchers and it contains almost half of Australia's bird species. The best time to see shorebirds is two hours before and after high tide.

Crab Creek Road, 25km from Broome.
☎ *(08) 9193 5600.*
Website *www.birdsaustralia.com.au.*
Admission *$5.*
Open *Dry Season 8am-6pm daily; Wet Season Tue-Sun 8am-6pm.*

Broome Historic Society

This small museum has exhibits on the history of Broome.

Hammersley Street, Broome.
☎ *(08) 9192 2075.*
Admission *$5.*
Open *Jan-May 10am-1pm daily; Jun- Oct Mon-Fri 10am-4pm, Sat-Sun 10am-1pm; Nov-Dec 10am-1pm daily.*

Cable Beach

Broome's main attraction is this pristine 22km long beach. There are several companies that offer camel rides along the beach with prices starting at $10 for a 15-minute ride.

Cable Beach Road, 5km from the town centre.

☐ *Town Bus.*

Gantheaume Point

The point at the southern extremity of Cable Beach is worth visiting at low tide if you want to search for the 130 million-year-old dinosaur footprints.

Malcolm Douglas Crocodile Farm

This crocodile farm at Cable Beach gives you the opportunity to see some really big crocodiles. It is best to visit for one of the feeding tours.

Cable Beach Road, Cable Beach.

☐ *Town Bus.*

☎ *(08) 9192 1489.*

Admission *$15 ($12 ISIC/VIP/YHA).*

Open *Apr-Nov Mon-Fri 10am-5pm, Sat-Sun 2pm-5pm; feeding tours Wed-Sun 3pm.*

Pearl Luggers

This attraction features exhibits on Broome's pearling history including a couple of restored boats. Rather than walk around at your own pace, visitors are given a tour by a pearl diver.

44 Dampier Terrace, Broome.

☎ *(08) 9192 2059.*

Admission *$18.50.*

Tours *Mon-Fri 11am, 2pm; Sat-Sun 11am.*

Sun Pictures Outdoor Cinema

The world's oldest outdoor cinema is right in the centre of Chinatown and has a brilliant atmosphere under the stars on a balmy tropical night.

Carnarvon Street, Broome.

☎ *(08) 9192 1077.*

Admission *$13.*

Derby

There's not a real lot to make you take the turnoff from the main highway to visit this dusty and muddy town. Derby's attractions include a prison built from a boab tree that has a girth of 14.7 metres and Myall's bore, a 120-metre-long cattle trough, which is the longest in the southern hemisphere. Derby's 11-metre tides are the highest in Australia.

Practical Information

Derby Visitors Centre

2 Clarendon Street, Derby.

☎ *(08) 9191 1426.*

Website *www.derbytourism.com.au.*

Open *Jan-Mar Mon-Fri 8.30am-4.30pm, Sat 9am-noon; Apr-May Mon-Fri 8.30am-4.30pm, Sat-Sun 9am-1pm; Jun-Aug Mon-Fri 8.30am-4.30pm, Sat-Sun 9am-4pm; Sep Mon-Fri 8.30am-4.30pm, Sat-Sun 9am-1pm; Oct-Dec Mon-Fri 8.30am-4.30pm, Sat 9am-noon.*

Accommodation

Spinifex Hotel

Basic backpackers' accommodation is available in four-bed dorms above the "Spinny" pub. It's in the centre of Derby and McCafferty's/Greyhound buses stop outside.

Clarendon Street, Derby.

☎ *(08) 9191 1233.*

Dorm bed *$20.*

Not yet rated

Fitzroy Crossing

Fitzroy Crossing is not much more than a roadhouse, a couple of motels, a pub and a welfare office, but it's a convenient base for exploring the surrounding region that includes Geikie and Windjana Gorges.

Practical Information

Fitzroy Crossing Tourist Bureau

Forrest Road, Fitzroy Crossing.

☎ *(08) 9191 5355.*

Open *Jan-Mar Mon-Fri 9am-5pm, Sat 9am-1pm; Apr-Sep 8am-5pm daily; Oct-Dec Mon-Fri 9am-5pm, Sat 9am-1pm.*

Sights

Geikie Gorge National Park

The best way to explore the gorge is to take one of the cruises on the river, although there are also some good walks along the gorge and elsewhere in the national park. The gorge features some nice picnic and barbecue sites and is home to plenty of freshwater crocodiles. It is worth the visit if you're driving although it's otherwise a bit difficult to get to.

17km northeast of Fitzroy Crossing.
☎ *(08) 9191 5121.*
Cruises *$17.50.*
Cruises depart *Apr-Nov 8am & 3pm daily.*
Park open *Apr-Nov 6.30am-6.30pm daily; entry restricted during Wet season (Dec-Mar).*

Halls Creek

The site of Western Australia's first gold rush in 1885, Halls Creek has a bit more to offer than Fitzroy Crossing, but not by much. There's not much reason to stop here except to fill the car with fuel and grab a bite to eat.

Purnululu (Bungle Bungle) National Park

Purnululu National Park is best known for the spectacular Bungle Bungles – a unique mountain range with the appearance of an upside-down egg carton. The Bungle Bungles are best experienced by a scenic flight, although this can get a little too pricey for most backpackers.

You will need a four-wheel-drive to actually explore the national park from the ground and for most people this means an even more expensive 4WD tour. Several companies in Kununurra, including Kununurra Backpackers organise 4WD tours for the Bungle Bungles. If you have access to a 4WD you can get to the trailhead of a number of hiking tracks including hikes to Cathedral Gorge, Echidna Chasm and the longer overnight hike to Piccaninny Gorge.

The park is closed during the wet season (between January and March).

Kununurra

Kununurra is a fairly modern town, coming into existence in the 1960s to serve as a base for the Ord River irrigation project. The town is now a modern regional centre for the surrounding farming regions and a popular spot with travellers as a base for exploring the Bungle Bungles, Hidden Valley and Lake Argyle.

Mirima (Hidden Valley) National Park is the most accessible of the national parks – you can even walk here from the centre of town. This park offers similar features to the Bungle Bungles for a fraction of the cost. There are several short walks in this park that make it an ideal daytrip from Kununurra.

Created in the 1970s as part of the Ord River Irrigation Project, the massive Lake Argyle is worth a visit. Located 35km south of town, Lake Argyle offers cruises, canoeing and camping.

The surrounding area is very fertile and there is plenty of work on farms between June and November and you may be able to arrange some of this through the local hostels.

Be very careful swimming around here, the rivers and lakes in this region are home to saltwater crocodiles.

Practical Information
Visitors Information Centre
Coolibah Drive, Kununurra.
☎ *(08) 9168 1177.*
Open *Mon-Fri 9am-4pm, Sat 9am-noon.*

Department of Conservation & Land Management (CALM)
Messmate Way, Kununurra.
☎ *(08) 9168 2000.*
Open *8am-5pm daily.*

Coming & Going
Kununurra is surprisingly well connected for a remote small town.

McCafferty's/Greyhound operate a daily coach service to Broome and Darwin via Katherine. Buses stop at the BP service station on Messmate Way.

The airport 5km north of town has daily flights on Air North (*website* www.airnorth.com.au) to Broome and Darwin. Flying can work out only about $40 more expensive than the bus, if you buy a ticket 48 hours before your flight.

Accommodation
Kimberley Croc Backpackers YHA
Kununurra's YHA hostel has a good range of facilities including a good kitchen, an outdoor TV lounge and a nice swimming pool, but the accommodation is fairly basic. It's the closest hostel to the town centre.
Corner Konkerberry Drive & Tristania Street, Kununarra.
☎ *(08) 9168 2702.*
Dorm bed *$21.50-23.50 ($18-20 YHA);* **double/twin room** *$55 ($48 YHA).*
Credit cards *MC, Visa.*
Reception open *6.30am-8pm daily.*
Not yet rated

Kununurra Backpackers Adventure Centre
This is a good hostel that offers short-term accommodation for travellers passing through and long-term accommodation for backpackers working in Kununurra. There are good facilities including Internet access, kitchen, a good TV lounge and a nice outdoor area with a barbecue and swimming pool. Accommodation is in small air-conditioned dorms. The staff know a lot about the local area and they run canoe safaris to the Bungle Bungles.
24 Nutwood Crescent, Kununurra.
☎ *(08) 9169 1998 or 1800 641 998.*
Dorm bed *$21;* **double/twin room** *$50.*
Not yet rated

Sights
Kellys Knob
Kellys Knob offers an excellent vantage point with views of the town and the surrounding area. Both hostels will drop you off near the summit so you only need to walk back down the hill.

Mirima (Hidden Valley) National Park
This small national park is only 2km from the centre of Kununurra and it offers similar features to the Bungle Bungles. Most travellers visit the park early in the morning before it gets too hot. It is a small park and two to three hours is sufficient time even if you walk every trail in the park.
Hidden Valley Road, Kununurra.
Admission *$9 per vehicle, free if you walk to the park.*

Index

Map Acknowledgements

Maps are created by BUG Backpackers Guide using data and base maps supplied by the following organisations: Department of Lands (NSW & ACT); Department of Infrastructure, Planning and Environment (NT); Department of Natural Resources and Mines (QLD); RAA (SA & NT); TASMAP (TAS); TUMAS (VIC); DLI (WA). Full map acknowledgements are as follows:

The following maps use base mapping reproduced with permission of the Department of Lands; Panorama Avenue, Bathurst NSW 2795 *(website www.lands.nsw.gov.au)*: Canberra (ACT), Byron Bay (NSW), Coffs Harbour (NSW), Katoomba (NSW), Newcastle (NSW), Port Macquarie (NSW) and Sydney (NSW).

The following maps use base mapping reproduced with permission of the Department of Infrastructure, Planning and Environment; Darwin NT 0801 *(website www.ipe.nt.gov.au)*: Alice Springs (NT) and Katherine (NT).

The following maps use base mapping reproduced with permission of Department of Natural Resources and Mines, Brisbane QLD 4000 *(website www.nrm.qld.gov.au)*: Agnes Water/Town of 1770 (QLD), Brisbane (QLD), Bundaberg (QLD), Cairns (QLD), Cardwell (QLD), Hervey Bay (QLD), Innisfail (QLD), Magnetic Island (QLD), Maroochydore (QLD), Noosa (QLD), Port Douglas (QLD), Rainbow Beach (QLD), Townsville (QLD) and Tully (QLD).

The following maps use base mapping reproduced with permission of the Royal Automobile Association of SA, Adelaide *(website www.raa.com.au)*: Adelaide (SA), Coober Pedy (SA) and Darwin (NT).

The following maps use map detail derived from TASMAP's Tasmanian Towns Street Atlas: Devonport (TAS), Hobart (TAS) and Launceston (TAS). To contact TASMAP phone 61 3 6233 3223, email tasmap@dpiwe.tas.gov.au.

The following maps were produced using TUMAUS *(website www.TUMAUS.com.au)*: Great Ocean Road (VIC), Lorne (VIC), Melbourne (VIC), Mildura (VIC), Port Campbell (VIC) and St Kilda (VIC).

The following maps are reproduced with permission of Department of Land Information, Perth, Western Australia *(website www.dli.wa.gov.au)*, Copyright Licence 64/2003: Broome (WA), Fremantle (WA) and Perth (WA).

The Australia map and individual state maps are based on data and base maps supplied by TUMAUS with additional information supplied by various tourist offices.

Get your travel gear online

Do you need a sleeping bag, backpack, Swiss Army knife or an adaptor for those funny Australian powerpoints?

You can get all this, and more, online at **travelgear.com.au**.

Tek Towel
This amazing microfibre towel features a terry towelling finish. It is super compact, taking up a fraction of the packing space required by a conventional towel. Essential if you want to travel light.
Regular A$19.95
Large A$29.95

Multi Adaptor for Australia/New Zealand
This ingeniously designed adaptor allows visitors to Australia and New Zealand to use appliances from Europe, the Americas, Asia and Great Britain.
A$12.50

UK/USA to Australia/New Zealand Adaptor
This compact electrical adaptor suits travellers with earthed appliances from North America, United Kingdom and parts of Europe. It will allow these appliances to be used in Australia, Fiji and New Zealand.
A$10.95

Travel Pillow
This Travel Pillow differs from others in the fact that it is not an inflatable pillow, but instead a real pillow with a durable polyester fibre filling and a brushed cotton face fabric. It features a compression draw cord that easily folds the pillow down to a compact size for packing.
A$24.95

The above products are an example of the large range of travel accessories available from **travelgear.com.au**.

Prices are quoted in Australian dollars, which is practically peanuts when you convert it into pounds or euros.

Worldwide delivery is a low A$8 for up to five items. Shipping is free for orders sent within Australia.